JESUS OF NAZARETH

JESUS OF NAZARETH

An Independent Historian's Account of His Life and Teaching

MAURICE CASEY

t&t clark

Published by T&T Clark International
A Continuum Imprint
The Tower Building, 11 York Road, London SE1 7NX
80 Maiden Lane, Suite 704, New York, NY 10038

www.continuumbooks.com

British Library Cataloguing-in-Publication Data
A catalogue record for this book is available from the British Library

ISBN 13: 978-0-567-10408-3 (Hardback)
           978-0-567-64517-3 (Paperback)

Typeset by Pindar NZ, Auckland, New Zealand
Printed and bound in Great Britain by the MPG Books Group

This book is dedicated to
Stephanie Louise Fisher
and
James Crossley,
brilliant colleagues with completely independent minds,
and wonderful friends

Contents

Preface

This book was effectively written over a period of many years. I began research into the life and teaching of Jesus, his Jewish environment, and fruitful methodology, by reading for a doctorate on aspects of the 'Son of man' problem at Durham University under Professor C. K. Barrett, whose extraordinary combination of learning and helpfulness with lack of bureaucracy or interference remains a model to which one can only aspire. My work on methodology, especially on the use of Aramaic to unravel and interpret accurate Gospel sources, and distinguish them from secondary material, was greatly facilitated by the award of a British Academy Research Readership 1994–96, when I worked on Aramaic sources of Mark's Gospel and of the 'Q' material, and a Leverhulme Major Research Fellowship 2001–4, when I worked on the 'Son of man' problem. I am also grateful to scholars who discussed with me over the years the many and difficult problems of method and detail which work on a life of Jesus has involved. I would particularly like to thank Dr R. D. Aus, the late Professor M. Black, Professor R. Bauckham, Professor G. J. Brooke, Professor B. D. Chilton, Professor J. A. Fitzmyer, Professor R. Kearns, the late Professor B. Lindars, Professor M. Müller, and Professor M. Wilcox. I would also like to thank members of the Aramaic Background and Historical Jesus seminars at SNTS, the Jesus seminar at meetings of British New Testament scholars, and an annual seminar 'The Use of the Old Testament in the New' now generally held at St Deiniol's Library, for what I have learnt from them.

An earlier version of parts of Chapter 1 was read as a conference paper at the University of Nottingham, and subsequently published as 'Who's Afraid of Jesus Christ? Some Comments on Attempts to Write a Life of Jesus', in J. G. Crossley and C. Karner (eds.), *Writing History, Constructing Religion* (Aldershot: Ashgate, 2005), pp. 129–46. I am grateful for permission to republish this material.

For many years, I had the absolute delight of working with students of Nottingham University on all the less technical aspects of this book. I am extremely grateful to them, especially those who took the trouble to work through New Testament Texts in Greek, for their careful work and sharp questions. I am grateful to Sian my daughter, who ploughed through the opening chapters on behalf of the general reader, asked interesting questions and noted for me the points at which I became incomprehensible. I would like to thank Dr. Jim West, who read a draft of most chapters of this book and made helpful comments throughout. I am grateful to doctoral students who wrote outstanding work on different topics, not all of it published, because they went on to do different things. I particularly learnt much from Sandie Schagen (resurrection and immortality), Jonathan Stock-Hesketh (Law in Jewish Apocalyptic), and Richard Burridge (Gospel genre and Graeco-Roman biography), all of whom provided many interesting and sometimes broad-ranging discussions, as well as excellent completed theses.

This brings me to the two outstanding students, friends and colleagues to whom this book is dedicated, without their permission, as far as I remember. James Crossley was a shipyard electrician who came to Nottingham to read a first degree in English and Theology, switched to Theology, and after a Master's degree, completed an outstanding doctorate on the date of Mark's Gospel. At this stage, he and Caroline his partner became good friends. He now lectures at the University of Sheffield. He read carefully through an earlier version of this book, and made many helpful comments. Since then, he has taken part with me in a variety of helpful discussions on topics relevant to the present version of this book, as well as giving me publications in which he has made a significant contribution to knowledge. After a varied life and a first degree in Religious Studies at Victoria University, Wellington, Stephanie Fisher came 12,000 miles to work with me on her doctorate on the 'Q' material. She has worked meticulously through every word of more than one draft of this version of this book, has made many helpful suggestions, and taken part in many helpful discussions. She has also become a wonderful friend, and on several occasions it has been a great delight to have James and Stephanie together for helpful discussions and other entertainment, especially dinner with lots of champers.

Finally, I am grateful to the British Library and to SOAS library for facilities essential for complex scholarly work in this area. I am also grateful to Alistair Sabin, of ADS Computers, for setting up, and subsequently working on, my word-processing facilities at home, on which most of this book was written.

Abbreviations

AB	Anchor Bible
ABRL	Anchor Bible Reference Library
Adv. Haer.	Adversus Haereses
AGJU	Arbeiten zur Geschichte des antiken Judentums und des Urchristentums
ANRW	H. Temporini and W. Haase (eds), *Aufstieg und Niedergang der römischen Welt* (many vols, Berlin: W. De Gruyter, 1972–)
Ant.	*Antiquities of the Jews*
Ant. Bib.	Biblical Antiquities
Ass. Mos.	*Assumption of Moses*
b.	Babylonian Talmud
2 Bar.	*2 Baruch*
Ber.	Berakhot
Bes.	Beṣah
BFChT	Beiträge zur Forderung christlicher Theologie
BQ	Baba Qamma
CBQ	*Catholic Biblical Quarterly*
CD	The Damascus Document
CIL	Corpus Inscriptionum Latinarum
Col.	Colossians
1 Cor.	1 Corinthians
Dan.	Daniel
Dec.	*De Decalogo*
Dem.	Demai
Dem. *Or.*	Demosthenes, *Orationes*
Deut.	Deuteronomy
De Vir. Ill.	*De Viris Illustribus*
Dial.	*Dialogue*
Did.	Didache
Diog. L.	Diogenes Laertius
Ed.	Eduyot
1 En.	1 Enoch
Epiph.	Epiphanius
Est.	Esther

Est.R.	Esther Rabbah
ET	English Translation
Eus.	Eusebius
Exod.	Exodus
ExpT	*Expository Times*
Ezek.	Ezekiel
FB	Forschung zur Bibel
FRLANT NF	Forschungen zur Religion und Literatur des Alten und Neues Testaments, Neue Folge
Gal.	Galatians
GCS	Die griechische christliche Schriftsteller der ersten drei Jahrhunderte
Gen.	Genesis
Gen.R.	Genesis Rabbah
G.Pet.	Gospel of Peter
Hab.	Habakkuk
Hag.	Hagigah
H.E.	*Historia Ecclesiastica*
Hipp.Th.	Hippolytus of Thebes
HJC	*History of Joseph the Carpenter*
Hos.	Hosea
HSM	Harvard Semitic Monographs
HThR	*Harvard Theological Review*
Hul.	Hullin
IG	Inscriptiones Graecae
Iren.	Irenaeus
Isa.	Isaiah
Jas	James
JBL	*Journal of Biblical Literature*
Jer.	Jeremiah
Jn	John
Jos.	Josephus
Josh.	Joshua
JRA.SS	Journal of Roman Archaeology. Supplementary Series
JSHJ	*Journal for the Study of the Historical Jesus*
JSJSup	Supplements to the Journal for the Study of Judaism
JSNT	*Journal for the Study of the New Testament*
JSNTSup	*Journal for the Study of the New Testament*, Supplement Series
JSOTSup	*Journal for the Study of the Old Testament*, Supplement Series
Jub.	*Jubilees*
Judg.	Judges
KEKNT	Kritisch-exegetischer Kommentar über das neue Testament
Kel.	Kelim
Ket.	Ketuboth

1 Kgs	1 Kings
2 Kgs	2 Kings
Lam.	Lamentations
LCL	Loeb Classical Library
Leg. ad Gaium	*Legatio ad Gaium*
Lev.	Leviticus
Lk.	Luke
LNTS	Library of New Testament Studies
LXX	Septuagint
m.	Mishnah
Maas.	Ma'aseroth
1 Macc.	1 Maccabees
2 Macc.	2 Maccabees
3 Macc.	*3 Maccabees*
4 Macc.	*4 Maccabees*
Mal.	Malachi
Meg.	Megillah
Men.	Menaḥoth
Mic.	Micah
Mk	Mark
Mt.	Matthew
Ned.	Nedarim
Neh.	Nehemiah
Neof I	Neofiti I
NovT	*Novum Testamentum*
NRSV	New Revised Standard Version
NTS	*New Testament Studies*
NT.S	Novum Testamentum. Supplements
Num.	Numbers
Pan.	*Panarion*
Pes.	Pesaḥim
1 Pet.	1 Peter
Phil.	Philippians
Prov.	Proverbs
Ps.	Psalm
Ps-J	Pseudo-Jonathan
Pss.	Psalms
Qid.	Qiddushin
R.	Rabbi
Rev.	Revelation
Rom.	Romans
RSV	Revised Standard Version
1 Sam.	1 Samuel
2 Sam.	2 Samuel
San.	Sanhedrin
SBLDS	SBL Dissertation Series

SBT	Studies in Biblical Theology
Sem.	Sᵉmāḥōth
Shab.	Shabbat
Shevu.	Shevu'ot
Sim.	Similitude
Sir.	Sirach
SJHC	Studies in Jewish History and Culture
SNTSMS	Society for New Testament Studies Monograph Series
Sot.	Sotah
Spec.Leg.	*De Specialibus Legibus*
Suet.	Suetonius
Sukk.	Sukkah
T.	Tosefta
Ta'an.	Ta'anith
Tanḥ.	Tanḥuma
T.Ephraem	*Testament of Ephraem*
Tg.	Targum
1 Thess.	1 Thessalonians
ThHNT	Theologischer Handkommentar zum Neuen Testament
Tob.	Tobit
Toh.	Toharot
2 Tim.	2 Timothy
Trans.	Translated by
TSAJ	Texts and Studies in Ancient Judaism
TU	Texte und Untersuchungen
TWNT	*Theologische Wörterbuch zum Neuen Testament*
Vit. Cont.	*De Vita Contempliva*
WUNT	Wissenschaftliche Untersuchungen zum Neuen Testament
y.	Yerushalmi (= Jerusalem/Palestinian Talmud)
Zab.	Zabim
Zech.	Zechariah
ZThK	*Zeitschrift für Theologie und Kirche*

CHAPTER 1

The Quest of the Historical Jesus

1. *Introduction*

Jesus of Nazareth is a major symbol in our culture. Most of us belong to social
subgroups which have a definite view of him. Some people belong to evangelical
Christian groups who believe in the literal truth of all four Gospels in their sacred
text, the New Testament. Many Christians believe that Jesus is the second person
of the Trinity, God the Son, and when he lived his life on earth he performed
miracles, knew everything and never made any mistakes. He died for the sins of
the world, and rose from the dead. Our society as a whole, however, is barely
Christian. Many people believe that none of the miracle stories are true, and
some non-religious people imagine that Jesus was not a historical character at
all. Jewish people generally believe that, whatever else he may have said or done,
Jesus was not the Messiah, and God did not raise him from the dead. They are
also convinced that no man can be God, and that the Christian doctrine of the
Trinity violates the monotheism which God revealed to them, his chosen people.
In accordance with their own traditions, the vast majority of Muslims believe
that Jesus did not die. This is what one short passage of the Qur'an is believed
to say, and it is part of the narrative of a mediaeval forgery known as the Gospel
of Barnabas.[1]

There is a second reason why it is difficult to discuss the earthly life which
Jesus lived 2,000 years ago. Our main historical sources are the four Gospels
which are now found in a Christian book, the New Testament. These Gospels
were written for Christian churches some time after Jesus' death, in Greek rather
than in the Aramaic which he spoke, by Christians who included those aspects

---

1 On this see D. Sox, *The Gospel of Barnabas* (London: Allen & Unwin, 1984). For Muslim
views of Jesus see more generally O. Leirvik, *Images of Jesus Christ in Islam: Introduction,
Survey of Research, Issues of Dialogue* (Uppsala: Swedish Institute of Missionary Research,
1999); and more generally still, H. P. Goddard, *Muslim Perceptions of Christianity* (London:
Grey Seal, 1996).

1

of his life and teaching which they found most significant. Mark and Luke show significant signs of Gentile self-identification, whereas Jesus and his first followers were Jewish. Matthew, who was at least culturally Jewish himself, shows significant signs of assimilation into the Gentile world. The Gospel attributed to John, which is very different from the other three, appears to have been largely written by Gentile Christians, and in parts it is vigorously anti-Jewish.

The purpose of this book is to engage with the historical Jesus from the perspective of an independent historian. I do not belong to any religious or anti-religious group. I try to use evidence and argument to establish historically valid conclusions. I depend on the best work done by many other scholars, regardless of their ideological affiliation. I also make abundant use of one relatively recent discovery which should help us to go further than ever before in reconstructing the Jesus of history in his original cultural context. That is the discovery of the Dead Sea Scrolls, and above all the eventual publication of all those which are written in Aramaic, the language which Jesus himself spoke. In two complex technical books, I have shown how genuine sayings of Jesus, and the earliest narrative reports of his deeds, can be reconstructed in their original Aramaic versions in a manner unthinkable before the publication of the Aramaic scrolls.[2] As all students of language and culture in general are very well aware, language is a central part of culture. Accordingly, the reconstruction of the Aramaic sources of the synoptic Gospels is an essential step in understanding him against the background of his own culture, that of first-century Judaism. All the details of this technical work cannot be presented in this book, but it lies behind it, and I present Aramaic reconstructions of the Lord's Prayer and of Jesus' words interpreting the bread and wine at the Last Supper, so that everyone can see what this work looks like, and experience something of what he really said. I also refer to this kind of work at other crucial points.

Attempts to see Jesus against the background of first-century Judaism have been made before, notably by Albert Schweitzer, Geza Vermes, and Ed Sanders. Six scholars, Tom Wright, Bruce Chilton, Jimmy Dunn, J. P. Meier, and Martin Hengel with Anna Schwemer, are notable among those who have tried again recently, at a time when seeing the historical Jesus as Jewish has become politically correct in Christian churches.[3] No one has quite succeeded, however, and

---

2   P. M. Casey, *Aramaic Sources of Mark's Gospel* (SNTSMS 102. Cambridge: CUP, 1998); *An Aramaic Approach to Q: Sources for the Gospels of Matthew and Luke* (SNTSMS 122. Cambridge: CUP, 2002).

3   A. Schweitzer, *Von Reimarus zu Wrede. Eine Geschichte der Leben-Jesu-Forschung* (Tübingen: J. C.B. Mohr (Paul Siebeck), 1906; 2nd edn, 1913): ET *The Quest of the Historical Jesus: A Critical Study of its Progress from Reimarus to Wrede* (trans. W. Montgomery. London: A&C Black, 1910): 2nd ET *The Quest of the Historical Jesus: First Complete Edition* (ed. and trans. J. Bowden *et al*. London: SCM, 2000); G. Vermes, *Jesus the Jew: A Historian's Reading of the Gospels* (London: Collins, 1973); G. Vermes, *Jesus and the World of Judaism* (London: SCM, 1983); G. Vermes, *The Religion of Jesus the Jew* (London: SCM, 1993); E. P. Sanders, *Jesus and Judaism* (London: SCM, 1985); E. P. Sanders, *The Historical Figure of Jesus* (London: Penguin, 1993); J. P. Meier, *A Marginal Jew. Rethinking the Historical Jesus* (ABRL. 4 vols so far. New York: Doubleday, 1991–); N. T. Wright, *Jesus and the Victory of God* (London:

insufficient study of Jesus' language is one reason for this. Another fundamental reason is the cultural background of scholars themselves. The vast majority of scholars have belonged to the Christian faith, and their portrayals of Jesus have consequently not been Jewish enough. Most other writers on Jesus have been concerned to rebel against the Christian faith, rather than to recover the Jewish figure who was central to Christianity in its earliest period. This is one reason why a fresh attempt to recreate the Jesus of history is essential. The history of scholarship is however very instructive, especially that since the fundamental work of Albert Schweitzer. For Schweitzer demonstrated how essential it is to see Jesus against his own cultural background in first-century Judaism, and that was in 1906. It was the 1910 ET of this book, *The Quest of the Historical Jesus*, which gave the quest its name. Throughout the twentieth century, however, scholars repeatedly failed to follow Schweitzer's example.

Of especial importance is the framework of Jewish apocalyptic, within which Schweitzer placed Jesus. Jewish apocalyptic claimed to be a literature of divine revelation. It was written by Jews who felt that they lived in such disastrous circumstances that God was bound to intervene in the near future to deliver them. Following the work of Weiss at the end of the nineteenth century, Schweitzer argued that Jesus predicted the immediate coming of the kingdom of God, and with it the end of normal human history.[4] This however did not happen. The notion that Jesus might have made a mistake, however natural for the interpretation of a vigorous first-century Jewish prophet, did not fit with Christian Christology. Whether explicitly or as part of a hidden agenda, this has been a significant aspect of attempts to avoid the Jewishness of Jesus ever since. Avoiding the Jewishness of Jesus is not of course a purely recent or simply scholarly concern. In a fine discussion of Jesus books in the period before Schweitzer, Charlotte Allen correctly commented on nineteenth-century liberal lives of Jesus:

> Underlying all the biographies was a universal condemnation of the Jews. In the minds of the liberal Protestants, first-century Judaism was a stand-in for Catholicism and other forms of orthodox religion. Ritualistic, legalistic, and censorious, it had been based on the doctrine of justification by works (obedience to Torah) à la Catholicism, in contrast to the Protestant doctrine of justification by faith.[5]

In spite of this, scholars of the Victorian era made one major critical advance which is essential for recovering the Jesus of history. They showed between them

SPCK, 1996); B. Chilton, *Rabbi Jesus: An Intimate Biography: The Jewish Life and Teachings that Inspired Christianity* (New York: Doubleday, 2000); J. D. G. Dunn, *Christianity in the Making*. Vol. 1, *Jesus Remembered* (Grand Rapids: Eerdmans, 2003); M. Hengel and A. M. Schwemer, *Jesus und das Judentum* (Geschichte des frühen Christentums, Band 1. Tübingen: Mohr Siebeck, 2007).

4   J. Weiss, *Die Predigt Jesu vom Reiche Gottes* (Göttingen: Vandenhoeck & Ruprecht, 1892); *Jesus' Proclamation of the Kingdom of God* (trans., ed. and with introduction by R. H. Hiers and D. L. Holland. London/Philadelphia: SCM/Fortress, 1971); Schweitzer, *Quest*.

5   C. Allen, *The Human Christ. The Search for the Historical Jesus* (Oxford: Lion, 1998), p. 169.

that the Gospel attributed to John is not literally true. While this result has not been welcome in the churches, critical scholars, whether Christian or not, have rightly seen it as fundamental. All serious scholarly lives ever since have been based on the Gospels of Matthew, Mark and Luke.

2. *The Nazi Period*

The years after Schweitzer's major contribution form the most disreputable part of the story of the quest, and one of the most illuminating episodes in the history of scholarship. This is however being concealed by an academic myth, according to which scholars are now working on the third quest for the historical Jesus. The first quest was supposedly torpedoed by Schweitzer in 1906, when he showed that the liberal quest of the historical Jesus essentially consisted of scholars looking in a mirror and finding in Jesus an image of themselves. Schweitzer's demolition of the first quest was so devastating that it brought the quest to a halt. The second quest was begun by Käsemann in a 1953 lecture, published in 1954. It therefore seems at first sight reasonable that we should call the period between Schweitzer and Käsemann the period of 'no quest'.[6]

Reasonable though this may seem at first sight, it is not accurate. In the first place, while Schweitzer's strictures were from an intellectual point of view so severe that they should have ended the first quest, they did not do so. Conventional lives of Jesus, not seriously different from liberal lives in the nineteenth century, continued to be written. Such included for example those of the Anglican Bishop A. C. Headlam in 1923, and the French scholar Guigenebert in 1933.[7] Moreover, another major critical advance was made, which is essential for recovering the Jesus of history. The priority of Mark was basically established. In 1924, Streeter gathered together the evidence that the Gospel According to Mark is our oldest source for the life and teaching of Jesus, and that it was copied and edited by Matthew and Luke.[8] He also presented a view of 'Q', one or more conjectural sources which scholars have inferred from the non-Markan material used by both Matthew and Luke. Ever since, most serious scholarly lives of Jesus have paid especially careful attention to the Gospel of Mark and to the 'Q' material.

The second major feature of the scholarship of the supposedly 'no quest' period was the radical and anti-Jewish work produced by learned scholars in Germany. As Nazi control of Germany increased in the run-up to the Holocaust,

---

6 Cf. S. Neill and T. Wright, *The Interpretation of the New Testament, 1861–1986* (Oxford: OUP, [2]1988), pp. 379–403; Wright, *Jesus and the Victory*, esp. pp. 21–23; B. Witherington, *The Jesus Quest: The Third Search for the Jew of Nazareth* (Carlisle: Paternoster, 1995).

7 A. C. Headlam, *The Life and Teaching of Jesus the Christ* (London: Murray, 1923, [3]1936); C. Guignebert, *Jésus* (Paris: Renaissance du Livre, 1933): *Jesus* (trans. S. H. Hooke. London: Kegan Paul, Trench, Trubner, 1935).

8 B. H. Streeter, *The Four Gospels: A Study of Origins* (London: Macmillan, 1924).

attempts to show that Jesus was not Jewish became more and more widespread. Such attempts were not new. Many Germans had already argued that Jesus was Aryan, not Jewish, but such Germans had not previously been New Testament scholars. In the nineteenth century, one of the most famous was the composer Richard Wagner. Perhaps the single most influential book was the 1899 work of H. S. Chamberlain, later translated into English as *The Foundations of the Nineteenth Century*.[9]

Chamberlain was originally English, but he settled in Germany, and became a naturalized German citizen. Like Wagner, he sought to understand the whole of Western civilization since the Greeks in terms of a racial struggle. The Aryans were the superior race. Only Aryans were capable of creative culture. The Germans were the finest representatives of the Aryan peoples, and best placed to establish a new European order. Chamberlain's argument that Jesus was not Jewish was based on racist principles. He considered the racial settlement of Galilee centuries previously, when it might be thought that Galilee was re-settled with Gentiles after the deportation of Israelites to Assyria. It was in the light of this that, despite confessing that Jesus was Jewish in religion and education, he declared: 'The probability that Christ was no Jew, that he had not a drop of genuinely Jewish blood in his veins, is so great that it is almost equivalent to a certainty.'[10] With that point made, and an Aryan Jesus apparently established, Chamberlain went on to picture Judaism very negatively, in contrast to the religion of Christ. This enabled him to see Christ as totally opposed to Judaism: 'His advent is not the perfecting of the Jewish religion but its negation.'[11]

This book was popular because it satisfied the needs of German people who were conditioned by centuries of Christian anti-Semitism. In the 1930s, the influence of this culture on biblical scholars was extensive.[12] I consider two works as significant examples of the scholarship of the supposedly 'no quest' period, one by the distinguished elderly scholar Paul Fiebig, the other by the up and coming Walter Grundmann, who had a 'distinguished career', both during and after the war.

Fiebig first came to scholarly notice with his 1901 monograph on the use of the term 'Son of man'. His subsequent publications included books on Jewish material relevant to understanding the Sermon on the Mount (1924), and on the Lord's Prayer (1927).[13] In 1935, he delivered three lectures under the title

9 H. S. Chamberlain, *Die Grundlagen des neunzehnten Jahrhunderts* (2 vols. München: Bruckmann, 1899, [29]1944): ET *The Foundations of the Nineteenth Century* (trans. J. Lees, 2 vols. London/New York: Lane/Bodley Head, 1910. Repr. New York: Fertig, 1968).

10 *Foundations*, pp. 211–12: ET from *Grundlagen*, pp. 218–19.

11 *Foundations*, p. 221: ET from *Grundlagen*, p. 227.

12 A history of anti-Semitism in German biblical scholarship has now been provided by A. Gerdmar, *Roots of Theological Anti-Semitism: German Biblical Interpretation and the Jews, from Herder and Semler to Kittel and Bultmann* (SJHC 20. Leiden: Brill, 2009).

13 P. Fiebig, *Der Menschensohn: Jesu Selbstbezeichnung* (Tübingen: J. C.B. Mohr (Paul Siebeck), 1901); *Altjüdische Gleichnisse und die Gleichnisse Jesu* (Tübingen: J. C.B. Mohr (Paul Siebeck), 1904); *Die Gleichnisreden Jesu im Lichte der rabbinischen Gleichnisse des neutestamentlichen Zeitalters* (Tübingen: J. C.B. Mohr (Paul Siebeck), 1912); *Jesu*

Neues Testament und Nationalsozialismus. Drei Üniversitätsvorlesungen über Führerprinzip – Rassenfrage – Kampf, which one might translate *New Testament and National Socialism. Three University Lectures on the Leader Principle – the Racial Question – Struggle*.[14] The preface is programmatic for the whole book: 'The Führer of each Christian is Jesus Christ, the Führer of each German is in the present time Adolf Hitler'.[15] The lectures carry through this comparison, much in favour of both men. For this purpose, it would not do for Jesus to be too Jewish. Fiebig drew a picture of Jesus as opposed to the Judaism of his time, opposed to his family, opposed to scribes and Pharisees, opposed to the chief priests. He was of course able to use real evidence of conflict. His major distortion was to regard Jesus' opponents as Judaism, while Jesus and his disciples were presented as not Judaism. This is the frame of reference, and it is not one required by the primary source material. The Racial Question was the only point at which Fiebig did not quite present the picture that German Christians needed. He admitted that Jesus was of Jewish birth on his mother's side. However, he argued that this did not matter. Jesus was God incarnate, born of a virgin, so God was his real father, and his mother was part of the opposition to him.

The continuing importance of Fiebig's work is that it helps us to see with clarity the nature of the quest of the historical Jesus. There are three main points. First, whereas the quest has had the *formal aim* of *finding* the historical Jesus, it has frequently had the *social function* of *avoiding* him. Fiebig's whole presentation includes the vigorous avoidance of Jesus' Jewishness. The social function of the conventional quest is especially clear in Fiebig's work, precisely *because* it was also his formal aim. Secondly, it is not a question of merely avoiding what is inconvenient. The quest has been carried through by means of a series of cultural circles with the lives of investigators. In avoiding Jesus' Jewishness, Fiebig partly satisfied the need of German Christians to believe in a non-Jewish Jesus. But he went further than that. In propounding an entirely favourable comparison between Jesus and Hitler, he sought to build a bridge between German Christians and the Nazi Party, some of whose members were not favourable to Christianity. In this way, he reinforced a form of German identity well adapted to Germany's cultural and imperialistic needs. In short, his presentation of Jesus in comparison with Hitler formed a massive cultural circle with his (Fiebig's) own life in service to the community to which he belonged. Thirdly, in analysing this situation, we need the traditional distinction between the Jesus of history and the Christ of faith. What Fiebig did was to replace the Jesus of history with the Christ of his faith. This has been a major feature of the quest throughout its history. This is

Bergpredigt. Rabbinische Texte zum Verständnis der Bergpredigt, ins Deutsche übersetzt, in ihren Ursprachen dargeboten und mit Erläuterungen und Lesarten versehen (FRLANT NF 20. Göttingen: Vandenhoeck & Ruprecht, 1924); *Das Vaterunser. Ursprung, Sinn und Bedeutung des christlichen Hauptgebetes* (BFChT 30. Gütersloh: Bertelsmann, 1927).

14   P. Fiebig, *Neues Testament und Nationalsozialismus. Drei Üniversitätsvorlesungen über Führerprinzip – Rassenfrage – Kampf* (Schriften der Deutschen Christen. Dresden: Deutschchristliche Verlag, 1935). There is no ET.

15   Fiebig, *Neues Testament und Nationalsozialismus*, p. 5: 'Der Führer jedes Christen ist Jesus Christus, der Führer jedes Deutschen ist in der Gegenwart Adolf Hitler.'

the more devastating reason why we must suppose that Schweitzer did not end the first quest of the historical Jesus. It continued throughout the immediately succeeding period of history, with the replacement of the Jesus of history with the Christ of German faith.

In describing this situation, I use the term 'cultural circle' in an unusual way to make a point, so some explanation is necessary. The term 'hermeneutical circle', which I used to use, is conventionally used to describe the experience of an interpreter of a text.[16] Interpreters generally approach the detailed study of texts with some kind of pre-understanding of the text and its author(s). This understanding is modified by detailed study of the text. This constant process of interaction between a general understanding of the situation of the text and detailed study of it is what is normally known as a 'hermeneutical circle'. It has however often been observed that this process does not necessarily lead to an understanding of the text closer to that of an original author, nor to an understanding which may be said to be in any reasonable sense more truthful or accurate. It may rather be a process which contains a significant element of distorting the text in the interests of the interpreter's life, whether an interpreter's personal life, or the life of a community to which the interpreter belongs. The point which is of central importance in understanding the quest of the historical Jesus is that this way of distorting the evidence is normal in it. Detailed study of Gospel texts frequently leads people to understand them in accordance with the needs of the community to which they belong. Less frequently, but equally importantly, a need to oppose the beliefs of a community which the interpreter does not belong to, or has left, may be an equally effective form of distortion. The process normally denoted by the term 'hermeneutical circle' is so central to this process of distortion that it seems to me that we need a term to describe it.

Fiebig is a particularly clear example of this process. When the Nazis came to power, he was a distinguished and experienced scholar, well versed in the detailed interpretation of New Testament texts. When he delivered his 1935 lectures, he used the Nazi frame of reference announced in the preface. Into this frame of reference he fitted the interpretation of texts which he had been studying in detail for a lifetime. I therefore use the term 'cultural circle' to refer to this distorting effect of the detailed study of texts. I start with Fiebig and Grundmann, because they are such clear examples of it.

Grundmann joined the Nazi Party on 1 December 1930 (membership no. 382544), and became active in the Deutsche Christen movement.[17] The

---

16   In a discussion of the term 'hermeneutical circle' in a seminar at the University of Nottingham, Prof. A. C. Thiselton argued that this term could be misleading, because it is so different from the positive way in which the term 'hermeneutical circle' is normally used by experts in hermeneutics. The other terms suggested by members of the seminar were however less clear than the above discussion is intended to be. I cannot see that 'hermeneutic of interest' and/ or 'contextual pragmatism' would enable me to better make the main point that important 'results' supposedly obtained by scholarly research are really driven by the lives of scholars in communities which provide the real driving force of their interpretations. I have accordingly used the term 'cultural circle', and I hope that my use of it is sufficiently clear.

17   On Grundmann and his environment in Germany see especially now S. Heschel, *The Aryan*

term 'Deutsche Christen' is difficult to translate into English. A literal translation would be 'German Christian', but the Deutsche Christen movement was more specific than this.[18] It was a deliberate attempt to produce a form of Christianity which maintained a Nazi ideology too. It was well known that some Nazis, including some of the most prominent, were very anti-Christian. Though it was internally motivated by people whose German and Christian identities were intertwined, one of the tasks of the movement was to produce a form of Christianity to which most Nazis would not object. Consequently, it was opposed by those German Christians who formed the 'Confessing Church' in opposition to it. Members of the 'Confessing Church' included three of the most important Christian theologians of the twentieth century, Barth, Bonhoeffer and Bultmann. Grundmann's activities in the Deutsche Christen movement accordingly place him on the Nazi right of Christianity.

Grundmann also served as assistant to the notoriously anti-Semitic Gerhard Kittel from 1930–32, preparing the *Theologisches Wörterbuch zum Neuen Testament*, still the standard *Theological Dictionary of the New Testament* found in theological libraries and used by students all over the world as if it were nothing but a standard work of reference.[19] On 1 April 1934, Grundmann became a supporting member (förderndes Mitglied) of the SS (Membership no. 1032691). In 1936, he became a professor at Jena. He had not written a *Habilitationsschrift*, the standard German qualification for promotion to professor. Hitler nonetheless signed the papers for his appointment, following a recommendation in which the Nazi rector of the university said that the Faculty wanted to become a stronghold of National Socialism, so that Grundmann's scholarship could be path-breaking for a National Socialist perspective in the realm of theology. In 1939, the Deutsche Christen movement opened the Institut zur Erforschung und Beseitigung des jüdischen Einflusses auf das deutsche kirchliche Leben (Institute for the Study and Eradication of Jewish Influence on German Church Life), with Grundmann as its academic director. His address at the opening, on 6 May 1939, was programmatic: 'The Dejudaization of the Religious Life as the Task of German Theology and Church'.[20] This declared that the elimination of Jewish influence on German life was an urgent task, a task vigorously pursued by Grundmann and by other members of the Institute.

Jesus: Christian Theologians and the Bible in Nazi Germany (Princeton: Princeton Univ., 2008). He is one of the scholars discussed by Gerdmar, *Roots of Theological Anti-Semitism*, pp. 531–76. Of the increasing secondary literature in German, the most important I have seen is R. Deines *et al.* (eds), *Walter Grundmann: Ein Neutestamentler im Dritten Reich* (Leipzig: Evangelische Verlagsanstalt, 2007). I am very grateful to Prof. Deines for giving me a copy of this book.

18 See in general D. L. Bergen, *Twisted Cross: The German Christian Movement in the Third Reich* (London/Chapel Hill: Univ. of North Carolina Press, 1996).

19 P. M. Casey, 'Some Anti-Semitic Assumptions in *The Theological Dictionary of the New Testament*', *NovT* 41 (1999), pp. 280–91; on Kittel see especially Gerdmar, *Roots of Theological Anti-Semitism*, pp. 417–530.

20 W. Grundmann, *Die Entjudung des religiösen Lebens als Aufgabe deutscher Theologie und Kirche* (Weimar: Verlag Deutsche Christen, 1939). There is no ET.

There is accordingly no doubt about Grundmann's central life-stance: he was a committed anti-Semitic Nazi. His contributions to falsehood included his 1940 book, *Jesus der Galiläer und das Judentum*. There is no English translation: the title means 'Jesus the Galilaean and Judaism'.[21] Like Chamberlain, Grundmann argued that not only was Jesus completely opposed to the Judaism of his time, he was not Jewish in any sense at all. Like Chamberlain, Grundmann did this by going back into the history of Galilee centuries previously and by using a racist theory of identity. In this way, the possibility that Galilaeans might have been descended ultimately from Gentiles overrode the fact that at least the majority of Galilaeans at the time of Jesus, including Jesus and all his first disciples, were culturally Jewish. When discussing the second century BCE, he commented '*C.150 B.C., therefore, Galilee is literally free of Jews.*'[22] He used the term 'Galilaean' rather than 'Aryan' because it was a respectable scholarly term, and he wished to present the Institute as a place of serious scholarship, not political propaganda.

Thus Grundmann avoided the Jesus of history even more comprehensively than Fiebig had done, and completed an even more effective cultural circle with the society in which he lived. Once more, the Jesus of history was replaced with a quite specific version of the Christ of faith. Once more, this was done by a professional scholar deeply involved in the study of relevant texts. When I first attended New Testament conferences in the early 1980s, some scholars recommended me to use the commentaries of Grundmann on the Gospels of Matthew, Mark and Luke, because of their supposedly excellent *theological* qualities.[23] None of them mentioned his Nazi record, or his Jesus book. What their judgement reflected, however, was that Grundmann spent his whole life in detailed exegesis.

3. Radical Form Criticism

In this light, we may look back from the 1930s to the social function of a major scholarly movement in the preceding years, that of Form Criticism, or *Formgeschichte*, as it was originally known. This movement began in Germany. It has flourished there ever since, and has spread to other countries too. Its major 'result' was to suppose that most of the material in the synoptic Gospels was created by the early church, leaving us with very little information about the historical Jesus.

For example, in his classic 1921 work on the history of the synoptic tradition, Bultmann discussed the narrative of Mk 2.23-28. This is a story of disciples going

---

21   W. Grundmann, *Jesus der Galiläer und das Judentum* (Leipzig: Wigand, 1940, ²1941).
22   Grundmann, *Jesus der Galiläer*, p. 169, 'Um 150 v. Chr. ist also Galiläa vom Juden im eigentlichen Sinne frei' (his emphasis).
23   W. Grundmann, *Das Evangelium nach Matthäus* (ThHNT 1. Berlin: Evangelische Verlagsanstalt, 1968, ⁴1975); *Das Evangelium nach Markus* (ThHNT 2. Berlin: Evangelische Verlagsanstalt, 1959, ⁷1977); *Das Evangelium nach Lukas* (ThHNT 3. Berlin: Evangelische Verlagsanstalt, 1961, ⁸1978). There are no ETs.

through the fields plucking grain on the sabbath. Some Pharisees objected to them doing this, assuming that plucking grain should be regarded as work, which everyone agreed was prohibited on the sabbath (Exod. 20.8-11//Deut. 5.12-15). Jesus defended his disciples with two arguments, which presuppose that poor and hungry people are not to be regarded as working if they pluck grain left for them at the edges of fields. His first argument was by analogy from the behaviour of David, who obtained and ate the shewbread in the Temple and gave it to his companions when they were hungry, an incident which is assumed to have taken place on the sabbath. His second argument was more fundamental, deriving his decision from the intention of God when He created the sabbath for the benefit of people. Underlying Jesus' arguments is the natural assumption that work is ploughing, carpentry and the like. Underlying the question from his opponents is the practice of expanding the biblical regulations as they are applied to the whole of life. This practice was widespread in the Judaism of the time. These points were thus natural in the life of the historical Jesus, and do not meet the needs of the early church.[24]

Bultmann argued that this story was entirely the product of the early church, and gives us no information about the historical Jesus.[25] Bultmann's first point is that Jesus is questioned about his disciples' behaviour rather than his own. Bultmann does not however discuss why the disciples might be going through fields plucking grain, so no reason for the difference between the behaviour of Jesus and that of his disciples could possibly emerge. Bultmann next declares that the church ascribes the justification of her sabbath customs to Jesus, but he does not discuss the absence of all such disputes from Acts and the epistles. Nor does Bultmann discuss whether this kind of legal dispute is typical of early Judaism, which it is, to the point that the historicity of such stories is very probable. Bultmann suggests that the scriptural proof, the use made by Jesus of the story of David, was used apart from its present context in the controversies of the early church, but he does not discuss the absence of any evidence that the early church had such controversies, nor the appropriateness of such an argument in Jesus' Jewish culture. He declares the final argument from man as Lord of the sabbath an originally isolated saying on the ground of the typical connecting formula 'and he said to them': he does not however show that this expression usually does indicate the addition of secondary material, nor does he discuss how natural it is as part of a continuous narrative in Aramaic, the language which Jesus spoke and in which the earliest traditions were transmitted. At no stage does he make any attempt to uncover a coherent argument in the passage.

Moreover, Bultmann's treatment of this passage is typical. Again and again he and other form critics made arbitrary declarations that material uncharacteristic of the early church was created by the early church: again and again they refused to read texts as consecutive wholes: again and again they refused to even examine

---

24   See pp. 321–24.
25   R. K. Bultmann, *Die Geschichte der synoptischen Tradition* (FRLANT 29, NF 12. Göttingen: Vandenhoeck & Ruprecht, 1921), p. 14; ET *The History of the Synoptic Tradition* (trans. J. Marsh. Oxford: Blackwell, 1963), p. 16.

Gospel passages as if they might derive from Jesus within the environment of Second Temple Judaism. Moreover, this process was carried through by scholars who spent their whole lives in detailed study of the texts which they so drastically failed to understand. It is no wonder that more conservative scholars coined the phrase 'form-critical circle', to denote the repeated assumption that a narrative has been created by the early church, when the passage itself is the only evidence that the early church was interested in the matter. What went wrong?

It is at this point that the work of Fiebig and Grundmann is so illuminating, because it enables us to home in on the *social function* of the work of Bultmann and others. The *effect* of their radical criticism was to ensure that out from under the synoptic Gospels there could never crawl a Jewish man. If moreover we can become convinced that we do not know anything much about the Jesus of history, the Christ of faith can continue unhindered. We can see this in Bultmann's 1926 book *Jesus*, translated into English as *Jesus and the Word*.[26] This contains not one single episode in which Jesus is immersed in detailed discussion of the practice of the Law. This is supposed to be for critical reasons. In fact, however, it is the effect of a cultural circle in which Bultmann removed an indelibly Jewish aspect of Jesus, an effect of working in a German environment in which Jewishness was so unwelcome. This was moreover done by means of a process of detailed exegesis, in which Bultmann engaged existentially with the biblical texts throughout his life.

This is well indicated by his vigorous presentation of the Matthaean antitheses (Mt. 5.21-48), the nearest Bultmann gets to detailed discussion of the practice of the Law. In each case, the Matthaean version of Jesus' teaching begins with something on the lines of 'you have heard that it was said', to which Jesus responds with authoritative teaching beginning 'but I say to you'. It is however notorious that most of the content of the Matthaean antitheses is paralleled in Luke, whereas the actual form of the antithesis, with the authoritative 'but I say to you', is unique to Matthew. For example, Mt. 5.31-32 presents Jesus' remarkable prohibition of divorce as follows:

Now it was said, 'Whoever divorces his wife, let him give her a certificate' [cf. Deut. 24.1]. But I say to you that everyone who divorces his wife, except for the reason of her having sex with another man, makes her commit adultery, and whoever marries a divorced woman commits adultery.

The version at Lk. 16.18 is simpler, and typically lacks the Matthaean rhetoric:

Everyone who divorces his wife and marries another woman commits adultery, and he who marries a divorcee commits adultery.

It is therefore most unlikely that the Matthaean antithesis form is original, and it is certainly much less well attested than some of the disputes between Jesus

---

26 R. K. Bultmann, *Jesus* (Berlin: Deutsche Bibliothek, 1926): ET *Jesus and the Word* (trans. L. P. Smith and E. H. Lantero. London: Collins, 1934).

and his opponents over details of the Law. Bultmann concludes that 'Jesus . . . opposes the view that the fulfilment of the law is the fulfilling of the will of God.'[27] That conclusion is clean contrary to the teaching of Jesus. It was however just what German Christians needed from the Christ of their faith, for it bluntly contradicts the centre of Judaism. It was moreover produced by means of detailed exegesis of selected texts. It also illustrates the centrality of anti-Judaism in the work of a distinguished member of the Confessing Church, the opposite wing of the German churches from the Deutsche Christen movement. Bultmann's general cultural environment led him to write Judaism out of the teaching of Jesus, using spurious intellectual arguments which wrote most of Jesus of Nazareth out of history altogether. He was left with the Christ of his faith in the guise of a historical figure about whom little can be known.

4. *Not the Second and Third Quests*

A few years after the Second World War, some attempts were made to restart the quest of the historical Jesus, what is sometimes known as the second quest. It is generally dated from a lecture delivered by Käsemann in 1953, and published in 1954.[28] This was genuinely a new start after the Nazi period, but not the first thing to have happened since Albert Schweitzer. I draw attention to one book, the 1959 work of J. M. Robinson, *A New Quest of the Historical Jesus*.[29] The title of this book recognizes the new start made by Käsemann. In this light, the whole book is devoted to justifying the basic idea of having a quest for the historical Jesus. It moves entirely within a Christian frame of reference, especially one which reflects German concerns. Robinson correctly believed that the French and Anglo-Saxon quests were an untroubled continuation of the nineteenth-century quest. He noted for example Guignebert's *Jésus*, published in 1933, and Vincent Taylor's 1954 book, *The Life and Ministry of Jesus*.[30] Robinson accepted however German concerns that a Jesus of history might become a result of man's striving before God, and therefore illegitimate. Robinson himself argued that the Incarnation, the Gospels and the kerygma demanded that the historical Jesus be taken note of, and that the historical-critical method would be necessary to fulfil this task. What is interesting is that this argument should have been necessary. The profound irony of the standard German concern is that it is so remote from the *social function* of not having a historical quest for the historical Jesus, which remained what it had been for Bultmann, Fiebig, Grundmann and others, avoiding a Jewish man.

By 1987, enough new work had been done for some scholars to feel that

---

27   *Jesus and the Word*, p. 70.
28   E. Käsemann, 'Das Problem des historischen Jesus', *ZThK* 51 (1954), pp. 125–53: ET 'The Problem of the Historical Jesus', in *Essays on New Testament Themes* (trans. W. J. Montague; SBT 41. London: SCM, 1964), pp. 15–47.
29   J. M. Robinson, *A New Quest of the Historical Jesus* (SBT 43. London: SCM, 1959).
30   Guignebert, *Jésus*; V. Taylor, *The Life and Ministry of Jesus* (London: Macmillan, 1954).

another new start to the quest of the historical Jesus had been made, and this was clearly articulated by Tom Wright, in a paper read to a meeting of British New Testament scholars that year. He made three points which seemed plausible to many of us at the time.[31]

1   Standards of proof have risen. Of particular importance at the time was Morna Hooker's demolition of the criterion of dissimilarity in her 1971 paper.[32] This criterion had been in use for many years, but it was not properly labelled and described until the 1960s. When clearly described, it states that anything in the Gospel accounts of the life and teaching of Jesus which is paralleled in Judaism or the early church must be attributed to the church, rather than to Jesus. This produces a quite unique Jesus, who cannot be connected with the Judaism of his time, and who is so remote from the early church as to make it impossible to see how Christianity started. Hooker was therefore right to argue that we should stop using this criterion. The criterion of multiple attestation was of major positive importance. As used at the time, it asserted that anything attested more than once in our oldest sources was likely to be true. For example, there is clear evidence that the controversy over Jesus casting out demons by the power of the devil was featured both in Mark (3.22-30) and in 'Q' (Mt. 12.22-32//Lk. 11.14-23; 12.10). This was taken to be strong evidence that the controversy really took place. Again, multiple attestation by form was important: so when we find exorcisms in narratives, summaries, parabolic sayings and controversy, that was very strong evidence that Jesus performed exorcisms.

2   Wright's second point was that the quest is being carried out by people who have different perspectives. The work of the Jewish scholar Geza Vermes was especially important, and I had been seeking to make some technical contributions from a non-religious perspective. In 1987 we seemed to be part of a welcome trend.

3   Wright's third point was that increased attention has been paid to Jesus' cultural background. This again seemed obvious in many people's work at the time. Two scholars, Geza Vermes and E. P. Sanders, had been conspicuously successful in portraying Jesus as belonging to first-century Judaism, and they continued to do so in subsequent years. I therefore consider briefly the main points of their work.

5. *Vermes and Sanders*

Vermes came in from an overtly Jewish perspective. The great strengths of his work are his complete knowledge and profound understanding of the Jewish

---

31   The following account is based on notes which I made at and shortly after the lecture. Cf. Neill and Wright, *Interpretation of the New Testament*, pp. 379–403.

32   M. D. Hooker, 'Christology and Methodology', *NTS* 17 (1970–71), pp. 480–87.

primary source material, and the sober and judicious manner in which he locates Jesus within the Judaism of first-century Galilee. Noteworthy achievements include an illuminating comparison between Jesus and other Galilaean holy men, or *ḥasīdīm*, devout Jews of a generally unconventional kind about whom miracle stories were told. Vermes discussed particularly Honi the Circle-Drawer, who successfully prayed for rain during a drought, and Ḥanina ben Dosa, who was said to have cured Gamaliel's son at a distance.[33] In discussing them and Jesus, Vermes also made fruitful use of the modern category of 'charismatic'. At a different level, Vermes wrote a seminal paper on the 'Son of man' problem,[34] which is from a technical point of view one of the most difficult problems in New Testament studies. He was able to bring new evidence to bear on this problem because of his thorough knowledge of rabbinical literature and his careful analytical technique. In general Vermes always handles rabbinical literature in a careful and critical way, never taking it for granted that late material must represent Judaism at the time of Jesus. His work on the Dead Sea Scrolls also enabled him to contribute with great methodological skill to discussions of the relative importance of the Scrolls and of rabbinical literature for our understanding of Jesus. He also made significant contributions to particular aspects of the teaching of Jesus, notably the Fatherhood of God. It is only regrettable that Vermes has not written a complete life of Jesus. In spite of this, his contributions have been so extensive and wide-ranging that every scholar trying to contribute to our knowledge of the historical Jesus should benefit from Vermes' work.

Nonetheless, Vermes' work is not without fault, and it is instructive to see what goes wrong when something does. The major difficulty is that Vermes has not been able to give a convincing explanation of why Jesus was crucified. Vermes of course knows the relevant texts very well, having spent his whole life in detailed exegesis of both Jewish and Gospel texts, and he has seen the importance of the Cleansing of the Temple (Mk 11.15-18). But he belongs to the Jewish community, whose members were persecuted for centuries partly on the grounds of deicide, a charge which held them responsible for crucifying Jesus and thereby killing God. This appears to be what has prevented Vermes from understanding the fundamental nature of Jewish opposition to Jesus, and its importance as a cause of the crucifixion. Thus Vermes' own life, and especially his membership of the Jewish community, has caused the same kind of distortion familiar to us from the work of Christian scholars.

A second problem lies in instances where Vermes uses conventional scholarship to discount the historicity of parts of our oldest sources. Like many other scholars, he got into difficulties over Mk 9.1: 'Amen I say to you that there are some of those standing here who will not taste of death until they see the kingdom of God come in power.' This saying predicts the coming of the kingdom of God within a short time. Unable to fit this into the teaching of Jesus, Vermes turned to

---

33 Vermes, *Jesus the Jew*, pp. 69–78.
34 G. Vermes, 'The use of *bar nash/bar nashā* in Jewish Aramaic', app. E in M. Black, *An Aramaic Approach to the Gospels and Acts* (Oxford: OUP, 3rd edn, 1967), pp. 310–28; repr. in G. Vermes, *Post-Biblical Jewish Studies* (Leiden: Brill, 1975), pp. 147–65.

Bultmann for the view that it is a Christian 'community formula of consolation in view of the delay of the Parousia'.[35] Yet the term 'kingdom of God', which is central to this saying, was central to the teaching of Jesus, and this saying does not mention the parousia. Accordingly, the saying fits perfectly into the teaching of Jesus, and it is not expressed in terms appropriate for Bultmann's 'formula of consolation'. Given Bultmann's lack of understanding of Judaism, it is deeply ironical that Vermes should resort to him at times.

As a result of his knowledge of ancient Judaism, as well as his own Jewish identity, Vermes' picture of the Jesus of history is more Jewish than that generally produced by Christian scholars. This led Vermes to launch an entirely proper challenge to orthodox Christian belief. Correctly using the traditional distinction between the Jesus of history and the Christ of faith, Vermes pointed out that the historical Jesus the Jew is not consistent with the deified second person of the Christian Trinity. Christian scholarship has not met this challenge, though it is a scholarly version of a complaint made by persecuted Jews for centuries. This illustrates the domination of a supposedly academic 'field' of 'study' by members of a single religion, who usually set the agenda and determine what is to be commented on.[36]

The other most important contributor to our knowledge of the historical Jesus during the last century was E. P. Sanders. His most significant contribution in scholarly terms was his 1985 book *Jesus and Judaism*, perhaps the most brilliant book on Jesus written so far. In 1993, he also contributed what is arguably the best single-volume life of Jesus so far written, *The Historical Figure of Jesus*. One of the major reasons that Sanders was able to make such an important and wide-ranging contribution to our knowledge of Jesus was his understanding of Second Temple Judaism, expounded at greater length in other books and articles.[37] Christian control of otherwise respectable scholarship in this field has been so extensive that one of Sanders's first tasks was to demolish Christian prejudices about Judaism, a task which he achieved with intellectual brilliance and incisiveness. For example, in his excellent introduction to *Jesus and Judaism*, Sanders repeatedly shows how twentieth-century scholars put forward a view of Judaism which was dependent on their need to regard Judaism as inferior to Christianity, rather than on their understanding of Jewish source material. In particular, Judaism was held to be legalistic, nationalistic and with a remote God, so that Jesus could be portrayed as bringing love, universalism and nearness to God. Among numerous advances at a detailed level, Sanders showed that the common scholarly discussion of Mt. 12.28//Lk. 11.20 was distorted by ideological

---

35 Vermes, *Religion of Jesus the Jew*, p. 141, quoting Bultmann, *History of the Synoptic Tradition*, p. 121.

36 Vermes, *Jesus the Jew*, pp. 15–17, 223–25; Vermes, *Religion of Jesus the Jew*, pp. 208–15. Cf. further G. Vermes, *The Changing Faces of Jesus* (London: Penguin, 2000).

37 Sanders, *Jesus and Judaism*; Sanders, *Historical Figure*; and especially E. P. Sanders, *Paul and Palestinian Judaism* (London: SCM, 1977), pp. 1–428; *Jewish Law from Jesus to the Mishnah: Five Studies* (London/Philadelphia: SCM/Trinity Press International, 1990); *Judaism: Practice and Belief 63 BCE–66 CE* (London/Philadelphia: SCM/Trinity Press International, 1992).

motivation: 'the kingship of God has come upon you' is an important comment on Jesus' exorcisms, but customary Christian moves to 'the *uniqueness of Jesus' self-consciousness or claim*' are not justified by the primary source material.[38] Sanders's extensive demolition of contemporary prejudice is doubly remarkable because Sanders himself came in from a perspective of Christian commitment. In addition to purely scholarly brilliance, therefore, this is one of the most remarkable examples of a critical scholar transcending his ideological background in order to produce, by means of evidence and argument, correct new results.

Sanders's first positive achievement was to direct attention away from sayings of Jesus to the prime importance of facts which can be established beyond reasonable doubt. At the beginning of his excellent outline of Jesus' life for general readers, he listed the following:

- Jesus was born c.4 BCE, near the time of the death of Herod the Great;
- he spent his childhood and early adult years in Nazareth, a Galilaean village;
- he was baptized by John the Baptist;
- he called disciples;
- he taught in the towns, villages and countryside of Galilee (apparently not the cities);
- he preached 'the kingdom of God';
- about the year 30 he went to Jerusalem for Passover;
- he created a disturbance in the Temple area;
- he had a final meal with the disciples;
- he was arrested and interrogated by Jewish authorities, specifically the high priest;
- he was executed on the orders of the Roman prefect, Pontius Pilate.[39]

In retrospect, this may look both obvious and not much. Its importance in 1993, and of the earlier version already in Sanders's 1985 book, was the certainty with which these points can be established. Sanders showed that the main points of Jesus' ministry ought not to be in doubt.

Into this outline Sanders fitted a considerable amount of material in a logically ordered and culturally appropriate manner. Among many good points was his treatment of miracles. Chapter 10 of *The Historical Figure of Jesus* begins with an excellent treatment of the ancient perspective on miracles, which has so often been ignored in modern treatments of them. In particular, Sanders noted that ancient people 'saw miracles as striking and significant, but not as indicating that the miracle-worker was anything other than fully human'.[40] One of the reasons for this was the occurrence of healings which were not understood, to the point that they were taken to be the action of a healer or of the God prayed to. Sanders noted particularly the healings reported by devotees of Asclepius,

38 Sanders, *Jesus and Judaism*, p. 137.
39 Sanders, *Historical Figure*, pp. 10–11; cf. *Jesus and Judaism*, p. 11.
40 Sanders, *Historical Figure*, p. 132.

reports in which possible and impossible healings stand side by side. Accordingly, stories also include 'nature miracles': for example, Honi the circle-drawer, already known to us from Vermes, was held to have successfully prayed for rain, while a prophet called Theudas was followed into the wilderness by many people who evidently believed that the waters of the Jordan would part before him.[41] Finally, Sanders noted that exorcisms and other healings lay within the culture of Second Temple Judaism.

All this enabled Sanders to take a more informed perspective on Jesus' exorcisms and other healings than is usually found. He situated them within Jesus' ministry, as events which were important to him but which were not events of such power and uniqueness that they persuaded most Jews to follow him. This is much the best treatment of these stories that I have seen. Sanders was more puzzled by the so-called 'nature miracles'. He did not have available to him the work of Roger Aus, who has shown that most of them are basically Jewish Haggadah.[42] The difficulty of carrying out such work indicates that we cannot expect to explain the origin of every story when all we have is a story, and no indication of why it might have originally been told.

The good sense which informs Sanders's treatment of miracles pervades all his work. It is reasonable to consider his combination of learning and sanity as a reasonable summary of what has made his work better than that of anyone else so far.

Nonetheless, with Sanders as with everyone else, we have to see what goes wrong when something does. The twofold answer highlights two major faults of scholarship as a whole: resorting to radical criticism when stuck, and inadequate appreciation of Jesus' use of Aramaic. Like Vermes, Sanders cannot quite cope with the conflicts between Jesus and his opponents. When he discusses the dispute between Jesus and the Pharisees over the disciples plucking grain on the sabbath (Mk 2.23-28), he invokes Bultmann, for Bultmann argued that such disputes are so unrealistic that they could not have taken place.[43] We have however seen that Bultmann's discussion of this passage is unsatisfactory because of its arbitrary and dogmatic nature, and we shall see that the passage fits perfectly into Jesus' ministry in first-century Judaism.[44] Moreover, the *social function* of Bultmann's

---

41   Sanders, *Historical Figure*, pp. 135–40.

42   Sanders, *Historical Figure*, pp. 154–57. Cf. R. D. Aus, *Samuel, Saul and Jesus: Three Early Palestinian Jewish Christian Gospel Haggadoth* (Atlanta: Scholars, 1994), ch. 3, esp. pp. 134–57; '*Caught in the Act', Walking on the Sea, and the Release of Barabbas Revisited* (Altanta: Scholars, 1998), pp. 51–133; *The Stilling of the Storm: Studies in Early Palestinian Judaic Traditions* (New York: Binghamton University, 2000), pp. 1–87; *My Name is 'Legion': Palestinian Judaic Traditions in Mark 5.1–20 and Other Gospel Texts* (Lanham: University Press of America, 2003), pp. 1–99; *Feeding the Five Thousand: Studies in the Judaic Background of Mark 6.30–44 par. and John 6.1–15* (Lanham: University Press of America, forthcoming, 2010). I am grateful to Dr Aus for sending me a copy of the ms in advance. See further pp. 341–42, 402, 418 n.22, 447–48, 474–75, 482–84.

43   Sanders, *Jesus and Judaism*, p. 265, invoking Bultmann, *History of the Synoptic Tradition*, p. 39.

44   See pp. 9–10, and pp. 321–24.

discussion was to remove Jesus from a Jewish environment. This is profoundly ironical, because Sanders was coming in from a liberal Christian perspective disturbed by the evidence of Jesus' ferocious conflicts with some of his fellow Jews. The reasons why Sanders could not cope with the evidence of these severe conflicts were accordingly almost the opposite of those which affected Bultmann.

Jesus' opponents also objected to him associating with 'sinners'. Sanders believed that these people were really 'the wicked', because he supposed that behind the Greek word *hamartōloi*, which means 'sinners', there lay the Hebrew *reshā'īm*, which means 'the wicked', or its Aramaic equivalent.[45] This is a standard mistake. The texts about the sinners are difficult. Instead of trying to reconstruct possible Aramaic sources, Sanders altered the meaning of these Greek texts by substituting one different word in Hebrew. In his more learned book, he should have offered complete Aramaic reconstructions, and proper philological discussion of the semantic areas of the relevant Greek, Hebrew and Aramaic words for 'sinner', 'wicked' and the like.

It would be wrong to end this discussion of Sanders on such a note. His great learning and good sense have enabled him to make the most important contribution of all to our understanding of the historical Jesus. If most scholars had worked like Vermes and Sanders, there would be no doubt that the quest of the historical Jesus is a quest to find him, and it would have been a great deal more successful than it has generally been.

6. *Crossan and the American Jesus Seminar*

When Wright read his 1987 paper, the outlook for the quest was very hopeful. Since 1987, however, a lot of unfortunate work has been done. Wright's 1996 history of scholarship in *Jesus and the Victory of God* tries to draw a somewhat wiggly line down the centre of the scholarship of his time, with work that belongs to the third quest on one side, and work of the same period which does not belong to the third quest on the other side. On the wrong side of the line is Crossan's enormous 1991 book *The Historical Jesus*, with its subtitle *The Life of a Mediterranean Jewish Peasant*.[46] Though he regards it as 'a book to treasure for its learning, its thoroughness, its brilliant handling of multiple and complex issues, its amazing inventiveness', Wright feels he has 'to conclude that the book is almost entirely wrong.'[47] This is correct. Crossan presents Jesus as 'a peasant Jewish Cynic'.[48] This is inconsistent with the fact that the Gospels do not mention philosophy, cynics, major cynic philosophers such as Diogenes, nor cynic peculiarities such as living in a barrel. Moreover, there is insufficient evidence

45   Sanders, *Jesus and Judaism*, p. 177.
46   J. D. Crossan, *The Historical Jesus: The Life of a Mediterranean Jewish Peasant* (Edinburgh/San Francisco: T&T Clark/HarperSanFrancisco, 1991).
47   Wright, *Jesus and the Victory*, p. 44; see further pp. 44–65.
48   For what this may mean see especially Crossan, *Historical Jesus*, pp. 421–22.

that cynic philosophy had penetrated Judaism in Israel: Jesus lived in a different culture from cynic philosophers.

Most of the time Crossan works with five primary sources: Mark, 'Q', the rest of Matthew or Luke, John, and the Gospel of Thomas. He does not admit the authenticity of material unless it is independently attested twice. This may look at first sight like a reasonable development of the criterion of multiple attestation, but its effects are quite destructive. If anything is attested by our oldest Gospel, Mark, Crossan will accept it only if it is independently attested. So out goes the whole of Mk 1.16-38, with the call of the first disciples and an early exorcism on the sabbath, as 'a Markan creation'. Yet this passage has many features of authentic tradition. One of the most notable is that people wait until the end of the sabbath before bringing other people to Jesus to be healed (Mk 1.32). This is because they obeyed their natural interpretation of the Law prohibiting the carrying of burdens on the sabbath (Jer. 17.21-22), a point which Mark did not need to mention.[49] If Mark had created this passage after a successful Gentile mission, he would have had to explain it, though he would have had no rationale for making it up in the first place.

Equally, Jesus' teaching that it is difficult for a rich person to enter the kingdom of God (Mk 10.23f.) is accepted only because it turns up also in the Shepherd of Hermas (Sim. 9.20.2b-3). Yet the repetition of only one aspect of this Markan passage in a second-century Christian source is irrelevant to whether Jesus said it. It is more important that it fits into Jesus' teaching, that the disciples' amazement reflects the natural assumptions of more conventional Jews, and that it is not the kind of thing that the early church was interested in. We may therefore be quite sure that the incident really took place.[50] In practice, therefore, good early tradition which fits perfectly into the life and teaching of Jesus is excluded unless later Christian tradition repeats it. Later Christian tradition may however be acceptable, if it is independently repeated. Hence the high proportion of parables and wisdom material accepted by Crossan.

There is also serious distortion of one of the central concepts of the teaching of Jesus, the kingdom of God. On pp. 284–87, Crossan discusses the *apocalyptic* kingdom of God. He gives appropriate quotations from the *Psalms of Solomon*, the *Testament of Moses* and the *Similitudes of Enoch*, all documents written in Israel at about the right time. Such documents provide the cultural background within which Jesus preached the coming of the kingdom. On the following pages, however, Crossan discusses the *sapiential* kingdom of God. His evidence is taken from Philo, the *Wisdom of Solomon* and the *Sentences of Sextus*. All these sources were written outside Israel, and resulted from far too much Greek influence to be helpful in understanding the ministry of Jesus. Under the general notion that Hellenization had penetrated Israel, however, these documents are taken to provide a serious cultural framework for the ministry. Once this has been done, Crossan declares that he will locate Jesus' kingdom as sapiential and peasant. There is no proper discussion of sayings such as Mk 9.1: 'Amen I say to

---

49 Crossan, *Historical Jesus*, pp. 346–47; see further pp. 72, 106, 268.
50 Crossan, *Historical Jesus*, pp. 274–75; see pp. 224, 287, 307.

you that there are some of those standing here who will not taste of death until
they see the kingdom of God come in power.' From Crossan's point of view, a
saying like this is attested only once, since Mt. 16.28 and Lk. 9.27 both resulted
from editing and copying Mk 9.1. Such sayings are therefore not acceptable,
not even if they have an excellent setting in the ministry of Jesus, a doubtful one
in the early church and none at all in later documents like the Gospels of John
and of Thomas.

The overall result of this process has the same social function as most scholarship on the Jesus of history: it reduces his Jewishness. Moreover, the depiction of
Jesus as a cynic forms a cultural circle with Crossan's intellectual environment.
Crossan's work also includes massive evidence of the detailed exegesis of texts.
At this point, moreover, we encounter a change in the nature of some of the
controlling cultural circles consequent upon the development of our massive
academic bureaucracies. A circle may be formed with recent trends which are
found attractive in academia, not only with major ideologies or opposition to
them. There has been a lot of recent work on peasants, some of it very fruitful.
Crossan has read this work. This led him to the extraordinary view that Jesus was
illiterate.[51] Thus his book illustrates the major faults of the quest of the historical
Jesus: its picture of Jesus is dependent on Crossan's own social environment and
consequently, Jesus does not emerge as a plausible first-century Jewish leader.

At this point we must consider the work of the American Jesus Seminar as a
whole. The Seminar was set up by Robert Funk with good intentions. Funk was
distressed by the significant role played in American life by Christian fundamentalism, a version of the Christian faith which he himself had left. Funk set up the
Jesus Seminar to tell the truth about Jesus, and to do so with people who had the
authority of critical scholarship behind them. In 1996 he wrote a book entitled
Honest to Jesus, which correctly reflects his intentions.[52]

The methods adopted by the Seminar were however sufficient to prevent these
aims from being achieved. In the first place, some of the best scholars in the USA,
such as E. P. Sanders, J. A. Fitzmyer and Dale Allison, were not members of it.
The absence of these scholars was compounded by the actual membership, and by
the method of deciding whether material in the Gospels was historically accurate.
A number of 'Fellows' of the Seminar had only recently completed doctorates
at American institutions, and the Seminar decided the authenticity of material
about Jesus by majority vote, averaged out as the 'Fellows' did not agree with
each other. In practice, this meant an averaged majority vote by people who were
not in any reasonable sense authorities at all.

In a published version of some of their results, one version of the coloured
beads with which they voted was given like this:

Red:　　Jesus undoubtedly said this or something very like it.
Pink:　　Jesus probably said something like this.
Gray:　　Jesus did not say this, but the ideas contained in it are close to his
　　　　　own.

51　See further pp. 158–62.
52　R. W. Funk, *Honest to Jesus: Jesus for a New Millennium* (New York: Polebridge, 1996).

Black: Jesus did not say this; it represents the perspective or content of a later or different tradition.

This is from the introduction to a 1993 book appropriately entitled *The Five Gospels*.[53] This is because of the exaggerated importance which they have attributed to the Gospel of Thomas, their addition to the canonical four. Their voting was so bizarre that they ended up with more red in that Gospel than in our oldest genuine source, the Gospel of Mark. Moreover, this is another example of a cultural circle. For all its limited learning, the Jesus Seminar consists of professional academics who spend their whole lives in detailed examination of these primary texts, including detailed exegesis of the Gospel of Thomas. The result of this process is that they have ended up with a figure whom they are happy with. In particular, he is much like a cynic philosopher, which suits their intellectual ambience, and has nothing to do with the apocalyptic and eschatological concerns which characterize American fundamentalism. It is ironically appropriate that the major recent attempt to reinstate Jesus as a millenarian prophet should have been made by Dale Allison, one of the most brilliant scholars who conspicuously did not belong to their group.[54]

7. From Bad to Worse

The effect of the American Jesus Seminar on conservative American Christians has been just as disastrous as the work of Seminar itself. Some of them write books which appear to assume that, if they can demonstrate that the Jesus Seminar is wrong, they thereby demonstrate the absolute truth of Protestant fundamentalism or Catholic orthodoxy, whichever the perspective from which the author is writing. For example, as early as 1995, Wilkins and Moreland edited a collection of essays devoted to refuting radical scholarship, under the title *Jesus under Fire*. The vast majority of its criticisms are fired back at the American Jesus Seminar, and its own life-stance wobbles between conservative and fundamentalist, including feeble defences of the historicity of the Fourth Gospel in general and the Raising of Lazarus (Jn 11.1-45) in particular.[55] Within quite a short space of time, therefore, the effect of the American Jesus Seminar was the opposite of its intentions. On the one hand, it grievously misled anyone who believed what it said. Equally, it did not correct the views of Christians who look at the world

---

53 R. W. Funk, R. W. Hoover and the Jesus Seminar, *The Five Gospels: The Search for the Authentic Words of Jesus* (Sonoma: Scribner, 1993; repr. New York: Macmillan, 1996), p. 36.

54 Dale C. Allison, *Jesus of Nazareth: Millenarian Prophet* (Minneapolis: Fortress, 1998); see also B. D. Ehrman, *Jesus: Apocalyptic Prophet of the New Millennium* (Oxford: OUP, 1999).

55 J. Wilkins and P. Moreland (eds), *Jesus under Fire: Modern Scholarship Reinvents the Historical Jesus* (Grand Rapids: Zondervan, 1995), esp. pp. 38–39, 131.

from inside extreme dogmatic blinkers. It rather encouraged them to imagine that all their dogmatism is right, because they can see with perfect clarity that the Gospel of Thomas is not a major source for the historical Jesus, and Jesus was not an imitation cynic philosopher.

As time has passed, the American debate about Jesus has got worse and worse. For example, in 1999, R. J. Miller launched a defence of the American Jesus Seminar, under the title *The Jesus Seminar and its Critics*.[56] At times, Miller does not seem to realize what a feeble defence he is conducting. For example, he notes that most 'Fellows' of the Seminar 'have the modest publication records typical for college or seminary professors who are full-time teachers' and alleges that 'a few prominent gospel scholars declined to participate in the Seminar because of its democratic organization'.[57] This is one of the weirdest outbursts of democracy that I have encountered. The mediocre quality of the 'Fellows', and the absence of the most able independent critical American scholars from the Seminar, are two major reasons for the poor quality of its work, and no explanation of how this regrettable situation came about suffices to remedy it. Again, Miller declares that 'some scholars who make confident claims about the Gospel of Thomas cannot read Coptic, the language in which the only extant copy of this gospel is preserved.'[58] What Miller does not say is that at least the vast majority of the 'Fellows' cannot read Aramaic, the language which Jesus spoke, and that this is one factor in their rejection of major facets of the life and teaching of the historical Jesus, and in their inability to fit him into his first-century Jewish culture.

Miller does however cast light on the appalling quality of American debates about Jesus. He alleges that a few members 'have been pressured by their institutions to resign from the Seminar', two have been fired and one tried for heresy, apparently because even attending the Seminar is seen as inconsistent with holding a position in a conservative Christian institution.[59] This should be scandalous, provided that it is true. What the current situation requires above all is genuine debate between scholars of different convictions and opinions. The presence of conservative Christian scholars in the seminar should have enhanced its work greatly, provided that everyone was willing to participate in genuinely independent scholarly debate. Miller also quotes opinions about the Seminar's work which go beyond legitimate scholarly criticism into unscholarly polemic. For example, he quotes this criticism from Witherington in 1995: 'Too often scholars . . . assume they know better than the early Christians who preserved and collected the sayings of Jesus and composed the Gospels what Jesus was or was not likely to have said. This assumption is founded on hubris.'[60] Miller is right to see this as rejection of critical scholarship, not just a critique of this Seminar's work.

Witherington, whose PhD qualified him to teach at an independent university, wrote these comments when he taught at Ashland Theological Seminary,

---

56   R. J. Miller, *The Jesus Seminar and its Critics* (Santa Rosa, California: Polebridge, 1999).
57   Miller, *Jesus Seminar*, p. 18.
58   Miller, *Jesus Seminar*, p. 69.
59   Miller, *Jesus Seminar*, pp. 19–20.
60   Miller, *Jesus Seminar*, p. 112, quoting Witherington, *Jesus Quest*, p. 48.

whose 'Core Values' include the belief that the Old and New Testaments are 'God's infallible message for the church and the world', and whose 'Statement of Faith' calls them 'the infallible record of the perfect, final and authoritative revelation of his work and will.'[61] In 1995, he was appointed as 'Amos Professor of New Testament for Doctoral Studies' at Asbury Theological Seminary, whose 'Statement of Faith' describes the Old and New Testaments as 'the only Word of God, without error in all that it affirms . . . the only infallible rule of faith and practice.' Its trappings of scholarship can be seen at the inauguration of Dr Timothy C. Tennent as its eighth President on 9 November 2009, replete with lots of distinguished-looking academic gowns.[62] All these statements illustrate the hollowness of the trappings, because they ensure that independent critical thought is not allowed. Witherington illustrated this especially well in 2009 when he made a malicious and mendacious attack on the Department of Biblical Studies at the University of Sheffield. When the department was threatened with the closure of its undergraduate department, and being turned into a 'research centre', which did not seem likely to work, its students protested, and the university received a massive quantity of letters of support for the department from all over the world. The situation was rapidly reviewed, the department was saved from this drastic damage, and it was promised that new staff would be appointed. Witherington, however, was quoted in *Christianity Today*:

> Other faculty [at Sheffield] were 'bent on the deconstruction of the Bible, and indeed of their students' faith,' according to Ben Witherington, a New Testament scholar at Asbury Theological Seminary.

Apart from its unacademic use of the technical term 'deconstruction', this accusation is false. In the subsequent debate on blogs, Witherington further alleged, 'Sheffield has deliberately avoided hiring people of faith.' This allegation is false too.[63] Unlike American theological seminaries, independent British universities like Sheffield do not discriminate on grounds of religion, any more than race, gender or colour, when making appointments. Independent critical thought is encouraged, whether from a Christian perspective or not.

Witherington thus demonstrated not only that he does not understand independent British universities, but that he does not always tell the truth, the most fundamental requirement of independent critical scholarship. This shows how right Funk was to set up the Jesus Seminar with the intention of telling the truth about Jesus: too many people in American theological seminaries do not do so. This also explains how Miller came to locate the opposition central to the Seminar's concerns. For example, he comments with reference to two of the Seminar's major publications: 'The analysis in *The Five Gospels* and *The Acts of Jesus* is an alternative to the fundamentalism and naive literalism so entrenched in

61   See http://seminary.ashland.edu
62   See http://www.asburyseminary.edu
63   An account of the debate by Stephanie Fisher, with subsequent comments by others, was posted at http://dunedinschool.wordpress.com/ on 12 November 2009.

our society.'[64] This accurately labels two major anti-scholarly faults in American society, faults to be found abundantly in American theological seminaries which offer students the opportunity to be processed in American fundamentalism, and call it 'Christian education'.

In 2005, Kloppenborg edited a collection of essays which originated in a symposium held in 2003, when some members of the American Jesus Seminar debated with outsiders, including two outstanding American scholars, Dale Allison and Paula Fredriksen.[65] Kloppenborg describes their aim as 'not to debate, yet again, whether the historical Jesus ought to be thought of as an apocalypticist of some variety, or to discuss the particular location within Second Temple Judaism that he and his immediate followers occupied. Instead, it was to ask why these issues are seen to matter as topics of intellectual inquiry and matter so acutely.'[66] This puts aside two major faults of the Seminar, and prepares for the essays of Arnal, Kloppenborg and Miller, which seek to reject criticisms of the American Jesus Seminar without sufficient scholarly discussion of the main primary sources and cultural background.

For example, Kloppenborg raises the question of 'the *kind of Jew* that Jesus was', in the context of what the limits of Judaism might be. He comments: 'this issue is seen most acutely in the criticism leveled at Burton Mack and John Dominic Crossan for their characterizations of Jesus as a "Jewish cynic" – criticism that appears often to rest on an unargued, indeed probably unarguable, assertion that "Jewish" and "cynic" are mutually exclusive conceptual categories.'[67] Kloppenborg offers no documentation for his view that this underlies scholarly critiques of Mack and Crossan, nor does he discuss the more obvious points that our primary sources for Second Temple Judaism do not discuss Jewish cynics, and the Gospels do not mention philosophy, cynics or anything of this kind. Arnal suggests that outstanding American scholars such as Chilton, Fredriksen and Sanders conform Jesus to the figure of an 'Eastern European Jew' to distance themselves from anti-Semitism and anti-Judaism in previous scholarship. He objects to 'a Jesus who was circumcised, who had a recognizably Jewish name . . . i.e. Yehoshua or Yeshua . . . If multiple attestation tells us anything, it is that Jesus' name was, in fact, *Jesus*.'[68] This is exactly the sort of rejection of Jesus' Jewishness to which scholars such as Fredriksen and Sanders have properly objected, and Arnal's use of the criterion of multiple attestation is quite bizarre. With arguments of this kind, Arnal's allegation that outstanding scholars have the 'Eastern European Jew' at the centre of their reconstructions of the historical Jesus never appears plausible.

---

64 Miller, *Jesus Seminar*, p. 47, referring to Funk *et al.*, *Five Gospels*, and to R. W. Funk and the Jesus Seminar, *The Acts of Jesus: The Search for the Authentic Deeds of Jesus* (San Francisco: HarperSanFrancisco, 1998).

65 J. S. Kloppenborg with J. S. Marshall (eds), *Apocalypticism, Anti-Semitism and the Historical Jesus: Subtexts in Criticism* (JSNTSup 275. London: T&T Clark, 2005).

66 Kloppenborg, *Apocalypticism*, p. vii.

67 Kloppenborg, *Apocalypticism*, p. 2.

68 W. Arnal, 'The Cipher "Judaism" in Contemporary Historical Jesus Scholarship', in Kloppenborg, *Apocalypticism*, pp. 24–54 (29 with n. 17).

In response, the essays of Fredriksen and Dale Allison restate some basic points. For example, Fredriksen prefers 'to judge the adequacy of our reconstructions of Jesus not by criteria of ethical or theological utility, but by the usual standards by which any historian judges a historical description.' Allison comments on the centre of the lives of our most outstanding critical scholars, 'surely the desire to find the truth of some things of interest really does partly animate some of us.'[69] It is a regrettable comment on the current state of American scholarship that such basic points need restating.

Conservative Christians and fundamentalists have continued to respond vigorously to the work of the American Jesus Seminar. Moreover, they have broadened their target so extensively that there is a danger of serious critical scholarship getting lost to view in a plethora of publicity. There have been two major additional targets. One is the discovery of additional Gospels. The two most notable have been the Gospel of Judas and the Gospel of Mary. These are both Gnostic works written in the second century, and neither of them contains any significant historical information about Jesus, or Judas Iscariot, or Mary Magdalene.[70] Nonetheless, both of them have been given such exaggerated publicity that responsible conservative scholars such as Craig Evans have felt obliged to include discussion of them in books which seek to reassure the faithful that they should not be taken in by what are seen as scholarly attacks on the faith. Indeed, Evans devotes two whole chapters to 'Questionable Texts', one of them entirely devoted to the Gospel of Thomas. Yet the subtitle of his book accurately portrays his main target: '*How Modern Scholars Distort the Gospels*'.[71] It is tragic that he can accurately describe the people at whom he fires as 'modern scholars'. It is tragic that he can describe going to meetings of the Society of Biblical Literature and finding New Testament scholars who 'had only the feeblest ability with Hebrew and Aramaic (if at all). Most knew little of early rabbinic literature and the Aramaic paraphrases of Scripture.' Evans goes on to suggest that this 'helps explain the oddness of much of the work of the Jesus seminar'.[72]

Another major unscholarly feature of recent debate has been a novel by Dan Brown! *The Da Vinci Code* was published in 2003.[73] One of the major characters in it is Sir Leigh Teabing, who declares in an authoritative manner a lot of inaccurate things about the origins of Christianity. For example, Jesus was married

---

69 P. Fredriksen, 'Compassion is to Purity as Fish is to Bicycle and Other Reflections on Constructions of "Judaism" in Current Work on the Historical Jesus', in Kloppenborg, *Apocalypticism*, pp. 55–67 (63); Dale Allison, 'The Problem of Apocalyptic: From Polemic to Apologetics', in Kloppenborg, *Apocalypticism*, pp. 98–110 (109).

70 See further pp. 534–37.

71 E.g. Craig Evans, *Fabricating Jesus: How Modern Scholars Distort the Gospels* (Downers Grove, Illinois, 2006), ch. 3: 'Questionable Texts – Part I: The *Gospel of Thomas*; ch. 4: 'Questionable Texts – Part II: The *Gospel of Peter, the Egerton Gospel, the Gospel of Mary and the Secret Gospel of Mark*, including pp. 92–94, 'The *Gospel of Mary*'; pp. 240–45, app. 2, 'What should we think about the *Gospel of Judas*?'.

72 Evans, *Fabricating Jesus*, p. 12.

73 Dan Brown, *The Da Vinci Code* (London: Bantam, 2003).

to Mary Magdalene and fathered her child, Sarah. More than 80 Gospels were considered for inclusion in the New Testament. All such 'facts' were covered up. Jesus was not considered divine until the Council of Nicaea. By officially endorsing Jesus as the Son of God, the emperor Constantine turned Jesus into a deity. He 'commissioned and financed a new Bible, which omitted those gospels which spoke of Christ's *human* traits and embellished those gospels that made Him godlike. The earlier gospels were outlawed, gathered up, and burned.'[74] All this is from a historical view such nonsense that it is quite amazing that anyone should believe it. The name 'Leigh Teabing' is derived from the names of two of the authors of *The Holy Blood and the Holy Grail*, a supposedly scholarly work from which Dan Brown obtained a significant part of his supposedly factual material.[75] From a scholarly, historical perspective, this work is so discredited that it is only a little less surprising that anyone has believed any of it either. Yet these works have been so influential that a sane and highly respected scholar, Bart Ehrman, must be considered to have performed a service to decent scholarship in 2004 by devoting a whole book to truth and fiction in *The Da Vinci Code*. Others did the same.[76]

With this massive debate bizarrely caused by the publication of a novel, it is only natural that *The Da Vinci Code* is a target in Craig Evans's sights too.[77] When a New Testament professor at Dallas Theological Seminary, together with two of its former students similarly employed, sought to defend their faith in 2006 with the book *Reinventing Jesus*, they used the subtitle *What THE DA VINCI CODE and Other Novel Speculations Don't Tell You.*[78] What is so misleading about this book and others like it is that, in firing almost indiscriminately at this novel, a selection of late inaccurate Gospels, the American Jesus Seminar and a selection of decent critical scholarship, it gives the impression of scholarly respectability when it is in effect a fundamentalist tract. For example, the introduction concludes with the story of Thomas from Jn 20.24-28 as if it were literally true. While differences between the synoptic Gospels and John are noted, the discussion of the significant work of Gerhardsson in defence of

---

74 Brown, *Da Vinci Code* (London: Corgi, 2004), p. 317.

75 M. Baigent, R. Leigh and H. Lincoln, *The Holy Blood and the Holy Grail* (London: Cape, 1982; 2nd edn, Arrow, 1996; 3rd edn, Century, 2005). The American editions seem to have been most influential, beginning with *Holy Blood, Holy Grail* (New York: Delta, 1982).

76 B. D. Ehrman, *Truth and Fiction in The Da Vinci Code: A Historian Reveals What We Really Know about Jesus, Mary Magdalene, and Constantine* (Oxford: OUP, 2004). I have noted also R. Abanes, *The Truth behind the Da Vinci Code* (Eugene: Harvest House, 2004); D. L. Bock, *Breaking the Da Vinci Code* (Nashville: Nelson, 2004); M. Haag and V. Haag, *The Rough Guide to The Da Vinci Code: An Unauthorized Guide to the Book and the Movie* (London: Rough Guides, 2004); C. E. Olson, *The Da Vinci Hoax* (San Francisco: Ignatius Press, 2004); see further nn. 77–78.

77 Evans, *Fabricating Jesus*, esp. pp. 210–13.

78 J. E. Komoszewski, M. J. Sawyer and D. B. Wallace, *Reinventing Jesus; What* The Da Vinci Code *and Other Novel Speculations Don't Tell You* (Grand Rapids: Kregel, 2006); cf. also B. Witherington III, *The Gospel Code: Novel Claims about Jesus, Mary Magdalene and Da Vinci* (Downers Grove: IVP, 2004); M. Green, *The Books the Church Suppressed: Fiction and Truth in* The Da Vinci Code (Oxford/Grand Rapids: Monarch, 2005).

accurate transmission of oral tradition simply assumes that this work may be used in defence of the accuracy of all four canonical Gospels. The defence of the authenticity of Jesus' unusual and probably unique use of 'Amen' at the beginning of some synoptic sayings proceeds as if the authenticity of Johannine sayings which begin 'Amen, amen . . .' is thereby defended too.[79] Yet for more than a century critical scholarship has based historical work primarily on the Gospel of Mark and the so-called 'Q' material because these are our earliest sources, whereas the Gospel of John is a relatively late theological document which contains hardly any accurate historical information that is not already to be found in Matthew, Mark and Luke.

It is accordingly almost to the credit of Craig Blomberg that he did at least write a book in defence of the historicity of the Gospel of John.[80] His main targets are the American Jesus Seminar and my 1996 book, *Is John's Gospel True?*.[81] These are natural enough targets: the American Jesus Seminar because it is so famous/notorious, *Is John's Gospel True?* because it is the only book in which all the main arguments against the historicity of John's Gospel are conveniently laid out. What is more remarkable is the virtual omission of all the most important scholarly lives of Jesus. The works of Bornkamm, Sanders and other critical (Christian!) scholars had been well known for years, and by 2001 Wright's *Jesus and the Victory of God* was also well known, and none of them makes significant use of the Gospel of John.[82] A fair debate should therefore have meant a vigorous attack on them too.

Moreover, Blomberg's arguments are extraordinarily feeble. For example, he seeks to defend the historicity of the uniquely Johannine story of the wedding at Cana in Galilee, in which Jesus is said to have turned water into wine (Jn 2.1-11).[83] In *Is John's Gospel True?*, I put forward a complete and largely conventional argument of cumulative weight against the historicity of this incident. Blomberg begins his response by raising the question of miracles, commenting that 'if one takes the position of Casey (1996: 52) that they are impossible, then further discussion proves fruitless.' But this is not the position which I took. I drew attention to the obvious fact that changing water into wine 'is, in normal circumstances impossible', whereas Jesus does it abundantly, producing no less

---

79 Komoszewski *et al.*, *Reinventing Jesus*, pp. 18, 34–35, citing B. Gerhardsson, *Memory and Manuscript: Oral Tradition and Written Transmission in Rabbinic Judaism and Early Christianity* (trans. E. J. Sharpe. Lund: Gleerup, 1961), as reprinted with *Tradition and Transmission in Early Christianity* (Lund/Copenhagen: Gleerup/Munkgaard, 1964), (Grand Rapids: Eerdmans, rev. edn, 1998), pp. 41–42.

80 C. L. Blomberg, *The Historical Reliability of John's Gospel: Issues and Commentary* (Leicester/ Downers Grove: IVP, 2001).

81 Maurice Casey, *Is John's Gospel True?* (London: Routledge, 1996).

82 G. Bornkamm, *Jesus of Nazareth* (1956, 111977. Trans. I. McLuskey and F. McLuskey with J. M. Robinson. London: Hodder & Stoughton, 1960, 21973); Sanders, *Jesus and Judaism*; Sanders, *Historical Figure*; Wright, *Jesus and the Victory*; J. Gnilka, *Jesus of Nazareth: Message and History* (1993. Trans. S. S. Schatzmann. Peabody: Hendrickson, 1997); J. Becker, *Jesus of Nazareth* (1995. Trans. J. E. Crouch. New York: de Gruyter, 1998).

83 Blomberg, *John's Gospel*, pp. 85–87.

than 120 gallons. I also drew attention to analogous incidents in stories to do with Dionysus, which Blomberg omits, and which he is in not in any danger of believing, because they are not part of his sacred text, a major point about miracles which he leaves out. Moreover, I noted the division of people into 'the Jews' (Jn 2.6) and 'his disciples' even though all Jesus' disciples were Jewish. I attributed this to the Gentile self-identification of the Johannine community in conflict with 'the Jews'. The fact that the chief steward is known only from sources concerned with Gentile weddings rather than Jewish ones also indicates the Gentile origin of the story. I concluded that all my points, taken together, 'form a devastating argument of cumulative weight against the historicity of the story.' Blomberg does not answer most of these points. His positive arguments include the supposed 'historical verisimilitude' of Nathanael coming from Cana at John 21.2, 'so it would be natural for Jesus and his small group of followers to go there (2.1).' But neither Nathanael nor Cana is found in the synoptic Gospels, and 'natural' items are characteristic of fiction and of rewritten history as well as of true stories, so much so that they are often termed 'reality effects'.

Blomberg goes on to defend the historicity of John's version of the Cleansing of the Temple (Jn 2.13-22), which is not miraculous.[84] Jesus really did cause a major incident in the Temple at the end of his ministry, and we shall see from Mark's accurate account (Mk 11.15-17) that this was an important event which led directly and understandably to his death.[85] Matthew and Luke repeated the story with some elaborations and omissions (Mt. 21.12-14; Lk. 21.45-46). John rewrote this story and moved it to the beginning of the ministry as part of his replacement symbolism according to which Christianity has replaced Judaism, symbolism which marked the previous story too. Blomberg's view of scripture is so uncritical that he is still inclined to believe all four versions, and since the Johannine version is at the beginning of the ministry and the synoptic versions at the end, that would leave him following the fundamentalist tradition that Jesus cleansed the Temple twice! *None* of the Gospels says this. Blomberg comments, 'these two accounts do not contradict each other at any point and can be combined to form a plausible, harmonious whole'.[86] This is neither historical criticism nor obedience to God's Word. It is an uncritical tradition which rejects historical research altogether.[87]

Americans do not however have a monopoly of regrettable recent work on Jesus. A recent European example was produced by the Pope.[88] One of its outstanding features is a whole chapter devoted to a defence of the historicity of John, and an exposition of its theology. Its historical arguments are basically circular. For example, the Pope comments on the uniquely Johannine event of a soldier piercing the side of Jesus when he was crucified:

---

84   Blomberg, *John's Gospel*, pp. 87–91.
85   See pp. 411–17.
86   Blomberg, *John's Gospel*, p. 90.
87   See further pp. 511–25, 'The Gospel of John'.
88   J. Ratzinger, Pope Benedict XVI, *Jesus of Nazareth: From the Baptism in the Jordan to the Transfiguration* (trans. A. J. Walker. London: Bloomsbury, 2007).

'and at once there came out blood and water' (Jn 19.34). These weighty words immediately follow: 'He who saw it has borne witness – his testimony is true, and he knows that he tells the truth – that you also may believe' (Jn 19.35). The Gospel traces its origins to an eyewitness, and it is clear that this eyewitness is none other than the disciple who, as we have just been told, was standing under the Cross and was the disciple whom Jesus loved (cf. Jn 19.26).[89]

This argument presupposes its result, for if we do not believe that this Gospel is literally true from beginning to end, we have no reason to believe this claim, and good reasons, which the Pope omits, not to do so. For example, the whole incident is omitted from the synoptics; Jesus' side is omitted from the recognition scene at Lk. 24.39-40, where the risen Christ identifies himself only by his hands and feet; the group standing under the cross is quite impossible and contrary to our oldest source, according to which the disciples fled (Mk 14.50-52); Peter alone made it to the high priest's house where he was in mortal danger (Mk 14.54, 66–72) and female followers watched from a long way off (Mk 15.40-41), the only safe place; and the 'disciple whom Jesus loved' is absent from the synoptic Gospels and from the public ministry in John.

The Pope is however aware that many Christian scholars do not believe in the literal historicity of this Gospel, and regard the 'beloved disciple' as an ideal rather than a historical figure. Contradicting the arguments of the respected Christian scholar Ulrich Wilckens to this effect, he comments:

> If the favorite disciple in the Gospel expressly assumes the function of a witness to the truth of the events he recounts, he is presenting himself as a living person. He intends to vouch for historical events as a witness and he thus claims for himself the status of a historical figure. Otherwise the statements we have examined, which are decisive for the intention and the quality of the entire Gospel, would be emptied of meaning.[90]

This is also circular, for it is only if we believe that this Gospel is literally true that we are dealing with 'the favorite disciple in the Gospel'. Otherwise, we may be dealing with a narratively convenient ideal figure, who is introduced occasionally when the authors needed him, after the public ministry was over. The notion that in such a case the statements referred to 'would be emptied of meaning' is entirely a matter of opinion, since a different meaning could be attributed to them, albeit a meaning not sufficient for the Pope's view of what Christian scripture ought to have said.

The Pope's book has generated a massive amount of discussion, especially in his native Germany.[91] This is due to the fact that it was written by a major

---

89 Benedict, *Jesus of Nazareth*, p. 222.
90 Benedict, *Jesus of Nazareth*, p. 223, referring to U. Wilckens, *Theologie des Neuen Testaments* (Neukirchen-Vluyn: Neukirchener, 2005), vol. I, pt 4, pp. 155–58.
91 For discussion in English see A. Pabst and A. Paddison (eds), *The Pope and Jesus of Nazareth:*

religious leader. If this book had been written by a New Testament scholar, it would have attracted very little attention.

As this book was being written, two more American social subgroups produced, or threatened to produce, further misleading work on Jesus. One is the first life of Jesus to emerge from the Context Group. This is a group of American Catholics, with enough foreign and non-catholic members to describe itself as a 'working group of international scholars committed to the use of the social sciences in biblical interpretation.'[92] A South African member, Pieter Craffert, recently produced *The Life of a Galilean Shaman*.[93]

Craffert begins with a lengthy caricature of critical scholarship. He criticizes its lack of consensus on aims and methods. However, Craffert includes Sanders, who did so much to advance our knowledge of the historical Jesus, together with scholars such as Burton Mack, whose work is almost completely wrong. Accordingly, this lack of consensus is neither surprising nor significant. Craffert declares, 'The basic *assumption*' (my emphasis), 'which functions as programmatic structure for most of historical Jesus research, is that the historical figure was different from the Jesus (or *Christ*) portrayed in the Gospels'.[94] This is not an *assumption* at all. It is a conclusion drawn from a large quantity of research, which the best scholars always assess critically. It should moreover be obvious that the picture of Jesus in the Fourth Gospel is so different from that in the synoptic Gospels that all four cannot be altogether right.

Craffert rejects basic historical research in favour of 'cultural bundubashing'. He says this metaphor is 'taken from off-road driving'.[95] Its crudity correctly represents Craffert's work: he rejects critical scholarship, and bashes it as hard as he can.

Freed from the constraints of critical scholarship, Craffert creates his shamanic figure by means of creative and uncritical use of whichever pieces of evidence suit him. After early work by Jung, and a highly influential book by Eliade, shamanism has been widely discussed by anthropologists, some of whom have used it very broadly.[96] Craffert majors on 'ASC experiences', that is, altered

---

Christ, Scripture and the Church (London: SCM, in association with the Centre of Theology and Philosophy, University of Nottingham, 2009), especially pp. 199–232, R. Deines, 'Can the "Real Jesus" Be Identified with the Historical Jesus? A Review of the Pope's Challenge to Biblical Scholarship and the Ongoing Debate', which gives an account of scholarly reaction to the Pope's book, especially in Germany.

92   http://www.contextgroup.org (I quote from their home page on 11 November 2009).

93   P. F. Craffert, *The Life of a Galilean Shaman: Jesus of Nazareth in Anthropological-Historical Perspective* (Matrix. The Bible in Mediterranean Context, 3. Eugene, Oregon: Cascade, 2008).

94   Craffert, *Life of a Galilean Shaman*, p. 43.

95   Craffert, *Life of a Galilean Shaman*, pp. xvii; 77 with n. 1.

96   I am grateful to Stephanie Fisher for helpful discussions, especially of the earlier work. See M. Eliade, *Shamanism: Archaic Techniques of Ecstasy* (1951. Rev. edn trans. W. R. Trask. New York/London: Bollingen Foundation/Routledge & Kegan Paul, 1964). Helpful introductions to recent work on shamanism are provided by F. Bowie, *The Anthropology of Religion* (Oxford: Blackwell, 1999. 2nd edn, 2006), ch. 7; B. Morris, *Religion and Anthropology: A Critical Introduction* (Cambridge: CUP, 2006), ch. 1.

states of consciousness experiences, which are very important to genuine shamans in their own cultures. Craffert begins with Jesus' baptism, the best place to start, because Jesus really did have a vision, a Jewish experience which fits into the more general category of ASC experiences. Moreover, the spirit drove him into the wilderness, where he was tempted by Satan, and angels ministered to him (Mk 1.12-13). These are all Jewish experiences which may reasonably be interpreted within the more general category of ASC experiences. Almost at once, however, Craffert starts to push the evidence too far. Apart from describing the angels as 'sky messengers', thereby turning a Jewish element into something more congenial to Gentile anthropologists, he suggests that Jesus being 'with the beasts' (Mk 1.13) was 'most likely also the product of a visionary experience . . . rather than an encounter with real desert animals', which goes beyond the evidence of our primary sources.[97]

At this point, Craffert's discussion leaves the ground altogether. Since many shamans are supposed to go on soul flights, or sky journeys, Craffert presents texts in which he supposes that Jesus does the same.[98] He begins with a 'middle-world journey': 'Guided by Satan, Jesus journeyed to the Temple in Jerusalem and to the top of a high mountain (Mt. 4.5, Luke 4.5, 9).'[99] For Craffert, this is also an ASC experience: it is of no concern to him that Mt. 4.3-11a//Lk. 4.3-13 might be a midrash created after the event.

Craffert finds further evidence of Jesus' sky journeys at Jn 3.13, where, according to the shorter text, which Craffert translates, Jesus tells Nicodemus 'No-one has ascended into heaven except the one who descended from heaven, the Son of Man.' This has nothing to do with sky journeys by the earthly Jesus: it refers to his pre-existence in heaven as the eternal Word, followed by his birth, and, as the longer text makes clearer, his ascension after his earthly life. The longer text reads '. . . the Son of Man, who is in heaven', which sets the discourse in the Johannine community long after the earthly life of Jesus, as should be clear from its use of the purely Hellenistic concept of rebirth, and its indirect exposition of the theology of Christian baptism (Jn 3.3-8).

Craffert also declares that 'During his lifetime, members of Jesus's disciple group often experienced ASCs.'[100] For these supposedly frequent events, he has only three pieces of evidence. His second example, following his wondrously anthropological reminder that in some Pygmy groups in the Ituri rain forest in the Democratic Republic of the Congo, all adult men can easily switch into their culturally approved ASCs, is from the Fourth Gospel, where 'Jesus promised Nathanael that he "will see heaven opened and the angels of God ascending and descending upon the Son of Man" (1.51). The casual way in which this is reported suggests that everybody accepted such visionary practices as culturally possible and likely.'[101]

---

97 Craffert, *Life of a Galilean Shaman*, p. 216.
98 Craffert, *Life of a Galilean Shaman*, pp. 217–20.
99 Craffert, *Life of a Galilean Shaman*, p. 219.
100 Craffert, *Life of a Galilean Shaman*, p. 225.
101 Craffert, *Life of a Galilean Shaman*, pp. 225–26.

Everything is wrong with this. The saying, which cannot be reconstructed in satisfactory Aramaic, is part of an extensive passage consisting of creative Johannine rewriting of synoptic tradition in the light of the faith of the Johannine community. Thus, for example, John the Baptist confesses Jesus as 'the Lamb of God who takes away the sin of the world' (Jn 1.29), which the historical John the Baptist did not do.[102] Jesus says of Nathanael, a character absent from the synoptic Gospels, 'Look! truly an Israelite in whom there is no deceit' (Jn 1.47), a striking contrast to Jacob/Israel (Gen. 27.35). Nathanael makes a sound Johannine confession, which is also absent from the synoptic Gospels: 'Rabbi, you are the son of God, you are the king of Israel' (Jn 1.49). Jesus' response is a midrash which uses the story of angels ascending and descending on Jacob's ladder in Gen. 28.12 to avoid all the problems of Mt. 26.64 and similar texts, according to which Jesus predicted that '. . . you will see the Son of man . . . coming on the clouds of heaven', and the like. Jn 1.51 itself has caused a lot of problems to interpreters who have taken it too literally.[103] Much the most probable interpretation was given long ago by Lightfoot: 'the meaning of this important verse is like that of I[14] and I[18]; it is a description of the coming ministry in which His disciples will witness their Lord's unbroken communion with the Father and will themselves partake in it.'[104] Accordingly, Jn 1.51 does not provide evidence for Craffert's assertion that 'members of Jesus's disciple group often experienced ASCs.'[105]

This illustrates Craffert's failure to fit Jesus into some of the main points of the experiences of a 'shamanic figure'. The remainder of the book contains many lamentable examples of pushing Jesus into this category. For example, Craffert suggests that Jesus' 'use of "Amen" to introduce particular sayings', and 'the formula "I say to you" . . . often found in antitheses . . . is the style of someone claiming to talk with a personal authority – a feature typical of shamanic figures . . .'.[106] That Jesus spoke with authority is not to be doubted, but the Matthaean antitheses are due to Matthew's editing, and 'Amen' is obviously Jewish, and more appropriately seen in the tradition of authoritative Jewish prophets than shamanic figures imported from other cultures.

Despite its unique features, this book illustrates the worst features of the quest of the historical Jesus: Craffert's Jesus is not recognizably Jewish, and he fits into Craffert's social subgroup, the Context Group. For example, Pilch has written on 'Altered States of Consciousness in the Synoptics', proposing that 'Jesus clearly fits the social scientific figure of a shaman', and giving Jesus' baptism, and 'Testing' among examples of Jesus' ASC experiences.[107] Elliot has proposed

102 Cf. pp. 173–83, 514–15.

103 For critical discussion, P. M. Casey, *The Solution to the 'Son of Man' Problem* (LNTS 343. London: T&T Clark International, 2007), pp. 277–81.

104 R. H. Lightfoot (ed. C. F. Evans), *St. John's Gospel: A Commentary* (Oxford: Clarendon, 1956), p. 99.

105 Craffert, *Life of a Galilean Shaman*, p. 225.

106 Craffert, *Life of a Galilean Shaman*, p. 344.

107 J. J. Pilch, 'Altered States of Consciousness in the Synoptics', in W. Stegemann, B. J. Malina and G. Theissen (eds), *The Social Setting of Jesus and the Gospels* (Minneapolis: Fortress, 2002), pp. 103–13.

that we should stop using the term 'Jew' for the people of the time of Jesus, and 'eliminate the term "Judaism" altogether'.[108] He also adds a dose of moralizing, as if other scholars use the terms 'Jew' and 'Judaism' because we are ignorant and immoral. This is accordingly the appropriate social subgroup from which Craffert's bizarre discussion might emerge.

The formation of another American social subgroup was recently announced, but when this was written it was not clear that it would go ahead. This was the Jesus Project. Its Chair was R. Joseph Hoffman, and one of his co-chairs was R. M. Price, who does not believe in the existence of the historical Jesus. The question 'Did Jesus exist?' seemed likely to be of central importance to it, though professional scholars generally regard it as having been settled in serious scholarship long ago.[109] Since however the view that Jesus did not exist keeps being promoted, I discuss the main arguments which are still being repeated. I have taken the first ones from Price's book *The Incredible Shrinking Son of Man: How Reliable is the Gospel Tradition?*[110]

Price proposes ludicrously late dates for the Gospels, a major feature of arguments against the historicity of Jesus. For example, he suggests that Mark 13, which predicts the destruction of the Temple, must have been written after the destruction of Jerusalem in 70 CE, on the assumption that apocalypses are *always* written after the events which they are supposed to predict.[111] We shall however see that Mark's predictions are not accurate enough to have been written after the event.[112] Moreover, predicting the destruction of Jerusalem is not what makes Mark 13 rather like an apocalypse: as we shall see, anyone living under Roman rule when Gaius Caligula threatened to set up his statue in the Temple might well have predicted a revolt followed by the destruction of the Temple, an event which had happened in real history before.[113] What makes it more like

---

108 J. H. Elliot, 'Jesus the Israelite Was neither a "Jew" nor a "Christian": On Correcting Misleading Nomenclature', *JSHJ* 5 (2007), pp. 119–54; I quote from p. 153. Cf. further pp. 512–13, 519–23: J. G. Crossley, 'Jesus the Jew since 1967', in H. Moxnes *et al.* (eds), *Jesus beyond Nationalism: Constructing the Historical Jesus in a Period of Cultural Complexity* (London: Equinox, 2009), pp. 119–37; J. G. Crossley, '"Forgive them: for they do not know what they are doing!" Bruce Malina, the Holocaust and a Rotten Core of Anthropological Approaches in New Testament Studies', in E. Pfoh (ed.), *Anthropology and Biblical Studies* (Piscataway, NJ: Gorgias Press, forthcoming 2010). I am grateful to Dr Crossley for advance copies of these essays, and for helpful discussions of these issues.

109 The major monographs were S. J. Case, *The Historicity of Jesus: A Criticism of the Contention that Jesus Never Lived, a Statement of the Evidence for His Existence, an Estimate of His Relation to Christianity* (Chicago: University of Chicago, 1912; 2nd edn, 1928); M. Goguel, *Jesus the Nazarene: Myth or History?* (1925. Trans. F. Stevens. New York: Appleton, 1926. With a new introduction by R. Joseph Hoffmann, Amherst, New York: Prometheus, 2006). It is perhaps more important that the standard treatments of the primary sources, in lives of Jesus and in commentaries, were generally regarded as decisive.

110 R. M. Price, *The Incredible Shrinking Son of Man: How Reliable is the Gospel Tradition?* (Amherst, New York: Prometheus, 2003).

111 Price, *How Reliable?*, p. 32.

112 See p. 69.

113 See pp. 69–71.

apocalyptic is events such as the stars falling from heaven and the Son of man coming on the clouds followed by the gathering of the elect from the four winds (Mk 13.24-27), events which were obviously predicted since they have still not happened. Furthermore, apocalypses were *not* written after *all* the events which they predicted. For example, the book of Daniel was written after the beginning of the persecution of Jewish people led by Antiochus Epiphanes, which is mentioned by means of symbolic predictions (e.g. Dan. 7.8, 19–21; 8.9-14), whereas its predictions of, for example, the kingdom being given to the people of the saints of the Most High for ever (Dan. 7.27) and the resurrection of the dead (Dan. 12.2-3) are genuine predictions, which have still not been fulfilled.[114] Mark's Gospel is not like this. Most of it is an account of the ministry of Jesus, and Mark 13 is a collection of genuine predictions.

Price's supporting arguments are also very weak. For example, Price discusses Mk 9.1: 'Amen I say to you that there are some of those standing here who will not taste of death until they see the kingdom of God come in power.' Price says that 'all interpreters admit this prediction must have the Parousia in mind (the apocalyptic coming of the Son of man at the end of the age) . . .' *All* interpreters have not adopted this incorrect exegesis,[115] for the very good reason that this saying mentions the kingdom of God, an important feature of the teaching of Jesus, whereas belief in the parousia was created by the early church after Jesus' death.[116] Price then interprets Mark's placing of the Transfiguration next in his narrative (Mk 9.2-8) to mean that he really wrote after the death of *all* Jesus' original disciples, which is contrary to the content of the saying. Supposing that John the Apostle died at the end of the first century, which he sees reflected at Jn 21.20-23, Price therefore dates the Gospel of Mark in the second century. Then he suggests that we should perhaps date it even later on the ground that it reflects the destruction of Jerusalem after the Bar Kochba revolt in 132 CE, citing an article by Detering, a named Fellow of the Jesus Project.[117]

Like Price, Detering presupposes that Mark 13 cannot contain any predictions of historical events in Jewish and Roman history, not even inaccurate predictions. For example, he objects to the correct dating of Mark 13 at about the time of emperor Gaius Caligula's threat to have a statue of himself set up in the Temple, on the ground that 'the actual erection of this desolating sacrilege . . . was never carried out.'[118] Indeed it was not, but this is because Mk 13.14 was a prediction which was not fulfilled as expected, not because it was a prophecy after the event. Unlike Price and many American scholars, however, Detering noticed that Mark 13 does not fit the destruction of Jerusalem in 70 CE very well. This is his

---

114 Cf. pp. 216–18.

115 Cf. e.g. M. D. Hooker, *The Gospel According to St Mark* (BNTC. London: A&C Black, 1991), p. 212.

116 See pp. 212–16, 374–77, 384, 389, 484, and on this saying, pp. 219–21.

117 Price, *How Reliable?*, pp. 32–33, referring to H. Detering, 'The Synoptic Apocalypse (Mark 13 par): A Document from the Time of Bar Kochba', *Journal of Higher Criticism* 7 (2000), pp. 161–200.

118 Detering, 'Synoptic Apocalypse', p. 181.

main argument for dating it after the emperor Hadrian set up a statue of himself in the Temple of Jupiter Capitolinus, which he built to replace the Temple in Jerusalem, which he rebuilt as Aelia Capitolina. Detering sees this as the reason for the 'prediction' of the Abomination of Desolation (Mt. 24.15//Mk 13.14).[119] One of the main reasons why he is wrong is that all his arguments depend on the same assumption, that none of Mark's predictions could be genuine predictions. The other reason is that, like Price, he omits all the positive arguments for an earlier date.[120]

The point of these unconvincingly late dates is to allow Price to argue that the Gospels are fictional, which, on the face of it, may seem more plausible the later they are dated.

One of the most important arguments in favour of the historicity of parts of the synoptic Gospels is that they contain a number of things which the early church would never have wanted to invent. One is the baptism of Jesus by John the Baptist, which might seem to make Jesus inferior to John, and which was a historical event of profound importance, when Jesus had a vision which was the equivalent of the call visions of the prophets.[121] Price suggests that John may not have been a historical figure at all, citing from the German philosopher Arthur Drews a century ago the extraordinary view that John (Greek *Iōannes*) was a historicized version of the ancient pagan fish God *Oannes*.[122] This arbitrary plucking of a dissimilar event from a pagan myth is another characteristic of arguments against the historicity of Jesus.

Another obvious objection is that there is a brief account of John's historical ministry and death in the Jewish historian Josephus (*Ant.* XVIII, 116–19). Price therefore finds spurious grounds for regarding this as a late interpolation into Josephus.[123] Price invents a mythical 'Christian (or Baptist) who was trying to correct Mark by interpreting what he said about a "baptism for the forgiveness of sins" in a nonsacramental direction.'[124] But Mark actually reported that John was preaching 'baptism *of repentance for* forgiveness of sins' (Mk 1.4//Lk. 3.3), when Jewish people believed that God invariably forgave repentant sinners. Mark also reports that people were baptized by John in the Jordan 'confessing their sins' (Mk 1.5//Mt. 3.6). This is perfectly correct, as we shall see, and means that John's baptism *symbolized repentance*, and that it was people's *repentance* which enabled God to forgive their sins.[125] This is not 'sacramental', as Christian baptism became. Moreover, writing this passage *into Josephus* to correct *Mark* is too bizarre and improbable a procedure for it to be plausible to suppose that this is

---

119 Detering, 'Synoptic Apocalypse', pp. 186–209.
120 For these arguments see pp. 65–74.
121 See pp. 176–77.
122 Price, *How Reliable?*, p. 102, with p. 128 n. 2, citing A. Drews, *The Christ Myth* (trans. C. Leslie Burns. Amherst, New York: Prometheus, 1998, pp. 120–22). This was originally a 1910 translation by C. DeLisle Burns (London: Unwin, 1910) of the third edition of a book published in German in 1909.
123 Price, *How Reliable?*, pp. 103–4.
124 Price, *How Reliable?*, p. 103.
125 See pp. 173–76.

a reason for an 'interpolation' into Josephus. It is however entirely reasonable to suppose that the Jewish author Josephus had heard of Christians being baptized 'in the name of Jesus for the forgiveness of your sins' (Acts 2.38), and perhaps even being 'baptised into Christ Jesus' (Rom. 6.3). He therefore made sure that John's baptism was interpreted within its original Jewish frame of reference, as Mark had done in a slightly different way.

Price further suggests that there is a 'redactional seam, a telltale sign of a copyist stitching in new material'.[126] His only reason for this is that the opening of Josephus' account says that the destruction of Herod Antipas' army in 36 CE by the Nabatean king Aretas was interpreted by some Jews as God's punishment of Herod for putting John to death, and Josephus repeats this at the end of the passage, before passing to his account of Vitellius' abortive preparations for a Roman attack on Aretas and his successful visit to Jerusalem with Herod Antipas. Price's conjecture is no more than arbitrary invention, caused by what Price does not wish to believe. Josephus' passage makes perfect sense as all his own work, and the passage about John fits perfectly where it is. It does not mention Jesus, and it is in no way particularly Christian.

Ancient texts should not be tampered with like this, and the removal of inconvenient evidence in this way is another significant characteristic of attempts to show that the historical Jesus did not exist.

Price proceeds to make fun of Jesus' vision when he was baptized by John. During this vision, Jesus heard a heavenly voice saying 'You are my beloved son, in you I am well pleased' (Mk 1.11). Price claims that this speech was put together from scriptural texts, and that 'The fictive character of this brief speech is evident from its scribal nature.'[127] Price supports this by chopping this short speech into very small pieces. His first piece is 'You are my son', which he derives from Ps. 2.7, 'You (are) my son', which is at least similar, though it does not have the word 'beloved', and what it does have in common is too short for this derivation to be obvious or necessary. Price says that the 'second scripture fragment' is Isa. 42.1. Here, however, for 'in you I am well pleased' (Mk 1.11) he reads 'whom' rather than the much better attested 'you' and he quotes the end of Isa. 42.1 as 'in whom my soul delights'. But he has added 'in whom' to the text of Isa. 42.1 from translations, citing the Greek translation at Mt. 12.18, so he has made a small part of Mk 1.11 more like Isa. 42.1 than it originally was, whereas 'in you I am well pleased' (Mk 1.11) is not sufficiently like 'my soul delights' (Isa. 42.1) for the derivation to be plausible. Price's third fragment is 'beloved son' from the (Greek) Septuagint description of Isaac as 'your beloved son' by an angel of the Lord addressing Abraham at Gen. 22.12, *as well as* from 'behold two chosen ones' in unspecified (Aramaic) Targums. This is a mistranslation from a massive Targumic insertion first found in Targum Neof I at Gen. 22.10, which includes a heavenly voice (*bath qōl*) saying of Abraham and Isaac, 'come see two unique ones [*yḥīdhīīn*]'. This cannot be earlier than the third century CE, is probably much later, and has many parallels in very late Jewish sources, so

126 Price, *How Reliable?*, p. 103.
127 Price, *How Reliable?*, p. 120.

it cannot possibly have been known to Mark. Price has simply depended on a discussion by Stegner, who cites the Targums in English in an associative manner without properly learned references or sufficient discussion of the dates of the traditions in them.[128]

Assuming *all* these scriptural derivations, Price declares Mark's heavenly voice 'not historical, unless one wishes to imagine God sitting with his Hebrew Psalter, Greek Septuagint, and Aramaic Targum open in front of him, deciding what to crib. Only then does it come to seem ridiculous.'[129] But it is Price who has manipulated it to make it seem ridiculous. The whole speech makes perfect sense as part of the vision of a first-century prophet. Imagining that one word comes from the Septuagint is, in Price's hands, simply destructive: 'beloved' is a perfectly reasonable translation of the Aramaic *ḥabbîbh*. It is difficult to avoid the impression that Price is caricaturing scholars who see Mark's use of scripture both where they should and where they should not, whether they believe this comes from God, or reflects the use of scripture by Mark in a more learned manner than he was capable of. It is symptomatic of Price's lack of learning that he cites Stegner, without noting that he sought to describe the work of Mark rather than God, instead of interacting with a learned scholar such as Marcus, who made a genuinely learned case for Mark putting together different texts, which is in no way ridiculous.[130]

Finally, leaving aside Price's destructive claim that one word comes from the Septuagint, there would be nothing wrong in supposing that a first-century Jew, as soaked in the scriptures as Jesus, would have a vision in which a heavenly voice spoke in scriptural terms. Visions were much commoner among normal people in their culture than in ours.[131] Heavenly voices are often reported in them, as for example in Peter's vision at Acts 10.13, 15, and Paul's vision at Acts 9.5-6; 22.7-8; 26.14-15. All that is needed for a heavenly voice to speak in scriptural terms, amalgamating different texts, is for the person experiencing the vision to be as soaked in the scriptures as Jesus was. What Price has done is to remove from history part of a fundamental human experience which he holds in contempt.

Price finally suggests parallels to Jesus' baptism and temptations in a variety of mythical figures. He suggests that the most important is the story of Zoroaster, who waded into a river to obtain water for the *haoma* ceremony, and returning to the riverbank after immersing himself, beheld in a vision the archangel Vohu Mana.[132] This is not the same as being baptized, Jesus did not see an angel in his baptismal vision, and Zoroaster was not tempted until later, when the evil

128 Price, *How Reliable?*, p. 130 n. 39, cites only W. R. Stegner, 'The Baptism of Jesus: A Story Modeled on the Binding of Isaac', in H. Shanks (ed.), *Abraham and Family: New Insights into the Patriarchal Narratives* (Washington: Biblical Archaeology Society, 2001). It is at pp. 57–66, reprinted from *Bible Review* 1 (1985), pp. 36–46.

129 Price, *How Reliable?*, pp. 120–21.

130 Cf. J. Marcus, *The Way of the Lord: Christological Exegesis of the Old Testament in the Gospel of Mark* (Edinburgh: T&T Clark, 1992), pp. 48–79, with massive and properly learned bibliography. I find it unconvincing, largely for the reasons given above.

131 Cf. pp. 488–90.

132 Price, *How Reliable?*, p. 125.

Ahriman sought to avert him from this mission. This imaginative use of pagan traditions which are not much like the Jewish traditions in our Gospels to posit them as the origins of Gospel stories is very widespread among opponents of the existence of Jesus, and should be regarded as completely unconvincing.

Another major argument concerns what is not said in the Pauline epistles. For example, Wells, the main recent British proponent of the view that Jesus did not exist, declares that the extent of Paul's silence is 'truly staggering'. His epistles 'mention neither John the Baptist . . . nor Judas, nor Peter's denial of his master . . . They give no indication of the time or place of Jesus' earthly exist-ence. They never refer to his trial before a Roman official, nor to Jerusalem as the place of his execution.'[133] All this means is that Paul wrote epistles about the problems which he found in his (largely Gentile) churches in the Graeco-Roman world, not an account of the life of Jesus, which the epistles take for granted. Consequently, they mention only a few main points, mostly when there was some point of controversy. For example, in writing to the Corinthians, Paul mentions Jesus' crucifixion at the centre of the Gospel: 'Christ crucified, a scandal to Jews, foolishness to Gentiles, but to those who are called, Jews and Greeks, Christ power of God and wisdom of God' (1 Cor. 1.23-24). Again, in dealing with the controversial issue of divorce, Paul quotes Jesus' prohibition of divorce as absolutely authoritative, distinguishing it from his own recommendations about the new situation of believers married to unbelievers (1 Cor. 7.10-16). That the churches would invent the points listed by Wells would be 'truly staggering', as would their absence from the Gospels. Their absence from the epistles is nothing more remarkable than a definition of what kind of documents they are.

In *The Jesus the Jews Never Knew* (2003), Zindler, an atheist who is not a qualified New Testament scholar but who is nonetheless another Fellow of the Jesus Project, contributed further destructive arguments which are remote from the environment of Jesus and the first Christians.[134] In a subsequent lecture to the Jesus Project, Zindler, who was a scientist, claimed that 'we should be as scientific as possible in our inquiry into the historicity of Jesus of Nazareth.'[135] With this as his excuse, he does not employ *historical* methods, but uses the requirements of proof proper to the natural sciences as a cloak for rejecting everything which, as a committed atheist as biased as a Christian fundamentalist, he does not wish to believe. A good example is the caricature with which his book opens.

> We can be quite certain that the miracle-working Jesus described in the New Testament never existed. Even if we disregard the fact that from a scientific point of view his magic-mongering can be ruled out *a priori*, if he really had 'cleansed' all those lepers, given sight to the congenitally blind, catered

---

133   G. A. Wells, 'The Historicity of Jesus', in R. Joseph Hoffmann and G. A. Larue (eds), *Jesus in History and Myth* (Amherst, New York: Prometheus, 1986), pp. 27–45 (31).

134   F. R. Zindler, *The Jesus the Jews Never Knew: Sepher Toldoth Jeshu and the Quest of the Historical Jesus in Jewish Sources* (Cranford, NJ: American Atheist Press, 2003).

135   F. R. Zindler, 'Prolegomenon to a Science of Christian Origins', delivered to the Jesus Project on 6 December 2008, p. 1.

a large mob with a bit of fish bait and pigeon snacks, restored locomotion to the halt and the lame . . . at least *someone* would have recorded it at the time . . .[136]

Everything is wrong with this tendentious description. First, 'magic-mongering' is an inaccurate, hostile and unscientific description of Jesus, who is not recorded in the New Testament to have done any magic. What Zindler has really done is to rule out *a priori* from the historical Jesus anything which any of his followers regard as miraculous. Secondly, Zindler's summary lumps together real events in the life of Jesus with secondary developments in an unscholarly way which appears to presuppose that his target is American fundamentalism rather than critical scholarship. For example, there is every reason to believe that Jesus cleansed or healed the man with a skin disease at Mk 1.40-45, a narrative translated from an Aramaic source, an aspect of the evidence which Zindler always omits because he is not learned enough to see it.[137] The historical truth of Mk 1.40-45 is in no way affected by the improbability of the story of the instantaneous healing of ten lepers in Luke alone (Lk. 17.12-19), as Zindler's comments seem to presuppose. Again, there is every reason to believe that Jesus healed a blind man from Bethsaida who had previously been able to see (Mk 8.22-26, also based on an Aramaic source), whereas the Johannine story of his healing a man blind from birth (Jn 9.1-7) has been at least written up secondarily.[138] Many Christian scholars have cast doubt on the historicity of the story of the feeding of the 5,000 (Mk 6.30-44), but Zindler never refers to such work, and there is no excuse for his uncomprehending description of this piece of midrash Haggadah as 'catered a large mob with a bit of fish bait and pigeon snacks'. His comment 'restored locomotion to the halt and the lame' is equally uncomprehending. There is every reason to believe most of Mark's story of the healing of a paralytic (Mk 2.1-12), but not, for example, Matthew's insertion of an extra piece into Mark's account of the Cleansing of the Temple, beginning with Jesus healing blind and lame people in the Temple (Mt. 21.14-16).[139]

Finally, several people did record events from Jesus' ministry at the time and not much later. We shall see that there were several Aramaic sources underlying parts of Mark and the 'Q' material and some pieces found in Matthew or Luke only.[140] I first wrote this up for some pieces of Mark in 1998, and I cannot be regarded as a Christian apologist since I left the Christian faith in 1962. I suggested that the Jewish nature of the material implied an early date for these sources, perhaps c.40 CE.[141] Zindler omits all work of this kind. His contemptuous summary of aspects of Jesus' supposed miracles also underlines his omission of scholars such as Sanders and Vermes.

---

136 Zindler, *Jesus the Jews Never Knew*, p. 1.
137 See pp. 266–68.
138 See pp. 270, 240–41, 521.
139 See pp. 256–62, 241.
140 See pp. 74–76, 82–92, 96–97.
141 Casey, *Aramaic Sources of Mark's Gospel*.

In his lecture to the American Jesus Project, Zindler further claimed that his book 'showed that the ancient Jews had never heard of "Jesus of Nazareth".'[142] This claim, which is a major feature of his book, is contrary to fact. Zindler appears to have assumed, without discussion, that no Christians can have been Jews. The most important Jews who proclaimed the Gospel centred on Jesus were Matthew the Evangelist and St Paul. Paul describes himself as 'circumcised on the eighth day, of the people of Israel, of the tribe of Benjamin, a Hebrew of the Hebrews, according to the Law a Pharisee, according to zeal persecuting the church, according to the righteousness in the Law become blameless' (Phil. 3.5-6). This is a perfectly intelligible description of Paul by Paul himself, and one which later Christians would have no reason to make up. Moreover, we have seen that while Paul did not have reason to cite the life and teaching of Jesus very often in epistles written to deal with problems in (mostly Gentile) churches, major points such as Jesus' crucifixion were extremely important to him, and he evidently regarded Jesus' teaching as authoritative.

Inferring the Jewish identity of the Gospel attributed to Matthew is more complicated, but a complete argument of cumulative weight should not leave any doubt. The major arguments were fully discussed by Davies and Allison in 1988.[143] The main point is that, although Matthew's Gospel is a Christian work which vigorously approves of the Gentile mission (Mt. 28.16-20), it clearly argues that Christianity ought to remain within the bounds of Judaism. For example, in the programmatic opening to the Sermon on the Mount, Matthew has Jesus say, 'So whoever sets on one side one of the least of these commandments and teaches people thus, shall be called least in the kingdom of Heaven, but whoever does and teaches (them), he shall be called great in the kingdom of Heaven' (Mt. 5.19). It follows that Gentile Christians who do not take on the observance of the Law will still be saved, but that this position is not to be approved of. That is intelligible only in a Christian who lives within Judaism. Furthermore, a number of Matthew's comments show a profound understanding of Jewish observance of the Law. For example, when he edited Mark's prediction of the destruction of the Temple, Matthew added the instruction to pray that the flight of 'those in Judaea' (Mt. 24.16) might not happen 'on a Sabbath' (Mt. 24.20). This shows great concern for, and understanding of, the observance of Jewish Law. There should therefore be no doubt that Matthew was Jewish, an ancient Jew who had not merely heard of Jesus, but who went to massive trouble to revise the First Gospel with masses of additional material, because he regarded Jesus as such an important historical figure.[144]

Zindler omitted all those Jews who wrote in Greek and whose work was so prized by Christians in general that they later included them in the New Testament. That is not a scholarly procedure. Nor does Zindler offer any satisfactory

---

142 Zindler, 'Prolegomenon to a Science of Christian Origins', p. 3.
143 W. D. Davies and Dale C. Allison, *A Critical and Exegetical Commentary on the Gospel According to Saint Matthew* (ICC. 3 vols. Edinburgh, T&T Clark, 1988–97), vol. 1, pp. 7–58.
144 See further pp. 86–93.

discussion of later Jewish believers in Jesus: on the contrary, he deliberately excludes evidence of Jews who knew a lot about Jesus on the ground that they were Christians.[145]

Zindler sets up quite unrealistic expectations as to what non-Christian Jewish sources would have said if Jesus did exist. For example, he concludes, quite correctly, that Jesus is not mentioned in the Mishnah, a major codification of Jewish Law written down c.200 CE.[146] Why should a major codification of Jewish Law mention the centre of what was by then a largely Gentile religion of Christians who rejected Judaism? Zindler proceeds to discuss late Jewish sources which are as maliciously critical of Christianity as he is. This is also because of the split between Judaism and Christianity, on account of which surviving late non-Christian Jewish sources are full of unrealistic falsehood.[147]

Zindler excludes large quantities of evidence from primary sources of different kinds by means of arbitrary hypotheses of interpolations. For example, he alleges numerous Christian interpolations into Josephus.[148] These include the whole of his short passage about Jesus (*Ant.* XVIII, 63–64), the passage about John the Baptist (*Ant.* XVIII, 116–19), and the passage about the death of Jesus' brother Jacob (*Ant.* XX, 200).[149] Zindler's criteria are uniformly unsatisfactory, with no adequate literary or historical reasons. He has a massive diatribe against Christian forgery, for which he uses many genuinely inaccurate statements which are however found in phenomenally late sources (as well as a forged passage which he wrongfully attributes to Augustine so that he can accuse him of an astonishingly stupid lie).[150] He uses this to cast doubt on the authenticity of these brief and relatively early reports, only one of which, the one about Jesus, shows any sign of the text being tampered with. For example, the passage about Jesus' brother Jacob says entirely reasonably that the high priest Ananus, a son of Annas, whose son-in-law Joseph Caiaphas handed Jesus over to Pilate, convened a Sanhedrin which accused 'the brother of Jesus who is called Christ, Jacob by name, and some others' of transgressing the Law, and had them stoned, which led to protests by Jewish people, all of whom can hardly not have known anything about Jesus. Because of this, King Agrippa dismissed Ananus from the high priesthood (*Ant.* XX, 200–3). Zindler uses comments on this passage by the *Christian* writer Photius in the *ninth century* CE, in which Photius naturally referred to Jacob as 'the brother of the Lord' as some Christians from Paul (Gal. 1.19, cf. 1 Cor. 9.5) onwards had done for centuries (e.g. Eus. *H.E.* II, 1, 2; Epiph. *Pan.* 29.3.8; Jer. *De Vir. Ill.* II; Hipp.Th. frg. I, 6), not least because

---

145 Cf. Zindler, *Jesus the Jews Never Knew*, pp. 329–43; and for proper scholarly discussion of Jewish Christians in and outside the New Testament, O. Skarsaune and R. Hvalvik (eds), *Jewish Believers in Jesus: The Early Centuries* (Hendrickson: Peabody, Massachusetts, 2007).

146 Zindler, *Jesus the Jews Never Knew*, p. 136.

147 Cf. especially W. Horbury, *Jews and Christians in Contact and Controversy* (Edinburgh: T&T Clark, 1998); P. Schäfer, *Jesus in the Talmud* (Princeton: Princeton Univ., 2007).

148 Zindler, *Jesus the Jews Never Knew*, pp. 75–102.

149 On Josephus, including his brief report about Jesus see pp. 120–21.

150 Zindler, *Jesus the Jews Never Knew*, p. 34.

the Pauline occurrence became canonical. Zindler simply assumes that Photius must therefore have read 'the brother of the Lord' *in his text of the Jewish author Josephus*, which was accordingly interpolated by a Christian![151] This shows a total lack of historical sense.

Zindler even finds interpolations in the Gospel of Mark, as part of his attempt to remove evidence of John the Baptist from the earliest Gospel. He begins with Mk 8.27-28, part of a passage which is largely secondary.[152] It records the views of people in response to Jesus' (surely secondary) question, 'Whom do men say that I am?' The first response is 'John the Baptist'. Zindler correctly treats this confusion between the two most important prophets of the time as a 'snippet of gossip', but nonetheless regards it as *absolutely reliable* evidence that 'John the Baptist could not have been a contemporary of Jesus', even though all the evidence indicates that they were contemporaries. He assumes it means that Jesus was 'thought of as the reincarnation of John the Baptist'.[153] He seems oblivious to the fact that reincarnation was not a Jewish idea. We should rather suppose that Mark's report reflects gossipy confusion among people who knew neither Jesus nor John.

Zindler then seeks to remove Mk 1.2-14a as an interpolation, but his arguments amount to little more than pouring scorn on the text. He removes Mk 1.14a, oddly translated 'Now after that John was put in prison', rather than 'And after John was arrested', on two grounds. First, he describes it as 'the jarring beginning of verse 14', because he finds it 'hard to believe that "Mark" could have assumed his readers would already know the tale of the imprisonment and execution of the Baptist'. This misinterprets the circumstances in which Mark's Gospel was written. It was the first Gospel *written in Greek for Christian churches*, many of whose members had heard lots of the story before, and who might well know of John the Baptist's arrest and execution. It would be read aloud at Christian meetings by someone who knew the story better than most people, and who would explain anything like this which the less knowledgeable members of the audience did not know, an unavoidable feature of some church meetings. Moreover, it was already known in the ancient period that Mark's Gospel was not written down in order, which indeed it was not.[154]

Zindler then objects that at Mk 1.9, 'Jesus came from Nazareth in Galilee', and at Mk 1.14, 'Jesus came into Galilee'. He claims that this 'has forced apologists to draw the implausible inference that "the wilderness" in which Jesus contested with Satan was not in Galilee.'[155] This is completely misleading. John the Baptist conducted his ministry much further south, in a general area correctly described by Matthew as 'in the desert of Judaea' (Mt. 3.1). This is how it came about that people from Judaea and Jerusalem went out to be baptized by him in the Jordan (Mk 1.5//Mt. 3.5-6). Just the other side of the Jordan was Antipas'

---

151 Zindler, *Jesus the Jews Never Knew*, pp. 50, 80.
152 Cf. pp. 188–89, 395.
153 Zindler, *Jesus the Jews Never Knew*, p. 89.
154 See pp. 66–69.
155 Zindler, *Jesus the Jews Never Knew*, pp. 90–91.

territory of Peraea, dangerously near Nabataea, the territory of Aretas, father of Herod's wife, whom Herod divorced, thereby causing a war. John will have been arrested in Peraea, before he was executed in the fortress of Machaerus (Jos. *A.J.* XVIII, 119), further south in Peraea. This is how it came about that Jesus went to be baptized by him where he was baptizing, miles south in Judaea, with the result that his experience of being tempted by Satan was not in Galilee at all.[156] Zindler has again dismissed 'apologists' without noting the work of decent critical scholars.

Zindler further claims that Jesus coming from Judaea 'only heightens the incongruity: Why doesn't the Greek text say that Jesus "came *back* into Galilee?"'[157] This is because Mark wrote the First Gospel by piecing together different traditions, and the tradition of Mk 1.14-15 is not likely to have come from the same source as Mk 1.7-13. It refers to the extraordinary fact that after John's arrest, Jesus went into Herod Antipas' territory in Galilee and preached openly, when he might have laid low or even fled. This is a completely different event from Jesus' baptism by John. For all we can tell, this important tradition may have been etched in Mark's memory from repeated oral retellings, rather than in a written source. Zindler does not say which word Mark might have used for 'came back'. This matters because Mark uses 'come' (*erchomai*) no less than 86 times, and hardly uses any of the possible words for 'come back'.[158] Mark's Greek makes perfect sense for anyone who appreciates normal Hellenistic Greek or Aramaic (a written Aramaic source might have said '*thā*', which would have made perfect sense, as Mark's text does). Zindler has simply invented his criticism on the basis of his English, instead of studying Mark's Greek or the possible effects of Aramaic sources. His work does not show any proper understanding of Greek or Aramaic.

Zindler also claims that various places where Jesus conducted his ministry did not exist at the time. We shall see that archaeological evidence for the main places in the ministry is perfectly adequate.[159]

Finally, people who deny Jesus' existence leave most of the main points out, and in that sense the whole of this book is required to refute them, not just this section. In Chapter 2, I establish the relatively early dates of the Gospels of Mark and Matthew, in Chapter 3 I discuss methodology, and the whole of the rest of this book puts the historical story of Jesus firmly in Israel in the early first century CE. Nothing less is required to do so, together with all the other scholarship which undergirds it and which I cannot repeat in a single volume. This is all genuine critical scholarship, whereas Price, Zindler and others seem to be firing at fundamentalist Christians without any proper awareness of what critical scholars have achieved.

---

156 See further pp. 173–81.
157 Zindler, *Jesus the Jews Never Knew*, p. 91.
158 He uses *anachōr(e)ō* once, but meaning 'withdrew' (3.7); *epistrephō* four times, but only once meaning 'go back' (13.16); and does not use *anakomizō* (in the passive), *epanerchomai*, *komizō* (in the passive) or *hupostrephō*.
159 See pp. 128–32, 164–67.

Meanwhile, conservative work continues to pour off the press. Paul Barnett, the former Anglican Bishop of North Sydney, now a Visiting Fellow at Macquarie University and still teaching at Moor College in Sydney and Regent College in Vancouver, argues in *Finding the Historical Christ* (2009) that the Jesus of history *was* the Christ of Christian faith.[160] He defends the historicity of John as the most conservative Christians do. For example, after commending Blomberg, he suggests the term 'chief-steward' at Jn 2.9 and the raising of Lazarus as authentic-sounding details in favour of the historicity of this document.[161] Yet the term 'chief-steward' is otherwise known only at Gentile weddings, and the story of the raising of Lazarus is full of specifically Johannine theology, the absence of which from the synoptic Gospels cannot be explained if it is attributed to the historical Jesus. Moreover, Lazarus is never mentioned in the synoptic Gospels, whereas in the Fourth Gospel Jesus' amazing miracle is the trigger of the passion, replacing in this respect the Cleansing of the Temple. Barnett does not offer proper critical discussion of such points, but relies on the uncritical discussion of Blomberg.

On the basis of a selective discussion of the authoritative use of sayings of Jesus in the epistles, Barnett announces that 'the leaders in early Christianity did not invent sayings of the Lord.'[162] This makes it impossible to explain the origin of synoptic sayings about Jesus' second coming, and Johannine discourses.[163] Barnett further announces, with especial reference to the gospel writers, they '*did not omit any saying of the Lord*'.[164] This is not consistent with the omission of most synoptic sayings from the Fourth Gospel, and since Barnett believes in the historicity of the Fourth Gospel, it is not consistent with the omission of the Johannine discourses from the synoptic Gospels either. Nor is it consistent with the omission of Markan sayings by Matthew and Luke: for example both omit from the story of the plucking of the grain – 'The sabbath was made for man, and not man for the sabbath' (Mk 2.27). Moreover, the Gospels are too short for us to suppose that the Gospel writers did not omit any sayings of Jesus.

On this uncritical basis, Barnett offers some discussion of the criteria of authenticity. The most remarkable is the 'criterion of inclusion'. This 'points to the likelihood of authenticity based on the simple reality that a saying included in the canonical gospel is more likely than not to be authentic.'[165] If adopted, this would render all other criteria irrelevant. It is not a historical criterion at all. Barnett's whole presentation is the outworking of his commitment to a particular conservative view of Christian tradition, not a genuinely historical presentation.

---

160 P. Barnett, *Finding the Historical Christ* (Grand Rapids: Eerdmans, 2009).
161 Barnett, *Historical Christ*, pp. 156–57, 161. On Blomberg and on Jn 2.1-11, cf. pp. 27–28, and on the raising of Lazarus pp. 513–14.
162 Barnett, *Historical Christ*, p. 211.
163 Cf. pp. 374–77, 383–87, 389, 511–25.
164 Barnett, *Historical Christ*, p. 214.
165 Barnett, *Historical Christ*, p. 223, with n. 12 citing N. T. Wright, *Jesus and the People of God* (London: SPCK, 1992), pp. 104–7 as if Wright supports what Barnett says, which he does not. Wright does not discuss the 'criterion of inclusion', which I do not remember from anywhere else. Nor does he believe in the historicity of the Fourth Gospel.

This section illustrates the unsatisfactory state of public debate about Jesus. It is remarkable that, with the exception of Dan Brown, everyone whom I have discussed is regarded by a significant number of relatively well educated people as a serious professional scholar. This is no guarantee of adequate qualifications, learning or good sense.

I turn finally to recent attempts to write a life of Jesus. I begin with the Bishop of Durham, who belongs to the wonderful line of scholar bishops who have recently occupied this see, a welcome change from the Norman barons who were the first Prince Bishops of Durham!

8. *Recent Lives of Jesus*

Together with the work of Vermes and Sanders, Tom Wright's 1996 book *Jesus and the Victory of God*, written before he occupied the see of Durham, must rate as one of the best books on Jesus so far.[166] It is distinguished by a lengthy history of scholarship. Despite its regrettable classification of the quest into three stages with a huge gap, Wright's history of scholarship contains many useful analytical comments. His demolition of recent American books on Jesus, including the Jesus Seminar, Mack and Crossan, is especially careful and effective. On the positive side, he gives a clear discussion of method, and especially how Jesus is to be related to the Judaism of his time. The substantive discussion takes seriously the categories of the primary source material, with lengthy discussion of Jesus as prophet, and it engages with the variety of material which is related to the kingdom of God, including the function of judgement. The discussion includes major events, in particular a whole section attempting to explain why Jesus was crucified. The discussion of sayings of Jesus does not isolate one or two single sayings as central but attempts to take an overall view of the synoptic tradition. The result is a logically coherent presentation of Jesus as the Messiah of Israel.

Nonetheless, there are serious problems with this book. One is the misunderstanding of apocalyptic and eschatological language as metaphor. This is done without satisfactory discussion of the nature of metaphor. For example, an important saying is Mk 9.1, which we have already seen dismissed by Crossan, causing trouble for Vermes, and misinterpreted by Price: 'Amen I say to you that there are some of those standing here who will not taste of death until they see the kingdom of God come in power.' Wright first reduces this to a 'clear promise of future victory and vindication', then expands it to such things as 'return from exile' and 'rebuilding of the Temple'.[167] This replaces what the text says with something more congenial. The most notorious feature of this saying is that it indicates that the kingdom of God would come very soon, and this did not happen. This is a natural mistake by a first-century Jew, but any mistake at all by Jesus is inconsistent with orthodox Christian Christology. The driving force

---

166 On Vermes and Sanders see pp. 13–18; Wright, *Jesus and the Victory*.
167 Wright, *Jesus and the Victory*, p. 470.

of Wright's interpretation is a cultural circle with which the mistaken Jesus of history is replaced by the infallible Christ of faith. But there is a second feature of equal importance in understanding why Wright holds a view which entails so much alteration of the text, and that is the bureaucratization of academia. Wright is repeating the view of his teacher G. B. Caird.[168] He has not taken seriously criticisms of Caird from outside Oxford, nor has he made sufficient use of modern linguistics.

Another unsatisfactory aspect of Wright's attitude to language is the conventional fault of not discussing genuine sayings of Jesus in Aramaic, the language which Jesus spoke. As so often, this is most regrettable with the term 'Son of man', because genuine uses are virtually untranslatable, with the result that examples of this expression shift significantly in meaning when attempts are made to translate them into Greek, English, German or the like.[169] Wright declares the expression 'notoriously ambiguous, even cryptic',[170] without any attempt to reconstruct an Aramaic sentence and explain what is ambiguous or cryptic about it, and without answering the classic point that the synoptic tradition does not show any signs of difficulty in understanding this expression. He suggests that those with ears to hear would understand this term in Mk 2.28 in the light of its Danielic context. I published a reconstruction of Mk 2.23-28 in 1988, with full critical discussion.[171] Wright should have explained how this could have been intended to call up a particular Danielic context, or offered an alternative reconstruction which does. Here again, we have dependence both on a cultural circle which pushes this expression as far as possible in the direction of being a Christological title found in Scripture, and on an academic habit. Scholars in several fields, Translation Studies above all, have noticed what a massive difference is made to our understanding of written texts by the language in which they are transmitted. New Testament scholars have however traditionally ignored this in their detailed examination of sayings of Jesus in Greek, and Wright has ignored it too.

A third problem is the interpretation of Gospel texts in the light of later Christian understanding of them. For example, it is important that John the Baptist offered a baptism of repentance in a culture where God was believed to forgive the sins of people who repented, thereby leading a renewal movement within Judaism which caused many people to accept him as a prophet. Wright describes this not unreasonably as 'water-baptism for the forgiveness of sins', but paraphrases its significance as 'you can have, here and now, what you could normally get through the Temple cult', and further declares that John 'presented a clear alternative to the Temple'.[172] This is *not* supported by the primary source

---

168 Cf. G. B. Caird, *The Language and Imagery of the Bible* (London: Duckworth, 1980), pp. 244–71.

169 See pp. 358–88.

170 Wright, *Jesus and the Victory*, p. 394.

171 P. M. Casey, 'Culture and Historicity: The Plucking of the Grain (Mark 2.23-28)', *NTS* 34 (1988), pp. 1–23. See now Casey, *Aramaic Sources of Mark's Gospel*, ch. 4.

172 Wright, *Jesus and the Victory*, pp. 160–61.

material. It may however be congenial to people within the Christian tradition, for whom it is very important that they have forgiveness of sins, who think of the Temple cult as obsolete, and Christianity as superseding Judaism.

It follows that despite Wright's learned and genuine attempt to set Jesus in his original cultural context, he cannot be said to have altogether succeeded in this task.

The next significant attempt to write a life of Jesus was Bruce Chilton, *Rabbi Jesus: An Intimate Biography*.[173] Chilton is one of the best qualified people in the world to write a life of Jesus. While he comes in from a Christian perspective himself, he is fully familiar with the Judaism of the time of Jesus, and he reads all the ancient sources in their original languages, including Aramaic. Consequently, this book contains a lot of accurate information about the Judaism of Jesus' time. This begins on the first page with the importance of his circumcision on the eighth day of his life, and the Aramaic language spoken by him because it was the normal language of Jews in Israel at the time. This positive aspect of Chilton's work continues throughout his book.

Chilton has however endeavoured to write what he calls a 'narrative', and this involves him in conjectural episodes some of which are more like a historical novel than a work of scholarship. Some conjectures are reasonable. For example, Chilton follows a handful of scholars in supposing that Jesus was born at Bethlehem in Galilee. We shall see that the stories of Jesus' birth at the traditional site of Bethlehem in Judaea are not literally true. They might have been sparked off by his birth at a place called Bethlehem not far from Nazareth, modified by searching the scriptures and finding Mic. 5.2-4. As the book goes on, however, Chilton's conjectures and narrative become more and more unlikely. He presents the so-called 'hidden years' as years during which Jesus rejected his family and lived apart from them. There is no evidence of this, and it can hardly be considered probable. By the time he gets to the mysterious man with the water pot who helped with the arrangements for Jesus' final meal (Mk 14.13), we find ourselves in the presence of Barnabas, supposedly Jesus' close associate for years. He was a wealthy man, in whose crowded house the last of many 'Eucharistic' meals before Passover took place.[174] By this stage, Chilton is writing a mixture of fact and fiction.

Another important life of Jesus is that of J. D. G. Dunn, *Jesus Remembered*.[175] The first part, 'Faith and the Historical Jesus', is effectively a history of the quest of the historical Jesus, together with extensive discussion of the philosophical and hermeneutical problems involved. This discussion contains much correct information, and some reasonable opinions. Dunn is especially good at seeing the cultural presuppositions of recent work by scholars such as Crossan, Funk and

173 Bruce Chilton, *Rabbi Jesus: An Intimate Biography: The Jewish Life and Teachings That Inspired Christianity* (New York: Doubleday, 2000).
174 Chilton, *Rabbi Jesus*, pp. 32–43, 71–73, 250–56.
175 J. D. G. Dunn, *Christianity in the Making*. Vol. 1. *Jesus Remembered* (Grand Rapids: Eerdmans, 2003).

the American Jesus Seminar.[176] It is however regrettable that, despite questioning the description of recent work as a third quest, Dunn describes the 40 years after the outbreak of the First World War as a 'hiatus' or 'diversion' in life of Jesus research, and discusses very little work done during that period, apart from a section on Bultmann and Form Criticism. He declares that the period was dominated by Barth and Bultmann, and omits scholars such as Fiebig and the very influential Nazi scholar Walter Grundmann, while a stray remark shows some awareness of what he did not discuss.[177]

Part II, 'From the Gospels to Jesus', discusses the main source material, with many remarks on appropriate methodology. Dunn follows the conventional view that the Gospel of Mark is our oldest and most reliable surviving written source, and what he calls a 'very large consensus of contemporary scholarship' in dating it 65–75 CE.[178] This obscures serious disagreements between scholars who date it before or after the fall of Jerusalem (in effect 65 *or* 75 CE), and Dunn offers no discussion of the reasons conventionally given for each of these different positions. He regards 'Q' as a Greek document, but he contemplates a wide variety of possible dates.[179] This entails a long period of transmission for the Gospel of Mark, and possibly for 'Q'.

In what is effectively the centre of this book, Dunn argues that the Jesus traditions were transmitted orally.[180] The case for such widespread orality is not however adequately made. For his theoretical orientation, Dunn seeks to apply to the Gospels the work of his fellow evangelical Ken Bailey on oral traditions in the modern Middle East.[181] Bailey's work among Arab Christians is a very limited study of a different culture at a different time, and therefore could not be determinative for understanding first-century Judaism, even if it were independently verified. When Weeden pointed this out, together with some evidence that oral traditions are not necessarily accurate even among modern Arab Christians, Dunn responded with scholarship no better than that of Bailey.[182] For example, he comments that 'the social habits and modes of passing on tradition in Middle Eastern villages I suspect have differed very little over the centuries', and asks 'Are personal experiences stretching over several decades to be dismissed simply because they are recorded with an anecdotal casualness that the scientific mind abhors?'[183] What sort of scholarship is that supposed to be? It is no excuse for

---

176   Dunn, *Jesus Remembered*, esp. pp. 58–65.

177   Dunn, *Jesus Remembered*, esp. pp. 85–86, 52, 298; cf. pp. 4–9.

178   Dunn, *Jesus Remembered*, p. 146.

179   Dunn, *Jesus Remembered*, p. 159.

180   Dunn, *Jesus Remembered*, pp. 192–254.

181   K. E. Bailey, 'Informal Controlled Oral Tradition and the Synoptic Gospels', *Asia Journal of Theology* 5 (1991), pp. 34–54; repr. *Themelios* 20 (1995), pp. 4–11; K. E. Bailey, 'Middle Eastern Oral Tradition and the Synoptic Gospels', *ExpT* 106 (1995), pp. 363–67.

182   J. D. G. Dunn, 'Kenneth Bailey's Theory of Oral Tradition: Critiquing Theodore Weeden's Critique', *JSHJ* 7 (2009), pp. 44–62, responding to T. J. Weeden, 'Kenneth Bailey's Theory of Oral Tradition: A Theory Contested by Its Evidence', *JSHJ* 7 (2009), pp. 3–43.

183   Dunn, 'Kenneth Bailey's Theory', pp. 46, 48.

following the unverified conjectures of an evangelical amateur who has taught modern Arab Christians, and applying them to first-century Jews.

From a practical perspective, Dunn's presentation of the Gospel evidence does not always support his view. For example, in his discussion of 'Jesus' last supper with his disciples', Dunn declares that in his A tradition (Mt. 26.26-29 and Mk 14.22-25) Jesus blesses 'the bread'. He does not however discuss what an Aramaic tradition might have said, so he does not consider the possibility that in Mark's source Jesus might have blessed God. He has the variation from his B tradition (Lk. 22.17-20 and 1 Cor. 11.23-26) 'most obviously' explained 'in terms of two slightly variant liturgical practices', for it would be 'somewhat farcical to assume that this tradition was known to the various writers only as written tradition'. But this rhetoric of obviousness demonstrates nothing, and Dunn does not answer arguments for supposing that Mark's account of the Last Supper is a translation of a *written* Aramaic source, and that Paul deliberately *rewrote* the tradition in order to control the riotous behaviour of Corinthian Christians at common meals, in parts of what are obviously *written documents*.[184]

This means that Dunn's book is seriously defective in its attempt to show that the oral transmission of Jesus tradition was as widespread as Dunn thinks, and the immediate source of our *written* documents. At the same time, however, when Dunn sketches 'the likely process of traditioning', he offers reasonable conjectures which might help to explain how *some* of the Jesus traditions were transmitted orally.[185] For example, he discusses Mt. 22.1-14 and Lk. 14.15-24, stories which have central common elements including a man inviting to a feast guests who did not come, but major differences such as whether he was a king, whether it was a wedding feast and what if anything happened to the absent guests.[186] These stories may well have emerged from repeated oral retelling.

The rest of the book works methodically through Jesus' mission, his 'self-understanding', and the climax of the story in his death and Resurrection. Here Dunn seeks to build up a picture of Jesus as remembered from orally transmitted traditions about him. Apart from his conviction that the traditions were all orally transmitted, Dunn's discussions of some points are very good. For example, he provides an excellent discussion of the place of faith in God in Jesus' ministry.[187] This makes all the main points accurately, including the interpretation of key Greek, Hebrew and Aramaic words, transliterated into English letters so that the discussion should be comprehensible to the general reader. He also provides a fine discussion of Table Fellowship, which makes the most important points with clarity.[188] Sections such as these, together with many parts of the opening section, make this book a genuine contribution to knowledge.

---

184 Dunn, *Jesus Remembered*, pp. 229–30, conspicuously not answering Casey, *Aramaic Sources of Mark's Gospel*, ch. 4; cf. pp. 429–38.
185 Dunn, *Jesus Remembered*, pp. 238–54.
186 Dunn, *Jesus Remembered*, pp. 234–36.
187 Dunn, *Jesus Remembered*, pp. 500–3.
188 Dunn, *Jesus Remembered*, pp. 599–605.

Other sections are problematic. For example, the section on Messiahship is out of date.[189] Dunn formulates the questions in terms of royal Messiahship, and does not offer adequate discussion of the Hebrew *(ham)mashīaḥ* or the Aramaic *mᵉshīḥ(ā)*, both of which mean 'anointed' as well as 'Messiah', and are consequently used of the high priest and of other figures. Dunn is inclined to vote in favour of the historicity of Peter's confession 'You are the Messiah' (cf. Mk 8.31), and the high priest's question, 'Are you the Messiah, the son of the blessed' (cf. Mk 14.61), both of which are difficult partly because of the range of meaning of the Aramaic *mᵉshīḥ(ā)*, which cannot function as a title in this simple way.[190] The section on 'Son of man' is also problematic. Dunn declares that Jesus used the term 'the Son of Man' of himself, and he further supposes that the 'articular form' may be rendered 'that son of man'. There is however no independent article in Aramaic, and Dunn offers no proper discussion of the definite and indefinite states, which are often thought to be equivalent to the presence and absence of the English definite article, nor of the Aramaic *bar* *(ᵉ)nāsh(ā)*. This is serious, because the Aramaic *bar* *(ᵉ)nāsh(ā)* cannot function as a title.[191]

Given that both these sections are concerned with the maintenance of traditional Christian interpretations of Christological titles, we must suspect the influence of a cultural circle formed with Dunn's Christian life, and this is made certain by this book's extraordinary conclusion.

> In short, *through the Jesus tradition the would-be disciple still hears and encounters Jesus* as he talked and debated, shared table-fellowship and healed. In hearing the Jesus tradition read from pulpit or stage, in sacred space or neighbour's sitting-room, we sit with the earliest disciple and church groups as they shared memories of Jesus . . . Through that tradition it is still possible for anyone to encounter the Jesus from whom Christianity stems, the remembered Jesus.[192]

This is culturally inaccurate. The earliest disciple groups were Jewish, and modern Christian groups are almost entirely Gentile. The passage of almost 2,000 years has involved other major cultural changes. Consequently, 'the would-be disciple' never encounters a first-century Jewish prophet and teacher. Dunn has concluded by replacing the Jesus of history with the Christ of faith, who is encountered in church and evangelical Bible study sessions in neighbours' sitting rooms.

Another important life of Jesus is that of Hengel and Schwemer, which I discuss briefly because it is not at present available in English, and it is heavily immersed in German rather than English-language secondary literature.[193] This is regrettable, because it is very learned and contains a lot of correct and relevant

---

189 Dunn, *Jesus Remembered*, pp. 617–55.
190 See pp. 392–99.
191 Dunn, *Jesus Remembered*, pp. 739, 741 n. 151, 759; see further pp. 358–88.
192 Dunn, *Jesus Remembered*, p. 893.
193 M. Hengel and A. M. Schwemer, *Jesus und das Judentum* (Geschichte des frühen Christentums, Band I. Tübingen: Mohr Siebeck, 2007).

information. This is especially true of the opening section on Judaism at the time of Jesus. The section on the sources has a very strong argument, based mostly on the Pauline epistles, for supposing that early Christian preaching would have required a lot of information about Jesus. They have a properly chaotic model of the 'Q' material, with an appreciation of the importance of the witness of Papias that the apostle and tax-collector Matthew wrote down Jesus traditions in Aramaic.[194]

After an appropriate section on John the Baptist, Hengel and Schwemer work through all the most important aspects of the ministry of Jesus. Some of this discussion is excellent. For example, they have a clear understanding of the kingship of God being seen as both present and future.[195]

Despite the great learning shown in many excellent discussions, this book suffers from two serious problems characteristic of the quest as a whole. One is its religious enthusiasm, shown especially in their discussion of Jesus' unparalleled *Messianic authority* (the best I can do to translate the quintessentially German '*messianischen Vollmacht*').[196] Their discussion of this is seriously out of date, especially in their view of recent discussion, so that the work of Martin Karrer is dismissed as if it were no better than the old view of German scholars such as Wrede and Bultmann that Jesus' ministry was 'non-messianic'.[197] Secondly, they do not make proper use of the Aramaic level of the tradition, and this is conspicuous, as so often, in their treatment of the term 'son of man'. They offer a quite inadequate discussion of the Aramaic term *bar* (*ᵉ*)*nāsh*(*ā*), and rely heavily on the discussion of their German colleague Colpe, which was outstanding when it was written in 1969, but is now out of date.[198] They do not discuss the work of the Jewish scholar Vermes, nor the work of Lindars and myself, all of whom write in English.[199]

In short, the work of Hengel and Schwemer has all the virtues and faults of the best of existing scholarship. On the one hand, it is a genuine attempt to recover the historical Jesus in his original Jewish environment, and much of the time it does so with great learning. On the other hand, it is biased by the cultural environment of the authors, and even their great learning lets them down at points where this really matters to them.

The potentially most important life of Jesus has been thought to be J. P. Meier, *A Marginal Jew*, in four large volumes so far.[200] The first volume is mostly

---

194 On the 'Q' material see pp. 78–86, and on Papias, pp. 86–89.

195 Hengel and Schwemer, *Jesus und das Judentum*, pp. 406–11. See further pp. 212–26.

196 E.g. Hengel and Schwemer, *Jesus und das Judentum*, p. 502, arguing that the difference between Jesus and his contemporaries 'wird vielmehr gerade *in der besonderen Form* seiner unableitbaren *messianischen Vollmacht* sichtbar.' No English word can adequately represent '*Vollmacht*'.

197 Hengel and Schwemer, *Jesus und das Judentum*, e.g. pp. 498–99, with n. 4. See further pp. 392–99.

198 Hengel and Schwemer, *Jesus und das Judentum*, p. 526, quoting C. Colpe, *ho huios tou anthrōpou*, *TWNT* VIII (1969), pp. 400–77, at 406.

199 See further p. 14, pp. 358–88.

200 J. P. Meier, *A Marginal Jew: Rethinking the Historical Jesus* (ABRL. 4 vols so far. New York: Doubleday, 1991–2009).

about background and methodology. It contains some exemplary discussions. For example, the discussion of the Gospel of Thomas is eminently sober, and properly presents it as a relatively late source which can be fitted into second-century Christianity. The discussion of the criterion of multiple attestation is equally exemplary. Meier applies it soberly to New Testament sources, and notes that it applies to forms as well as to sources. He also notes that if used mechanically it is not infallible, since secondary material might originate so early as to be repeated in more than one strand of tradition, and genuine material was not always repeated by the early church.[201] The quality of these discussions made this book an essential resource.

Nonetheless, some problems can be seen ready to emerge. The most serious is Meier's attitude to Aramaic, which begins to emerge in a section headed 'Secondary (or Dubious) Criteria' beginning with '6. The Criterion of Traces of Aramaic.'[202] This consists almost entirely of negative comments, and while these are largely justified in themselves, Meier does not discuss more promising recent developments.

The second volume moves on to John the Baptist and then to Jesus himself. Here again, there is some fine scholarship. For example, Meier supplies a very careful and fully critical discussion of John the Baptist and his baptism, correctly presented as emerging from the customs and symbolism of Jewish washing.[203]

On the other hand, it is not probable that Meier's extensive discussion of Jesus' miracles will satisfy anyone. For example, the healing of a man with a supposedly withered hand at Mk 3.1-6 is treated as indefinable, inexplicable, involving improbable argumentation and leading to a quite incredible conclusion, a plot to put Jesus to death. After all that, Meier sits on the fence on the historicity of the actual miracle story.[204] What is worse, Meier's comments on this story have two major faults. First, he ignores any possible Aramaic level of the tradition. So his discussion of Jesus' argument about saving life (Mk 3.4) proceeds as if the text says 'life', without any consideration of the Aramaic *n*ᵉ*phash*, which means 'person' as well as 'life'. Secondly, Meier rejects aspects of Judaism. For example, he decides that in the actual healing, 'Jesus *performs no action*', so that 'in no sense can he be said to break the Sabbath by working', an important point in his view that the story cannot be historically accurate.[205] This shows no understanding of the flexibility of Torah interpretation within Jewish culture, which allowed Jesus' most serious opponents to expand the commandment not to work on the sabbath more extensively than Meier is willing to contemplate.

Meier's third volume, 'Companions and Competitors', has many excellent features. The first part has separate chapters on the crowds, the 'disciples', the Twelve and individual members of the Twelve. Each chapter contains fine

---

201 Meier, *Marginal Jew*, vol. 1, pp. 124–39, 174–75.
202 Meier, *Marginal Jew*, vol. 1, pp. 178–83, with Aramaic at pp. 178–80.
203 Meier, *Marginal Jew*, vol. 2, pp. 42–56.
204 Meier, *Marginal Jew*, vol. 2, pp. 681–84, 730–33.
205 Meier, *Marginal Jew*, vol. 2, p. 683.

discussion of what we really know about these groups and their relationships with Jesus. Anything which disturbs some people, such as that there is not much information about the Twelve, or that the word 'disciple' is not used of women, is squarely faced and discussed. Meier is also exceptionally effective in demolishing some regrettable opinions which are left over from the last generation of criticism. Thus he defends the existence as well as the main functions of the Twelve, and does so excellently.

The second half of the book discusses Pharisees, Sadducees, Essenes, Samaritans and other groups. At one level, these discussions are learned and fully critical in orientation. At the same time, problems continue to emerge, especially when Meier deals with Jesus' conflicts with his opponents. For example, Meier's discussion of Mk 2.1–3.6 is heavily dependent on the work of Dewey, who envisaged Markan patterns.[206] He declares that 'the cycle of Galilean dispute stories in Mark 2.1–3.6 is carefully composed to create an artistic and theological pattern', and describes it as 'from Mark's redactional hand'.[207] Throughout his discussion, Meier ignores Aramaisms as indications of pre-Markan tradition. His comments on Mk 3.1-6 repeat the faults in his more detailed discussion of this passage in volume 2.[208] He ignores the signs of authenticity of Mk 2.23-28, which he discusses in detail in volume 4.[209] Instead, he comments for example that 'the stories are driven by an ever increasing tone of antagonism and an ever more direct attack on Jesus himself.'[210] He does not seriously consider the possibility that this reflects increasingly hostile opposition to Jesus as the historic ministry continued.

The fourth volume, 'Law and Love', is deeply flawed. Meier begins with worthy aims, declaring that a 'basic insight' which will emerge is that 'the historical Jesus is the halakic Jesus'.[211] Most of the first substantial chapter (Chapter 31) is devoted to the Torah, or Law, and serious problems begin to emerge here. For example, Meier finds it 'startling' that the Law of Moses was believed to contain 'important commandments that, from our historical-critical perspective, simply are not there in the text.'[212] Students of the Torah within Jewish culture should not find this startling. Texts frequently imply cultural assumptions which their authors do not need to state. People who lived the whole of their lives in accordance with the Torah believed that its general commandments entailed details which it did not state explicitly.

Nowhere is this more obvious than with Meier's example, sabbath observance. During the Maccabaean revolt (167–164 BCE), some Jews died rather than fight on the sabbath (1 Macc. 2.29-38), and Mattathias and his supporters made the obvious decision that they should fight on the sabbath (1. Macc. 2.39-41).

---

206 Meier, *Marginal Jew*, vol. 3, pp. 332–33, with p. 385 n.164, citing J. Dewey, *Markan Public Debate* (SBLDS 48. Chico: Scholars, 1980), presumably meaning pp. 181–93, as at vol. 2, p. 728 n. 6.
207 Meier, *Marginal Jew*, vol. 3, pp. 560–65.
208 Meier, *Marginal Jew*, vol. 2, pp. 681–84, 730–33.
209 Meier, *Marginal Jew*, vol. 4, pp. 267–93, 319–41; on this incident see pp. 321–25.
210 Meier, *Marginal Jew*, vol. 3, p. 333.
211 Meier, *Marginal Jew*, vol. 4, p. 8.
212 Meier, *Marginal Jew*, vol. 4, p. 32.

Meier comments, 'Remarkably, the issue is never explicitly raised in the Jewish
Scriptures', adding that there are numerous examples of Israelites fighting on the
sabbath, with the caveat that 'an argument from silence is always perilous.'[213]
This is not in the least remarkable, and arguments from cultural assumptions
should not be confused with arguments 'from silence'. The centre of the Torah is
God's covenant with Israel. So Moses commanded Israel, 'obey the statutes and
the ordinances which I teach you to do, so that you may live' (Deut. 4.1). Again,
'For if keeping you will keep all these commandments which I command you to
do, to love YHWH your God to walk in all his ways and to cleave to him, YHWH
will drive out all these nations from before you . . .' (Deut. 11.22-23). This means
that God will fight Israel's battles, so he was known as 'YHWH of hosts, God
of the battle array of Israel' (1 Sam. 17.45). Any notion that God's heavenly and
earthly hosts would stop fighting one day a week was quite ludicrous. Mattathias
and his followers took this for granted, because it was a cultural assumption at
the heart of their relationship with God.

Meier describes the decision of Mattathias and his followers to defend themselves on the sabbath as a result of 'appealing to common sense rather than
to subtle legal reasoning', and he believes that they saw no need to appeal to
'particular Scripture passages or legal reasoning based on Scripture.'[214] This is
misleading in two ways. First, the account of this decision is only two verses long
(1 Macc. 2.40-41). We have no idea of the extent to which Mattathias and his
followers may have discussed particular passages of the Torah as well. Meier has
assumed that what is not mentioned in a very brief text did not happen, an 'argument from silence' which is 'often perilous', but which he often uses. Secondly,
the decision to fight in self-defence on the sabbath did not require 'subtle legal
reasoning' or 'particular Scripture passages' because it was based on the centre
of God's covenant, which brought Israel life, not genocide.

Nor does Meier understand 'one stringently observant group', who refused
to defend themselves when attacked on the sabbath. He observes, 'The predict-
able result was total slaughter', and correctly sees their decision reflected in the
halakhah of the book of *Jubilees*, whose expanded list of sabbath prohibitions
concludes with waging war. He comments, 'In the mind of the author of *Jubilees*,
the Torah does deal directly with fighting on the sabbath, and it totally forbids
it.'[215] Meier offers no explanation of this, and it is central to understanding the
development of Jewish Law. The persecution of Antiochus IV Epiphanes was part
of an ongoing Hellenizing movement which reached a climax in the attempt of
Antiochus' Greek government to prevent the observance of the Torah. In response
to that movement, many Jewish people reinforced their Jewish identity not only
by observing the Torah as they had before, but by expanding its ordinances, so
that more and more things they did were distinctively Jewish. Thus the authors of
Jubilees rewrote part of the Pentateuch to include their expanded sabbath regulations, all revealed to Moses on Mount Sinai. That is also why the immediately

213 Meier, *Marginal Jew*, vol. 4, p. 32.
214 Meier, *Marginal Jew*, vol. 4, p. 33.
215 Meier, *Marginal Jew*, vol. 4, pp. 33–34.

succeeding period saw the emergence of orthodox groups of Pharisees, Essenes and the Dead Sea sect. This same trend is a fundamental reason for the eventual emergence of Jesus' opponents among scribes and Pharisees.

After failing to understand the decision of Mattathias and his followers, Meier describes it as 'not the most startling point. What is truly astounding' is that 'Josephus states flatly that "the Law [*ho nomos*] permits [Jews on the sabbath] to defend themselves against those who begin a battle and attack them, but it does not allow [Jews] to fight their military opponents if the latter are doing anything else"'.[216] What Meier appears to regard as 'truly astounding' is the 'equating of a relatively recent rule with "the Law"', for he proceeds to further examples of development. He cites for example passages of Philo and Josephus which 'affirm that Moses *commanded* in the *written* Law that Jews should study Torah (Philo: "to philosophize" in "prayer houses") and/or to attend synagogue (Josephus: "to come together") on the sabbath', adding that Ps-Philo, 'goes so far as to include communal worship on the sabbath in his list of the Ten Commandments' (Ant. Bib. XI, 8).[217] All this reflects Meier's failure to understand the nature of Torah. The Torah was a *living* text, at the centre of the daily life of Jewish people, and at the centre of God's relationship with Israel. That is why it could be expanded to clarify for Jewish people how it was to be observed.

With such fundamental mistakes at the heart of Meier's attitude to the Torah, every subsequent chapter contains serious mistakes. The worst examples are in Chapter 34, 'Jesus and the Sabbath'. For example, Meier refuses to believe in the historicity of Jesus' first reported exorcism, in a Capernaum synagogue one sabbath (Mk 1.23-27). His reasons are that the exorcism and Jesus' teaching provoke astonishment, but there is no dispute about Jesus exorcizing a demoniac on the sabbath, and previous scholarship often portrayed Mk 1.23-34 as an 'ideal scene'.[218] As before, Meier ignores all signs of transmission of the material in Aramaic, and the perfect setting of the incident in the life of Jesus. He does not take seriously the obvious possibility that the absence of dispute is due to the absence of scribes and Pharisees. He also ignores the fact that the early church had no interest in creating such stories, and interprets the recurrence of some features of the story elsewhere in Mark as evidence of Markan creativity.[219]

In preparation for further comments on Mk 3.1-6, Meier stresses *repeatedly* that Jewish *texts* do not prohibit healing on the sabbath. For example, he comments on Philo: 'Nowhere is there any mention of prohibiting the healing of illnesses, the only action Jesus ever directly does that supposedly violates the sabbath.'[220] He draws all such comments together as an argument against the historicity of the incident, commenting, 'no Jewish document prior to A.D. 70 gives the slightest indication that an act of healing was considered a violation of the sabbath rest.' Yet Meier makes this claim while considering Mk 3.1-6,

---

216 Meier, *Marginal Jew*, vol. 4, p. 35, with his translation from Jos. *Ant.* XIV, 63.
217 Meier, *Marginal Jew*, vol. 4, pp. 35–36.
218 Meier, *Marginal Jew*, vol. 4, p. 252, with p. 311 nn. 63–64 and vol. 2, pp. 648–49.
219 On this incident see pp. 247–49.
220 Meier, *Marginal Jew*, vol. 4, p. 246.

which *is* the vital piece of evidence to the contrary. He adds that in the much later Mishnah, 'in the full flowering of lists of acts prohibited on the sabbath, healing is absent.' He argues again that 'Jesus *does* nothing, he does no "work"'.[221]

All this shows again Meier's lack of understanding of the development of Jewish Law. In general, the halakhic judgements made by scribes and Pharisees who opposed Jesus were stricter than those of most other Jews. Pharisees separated themselves from other Jews and tried to live in a state of purity.[222] Other orthodox Jews, who included Essenes and the Qumran sect, also made halakhic decisions which were stricter than those of most Jews. For example, Josephus records that the Essenes would not defecate on the sabbath (*War* II, 147), and the book of *Jubilees* prohibits sex on the sabbath (*Jub.* 50.8). These judgements are quite different from the views of later rabbis, who wrote the Mishnah and other collections of Jewish Law. The rabbis did not separate themselves from other Jews, but sought to legislate for all Israel after the disastrous defeat of the Roman war (66–70 CE). This is what is so pointless about Meier's repeated stress on the absence of a prohibition of healing on the sabbath from Jewish *texts*. Jesus' opponents did not leave any written texts, which is why this prohibition is absent from other *texts*. Equally pointless are Meier's repeated declarations that in this healing Jesus did no 'work'. This is Meier's opinion, and it may have been widespread, but Mark's text is straightforward evidence that it was not the opinion of Jesus' opponents.

Two other major faults reinforce these mistakes. Meier is extraordinarily reluctant to believe that Jesus' opponents in this passage were Pharisees, apparently because they are not mentioned at Mk 3.2, and he attributes too much to Markan redaction. He comments for example, '*In Mark's mind*, the adversaries are probably to be identified with the Pharisees in 2.24' (my emphasis), and again refers to the 'clearly redactional conclusion to the dispute in 3.6 (the Pharisees consult with the Herodians on how to destroy Jesus)'.[223] The removal of these important points from the level of history to that of redaction is quite arbitrary. These verses *are* the evidence that the Pharisees were the opponents in Mk 3.1-6. Mark's failure to repeat the subject in 3.2 is due to Mk 2.23–3.6 being a literal translation from an Aramaic source which I reconstructed with full critical discussion in a 1998 book which is not even mentioned in Meier's extensive bibliographical footnotes.[224] Aramaic stories often change subject without marking the change, and frequently do not repeat subjects either. I also showed how appreciation of Mark's Aramaic source makes it possible to explain the peculiarities of his narrative, and I fitted the whole narrative into the historic ministry of Jesus.[225] Meier does not consider any of this.

Similar faults recur throughout the chapter. Consequently, Meier's treatment of Jesus and the sabbath cannot be regarded as reasonable historical research.

---

221 Meier, *Marginal Jew*, vol. 4, p. 255.
222 See pp. 315–19.
223 Meier, *Marginal Jew*, vol. 2, p. 682; vol. 4, p. 254.
224 Casey, *Aramaic Sources of Mark's Gospel*, pp. 138–92.
225 For discussion of the main points see pp. 321–24.

Chapter 35, 'Jesus and Purity Laws', has similar weaknesses. For example, in rejecting the historicity of Mk 7.1-23, Meier argues that 'the scriptural debate presented by Mark in 7.6–8 is not conceivable as an event in the life of the historical Jesus', because Jesus' argument 'demands the LXX of Isaiah . . . slightly tweaked by Mark.'[226] That Mark quotes the LXX of Isa. 29.13, as he quotes the LXX elsewhere, is to be explained by the position of the LXX as the Bible of the Greek-speaking churches for whom he wrote. Meier also quotes Isa. 29.14, which Jesus did not, and stresses the absence from the LXX of 'because' at the beginning of Isa. 29.13. If a major prophet quoting another major prophet to denounce hypocritical opponents did not wish to quote his opening conjunction he did not have to, doubly so because he is likely to have spoken in Aramaic, rather than quote the original text in Hebrew. Once again, Meier has no idea about the parameters within which first-century Jews could interpret scripture, nor does he take seriously the fact that we have before us the result of the work of a *translator* who has used the LXX to make perfect sense of Jesus' argument. What we lack is the *exact Aramaic* words of the historical Jesus, of which Mark may have given us a precise or approximate translation.

Meier also discusses Mk 7.15, which he translates as follows:

There is nothing outside a man that, by entering into him, can defile him; but those things that come out of a man are the things that defile the man.

Meier discusses this in the context of Mk 7.14-23, and simply assumes that it overthrows the Jewish food laws, so he argues that it does not go back to the historical Jesus.[227] He does not consider the opinion of scholars who believe that 'This is the ultimate answer to the question of the Pharisees and scribes as to why Jesus' disciples eat with unwashed hands.'[228]

Meier then argues that the introduction in Mk 7.1-5, in which Pharisees and some of the scribes who came from Jerusalem ask why Jesus' disciples eat with unwashed hands, cannot be authentic because 'there is no historical Jesus tradition for which vv 1–5 can serve as the introduction.'[229] He adds his own scepticism to the whole idea that handwashing before meals was practised as early as this, again discounting Mark as evidence and failing to see that Jesus' opponents were especially strict. The sophisticated discussion of Crossley, who argues for the authenticity of the incident and separates out Markan redaction towards the end of the passage, is not even mentioned in Meier's massive bibliographical footnote.[230]

---

226 Meier, *Marginal Jew*, vol. 4, pp. 369–76; I quote from Meier's conclusion on p. 376.
227 Meier, *Marginal Jew*, vol. 4, pp. 384–99.
228 J. Marcus, *Mark 1–8: A New Translation with Introduction and Commentary* (AB 27. New York: Doubleday, 1999), p. 446.
229 Meier, *Marginal Jew*, vol. 4, pp. 399–405 (400).
230 J. G. Crossley, *The Date of Mark's Gospel: Insight from the Law in Earliest Christianity* (JSNTSup 266. London: T&T Clark International, 2004), pp. 183–205, 'Dating Mark Legally (II): Mark 7.1-23'; see further pp. 326–31.

The 'halakic Jesus' could not possibly emerge from such destructive scholarship. Moreover, when a Christian scholar does not understand Judaism, Jesus' teaching is seen at some point to contradict Torah. Meier does this twice, with divorce and with oaths.[231]

On oaths, it is evident that the main passage (Mt. 5.33-37) has suffered some secondary editing, but Meier's discussion completely fails to sort this out. He does not consider any possible Aramaic underlay. He therefore takes seriously 'at all' in Mt. 5.34, so that Jesus may have said, 'Do not swear at all'. There is however no Aramaic expression for 'at all', so Jesus cannot have said that. Treating Jas 5.12 as an alternative version of the same tradition, which it does not claim to be, Meier supposes that an alternative version of the tradition was 'Do not swear by heaven or by earth or by any other oath', which is supposed to 'make it fairly certain that the primitive tradition contained some way of stressing the absolute nature of the prohibition.'[232] Meier also finds spurious reasons for not attributing to Jesus most of his examples of the oaths which he criticized. For example, noting the absence of most examples from Jas 5.12, which does not claim to reproduce Jesus' teaching, let alone *all* of it, Meier claims that 'almost all critics identify Matt 5.36 ("do not swear by your head . . .") as a secondary accretion' also because it 'breaks the pattern seen . . . in Matt 5.34c-35d' because it is so different from swearing by heaven, earth or Jerusalem, 'all names of places important in Israel's sacred traditions'.[233] This is irrelevant: Jesus objected to people swearing to each other by anything. Nor does Meier give adequate consideration to Jesus' further criticism of oaths in Mt. 23.16-22.[234] This leaves Meier attributing to Jesus a blanket prohibition of oaths with precious few examples. This is essential for Meier to reach the conclusion, which he does not sufficiently discuss, that 'Jesus is abrogating an important social and legal institution that is permitted and regulated by the Torah.'[235] Jesus' teaching nowhere discusses the very infrequent occasions on which the Torah prescribes an oath, as for example when a man's animal kept by a neighbour dies or is hurt or is driven away without anyone seeing it (Exod. 22.10-11). Once again, Meier's methodology has prevented the emergence of the halakhic Jesus.

Meier's enormous book began promisingly, but each volume has problems, and volume 4 is an unmitigated disaster. He is not sufficiently sympathetic to ancient Judaism to conduct accurate historical and cultural research in this area. Consequently, he has adopted destructive methods, a fact which was not to be expected from his discussion of methodology in volume 1. This has combined with his lack of understanding of ancient Judaism to remove from the historical Jesus a large portion of his words and deeds. Meier's refusal to make proper use of Aramaic is central to this. Its effect is that the picture of Jesus which emerges from Meier's work is not that of a first-century Jew immersed in Judaism.

---

231 Meier, *Marginal Jew*, vol. 4, pp. 74–234.
232 Meier, *Marginal Jew*, vol. 4, pp. 193–94.
233 Meier, *Marginal Jew*, vol. 4, pp. 191–92.
234 There are a few brief comments in Meier, *Marginal Jew*, vol. 4, p. 200, with 225–26 n. 64.
235 Meier, *Marginal Jew*, vol. 4, p. 233 n. 90.

This is an appropriate place to end this survey of modern scholarship. Meier made a genuine critical attempt to recover the historical Jesus from our earliest sources. In the end, however, a Catholic priest came to grief because he cannot understand Jewish Law. Moreover, his basic refusal to take seriously the Aramaic level of the tradition is at the heart of this failure. These are central faults in the quest of the historical Jesus. Jesus was not a 'marginal' Jew, and he did not seek to contradict Torah. The first traditions about him were written down in Aramaic, and have to be recovered from the synoptic Gospels and interpreted in the light of the Jewish assumptions which they made.

9. Conclusions

It is evident from the above discussion that the quest of the historical Jesus has been a difficult enterprise. Not only is the source material difficult to handle, the quest has suffered badly from the religious, and sometimes anti-religious, convictions of scholars. The time is now ripe to succeed in the task attempted by Schweitzer, Vermes, Sanders, Wright, Chilton, Dunn, Hengel and Schwemer, and Meier, by setting Jesus in his original cultural context. For this purpose, I use our oldest sources, which make clear that this cultural context was first-century Judaism.

As part of our renewed efforts to set Jesus in his original cultural context, I have begun the task of reconstructing the sources of Mark and of 'Q', and a few passages of Matthew and Luke, in their original language, Aramaic. The past history of work of this kind has not been good, but the publication of all the Aramaic Dead Sea Scrolls has put us in a position to revolutionize this work. This is the work which I have begun in recent years, and all the following chapters have benefited from it. Jesus' language has been a missing link which should now help us to reconstruct his whole ministry against its original background.

It is with this Judaism, the Judaism of the first century CE, that we must carry through the task of finding the historical Jesus. First, however, we must consider the nature of the primary source material which is available to us. Until recently, all critical scholars agreed that our oldest sources are the Gospel of Mark, and the so-called 'Q' material, and that some further historically accurate material is to be found in the Gospels of Matthew and Luke. As we have seen in this chapter, however, this consensus has not been maintained. Apocryphal Gospels have been considered equally important, especially the Gospel of Thomas, and there has been a resurgence of conservative scholars who treat the Gospel of John as a serious historical source. Moreover, there is no longer anything like general agreement as to the methods which we must use. I have therefore written two further introductory chapters, one to establish our oldest primary sources, and one to discuss method. I discuss other Gospels, including those attributed to John and to Thomas, in the Appendix.

CHAPTER 2

Historically Reliable Sources

1. *Introduction*

The most important sources for the life and teaching of Jesus are in my view the first three Gospels in the New Testament, the Gospels of Matthew, Mark and Luke. Until recently, there was a widespread consensus among critical scholars that our oldest and most reliable sources are the oldest of these three, the Gospel of Mark, and what scholars call 'Q', material which is found in both Matthew and Luke, but not in Mark. This consensus is no longer maintained. Some scholars argue that there is very little reliable material in the Gospel of Mark. Some consider that the 'Q' material was a single Greek document, the first Gospel. It was written by Christians who did not attach much importance to things which are not found in it, and since it has neither a passion narrative nor any Resurrection stories, that makes them seriously different from any traditional picture of the earliest Christians. On the other hand, the traditional Christian view that John's Gospel contains historically reliable material has been seriously revived by conservative Christian scholars.

Outside the New Testament, the Gospel of Thomas is regarded by some scholars, notably members of the American Jesus Seminar, as an essential source of information about the historical Jesus. Some scholars even consider one or more of the other apocryphal Gospels to be of crucial importance, especially the Gospels of Peter, Judas, and Mary.

The purpose of this chapter is to discuss the first three Gospels, and to give reasons for maintaining something like the original consensus, that Mark and the 'Q' material are our oldest and most reliable sources, to be expanded with judiciously selected material from Matthew and Luke. Contrary to any consensus, however, I argue for an unconventionally early date for Mark, and for a quite chaotic model of the varied material known as 'Q'. I discuss other Gospels, which between them contribute hardly any further knowledge of the historical Jesus, in the Appendix, 'Other Gospels'.

2. *The Gospel According to Marcus*

The Gospels of Matthew, Mark and Luke are closely related to each other in many passages. This relationship is sometimes so close, both in verbal agreement and in common order, that there is still an almost universal consensus that there is some kind of literary relationship between them.

Most scholars believe that this close literary relationship is due to Matthew and Luke independently copying Mark. This differs from the view, first clearly stated by St Augustine, that Mark abbreviated Matthew. This view reflects Matthew's position as the first Gospel in the canon of the New Testament and the most popular Gospel in the churches, as well as the tradition that it was written by the apostle Matthew, one of the Twelve. This view was taken up by Griesbach in 1783, when he made famous the view that Mark abbreviated both Matthew and Luke. This is now known as the 'neo-Griesbach hypothesis', or the 'Two-Gospel Hypothesis', most vigorously put forward in recent years by William Farmer.[1]

A straightforward example of the relationship between Matthew, Mark and Luke is found in a story in which Jesus heals a paralytic. At the crucial point he makes the following speech, first to his opponents and then to the paralyzed man:

What is easier, to say to the paralytic, 'your sins are forgiven', or to say, 'get up and pick up your mattress and walk'? But so that you may know that the Son of man has power to forgive sins on earth, – he says to the paralytic – I'm telling you, get up, pick up your mattress and go to your house. (Mk 2.9-11)	For what is easier, to say 'your sins are forgiven', or to say, 'get up and walk'? But so that you may know that the Son of man has power on earth to forgive sins, – then he says to the paralytic – get up, pick up your bed and go to your house. (Mt. 9.5-6)	What is easier, to say 'your sins have been forgiven', or to say, 'get up and walk'? But so that you may know that the Son of man has power on earth to forgive sins – he said to the paralysed (man) – I'm telling you, get up, pick up your little bed and go to your house. (Lk. 5.23-24)

This is obviously the same story, and it is told in almost the same words, the crucial indicator that there is a literary relationship between Matthew, Mark and Luke. The narrative interpolation into Jesus' speech is especially significant here: '(then) he says/said to the paralytic/paralysed'. The chances of three independent

---

1   W. R. Farmer, *The Synoptic Problem: A Critical Analysis* (New York: Macmillan, 1964); *New Synoptic Studies: The Cambridge Gospel Conference and Beyond* (Macon: Mercer, 1983); *The Gospel of Jesus: The Pastoral Relevance of the Synoptic Problem* (Louisville: Westminster John Knox, 1994).

writers making this almost identical narrative interpolation at the same point are negligible. One of the small variants in the passage is also significant, though difficult to translate into English. Mark called the thing on which the man lay to be carried to Jesus *krabaton*, a crude Greek word which I have translated as 'mattress'. Matthew and Luke each altered this to a better Greek word, Matthew to *klinē*, Luke to *klinidion*. This is a small indication of the normal way in which Matthew and Luke depend on Mark. It is understandable that Matthew and Luke should each seek to improve on Mark's crude Greek word, whereas Mark would have had no reason to alter Matthew's *klinē*, if he had been copying Matthew.

This is typical of the relationship between these three Gospels. Moreover, a number of changes are more dramatic than this, especially where Mark's Greek is strange. For example, Mk 1.40-45 tells the story of how Jesus healed a man who suffered from a skin disease. There is a notorious crux at Mk 1.41, where the original text of Mark appears to say that Jesus was angry when the man approached him.

And being angry, having stretched out his hand he touched him, and says to him, 'I am willing, be cleansed.' (Mk 1.41)	And having stretched out his hand he touched him, saying, 'I am willing, be cleansed.' (Mt. 8.3a)	And having stretched out his hand he touched him, saying, 'I am willing, be cleansed.' (Lk. 5.13a)

Here Matthew and Luke both left out 'being angry' (*orgistheis*) because it is obviously unsuitable. Christian copyists of Mark's Gospel did not like it either, so they altered it, with the result that most manuscripts of Mark read 'having compassion' (*splanchnistheis*), which fits our image of Jesus much better. We must however follow the more difficult reading, because we can understand it only if it is original, and it explains why both Matthew and Luke independently left the same word out. Moreover, here as so often, Mark's Greek is perfectly comprehensible as a literal and unrevised translation of an Aramaic source which gave a perfectly accurate albeit very brief account of an incident which really took place. The Aramaic source will have read *regaz*. This word often does mean 'be angry', which is why Mark translated it with *orgistheis*. But the Aramaic *regaz* has a wider range of meaning than 'be angry', including 'tremble' and 'be deeply moved'. Accordingly, Mark did not mean that Jesus was angry. He was suffering from interference, the influence of one of his languages on another. All bilinguals suffer from interference, especially when they are translating, because the word which causes the interference is in the text which they are translating. In Mark's mind, the Greek word for being angry (*orgistheis*) also meant 'tremble' or 'be deeply moved', because this was the range of meaning of the normally equivalent Aramaic word in front of him.

Accordingly, this example makes sense only if Matthew and Luke were copying Mark, which is therefore the oldest of the synoptic Gospels. It also provides evidence that Mark is an unrevised literal translation of an Aramaic source, and this at a point where there is every reason to believe that the story is literally true.[2] This means that our oldest source is sometimes perfectly accurate, because parts of it were originally written by people who were in close touch with the events of the historic ministry. This is only one short step away from eyewitness testimony. Furthermore, as often in Aramaic narratives, the subject is not always clear. Was Jesus 'deeply moved', or did the man 'tremble'? Who stretched out his hand and touched whom? Clearly it was Jesus who said, 'I am willing, be cleansed.' Matthew and Luke sorted that out too. Jesus is the subject all along. This too makes sense only if Matthew and Luke were copying Mark.

Some examples are more extreme than this, in that they contain mistakes due to slight misreadings of an Aramaic source. For example, Mark's story of the disciples going through the fields on the sabbath plucking ears of corn begins somewhat as in the following table, though it is difficult to translate into English, because it is not satisfactory Greek.[3] Matthew and Luke naturally altered it, with the following results.

And it came to pass that on the Sabbath he was passing through the cornfields, and his disciples began to make a path, plucking the ears. (Mk 2.23)	And at that time Jesus went, on the Sabbath, through the cornfields. But his disciples were hungry and they began to pluck the ears and to eat (them). (Mt. 12.1)	Now it came to pass on a Sabbath that he was going through cornfields, and his disciples were plucking and eating the ears, rubbing (them) in their hands. (Lk. 6.1)

It is obvious from the subsequent dispute with the Pharisees that the objection of the Pharisees was to the disciples' behaviour in plucking the ears of corn. This is a very intelligible subject of dispute. Poor people were entitled to walk on the paths through other people's fields plucking the grain deliberately left for them. It was a custom known as leaving and taking *Peah*, and it is laid down in the Bible (Lev. 23.22). The Bible does not however say whether the poor, for whom this grain was left, might or should not take it on the sabbath. It is entirely logical that the Pharisees should think that this was work, which everyone agreed was prohibited on the sabbath, and that Jesus and his disciples should think it was not work.

Mark's Greek, however, says that the disciples were *making* a path, a serious offence which does not figure in the subsequent dispute. Hence neither Matthew nor Luke repeats it. Mark's Greek is however easy to understand as a slight misreading of a single Aramaic word. Mark's Aramaic source will have read *lema'ebhar*, so they began 'to go along' a path, which everyone was perfectly entitled to do on the sabbath, so the Pharisees had no reason to object to this. This has been slightly misread as *l^ema'ebhadh*, 'to make', with 'd' (ד) rather than 'r' (ר) as the final letter, by a translator who was again suffering from interference.

---

2 See further pp. 266–68.
3 On this story see further pp. 321–23.

Mark will have had a text written on something like a wax tablet or a sheet of papyrus, and these could be difficult to read. Moreover, in Aramaic, the letters 'r' (ר) and 'd' (ד), very similar in the square script which I have printed here, were often virtually indistinguishable in an ancient written text. This is how the translator came to misread the text. Similar mistakes occur in the Septuagint, the only surviving translation of the whole Hebrew Bible into Greek.

The importance of this is threefold. First, this is another passage in which Mark's Greek is peculiar because it has resulted from a literal and unrevised translation from a source which was written in Aramaic. Moreover, mistakes like this occur in passages where there are other good reasons to believe that Mark's account, albeit abbreviated, is otherwise literally accurate. Secondly, the fact that the translation has not been revised makes it extremely probable that Mark himself did the translating. If Mark inherited the translation, he would surely have improved it as he wrote his Gospel. Thirdly, Matthew and Luke were altering Mark. Both of them omit the expression 'make a path'. They both then proceed to the actual source of the dispute, the fact that, as Mark says, the disciples were plucking the ears of corn. Moreover, both evangelists proceed to explain this. Matthew explains that the disciples were hungry, so they were eating the grains then and there. Luke does not say they were hungry, but he explains not only that they were eating the grains, but also how they could do so, by first rubbing them in their hands.

There are many passages of the synoptic Gospels which are related in a similar way. It follows that the conventional critical view of the relationship between the Gospels of Matthew, Mark and Luke is the correct one. Mark is the oldest Gospel, and it normally contains the most primitive account of stories and sayings which are transmitted by all three.

The next question is the date of the oldest Gospel. There are *two different* conventional dates in scholarship. Some scholars, especially in Europe, date it c.65–69 CE, not long before the destruction of Jerusalem by the Romans in 70 CE, whereas others, especially in the USA, date it c.75 CE, not long after the same event. A consequence of such late dates is, necessarily, even later dates for the Gospels of Matthew and Luke. Earlier dates have occasionally been suggested, but mostly by scholars whose conservative convictions were strong enough to damage the plausibility of their arguments. All this should now be changed in the light of a brilliant book by James Crossley, *The Date of Mark's Gospel*.[4] Crossley has proposed a date c.40 CE. I therefore examine the basic arguments for each of these dates.

The later dates are based primarily on the witness of some Church Fathers, and on a possible interpretation of the predictions in Mark 13. The earliest piece of evidence from the Church Fathers is a quotation attributed to Papias, who was bishop of Hierapolis, in Asia Minor, in the early second century. All his writings have disappeared, but fragments of his work are preserved in the Ecclesiastical

---

4   J. G. Crossley, *The Date of Mark's Gospel: Insight from the Law in Earliest Christianity* (JSNTSup 266. London: T&T Clark International, 2004). I am grateful to Dr Crossley for giving me a copy of this book.

History written by Eusebius, bishop of Caesarea in the early fourth century. Papias claimed to have met not the first disciples from the historic ministry, but the next generation of Christians, including the mysterious figure of John the Elder, sometimes identified as the author of the Johannine epistles, and even as the author of the Fourth Gospel. Eusebius quotes Papias attributing the following comments to John the Elder:

> Mark, having become an interpreter of Peter, wrote down accurately whatever he remembered, what was said or done by the Lord, not however in order. For he neither heard the Lord nor followed him, but later, as I said, (he followed) Peter.
>
> (Eus., *H.E.* III, 39, 15)

Papias goes on to explain that Mark heard Peter teaching, which is why the material is not in order, and he stresses that Mark's writing of this was very accurate, to the point where it is not clear whether some of his comments are due to John the Elder or not. The term 'later' is not defined by Papias, and would make perfect sense if Mark had heard Peter teach at any date.

The same kind of connection between Mark and Peter is indicated by Justin Martyr, writing in the middle of the second century. Justin refers not to the Gospel According to Mark, but to the 'memoirs' of Peter. One reference to Peter's memoirs has the sons of Zebedee called 'Boanerges, which is "sons of thunder"' (*Dial.* 106). The word 'Boanerges' is known only from Mk 3.17, where Mark says that Jesus gave Jacob and John, the sons of Zebedee, 'the name "Boanērges", which is "sons of thunder"'. This reference is not merely unique. The term 'Boanerges' is a *mistaken* attempt to transliterate into Greek letters the Aramaic words $b^e n\bar{e}$ $r^{e'}em$, which mean 'sons of thunder'.[5] The possibility that two independent sources made *almost identical mistakes* in the transliteration of these words is negligible. It follows that by 'the memoirs of Peter' Justin meant the Gospel of Mark. He does not say anything to indicate when Mark wrote his Gospel, nor how much of it was derived from Peter.

Papias' comments have frequently been interpreted in the light of later church traditions. The next one to have survived is the so-called anti-Marcionite prologue, which must be dated c.160–80 CE. This repeats that Mark was an interpreter of Peter, and adds that he wrote his Gospel after Peter's death, in the regions of Italy. According to early and apparently accurate church tradition, Peter was martyred in Rome in 64 CE, during the persecution of Christians instigated by the emperor Nero. Irenaeus, bishop of Lugdunum in Gaul, now Lyons in France, repeated all this c.177 CE, in terms which imply that Mark wrote in Rome (Adv. Haer. III, 1, 1). Thus the dominant church tradition was established by the end of the second century, and since Mark is supposed to have written after Peter's death in 64 CE, the earliest possible date for his Gospel is 65 CE.

Some aspects of this tradition must be true, but not all of them. First, the

---

5 See pp. 189–90.

author was certainly Mark. Our name Mark is the Greek *Markos* without its ending, and this is the Greek form of the Latin *Marcus*, one of the commonest names in the Roman empire. Secondly, Papias must be right in supposing that Marcus 'neither heard nor followed the Lord'. The early church would not have attributed its first Gospel to someone called simply Marcus, who was not a follower of Jesus, unless both points were known facts.

Problems arise with Papias' use of the tradition that Mark heard Peter teach to establish the accuracy of the whole Gospel, despite the fact that it is not in the order of a historical outline. This indeed it is not, apart from the Cleansing of the Temple and the Passion narrative at the end. An undue proportion of conflict stories are placed together (Mk 2.1–3.6). A high proportion of parables are placed together in Chapter 4, complete with the quite unconvincing theory that they were told to conceal the mystery of the kingdom of God (Mk 4.10-12), a view contrary to the nature of Jesus' ministry, but one which has an excellent setting in the life of Christians who found the parables difficult to understand. This wondrous theory is immediately followed by a secondary allegorical interpretation of the parable of the sower (Mk 4.14-20), which cannot possibly have been derived from the teaching of Peter. A high proportion of Mark's eschatological teaching is collected into Chapter 13, and some of that is evidently secondary too.[6] It follows that Papias drastically overplayed his hand. While Mark may well have heard Peter teach, and this may have been the source of some of some of his perfectly accurate material, the *whole* of his Gospel cannot possibly have been derived from this source. Papias has produced a legitimating tradition. Faced with the fact that this Gospel was written by an unknown man called Marcus who never encountered the historical Jesus, he has sought to legitimate the accuracy of the whole of Mark's Gospel by associating it as closely as he could with the leader of the Twelve during the historic ministry.

Nor has Papias provided a sound explanation as to *why* Mark's material is not in a convincing historical order. Suppose that Mark heard Peter teach often enough for this to be his main source for the life and teaching of Jesus in his Gospel, why did he never ask Peter to provide him with the chronological outline which his Gospel so obviously lacks? Even if he did not actually write his Gospel until after Peter was martyred, anyone knowing that he had some intention of producing the first Gospel would surely have asked for any information that he did not possess, provided only that he saw a lot of Peter, and did not just hear him once or twice before he had decided to write. The associated tradition that Mark wrote in the centre of the Roman empire shows every sign of being secondary too. By the time of Irenaeus, the authenticity of 1 Peter was accepted, and at its end Peter, be this originally the famous apostle himself or a pseudonym, sends greetings from people in 'Babylon', a cipher for Rome, and from 'Mark my son' (1 Pet. 5.13). How easy it is to add in some details for the increasing witness of the Church Fathers! It is possible that this was a major cause of the tradition known to us from Papias. According to Eusebius, it was quoted by Origen in the

6   See further pp. 69–71, 374–75, 382.

third century, in support of his view that Mark wrote in accordance with Peter's instructions (Eus. *H.E.* VI, 25, 5).

It has naturally been tempting to identify Mark the Evangelist in other New Testament references as well, so much so that Taylor commented in 1959, 'Today this view is held almost with complete unanimity and it may be accepted as sound.'[7] A critical review of the evidence suggests otherwise. At Acts 12.12, Peter goes to the house of Mary, 'the mother of John, also named Marcus'. This associates Peter and Mark, but if this is Mark the Evangelist, it is surprising that church tradition does not call him John Mark. While John was a common enough Jewish name, the double name John Mark is far more distinctive than the simple Marcus. At Acts 12.25, where Barnabas and Saul take him with them to Jerusalem, he is again called 'John, also named Marcus'. At Acts 13.5, where he still accompanies Barnabas and Saul, he is simply referred to as 'John', as also at Acts 13.13, where he leaves 'those around Paul' and returns to Jerusalem. This incident led to subsequent disagreement between Barnabas, who again wanted to take 'John, called Marcus' (Acts 15.37), which Paul refused to do, so they parted company and Barnabas took him, now for the only time in Acts simply called 'Marcus' (Acts 15.39), to Cyprus. It is therefore probable that he is the same person as is referred to by Paul as 'Marcus, the cousin of Barnabas' (Col. 4.10), where 'the cousin of Barnabas' tells us which Marcus is meant. At Philemon 24, someone simply called 'Marcus' is among Paul's co-workers whose greetings he sends, and at 2 Tim. 4.11, which is probably pseudonymous, Paul asks for 'Marcus' to be brought to him. It is by no means clear that these last two passages refer to the same person. All the other references make quite clear which Mark is being referred to. It is even less probable that all these references mean Mark the Evangelist, since Luke nowhere mentions him composing a Gospel, let alone the one which provided him with so much material, and the earliest traditions in Papias and others do not mention his being the well-known John Mark, cousin of Barnabas.

Nor should we believe the alternative tradition among other Church Fathers, according to which Mark wrote during Peter's lifetime, and either wrote in, or at least went to, Alexandria. According to Eusebius, he preached the Gospel, which he had already written, in Egypt and founded churches in Alexandria, and Eusebius could be understood to mean that Mark was bishop there (*H.E.* II, xv, 1; xxiv, 1). At the end of the fourth century, John Chrysostom says that he actually wrote the Gospel in Alexandria (*Homily 1 on Matthew*, 7). By the time of Jerome in the early fifth century, Mark the Evangelist clearly is the first bishop of Alexandria (*Commentary on Matthew*, Prooemium 6). This tradition is too late and too poorly attested to be taken seriously as historical fact.

We must therefore treat the witness of the Church Fathers with caution. The evidence of Papias shows that the Gospel of Mark was written by an unknown Christian called Marcus, who was not present during the historic ministry of Jesus. It is probable that Marcus heard Peter preach, but it is most improbable

---

7 V. Taylor, *The Gospel According to St. Mark: The Greek Text with Introduction, Notes and Indexes* (London: Macmillan, 1959), p. 26.

that he heard him often, and out of the question that he knew him well. We cannot tell from the evidence of the Fathers when or where Marcus wrote his Gospel, because the relatively early external evidence consists of unreliable legitimating traditions.

The evidence provided by Mark 13 is by no means straightforward either. Here Jesus predicts the destruction of the Temple, declaring that 'there shall not be left here a stone upon a stone that shall not be destroyed' (Mk 13.2). The destruction of the Temple in 70 CE was an event of such importance that it is understandable that Christians have interpreted it as a fulfilment of Jesus' prophecy. When people believe predictions like this, they tolerate a certain degree of difference between the prophecy and its fulfilment. If however we are to treat Mark 13 as a pseudo-prophecy written after the destruction of Jerusalem, it becomes important that such differences cannot be explained. It is not literally true that not one stone was left standing upon another: some stones are *still* standing, and they are famous as the 'Wailing Wall', where observant Jews still worship. Moreover, one of the most famous aspects of the destruction of the Temple was that it was burnt down (Jos. *War* VI, 250–84). It is accordingly inconceivable that a pseudo-prophecy written *after* these dramatic events should make an incorrect statement about the stones and omit the centre of the drama, the burning down of the whole Temple. Furthermore, Mark predicts that they will see 'the abomination of desolation standing where (he/it) should not' (Mk 13.14): there was no such event in 70 CE. When this non-event happens, Jesus urges them to flee to the mountains, which did not happen either. It follows from all this that Mark 13 was not written after the events of 70 CE: it is a genuine prediction written before them.

This is sufficient to exclude the latest dates proposed for the composition of Mark's Gospel, but it does not tell us *how long* before 70 CE it was written. At this point it becomes important that a quite different event might have inspired these predictions: the Caligula crisis of 39 CE. At that time, the emperor Gaius, often known by his nickname Caligula, ordered that a statue of himself should be set up in the Temple in Jerusalem. From a Jewish perspective, that would have been idolatry in the centre of the Jewish faith, strongly reminiscent of the Maccabaean crisis, when the Greek king Antiochus Epiphanes set up a statue of himself in the Temple. It was this event which led to the pseudo-prophecy of the book of Daniel, which says of Antiochus' persecution:

> He shall make a strong covenant with many for one week, and for half of the week he shall make sacrifice and offering cease: and on a wing shall be an abomination that desolates, until the decreed end is poured out upon the desolator.
>
> (Dan. 9.27)

Here the 'abomination that desolates' is the statue of Antiochus Epiphanes in the Temple. The prediction that the persecution would end after 'one week', i.e. one week of years = seven years, that the cessation of the sacrifice and offering would last half of the week = three and a half years, and that the 'decreed end' would be 'poured out upon the desolator', all this is genuine prediction, and many interpreters, including in due course the whole of the Syriac-speaking church, saw this fulfilled in the defeat of Antiochus and the rededication of the Temple. Most interpreters in the west, however, have continually pushed it forwards as a prophecy of the future, and it is to this tradition that Mark belonged.[8]

This is why Mk 13.14 runs as it does:

> Now when you see the 'abomination of desolation' standing where (he/it) ought not (let the reader understand), then let those in Judaea flee to the mountains . . .

Here the 'abomination of desolation' is a reference back to the prophecy of Dan. 9.27 (referred to also in the prophecies of Dan. 11.31, 12.11: at 12.11, the LXX has the exact phrase used by Mark). This reference was inspired by Caligula's instructions to have a statue of himself placed in the Temple, which would have been seen as a fulfilment of that prophecy. This also explains a peculiarity in Mark's Greek. The Greek word for 'abomination' (*bdelugma*) is neuter, but the word for 'standing' (*hestēkota*) is masculine, whereas in grammatically correct Greek it would be neuter, because it refers to the 'abomination'. It is masculine because it refers to a masculine person (Caligula), and the Greek word for statue (*andrias*) used for Caligula's statue by both Philo (*Leg. ad Gaium* 188, 203, etc.) and Josephus (*Ant.* 261, 269, etc.) is masculine too.

The stage direction 'let the reader understand' refers to the situation when Mark's Gospel would be read at Christian meetings, and the person who read it out would explain what it meant, including the reference back to Dan. 9.27 and to Caligula's threat to put his statue in the Temple in Jerusalem, and to the normally incorrect Greek grammar. It follows that this prophecy originated during the Caligula crisis, c.40 CE. Moreover, it makes much better sense then than at any other time, because as far as we know this threat was not repeated subsequently. This also explains the editing of the prophecy by the other synoptic evangelists. Matthew, writing not very much later, clarified the prediction, but corrected the grammar:

> When therefore you see the 'abomination of desolation' spoken of through Daniel the prophet standing in a holy place (let the reader understand) . . .
>
> (Mt. 24.15)

Luke however, genuinely writing after the fall of Jerusalem, altered it completely:

> Now when you see Jerusalem surrounded by armies, then know that its desolation is at hand.
>
> (Lk. 21.20)

---

8   On these exegetical traditions see further pp. 216–18, and for more detailed discussion, P. M. Casey, *Son of Man: The Interpretation and Influence of Daniel 7* (London: SPCK, 1980), chs 3–4.

Of course, as Matthew shows, once the prophecy was written it might be repeated even if there was no specific threat from the current emperor, and the Roman historian Tacitus confirms continued Jewish fears that a later Roman emperor would repeat Caligula's threat (*Annals* XII, 54). Nonetheless, the Caligula crisis makes much the best sense of the origins of the prophecy, and the whole of Mark 13, secondary as much of it is, makes excellent sense at this time too.

The prophecy of the destruction of the Temple (Mk 13.2) takes off from Jesus' preaching on Jeremiah 7 in the Temple.[9] Mark quotes 'den of robbers' from Jer. 7.11 (Mk 11.17), and the Jeremiah context is also important. Criticizing sinful people who worshipped in the Temple, Jeremiah has God threaten to do to the Temple 'as I did to Shiloh' (Jer. 7.14). Everyone believed that God had destroyed Shiloh (Ps. 78.60, cf. Jer. 7.12), so this means that Jesus made a conditional threat of the destruction of the Temple too. This was naturally remembered, and will have seemed especially real when the Caligula crisis loomed. It was therefore rewritten into the definite prediction of the destruction of the Temple with which Mark's eschatological discourse begins.

With the destruction of the Temple set up at the beginning of Mark 13, Mark moves Jesus and his disciples from the Temple across to the Mount of Olives, a traditional eschatological site. He brings forward the inner group of three, Peter, Jacob and John, together with Andrew, Peter's brother and another member of the Twelve, to ask the vital question, 'When will these things be, and what (will be) the sign when all these things are about to be completed?' (Mk 13.3-4). The resulting discourse has numerous indications of the influence of the early church, as for example the reference to persecutions with the central piece of information, 'And first the Gospel must be preached to all the nations' (Mk 13.10). The climax is entirely based on scriptural passages. Some of them are difficult to identify, but there is no doubt about the centre of the hope of the early church: 'And then they shall see the Son of man coming in clouds with much power and glory' (Mk 13.26). This is a clear reference to the second coming of Jesus seen as predicted at Dan. 7.13. We shall see that it does not fit into the teaching of the historical Jesus, for he hoped that God would establish his kingdom without Jesus having to die first.[10] Jesus' second coming was however central to the hopes of the early church. They searched the scriptures to find it, and the climax of Mark's eschatological discourse is a result of this. Hence for example the gathering of the elect at Mark 13.27, part of traditional Jewish expectation found in scriptural passages such as Deut. 30.4 and Zech. 2.10 (LXX).

This makes the discourse later than the time of Jesus, but not necessarily *much* later. The spread of the Gospel to the Gentiles and the hope for Jesus' second coming were both well established features of early Christianity by the time of the Caligula crisis. The whole discourse could therefore have been written at the time of the Caligula crisis, when the threat of his statue being set up in the Temple was a real one, Jewish opposition to it might well lead to the destruction of the Temple, and Christians hoped that Jesus would return in triumph.

9   See pp. 411–15.
10   See pp. 214–24, 435–39.

Mark's view of the Law fits in perfectly with such a date. He makes a number of comments which *presuppose* knowledge of Jewish Law perfectly possible at a relatively early stage of the Gentile mission, and increasingly improbable as time went on. I have noted the dispute between Jesus and some Pharisees at Mk 2.23-28, arising from the disciples going through other people's fields plucking grain on the sabbath.[11] Mark takes it for granted that his audience will know that the disciples must have been poor people taking *Peah*, the grain left for poor people at the edges of every field, in accordance with Lev. 23.22, and that if anyone at a church meeting did not know this, the reader would be able to explain it. Similarly, when Jesus had performed an exorcism in the synagogue at Capernaum one sabbath, and healed Simeon Peter's mother-in-law at home, people brought other sick people and demoniacs to Jesus so that he could heal them (Mk 1.21-34). Mark's note of the time at which they did so is very careful: 'in the evening, when the sun had set'. This presupposes the knowledge that the Law prohibits the carrying of burdens on the sabbath (Jer. 17.21-22), which ends when darkness falls, as well as the obvious fact that sick people who have to be carried are heavy enough to be burdens.[12]

The dispute at the beginning of Mark 7 has been more controversial, and it is more difficult to sort out.[13] It differs from the two previous examples in that Mark does explain the situation, and it has often been suggested that he did not do so correctly because he was out of touch with Jewish customs. This dispute was begun by Pharisees and some scribes from Jerusalem, who wanted to know why Jesus' disciples ate food with their hands not in a state of purity, that is to say, without washing them first, as Mark correctly explains. They asked, 'Why do your disciples not walk according to the tradition of the elders, but eat food with profane hands?' (Mk 7.5). Accordingly, what the disciples violated was not the written Torah, but an oral tradition of orthodox Jews, and this is why Mark has felt it necessary to explain the situation.

Mark's further explanation has often been thought to be partly wrong:

> For the Pharisees and all the Jews, unless they wash their hands with a fistful [of water] do not eat, adhering to the tradition of the elders, and [when they come] from the market-place, they do not eat without immersing, and there are many other [traditions] which they have received to adhere to, immersions of cups and pots and bronze kettles and dining couches.
>
> (Mk 7.3-4)

This is a perfectly accurate account of the behaviour of Pharisees and other orthodox Jews, who adhered to many expansions of the written Torah. It is full of technical terminology, including the basic terminology for the handing down and receiving of traditions, as well as details on account of which I have added some bracketed words so that it makes sense in normal English. One point is

---

11   See pp. 9–10, and pp. 312–15.
12   See further pp. 106–7, 268.
13   See further pp. 326–31.

exaggerated, the attribution of these customs to 'all the Jews'. This exaggeration is however more characteristic of observant Jews being hopeful about what Jews ought to do, than of Gentiles who do not understand Jewish customs. For example, the *Letter of Aristeas* says of the Jewish people involved in translating the Hebrew Bible into Greek, 'following the custom of *all the Jews*, they washed their hands in the sea in the course of their prayers to God' (*Aristeas* 305). Handwashing among Jews during prayers was not universal in the second century BCE, but this unimpeachably knowledgeable Jewish author would like us to imagine that it was, and this is the same kind of exaggeration as we find in Mark. We must therefore conclude that Mark has accurately described the oral Law of orthodox Jews in considerable detail, which is easier to envisage when Christianity was still partly a Jewish movement, than later when Greek-speaking churches were more and more Gentile.

After his account of Jesus' response to the scribes and Pharisees, Mark concludes by attributing further teaching to Jesus, some of which is of doubtful authenticity. The first saying is at Mk 7.15:

> There is nothing outside a man going into him which can make him unclean, but the (things which) come out of a man are what make the man unclean.

Mark has that addressed to 'the crowd', and gives Jesus' subsequent attempt to explain this to the disciples in 'the house away from the crowd', which is often suspected to be a deliberate indication that this is a secondary explanation for the benefit of the church. Be that as it may, it is clearly accompanied by Mark's own comment:

> Do you not understand that everything outside going into a man cannot make him unclean, because it does not go into his heart but into his stomach and goes out into the latrine (cleansing all foods) . . .
>
> (Mk 7.18-19)

Here the comments attributed to Jesus himself make perfect sense in the original context of Jewish purity law. In the first place, and central to the original dispute, whatever is on your hands when you have not washed them, will not make you unclean when you pick up food in your hands to eat it, because nothing outside a person can make that person unclean when it enters them, that is, when they eat or drink it. Since you might have touched all sorts of unclean things with your hands before you picked up your food to eat it, Jesus expressed himself in this very general way, 'There is nothing outside a man going into him which can make him unclean . . .'. Secondly, the Torah says very clearly, forcefully and repeatedly, that God has forbidden his people to eat unclean food. For example,

> These you shall detest among the birds; they shall not be eaten, they are an abomination: the eagle and the vulture and the osprey and the kite and the falcon of every kind, every raven of any kind . . .
>
> (Lev. 11.13-15)

Since, however, you are forbidden to eat these creatures, the Torah does not tell you how to cleanse yourself if you do eat them. It does tell you what to do if, for example, you carry the carcass of such an animal when it is dead: he 'shall wash his clothes and be unclean until the evening' (Lev. 11.25). Since you do not eat unclean animals, Jesus could make the very general statement that 'There is nothing outside a man going into him which can make him unclean . . .'.

It was different with all sorts of bodily discharges, which do make you unclean. The Torah defines these, and gives instructions for dealing with them. For example, 'If a man lies with a woman and has an emission of semen, they shall bathe in water and be unclean until the evening' (Lev. 15.18). Hence the second part of Jesus' saying at Mk 7.15: 'the things which come out of a man are what make the man unclean.' The second version at Mk 7.18-19 is more dubious as a saying of Jesus, because its rationale would allow the eating of unclean foods, since what goes into your stomach and out into the latrine brings to mind food rather than dirt or any sort of uncleanness on your hands. Mark's gloss is accordingly reasonable: 'cleansing all foods'. Some scholars are also right to see here Gentile influence, but it does not follow that Mark was personally Gentile or that his Gospel is to be dated later than c.40 CE. The Gentile mission began early. St Paul retained his Jewish identity, but he considered it right in principle to eat unclean food, and qualified this only through concern for weaker brethren, especially if food was known to have been sacrificed to idols (e.g. Rom. 14.1-4, 14–21; 1 Corinthians 8). This was a necessary part of a successful Gentile mission, the only possible context for a Gospel written for Greek-speaking Christians. Mk 7.18-19 locates Mark in that cultural context, but it does not tell us whether he was personally Gentile, nor does it imply a late date for the composition of his Gospel.

I therefore conclude that Crossley is right: Mark's Gospel was written c.40 CE. *It was not however finished*. It is remarkable that only one piece of evidence for this important conclusion has been generally noted, and that has been disputed – this Gospel does not have a proper ending, it just stops. It is more important that the *whole* of it is unfinished. It contains many features which cry out for revision, including both Aramaisms and other mistakes, such that any decent literate Greek speakers would alter it, as Matthew and Luke did abundantly. For example, the Gospel begins with a programmatic citation, 'as it is written in Isaiah the prophet', but the quotation begins with Mal. 3.1 before proceeding to Isa. 40.3, followed by the ministry of John the Baptist. This is because Jesus himself saw both texts fulfilled in John's ministry (cf. Mk 9.11-13; Mt. 11.10// Lk. 7.27).[14] This has led them to be amalgamated, as scriptural passages often were, and the result has been attributed to Isaiah, the more important prophet with the most easily recognizable quotation. It is wrong, however, and Matthew and Luke both corrected it by quoting from Isaiah only, while copyists of Mark corrected the reference to 'in the prophets'.

We have seen that at Mk 1.41, Mark has Jesus be angry (*orgistheis*). This is inappropriate, and it happened because Mark was translating the Aramaic *regaz*

14 See further pp. 178–80.

and suffering from interference. Matthew and Luke left it out, and copyists of Mark altered it so that Jesus had compassion instead. We have also seen that at Mk 2.23, Mark has the disciples 'make' a path, which is not appropriate either. Mark's Aramaic source will have read *lᵉma'ᵉbhar*, so they began 'to go along' a path, which everyone was entitled to do on the sabbath. This has been slightly misread as *lᵉma'ᵉbhadh*, 'to make', with 'd' (ד) rather than 'r' (ר) as the final letter, by a translator who was again suffering from interference. Matthew and Luke both corrected this by leaving out 'make a path'.[15] Some copyists of Mark left it out too, while others produced variant readings, one of which simply means that the disciples were 'walking', so this was felt to be an improvement. According to Mk 7.31, Jesus, 'coming out from the regions of Tyre, went through Sidon', some 20 miles to the North, 'to the sea of Galilee', miles to the south-east of Tyre. This is not a sensible way to describe a journey. Most manuscripts of Mark read instead the much easier 'Jesus, coming out from the regions of Tyre and Sidon went to the sea of Galilee'. Matthew omitted Sidon in a perfectly reasonable description of Jesus' return from Tyre to the sea of Galilee (Mt. 15.29) (Luke omitted Mk 6.45–8.26).

At Mk 12.4, Mark has a new Greek word, a verb formed from the common Greek word for 'head'.[16] Common translations, such as 'beat over the head' (NRSV), correctly represent what Mark meant. I suggest that Mark had in front of him Jesus' rare and colourful Aramaic *r'shīn*, which means 'pound, bray', so this is another word for 'beat up'. Mark did not recognize it, but he did recognize the first three letters (*r' sh*) as the normal Aramaic and Hebrew word for 'head'. This is why he made up a new word, under the influence of the text which he was translating. Translators often behave like this when they get stuck. Matthew and Luke both omitted this word as they rewrote the passage. Copyists of Mark were also troubled. Most used another word related to 'head' which ought to mean 'summarized', but which is at least a normal Greek word, and most of them also added 'stoning' from Mt. 21.26 to make the meaning clear.

At Mk 14.25, straight after his interpretation of the cup at the last supper, Jesus told his followers 'we will not add to drink from the fruit of the vine until . . .'. Here, with the words 'we will not add to drink', I have translated the most difficult reading, that of ancient Greek manuscripts which have preserved the idiom of Jesus' original, and perfectly normal, Aramaic. He meant, 'we will not drink again', and Mark translated his Aramaic source literally. Most scribes, however, altered it because it is exactly as peculiar in Greek as it is in English, and that is why most manuscripts read normal Greek for 'I will not drink' or 'I will not drink again'. Matthew and Luke made similar alterations (Mt. 26.29; Lk. 22.18).[17]

At the end of his account of Peter denying Jesus, Mark says 'throwing, he wept' (Mk 14.72). In Greek this is nonsense, but in Aramaic people could 'throw' (*shedhā*) threats and curses, much as in English people can 'hurl' abuse, and this

15 See further pp. 64–65.
16 See further pp. 418–19.
17 On this verse see further p. 435.

is exactly what Peter had just been doing. That is what Mark meant. He will however have misread the Aramaic *shr'*, 'began', as *shd'*, a difference of one let-ter, reading 'd' (ד) rather than 'r' (ר), so this is similar to Mk 2.23. The source read, 'And he began to weep'. Moreover, Matthew and Luke were so puzzled by 'throwing, he wept' that they consulted another source for the same event, or Matthew did so, and Luke copied Matthew. After copying Mark as usual, they have a run of five identical words instead of Mark's mistake: 'And going outside, he wept bitterly' (Mt. 26.75//Lk. 22.62).[18] Three important manuscripts, which often *preserve* correct readings where Mark has Aramaisms, put 'and he began to weep'. They must have realized what had happened, and wrote something more correct than Mark's own text!

I hope these examples illustrate the main point. Mark's Gospel contains so many peculiarities like those listed here that it must be regarded as a first draft. I do not of course mean that, had he lived to revise it, his Greek would sud-denly have become as good as that of Matthew, let alone Luke. For example, it would be no surprise to find that, however often he revised it, he still used 'and', 'immediately', 'again' and the historic present more often than a writer of good Greek, and that Matthew and Luke still had cause for extensive revisions. What I do mean is that the number of mistakes like those which I have just listed is so great that he would have revised at least the majority of them, and that we should infer from them that this is an unfinished first draft of his Gospel.

It is in this light that we should consider the ending.[19] Mark has Jesus tell his followers, after the Last Supper, that after his Resurrection, 'I will go before you into Galilee' (Mk 14.28). Later, the angel in the empty tomb tells the three women to tell his disciples and Peter, 'he is going before you into Galilee. There you will see him, as he told you.' Instead of recounting this, however, Mark concludes,

> And going out, they fled from the tomb, for trembling and amazement held them. And they said nothing to anyone, for they were afraid.
>
> (Mk 16.8)

In the ancient world, this satisfied no one. Matthew and Luke replaced it with their own endings. Ancient copyists of Mark added two different endings, known as the Shorter Ending and the Longer Ending, which is found in the majority of manuscripts. This shows how widespread was the feeling in the ancient churches that Mark needed a proper ending.

It has been suggested that the ending was lost, a view which may be supported by pointing out that an ancient scroll could easily be damaged in such a way that the ending, which was literally on the outside of the scroll, was the part which was lost.[20] This is true, but it does not explain why the rest of the document appears unfinished, nor why there was only one copy, nor why Mark could not

---

18   On this passage see further pp. 442–43.
19   See further pp. 435, 477–78.
20   E.g. recently B. Witherington III, *The Gospel of Mark: A Socio-Rhetorical Commentary* (Grand Rapids: Eerdmans, 2001), pp. 47–49.

be contacted to write a replacement ending. It has also been said that 'one may wonder why, if Mark was suddenly removed from the scene, a member of his community did not complete the Gospel for him.'[21] This should underline for us the extraordinary nature of Mark's achievement in writing the first Gospel.

Mark was not an author like Plutarch or Suetonius, well educated, experienced and writing another Life of Someone Famous. He was a bilingual Christian writing a Gospel for Greek-speaking Christian communities which needed a written Life of Jesus, and had no expert bilingual author to write it for them. Mark's best sources were in Aramaic. They were also written, and will have been written on wax tablets or perhaps sheets of papyrus, which were in widespread use.[22] These could be difficult to read, and Mark translated them as he went along, as we must infer from the same features as show that his Gospel is a first draft. If someone else had translated them for him, he would have been as likely to make corrections as Matthew, Luke and copyists of Mark can be seen to have done.

Wax tablets and sheets of papyrus were frequently fastened together, and some of Mark's sources may have been of some length. For example, it has often been suggested that Mk 2.1–3.6 was a single pre-Markan complex. For all we know, it may be a translation of an Aramaic source which reached Mark in one piece. It is possible that further research into the Aramaic background of this Gospel will cast more light on such questions. In any case, we should not underestimate the magnitude of Mark's achievement, simply because we can see that the result was not faultless. Without the training which modern translators receive, but simply on the basis of his knowledge of Aramaic and Greek, and perhaps the Hebrew Bible as well as the Septuagint, he made translations of at least some of those sources available to him. He also heard Peter preach to some extent, almost certainly in Aramaic too, whether in Antioch, Jerusalem or elsewhere. Mark will have known oral sources too, some of which will have been people talking to him, or at church meetings, in Greek. He put all this together into the first Gospel, an achievement which required him to do a considerable amount of editing as well. This was a massive achievement, for which he should be given every credit. His Gospel could not possibly have been completed by handing it over to another member of his local church. Most members of whichever local church this was could not have undertaken a task of this magnitude. A significant proportion of them will have been unable to write, let alone revise this work, or improve on the ending.

Moreover, anyone who had achieved this much will have been well known in many churches, for he wrote a Gospel for all Christians.[23] To do it, he must have travelled among the churches, and it is not probable that he obtained his

---

21 J. Marcus, *Mark 8–16: A New Translation with Introduction and Commentary* (AB 27A. New Haven: Yale UP, 2009), p. 1091.

22 For an excellent general account of all such matters see A. R. Millard, *Reading and Writing in the Time of Jesus* (The Biblical Seminar, 69. Sheffield: Sheffield Academic, 2000).

23 R. Bauckham (ed.), *The Gospel for All Christians: Rethinking the Gospel Audiences* (Edinburgh: T&T Clark, 1998), especially the fine opening essay of R. Bauckham, 'For Whom Were Gospels Written?'.

Aramaic sources without visiting Jerusalem or Galilee, or both. How long it took him to write his Gospel we do not know, but if he completed it c.40 CE, he can hardly not have begun work as early as c.35 CE. During this period, his efforts will have become well known in many churches, and his Gospel eagerly expected. To achieve so much and not complete his work, he must have been imprisoned, died or become too ill to continue. Persecution of Christians was enough to make imprisonment possible, death suddenly at any age was a normal feature of life in societies with no modern medicine, and hygiene in cities was vile enough to make some of us feel ill just reading about it. It would require a remarkable person to improve on his work. Such a man was duly found: we know him as Matthew the Evangelist, though we shall see that his real name is somewhat uncertain. He may already have been collecting material, but he used Mark's Gospel as his base narrative because it was much the best, or perhaps the only, one available.

In the meantime, for a period of perhaps some 10 or 15 years, Mark's Gospel was the only written Gospel available in the churches. This is why it was copied and widely distributed without delay. This is the explanation, and the only possible explanation, of the fact that it was held sacred enough to become canonical even after the Gospel according to Matthew was completed and distributed. At the same time, it was Matthew's Gospel which became the most popular in the churches. It is much better written, and it contains much more of Jesus' teaching, together with a proper ending.

The following conclusions may therefore be drawn. The Gospel of Mark was the first of the Gospels to be written. Both Matthew and Luke used it as the basis of their own outlines of the ministry of Jesus, copying and editing it as they went along. Mark's Gospel was written by an unknown Christian called Marcus. He wrote in Greek for Greek-speaking churches c.40 CE, and he used Aramaic sources, some of which were abbreviated but in all other respects literally accurate accounts of incidents from the life of Jesus and sayings which he spoke. His Gospel is accordingly the most important single source for our knowledge of the life and teaching of Jesus.

3. *The So-called 'Q' Material*

The Gospels of Matthew and Luke used other source material too. The other material used by both of them has often been thought to have been drawn from a single Greek document. Much of the early work on this was done in Germany in the second half of the nineteenth century, and this led to it being labelled 'Q', an abbreviation of the German word *Quelle*, which simply means 'Source'. Some scholars now regard the view that this was a single Greek document as the dominant theory, and some of them believe that John Kloppenborg has shown that it is correct.[24] It is important to realize that this hypothesis regards *one single*

---

24 J. S. Kloppenborg, *The Formation of Q. Trajectories in Ancient Wisdom Collections*

Greek document as the source of *all* the 'Q' material. Accordingly, despite the central fact that this document does not exist, a team of scholars have produced a 'critical edition' of it.[25]

The mainstream version of this view has one general problem, namely that the disappearance of 'Q' is difficult to explain. More extreme forms of this hypothesis regard 'Q' as the first Gospel, the product of a 'Q Community', who are often located in Galilee, and sometimes viewed as sort of cynic philosophers, and/or as not really Christian at all.[26] However, the more vigorous the community for which the 'first Gospel' is supposed to have been written, the more impossible it is to explain its disappearance. Moreover, if 'Q' is regarded as cynic and hardly Christian, it becomes difficult to explain why Matthew and Luke had anything to do with it, let alone copied some of it with exceptional accuracy, as the verbally identical parts of 'Q' show that they must have done. It is also difficult to connect it with Jesus in his original environment.

Other scholars believe that the 'Q' material was not source material used independently by Matthew and Luke, but that Luke copied parts of Matthew, editing as he went along.[27] This is generally known as the 'Mark without Q' hypothesis, since its adherents believe in the priority of Mark but not in the existence of 'Q'. The view that Luke used Matthew is also part of the neo-Griesbach hypothesis, which supposes that Mark used both Matthew and Luke.[28] It is important that the 'Mark without Q' hypothesis supposes not merely that Luke used the Gospel of Matthew, but that almost all the 'Q' material is to be explained by Luke's use of Matthew. They make an exception for Luke's use of independent oral traditions, such as for example his version of the Lord's Prayer (Lk. 11.2-4).[29] Lack of common order is one of the major problems of the 'Mark without Q' hypothesis,

---

(Philadelphia: Fortress, 1987); J. S. Kloppenborg Verbin, *Excavating Q. The History and Setting of the Sayings Gospel* (Minneapolis/Edinburgh: Fortress/T&T Clark, 2000).

25 J. M. Robinson, P. Hoffman and J. S. Kloppenborg (eds), *The Critical Edition of Q: Synopsis, including the Gospels of Matthew and Luke, Mark and Thomas, with English, German and French Translations of Q and Thomas* (Leuven: Peeters, 2000).

26 For some of these variations see notably A. D. Jacobson, *The First Gospel: An Introduction to Q* (Sonoma: Polebridge, 1992); B. L. Mack, *The Lost Gospel: The Book of Q and Christian Origins* (San Francisco/Shaftesbury: HarperCollins/Element, 1993); and L. E. Vaage, *Galilean Upstarts: Jesus' First Followers According to Q* (Valley Forge: Trinity Press International, 1994).

27 A. M. Farrer, 'On Dispensing with Q', in D. E. Nineham (ed.), *Studies in the Gospels: Essays in Memory of R. H. Lightfoot* (Oxford: Blackwell, 1955), pp. 55–88; M. D. Goulder, *Luke: A New Paradigm* (2 vols. JSNTSup, 20. Sheffield: Sheffield Academic, 1989); M. Goodacre, *Goulder and the Gospels: An Examination of a New Paradigm* (JSNTSup, 133. Sheffield: Sheffield Academic, 1996); *The Synoptic Problem: A Way through the Maze* (The Biblical Seminar, 80. Sheffield: Sheffield Academic, 2001); *The Case Against Q: Studies in Markan Priority and the Synoptic Problem* (Harrisburg: Trinity Press International, 2002).

28 Cf. p. 62, and e.g. A. J. McNicol, with D. L. Dungan and D. B. Peabody (eds), *Beyond the Q Impasse – Luke's use of Matthew: A Demonstration by the Research Team of the International Institute for Gospel Studies* (Valley Forge: Trinity Press International, 1996).

29 See for example Goodacre, *Case Against Q*, pp. 64–66.

because it makes it difficult to explain why Luke, following the order of Mark's Gospel, which was also followed by Matthew, moved so much of Matthew's 'Q' material into blocks instead of leaving it where it was in Matthew.[30] The proponents of this hypothesis have also failed to take sufficient account of genuine material about the Jesus of history as a source of what is now found in both these Gospels.

Some scholars are not convinced that all of the 'Q' material was a single document, nor that all of this material was transmitted to Matthew and Luke in Greek rather than in Aramaic, nor that Luke's use of Matthew provides a feasible explanation of most of the material which they have in common. I therefore propose what I call a 'chaotic model of "Q"'. This used to be implicit in the work of outstanding scholars who took seriously the Aramaic dimension of 'Q', but who did not write books devoted to establishing this model.[31] In 2002, I contributed *An Aramaic Approach to Q*, in which I examined in detail a small number of passages (Mt. 23.23-36//Lk. 11.39-51; Mt. 11.2-19//Lk. 7.18-35; Mk 3.20-30; Mt. 12.22-32; Lk 11.14-23 and 12.10), and argued that only a relatively chaotic model of the 'Q' material could explain all the varied evidence which it provides.[32]

It is astonishing that such a model has hardly been taken seriously in any other book written on 'Q' for many years, whereas it is sympathetically viewed by many New Testament scholars with whom I have discussed it at conferences. This is reflected in almost stray remarks in some books about Jesus. For example, Hengel and Schwemer comment briefly:

> The 'Q' hypothesis is much more complex and complicated than is generally supposed. Casey comes therewith [in *An Aramaic Approach to Q*] nearer to reality than the Q-hypothesis, which is often presented to-day as much too simple.[33]

Such opinions are widespread among New Testament scholars who have not recently written books and articles on the 'Q' material. I hope therefore that the forthcoming work of Stephanie Fisher will establish it beyond reasonable doubt as the normative view of New Testament scholars.[34] In the meantime, the

---

30   Adherents of this hypothesis do of course go to great lengths to explain this feature of the evidence. See for example Goulder, *Luke*, passim; Goodacre, *Case Against Q*, ch. 4, '"Unscrambling the Egg with a Vengeance"? Luke's Order and the Sermon on the Mount'.

31   E.g. C. K. Barrett, 'Q: A Re-examination', *ExpT* 54 (1942–43), pp. 320–23; M. Black, 'The Aramaic Dimension in Q with Notes on Luke 17.22 and Matthew 24.26 (Luke 17.23)', *JSNT* 40 (1990), pp. 33–41.

32   P. M. Casey, *An Aramaic Approach to Q: Sources for the Gospels of Matthew and Luke* (SNTSMS 122. Cambridge: CUP, 2002).

33   Hengel and Schwemer, *Jesus und das Judentum*, p. 225 n. 149 from p. 224: 'Die »Hypothese Q« ist sehr viel komplexer und komplizierter, als allgemein angenommen wird. CASEY kommt damit der Wirklichkeit näher als die heute oft als viel zu einfach vorgestellte Q-Hypothese.' For a brief assessment of this book see pp. 50–51.

34   Stephanie is writing a doctoral thesis on this at Nottingham University.

following discussion is intended to present the main evidence generally supposed to favour each of the three major hypotheses, concluding with decisive arguments in favour of the 'chaotic model'.

The two main arguments in favour of 'Q' being a Greek document are verbal identity and common order. Some passages of Matthew and Luke, which are not found in Mark, are almost verbally identical in Matthew and Luke. For example, both report more of John the Baptist's preaching than Mark does, including this:

Offspring of vipers, who warned you to flee from the coming Wrath? Do therefore fruit worthy of repentance, and do not think to say among yourselves, 'We have a father, Abraham'. For I'm telling you that God can raise up from these stones children for Abraham.	Offspring of vipers, who warned you to flee from the coming Wrath? Do therefore fruits worthy of repentance, and do not begin to say among yourselves, 'We have a father, Abraham'. For I'm telling you that God can raise up from these stones children for Abraham.
(Mt. 3.7-9)	(Lk. 3.7-9)

Here the verbal agreement between Matthew and Luke is so extensive that there must be a close literary relationship between them. Moreover, Matthew and Luke have this preaching in the same position relative to other material. There are only two reasonable explanations of this: either Matthew and Luke found this material in a Greek document, or one of them copied it from the other.

Another passage with a high level of verbal agreement contains Jesus' condemnation of cities in which he worked during the ministry:

Woe to you, Chorazin, woe to you, Bethsaida, for if the mighty works performed in you had been performed in Tyre and Sidon, they would have repented long ago in sackcloth and ashes. But I'm telling you, it will be more tolerable for Tyre and Sidon in the day of judgement than for you. And you, Capernaum, will you be exalted to heaven? You will be cast down to Hades!	Woe to you, Chorazin, woe to you, Bethsaida, for if the mighty works performed in you had been performed in Tyre and Sidon, they would have repented long ago, sitting in sackcloth and ashes. But it will be more tolerable for Tyre and Sidon in the judgement than for you. And you, Capernaum, will you be exalted to heaven? You will be cast down to Hades!
(Mt. 11.21-23)	(Lk. 10.13-15)

Here too the level of verbal agreement in Greek is so high that there must be a literary relationship between the two passages. Once again, either they are both dependent on a source which was written in Greek, or one evangelist has copied the other. Moreover, a reasoned case can be made for supposing that these passages are in the same order relative to the Gospels of Matthew and Luke, though this is less obvious than with the previous passage, for it depends on the view taken of several other passages.

However, for us to believe that the 'Q' material was a single document written in Greek, all of it would have to be like these two passages, whereas much of it is not. Some of it is not in common order, and, what is even more important, some of the material not in common order can be shown to have come from two independent translations from the original Aramaic. One of the most famous passages of this kind comes from Jesus' polemic against his opponents:

Woe to you, scribes and Pharisees, hypocrites, for you tithe mint and dill and cumin and omit the heavier things of the Law, justice and mercy and faith. It was necessary to do the latter and not omit the former. Blind guides, who strain out the gnat but swallow the camel! (Mt. 23.23-24)	But woe to you Pharisees, for you tithe mint and rue and every herb and pass over justice and the love of God. It was necessary to do the latter and not pass over the former. (Lk. 11.42)

These passages are not remotely in common order, and the level of verbal agreement is much lower than in the two passages which I have just discussed. The most important variations reflect alternative readings of one Aramaic source, while others are due to Luke's editing.

The cultural context is the behaviour of scribes and Pharisees, who have expanded the Torah's commandments to tithe for example grain, wine and oil (Deut. 14.23), in the light of its commandments to tithe for example 'the seed of the earth' and 'the fruit of the tree' (Lev. 27.30), to mean that they should tithe herbs as well as basic foods. The effect of this at the time of Jesus was to provide the priests in the Temple, who received the tithes, with herbs as well as basic foods, so they could perhaps make mint tea, eat dill with their fish, and flavour tasteless vegetables with cumin. Matthew's version of the herbs to be tithed is accordingly very sensible, but Luke's is not. In the first place, it was not true that orthodox Jews tithed 'every herb'. Secondly, Luke's 'rue' (*pēganon*) is a mistake. The Aramaic for dill was four letters written as *sh-b-th-ā*: Luke, or perhaps his translator, misread it as *sh-b-r-ā*, 'rue', so just one letter different (ת misread as ר), an easy mistake to make if he was reading a wax tablet or a single sheet of papyrus, on which the left-hand side of the letter, likely to be much squigglier than the square script printed here, had been wiped out or become too faint to see. Now *sh-b-r-ā* cannot be right, because it means *Syrian* rue, *peganum harmala*, which would not be eaten. The translation of *sh-b-r-ā* with *pēganon* was however natural: as one Greek writer put it, 'some call it "wild rue (*pēganon*)", but others call it *harmala*, but the Syrians (call it) *bēssasa*' (Dioscorides III, 46). Luke's readers and audiences may however have thought his *pēganon* was what people in our society call 'rue' if they use it, *ruta graveolens*, which was widely used in Italy and known in Greece, chiefly for medicinal purposes. Others may have thought of *ruta chalapensis* or the like. Such Christians will have varied in how stupid they thought the Pharisees were!

It follows from this particular difference that Luke was not copying Matthew, nor could Matthew have been copying Luke. Where Matthew has 'omit', Luke has 'pass over'. Either is reasonable, but Luke's is a more literal translation of the Aramaic *'br*, so Luke cannot have copied that from Matthew or from a common Greek source either. Where Matthew has 'mercy and faith', Luke has 'the love of God'. Either is reasonable, but now we know we are dealing with an Aramaic source we can see that Matthew correctly translated *rḥmthā*, 'mercy', which Luke misread as *rḥmyā*, 'love' and that is what he edited.

Luke's remaining variations are due to his editing the material for his Gentile Christian audiences. Jesus referred to 'justice and mercy and faith' as *hōmerayā*, literally 'heavies', an Aramaic and Hebrew technical term for important and/or stringent points of the Torah, and very difficult to translate into Greek, which had no equivalent term. Matthew did his best for his Jewish Christian audiences, editing it to 'the heavier things of the Law', knowing that the Greek word for 'heavy' was used in many other metaphorical ways. Luke, writing for Gentile Christian audiences for whom anything like that would be incomprehensible, left it out. He also omitted Jesus' wondrous joke: 'Blind guides, who strain out the gnat but swallow the camel!' Most people do not find this in the least bit comical, because one needs a very detailed knowledge of the intricacies of the expanded halakhah of scribes and Pharisees to understand it in the first place. Luke was accordingly very sensible to leave it out.[35]

This demonstrates that the two models of the 'Q' material commonest in recent scholarship on 'Q' are both historically implausible. The 'Q' material as a whole cannot have been taken from a single document written in Greek, and, even apart from occasional pieces transmitted orally, all Luke's 'Q' material cannot have been taken from Matthew. It remains possible that some of the 'Q' material was derived from a document of some length written in Greek, and it remains probable that Luke knew Matthew, as we shall see. We must however adopt a more chaotic model for the 'Q' material as a whole.

At this point we must return to the question of common order, for the use of the argument from common order to establish the most conventional model of 'Q' is also faulty. There are two things wrong with it. In the first place, too many passages which have a reasonably high level of verbal agreement in Greek are not in common order. For example, Matthew collected some eschatological material from 'Q' into his final eschatological discourse, Matthew 24. This is partly based on the eschatological discourse of Mark 13, and Matthew retains Mark's setting on the Mount of Olives, some time after the Cleansing of the Temple. Luke, however, while vigorously editing material from Mark 13 into his eschatological discourse at Luke 21, put some of the same sayings as we find in Matthew 24 into Jesus' teaching in Luke 17. This is part of a lengthy account of varied teachings of Jesus supposedly delivered during his final journey from Galilee to Jerusalem. Such sayings include the following:

35 See further pp. 331–34.

For as the lightning goes out from the East and shines to the West, so shall be the parousia of the Son of man. Wherever the corpse is, there the eagles/vultures will gather together.	For as the lightning, when it lightens, shines from under the heaven to under the heaven, so will the Son of man be in his day . . . Where the body is, there the eagles/ vultures will gather together to (it).
(Mt. 24.27-28)	(Lk. 17.24, 37b)

This saying is significantly different from the others just considered. While the versions of Matthew and Luke have enough in common to make it clear that they are two versions of the same saying, the level of verbal agreement is not as high as at Mt. 3.7-9//Lk. 3.7-9 or Mt. 11.21-23//Lk. 10.13-15. Secondly, while the two sayings here are in common order relative to each other, they are not in common order relative to the Gospels of Matthew and Luke as a whole. This is enough to conclude that we are not dealing with a single Greek document, the same one as at Mt. 3.7-9//Lk. 3.7-9 and Mt. 11.21-23//Lk. 10.13-15. Moreover, the 'Son of man' saying is not an authentic saying of Jesus, and cannot be reconstructed in feasible Aramaic. Jesus did not talk about his future coming in this way, and the Aramaic *bar* (*e*)*nāsh*(*ā*) cannot function as a title like this.[36] Like some other sayings, this one originated in Greek, created by someone in the early church trying to picture Jesus' second coming. This warns us that, while some 'Q' material is important for our knowledge of the historical Jesus, other 'Q' material is secondary. It is therefore essential to assess independently the authenticity of each piece of the 'Q' material.

The next point is to consider again a major facet of those sections of the 'Q' material which are in common order. Is there a possible explanation of this, other than that of a single Greek document? To a significant degree, this question must be answered in the affirmative, because of the major aspect of the synoptic Gospels with which this chapter began: Matthew and Luke copied and edited Mark. If they both inherited the 'Q' material in pieces, written on wax tablets or single sheets of papyrus, it would be entirely natural that they should insert some pieces in the appropriate places of Mark's narrative. Moreover, some places are so obviously appropriate that they would occur naturally to two authors who were independent of each other. The first passage discussed above, Mt. 3.7-9// Lk. 3.7-9, is a clear example of this. Both Matthew and Luke copied and edited Mk 1.2-8. It is entirely natural that they should both have inserted Mt. 3.7-9// Lk. 3.7-9 independently between Mark's account of John's ministry and his pre- diction of what all three of them saw as John's prediction of the coming of Jesus, and that Luke should have added further material of his own in the same place. This is doubly so if Luke knew Matthew, for he might well have remembered the material in Matthew, and could have checked up on it when he wished to. In these circumstances, he could have copied a passage such as Mt. 3.7-9 into Lk. 3.7-9 if he particularly liked it, even if this is not what he usually did.

All the passages which I have discussed are in some way typical. It follows

---

36   See further pp. 214–24, 358–88, 435–39.

that a chaotic model of the 'Q' material is the only realistic one. Matthew and Luke each inherited this material in pieces. Some pieces reached them written in Greek. Some parts which have a relatively high degree of verbal identity in Greek, and which contain authentic material about Jesus, were each derived from a single translation from the original Aramaic. Beyond their membership of Christian churches, there is nothing to connect the translators of these pieces with each other, except that they followed a common strategy in the translation of the term *bar* (ᵉ)*nāsh*(*ā*), 'Son of man'.[37] Other parts of the 'Q' material, which have a relatively high degree of verbal identity in Greek, but which were originally written by members of the earliest Christian communities, were written in Greek. In any particular case, a piece of this material may have been transmitted to Matthew, and copied from Matthew by Luke.

Other parts of the 'Q' material, which contain authentic material about Jesus, were translated from Aramaic into Greek more than once. These pieces may have reached each evangelist in a different translation, or they may have reached them in Aramaic, and were then translated either by Matthew and Luke themselves, or by one of their assistants. These different pieces were written down on wax tablets, single sheets of papyrus or the like. We know that such materials were in general use, and there were plenty of people who could write on them and read them.[38] The translators might however be bilingual people who were not accustomed to the difficult and skilful task of translation. This could be a major problem, especially with languages as different from each other as Aramaic and Greek. This is one factor in those passages where an Aramaic source has been misread, as for example Lk. 11.42, discussed above. When such source material reached Luke, perhaps c.75–85 CE, it may also have been difficult to read. The second factor involved at this point is the editorial work of each evangelist. We have seen that, while resulting partly from misreading the Aramaic source, Lk. 11.42 itself, complete with the omission of Mt. 23.24, is excellently adapted to the needs of the Gentile Christian churches for whom Luke wrote.

This chaotic model enables us to explain another major feature of the 'Q' material: it has not been preserved on its own. This is natural if it was a number of different pieces, independently collected by or for each of the two evangelists. If however it was a single Greek document, its disappearance cannot be explained. This is doubly so if it were the first Gospel, written in a 'Q' community, who would have had a particularly direct interest in keeping it, and who would not have given it up when Matthew and Luke edited it into their own Gospels. The fate of the Gospel of Mark is instructive at this point. Even though it was written by an unknown Christian called Marcus, cries out to be rewritten at various points, and has no proper ending, it was faithfully kept and venerated in the churches, even after it was rewritten by Matthew and Luke. Moreover, this was the fate of other complete documents in the Judaism of this period, but not of small sources used by historians. When part of Samuel-Kings was rewritten to produce 1 and 2 Chronicles, the books of Samuel and Kings were kept

---

37   On this see pp. 369–74.
38   Millard, *Reading and Writing in the Time of Jesus*.

to remain part of the sacred text. When part of the Pentateuch was rewritten c.166–165 BCE as the book of *Jubilees*, the Pentateuch was kept too, and both were copied at Qumran.

I have not yet mentioned patristic sources about 'Q', because this is not what they discuss. In the next section, however, I discuss a brief comment by Papias, preserved again by Eusebius, overtly about Matthew and interpreted by church tradition as if it were about the surviving Gospel According to Matthew (Eus. *H.E.* III, 39, 16).[39] I point out, however, that Papias originally referred to the transmission of Gospel traditions in general, and that his comments support a chaotic model of the 'Q' material. Papias attributed the collection of some Gospel traditions to the apostle Matthew, one of the Twelve, who wrote them down in Aramaic and everyone 'translated/interpreted (*hērmēneusen*)' them as well as they were able. There is every reason to believe this. It explains the high proportion of literally accurate traditions, mostly of sayings of Jesus, in the 'Q' material and in material unique to the Gospel of Matthew. It also explains the lack of common order, as well as the inadequate translations of some passages into Greek.

4. *The Gospel According to Matthew*

The Gospel of Matthew is usually dated c.75–85 CE, and its author is considered to be unknown. I propose that it should be dated much earlier than this, c.50–60 CE, and that its author was an unknown Jewish Christian, who may or may not have been called *Mattai* or the like. This name was used in more than one form. The Aramaic *Matt(h)ai* was transliterated into Greek as *Matthaios* or *Maththaios*. These are the forms which are found in New Testament manuscripts, and which led to the English name Matthew, which we use both for one of the original members of the Twelve, and for the Gospel writer. Forms such as the Hebrew *Mattiya* led to the Greek *Matthias* or *Maththias*. This is the English name Matthias, a name which we use of the man who replaced Judas Iscariot as one of the Twelve (Acts 1.23-26), and for Josephus' father. In one form or another, this was a standard Jewish name of this period.

Church tradition has for centuries held that the author of 'the Gospel According to Matthew' was the apostle Matthew, who is found in Mark's list of the Twelve (Mk 3.18). It has also been considered significant that whereas Mark relates the call of a tax collector whom he names Levi, son of Alphaeus (Mk 2.14), Matthew, in copying the story, names him 'Matthew' instead, and adds 'the tax collector' as a description of Matthew in his list of the Twelve (Mt. 9.9, 10.3). The church tradition has often been traced back to Papias, quoted by Eusebius continuing the passage about the authorship of Mark (Eus. *H.E.* III, 39, 15–16).[40] Papias records a traditional view that 'Matthew compiled

---

39   See pp. 86–88.
40   See pp. 65–69.

the sayings/oracles (*logia*) in a Hebrew language', which could mean either Hebrew or Aramaic, and certainly did not mean Greek. Papias also says that everyone 'translated/interpreted (*hērmēneusen*)' them as well as they were able. The way this was understood by later Church Fathers is already clear in the comments of Irenaeus c.177 CE, as quoted by Eusebius:

> Now Matthew published among the Hebrews in their language a writing of a Gospel, while Peter and Paul were in Rome evangelizing and founding the church.
>
> (Iren. *Adv. Haer.* III, 1, 1, quoted by Eus. *H.E.* V, 8, 1)

Later Church Fathers repeat this tradition and amplify it.

When applied to our Gospel of Matthew, this tradition is complete nonsense, as most scholars have recognized. Our Gospel is not only written in perfectly decent Greek, it was partly written by an author who was revising our Greek Mark into better Greek, including the removal of a number of features of Mark's Aramaic sources. It was therefore written in Greek. Moreover, one of the Twelve would not have had reason to copy Mark's outline in this way. On the contrary, he would have had very good reason to replace it with an accurate outline which included the length of the ministry.

The origin of this tradition naturally proved difficult to fathom. How could such a grossly confused view of our Gospel of Matthew have arisen? It has often been suggested that the transmission of the 'Q' material was a source of the confusion, and this should be accepted.[41] A significant part of the 'Q' material consists of perfectly accurate material about Jesus, almost all of it sayings, and all of it within the slightly wider range of the Greek word *logia*. It is entirely reasonable to suppose that one of the Twelve wrote at least some of it. The Gospel writer's view of the apostle Matthew was that he was a tax collector (Mt. 9.9, altering Mk 2.14; Mt. 10.3, expanding Mk 3.18), and he is most unlikely to have added this view to his Markan tradition, unless he had a good source for it. We should therefore accept this. As a tax collector, the apostle Matthew would be very experienced in writing information accurately and legibly on wax tablets. It is entirely natural that one of the Twelve, who was a tax collector, selected himself to write down material about Jesus during the historic ministry.

Some of this Gospel's 'Q' material and some of the material unique to it resulted from Matthew the tax collector's material being transmitted accurately and translated and interpreted in accordance with the original Jewish tradition. On its way to Luke, however, some of the material transmitted in Aramaic was translated and interpreted as well as someone else was able, not very accurately and in accordance with the needs of Gentile Christian congregations. I have discussed Mt. 23.23-24//Lk. 11.42, which provides excellent examples of these

---

41 See for example the influential discussion of T. W. Manson, *The Sayings of Jesus* (London: Nicholson and Watson, 1937, as Part II of H. D. A. Major *et al.* (eds), *The Mission and Message of Jesus*. Reprinted separately, London: SCM, 1949), pp. 17–20.

points.[42] Mt. 23.23-24 was translated as accurately as possible, though Matthew used the Greek word *barūtera*, literally 'heavier', in a novel sense, because the best he could do with the Aramaic technical term *ḥōmerayā* was to translate it literally. Luke, however, dropped it, misread the Aramaic *sh-b-th-ā*, 'dill', as *sh-b-r-ā*, 'rue', so he has one of the herbs wrong, and misread the Aramaic *rḥmthā*, 'mercy', as *rḥmyā*, 'love', so he has another word wrong. While some of the differences between Matthew and Luke are due to Luke's editing for his Gentile congregations, it is clear that Matthew the Gospel writer made, or had available to him, a much better translation than that used by Luke.

It follows that this is what Papias meant! It is genuinely true that the apostle Matthew 'compiled the sayings/oracles in a Hebrew language, but each (person) translated/ interpreted them as he was able.' Moreover, the Greek word *logia*, which I have translated 'sayings/oracles', has a somewhat broader range of meaning than this, and could well be used of collections which consisted mostly, but not entirely, of sayings. It would not however have been a sensible word to use of the whole Gospel of Matthew. It was later Church Fathers who confused Matthew's collections of sayings of Jesus with our Greek Gospel of Matthew.

I suggest that a second source of the confusion lay with the real author of this Gospel. One possibility is that he was also called Matthias or Matthew. These were common enough Jewish names, and different forms were similar enough to cause confusion, as identical forms more obviously could. There is accordingly nothing in the least improbable or peculiar in the author of one synoptic Gospel having more or less the same name as one of the Twelve.

Alternatively, we must bear in mind the nature of authorship in Second Temple Judaism. Composite authorship was common, and so was the attribution of documents to the fountainheads of traditions. So, for example, the final authors of the book of Isaiah were quite happy to leave the impression that it was the work of Isaiah of Jerusalem, even though they included the work of another major prophet (Isa. 40–55), who is consequently known to us only as Second Isaiah. They also included several other prophetic pieces, and they endeavoured to unify this massive compilation with their own editorial work. Similarly, when the authors of the book of *Jubilees* rewrote part of the Pentateuch, they attributed it to the angel of the presence, speaking on behalf of God to Moses on Mount Sinai.[43]

Whatever the personal name of the final editor of our Greek Gospel of Matthew, he may have been absolutely delighted to have his completed work known as the Gospel according to (the apostle) Matthew, a highly desirable designation in churches which already knew the Gospel of Marcus. Second only to Jesus himself, the apostle Matthew was the fountainhead of many authentic traditions now part of this Gospel. How many people translated and edited these traditions, we do not know, nor does it matter at this point. The final editor used their work, and included other material, such as the birth narratives.[44] Thus our

---

42   See pp. 82–83, and further pp. 331–34.
43   See further pp. 124–25, 132–41.
44   On these stories see pp. 145–51.

Greek Gospel of Matthew is of composite authorship in the same sense as many ancient Jewish works, such as the books of Isaiah and *Jubilees*. Most Christians would notice that, in accordance with ancient custom, the author of the Greek Gospel of Matthew made extensive use of the Gospel of Marcus, the only written Gospel previously available in Greek. He will have been very happy for everyone to know that significant portions of his other material had been transmitted directly from Matthew the tax collector, one of the Twelve. At this stage there would be no risk of confusion, because ancient Jewish habits of authorship were pervasive in Jewish communities. The title of this Gospel, though not included in the text of the work and known to us only from much later manuscripts, is likely to have been generally known when the work was first composed, and to have been written at the beginning or end of the first copies.

The third source of eventual confusion was that it was extremely helpful to the early church to imagine that the Gospel which it most loved was written by one of the Twelve. This is the overwhelming force which drove the mistakes of the Church Fathers from Irenaeus onwards. It will have been helped by assumptions about authorship normal in the Graeco-Roman world. However much sources were used by authors such as Livy, the pre-eminent Roman historian, and Plutarch, who wrote lives of Julius Caesar, Augustus and many other people in Greek, they each claimed the authorship of what they saw as their own work. When later Church Fathers inherited the tradition which we know from Papias, it would be natural for them to conclude that the apostle Matthew wrote our Gospel of Matthew. Hence the quite confused tradition that it was originally written in Aramaic or even Hebrew.

The great advantage of this hypothesis is that it explains both the real nature of this Gospel and the confusion of church tradition about it. That some of the 'Q' material and some material special to Matthew was written by one of the Twelve explains the presence of perfectly accurate material. Confusion between two men called Matthew or the like, the fact that one of them was one of the Twelve, and the need to believe in the apostolic authority of Gospels, is one possible explanation of how the early church tradition became confused. Equally, the final editor of the Gospel may have released it under the name of Matthew, because the apostle Matthew was his major source, apart from Mark. That the material transmitted in Aramaic was translated by several different people explains both the evidence which requires a chaotic model of 'Q', and the inaccuracies detectable in Lukan tradition. Accordingly, this hypothesis seems to me to make much better sense than any previous proposal.

I consider next the date of this Gospel. The traditional date c.75–85 CE is largely dependent on conventionally late dates for Mark, plus the perfectly correct view that Matthew copied Mark. It has several unsatisfactory features, the most important of which are Matthew's eschatology and his position within Judaism.

Mark already believed that the kingdom was at hand. Matthew often makes this clearer, whereas Luke was concerned to distance himself from any idea that the kingdom had been expected to come long ago. For example, Mark has Jesus predict 'that there are some of those standing here who will not taste death until they have seen the kingdom of God come in power' (Mk 9.1). Matthew edited this in accordance with his eschatology, so that Jesus predicted that they would not taste death 'until they have seen the Son of man coming in his kingdom' (Mt. 16.28). This makes absolutely clear the church's view that Jesus predicted his own second coming. Matthew has however retained the notion that some of the people present with Jesus at the time would see the event which Jesus predicted. This makes much better sense c.50–60 CE, when eschatological expectation was extremely vigorous, than after the fall of Jerusalem, when most of the people present during the historic ministry were dead. Matthew retains features of the prediction of the destruction of the Temple which did not come true. So he retains the prediction that 'there will not be left here a stone upon a stone which will not be thrown down' (Mt. 24.2, from Mk 13.2), and does not mention the Temple being burnt down. He not only retains, but also clarifies the reference to 'the abomination of desolation . . . standing in a holy place' (Mt. 24.15, editing Mk 13.14). He retains the instruction to flee to the mountains, and adds to Mark's instruction to pray that this may not happen in winter (Mk 13.18) 'or on a sabbath' (Mt. 24.20). All this entails a date before 70 CE, and makes perfect sense c.50 CE.

It is astonishing that many scholars have used Mt. 22.7 as an argument for a late date, supposing that it reflects the fall of Jerusalem in 70 CE. As recently as 2008, Snodgrass correctly represented the general state of scholarship on the parable to which this verse belongs:

> A common assumption is that Matthew has strongly allegorized his version so that the sending of the servants refers to the early and later prophets, the murder of the servants represents the murder of Jesus and the prophets, the burning of the city refers to the destruction of Jerusalem, and the third sending of the servants is understood as the mission of the church.[45]

The problem with this view, correctly characterized by Snodgrass as an 'assumption', is that Mt. 22.1-14 is a *parable*, generally known as the Parable of the Great Supper, or the like. It is often thought to be part of the 'Q' material because there is a parallel in Luke (14.15-24), as also in the Gospel of Thomas (Saying 64), neither of which has a proper parallel to Mt. 22.6-7, possibly because Matthew really did create these two verses. By this stage, the guests invited to the feast have declined to come when called by the slave (Luke, Thomas) or slaves (Matthew) of the man (Thomas), man/householder (Luke), or king (Matthew).

> But the others seized his slaves, maltreated them and killed them. Now the king was angry. He sent his troops, destroyed those murderers and burnt their city.
>
> (Mt. 22.6-7)

---

45   K. R. Snodgrass, *Stories with Intent: A Comprehensive Guide to the Parables of Jesus* (Grand Rapids: Eerdmans, 2008), p. 308.

Since this is a parable, the main point is surely that the burning of cities was a normal part of ancient practice, and consequently of ancient storytelling. For example, Joshua and his army are said to have burnt Jericho (Josh. 6.24), the men of Judah set Jerusalem on fire (Judg. 1.8), and Nebuchadnezzar's general Nebuzaradan 'burnt the house of the LORD and the house of the king and all the houses of Jerusalem' (2 Kgs 25.9). Mt. 22.6-7 is thus a perfectly natural part of a story, whether or not Matthew inserted it himself. He may or may not have thought of the sack of Jerusalem, but if he did, that was because it was predicted. This in no way implies that it had already happened. These verses are therefore not a reliable indication of the date when this Gospel was written.

When he edited Mark's prediction of the destruction of the Temple, Matthew added the instruction to pray that the flight of 'those in Judaea' (Mt. 24.16) might not happen 'on a Sabbath' (Mt. 24.20). This shows great concern for, and understanding of, the observance of Jewish Law. While mainstream Jews believed that saving life overrides the sabbath, some Jews did not. Indeed, the first known need to promulgate a decision to fight when attacked on the sabbath (1 Macc. 2.41) arose from an incident when 1,000 Jews died because they refused to profane the sabbath in order to save their lives. Matthew knew that if 'those in Judaea' had to 'flee to the mountains' on the sabbath, some would refuse, and all of them would be unable to observe the sabbath and would feel bad about it. His concern could be found only within Judaism.

Matthew was of course very much in favour of the Gentile mission. His concluding Resurrection appearance puts this in a nutshell, for Jesus instructs the 11 left of the Twelve, 'Go therefore and make disciples of all the nations, baptizing them in the name of the Father and the Son and the Holy Spirit, teaching them to keep everything which I have commanded you' (Mt. 28.19-20). What a beautifully condensed presentation of the needs of Christian churches as Matthew saw them![46] It begins with the Gentile mission, and continues with the central initiation rite of both Jewish and Gentile Christians. But we must consider the implications of 'teaching them to keep *everything* which I have commanded you.' The Gospel writer's ideal Christian was a 'scribe discipled for the kingdom of Heaven' (Mt. 13.52). His introduction to the Sermon on the Mount, his own edited collection of teachings attributed to Jesus, comments on the permanent validity of the Law:

> So whoever sets on one side one of the least of these commandments and teaches people thus, shall be called least in the kingdom of Heaven, but whoever does and teaches (them), he shall be called great in the kingdom of Heaven.
>
> (Mt. 5.19)

It follows that Gentile Christians who do not take on the observance of the Law will still be saved, but that this position is not to be approved of. Rather,

---

46   See further pp. 479–81.

they ought to take on the observance of the Law when they are converted to Christianity. This is not feasible after the fall of Jerusalem either, and the later we date Matthew after c.50 CE, the more difficult it becomes.

Matthew's profoundly Jewish understanding of the Law is all of a piece with this. For example, in editing Jesus' dispute with scribes and Pharisees in Mark 7, Matthew drops Mark's comment that Jesus 'cleanses all foods' (Mk 7.19), and adds his own conclusion, 'but eating with unwashed hands does not defile a man' (Mt. 15.20b). This editing makes certain that we keep this dispute within its original cultural context as a dispute about whether to follow the recent tradition of scribes and Pharisees who washed their hands before meals, and that we do not draw from it the exaggerated conclusion favoured by Mark.[47]

In view of all this, it is natural that some perfectly accurate material which presupposes Jesus in his original Jewish context is to be found in Matthew's Gospel only. For example, Matthew's Sermon on the Mount contains this:

> So whenever you do almsgiving, do not sound a trumpet before you, as the actors do in the synagogues and in the streets, so that they may be glorified by men. Amen, I'm telling you, they have their reward. But you, when you do almsgiving, do not let your left hand know what your right hand is doing, so that your almsgiving may be in secret. And your Father who sees in secret will reward you.
>
> (Mt. 6.2-4)

This has an excellent setting in the life of Jesus, and several characteristics of his teaching. In the first place, almsgiving was a major feature of Judaism at the time, the nearest thing there was to social security for the very poor. It was therefore of great importance to the community that the rich gave alms abundantly. Secondly, Jesus was very opposed to rich people in general, and loved to attack them, as he does here.[48] His description of them as 'actors', using the Greek word *hupokritai*, is especially polemical, because almsgiving was a Jewish custom, and actors were a Greek phenomenon to be found in Greek theatres. His description of them as sounding a trumpet before them in synagogues and on street corners is equally polemical. Jesus' instructions presuppose his concern for the poor, and his description of God as simply 'your Father' reflects a major aspect of his teaching.

It follows that material special to Matthew always requires independent assessment. While he was perfectly capable of secondary editing, he also preserved original material, and it should never be considered secondary only because it is attested just once. At this point, the brief comment of Papias is again important. When Matthew wrote his Gospel, Luke had not yet written his, so there could not be any difference between what we may think of as 'Q' material, which Luke used, and special Matthaean material which Luke did not use. Passages such as Mt. 6.2-4 may have been written down accurately in Aramaic on a wax tablet by Matthew, the apostle and tax collector.

---

47   See further pp. 326–31.
48   On the cultural context of this see pp. 305–8.

I conclude that the Gospel of Matthew is a major source for our knowledge of the life and teaching of Jesus.

5. *The Gospel According to Luke*

The Gospel According to Luke has major features in common with Matthew, as well as significant differences. We have seen that, like Matthew, Luke made significant use of Mark and of 'Q' material. Luke was however a highly educated Greek-speaking Gentile Christian, who wrote primarily for Gentile churches. The conventional date for the writing of his Gospel is c.80–90 CE, some time after the fall of Jerusalem, and this date is entirely reasonable.

Early church tradition is unanimous in supposing that this Gospel was written by Luke, a companion of Paul, who was not present during the historical ministry of Jesus. This part of church tradition should be accepted, because it is soundly based in the primary source material, as we shall see. Other aspects of later church tradition, such as that Luke came from Antioch, or that he was a constant companion of Paul and transmitted the Gospel which Paul preached, are full of imaginative conjectures, and are no more reliable than other legends and legitimating traditions.

The prologue to the Gospel contains important information about its author, though it does not name him. It is written in excellent Hellenistic Greek, as is the Gospel as a whole, by someone who was familiar with the tradition of writing prologues to literary Greek works, so the author was a highly educated Greek:

Since many (people) have set their hand to compiling an orderly account concerning the events which have been fulfilled among us, as the eyewitnesses from the beginning and those who became ministers of the Word handed down to us, it seemed good to me too, after following through everything from the beginning, to write it down for you accurately and in order, most excellent Theophilos, so that you might know the certainty of those things about which you were instructed.

(Lk. 1.1-4)

The opening of this prologue tells us that Luke had read several accounts of the ministry of Jesus. It distinguishes the author clearly from the eyewitnesses of the ministry, and from the next people who handed the material down. It follows that important material from this early period has been lost. The prologue also rules out any possibility of an early date for the completion of this Gospel. Since Matthew completed his Gospel c.50–60 CE, he was much the most conspicuous person to have written 'an orderly account concerning the events which have been fulfilled among us', using material 'handed down to us', including that from Matthew the apostle and tax collector, one of 'the eyewitnesses from the beginning'. We should therefore infer that Luke had read our Greek Gospel According to Matthew.

Secondly, the dedication of this educated work to 'most excellent Theophilos' shows that Luke had a rich, distinguished and well-educated Christian patron, who could be relied upon to provide for his needs. These might include for example scrolls of the Septuagint, the major translation of the Hebrew Bible into Greek. Between this and his membership of at least one major Greek Christian community, Luke will also have had access to such assistants as he may have needed. We should envisage them travelling to other churches and synagogues to collect information, reading source material to him, and copying his Gospel out as he dictated it. Communication between different churches and synagogues, though slow by our standards, was effective and frequent. An author of Luke's education and determination could have gained access to more material than we can envisage, and to oral sources as well as written ones. Moreover, if he were educated somewhere like Corinth or Thessalonica and did not know Aramaic, Luke could have gained access to people who would have translated Aramaic sources for him. How well they would do so is another matter, and he might have been able to control the suitability of the results for Gentile Christians, but not the degree of accuracy. Equally, if he really came from somewhere like Antioch, he may well have known some Aramaic and Hebrew, and have done some of this work himself.

After writing his Gospel, Luke wrote Acts, which is also dedicated to his patron Theophilos. The second part of Acts gives an account of the Gentile mission led by St Paul, and this contains the famous 'we' passages. These begin when Paul was in Troas, a Roman *colonia*, that is, a city which had been settled with veterans from the Roman army. Troas was in the north-west of Asia Minor, and there Paul had a vision of a man of Macedonia urging him 'come across into Macedonia and help us' (Acts 16.9). Luke's account continues:

Now when he had seen the vision, we immediately sought to go out to Macedonia, concluding that God had called us to evangelize them. Having set sail from Troas, we made a straight run to Samothrace, and on the next day to Neapolis, and from there to Philippi, which is a leading city of the district of Macedonia, and a colonia. Now we stayed in this city for some days.

(Acts 16.10-12)

This gets Luke in Paul's party at a major centre of the Pauline mission, c.49 CE. This narrative 'we' stops when Paul and Silvanus were arrested and subsequently thrown out of the city, so Luke presumably stayed there for some time preaching the Gospel. The narrative 'we' resumes after a matter of years, c.57 CE, when Paul and named Christians including Timothy 'went ahead and waited for us in Troas, but we sailed out from Philippi after the days of Unleavened Bread, and in five days we came to them in Troas, where we stayed for seven days' (Acts 20.5-6). This presupposes that Luke and others were still in Philippi, and now went to join Paul and his party in Troas.

Most scholars infer that, except for this story when 'we' went out to join Paul and others in Troas, Luke was with Paul's party when his narrative uses 'we', and not the rest of the time. This is an entirely natural interpretation of a major primary source written by an intermittent eyewitness.

Paul also mentions Luke at the close of two or three letters. At the end of the epistle to Philemon, written in the name of Paul and Timothy when Paul was in prison, so probably c.62 CE from Rome, he sends greetings from Luke, with Mark, Aristarchus and Demas, referring to them as 'my co-workers'. At Col. 4.14, also written in the name of Paul and Timothy when Paul was in prison, so again probably c.62 CE from Rome, he sends greetings from 'Luke the beloved physician' and Demas, in a context of many greetings, including those from 'Aristarchus my follow-prisoner and Mark the cousin of Barnabas', who are described as 'of the circumcision' (Col. 4.10-11), so Luke is assumed to be Gentile. Luke's presence in Rome c.62 CE is consistent with the narrative of Acts, in which the 'we' passages end with Paul's journey to Rome, when 'we came into Rome' (Acts 28.14-16). Luke is also mentioned at 2 Tim. 4.11, which is written in Paul's name to Timothy, but which is probably pseudonymous. For what it is worth, this says 'Luke alone is with me' (2 Tim. 4.11), though he is not among those from whom 'Paul' sends greetings, except under the general term 'all the brethren' (2 Tim. 4.21).

All this evidence is interlocking in a consistent manner. When Luke wrote his Gospel, he had been a committed Gentile Christian for over 30 years. He sometimes worked as an evangelist and missionary, and some of this work was done in specifically Pauline churches. While he was not one of Paul's closest co-workers like Timothy and Silvanus, he travelled round different Christian churches. Churches where he stayed for some considerable time included those in Philippi and in Rome, and Christian centres which he visited included Jerusalem. This put him in an ideal position to collect information for his Gospel, as well as for parts of Acts. He knew both Jewish and Gentile Christians, and was evidently capable of journeys which he has not told us about, to collect information from such people. For this purpose, he could use the contacts already traditional between different churches and indeed synagogues, and he could gain access to people who spoke Aramaic, and/or transmitted sources in Aramaic, as well as in Greek.

All this is consistent with the evidence of Luke's Gospel itself that it was written at a relatively late date. Here its eschatology is of prime importance. I have discussed the eschatological discourses of Mark 13 and Matthew 24, and we have seen that they could not possibly have been written after the fall of Jerusalem, and that a much earlier date, c.40 CE for Mark and c.50–60 CE for Matthew, is to be preferred.[49] Luke's discourse is significantly different. His most important change to Mark's eschatological discourse was to replace the prediction of the abomination of desolation, a prediction which was known not to have been fulfilled, with a different prediction:

> But when you see Jerusalem surrounded by armies, then know that her desolation is at hand . . . there will be great distress on the land and wrath against this people, and they will fall by the edge of the sword and be taken captive

---

49   See pp. 69–71, and further pp. 374–75.

to all the nations, and Jerusalem will be trampled on by Gentiles, until the times of the Gentiles are fulfilled.

(Lk. 21.20, 23–24)

Here Mark's predictions have been rewritten in the light of the fall of Jerusalem, and the subsequent taking of prisoners who were sold into slavery elsewhere. This is sufficient to date Luke's Gospel some time after the destruction of Jerusalem in 70 CE. The reference to the 'times of the Gentiles' being fulfilled is not precise, but this is evidently supposed to be some time before the coming of the Son of man in a cloud (Lk. 21.27).

Again, Luke altered Mark's prediction that 'there are some of those standing here who will not taste death until they have seen the kingdom of God come in power' (Mk 9.1). Luke dropped Mark's expression 'in power', so that any display of the kingship, or authority, of God could be seen as a fulfilment of this prediction. He then altered the immediately following introduction to the Transfiguration to read, 'Now it came to pass about eight days after these words . . .' (Lk. 9.27-28). Thus the prediction could be seen to have been fulfilled in the Transfiguration, and the original notion of the final coming of the kingdom has been removed, so that the prediction could no longer be seen to be false.

In addition to alterations removing predictions which had been falsified, Luke added pieces which made clear that the coming of the kingdom should never have been expected at an earlier time. For example, Luke introduces a *very* edited version of an earlier saying with an explicit piece of his own, fired at some of Jesus' most vigorous opponents:

Now being asked by the Pharisees when the kingdom of God would come, he answered them and said, 'The kingdom of God does not come with watching, nor will they say "Look here!", or "There!", for behold!, the kingdom of God is among you.'

(Lk. 17.20-21, cf. Mt. 24.23, Mk 13.21)

This makes it absolutely clear that any notion of the kingdom of God coming long ago was the province of Jesus' opponents, not part of Jesus' expectations.

All this evidence is completely consistent. As a culmination of many years' work as a committed Christian evangelist and inveterate collector of traditions about Jesus, Luke, with much help from other Christians, finally completed his Gospel c.80–90 CE.

It remains to note that, as an outstanding historian by ancient standards, Luke found some material about Jesus which does not turn up in other ancient Gospel sources. Perhaps the most outstanding example is Lk. 13.31-33. It contains several Aramaisms, and I offer here a translation of Luke's (literally translated) Aramaic source:

In that hour Pharisees went and said to him, 'Get out and go away from here, for Herod wants to kill you.' And he said to them, 'Go tell that jackal, "Look! I am casting out demons and performing healings to-day and to-morrow, and on the third (day) I am perfected. But I am going to proceed to-day and to-morrow and on the following day, for it would not be fitting for a prophet to perish outside Jerusalem.'''

Scholars have been extraordinarily reluctant to see this as a historical result of Mk 2.23–3.6, where some Pharisees took counsel with 'Herodians', followers of Herod Antipas, to have Jesus put to death, when he had merely defended poor disciples who were plucking grain on the sabbath, and healed a man with a paralyzed arm on the sabbath. They took counsel with Herodians because they could not get two violations of their own expansions of the Law to stand up in a normal court so as to obtain a conviction, whereas Herod had had John the Baptist executed, so he was a convenient choice as the powerful secular arm. Pharisees as such, however, were merely orthodox Jews, so it is entirely reasonable that some of them should have considered this action wicked, and a potential violation of the sixth commandment, 'You shall do no murder.' They may well have considered that to do this to a second prophet, who also brought normal Jews back to the Lord himself, was doubly wicked and clean contrary to the will of God.[50]

Thus this is a perfect example of authentic material, literally translated from Aramaic, transmitted to us by Luke alone. Who originally wrote it down we do not know, but it was someone who had access to authentic material which they wrote down briefly, so in any given instance, a passage like this might have been written down in Aramaic by the apostle Matthew. It follows that, however much we have to dismiss some items attested by Luke alone c.80–90 CE, we must never dismiss any piece of tradition only on the ground that it is transmitted to us by Luke alone. As noted above, he was an outstanding historian by ancient standards, and he had access to a wide variety of sources, so we must assess independently each piece of tradition attested by Luke alone.

I therefore conclude that the Gospel of Luke, like that of Matthew, is a major source for our knowledge of the life and teaching of Jesus.

6. *Conclusions*

The following conclusions may therefore be drawn. The oldest and most reliable of the Gospels is the Gospel According to Mark. It was written by an unknown Christian called Marcus, c.40 CE. Marcus was not himself present during the historic ministry of Jesus. He did hear Peter, the original leader of the Twelve, preach. He did not however know him well, and we do not know how much of Mark's Gospel is derived from Peter. Marcus may have inherited some of these pieces in Greek, but his best sources were in Aramaic, and he translated them as he went along. These sources, though abbreviated, were literally accurate

---

50 For detailed discussion of this passage, with an explanation of the Aramaisms see pp. 321–24.

accounts of incidents and sayings from the life and teaching of Jesus. We do not know who wrote these sources, but they were certainly in close touch with the ministry of Jesus, so this is just one short step away from eyewitness testimony. Thus Mark's Gospel is the single most important source for the life and teaching of Jesus.

The so-called 'Q' material is equally important for our knowledge of Jesus' teaching, and for some of his deeds. This material, however, was of several different kinds. Some of it was originally written down during or after the ministry of Jesus by the apostle and tax collector Matthew, who was already well accustomed to writing on wax tablets and the like. Various pieces were subsequently translated by different people. Some of them were translated very well, and some of these excellently translated pieces were used by both Matthew and Luke. Some other pieces were not so well translated, and ended up edited by Luke in accordance with the needs of Gentile Christian churches. It is possible that several pieces, well translated, with a high level of verbal identity and in the same order in both Gospels, were collected into one document in Greek, and that this document was independently used by both Matthew and Luke. If so, however, this does not account for a very high proportion of the so-called 'Q' material. Other parts are quite secondary, and were written in Greek by members of the early churches. Some parts may simply have been copied by Luke from Matthew. Thus some of the 'Q' material was originally written by one of the Twelve, so it goes back to a genuine and important eyewitness of the historic ministry. Some other parts are secondary, so that each piece of this material requires critical assessment to determine its authenticity.

The completed Gospels of Matthew and Luke are also important sources for the life and teaching of Jesus. The Gospel of Matthew was written c.50–60 CE by an unknown Jewish Christian who may or may not have been called Matthew. Its major source was the Gospel of Mark, which the evangelist Matthew copied and edited as he went along. This visible editing provides a lot of insight into the way that Matthew worked. Whether this Gospel was written by someone called Matthew or not, it was also or in any case named after the apostle and tax collector Matthew, who wrote its other important source material in Aramaic. This included some special Matthaean material, as well as some of the 'Q' material. This Gospel also includes new secondary material. This Gospel is also a crucial source for the life and teaching of Jesus, but secondary material has to be carefully separated from material which is old and derived from the apostle Matthew and other early witnesses.

The Gospel of Luke was written by a well-educated Gentile Christian called Luke, c.80–90 CE. Luke is well known for having been a companion of Paul, which he was for relatively short periods during the Pauline mission. When he wrote his Gospel, he had been a committed Gentile Christian for over 30 years. At least for some of this time he was an evangelist and missionary. Major churches in which he worked included those in Philippi and Rome. He was able to travel and collect information from churches and synagogues elsewhere. He had a rich Christian patron called Theophilos, and assistants to help him. All this put him in an ideal position to collect information for his Gospel. He researched carefully into the life and teaching of Jesus. He used the Gospel of Mark, which he copied and edited as he went along, as the basis of his own Gospel. He also read the Gospel of Matthew, and may have taken some material directly from it. He used 'Q' material, some parts well translated, other parts less well translated and edited by him with the needs of Gentile Christian churches in mind. Some of his special material, like some of the 'Q' material, shows every sign of being authentic material literally and accurately translated from Aramaic sources. Luke's Gospel also includes new secondary material. It follows that Luke's Gospel is also a crucial source for the life and teaching of Jesus, but that secondary material has to be carefully separated from material which is old and genuine.

I have borne all this carefully in mind while writing the rest of this book. I have used Mark, 'Q', Matthew and Luke as the main sources for the life and teaching of Jesus. I have tried to make full use of the old and authentic sources, some of which were written by eyewitnesses of the historic ministry, including the apostle Matthew, but surely including others too. I have paid much less attention to secondary material, which I have however discussed whenever it has been widely considered to be authentic, and at such points I have tried to offer some understanding as to why the secondary material was written down by these three major evangelists. I hope the result advances our understanding of the historic ministry, which I have also sought to illuminate from other remains of Jesus' first-century Jewish culture. How to do this is however a very controversial matter. I have accordingly devoted Chapter 3 to a discussion of the methods which should be carefully used to work out from these primary sources what the historical Jesus really said and did.

Historical Method

1. *Introduction*

As we have seen in Chapter 1, there is no general agreement as to the methods which scholars should use to uncover the Jesus of history. The purpose of this chapter is to explain the methods which I use, and how I employ them. I begin with a discussion of standard criteria which are, or have been, in widespread use. I then pass to Theissen and Winter's criterion of historical plausibility, which has rightly attracted a lot of attention in recent years, because it is extremely valuable. I proceed to fit the use of Aramaic into the criterion of historical plausibility. It is widely accepted that Jesus spoke Aramaic, but the use of Aramaic as a criterion of historicity has had a chequered if not altogether disastrous history. Since the discovery of the Aramaic Dead Sea Scrolls and other ancient Aramaic documents in the twentieth century, much more work has become possible. I propose carefully controlled methods for making the most of these resources.

The criterion of historical plausibility is dependent on our knowledge of Jesus' environment within the Judaism of his time. I therefore offer a brief summary of the documentary and archaeological resources available for this purpose, leaving more detailed discussion of individual matters scattered throughout this book at points where our knowledge of Judaism is particularly important for understanding aspects of Jesus' life and teaching.

Finally I discuss two aspects of Jewish literary sources which have been extensively studied in recent years by scholars who spend their whole lives studying ancient Judaism, but which have been rather neglected by mainstream New Testament scholars. One is the rewriting of history. Whereas some scribes copied sacred texts very accurately, other writers rewrote traditional Jewish sources to satisfy the needs of the communities in which they lived. This is important in understanding the Gospel writers, especially Matthew, Luke and John. Secondly, some people loved telling stories. Jesus himself was the most celebrated story-teller of all, but that is not a problem. When he told for example the parable of the Good Samaritan (Lk. 10.30-37), everyone knew that the story was fiction, presenting serious ethical teaching in story mode. Unfortunately for the historian, some of Jesus' followers loved telling stories about him too, and the Gospel writers wrote them down together with true stories about what he really did. As when they rewrote history, they did so to satisfy the needs of the communities in which they lived. In the substantive chapters of this book, I argue that the stories of his virgin birth and the empty tomb and Resurrection appearances are in this category. In this chapter I discuss how to find out which Gospel stories are creative fiction, and which ones are not. I argue that this affects even our oldest and most accurate source, the Gospel of Mark, so that telling the difference between accurate history and creative storytelling is an important task.

2. *Multiple Attestation*

Multiple attestation is a useful criterion when properly used. Its application is however limited, and there are serious pitfalls to avoid. In the first place, we have seen that some of our oldest sources contain a lot of perfectly reliable material. It follows that anything attested more than once *in our oldest sources* is likely to be true. For example, the controversy over Jesus casting out demons by the power of the devil is featured both in Mark (3.22-30) and in the 'Q' material (Mt. 12.22-32//Lk. 11.14-23; 12.10). This is strong evidence that the controversy really took place. Moreover, that is the correct and fruitful way to use the criterion of multiple attestation by source. The other important kind of multiple attestation is multiple attestation by form. For example, there is evidence of Jesus' exorcisms in narratives, summaries, parabolic sayings and controversy. These are different *kinds* of evidence, and taken together they also provide very strong evidence that Jesus performed exorcisms.

The major pitfalls are in the use of multiple attestation by source. It is essential to be careful about what the sources say, to be sure that they are independent of each other, and that none of them is too late, and contains too much secondary material, to be regarded as a reliable historical source. For example, Dunn claims that Jesus 'was condemned for claiming to be "the king of the Jews", as all four canonical Gospels agree (Mark 15.26 pars.)' and that there is 'no doubt that the key issue before Pilate was whether Jesus had claimed to be "the king of the Jews" (15.2 pars.).'[1] Dunn's comment 'as all four canonical Gospels agree' is clearly an attempt at multiple attestation by source. His first reference however, 'Mark 15.26 pars.', i.e. Mk 15.26//Mt. 27.37//Lk. 23.38; Jn 19.19, does not contain a *claim by Jesus* at all! It is simply the inscription which Pilate had placed on the cross. I do not doubt that it is an accurate account of what Pilate had put on the cross, because it is not something that either Jesus' Jewish opponents or the early church would have invented, whereas it is precisely how a Roman governor

---

1   Dunn, *Jesus Remembered*, pp. 628–29.

might describe a bandit whom he judged worthy of crucifixion.[2] But the fact that 'all four canonical Gospels' agree about that does not strengthen that evidence, because Matthew and Luke may be dependent on Mark, as they so often are, and John adds a completely secondary story, as befits a source which is too late and secondary to be used in multiple attestation at all.

At Dunn's second reference, Mark '15.2 pars.', i.e. Mk 15.2//Mt. 27.11// Lk. 23.3//Jn 18.34, Pilate's question is verbally identical in all four Gospels. Matthew and Luke appear to be copying Mark, and John's rewriting is evidently dependent on the same tradition. This underlines the point that John's evidence should never be brought into multiple attestation, because he is a late secondary source, and here too the following passage consists of creative fiction which belongs to a much later date.

This example illustrates what can go wrong when the criterion of multiple attestation by source is used by relatively conservative and orthodox scholars. When it is used by more radical scholars, different, equally inappropriate and even later sources may be used, notably the Gospel of Thomas, which several American scholars date much too early.[3] For example, Crossan lists under 'Double Independent Attestation' what he calls 'Seeking Too Late', citing Thomas 38.2 and Jn 7.34a, 36b.[4] He does not offer a detailed discussion, but he appears to mean this:

> The days will come (when) you will seek me (and) you will not find me.
> (Thomas 38, second part)

> You will seek me and you will not find (me) . . . you will seek me and you will not find (me).
> (Jn 7.34a, 7.36b)

Both these sayings are found in heavily secondary contexts in very late sources. The chances that a genuine saying of the historical Jesus underlies them are therefore negligible.

The other major problem with multiple attestation by source is also found in the work of Crossan, who casts doubt on the authenticity of anything which is *not* multiply attested. He comments on attestation:

> The final element is a *bracketing of singularity*. This entails the complete avoidance of any unit found only in single attestation even within the first stratum.[5]

---

2 See pp. 443–51.
3 See further pp. 525–34.
4 Crossan, *Historical Jesus*, p. 427, suggests that Thomas has two layers, one 'composed by the fifties C. E.', and a second layer 'added, possibly as early as the sixties or seventies', and he comments on 'Seeking Too Late' at pp. 438, 439.
5 Crossan, *Historical Jesus*, p. xxxii.

This is not satisfactory because of the nature of surviving primary sources. As we have seen, Matthew and Luke copied Mark, so most passages found in all three of our most important primary sources are not *independently* attested. This can never mean that nothing in Mark, copied by Matthew and Luke, is historically true. Rather, it means that other ways of assessing the historicity of Markan passages must be used.

It follows that the criterion of multiple attestation is of significant value when it is carefully used. It is however of limited application because too little of the surviving evidence about Jesus is independently attested more than once in our oldest sources.

3. *Dissimilarity, Coherence and Embarrassment*

The criteria of dissimilarity and coherence used to be widely used, but that of dissimilarity has rightly been severely criticized in recent scholarship, and that of coherence depends on it. When clearly described, as it often was not, the criterion of dissimilarity states that anything in the Gospel accounts of the life and teaching of Jesus which is paralleled in Judaism or the early church must be attributed to the church, rather than to Jesus. It was labelled and described with particular clarity by Perrin in 1967, and this led directly to its demolition by Morna Hooker in a classic paper soon afterwards.[6] Its central problem was that it artificially produced a quite unique Jesus. He could not be connected with the Judaism of his time, because anything in his life and teaching paralleled in Judaism was regarded as secondary on principle. Furthermore, he was so remote from the early church as to make it impossible to see how Christianity started, because anything in his life and teaching paralleled in the early church was also regarded as secondary on principle. Hooker was therefore entirely right to argue that we should stop using this criterion.

What was wrong with it, however, was the exclusion of material which is paralleled in Judaism or the early church. Despite gaps in our knowledge of both ancient Judaism and the early church, it remains true that anything not paralleled in either of them is authentic Jesus material. So, for example, there should be no doubt that Jesus taught 'Love your enemies' (Mt. 5.44//Lk. 6.27). This is not however to be regarded as more important or even more typical of Jesus than his teaching about the Fatherhood of God, which he took from Judaism and which was vigorously taken up by the early church. It follows that the criterion of dissimilarity is of very limited value, and it has generally caused more trouble than it is worth.

The use of the criterion of dissimilarity led not only to a quite unique Jesus, but also to a Jesus about whom very little was known. The criterion of coherence

---

6   N. Perrin, *Rediscovering the Teaching of Jesus* (London/New York: SCM/Harper & Row, 1967), pp. 40, 47; M. D. Hooker, 'Christology and Methodology', *NTS* 17 (1970–71), pp. 480–87.

mitigated this effect somewhat, by accepting as authentic material which was coherent with what emerged from use of the criterion of dissimilarity. It could be used with any other criteria too, but it was the use of the criterion of dissimilarity which gave it its real importance. Since I do not make any significant use of the criterion of dissimilarity, I shall not use the criterion of coherence either.

The criterion of embarrassment was correctly described and evaluated by J. P. Meier:

> . . . [it] focuses on actions or sayings of Jesus that would have embarrassed or created difficulty for the early Church. The point of the criterion is that the early Church would hardly have gone out of its way to create material that only embarrassed its creator or weakened its position in arguments with opponents.[7]

This is correct as far as it goes. Meier's first example is Jesus' baptism by John the Baptist, who proclaimed a 'baptism of repentance for the forgiveness of sins' (Mk 1.4). This is a sound example. The story could be interpreted to mean that Jesus was sinful, and inferior to John the Baptist. Whereas Mark simply passes on the historical tradition handed on to him, later Gospels can be seen struggling with these implications. For example, Matthew adds a conversation in which John the Baptist says that *he* needs to be baptized *by Jesus*, and Jesus tells him to proceed, 'for in this way it is fitting for us to fulfill all righteousness' (Mt. 3.14-15). The Gospel According to the Hebrews is more developed:

> Behold! The mother of the Lord and his brothers said to him, 'John the Baptist is baptizing for the remission of sins. Let us go and be baptized by him.' But he said to them, 'What sin have I committed, that I should go and be baptized by him? Unless perhaps what I have just said is ignorance'.
>
> (Jerome, *Against the Pelagians* III, 2, quoting from the Gospel According to the Hebrews)

These late sources illustrate how unlikely it is that the original story would have been invented by the early church.

This example shows that the criterion of embarrassment can be useful. Like the criterion of multiple attestation, it is of limited value because it is of limited application. The early church was originally centred on the life and teaching of Jesus, and very little that he said or did was embarrassing to it. It is however important in refuting the view of extremists that Jesus did not even exist, because it focuses attention on aspects of his life and teaching which would not be found in the Gospels if this were so.

---

7 Meier, *Marginal Jew*, vol. 1, p. 168.

4. *Historical Plausibility*

In a vigorous and excellent critique of the criterion of dissimilarity, Theissen and Winter have helpfully proposed to replace it with a criterion of historical plausibility.[8] This is a very useful cover-all term for the welcome tendency in recent scholarship to fit Jesus into his original historical context in first-century Judaism, and to assess the authenticity of Gospel traditions accordingly. This is a brief summary of their proposal:

> What Jesus intended and said must be compatible with the Judaism of the first half of the first century in Galilee . . . What Jesus intended and did must be recognizable as that of an individual figure within the framework of the Judaism of that time . . . What we know of Jesus as a whole must allow him to be recognized within his contemporary Jewish context and must be compatible with the Christian (canonical and noncanonical) history of his effects.[9]

All these points are of central importance. Our early primary sources are unanimous and unambiguous in placing Jesus within a context of first-century Judaism. It follows that our picture of Jesus should be comprehensible within that cultural framework, and further, when a piece of information about Jesus or those present during the historic ministry fits *only* there, that is a strong argument in favour of its historicity.

For example, after Jesus had performed an exorcism in a Capernaum synagogue one sabbath (Mk 1.23-27) and healed Peter's mother-in-law of a fever (Mk 1.30-31), Mark records this:

> Now when evening came, when the sun had set, (people) brought to him all those who were ill and those who were possessed of demons . . .
>
> (Mk 1.32)

Carrying burdens on the sabbath was against the Law (Jer. 17.21-22), and anyone who has tried to carry a sick person should understand that the person is so heavy and difficult to carry that bringing this under the prohibition of carrying burdens is almost inevitable. This is why Mark's note of time is so careful. The sabbath ended when darkness fell. 'When evening came' might not be clear enough: 'when the sun had set' settles it – his audiences would know that people carried other people only when the sabbath was over, so as not to violate the written Law. It follows that this report cannot be the work of the early church, who were not interested in such matters: it must go back to a real report transmitted during the historic ministry, when this observance of the written Law mattered, and everyone took this so much for granted that the careful note of time was sufficient

---

8   G. Theissen and D. Winter, *The Quest for the Plausible Jesus: The Question of Criteria* (1997. Trans. M. E. Boring. Louisville: Westminster John Knox, 2002).
9   Theissen and Winter, *Plausible Jesus*, pp. 211–12.

to bring it to mind. It is also therefore powerful evidence of Jesus' successful ministry of exorcism and healing.

This further illustrates that our picture of Jesus 'must be recognizable as that of an *individual* figure within the framework of the Judaism of that time'.[10] Placing him within ancient Judaism does not mean turning him into an ordinary or average first-century Jew. We shall see in Chapter 7 that Jesus was by far the most successful exorcist and healer of his time. That judgement is based on a massive amount of evidence in our oldest primary sources, critically assessed within the criterion of historical plausibility. The rest of this book is also devoted to allowing the emergence of a quite unique figure, yet a figure seen within his historical context in first-century Judaism. I also confront the opposition to Jesus, and how it led to his crucifixion. I have noted in Chapter 1 the difficulties which these aspects of Jesus' life posed for the outstanding but relatively liberal work of Vermes and Sanders.[11] This has always been a problem for liberal lives of Jesus. Charlesworth commented recently on the work of the outstanding German scholar Harnack at the end of the nineteenth century:

> Harnack claimed that Jesus was a revelatory genius who illustrated the fatherhood of God, the brotherhood of all men, and the binding ethic of love . . . But something was amiss. With such a nonthreatening philosophy it is impossible to explain why Jesus was judged and condemned to death on a cross.[12]

Harnack is only the most notorious example of a serious and recurring problem for lives of Jesus written from any kind of relatively liberal perspective. Historical plausibility demands that we take seriously the *whole* of Jesus' life in first-century Judaism, including the massive Jewish opposition to his ministry, which led to his crucifixion.

It is more difficult to ensure that a picture of Jesus is 'compatible with the Christian . . . history of his effects',[13] because tracking these out is a complex task in itself. It is however a very important task. Perhaps the most important aspect of it for a life of Jesus is to explain why the earliest Christians believed that Jesus had risen from the dead, a task which I attempt in Chapter 12. More generally, even if Jesus did not found the church, and however much Christological development took place after his death, we must be able to see the connections between the historical Jesus and the subsequent movement which regarded him as its central figure.

Furthermore, if 'what Jesus intended and said must be compatible with the Judaism of the first half of the first century in Galilee', it follows that anything attributed to him which is *not* compatible with first-century Judaism cannot be

---

10 Theissen and Winter, *Plausible Jesus*, p. 211 (my emphasis).
11 See pp. 14–15, 17–18.
12 J. H. Charlesworth, *The Historical Jesus: An Essential Guide* (Nashville: Abingdon, 2008), pp. 3–4.
13 Theissen and Winter, *Plausible Jesus*, p. 212.

authentic. The most outstanding example of this is his exposition of his deity in the Fourth Gospel. This is quite unJewish, for in Judaism no man can be God. Yet throughout the Fourth Gospel, Jesus is portrayed as conscious of his position as the incarnate Son of God who is co-equal with the Father. The classic declaration is 'I and the Father are one' (Jn 10.30), a declaration so provocative that 'the Jews' immediately take up stones to throw at Jesus. This completely external description of 'the Jews', repeated throughout the Fourth Gospel, also reflects its position outside Judaism, even though it is profoundly permeated with Jewish culture. At Jn 10.33, 'the Jews' give their reasons for threatening to stone Jesus: 'for blasphemy, and because, although you're a man, you make yourself God.' This is a perfectly Jewish reaction to a quite unJewish claim. Like the claim attributed to Jesus, this reaction is absent from Jesus' public conflicts with his opponents in the synoptic Gospels.

5. *Aramaic*

I now propose to make the use of Aramaic an important aspect of the application of the criterion of historical plausibility. Jesus taught in Aramaic, which was also the language spoken by his family and by all his followers during the historic ministry. Moreover, the synoptic Gospels, which are written in Greek, show many signs of their sources being transmitted in Aramaic. The use of Aramaic as a historical criterion in Jesus research has however had a very chequered history.[14] There were three reasons for this. One is that, until recently, there was not enough early Aramaic available for much careful work to be done. Secondly, and partly for this reason, the small minority of scholars who tried to make use of Aramaic for historical research did not have sufficient control over their methods. Thirdly, most New Testament professors who write academic books and articles about Jesus have never been able to handle the language Jesus spoke with any semblance of competence. This situation should now be regarded as quite scandalous, and ought to be brought to an end. Since the publication of the Aramaic Dead Sea Scrolls, and a variety of other Aramaic documents written in the ancient world, the present generation of scholars have had the opportunity to make massive progress. I have accordingly devoted two books, and parts of a third, to expounding controlled methods for fruitful use of Aramaic in research into the historical Jesus.[15] I now summarize the methods which lie behind all this research.

First, despite the Gospels being written in Greek, they attribute some Aramaic words to Jesus, and those in Mark, our oldest source, are found in narratives

---

14   For a basic critical survey see Casey, *Aramaic Sources of Mark's Gospel*, ch. 1, 'The State of Play'.

15   Casey, *Aramaic Sources of Mark's Gospel: Aramaic Approach to Q: Solution to the 'Son of Man' Problem*; further, P. M. Casey, 'The Role of Aramaic in Reconstructing the Teaching of Jesus', in S. E. Porter and P. Holmen (eds), *Handbook for the Study of the Historical Jesus* (4 vols. Leiden: Brill, forthcoming), vol. 2, pp. 1343–75.

which satisfy the rest of the criterion of historical plausibility too. For example, when Jesus healed a synagogue leader's daughter, Mark relates that he grasped her hand and said:

Talitha koum, which is in translation, little girl, I tell you, get up!

(Mk 5.41)

The first two words, *Talitha koum*, are Aramaic for 'little girl, get up', so Mark has correctly translated them into Greek for his Greek-speaking audiences, adding the explicitative comment 'I tell you', as translators sometimes do. Moreover, I have followed the reading of the oldest and best manuscripts. The majority of manuscripts read the technically correct written feminine form *koumi*, but there is good reason to believe that the feminine ending 'i' was not pronounced. It follows that *Talitha koum* is *exactly* what Jesus said.[16] In Chapter 7, I give reasons why there should be no doubt that the whole of this healing narrative is literally true, and that it is dependent ultimately on an eyewitness account by one of the inner circle of three of the Twelve, who were present throughout, and who accordingly *heard and transmitted exactly* what Jesus said.[17]

I deliberately propose to put the use of Aramaic under the general heading of historical plausibility, because fiction could be composed in Aramaic as well as in any other language, and Aramaic or Hebrew words could be placed in a Greek story by a storyteller seeking a reality effect. For example, at Jn 4.25, the Samaritan woman says to Jesus:

I know that Messiah (*Messias*) is coming, who is called Christ (*Christos*).

Here the word *Messias* is an obvious attempt to put into Greek letters the Aramaic *mᵉshīḥā*, which means 'anointed' or 'Messiah' (equivalent to the Hebrew *(ha) mashīaḥ*).[18] The Samaritan woman then supplies the Greek equivalent *Christos*. The Samaritans, however, did not call the figure whom they expected 'anointed' or 'Messiah'. They called him *Taheb*, which means 'Restorer'. Accordingly, this use of *Messias* has no historical plausibility at all. Nor does her use of the Christian term *Christos*, nor do some specifically Johannine features of the story, such as Jesus' ability to give her living water and eternal life (Jn 4.10-14).

These two examples illustrate how important it is to use Aramaic as part of the criterion of historical plausibility. We must not imagine that the *mere occurrence* of one or two Aramaic words is sufficient evidence of historical authenticity. We must always look for the historical plausibility of the narratives in which Aramaic words are embedded. We shall see that this criterion is satisfied in Mark's stories, and I argue that this is because our oldest Gospel is partly dependent on eyewitness accounts by Aramaic-speaking disciples.

---

16   For more technical discussion see P. M. Casey, 'Aramaic Idiom and the Son of Man Problem: A Response to Owen and Shepherd', *JSNT* 25 (2002), pp. 3–32 (9–10).

17   See pp. 268–69.

18   On these terms see pp. 392–99.

Secondly, the Gospels, especially Mark, have various peculiarities in Greek which can be explained by their use of Aramaic sources. The simplest examples are mistakes. I have noted for example a mistake at Mk 2.23.[19] This is a story of Jesus' disciples going through the fields on the sabbath plucking ears of corn. Poor people were entitled to take *Peah*, the grain left for them at the edge of fields (Lev. 23.22), and for this purpose they naturally had to *go along* the paths in between other people's fields. Hence the Pharisees do not complain at them doing so. Mark, however, says that they began to *make* a path. This is due to a simple misreading of his Aramaic source. Mark's Aramaic source will have read *lema'ebhar*, so they began 'to go along' a path, which everyone was perfectly entitled to do on the sabbath, and this has been slightly misread as *lema'ebhadh*, 'to make', with 'd' rather than 'r' as the final letter. In Aramaic, the letters 'r' and 'd' are always similar, now conventionally printed as ר and ד, which are obviously alike, and in the Dead Sea Scrolls they are often indistinguishable. Moreover, this mistake occurs in a story which in all other respects satisfies the criterion of historical plausibility, and this applies to all other examples of such mistakes in Mark's Gospel.

Similar mistakes in Luke's Gospel would be more difficult to uncover if we did not have Matthew's much more accurate version of some of the 'Q' material. I have discussed outstanding examples of this at Lk. 11.42:[20]

> But woe to you Pharisees, for you tithe mint and rue and every herb and pass over justice and the love of God. It was necessary to do the latter and not pass over the former.

If we did not have Matthew's version of the herbs to be tithed (Mt. 23.23), we would be puzzled by 'rue and every herb'. Since however Matthew has 'dill and cumin', we can see what has gone wrong. The Aramaic for dill was four letters written as *sh-b-th-ā*: Luke misread it as *sh-b-r-ā*, 'rue', i.e. Syrian rue (*peganum harmala*). This is just one letter different, an easy mistake to make if he was reading a wax tablet or a single sheet of papyrus. Luke then replaced 'and cumin' with 'and every herb'. Also, Matthew has 'mercy and faith', where Luke has the otherwise plausible 'the love of God'. Consequently, we can see that Matthew correctly translated *rḥmthā*, 'mercy', which Luke misread as *rḥmyā*, 'love', and that is what he edited.

In both these examples, my use of Aramaic has been carefully controlled. In each case there is a mistake in the text, 'make' at Mk 2.23, and 'rue' at Lk. 11.42, and Mt. 23.23-24 forms a control over the understanding of Lk. 11.42. We must not however alter the meaning of texts at the hand of Aramaic conjectures, an error of method widespread in the history of scholarship. There is a wondrous example of this in the Johannine prologue. Many Christians have been puzzled at the absence of the virgin birth from the Fourth Gospel. The Christian scholar

---

19　See pp. 64–65.
20　See pp. 82–83, and for more comprehensive discussion of the whole passage, pp. 331–34.

Burney made up an Aramaic source of Jn 1.13-14 in which it is duly to be found. The original text makes perfect sense. It comments on those who become the children of God because they believe in the Word of God, the true light coming into the world, and, having described those people who can perceive the Incarnation of the Word when they see Jesus of Nazareth, the prologue narrates the Incarnation of the Word:

> . . . those who believe in his name,[13]who were born not of blood, nor of the will of the flesh nor of the will of man, but of God.[14]And the Word (*logos*) became flesh and dwelt among us, and we beheld his glory . . .
>
> (Jn 1.12b-14a)

Burney reconstructed an Aramaic verb behind 'were born', which he placed last in the sentence, where the Greek verb 'were born' is naturally to be found. He reconstructed 'And', the first word of Jn 1.14, which is a single letter (*w*), and proposed that it had become accidentally doubled, thus turning an original 'was born' into 'were born', for that same letter makes the difference between the singular and the plural of the verb. He thus replaced the text of John with this:

> . . . to those that believe in His name; because He was born, not of blood, nor of the will of the flesh, nor of the will of man, but of God. And the Word was made flesh . . .

Burney thus presented the author as 'drawing out the mystical import of the Virgin-Birth for believers'.[21]

There are four serious mistakes here. First, the original text makes perfect sense. We should never alter texts which make perfect sense by making conjectures. Secondly, there are no good reasons to believe that there was an Aramaic source of any part of the Johannine prologue. In this, it is quite different from parts of Mark, the 'Q' material and some other parts of the Gospels of Matthew and Luke. Thirdly, Burney's Aramaic conjecture is extremely improbable, because he supposed that the Aramaic verb 'was/were born' was placed in its Greek position at the end of the sentence, where an Aramaic author is most unlikely to have put it. Fourthly, Burney's conjecture was motivated by his religious convictions. He believed in the virgin birth himself, and this is the fundamental reason why he sought to get it into the Johannine prologue.

A different and equally instructive mistake was made by the Jewish scholar Zimmermann. The deity of the Word Incarnate is naturally uncongenial to Jewish scholars. Zimmermann proposed that the Greek *logos*, usually translated 'Word', was a mistranslation of the Aramaic *'imrā*, which was intended to mean 'lamb'.[22]

---

21 C. F. Burney, *The Aramaic Origin of the Fourth Gospel* (Oxford; Clarendon, 1922), pp. 34–35, 41–42.

22 F. Zimmermann, *The Aramaic Origin of the Four Gospels* (New York: Ktav, 1979), pp. 167–70.

There are four serious mistakes here too. The first two are the same as in the work of Burney – the original text makes perfect sense, and there are no good reasons to believe that there was an Aramaic source of any part of the Johannine prologue. Thirdly, Zimmermann's Aramaic conjecture is extremely improbable, because it presupposes a theology of a pre-existent lamb which was made flesh, and Zimmermann made no reasonable attempt to expound this. Fourthly, although he made some attempt to give academic reasons for his judgement, such as that the *logos* is not used in the rest of the Gospel, whereas Jesus is presented as the Lamb of God (cf. Jn 1.29, 36; 19.36), it is clear that Zimmermann's conjecture was motivated by his ideological convictions, just as much as the conjecture of Burney.

I have selected these two examples from thousands of regrettable conjectures to make one central point of method. Misreadings and mistranslations of Aramaic sources should be proposed only in cases where they are at least part of an argument of cumulative weight for supposing that a document was partly based on one or more Aramaic sources. Secondly, the proposed Aramaic must be realistic, and so must any proposed misreading or mistranslation. These conditions are satisfied by all the proposals which I make in this book.

As well as simple mistakes, there are cases where Mark's Greek is unidiomatic, because Mark was suffering from interference from an Aramaic source in front of him, as translators often do. For example, Mark transmits John the Baptist's prediction of his successor in a form which may be literally translated as follows:

> The one stronger than me is coming after me, of whom I am not worthy to bend down and undo the latchet of the sandals of him.
>
> (Mk 1.7)

Here the meaning is unambiguous and correct, but 'of whom' followed by 'of him' is no more idiomatic in Greek than it is in English. The relative particle in Aramaic (*de* or *di*), the equivalent of the English 'who', 'what', etc., has to be picked up by another particle later in the sentence, in this case *delēh*, the equivalent of 'of him'. In Greek, this is not the case, just as in English, and once Mark had correctly put 'of whom', there was no need for him to put 'of him' at the end of the sentence. He did so because he had *delēh* at the end of the sentence in the text in front of him. This is very valuable evidence, because it shows that Mark was translating a written Aramaic source. There are more unidiomatic features of this kind in Mark's Gospel than in any of the others. Matthew and Luke have a natural tendency to alter such features in their attempts to write better Greek. In this case, Matthew has so many differences from Mark that it is difficult to know whether he was altering Mark, or shifting already to the 'Q' material from which he took the end of John the Baptist's prediction (Mt. 3.11-12, cf. Lk. 3.17). Luke, however, despite making some minor alterations, left 'of whom . . . of him' unchanged.

The Fourth Gospel has only one comparable example:

Among you stands one whom you do not know, the one who comes after me, of whom I am not worthy to undo of him the latchet of the sandal.

(Jn 1.26-27)

This same peculiarity, 'of whom . . . of him' is straightforward evidence that the Johannine community possessed Mark's Gospel, as is to be expected of a Christian community at the end of the first century CE. At the same time, they have rewritten the whole context so as to ensure that John bears unambiguous witness to Jesus, 'the lamb of God who takes away the sin of the world' (Jn 1.29). This is reflected at the end of Jn 1.26, an addition to Mark in which the words 'one whom *you* do not know' reflect John the Baptist's knowledge of Jesus, which he is about to reveal, clean contrary to the synoptic Gospels and historical reality.

This indicates again how careful we must be to fit evidence of Aramaic sources into historical plausibility as a whole. The peculiarity of the Greek of Mk 1.7 shows that he was translating an Aramaic source, and fits into the evidence of the historicity of the whole of Mark's Aramaic source. The same peculiarity in the Greek of Jn 1.27 indicates that he inherited Markan tradition, and is found in a context in which he has rewritten history in accordance with the needs of the Johannine community.

The phenomenon of interference also affects single words. A bilingual translator may use a word in an unfamiliar sense, because he is so used to using it as equivalent to a word in his source. I have drawn attention to an example of this, 'being angry' (*orgistheis*) used of Jesus at Mk 1.41 when he healed, or perhaps pronounced clean, a man with a skin disease.[23] Here again Mark's Greek is perfectly comprehensible as a literal and unrevised translation of an Aramaic source which gave a perfectly accurate albeit very brief account of an incident which really took place. The Aramaic source will have read *regaz*. This word often does mean 'be angry', which is why Mark translated it like this. But it has a wider range of meaning than this, including 'tremble' and 'be deeply moved'. Accordingly, Mark did not mean that Jesus was angry. He was suffering from interference, as all bilinguals do, especially when they are translating. In Mark's mind, the Greek word for being angry also meant 'tremble' or 'be deeply moved', because this was the range of meaning of the normally equivalent Aramaic word in front of him.

Translation also affects the frequency with which words are used. For example, Mark uses the Greek word for 'begin' 26 times, far more than one would expect in a Greek document, and Matthew and Luke have a very strong tendency to remove it, though they have other examples of their own. The word for 'begin' (*archomai*) is as normal in Greek as it is in English, but the Aramaic equivalent (*sheri*) is often used when to us it means nothing very much, and this is what Matthew in particular seems not to have liked. He kept only six of Mark's

23   See further p. 63, p. 267.

26 examples, and he has only 13 altogether. Examples include Mk 2.23, where the disciples 'began to make a path'. I have discussed 'make', and I pointed out that this is a mistake due to Mark's misreading of an Aramaic source.[24] There should be no doubt that in this instance Mark has translated *sheri* literally from his Aramaic source. Matthew omitted the incorrect 'make a path' and edited the narrative to read 'began to pluck the ears' (Mt. 12.1), while Luke omitted 'began to make a path' altogether. Mark's 26 examples should be attributed to his use of Aramaic sources. This is part of an argument of cumulative weight for the dependence of our oldest Gospel on written Aramaic sources.

Sometimes, a Greek word in a saying of Jesus can represent only one particular Aramaic word, which has a different meaning which fits much better into the criterion of historical plausibility. For example, some Pharisees are said to have warned Jesus that Herod Antipas wanted to kill him (Lk. 13.31). Jesus is said to have replied:

> Go and tell this fox, Look! I am casting out demons and performing healings to-day and tomorrow, and on the third I am perfected.

Jesus' apparent reference to Herod Antipas as a fox (Greek *alōpēx*) has led many scholars to describe Antipas as cunning, for foxes were commonly thought of in the Greek world as cunning.[25] This does not however make good historical sense, since Herod Antipas is not otherwise known to have been particularly cunning. Moreover, Jesus' Aramaic word can only have been *ta'alā*, which also means 'jackal' (*canis aureus*), and there seem to have been more jackals than foxes in Israel. Luke's translation of *ta'alā* with *alōpēx* was however virtually inevitable, because *ta'alā* does mean 'fox', whereas there was no standard Greek word for 'jackal', because there were no jackals in Greece.[26] We may therefore conclude that Jesus described Antipas as a jackal. That makes perfect polemical sense! The jackal was a noisy, unclean nuisance of an animal, a predator which hunted in packs. This is a beautiful description of one member of the pack of Herods, none of them genuinely observant Jews, some of them ruthless rulers who worked with packs of supporters to hunt down their opponents and kill them, as Antipas had hunted down and killed John the Baptist and was now hunting down Jesus himself. Thus the recovery of Jesus' original word *ta'alā* helps to fit this saying more accurately into its original cultural context.

One of the problems encountered by all translators is that words in their sources may have idiomatic meanings which do not have the same connotations in their target language. Many translators respond by translating literally. Lk. 13.32 has two examples of this as well. One is the last word, 'I am perfected'.

---

24   See pp. 64–65, 75, 110.
25   E.g. M. H. Jensen, *Herod Antipas in Galilee* (WUNT 2, 115. Tübingen: Mohr Siebeck, 2006), pp. 116–17, not mentioning the Aramaic reconstruction and discussion of Lk. 13.31-33 in Casey, *Aramaic Sources of Mark's Gospel*, pp. 188–89.
26   See further pp. 362–63; Casey, *Solution to the 'Son of Man' Problem*, pp. 170–72, with bibliography to foxes and jackals.

In Aramaic, this word (*sh^elam*) was used idiomatically with reference to death, so here Jesus referred idiomatically to his forthcoming death. The other idiomatic usages in this verse are the indications of time. Jesus' declaration that he was continuing his ministry of exorcism and healing 'to-day and to-morrow', more literally in Aramaic 'this day and another day', and that he would die 'on the third', are not to be taken literally. They refer to short intervals of time, as was normal in Aramaic but not in Greek.[27]

The most striking Aramaic idiom in the whole of the Gospels is the use of two words, *bar* (*^e)nāsh(ā)*, literally 'son of man'. I argue that Jesus used these words of himself in a particular Aramaic idiom, in which a speaker used a somewhat general statement to refer to himself, or himself and other people made obvious by the context.[28] These words were however difficult to translate, because there is no such idiom in Greek, so the translators adopted a strategy. They decided to render *bar* (*^e)nāsh(ā)* with the Greek *ho huios tou anthrōpou*, literally 'the son of (the) man', whenever it referred to Jesus, and to use other terms whenever it did not. In this way they produced a major Christological title, which we call 'the Son of man' in English. Mark found this term in scripture at Dan. 7.13, where the term is *k^ebhar ^enāsh*, 'one like a son of man', the same two words 'son' and 'man', but preceded by 'like' (*k^e*), and not used in the same idiom. Mark also rewrote one of Jesus' major predictions of his death and resurrection, and used it in different forms more than once. Matthew and Luke followed him in this. They also inherited sayings from the 'Q' material, and they were so happy with the Greek term *ho huios tou anthrōpou* as a Christological title that they used it in new sayings of their own.

This has left a very complex problem for modern scholars, and given that most New Testament professors cannot read the language Jesus spoke, it has been exceptionally difficult to solve. Every time that the Greek term *ho huios tou anthrōpou* occurs, it is an obvious Aramaism. Yet such was the delight of the Gospel writers in this new Christological title that it does not follow that all the 'Son of man' sayings are authentic sayings of Jesus – some are creations of the evangelists. The Aramaic criterion can still be used, but using it is very complicated. I begin with the particular Aramaic idiom, in which a speaker used a somewhat general statement to refer to himself, or himself and other people made obvious by the context. About a dozen examples of this idiom can be reconstructed from sayings of Jesus found in the Gospels, and all of them should be regarded as genuine.

For example, at his final Passover meal with his disciples, Jesus made the following comment on his forthcoming betrayal:

A/The son of man goes as it is written concerning him, and woe to that man by whose hand a/the son of man is betrayed/handed over.

(Mk 14.21)

---

27   Cf. pp. 379, 471–72.
28   See pp. 358–68, and for full discussion, Casey, *Solution to the 'Son of Man' Problem.*

Here the idiomatic Aramaic *bar 'nāsh(ā)*, literally 'son of man', cannot lose its level of generality, though this is not the main point of the saying. Jesus was in no doubt that he was going to suffer a humiliating death, and that this was to have a fundamental redemptive function. He therefore had good reason to state the prediction of his death in scripture, and the doom awaiting the traitor, by means of general statements. The Aramaic word 'goes' (*ᵃzal*) was a normal metaphor for 'dies', as the Greek word for 'goes' was not, so this is further evidence that Mark was translating an Aramaic source. Despite the general level of meaning, no one will have been left in doubt that Jesus' own death was primarily referred to. The doom pronounced on the traitor also has a general level of meaning, which helped to make it acceptable.[29] There should therefore be no doubt that this saying is genuine, and the same goes for all the other examples of this idiom that can be reconstructed from sayings of Jesus in the synoptic Gospels. All of them fit perfectly into the life and teaching of Jesus. Moreover, sayings in which Jesus uses this idiom are found in Mark, in the 'Q' material, and one of them is found in Luke's special material (Lk. 22.48), so this also satisfies the criterion of multiple attestation by source. While these examples are found in our oldest sources, there are no examples in the Fourth Gospel. This distribution is consistent with everything we know about the historical reliability of the Gospels.

At the other end of the spectrum, some 'Son of man' sayings which cannot be fitted into the ministry of the historical Jesus cannot be reconstructed in idiomatic Aramaic at all. For example, in one Johannine discourse, Jesus says:

> And no-one has gone up to heaven except he who came down from heaven, the Son of man who is in heaven.[14]And as Moses lifted up the serpent in the wilderness, so the Son of man must be lifted up,[15]so that everyone who believes may have eternal life.
>
> (Jn 3.13-15)[30]

These two 'Son of man' sayings have no general level of meaning, and cannot be reconstructed in Aramaic because the Aramaic term *bar* (*ᵉ)nāsh(ā)* is an ordinary term for 'man'. The first saying refers to Jesus' pre-existence, a Johannine idea which the historical Jesus never contemplated. The second makes obvious midrashic use of Num. 21.9, together with less obvious but equally important midrashic use of Isa. 52.13. This saying ends with Jesus' atoning death bringing eternal life to every believer, which goes much further than the historical Jesus ever did in understanding his death. Thus two sayings which cannot be reconstructed in Aramaic also present quite distinctive Johannine Christology.

Some 'Son of man' sayings in the Gospels of Matthew and Luke are equally impossible to reconstruct in Aramaic. For example, the Matthaean version of a 'Q' saying is as follows:

---

29   For general discussion of the whole passage see pp. 430–32.
30   For detailed discussion of this passage see Casey, *Solution to the 'Son of Man' Problem*, pp. 282–91.

For like the days of Noah, so shall the parousia of the Son of man be.

(Mt. 24.37, cf. Lk. 17.26)

Here Matthew's Greek term *parousia* refers to the second coming of Jesus. The term 'the Son of man' is a title of Jesus alone. A satisfactory Aramaic reconstruction cannot be made, because the Aramaic term *bar* (*e*)*nash*(*ā*) has a general level of meaning, which cannot be found in an Aramaic reconstruction of this verse. There is no natural Aramaic equivalent of Matthew's *parousia* either. Moreover, the reference to Jesus' second coming has no setting in the teaching of Jesus, who hoped for the coming of the kingdom and did not look into the distant future for his own return.

In these two groups of 'Son of man' sayings, therefore, the use of the Aramaic criterion is relatively straightforward. One group can be reconstructed in Aramaic, and Jesus said every one of them. The other group cannot be reconstructed in Aramaic, and Jesus did not say any of them.

Two other groups of sayings are more complicated. Some sayings make use of Dan. 7.13, where *kebhar enāsh*, 'one like a son of man', is found. Here the general level of meaning has nothing to do with the idiom discussed above, but simply means that this being is being compared to a man. Consequently, this text lent itself to interpretation of a single individual, with the result that in the Western tradition it was interpreted of the Messiah, and in the Western *Christian* tradition it was interpreted of Jesus.[31] This is the tradition to which Mark already belonged, and this tradition made it possible to use *bar* (*e*)*nash*(*ā*) in Aramaic with reference to a particular individual, provided that the context made sufficiently clear reference to Dan. 7.13. For example, at the climax of the largely secondary eschatological discourse in Mark 13, Jesus predicts his own second coming:

And then they will see the Son of man coming in clouds with much power and glory.

(Mk 13.26)

The dependence of this verse on Dan. 7.13 is almost universally recognized. It has the crucial terms 'Son of man' and 'come', the distinctive clouds, and the common elements of power and glory. Precisely because of its use of Dan. 7.13, it is perfectly possible to reconstruct a possible Aramaic source of this verse in which *bar* (*e*)*nash*(*ā*) refers to Jesus alone and has no general level of meaning.[32]

There are however other reasons to believe that this is not a genuine saying of Jesus. It is part of a largely secondary discourse. Jesus preached the coming of the kingdom of God in terms which barely left room for him to die and return. The coming of the Son of man is never predicted together with his death and resurrection. Nor is it predicted together with the coming of the kingdom. Matthew does however associate the two in his secondary editing (Mt. 13.41;

---

31   See further pp. 217–18, 374–78 and Casey, *Interpretation and Influence of Daniel 7*, especially ch. 4: 'The Western Tradition'.

32   See Casey, *Interpretation and Influence of Daniel 7*, pp. 165–78.

16.28), which shows how natural this association is for anyone who believes in both. Jesus' second coming is also abundantly predicted in Acts and the epistles, so it is something which the Gospel writers would be motivated to add to his authentic teaching. Jesus predicts it only in scriptural terms, using 'Son of man' from Dan. 7.13, whereas it is not generally characteristic of him to confine his teaching about anything to scriptural terms only. In short, this saying does not satisfy the criterion of historical plausibility in general, even though it could be seen to satisfy the Aramaic criterion. This illustrates again two basic points: the Aramaic criterion should never be used on its own, and should always be regarded as a subdivision of the criterion of historical plausibility.

The second complicated group of 'Son of man' sayings are those in which Jesus predicts his death *and* Resurrection. These cannot be reconstructed in their present form, because they have so many features which are particular to Jesus that they have no general level of meaning. This is the case for example with Mk 8.31:

> And he began to teach them that the Son of man must suffer many things, and be rejected by the elders and the chief priests and the scribes, and be killed, and after three days rise.

Here the problem is that the saying makes precise reference to 'the elders and chief priests and scribes', that is, to the circumstances of Jesus' death so specific as to preclude any general level of meaning. On the other hand, Peter is portrayed as understanding this saying very clearly, and reacting to it in an understandable way that the early church would have no reason to invent (Mk 8.32-33).

In Chapter 10, I discuss this saying in detail, and propose that it is possible to reconstruct from Mk 8.31 a somewhat shorter saying, and that there is every reason to believe that a prediction in this form is genuine:

> *ḥayyābh bar (ᵉ)nāsh(ā) lᵉmikēbh saggī' ūlᵉethbᵉsārāh ūlimᵉmāth ūlimᵉqām bāthar tᵉlāthāh yōmīn*

> A/the son of man is liable to suffer much and be rejected and die, and rise after three days.

This has a sound general level of meaning. At the same time, the idiomatic use of the Aramaic *bar (ᵉ)nash(ā)*, 'son of man', was so well established that the disciples will have been left in no doubt that Jesus intended to put himself in a position where he would be put to death. Other predictions of the Son of man's death and resurrection after three days (Mt.16.21//Lk. 9.22; Mk 9.31//Mt.17.22-23// Lk. 9.44; and Mk 10.33-34//Mt. 20.18-19//Lk. 18.31-33) are the result of the evangelists rewriting the same or one or more very similar predictions, as are a small number of other sayings (cf. Mk 9.9, 14.41; Mt. 26.2; Lk. 17.25; 24.7).[33]

---

33   See pp. 377–81.

In this case, therefore, the Aramaic criterion is perfectly viable, only rather complicated to use.

I therefore conclude that the use of the Aramaic criterion is essential to the solution of the problems posed by the Gospel title 'the Son of man'. It has to be used very carefully, however, and always within the more general confines of the criterion of historical plausibility.

With regard to the Aramaic criterion in general, there are two other points of method to make. One is that some passages which are certainly authentic do not show irrefutable signs of Aramaisms. For example, Mark's account of the Cleansing of the Temple (Mk 11.15-17) has no such signs. It does have 'and' no less than eight times, and one occurrence of Mark's overused 'began' (Mk 11.15), but neither of these is decisive. An Aramaic reconstruction is nevertheless valuable to scholars, because it confirms the possibility of an Aramaic source, and it makes it easier for us to see the narrative in its original cultural context.[34] In this particular case, for example, the opening of v. 17 runs 'And he was teaching, and he said'. Many scholars have argued that this introduction is 'Markan', and have inferred that the important scriptural texts on which Jesus preached (Isa. 56.7 and Jer. 7.11) were not part of Jesus' preaching, but were added by Mark.[35] One advantage of an Aramaic reconstruction is that it makes it obvious that these words are a natural part of a straightforward Aramaic narrative, not an indication that anything has been secondarily added.

The remaining point of method is that the mere fact that a Gospel saying can be translated into Aramaic does not show that it was a saying of Jesus, or even that there was an Aramaic version before it was translated into Syriac. For example, at Lk. 17.20-21, we read this:

> Now being asked by the Pharisees when the kingdom of God was coming, he answered them and said, 'The kingdom of God does not come with watching,[21]nor will they say, "Look, here!" or "There", for look! the kingdom of God is within/among you'.

There are good reasons to regard the whole of this passage as secondary, because it fits so well into Luke's need to make it clear that Jesus did not expect the kingdom of God to have come long ago.[36] This passage shows that such a concern was the province of Jesus' opponents, not part of Jesus' expectations. It does not however fit well into the teaching of Jesus. Nonetheless, after a careful scholarly discussion of the possible authenticity or otherwise of the passage, Meier cautiously offers an Aramaic reconstruction of vv. 20b and 21b.[37] This has one problem typical

---

34 See P. M. Casey, 'Culture and Historicity: The Cleansing of the Temple', *CBQ* 59 (1997), pp. 306–32.

35 Cf. e.g. Sanders, *Jesus and Judaism*, p. 66, with p. 367 nn. 40–41, citing M. Trautmann, *Zeichenhafte Handlungen Jesu* (FB 37; Würzburg: Echter, 1980), pp. 87–90; J. Roloff, *Das Kerygma und der irdische Jesus* (Göttingen: Vandenhoeck & Ruprecht, 1969), p. 93.

36 See p. 96.

37 Meier, *Marginal Jew*, vol. 2, pp. 423–30, 476–83, with an Aramaic reconstruction at p. 483

of attempts to translate secondary Gospel sayings into Aramaic: finding a word for the abstract noun 'watching'. Meier does come up with one (*manṭĕrāh*). This word is attested in Aramaic from before the time of Jesus, though Meier offers no real parallel to this example. It is rare, because abstract nouns were much less common in Aramaic than in Greek, or, say, English or German. They became more common in Syriac, a group of Aramaic dialects much influenced by Greek, including translations of the Gospels, and the Syriac versions of this verse use words very closely related to the one selected by Meier.

The main point of method is that Meier's translation of this saying into Aramaic does not affect the question of its authenticity. Many secondary sayings which were first written in Greek can be translated into feasible Aramaic because the Gospels were heavily influenced by Jewish culture in general and Aramaic in particular. Translating Gospel sayings into Aramaic is accordingly quite different from translating parts of *Hamlet* or *Lear* into Aramaic, which is basically not a feasible task.

I hope this discussion has shown how important the Aramaic criterion is, and how carefully it needs to be handled. Above all, it must be used as part of the criterion of historical plausibility, not as a criterion on its own. Work on the Aramaic level of the traditions about Jesus underlies all my comments on his life and teaching in this book.

6. *Jewish Source Material*

The criterion of historical plausibility can be used successfully partly because of our increasing knowledge of ancient Judaism in general and Galilee in particular. This is the cultural environment into which Jesus' life and teaching must be fitted, because that is where he belonged. Reconstructing that whole life-world is however a complex and difficult task which cannot be attempted in this book, for it would require several volumes, most of which would not be about Jesus! All I can do here is to draw attention to the most important documents surviving from that period, and the increasing evidence from archaeology. I use these sources throughout the rest of this book at points where they are relevant to understanding the life and teaching of Jesus.

The work of one significant contemporary historian of Judaism at the time of Jesus has survived. He was originally called Joseph son of Mattai, or Matthias. He was born in Jerusalem c.37–38 CE of priestly descent, and he served as a priest in the Temple in Jerusalem. He fought on the Jewish side in the war against Rome and was captured by the Romans in 67 CE. He brightly predicted that the general Vespasian would become emperor of Rome. When this happened, Vespasian set him free, and at the end of the war he was taken to Rome, where Vespasian granted him Roman citizenship. Hence his new name, Flavius Josephus. He was

n. 144, rather more enthusiastically embraced by Hengel and Schwemer, *Jesus und das Judentum*, p. 428 with n. 134.

granted a pension and estates, and this enabled him to write his major works, the *Jewish War* and the *Jewish Antiquities*, together with his *Life* and *Against Apion*. The Aramaic original of the *Jewish War* has not survived, so we have all Josephus' works in Greek. The Jewish community did not treasure his works, because they regarded him as a traitor who went over to the Romans, so all surviving manuscripts were copied by Christians. Nonetheless, the text appears to be generally reliable, except in the most contentious passage, a remarkably short passage about Jesus! The surviving text reads as follows:

> At this time there lived one Jesus, a wise man, if indeed one should call him a man. For he performed surprising deeds, and he was a teacher of men who gladly accept the truth. He won over many Jews and many of the Greeks. He was the Christ. When Pilate, on hearing him accused by men of the highest standing among us, had condemned him to the cross, those who first loved him did not stop. For he appeared to them on the third day, living again, for the divine prophets had foretold these and countless other marvellous things about him. And the tribe of the Christians, so called after this (man), has not died out to this day.
>
> (*Ant.* XVIII, 63–64)

It is obvious that something is the matter with this passage. If Josephus had believed that Jesus 'was the Christ', and that he 'appeared to them on the third day', he would have been a Christian, and his life and works would have been very different. Origen moreover says that Josephus did not believe in Jesus as the Christ (*Against Celsus* I, 47; *Commentary on Matthew*, X, 17, on Mt. 13.55). On the other hand, a Christian is not likely to have begun a complete interpolation 'At that time there lived one Jesus, a wise man', nor to have ended by saying that 'the tribe of Christians . . . has not died out to this day.' Accordingly, the usual scholarly view is that Josephus, who also recorded the trial and execution of Jacob, 'the brother of Jesus who is called Christ' (*Ant.* XX, 200), wrote a short piece about Jesus, and that it was edited by Christian scribes, who had inserted 'He was the Christ' already by the time of Eusebius, c.324 CE. These scribes may have omitted things as well as added them. The importance of this passage is therefore basic. Against people who still argue that Jesus was not a real historical figure, it is an important piece of non-Christian evidence that he was. For sober scholarship, however, Josephus' real importance lies in the massive quantity of evidence about first-century Judaism that he provides.[38]

The most important Jewish documents to have survived in copies written by the time of Jesus are the Dead Sea Scrolls, arguably the most important single archaeological discovery in recent times. They were deposited in caves beside

---

38 It is regrettable that a decent modern translation into English is not readily available. The best is still with the Greek text in H. St. J. Thackeray *et al.* (eds), *Josephus* (LCL, 9 vols. London/Cambridge, MA: Heinemann/Harvard University, 1926–65). A new translation and commentary is being produced, but in several expensive volumes: S. Mason (ed.), *Flavius Josephus: Translation and Commentary* (10 vols. Leiden: Brill, 2000–).

the Dead Sea, perhaps because they were the library of a group of Essenes who lived there, though this is still disputed. They provided a massive amount of new evidence about the Jews of the period, though many were in fragments, and some suffered damage from greedy people possessing and selling them. They provide valuable evidence about Jewish views of heaven, as well as earth. Some portray the worship of God by the highest angels on the sabbath, apparently synchronized with worship in the Temple in Jerusalem, including this for the sacrifice on the twelfth sabbath on the 21st of the third month:

> The [cheru]bim fall down before Him and bless. At their rising, the voice of the murmuring of *Elohim* [is heard] . . . The cherubim bless the image of the throne-chariot above the firmament [and] they praise [the splen]dour of the luminous firmament beneath His seat of glory. When the wheels advance, angels of holiness come and go.
>
> (4Q 405 20 ii 7b-9)

This is one of many passages in which *Elohim*, previously known as a word for God alone in the Hebrew Bible, is used of senior angels.

Down here on earth, a whole document (4Q MMT) was written, apparently to the high priest in Jerusalem, urging him to adopt the author(s)' interpretation of various aspects of the Law. It was probably written c.155 BCE, when the leader of the sectarian community on whose behalf it was written was the person known as the Teacher of Righteousness, the major figure in the history of the community who was probably viewed as the legitimate high priest. It includes the information that 'we have separated ourselves from the multitude of the peo[ple' (4Q MMT C 7), and it seems to have begun with an exposition of the 364-day solar calendar. This was enough to keep them out of synch with the dates of all the major festivals as practised in the Temple and by most Jews. They were thus a much more sectarian group than the Pharisees, who were formed as a sectarian group within Israel at about the same time. They were also very concerned with purity, as shown for example by this:

> [And] furthermore concerning liquid streams: we say that there is no purity in them, and that these streams do not separate between impure and pure. For the liquid of streams and of the receptacle are alike, one liquid.
>
> (4Q MMT B 55–58)

Elsewhere, there is further evidence of the importance of priests in the community. For example, the Community Rule is for those who volunteer

> . . . to separate from the congregation of the men of injustice, to become a community in Law and possessions, under the authority of the sons of Zadok, the priests who keep the Covenant, and under the authority of the multitude of the men of the Community who hold fast to the Covenant. On their authority goes forth every decision concerning law, property, and justice.
>
> (1QS V, 1–4)

Their eschatological beliefs reflect this. As well as hoping for a future king of Israel, they also hoped for an eschatological high priest, who would be the superior of the two:

> When [God] begets the Messiah/Anointed among them, he shall come [at] the head of the whole congregation of Israel with all [his brethren, the sons] of Aaron the Priests . . . And then [the Mess]iah/[Anoin]ted of Israel shall [come] . . . And [when] they gather for the [tab]le of community . . . let no man [stretch out] his hand over the first-fruits of bread and wine before the Priest . . . And afterwards, the Messiah/Anointed of Israel shall stretch out his hand over the bread . . .
>
> (1QSaII, 11–22, extracts)

Another aspect of their eschatological beliefs is of particular interest. They had expected the End to come, in accordance with their interpretation of scripture, but their expectation was naturally not fulfilled, and one of them recorded their reaction:

> 'For yet a vision for the appointed time. It will tell of the End and it will not lie' (Hab. 2.3a). Its interpretation is that the final age will be prolonged and exceed all that the prophets have said, for the mysteries of God are wonderful. 'If it tarries, wait for it, for it will surely come and not delay' (Hab. 2.3b). Its interpretation concerns the men of truth who do the Law, whose hands will not slacken in the service of truth when the final age is prolonged upon them. For all the ages of God reach their appointed end as He has determined for them in the mysteries of his prudence.
>
> (1QpHab VII, 5–14)

This illuminates the nature of eschatological hopes in the whole of the Judaism of this period. Faithful Jews hoped that God would deliver Israel, as did Jesus and his earliest followers. Some of them searched the scriptures, and believed that they found that this would happen soon. When it did not happen, they did not falter in their faith, but continued to hope.[39]

As befits such a learned and scripturally oriented group, the people at Qumran copied the scriptures. Most documents in our Hebrew Bibles have survived in fragments, and there is an especially magnificent scroll of Isaiah from Cave 1. The scrolls show that something very like the text of our Hebrew Bible was known at the time of Jesus, but also that there were more variant texts than scholars previously knew about. The documents in the Hebrew Bible are some of the most important documents from the time of Jesus, for they were the Bible to him, as to his followers and their Jewish opponents. It is moreover clear that the major works in our Bible, such as the Pentateuch, the prophets and writings such as the

---

39 The scrolls are now generally available, though some of them are still not published in satisfactory editions. The best English translation is G. Vermes, *The Complete Dead Sea Scrolls in English* (Penguin Classics. London: Allen Lane, 1997. Rev. edn, 2004).

Psalms, were sacred to them. They kept them in separate scrolls, not in a book, for books like ours had not yet been invented, and some people held sacred some books which are not in our Hebrew Bible.

Scholarly classification of other sacred books has tended to follow Western church canons, which had not been invented at the time of Jesus. Many of the books in our Apocrypha were already considered sacred by some people at the time of Jesus.[40] For example, the book of Sirach, or Ecclesiasticus, in the Apocrypha was originally written by *Yeshua'* son of Eleazar son of Sira, in Hebrew, in the early second century BCE. He is generally known as Jesus son of Sirach, after the Greek form of his name, because the version of this book in the Apocrypha is a translation of the Greek translation made by his grandson. Some fragments of the original Hebrew have survived from Qumran and Masada, and substantial parts from a Cairo Genizah (where worn out manuscripts of sacred texts were stored rather than being destroyed), so that some 68 per cent of the original Hebrew now survives. This shows that the original Hebrew was a sacred text, and the Dead Sea fragments show that it was already so by the time of Jesus.[41]

Many texts from this period were not kept sacred by the Jewish community in Israel, but have survived in Bibles elsewhere in the world. For example, the first book of Enoch has survived in its entirety only in Ethiopic in Ethiopia, where it was transmitted by Jews and is still part of the canon of the Ethiopian church. All the Ethiopic manuscripts are of very late date, the oldest known being probably no earlier than the fifteenth century CE! It is essentially a collection of many different pieces, some as early as the third century BCE. There are significant fragments of more than one copy of parts of it among the Dead Sea Scrolls, which shows that some parts of it were held sacred by some Jews before the time of Jesus. Moreover, one verse is cited, in Greek, as if it were a genuine prophecy of Enoch, in the epistle attributed to Jesus' brother Judah:

> Now Enoch, the seventh from Adam, also prophesied about these things, saying, 'Behold! The Lord came with his holy myriads to execute judgment on all . . .
>
> (Jude 14–15a, quoting 1 En. 1.9)

A Greek translation of some parts of 1 Enoch has also survived. The combination of all these witnesses shows that where more than one version survives, the Ethiopic is a reasonable representation of the text on the whole, but that it cannot be relied on for every detail, because the manuscripts are too late and corrupt.

---

40 One of the better translations is *The Holy Bible, containing the Old And New Testaments with the Apocryphal/Deuterocanonical Books: New Revised Standard Version* (London: Collins, 1989, and in other editions).

41 An English translation of the Hebrew is not readily available, because it is no longer in anyone's sacred text! There is an excellent English translation, with a full scholarly commentary: *The Wisdom of Ben Sira: A New Translation with Notes by P. W. Skehan: Introduction and Commentary by A. A. Di Lella* (AB 39. New York: Doubleday, 1987).

It is all the more regrettable that a whole section, generally known as the Similitudes (1 Enoch 37–71), has survived only in Ethiopic. This has been of the greatest interest to New Testament scholars, because three Ethiopic terms for 'Son of man' in the singular occur no less than 17 times, and they appear to refer to a heavenly figure, though he is identified as Enoch at the end of the work (1 En. 71.14). Had the original Aramaic text survived, it might have been clear that the Aramaic term for 'son of man', *bar* (*e*)*nāsh*(*ā*), was being used as a normal term for 'man', as it always is in Aramaic texts.[42]

1 Enoch is so called because it is written in the form of revelations granted to the ancient patriarch Enoch. Many other works written at about the same time were also attributed to ancient patriarchs. They include for example the *Testaments of the Twelve Patriarchs*, which survive only in Greek in a somewhat rewritten Christian form, or in translations of this Greek version. There are Aramaic fragments of a Levi document, of a Testament of Qahat (4Q542), and of Visions of Amram (4Q543–48), which are similar in form. These show that pseudepigraphal works of this kind were part of Judaism in Israel before the time of Jesus. The *Testaments of the Twelve Patriarchs* as we have them in Greek, may however have first been written in Greek in the Jewish diaspora. They purport to give the final words of each of the 12 patriarchs to their children. Similarly, the second book of Baruch, which survives only in Syriac, together with a Greek fragment, is dated at the destruction of Jerusalem in 587 BCE, and written in the name of Baruch. It was really written in Hebrew c.100 CE, and reflects the concerns of Jews of that period.

Since these works were attributed to major traditional figures who did not write them, they are generally known as the *Pseudepigrapha*. They are very important for understanding Judaism at the time of Jesus.[43]

The other major feature of Jewish evidence uncovered in recent years is due to a massive increase in archaeological excavations in Israel. Perhaps the most important finds for the life and teaching of Jesus are those which have been repeated on different sites. Many stone vessels have been found. Stone vessels were essential for maintaining the expanded purity laws previously known to us from literary sources (e.g. Jn 2.6). Many *mikwāōth* have also been found. These were stepped stone pools in which people could immerse themselves in order to live as far as possible in a state of purity. Mark reports Jews immersing themselves before eating when they have been to the marketplace (Mk 7.4), and Luke records a Pharisee being amazed that Jesus did not immerse himself before eating breakfast (Lk. 11.37-38). The *mikwāōth* confirm that such customs were widespread in Jewish cities. Excavations are now so extensive that a *negative* result is of similar importance. No pig bones have been found in any Jewish city. Given the quantity of bones of animals obviously used for food that have now been found, this implies that pork was not being generally eaten in Jewish

---

42 On the term 'son of man' see pp. 358–88.
43 The best collection of such documents in English is J. H. Charlesworth (ed.), *The Old Testament Pseudepigrapha* (2 vols. London: Darton, Longman & Todd, 1983–85).

cities. This in turn confirms that non-Jewish food would simply not have been available in Jewish areas.

Many detailed finds have cast light on small details of the background to the ministry of Jesus. The importance of these lies not so much in any one detail, as in the general increase of our understanding of the practical details of the daily lives of Jesus and his first followers. For example, Mark says that when four men brought a paralytic to Jesus to be healed, they could not get into his house in Capernaum in a normal way, so they took off the roofing and dug it out, and lowered him through the roof (Mk 2.4). It is clear from archaeological evidence that Capernaum houses could not generally support a second storey. The walls of houses were generally constructed with pieces of black basalt held together with clay, and these were not strong enough to stand the weight of a second storey.[44] It was normally possible to have a ladder to the roof. Roofs were normally made from wooden beams, placed at intervals, covered with branches or reeds which were plastered with clay. This is a kind of roof which could be dug through, and the gaps between the beams might well be large enough for a sort of mattress with a man on it to be lowered between them. Thus archaeological evidence shows that there is nothing implausible in the story, remarkable though it be. Luke altered it. He left out digging through the roof, and says they lowered the paralyzed man 'through the tiles' (Lk. 5.19). There were tiled roofs in the Hellenistic cities with which Luke was familiar. Here archaeological evidence also supports the abundant evidence of other kinds that Mark generally inherited accurate traditions, and the later evangelists often altered them.

Some pieces of archaeological evidence are of a more personal kind. For example, an ossuary found in Jerusalem and dated to the first century CE has an inscription 'Alexander (son of) Simon' in Greek on the front and back, and perhaps 'Alexander the Cyrenian' in Hebrew on the lid. Doubt about the word 'Cyrenian' is mitigated by adjacent ossuaries, which have names more characteristic of Jews from Cyrene than from Jerusalem. Mark says that the soldiers who led Jesus out for crucifixion compelled 'Simon a Cyrenian . . . the father of Alexander and Rufus' to carry his cross (Mk 15.20-21). Here the combination of archaeological and literary evidence enables us to infer that Simon, Alexander and Rufus were members of the Jerusalem church, that Simon was converted to Jesus as a result of his awful experience, and that Mark's account at this point goes back to a Christian eyewitness (cf. Acts 6.9, 11.20, 13.1).[45]

It follows from evidence of this kind that archaeological evidence is essential for historians who wish to locate Jesus within his original environment of first-century Judaism.[46]

---

44 J. L. Reed, *Archaeology and the Galilean Jesus: A Re-examination of the Evidence* (Harrisburg: Trinity Press International, 2000), p. 159.

45 See further pp. 445–47, and on the ossuary C. A. Evans, 'Simon of Cyrene', in J. H. Charlesworth (ed.), *Jesus and Archaeology* (Grand Rapids: Eerdmans, 2006), pp. 338–40.

46 For a very brief introduction, J. H. Charlesworth, *The Historical Jesus: An Essential Guide* (Nashville: Abingdon, 2008), ch. 7, 'Jesus and Archaeology'; for more details, J. J. Rousseau and R. Arav, *Jesus and His World: An Archaeological and Cultural Dictionary* (Minneapolis:

There are however two major pitfalls in the use of archaeological evidence which are sufficiently pervasive to be mentioned here. One is forgeries, in both the ancient and the modern worlds. A conspicuous mediaeval example is the Turin Shroud. This has been claimed to be the shroud in which Jesus was buried. The most important point is that the forgery of relics in the Syriac-speaking church, where the earliest relics of this kind known to me are first mentioned in literary sources, and in the West in the mediaeval period, when anything recognizable as the Turin Shroud itself is first mentioned, was widespread. Forged relics first turning up in the sixth century include the Image of Edessa, sometimes later associated with St Veronica, and sometimes even thought to have been the Turin Shroud folded up. The Turin Shroud itself was first exhibited in 1357, when it was denounced by the Bishop of Troyes as the work of an artist who had confessed to painting it. It is the only one of several forged shrouds of Jesus that anyone still believes in. In 1988, there was a scientific examination of very small samples in three independent laboratories. The radiocarbon dating of these gave a date of 1260–1390, which fits perfectly with the date when it was first exhibited. This has been challenged by devotees of this relic, and no further samples have been released for scientific examination. There is a massive specialized bibliography to it.[47] We shall see good reason to suppose that Jesus was not buried in a shroud, and that his grave was unknown.[48] That his shroud should survive, if he had been buried in one, would also be quite amazing, but there is no limit to what the piety of devotees of the Turin Shroud will believe.

Modern forgeries have more to do with corruption and greed in the Israeli antiquities market. A conspicuous example is the James Ossuary. The box itself, including its lid, is certainly from ancient Jerusalem, but it was not found *in situ*, that is, in an appropriate ancient tomb, an essential aspect of verifying the authenticity of ancient objects. Its owner, an antiquities dealer, claimed to have bought it from an Arab antiquities dealer years previously. His excuses for the delay are not convincing, and made it impossible to be precise about its origins. It was sent to an exhibition in Toronto, shockingly packed, and it arrived cracked, the biggest crack going right through the inscription, which is not helpful either. It was exhibited because it had an inscription in Aramaic, 'Jacob son of Joseph brother of *Yēshua*'. Scholars who originally examined it were deceived, but their work showed only that it was not a *clumsy ignorant* forgery, which indeed it

Fortress, 1995. London: SCM, 1996); Reed, *Archaeology and the Galilean Jesus*; J. D. Crossan and J. L. Reed, *Excavating Jesus: Beneath the Stones, behind the Texts* (Rev. edn, London/San Francisco: SPCK/ HarperSanFrancisco, 2001); Charlesworth (ed.), *Jesus and Archaeology*; J. L. Reed, *The HarperCollins Visual Guide to the New Testament: What Archaeology Reveals about the First Christians* (New York: HarperCollins, 2007).

47   Cf. e.g. I. Wilson, *The Turin Shroud* (London: Gollancz, 1978); W. C. McCrone, *Judgement Day for the Turin Shroud* (Chicago: Microscope, 1997); J. Nickell, *Inquest on the Shroud of Turin. Latest Scientific Findings* (New York: Prometheus, 1998); I. Wilson and B. Schwortz, *The Turin Shroud: The Illustrated Evidence* (London: O'Mara, 2000). Basic information is available from Wikipedia, and the believers' website is http://www.shroud.com

48   See pp. 448–53.

was not. The inscription was an extremely clever forgery, written on a genuinely ancient ossuary, and it was eventually traced to a forger's workshop.

Believers continue to take heart from the difficulty found by the Israeli antiquities authority in obtaining a conviction.[49] There are however three reasons for this, one good and two bad. The good reason is that courts in reasonably civilized countries rightly set a very high standard of scientific proof in cases of this kind, because wrongful convictions wreck the lives of innocent people. The second reason is that the Israeli legal process is not altogether satisfactory, which partly explains why the trial has taken so long. These two points taken together mean that some of the evidence noted above cannot be presented in court. Among other defects is that an Egyptian, accused of forging things for Oded Golan, the owner of the ossuary who is accused of forging the patina and the inscription on this ossuary, could not be extradited to testify, so his evidence was not admissible either. The third reason is that the defence can employ scientists who will not only poke reasonable holes in defective scientific arguments, but who will also challenge any other arguments. In this case, the important ones are the largely spurious arguments defending the authenticity of the patina on which the inscription was inscribed, and maintaining the plausibility of the writing itself being ancient.

Accordingly, these arguments do not mean that the inscription is authentic, only that purely 'scientific' proofs which are unchallengeable in this court of Israeli law are difficult to mount. There are thus many reasons for some people to maintain the authenticity of the inscription. At this point, there is also some connection with relics like the Turin Shroud, in that a lot of other people like to believe in the authenticity of inscriptions like this too. For example, Witherington, who believes in the virgin birth of Jesus and in the Turin Shroud, uses the ossuary in his attack on Catholic and Orthodox views of the perpetual virginity of Mary.[50] Their doctrines are just as spurious as he says they are, but a demonstration of this requires critical scholarship, not belief in a forgery.

The work of biased scientists is also important in assessing the second major pitfall of using archaeological evidence. This is to reject it, and to imagine that places significant in the ministry of Jesus did not exist, so he did not exist either. For example, Zindler has argued that Nazareth, Capernaum and other places significant in Jesus' life did not exist.[51] Nazareth and Capernaum are examples

---

49   The most important book proclaiming the authenticity of the inscription is H. Shanks and B. Witherington, *The Brother of Jesus: The Dramatic Story and Meaning of the First Archaeological Link to Jesus and his Family* (London/ San Francisco: Continuum/ HarperSanFrancisco, 2003). On the background in the Israeli antiquities market, the defects of the original presentation of the ossuary, and the legal proceedings see especially N. Burleigh, *Unholy Business: A True Tale of Faith, Greed and Forgery in the Holy Land* (New York: Smithsonian Books/Collins, 2008, and London: JR Books, 2009); R. Byrne and B. McNary-Zak, *Resurrecting the Brother of Jesus: The James Ossuary Controversy and the Quest for Religious Relics* (Chapel Hill: Univ. of North Carolina, 2009).

50   Witheringon, in Shanks and Witherington, *Brother of Jesus*, pp. 94–96, 199–209.

51   F. R. Zindler, 'Where, Jesus Never Walked', *American Atheist* 36 (1996–97), pp. 33–42, which I accessed at http://www.atheists.org in December 2009, and therefore cite by the

of quite different kinds. Nazareth was a very insignificant village, which explains Zindler's first point, that it is not mentioned in various ancient sources, including the basic Jewish sources, the Old Testament, Josephus and the Talmud. Given also that later building in the immediate area includes the modern town of 60,000 people, the absence of recoverable archaeological remains would not have been significant, had it been the case.

Zindler's second point is to make fun of Lk. 4.29-30, and of pilgrim traditions based on it. This is Luke's rewritten version of Jesus' visit to Nazareth, an accurate account of which is given at Mk 6.1-66 (cf. Mt. 13.53-58). According to Luke only, the inhabitants threw Jesus out and 'led him to the brow of the hill on which their city was built' (Lk. 4.29). Zindler uses this to argue that Nazareth did not exist, but critical scholars know that 'There is no site corresponding to the description in Luke 4.29' and that 'Luke expands Mark . . . *thirdly* by a redactional rounding off of the event . . .'.[52] Moreover, late pilgrim traditions are hopelessly inaccurate. Accordingly, Zindler's comments do not cast doubt on the existence of Nazareth or the accuracy of Mk 6.1-6, and illustrate again that he repeatedly ignores serious scholarship, and prefers to attack the piety of ignorant Christians.

Zindler proceeds to make fun of Franciscan excavations and of pious veneration of the supposed site of the Annunciation. There are genuine problems with pious excavators, as all critical scholars know, and most critical scholars do not believe in the stories of Jesus' birth, so there was indeed no site of the Annunciation.[53] It does not follow that there was no Nazareth.

A more thorough attempt to demonstrate that Nazareth did not exist at the time of Jesus has recently been made by Salm.[54] Salm got one point right: late pilgrim traditions, which believed Lk. 4.29 and accordingly assumed that there was a brow of a hill on which Nazareth was built, caused problems with the location of the site. This situation was made worse by the pious assumptions of early excavators, who interpreted what they found in accordance with what church traditions led them to believe should be there.[55] This does mean that the *precise* location of the settlement at the time of Jesus is somewhat uncertain. Moreover, absolutely precise information about the date of some finds is not always available, not least because some finds, such as shards and lamps, can be difficult to date with precision. However, there does not seem to be any serious doubt among competent investigators that some finds are of sufficiently early date, and that these include a vineyard with walls and a tower, which show that there was some sort of settlement, and shards which are said to date from the Herodian

page numbers of my printout. Cf. Zindler, *Jesus the Jews Never Knew*, pp. 1–2, 4, 72, which makes some of the same points more briefly. On this book see pp. 38–43.

52 Respectively, Rousseau and Arav, *Jesus and His World*, p. 214; G. Lüdemann, *Jesus after 2000 Years* (Trans. J. Bowden. London: SCM, 2000), p. 283.

53 On the birth stories see pp. 145–51.

54 R. Salm, *The Myth of Nazareth: The Invented Town of Jesus* (Cranford, NJ: American Atheist Press, 2008).

55 See especially the proper critical study of J. E. Taylor, *Christians and the Holy Places: The Myth of Jewish-Christian Origins* (Oxford: Clarendon, 1993), pp. 221–67.

period. Salm himself imagines that, when the settlement was restarted after 70 CE, it was on the Nazareth valley floor. He comments, 'One obvious lacuna in the archaeological record is that the Nazareth valley floor has never been excavated . . . is now heavily built over and will in all likelihood never be excavated.'[56] This is a main point. Its significance is that some absence of archaeological evidence is not evidence of the absence of Nazareth.

This underlines the importance of the literary evidence, which Salm handles with extraordinary incompetence and bias, which reflects his lack of relevant scholarly qualifications. He begins with the *Protevangelium of James*, which was written in the second half of the second century, and which consists of late inaccurate storytelling.[57] Its stories presuppose that Joseph and Mary lived in Judaea *before the birth* of Jesus, as Matthew seems to have believed (Mt. 2.19-23). Salm, however, misinterprets this to mean that the 'hometown' of *Jesus* was in Judaea, whereas this document is not about the life of Jesus, and does not even mention *his* hometown. Salm next misinterprets a passage of the Christian writer Julius Africanus (c.200 CE) quoted by Eusebius, claiming that he describes Nazara and Cochaba as 'villages of Judea' and quoting an antiquated American translation to this effect. Julius in fact described them as Jewish villages (*kōmōn Ioudaikōn*, Eus. *H.E.* I, 7, 14), so he meant Nazareth in Galilee, an interpretation which Salm describes merely as 'conceivable'.[58]

Salm proceeds to the *History of Joseph the Carpenter*, an even later legendary work, not written before the *fourth* century.[59] According to Salm, this text 'locates Nazareth in Judea and within walking distance of the temple.'[60] This is not true. It says that, after Herod's death, Joseph, Mary and Salome, obviously with Jesus, 'returned into the land of Israel, and lived in a city of Galilee which is called Nazareth' (*HJC* 9, cf. Mt. 2.19-23). When Joseph was near death at the age of 111, 'he rose up and went to Jerusalem' (*HJC* 12). After praying in the Temple, 'he returned to his own house in the city of Nazareth' (*HJC* 14). When he died, Jesus and Mary 'rent their clothes and wept. And indeed, the inhabitants of Nazareth and of Galilee, having heard of their lamentation, flocked to them, and wept from the third hour even to the ninth' (*HJC* 24–25). It should be obvious that this text locates Nazareth in Galilee, and the brevity of its spurious account of Joseph's final visit to the Temple should not be taken to indicate otherwise.

None of the other texts cited by Salm puts Nazareth in Judaea either. The whole idea has been invented by Salm, and is based on his misinterpretation of texts which are too late to establish anything for the time of Jesus. It is also extraordinary that, after his comments on the archaeology of the real Nazareth

---

56 Salm, *Myth of Nazareth*, p. 289, cf. 225–26.
57 For an ET see E. Hennecke and W. Schneemelcher, *New Testament Apocrypha* (Trans. R. McL. Wilson. Philadelphia: Westminster, 1963), vol. 1, pp. 404–17. Cf. pp. 151–52.
58 Salm, *Myth of Nazareth*, pp. 295–96.
59 I quote from the ET of A. Walker, in A. Roberts and J. Donaldson, *Ante-Nicene Christian Library*, vol. XVI (Edinburgh: T&T Clark, 1870), pp. 62–77.
60 Salm, *Myth of Nazareth*, p. 296.

in Galilee, Salm shows no concern about the absence of archaeological evidence of the existence of his invented Nazareth supposedly in Judaea.

Salm's conviction that Nazareth did not exist at the time of Jesus is obviously contrary to the evidence of Mk 1.9, 'Jesus came from Nazaret of Galilee.' In accordance with his conviction, Salm declares that 'the word *Nazaret* . . . is the interpolation of a later hand.'[61] While a few manuscripts read *Nazarat*, and many read the more conventional *Nazareth*, no ancient manuscripts omit this word, but we have seen atheists Price and Zindler remove inconvenient evidence in this arbitrary way too.[62] Salm's attempt to support this by the obvious fact that Mark treats Capernaum as Jesus' home *during the ministry* is quite wrong, and his citation of Mk 6.3 in support of his notion that Jesus' family resided in Capernaum makes nonsense of Mk 6.1-6. Here Jesus returns to his 'home town (*patris*)', and his reception by the inhabitants, who know his family and him as a carpenter, is not consistent with this place being the centre of his ministry.[63]

Salm proceeds to get in a muddle over the different forms of the name Nazareth, but he demonstrates only that he does not understand place names in Israel or the problems which arise from transliterating words from Aramaic and/ or Hebrew into Greek. For example, he imagines that Mark's four examples of the adjective 'Nazarene' applied to Jesus must mean something other than 'from Nazareth', apparently because he has removed 'Nazaret' from Mk 1.9, leaving no references to it in Mark. He then discusses the form 'Nazara', found for example at Mt. 4.13, which Salm oddly assumes is from 'Q', apparently because the same *form* 'Nazara' is also found in the otherwise quite different Lk. 4.16. Salm declares that this cannot be Nazareth in Galilee, because it 'did not exist before 70 CE, when the putative 'Q' document was compiled', so '*Nazara* in 'Q' must refer to some other place.'[64] He proceeds to locate it as the site which he has invented in Judaea, supporting this with further uncontrolled imagination.

Salm's work is accordingly of no value at all. His archaeological comments are too strict, and his work on texts is incompetent and destructive. He is just as full of inaccurate prejudice as the most conservative Christians whom he despises.

Capernaum is quite different from Nazareth. It was a town on the shore of the Lake of Galilee which seems to have been the major centre of Jesus' ministry. If there were no remains of it, that would be a serious matter, but it has been successfully excavated at a site known as Tell Ḥum.[65] Zindler dismisses the two occurrences of Capernaum in Josephus in order to claim that Capernaum is unknown outside the Gospels before the end of the first century.[66] In fact, however, Josephus says how he was injured and taken to a village called *Kepharnōkon* (*Life* 403–4 ms P, *Kapharnōmōn* ms W, other variants), which Zindler is quite sure is a different place from the Gospel town *Kapharnaoum*. Zindler takes no

---

61 Salm, *Myth of Nazareth*, p. 300.
62 See pp. 35–36, 41–43.
63 On this story see pp. 143–44.
64 Salm, *Myth of Nazareth*, pp. 300–1.
65 See further pp. 165–66.
66 Zindler, 'Where Jesus Never Walked', p. 6.

account of either differences in pronunciation or differences in transliteration of the Semitic *kphr nḥm* into Greek, which are sufficient to account for this. Moreover, Taricheae, to which Josephus was taken next, is the later name of Magdala, which was genuinely nearby.[67]

Zindler points out that the Gospels are not precise about exactly where near a shore of the sea of Galilee Capernaum was located. This is true, but it does not mean that anything is wrong with its identification with Tell Ḥum, which fits all the Gospel evidence perfectly. Zindler makes a lot of the absence of the site of Capernaum in Christian tradition for 'several centuries'. In fact, however, Capernaum became very well known before the end of the reign of Constantine (306–37 CE), when a church was built there, the earliest date at which this was possible. Zindler pours scorn on Franciscan excavation of the site. This was indeed faulty, but doubts about the identification of Peter's house should not lead us to undervalue the fact that the kind of house in which Peter would have lived has been found. Zindler declares that 'finding the remains of a first-century synagogue is a prerequisite for establishing any site as a candidate for the biblical Capernaum'.[68] There are two reasons why this is wrong. First, we do not know that the synagogue which Jesus attended was a sufficiently distinctive site for its remains to be identifiable as such. Secondly, a later synagogue covered the most promising site, so decisive excavation is most unlikely. This does not show that the site was not a first-century synagogue, let alone that the whole place is not Capernaum. Zindler does not say anything about what he thinks the site at Tell Ḥum was, which is of central importance because it is so perfectly suitable for having been Capernaum, and it was certainly there at the time.

It is regrettable that I have had to discuss what not to do with archaeology as well as how illuminating some of its results are. It will be clear that there are three basic reasons for this. One is Christian piety, which leads to false belief about various sites and objects. The second is that there are always 'scientists' available who are completely biased and/or not competent in archaeology or New Testament studies. The third is that there are atheists who are determined to oppose Christian piety, and who have therefore come up with negative comments which are no improvement on Christian piety. In the rest of this book I simply refer to positive results where these are available.

7. *Rewriting History, Telling Stories and Social Memory*

There are two major features of ancient Judaism to which I draw attention in this final section, because both are very well known to scholars who spend their lives in the study of ancient Jewish documents, but largely ignored by New Testament scholars. One is that when people wrote about Jewish history, they frequently rewrote it in accordance with the needs of the communities to which

---

67   On Magdala/Taricheaea see pp. 165, 193.
68   Zindler, 'Where Jesus Never Walked', p. 9.

they belonged. The other is that some people loved telling stories, and they did not always distinguish between history and fiction with the care that we consider appropriate. What is more, some Greek documents show similar features. All this is essential in the study of all four canonical Gospels, and without a careful appreciation of these points we cannot hope to distinguish with sufficient accuracy between what Jesus said and did, on the one hand, and what the evangelists attribute to him on the other.

In recent scholarly work, both rewriting history and telling stories about traditional figures have been drawn together into discussions of 'social memory'. In the most fruitful relevant work that I have seen, April DeConick, writing on the Gospel of Thomas, summarizes this as follows, using the term 'communal' rather than 'social':

> So the formation of communal memory is not a retrieval of past traditions and history. Rather it is the 'reconfiguration' of the past, making it conform to the present experiences and future expectations of the group. 'Remembering' is not a matter of recall, but a selection and reorganization of traditions so that the present can be better understood in light of its past and a sense of continuity between the present and the past is achieved. In this sense, it is best characterised as retrospective. These retrospective reconstructions of the past are largely achieved by adapting traditions and historical facts to the beliefs and spiritual needs of the contemporary group.[69]

Such work has great potential. It applies most obviously to the Gospels of John and of Thomas. It is however potentially helpful also in understanding secondary material in the synoptic Gospels.[70]

I now give a few examples, mostly Jewish. Josephus retells a lot of biblical tradition about King Solomon. He adds this:

> Now God granted him understanding of the skill used against demons for the help and healing of people. He also composed incantations by which diseases are alleviated and he left methods of exorcisms by which those who are entangled drive out demons so that they never return. And this healing is extremely powerful among us to this day . . .
>
> (*Ant.* VIII, 45–46)

This information about Solomon is absent from the biblical account. The final sentence, followed by an account of an exorcism which Josephus himself had witnessed, shows that Josephus' account reflects the customs of Jews at the time

---

69 A. D. DeConick, *Recovering the Original Gospel of Thomas: A History of the Gospel and its Growth* (LNTS 286. London: T&T Clark, 2005), p. 12.

70 More generally see especially D. Mendels, *Memory in Jewish, Pagan and Christian Societies of the Graeco-Roman World* (London: T&T Clark, 2004); L. T. Stuckenbruck *et al.* (eds), *Memory in the Bible and Antiquity: The Fifth Durham-Tübingen Research Symposium* (WUNT 212. Tübingen: Mohr Siebeck, 2007).

of Josephus, not an independent historical source about what had happened a millennium earlier. He concludes his account of the exorcism which he had witnessed:

> Now when this had happened, the clear understanding and wisdom of Solomon were shown. Because of this, we were induced to speak about these things, so that everyone might know the greatness of his nature and how God favoured him, and that the king's surpassing virtue of every kind might escape no-one under the sun.
>
> (*Ant.* VIII, 49)

This is an overt declaration that Josephus made this non-biblical report about Solomon because of its importance in the world in which he himself lived. His whole account is a perfect example of 'social memory'.

Historians in the Graeco-Roman world exercised particular freedom with speeches. For example, Livy records the ascension of Romulus. In an appearance from heaven, Romulus makes a speech in which he foretells that Rome will be the capital of the world and her armed forces irresistible, in accordance with the will of heaven (I, XVI). It is clear that Livy created this speech, in accordance with the needs of Rome in his own time, not because the speech was recorded in an ancient source. Moreover, Livy knew perfectly well what he was doing. As he put it, when dealing with a different matter long before his time, 'in matters so ancient, I should be content if what be like truth be accepted as true' (V, XXI, 9). Tacitus, with a speech of Claudius actually available to him in a written record, rewrote it when he could have quoted it. While he kept its main arguments, he reorganized it and altered its style, so that the resulting speech is one which Tacitus could have created (*Annals* XI, 24).[71]

Josephus, with a speech of Joseph available to him in the Torah (Gen. 45.3-13), rewrote it instead of quoting it (*Ant.* II, 161–65). I give the opening of the two versions side by side. In the text of Genesis, I have put '. . .' where there is a little narrative, and in the text of Josephus, I have placed what might be considered a narrative summary by Josephus of Joseph's opening words in brackets. There are no serious differences between the Hebrew text of Genesis and the standard Greek translation of it.

I am Joseph. Is my father still alive? . . . Come close to me . . . I am Joseph your brother whom you sold into Egypt. And now do not be distressed and do not be angry with yourselves because you sold me to	(he made himself known to his brothers and said) I praise you for virtue and goodwill towards our brother, and I find you better men than I expected from your plots concerning me, having done all this

---

71 The original speech was found on an inscription, CIL XIII, 1668, available in an English translation in N. Lewis and M. Reinhold (eds), *Roman Civilization Sourcebook II: The Empire* (New York: Columbia Univ., 3rd edn, 1990), pp. 54–55.

here, for God sent me before you to   to test your brotherly love. Nor do I
live. For the famine (has been) in the   think that you have been evil to me
land these two years, and there are   by nature, but by the will of God
yet five years in which there (will be)   working out the bestowal of good
no ploughing or harvest. And God   things for us now and hereafter, if he
sent me before you . . .   remains gracious to us . . .
                            (Gen. 45.3-6)   (*Ant.* II, 160–61)

If Josephus had wished, he could have copied Joseph's speech directly from
Genesis. Instead, he replaced it with a speech which he felt was more suitable
for his potential audiences.

The Torah itself, venerated as it was, could be rewritten as required, in a
culture in which rewriting the Torah for the Jewish community *was* a mode of
venerating it. Philo, an elder contemporary of Jesus in Alexandria, so writing
in Greek, begins his comments on the fourth of the Ten Commandments in an
obviously appropriate way:

> The fourth commandment is that concerning the sacred seventh (day), so that
> it should be observed in a reverent and holy way.
>
> (*Concerning the Ten Words*, 96)

In the Torah, there are two versions of the fourth commandment, which give different reasons for observing the sabbath (Exod. 20.8-11//Deut. 5.12-15). Philo's
next comments obviously have the Exodus version in mind, and I translate literally the Septuagint, the standard Greek translation which Philo used:

> Remember the day of the Sabbaths to sanctify it. Six days you shall work,
> and do all your works. But on the seventh day (is) the Sabbaths for the
> Lord your God. You will not do on it any work, you and your son and your
> daughter, your servant/slave and your female servant/slave, your ox and
> your yoked (animal) and every beast of yours, and the proselyte who dwells
> among you.
>
> (Exod. 20.8-10 LXX)

Philo does not quote this, apparently assuming that his audiences would know
the text of the Torah. He comments reasonably on people's need to work to provide the necessities of life, and God's provision of rest on 'the sacred sevenths'.
Then he adds this, with an apparent quotation:

> Now is not this an altogether excellent and most sufficient encouragement to
> turn to every virtue and most of all to piety? 'Follow', it says, 'always God.
> Let the one all-sufficient six-day period in which he created the world be for
> you a pattern of fixed time set apart for deeds. And (let) the seventh (day be
> for you) a pattern of your duty to philosophize/study wisdom, (the day) on
> which it is said that he surveyed what he had made, so that you yourself may
> meditate on the things of nature, and whatever of your personal things make

for happiness.' Let us therefore not pass over so great an archetype of the best
lives, the practical and the contemplative . . .

(*Concerning the Ten Words*, 100–1)

The apparent quotation is not in the Torah. Like Philo's other comments, which
are overtly presented as his comments, the apparently quoted part is his interpretation. In particular, the duty to philosophize/study wisdom (*philosophein*) is
an interpretation by a Jewish philosopher who wrote in Greek.

Other Jews added to the regulations in the written text. For example, the book
of *Jubilees* is in effect a rewritten version of part of the Pentateuch. It was written
in Israel c.166–165 BCE. It has survived complete only in Ethiopic, because, like
1 Enoch, it was part of the Bible in Ethiopia, but fragments of it in the original
Hebrew have survived among the Dead Sea Scrolls. The pseudepigraphical device
is presented in the opening words:

> This is the account of the division of the days of the law and of the testimony,
> of the events of the years, of their weeks, of their jubilees throughout all the
> years of the world, as the Lord said to Moses on Mount Sinai when he went
> up to receive the tablets of the law and of the commandment, according to
> the voice of God as he said to him, 'Come up to the top of the mountain'.

After a substantial introduction, God commands an angel of the presence to
write for Moses from the beginning of creation, and in Chapter 2 he begins this.
At *Jub.* 2.17-22 the angel records the creation of the sabbath day as a great sign,
and in the final chapter he records some of its regulations, and ends by repeating
the pseudepigraphical device:

> Six days you will work, but the seventh day is the Sabbath of the Lord your
> God . . . And let the man who does anything on it die. Every man who will
> profane this day, who will lie with his wife . . . let him die . . . And any man
> who does work on it . . . who fasts or makes war on the day of the Sabbath,
> let any man who does any of these on the day of the Sabbath die, so that the
> children of Israel might keep the Sabbath according to the commands of the
> Sabbaths of the land just as it was written in the tablets which He placed in
> my hands so that I might write for you the law of each time . . .

(*Jub.* 50.7, 8, 12–13)

The prohibitions of sex and war on the sabbath were never part of the halakhah,
that is, the legal observances, of mainstream Judaism. Nonetheless, they are presented here as part of the revelation of God to Moses on Mount Sinai.

These authors' rewriting of the Torah was not confined to the expansion
of the halakhah in regulations. It also included apparently factual information
and stories to recommend the maintenance of various aspects of the Torah. In
166–165 BCE, when the book of *Jubilees* was written in Israel, there was a severe
persecution in which circumcision was prohibited (1 Macc. 1.48, cf. 1.52, 60–61,
2.46). The author(s) accordingly declared that the two highest classes of angels

were created circumcised (*Jub.* 15.27). The author(s) also wished to encourage the celebration of the Feast of Weeks, as in the Torah at Lev. 23.9-21. This is one story to support this:

> And all of this feast was celebrated in heaven from the day of creation until the days of Noah, twenty-six jubilees and five weeks of years. And Noah and his children kept it for seven jubilees and one week of years until the day of the death of Noah.
>
> (*Jub.* 6.18)

That looks like information, and it is not found in the Pentateuch. After that, the feast was not observed properly, and its renewal in the days of Abraham is recounted in story mode:

> And it came to pass in the first week of this forty-fourth jubilee in the second year, that year in which Abraham died, that Isaac and Ishmael came from the Well of the Oath to Abraham, their father, to observe the feast of Weeks . . . And both of them came together, and Isaac slaughtered a sacrifice as a burnt offering and offered (it) up on the altar of his father which he built in Hebron. And he sacrificed a thank offering and made a feast of joy before Ishmael, his brother. And Rebecca made new round cakes of new grain. And she gave them to Jacob, her son, to take to Abraham his father, from the firstfruits of the land so that he might eat and drink and bless their creator before he died.
>
> (*Jub.* 22.1, 3–4)

This story is not found in the Pentateuch either. It has been elaborated with vivid details, but since it is not in the biblical canon in the West, conservative scholars do not argue that these details are due to an eyewitness account!

The story of Abraham's death, briefly related at Gen. 25.8, is massively elaborated in story mode. Abraham makes a lengthy final speech (*Jub.* 22.11-24), and there are many vivid details in the account of his death:

> And Jacob slept on the bosom of Abraham, his father's father . . . And he [Abraham] placed the two fingers of Jacob on his eyes and he blessed the God of gods. And he covered his face, and stretched out his feet and slept the eternal sleep, and he was gathered to his fathers . . . And Jacob awoke from his sleep and behold, Abraham was cold as ice, and he said, 'O father, father!' And none spoke, and he knew that he was dead. And he rose from his bosom and ran and told Rebecca, his mother. And Rebecca went to Isaac in the night and told him. And they went together and Jacob was also with them, and a lamp was in his hand. And when they went, they found Abraham lying dead.
>
> (*Jub.* 22.26; 23.1, 3–4)

This illustrates the great freedom of storytellers when they recounted the history of Israel, and the standard nature of attributing both halakhic details and entertaining stories to the perceived fountainheads of traditions, in this case the revelation of God to Moses on Mount Sinai.

Thus the whole book of *Jubilees* is a perfect example of the social memory of a social subgroup of the Jewish community.

Other Jews contributed many stories of different kinds. For example, the first book of Enoch includes accounts of Enoch's heavenly and earthly travels. After visiting Israel, portrayed as the centre of the earth, and the scene of the Last Judgement, Enoch travels further east:

> And from there I went towards the East into the centre of a mountainous part of the desert, and I saw the wilderness, and it was solitary, full of trees and plants, with water gushing forth on it from above, (then) being carried by a copious aqueduct approximately to the North-West, and from all sides it was taking up water and dew.
>
> (1 En. 28.1-3)

This contains perfectly accurate topographical information, referring to the Wadi Musa, and the famous aqueduct which ran into Petra. This illustrates the fact that accurate topographical information never entails the literal accuracy of stories, an especially important point in dealing with the historicity of the Fourth Gospel. The aqueduct was of course famous at the time of the author, who was not in the least concerned that it might not have been there as early as the time of Enoch!

That story was meant to be entertaining and rather marvellous. Some people loved telling stories in which normally impossible events are recounted. For example, in 1 Enoch 106, fragments of which survive in Aramaic from Qumran, Lamech's wife gives birth to a son:

> And when the child was born, his body was whiter than snow and redder than a rose. The tresses of the hair of his head were all white like white wool, and thick and glorious, and when he opened his eyes, the house shone like the sun. And when he was taken up from the hands of the midwife, he opened his mouth and spoke to the Lord of righteousness.
>
> (1 En. 106.2-3)

This birth is obviously intended to be miraculous in the strictest sense.[72] The entertaining story continues with Lamech going to his father Methuselah, who goes to his father Enoch 'at the ends of the earth where he had heard that I then was' (1 En. 106.8). Enoch reassures Methuselah that the child is genuinely Lamech's son, and that he and his three sons will survive a Flood, in which the rest of humankind will die. He instructs Methuselah to tell Lamech to call his son Noah. The truth of the story, including predictions of evil times leading up to the Flood, is guaranteed by Enoch's declaration that the Holy Ones have shown him and told him, and he has read it on the heavenly tablets (1 En. 106.19).

---

72   On miracles see further pp. 237–44.

This apparently personal legitimating device should be borne in mind in assessing what may appear at first sight to be eyewitness claims in the Fourth Gospel (Jn 19.35, 21.24).

Angels are important characters in the stories of this culture. For example, in the book of Tobit, fragments of which survive from Qumran, some in Hebrew and more in Aramaic, a major role is played by Raphael, the archangel in charge of healing. He appears in the guise of Azariah, son of Hananiah, and accompanies Tobias on his journey from Nineveh to Ecbatana in Media, for Raphael naturally knows the way! On the way, he gets Tobias to catch a large fish and keep its gall, heart and liver, on the ground that these are 'useful for medicine' (Tob. 6.5). When they get to Ecbatana, Tobias marries Sarah, whose previous *seven* husbands died in the bridal chamber because of a demon. Raphael, however, instructs Tobias to take some of the fish's liver and heart, and put them on the embers of the incense in the bedroom, for this will drive the demon away. Of course, they must also pray to the Lord of heaven (Tob. 6.17-18). This works, and the demon flees to southern Egypt, where Raphael binds him (Tob. 8.3).

Raphael, being able to move instantaneously anywhere, is shortly back in Ecbatana, where, as Azariah, he travels to Rages, and brings back Gabael with lots of money for Tobias. After wedding celebrations, Tobias returns to his father Tobit with Sarah, Raphael and lots of property (slaves, camels, money, etc.). When they are nearly there, Raphael instructs Tobias to cure the blindness of Tobit by smearing the fish gall on his eyes (Tob. 11.7-8). This works too, so Tobit sees his son Tobias, and greets his wife Sarah. Thus there was rejoicing among all the Jews who were in Nineveh (Tob. 11.17).

After more wedding celebrations, Tobit and Tobias decide to pay Raphael handsome wages for two cures and much other help. Raphael, however, after urging them at some length to bless God and be good, reveals himself, declaring his heavenly role and how it was God who had sent him, and concluding:

> I am Raphael, one of the seven holy angels who present the prayers of the saints and enter before the glory of the Holy One.
>
> (Tob. 12.15)

Tobias and Tobit fall down before him, and Raphael finally explains that he did not really eat and drink while he was with them. He tells them to get up and acknowledge God, to whom he is about to ascend. He also tells them to write down everything that has happened to them. Then he ascended and they no longer saw him (Tob. 12.20-21).

In general, the documents of this time set their stories in relatively ancient times. Sometimes, however, they were written about contemporary events. For example, in Daniel 8, Daniel sees a vision, which is dated in the time of King Belshazzar (Dan. 8.1). The archangel Gabriel is sent to interpret it for him (Dan. 8.15-26). He interprets the goat in the vision as 'the king of Greece', and its great horn as 'the first king', so that is Alexander the Great. Much of the interpretation is taken up with the little horn, which is interpreted as a wicked king who will destroy 'the people of the holy ones'. While this is couched in terms as indirect as the vision itself, there should be no doubt that this is Antiochus Epiphanes, whose destruction is foretold. This document was written c.166–165 BCE during that persecution, so it is really about contemporary events. It is set in ancient times so that the prediction of the deliverance of Israel can be made by an Israelite sage, who receives a vision interpreted by an archangel. That is a device for declaring the truth of the predictions, of which the deliverance of Israel from Antiochus Epiphanes was still a matter of further hope when the document was written.

Stories deliberately located in the present or the recent past were sometimes written too. For example, the second book of Maccabees was written in the name of 'the brethren the Jews in Jerusalem and those in the land of Judaea' to 'the brethren the Jews in Egypt' (2 Macc. 1.1). Its purpose was to encourage them to celebrate the new Feast of Hanukkah, and it appears to date itself c.124 BCE (2 Macc. 1.9). It refers back to the history of the Maccabaean wars of deliverance written in five books by Jason of Cyrene (2 Macc. 2.23), which have not survived. During the reign of the Greek king Seleucus IV Philopator (187–175 BCE), the finance minister Apollonius sent Heliodorus to Jerusalem to confiscate funds from the Temple treasury, which the high priest Onias III somehow managed to prevent. The narrative of 2 Maccabees tells us what 'really' happened. When Heliodorus arrived at the treasury with his bodyguard,

> There appeared to them a beautifully adorned horse with a fearsome rider, which rushed at Heliodorus and struck him with its front hoofs . . . Now two other young men appeared to him . . . who stood on each side of him and scourged him continually, inflicting many blows on him.
>
> (2 Macc. 3.25-26)

Heliodorus collapsed, and his bodyguard and retinue recognized the sovereign power of God and praised him. His friends begged Onias to call on the Most High. Onias therefore offered sacrifice for him. While he was making the atonement,

> the same young men appeared to Heliodorus . . . and said, 'Give many thanks to Onias the High Priest, for because of him the Lord has granted you life. Now you, having been scourged from heaven, announce to everyone the mighty power of God.' Now when they had said this, they disappeared.
>
> (2 Macc. 3.33-34)

Heliodorus did as he was told, bearing witness to the deeds of the supreme God, which he had seen himself.

This is a quintessentially Jewish story, relating the triumph of God over enemies of Israel. The two young men are what we otherwise call angels, who visit men in accordance with God's orders, as did Raphael in the book of Tobit, and Gabriel in the book of Daniel.

Of course, none of this demonstrates that angels do not exist, or that God does not send them according to his will. These stories do however demonstrate that angels were a natural part of Jewish fiction at the time of Jesus, and this should be borne in mind when considering the historicity of the stories of Jesus' birth and resurrection.

8. *Conclusions*

In this chapter, I hope to have made clear the methods which I use throughout this book to put forward the most accurate account of the life and teaching of Jesus that an independent historian can hope to achieve. The most important single criterion is that of historical plausibility. I seek to place Jesus within the framework of first-century Judaism, where he originally belonged. The most important new point is that, within this framework, I seek to take more seriously than previous scholars the evidence provided by the oldest primary sources of the Aramaic which Jesus spoke. For this purpose, I have made full use of the Aramaic documents discovered in relatively recent times, which permit much more fruitful work to be done now than was possible for previous generations of scholars.

To do this successfully, it is essential to have a clear grasp of which primary sources are the oldest and most reliable. I discussed this in Chapter 2, where I showed that our oldest single source is the Gospel of Mark. Much of the so-called 'Q' material is equally valuable, and so are parts of the Gospels of Matthew and Luke, each of whom inherited some perfectly reliable material too. When dealing with these sources, the criteria of multiple attestation and embarrassment are also of some value, though they are of limited application. The criterion of dissimilarity, though much abused in traditional Christian scholarship, is not altogether without value, in that unparalleled items attributed to Jesus in our oldest sources should be regarded as genuine.

To fit Jesus into his original cultural background in first-century Judaism, we must also be able to reconstruct that environment. I have therefore provided a summary of the main sources available to us, including recent archaeological work, and I refer to important points from this material throughout the rest of this book. To obtain an accurate picture of Jesus, it is also necessary to show that secondary material *is* secondary. I have therefore considered also the ways in which Jewish authors rewrote traditional accounts of events in the light of contemporary needs, and how they made up stories, for a combination of entertainment and for the presentation of serious theology in story mode. I noted how fruitful the concept of 'social memory' can be in understanding these points. Rewriting and storytelling were in effect ways of updating traditions for the benefit of the communities for which authors wrote. I take up these points throughout this book too. Secondary material of all kinds is abundant in later Gospels, which I discuss in the Appendix.

The task of distinguishing between historically accurate material and secondary material in the Gospels is the most difficult that a historian can face. I begin it in the next chapter with Jesus' birth and background.

CHAPTER 4

Family, Birth, Upbringing and Cultural Background

1. Family

Jesus was born in Israel, into an observant Jewish family. He was always said to have come from Nazareth, in Galilee, so there is no doubt that this is where he was brought up. Jesus' family in Nazareth are also known up to a point. His father was Joseph, called after a major patriarch who ruled over Egypt under the Pharaoh. Jesus' mother was Miriam, whom we call Mary, so she was called after Moses' sister. Jesus' own name, *Iēsous* in our Greek Gospels, is the Greek equivalent of *Yēshuaʿ*, which we usually render into English as Joshua. Thus Joseph and Miriam called Jesus after the major figure of Jewish history who succeeded Moses and led Israel across the Jordan into the promised land. At the time his name was understood to mean 'YHWH saves' or the like, with the name of God at the beginning, so effectively 'God saves'. Joseph, Miriam and Jesus must have been aware of this understanding of his name, and it is reflected at Mt. 1.21, where an angel of the Lord tells Joseph that Mary will bear a son 'and you will call his name Jesus, for he will save his people from their sins'.

Jesus had four brothers. The most famous was Jacob, whom we usually call James, who later led the Jerusalem church and became famous for his piety. He was called after the eponymous patriarch of the whole nation, Jacob who was also known as Israel. The other brothers were Judah, who was probably the author of what we call the epistle of Jude, Joseph and Simeon. Jesus had sisters as well (Mk 6.3), but we do not know their names. All the known names are major patriarchal names. Thus the names of the men in Jesus' family are straightforward evidence that he was born into a traditional Jewish family, who were expecting the salvation of Israel.

Christian tradition has supposed that Jesus' brothers and sisters were not born of Miriam, but Joseph's children by a previous wife, or even that they were Jesus' cousins. Neither situation would have given rise to the report of Mk 6.3:

> Is not this the carpenter, the son of Mary and brother of Jacob and Joses and
> Judah and Simon? And are not his sisters here with us?

This report assumes that Jesus, being called son of Mary and having named
brothers and unnamed sisters, was the brother of other children of Mary. Other
ideas are due to later Christian belief in the perpetual virginity of the Blessed
Virgin Mary, a piece of imaginative doctrine which has no place in historical
research, and no connection with the historical Miriam. We must prefer the
evidence of Mark: Miriam had several children.

The report of Mk 6.3 has another remarkable feature, from which we must
be careful to draw the correct conclusion. This is the reaction of the people of
Nazareth, when Jesus returned there. They did not welcome him as a remarkable religious figure because he was already known to them as a normal person,
and they stated this normality by referring to his job as well as his family. Their
term 'son of Mary' has caused difficulty to interpreters, who expect Jesus to be
called the son of his father, as he is called (the) son of Joseph (Lk. 4.22; Jn 6.42)
or the son of the carpenter (Mt. 13.55). Some people have seen here a reference
to the virgin birth, and others have thought that Jesus was so described because
he was believed to be illegitimate.[1] The virgin birth is never mentioned in Mark,
and the ordinary inhabitants of Nazareth certainly did not believe in it when
they rejected him. It follows that this cannot have been what they meant. As so
often, the problem arises from reading the passage with later traditions in mind,
instead of looking for its original setting in the life of Jesus. Miriam is found
during the ministry leading Jesus' brothers to seize him because he was out of
his mind (Mk 3.21, 31–35). Luke reports her continued presence after his death
(Acts 1.14). Joseph, however, is never mentioned. We should infer that Miriam
was a very vigorous woman at the time of the historic ministry, whereas Joseph
was long since dead. This is in no way improbable. If Jesus was about 30 at the
time of the ministry, Miriam will have been round about 45. Many people are
still vigorous at that age. On balance, Joseph is likely to have been older than
his wife, and many people who survived to be adults died before they were 50
or 60. Hence the description of Jesus as 'son of Mary', a natural description
in the circumstances, but unusual because popular descriptions of apparently
ordinary people whose fathers were dead are almost unknown. It was changed
by Matthew, Luke and John because Joseph was famous to them, and reference
to a person's father was conventional.

There is a biblical precedent for a man being called the son of his mother
rather than his father in Joab son of Zeruiah (e.g. 2 Sam. 2.13) and his brothers, for Zeruiah was the sister of David: we can assume that their unmentioned
father was unimportant and probably long dead too. Similarly a widow may be
said to have a son, without reference being made to his dead father (1 Kgs 17.17;
Lk. 7.12). There are other examples from later Jewish sources. Josephus refers to
Antipater as 'son of Salome' (e.g. *Ant.* XVII, 230). This is usually thought to be

---

1   See pp. 151–58.

because Salome was important at Herod's court, and this explanation is surely correct. Josephus also refers to a high priest as Simon son of Kamith (*Ant.* XVIII, 34), and later sources, describing him as 'Simeon son of Qmḥīth', discuss the virtues of his mother Qimḥīth (e.g. y.Yoma 1, 1/33 (38d)). He was obviously not born of a virgin, and had there been doubts about his parentage, he could not have been high priest. Another example is found at b. Ket. 87a, which discusses opinions attributed to, or discussed by, a rabbinical sage called 'Abba Saul son of Imma Miriam'. It follows that there had to be a reason for a man to be described as the son of his mother rather than his father. There could be a variety of reasons for this, and none of the other examples are known to have been caused by either virgin birth or illegitimacy.

If Jesus was the first of the children of Miriam and Joseph, Joseph's death is likely to have left him with a kind of leadership role within the family, as the eldest child. While Miriam will have remained in overall control, Jesus is likely for example to have been in charge of the carpentry business, ensuring that it remained prosperous. This period may have lasted for several years. Jesus is not said to have married, nor are any children recorded. It is therefore virtually certain that he did not marry, and absolutely certain that he had no wife at the time of his ministry, and that he never had any children. Most attempts to present Jesus as married do not belong to serious scholarship. The most respectable that I have seen is that of Phipps, who overinterprets Jewish views that men should marry and applies them to Jesus. He is obviously motivated by a proper and natural concern for normal human sexuality in the Christian churches, but he has retrojected this concern onto Jesus in much the same way as the celibate clerics whom he criticizes have retrojected their particular tradition. This debate is virtually a paradigm of what is wrong with the whole quest of the historical Jesus, acted out on a single topic.[2]

None of our sources consider the fact that Jesus was unmarried worthy of mention. It follows that it was either less unusual than some people have suggested, or the fact of his vigorous prophetic ministry was an obvious explanation for his remaining single, like John the Baptist, or both.

2. *Birth*

Christian tradition, based on the birth narratives in the Gospels of Matthew and Luke, has supposed that Jesus was born in Bethlehem, in Judaea. Critical scholars have however known for a long time that these entertaining stories are not literally true. As Hans Küng put it, 'today of course it is admitted even by Catholic exegetes that these stories are a collection of largely uncertain, mutually

---

2   W. E. Phipps, *Was Jesus Married? The Distortion of Sexuality in the Christian Tradition* (New York: Harper & Row, 1970); *The Sexuality of Jesus* (New York: Harper & Row, 1973). Marriage to Mary Magdalene is presented e.g. in *The Da Vinci Code*: cf. pp. 25–26, and pp. 192–97. For sober historical discussion see Meier, *Marginal Jew*, pp. 332–45.

contradictory, and strongly legendary and ultimately theologically motivated narratives, with a character of their own.'[3] Since so many people persist in believing that they are literally and historically true, I give reasons for not doing so.

The birth narratives of Matthew and Luke are written in story mode, and if they are interpreted literally, they are inconsistent with each other. The announcements of the birth are not so much inconsistent as unconnected. In Matthew, an angel of the Lord appears in a dream to Joseph, but not to Miriam. Joseph is apparently unaware of the forthcoming event *after* Miriam has become pregnant, so much so that he considers divorcing her quietly (Mt. 1.19), an episode not found in Luke. The angel tells Joseph to proceed from betrothal to marriage, for Miriam's child has been begotten by the Holy Spirit (Mk 1.20). In Luke, the angel Gabriel is sent to Miriam herself, and tells her that she will give birth to Jesus by the power of the Holy Spirit (Lk. 1.26-38). At this stage Miriam is betrothed but not married, and certainly not pregnant, for she objects that she does not know a man (Lk. 1.34).

The birth in Bethlehem produces equally dissociated features of a dramatic kind. Luke explains it with an inaccurate report of a Roman census (Lk. 2.1-7). The census under Quirinius did not take place until some years later, and did not require people to leave the places where they normally lived to return to their ancestral homes. Luke's report is a narrative device to get Joseph and Miriam to Bethlehem in Judaea, so that Jesus can be born there, in a city of David.[4] This inaccurate narrative device is naturally unmentioned by Matthew, who appears to believe that Joseph and Miriam lived in Bethlehem (cf. Mt. 2.21-23). Matthew, therefore, needs a different narrative device to get the family from Bethlehem to Nazareth. He has a story of astrologers who come looking for the 'king of the Jews' because they have seen his star in the East. This is not a very realistic story, and their appearance has a dire effect on Herod, who proceeds to kill all male children under two in the area around Bethlehem (Mt. 2.16-18, using Jer. 31.15). Herod was cruel, but he was not so foolish as to launch such a pointless attack on his own people, and the absence of this atrocity from Luke and from Jewish sources must mean that it did not occur. The story will have been sparked off in someone's imagination by the story of Pharaoh ordering the deaths of all male Hebrew babies, with the escape of Moses in Egypt (Exod. 1.15–2.15). This story gives Matthew a reason for his account of the flight of the family into Egypt (Mt. 2.13-15), which is also unmentioned by Luke. Matthew legitimates it with Hos. 11.1, 'Out of Egypt I called my son' (Mt. 2.15). This enables Matthew to get the family to Nazareth (Mt. 2.19-23), where Luke correctly believed that they had previously been living (Lk. 1.26; 2.4, 39). The Matthaean story is a tale based on scripture from beginning to end.

The background culture was perfectly capable of producing such stories. Stories of angels appearing were widespread. Sometimes they foretell important events. For example, the angel Gabriel appears to Daniel in Daniel 8. He predicts

---

3   H. Küng, *On Being a Christian* (1974. Trans. E. Quinn. New York/London: Doubleday/ Collins, 1976–77), p. 451.
4   See e.g. Fitzmyer, *Luke*, pp. 392–94, 399–407.

the rise of the Macedonian kingdom and, in less direct terms, the rise of the Greek king Antiochus Epiphanes, his persecution of Israel in 171–164 BCE, and his fall. Other announcements are more personal, as at Josephus *Ant.* I, 196–98, where three angels announce the forthcoming birth of a child to the 90-year-old Sarah (cf. Gen. 18.1-15). This is hardly less miraculous than virgin birth, and it was caused by direct divine intervention. This kind of connection is made especially clear by Luke. When the angel Gabriel appears to Jesus' mother Miriam to announce her pregnancy by God's power while she was still a virgin, he also tells her that her kinswoman Elizabeth has become pregnant in her old age, even though she was believed to be sterile (Lk. 1.36). The underlying point is that people believed that God intervened in *all* births, so they prayed for all women who were or wished to become pregnant. Of course they knew that you had to have sex to have children, but they also knew that this did not always work, that mothers could die in pregnancy or childbirth, and that children could be born with all manner of defects, and could be born prematurely and die. They did not understand why, and assumed that God was in charge of this process. Hence, following the birth of Cain, the first man to be born rather than created, Eve says 'I have got a man with YHWH', even though the Bible has also reported 'And Adam knew Eve his woman' (Gen. 4.1). Sex was essential, but it was not enough. Thus a virgin birth, and a birth to an old woman believed sterile, were both less different from a normal birth in the stories of their culture than they are in the reality of ours.

There are several stories of remarkable births from the Mediterranean world. For example, Plato's nephew Speusippus and others are reported to have related the story that Plato was the child of Perictione by Apollo (Diog. L. III, 1–3, 45). Nearer to the time of Jesus, Apollo was said to have fathered the emperor Augustus (e.g. Suet. *Divus Augustus*, XCIV, 4).[5] These stories are not very similar to the birth stories of Matthew and Luke. We must however remember that when the Gospels of Matthew and Luke were written, many Gentiles had joined the Christian communities. Those familiar with the stories of divine births in the Gentile world may have felt that more entertaining and more Jewish stories about the birth of Jesus would be appropriate. Plutarch (*Num.* 4) also records an Egyptian belief that it is not impossible for the Spirit of God to draw near to a woman and to beget in her the beginnings of birth. Again, this is not the same as our stories, but it could spark off an interest in telling them.

There are three particularly relevant stories in the Jewish sources of our period. The miraculous birth of Melchizedek in 2 Enoch 71 is not a virgin birth, but it is a birth without a human father. Sothonim was an old and sterile woman, and when Nir her husband found out she was pregnant he was so angry that she fell down dead. It is clear that they had not recently had sex together. Melchizedek was born from Sothonim's womb nonetheless, fully developed like a 3-year-old, speaking and blessing the Lord. He also had the badge of priesthood on his chest. In this case sex was not necessary because Nir and Melchizedek

---

5   For these and other such stories see R. J. Miller, *Born Divine: The Births of Jesus and Other Sons of Gods* (Santa Rosa: Polebridge, 2003), pp. 133–53: 'Hellenistic Infancy Narratives'.

were non-Jewish priests, and Nir and Sothonim could be thought of as pure in refraining from sex after Nir became a priest.

Other stories concern the birth of Noah (1QapGen II–V: 1 Enoch 106–7). As the story turns out, his conception was partly due to normal human sex between his parents, but his birth was so unusual that Lamech suspected that conception was by one of the Watchers and the Holy Ones, the Jewish equivalent of Greek gods having sex with human women. His wife Bitenosh reminded him of how they had sexual intercourse, and declared that the father was no stranger or Watcher or Son of Heaven (1QapGen II, 16). Both stories treat these miraculous births as Matthew and Luke treat the virgin birth, as a great sign rather than as something to be kept a modest secret. Before the event is known to be a great sign, however, they express feelings of shame and modesty, and concern that the mother has been immoral. These stories were meant to be entertaining, and since they did not make it to mainline Jewish or Christian scriptures, no one takes them literally now.

The birth of Moses was also further developed beyond the biblical account. According to Josephus, one of the sacred scribes, referred to in other Jewish sources as 'astrologers', announced to 'the king' that 'there would be born to the Israelites at that time one who would bring down the rule of the Egyptians and exalt the Israelites.' It was because 'the king' was 'afraid' at this, that he ordered that every male child born to the Israelites should be killed (*Ant.* II, 205–6). The Egyptians are said to have been afraid too (*Ant.* II, 215, 235). Moses' father, Amram, is described in several Jewish sources as 'righteous'. For example, at b. Sot. 12a, Amram responds to the decree of the 'wicked Pharaoh' by divorcing his wife, and all the Israelites followed suit. His daughter Miriam, later Moses' sister, found fault with him, noting that his decree would be fulfilled because he was a righteous person. He therefore took his wife back, and all the Israelites followed suit again.

In Josephus, Amram was concerned about the King's murderous order, so he naturally prayed to God. God himself appeared to him when he was asleep, and in a lengthy speech he assured him that his child 'will deliver the race of Hebrews from bondage among the Egyptians' (*Ant.* II, 216). According to Pseudo-Philo, the spirit of God fell upon Moses' sister Miriam at night, and she saw a dream in which an angel declared 'I will do signs through him, and I will save my people' (Ps-Philo, *Ant. Bib.* IX, 10). Moses was born circumcised (IX, 13), another miracle due to divine intervention. He survived Pharaoh's orders to kill all male Hebrew children (Exod. 1.15–2.10).

These stories show that once a human being was sufficiently highly thought of, secondary stories of his birth might arise within Judaism. Moreover, some of these traditions were directly influential, especially the stories of Moses' birth on the people who told the stories which we now find in Matthew.[6] Against this cultural background, the absence of the virgin birth from most New Testament

---

6   See especially R. D. Aus, *Matthew 1–2 and the Virginal Conception in Light of Palestinian and Hellenistic Judaic Traditions on the Birth of Israel's First Redeemer, Moses* (Lanham: University Press of America, 2004).

documents, combined with the inconsistent and storytelling nature of the two major sources in which it is found, shows that the virgin birth of Jesus is a secondary development rather than an historical fact. Stories about Jesus' birth arose because Jesus was the central figure of the Christian community, a man already associated with miracles performed by God through him and upon him.

In view of the proportion of Gentiles in the Christian churches when the Gospels of Matthew and Luke were written, it remains important that these stories have so many basic Jewish elements. The people involved around Jesus are all Jewish: Gentiles either come from afar, as the astrologers do, or they belong far away, as the Roman emperor Augustus does. The stories are dominated by the action of the one God. Other distinctively Jewish features include angels, circumcision, the fulfilment of purity Law in the Temple at Jerusalem, and the celebration of the major feast of Passover every year. The importance of the Gentile mission to both Matthew and Luke could not lead them to abandon the tradition that Jesus lived entirely within Judaism, not even when they were writing in story mode. This is because the traditions which placed Jesus entirely within Judaism were pervasive.

The presence of Gentiles in the churches is essential in understanding why the stories of Jesus have him born of a virgin.[7] To see this, we must consider first the stories of births to the major matriarchs, wives of Abraham, Isaac and Jacob. Sarai did not have children, and said to Abraham, 'YHWH has prevented me from bearing (a child)' (Gen. 16.2). After the birth of Ishmael to Hagar, God renamed Sarai Sarah, explaining to Abraham 'I will give you a son from her' (Gen. 17.16). The references to Abraham's great age (Gen. 17.17; 18.11-12; 21.2, 5) imply the sex necessary for this birth, so that God could fulfil his promise to establish his covenant 'between me and you and your seed' (Gen. 17.7). God's intervention is nonetheless recorded:

> YHWH visited Sarah . . . and Sarah conceived and bore a son to Abraham . . . and Abraham called the name of his son whom Sarah bore him Isaac.
>
> (Gen. 21.1-3)

Thus God's intervention in this major birth is clearly recorded and sex is taken for granted both because it is normal and because the Jewish community is bounded by genealogy.

The same is true of the birth of Jacob, or Israel, to Isaac. Isaac married Rebecca: 'And Isaac entreated YHWH for his wife, because she was barren, and YHWH granted his prayer and Rebecca his wife conceived' (Gen. 25.21), and produced Esau and Jacob. Sex between Isaac and Rebecca is taken for granted, for this is how Rebecca was known to be barren in the first place. Equally clear, however is God's direct intervention in response to Isaac's prayer, so God was directly responsible for the birth of Jacob/Israel.

---

7   I am grateful to Rabbi Prof. Seth Kunin and to Caroline Penney for fruitful discussion of this and related issues. We owe the central idea to Seth, but I am responsible for what I have written here.

The story of Jacob and Rachel is more complicated. Sex is in the first place explicit: 'And he [i.e. Jacob] went in to Rachel too . . .' (Gen. 29.30). Divine intervention is also explicit, for YHWH opened Leah's womb, whereas Rachel was barren. When Rachel complained to Jacob he had a tiff with her, and said, 'Am I in place of God, who has withheld from you the fruit of the womb?' (Gen. 30.2). Evidently Jacob went on having sex with Rachel, who was prevented from bearing children by the intervention of God. After the birth of further children to Jacob by Bilhah, Zilpah and Leah, 'And God remembered Rachel and God listened to Rachel and opened her womb' (Gen. 30.22). The result was the birth of Joseph.

These stories are biblical, so they would have been generally known. Jesus' position relative to the early Christian community was just as great as that of the major patriarchs relative to Israel. In a community which produced stories of the miraculous births of Noah and Melchizedek, as well as further developments of the story of the birth of Moses, stories of Jesus' birth were inevitable. There was however one major change. The Jewish community was bounded by genealogy. The Christian movement was not so bounded. Already by the time of the Gospel of Matthew, when stories about the birth of Jesus are first attested, the Gentile mission was flourishing. The major patriarchs have sex with their wives to maintain the genealogy of the Jewish community. Mary did not have sex with Joseph before the birth of Jesus because Jesus was the centre of a movement created by God without genealogy. The genealogy with which Matthew opens his Gospel makes this especially clear. After mentioning various men from Abraham onwards who fathered the succeeding man, with just an occasional mention of a mother as well, it concludes:

. . . now Jacob fathered Joseph the husband of Mary, from whom Jesus called Christ was born.

(Mt. 1.16)

The virgin birth was however a new departure, so it is presented with the two modes of legitimating revelation characteristic of ancient Judaism: scriptures, and dreams or visions. Matthew has an angel of the Lord appear in a dream to Joseph, to tell him and the Christians who heard the story that the virgin birth was due to the Holy Spirit. The Holy Spirit was a metaphor for God in action, so this is direct divine intervention in a major birth again. Matthew also declares this to be the fulfilment of Isa. 7.14, which he quotes in Greek: 'Behold, the virgin (*parthenos*) shall have in womb and bear a son' (Mt. 1.23). The original Hebrew does not have the term 'virgin', but an ordinary Hebrew word which means 'young woman' (*'almāh*), so this use of scripture was only possible when Christianity was Greek-speaking. Luke does not have the quotation from Isa. 7.14, though Gabriel's announcement at Lk. 1.31 will have reminded some people of it. He has more supernatural events, and more speeches by people who were inspired by the spirit. His narrative is also very much inspired by the scriptures, including the stories of the birth of Samuel to Hannah, and of the birth of Samson to

Manoah and his wife.[8] Like the major matriarchs, both Hannah and Manoah's wife were barren, and YHWH intervened directly to bring about the births of Samuel and Samson. These stories also inspired Luke's story of the birth of John the Baptist, which is due to direct divine intervention in the lives of a couple who do have sex together, and who produced an important prophet who remained within Judaism. This contrasts with the virgin birth of Jesus, the central figure of a largely Gentile religion which was not bounded by genealogy.

One aspect of the birth narratives which could possibly be right is Jesus' Davidic descent through Joseph. There is very little sign of Jesus' Davidic descent in Mark. The son of Timaeus hails him as 'son of David' (Mk 10.47-48), but it is not clear that this should be interpreted literally. In the very next story, the crowd look forward to the coming kingdom of 'our Father David' (Mk 11.10), and that is because they were Jews hoping for the coming kingdom, not because all of them were literally of Davidic descent. The Davidic kingship of Jesus is developed in both Matthew and Luke. Matthew has the term 'son of David' eight times of Jesus. Among their birth narratives, both Matthew and Luke have actual genealogies which run back through David (Mt. 1.1-17; Lk. 3.23-38), but their secondary nature is revealed by their comprehensive lack of agreement about Jesus' immediate ancestry. In Matthew, Joseph's father is Jacob, whereas in Luke he is Eli, and the two evangelists do not agree on anyone between Joseph and the famous sixth-century Davidic Zerubbabel. Davidic descent is confirmed by St Paul, who appears to be quoting an old formula (Rom. 1.3, cf. 15.12). It is therefore possible that Jesus was of Davidic descent through Joseph, and that this aspect was further developed after his death. It may however be that it is an entirely secondary result of applying to him the category of Davidic kingship.

Given that the birth stories are not literally true, it has periodically been suggested that Jesus was really born at Bethlehem in Galilee, and this suggestion has recently been revived by Chilton.[9] Bethlehem in Galilee is just a few miles from Nazareth. It is conceivable that Jesus was born such a short distance from his home village, and that this sent imaginative people to the scriptures, where they found the prediction of Mic. 5.2-4, and that this sparked off stories of Jesus' birth at Bethlehem in Judaea. This is in short a feasible conjecture, which we are in no position to confirm or deny. It is not a necessary conjecture, in that the telling of these stories makes perfectly good sense without it.

Moreover, Chilton's reasons for believing in this conjecture are not strong enough. He declares that Joseph was a widower from Bethlehem, and 'a journeyman (a *tekton*, not a carpenter)'.[10] There is no evidence that Joseph was a widower before the wildly imaginative storytelling of the *Protevangelium of James*.[11] This document was written in the second half of the second century.

---

8   For more details see e.g. E. D. Freed, *The Stories of Jesus' Birth: A Critical Introduction* (Sheffield: Sheffield Academic, 2001), pp. 87–90.

9   Chilton, *Rabbi Jesus*, pp. 6–9.

10   Chilton, *Rabbi Jesus*, p. 6, with n. 4.

11   For an ET of this document see E. Hennecke and W. Schneemelcher, *New Testament*

According to one of its stories, an angel of the Lord appeared to Zacharias the high priest, who followed his instructions to assemble the widowers of the people. The widowers came to the high priest with rods. When the rods were given back to them, Joseph received the last rod, and a dove came out of the rod and flew onto Joseph's head. In view of this sign, the high priest told him that he would receive 'the virgin of the Lord'. Joseph at first protested that he was old and already had sons, but he naturally gave in to the will of the Lord, and took Mary as his wife. The story of her pregnancy is much elaborated too. It should be obvious that this is not a sound historical source.[12] The notion that Jesus' brothers and sisters were his children by a previous wife were taken up into the doctrine of Mary's perpetual virginity, and this particular view was especially associated with the fourth-century Church Father Epiphanius. For historical reasons, it is regrettable that such views are still taken seriously.[13]

There is no evidence that Joseph came from Bethlehem in Galilee either. The Greek word *tektōn*, used to describe Jesus at Mk 6.3, altered to describe Joseph at Mt. 13.55, may mean more than a carpenter, and both Joseph and Jesus may have worked as builders and stonemasons as well. Moreover, the underlying Aramaic *naggārā*, like the Akkadian *naggārū* from which it was originally borrowed, has a similar range of meaning. None of these words, however, means 'journeyman', an assertion which Chilton does nothing to justify, and we have no idea as to what extent, if any, Joseph and Jesus would have had to work outside Nazareth to run a profitable business. In short, Chilton's imagination has outrun the evidence, and we shall see this again with his imaginative conjecture that Jesus was thought to have been illegitimate.

This brings us to three conjectures, each of which presupposes that the birth stories are covering something up. The foundational one is a story found in some ancient Jewish sources, according to which Jesus was illegitimate, and his real father was a Roman soldier called Pantera. The historicity of this story has recently been defended with great vigour by James Tabor.[14] The Jewish sources themselves are not early, and they have proved difficult to interpret. It is however now quite clear, especially from the new discussion of Peter Schäfer, that the Jewish sources themselves were formed from outright and vigorous hostility to Christianity.[15] Portraying Jesus as illegitimate was a deliberately hostile Jewish reaction to Christian stories of his virgin birth.

Moreover, the evidence of Origen shows that the story of Jesus' father being a Roman soldier called Panthera originated not later than the second century. In the middle of the third century, Origen wrote an important polemical work *Against*

Apocrypha (Trans. R. McL. Wilson. Philadelphia: Westminster, 1963), vol. 1, pp. 404–17.

12   For brief discussion of the main points see e.g. G. Parrinder, *Son of Joseph: The Parentage of Jesus* (Edinburgh: T&T Clark, 1992), pp. 85–90.

13   Chilton, *Rabbi Jesus*, p. 6. n. 4, cites Epiphanius as if he were right, citing also R. Bauckham, 'The Brothers and Sisters of Jesus: An Epiphanian Response to John P. Meier', *CBQ* 56 (1994), pp. 686–700.

14   J. D. Tabor, *The Jesus Dynasty: Stunning New Evidence about the Hidden History of Jesus* (London: HarperElement, 2006).

15   P. Schäfer, *Jesus in the Talmud* (Princeton: Princeton Univ., 2007), esp. pp. 15–24.

Celsus. Celsus was a pagan critic of Christianity, whose work has long since been lost, probably because it was destroyed by Christians. Origen claims to have written long after the death of Celsus, who evidently published his critique of Christianity c.180 CE. Origen quotes this work extensively. It is clear from these quotations that Celsus had a Jewish source, according to which Jesus invented the story that he was born of a virgin. This source said that Jesus' mother 'was driven out by the carpenter who was betrothed to her, having been convicted of adultery and become pregnant by a soldier whose name was Panthera' (Origen, *Against Celsus* I, 32). Unlike later Jewish sources, this has the merit of absolute clarity. Moreover, Panthera was a common name among Roman soldiers. This is therefore a story which could be believed by members of the Jewish community, who rejected Christianity. As a historical source about the origins of the historical Jesus, however, it should not be taken seriously.

Tabor sets the scene with true facts about the cultural background. However, he says that the Romans occupied Galilee, which they did not. They ruled it by means of a client king, Herod the Great, which means that Herod was in charge of the place, and in normal circumstances Roman soldiers were not to be found in Galilee. Tabor correctly delineates the situation at Herod's death in 4 BCE, when there were a lot of rebellious upsets in Israel. The situation was so serious that Publius Quinctilius Varus, the Roman governor of Syria, did bring three legions down to Israel. Varus sacked Sepphoris, just 4 miles over the hill from Nazareth, and enslaved its inhabitants.[16] In this situation there were many Roman soldiers in Galilee, and they will have included seduction and rape among their achievements.

After retailing the story of Panthera from Celsus and other sources, Tabor discusses a genuine first-century inscription found at Bingerbrück, near Bad Kreuznach, in Germany.[17] This inscription is on the gravestone of a Roman soldier, Tiberius Julius Abdes Pantera, an archer who came from Sidon, an ancient Phoenician city on the East Mediterranean coast. Sidon was basically a pagan city, and by the time of Pantera it was very Hellenized. His first two names, Tiberius and Julius, indicate his Roman citizenship. His third name, Abdes, is Semitic, as is appropriate for a man from an ancient Phoenician city. It is therefore probable that he spoke Aramaic, the same language as Jesus and Jesus' mother Miriam. Tabor also notes a first-century ossuary from not far north of Jerusalem. Its inscription is in Greek and indicates that it held the bones of Pentheros and Josepos (i.e. Joseph). There is thus sufficient evidence that Panthera was a name in use among Jews.

Tabor fastens secondly on Mk 7.24: 'Now he [i.e. Jesus] got up from there and went away to the regions of Tyre.' Some ancient manuscripts read 'Tyre and Sidon', probably because they were following the parallel passage Mt. 15.21, but Tabor simply accepts this longer reading. He also notes that following the next incident, Mark records that Jesus 'going out from the regions of Tyre went through Sidon to the sea of Galilee', a strange description on which Tabor

16   Tabor, *Jesus Dynasty*, pp. 34–36.
17   Tabor, *Jesus Dynasty*, pp. 58–62.

comments mildly 'not the most direct route'.[18] The rest of Mk 7.24 is as mysterious as Tabor says it is: 'And going into a house he did not want anyone to know, and he was not able to keep it quiet.' The healing of the daughter of a woman who was 'Greek, Syrophoenician by race' is narrated next. We simply do not know what Jesus was doing so far from Israel, whose house it was, or why he wanted it kept quiet. It does not however follow that Jesus was really visiting the home of his biological father! We must make more sober and plausible conjectures if we think we have no alternative but to make some. I suggest the following.

There were Jewish communities in many Greek and pagan cities. Jesus went this far from Israel, walking as one did in those days, to preach to and teach Jews who were, or might become, favourable to his ministry. He went to the house of such Jews, and he wanted it kept quiet so he could have a bit of a rest in the middle of an exhausting trip. There he met a Godfearer, a Gentile woman who worshipped the one God of Israel and observed as much of his Law as she reasonably could. He announced that a demon had left her daughter, and she went home sufficiently reassured to believe that this was the case. This is the reason why this story was transmitted to Mark, without any further details of an otherwise unremarkable trip. All this makes excellent sense of the facts reported by Mark.

We must adopt two conclusions. First, the story of Jesus' illegitimate birth from a soldier called Panthera originated as Jewish polemic against Christianity, polemic which has no historical plausibility at all. Secondly, Tabor's attempt to give credence to this story is to be regretted and rejected.

The story of Jesus' illegitimate birth is part of the background to the modern feminist story that Jesus' mother Miriam was seduced, or more probably raped, by a man other than Joseph. This view has been vigorously put forward by Jane Schaberg.[19] Schaberg's interpretation of the birth narratives in Matthew and Luke is faulty from beginning to end. Very early in her book, she draws attention to the obvious fact that, if they narrate a virgin birth, the Infancy narratives are seriously different from Jewish and pagan stories alike. From this alone, she already draws the conclusion that the texts are not about a virginal conception, but an illegitimate conception.[20] This shows a lack of respect for what the text says. Moreover, one of the most important known facts about early Christianity is that it was significantly different from Judaism, so much so that in due course it became separate from Judaism. The requirement that the birth stories somehow must be the same as other stories is contrary to this as well. Moreover, the majority of such stories are not about illegitimate births. Schaberg also seeks to discount the importance of the story of the birth of Melchizedek in 2 Enoch 71 on the ground that it is not virginal, and does not narrate the conception of a real

18   Tabor, *Jesus Dynasty*, pp. 64–65; cf. p. 75.
19   J. Schaberg, *The Illegitimacy of Jesus: A Feminist Theological Interpretation of the Infancy Narratives* (San Francisco: Harper & Row, 1987; repr. Sheffield: Sheffield Academic, 1995; 2nd edn. Sheffield: Sheffield Phoenix, 2006).
20   Schaberg, *Illegitimacy of Jesus*, p. 19; likewise, e.g. p. 67.

human being.[21] This is not satisfactory, because the birth of Melchizedek took place without sex between his parents, and the miraculous nature of his birth should not be used to argue that this amazing figure was not human.

All Schaberg's supporting arguments are equally weak. For example she proposes that phrases in Mt. 1.18, 20 'should be read in a figurative or symbolic, not a literal sense'.[22] This is contrary to the plain meaning of the text. When Matthew says that Mary was found to be pregnant before she was married, he immediately says 'of holy spirit' (Mt. 1.18). An angel of the Lord repeats this to Joseph, instructing him to take Mary to wife, and Matthew explains this by means of a prophecy that a *virgin* will conceive and bear a son (Mt. 1.20, 23), an impossibly strange way of Matthew and the angel telling us that Mary had been seduced or raped. Any such thought is so far from the text that Schaberg is reduced to claiming that 'It is necessary to imaginatively "read the silence" as indication of that about which Matthew does not speak directly.'[23] This is no excuse for reading into the text what is not there.

Luke's birth narrative has more often been thought not to state clearly that Jesus was born without sex between Mary and Joseph, but Schaberg's notion that it too presupposes that Mary was seduced or raped by another man is no improvement on her treatment of Matthew's story. Some of her arguments are based on detailed linguistic study of a traditional kind which has long since been discredited. For example, the angel Gabriel is sent to a virgin called Miriam (Lk. 1.27), a great improvement on Matthew's angel of the Lord going only to Joseph! Gabriel foretells the birth of Jesus, 'Holy Spirit will come upon you and the power of the Highest will overshadow you: therefore the holy (child) born will be called son of God' (Lk. 1.35). In its context, this makes clear that this child will be born without normal sex between two parents. Miriam therefore got up and went 'with haste' (*meta spoudēs*) to see Elizabeth (Lk. 1.39). It is obvious from the flow of the narrative that this is an extremely joyful occasion. Schaberg however considers briefly passages of the Greek Bible in which people hurry because they are anxious, perturbed, dismayed or terrified, and suggests that Luke's 'with haste' 'points toward a situation of violence and/or fear in connection with Mary's pregnancy, or at least to the idea that she is depicted as reacting with anxiety or inner disturbance to the pregnancy.'[24] This interpretation has nothing to recommend it. It consists of reading into this passage the connotations of one word in quite different contexts.

Similarly, Schaberg fastens on the word 'humiliation' in the Magnificat, Mary's wonderful outburst of thanks to God (Lk. 1.46-55). This is somewhat overblown at times because it is based on traditional biblical sources, such as the prayer of Hannah, when she took her son Samuel to serve in the Temple, hav-

---

21   Schaberg, *Illegitimacy of Jesus*, p. 192 n. 202. Schaberg refers to 2 Enoch 23: this is the same
        passage, differently numbered by different editors.
22   Schaberg, *Illegitimacy of Jesus*, p. 68.
23   Schaberg, *Illegitimacy of Jesus*, p. 75.
24   Schaberg, *Illegitimacy of Jesus*, p. 87.

ing been barren until the Lord remembered her (1 Sam. 2.1-10).[25] Hence Mary
rejoices in God 'because he has looked upon the humility (*tapeinōsin*) of his
maidservant' (Lk. 1.48). Schaberg interprets this as a reference to Mary's sexual
humiliation, and suggests that Luke inserted a

> Jewish Christian hymn for use as Mary's canticle . . . to communicate the
> tradition he received: that she had been violated and made pregnant, but
> that God vindicated her, protecting her and her child . . . Hannah's canticle
> is appropriate as a model for Mary's because Mary, in the tradition Luke
> inherited, experienced a disaster worse than barrenness; sexual violation.[26]

There is no sign of this in the text of Luke either.

None of Schaberg's arguments are any more convincing than the ones which
I have discussed. Her views should therefore be rejected. Like the view that
Jesus was married, her view illustrates the central fault of the whole quest of the
historical Jesus, that of imposing on the primary sources the concerns of herself
and her own social subgroup.

Chilton has suggested that Jesus was a *mamzer*. This term is difficult to define,
because there is so little biblical or contemporary interpretation of it. Chilton
defines it as 'an Israelite of suspect paternity'. He argues,

> The fundamental issue was not sex before marriage (which was broadly
> tolerated) but sex with the wrong person . . . Mary's sexual relations with
> Joseph had not been prohibited, but given that Joseph had lived in Bethlehem
> and she in Nazareth when she became pregnant, it was virtually impossible
> for her to prove that he was the father. In the absence of proof, Jesus was
> considered a *mamzer* . . .[27]

Chilton has effectively made the same mistake as Tabor and Schaberg, imagining
that the stories of Jesus' virgin birth are covering up his birth out of wedlock,
only Chilton supposes that his father was in fact Joseph, who was allowed to
have sex with Miriam before marriage. He has combined this with Jesus' birth in
Bethlehem near Nazareth, and with his imaginative story about what happened
when Joseph was a journeyman.

Chilton's imaginative story has two regrettable consequences. One is over-
interpretation of two New Testament passages, Mk 6.3 and Jn 8.41, in the
context of a serious mistake. He declares:

> The charge that he was illicitly conceived plagued Jesus all his life. Even far
> from his home, during disputes in Jerusalem after he had become a famous
> teacher, Jesus was mocked for being born as the result of 'fornication'

---

25 More detailed discussion is provided e.g. by Fitzmyer, *Luke*, pp. 358–62, 366–69.
26 Schaberg, *Illegitimacy of Jesus*, p. 91.
27 Chilton, *Rabbi Jesus*, pp. 12–13.

(John 8.41). The people of his own village called him 'Mary's son', not Joseph's (Mark 6.3).[28]

These passages are not sufficient evidence that any such charge 'plagued Jesus all his life'. We have seen that a person might be called a son of his mother rather than his father if there were sufficient reason for this, and that whereas Mary was still a vigorous figure during the historic ministry and Joseph is no more mentioned, it is a sober and reasonable hypothesis that Joseph was dead and that this is why Jesus was called 'son of Mary'.[29] While the reception of his teaching and healing ministry in his home town of Nazareth was somewhat hostile, there is no indication that this was due to stories about his birth.

John 8.41 is part of a completely unhistorical discourse which tells us about the situation of the Johannine community towards the end of the first century – it does not record the ministry of the historical Jesus.[30] It begins with Jesus declaring 'I am the light of the world' (Jn 8.12), one of the 'I am' sayings with which this Gospel indicates the deity of Jesus, and ends with Jesus saying, 'Amen, amen I'm telling you, before Abraham was born, I am' (Jn 8.58), which indicates Jesus' pre-existence and therefore, again, his deity. Such declarations are absent from the synoptic Gospels because they were no part of the ministry of the historical Jesus. They frame a dispute with 'the Jews', during which Jesus accuses them of being the children of the devil (Jn 8.44), to which they respond by calling him a Samaritan (Jn 8.48). In the midst of this ferocious polemic, the Jews comment, 'We were not born of fornication: we have one father, God' (Jn 8.41). It is possible that this is a response to the Gospel stories of the virgin birth, since the Matthaean stories were certainly well known by the end of the first century, and Luke's stories may have been known too. If so, however, that is what this evidence indicates: towards the end of the first century, the Johannine community were in the midst of a ferocious dispute with 'the Jews', who were already responding polemically to these stories with their own story that Jesus was illegitimate, a reaction which I have noted in sources from the second century onwards. This is not evidence of what happened during the historic ministry.

Accordingly there is no evidence that 'The charge that he was illicitly conceived plagued Jesus all his life.'

At this point, Chilton's storytelling leaves the ground altogether:

> As a *mamzer*, Jesus was ostracised by the elders of Nazareth . . . His fellow villagers kept him from the elders' gathering, while his brother James (Joseph's eldest son from his first marriage) emerged as an authority in the congregation . . . Insults such as exclusion from the synagogue were a regular part of Jesus' childhood . . . Jesus must have spent much of his time alone . . .[31]

---

28 Chilton, *Rabbi Jesus*, p. 6.
29 See pp. 144–45.
30 See further pp. 511–25.
31 Chilton, *Rabbi Jesus*, pp. 15, 16, 17.

These comments on Jesus' childhood have no basis in our texts.

There is accordingly very little genuine historical information to be gleaned from the stories of Jesus' birth. He was not born of a virgin, his mother was not raped, and he was not an ostracized *mamzer*. The Gospel accounts have resulted from storytelling which became inevitable because of his position at the centre of early Christianity, a movement which was not bounded by genealogy. The original alternative accounts resulted from Jewish polemic against Christianity. Modern alternatives have not taken properly on board either of these major points, and they have reacted to the ancient stories with insufficiently controlled imagination.

3. *Upbringing*

We have seen that Jesus was born into an observant Jewish family. He had brothers and sisters, and his mother Miriam was still active at the time of the historic ministry, whereas Joseph seems to have been dead. We can glean some further information about his background and upbringing. At home, Jesus was brought up speaking Aramaic, as all his family did. Aramaic was the main language universally spoken throughout Israel at that time, and the only language used in the Galilaean countryside.[32] Aramaic was therefore the language which Jesus had to use to teach ordinary Jews in Galilee, where his ministry of preaching and teaching did not take him into cities which were, or may have been, more influenced by Greek culture. Moreover, the Gospels confirm that Aramaic was the language which Jesus himself spoke. Though they are written in Greek for Greek-speaking churches, the Gospels contain Aramaic words the presence of which can only be explained if Jesus himself spoke Aramaic. The most striking is *Abba*, an ordinary term for 'father' which he used to address God.[33] Others include *talitha qum*, 'girl, get up', words with which he aroused a 12-year-old girl who was thought to be dead (Mk 5.41).[34] Other sayings of Jesus, though transmitted to us in Greek, contain features which can only be explained if they were originally spoken in Aramaic. The most striking is the term 'Son of man', which is not natural Greek and which originated in authentic sayings of Jesus as a translation of the Aramaic *bar* (*e*)*nash*(*ā*).[35]

We must also infer that Jesus read the scriptures in Hebrew, though the arguments by which we can establish this are more complicated, and the situation has been misrepresented in some recent scholarship. For example, Crossan comments 'since between 95 and 97 per cent of the Jewish state was illiterate at the

---

32 The evidence of this has often been presented. See further pp. 108–20, and for a recent summary, Casey, *Aramaic Sources of Mark's Gospel*, pp. 76–86.
33 See further pp. 204–12.
34 See further p. 109, 268–69.
35 See pp. 115–19, 358–74.

time of Jesus, it must be presumed that Jesus also was illiterate.'[36]

The figure of 95–97 per cent is too high when it is a guess about the Gentile world, the real origin of Crossan's figure. In his books about Jesus, he gives no source for his figures, but in *The Birth of Christianity* he does so.[37] He refers firstly to the classic work of Harris on literacy in the Graeco-Roman world, from which he gets a figure of less than 10 per cent literacy.[38] Harris however offered a minimalist reading of the Graeco-Roman evidence, and responses by other scholars provided solid evidence for a higher degree of literacy in the Graeco-Roman world.[39] The application of this to Judaism is moreover a major cultural mistake. Crossan refers next to a regrettable article by the Israeli scholar Bar-Ilan, which is mostly about illiteracy in modern non-Jewish societies.[40] Bar-Ilan suggested that the total literacy rate of Jewish people in Israel was 'probably less than 3%', but his guesswork is based on his modern non-Jewish evidence and one rabbinical saying which legislates for a situation in which, according to him, only one person in a town or synagogue can read (*Soferim* 11.2//T. Meg. 3.12).[41] Both versions of this saying were written down very late, when rabbis were legislating for any possible situation that could arise in Jewish communities. The earlier version of this saying, written down in the fourth rather than the eighth century CE (T. Meg. 3.12 rather than *Soferim* 11.2), may be literally translated as follows:

> The sons of the synagogue who have none who will read except one, (he) stands reads and sits, stands reads and sits, even if seven times.

This shows that there might be a situation in which a synagogue might have only one person who was willing to read from the Torah in Hebrew, but it does it not tell us when or where such a situation might reasonably be expected. It could

---

36 J. D. Crossan, *Jesus: A Revolutionary Biography* (New York: HarperSanFrancisco, 1994), p. 25.

37 J. D. Crossan, *The Birth of Christianity: Discovering What Happened in the Years Immediately after the Execution of Jesus* (Edinburgh: T&T Clark, 1998), pp. 234–35.

38 W. V. Harris, *Ancient Literacy* (Cambridge, MA: Harvard UP, 1989).

39 See especially M. Beard *et al.*, *Literacy in the Roman World* (JRA. SS 3. Michigan: Ann Arbor, 1991).

40 M. Bar-Ilan, 'Illiteracy in the Land of Israel in the First Century c.e.', in S. Fishbane *et al.* (eds), *Essays in the Social Scientific Study of Judaism and Jewish Society* (2 vols. Hoboken: Ktav, 1992), vol. II, pp. 46–61.

41 The major minimalist treatment of literacy in Judaism at the time of Jesus is now C. Hezser, *Jewish Literacy in Roman Palestine* (TSAJ 81. Tübingen: Mohr Siebeck, 2001). Hezser was originally inspired by Harris, *Ancient Literacy*. She has a thorough scholarly knowledge of the primary sources and secondary literature, including a much more scholarly treatment of the above passages and others which might be considered to have similar implications. In my view, however, she is consistently too sceptical. Her opinion that the average literacy rate among Palestinian Jews was 3 per cent 'or slightly higher' is not convincing, and her 'first reason', 'the largely rural character of Palestine throughout antiquity' (p. 496), is, again, despite her thorough knowledge of Jewish source material, too dependent on general work on rural societies, most of which were not Jewish. The best work I have seen is Millard, *Reading and Writing in the Time of Jesus*.

happen if most of a congregation were illiterate, or if there was a small Jewish community in a Greek city, where most of them spoke Greek and hardly anyone could read Hebrew. It is doubtful whether this should be read back into the time of Jesus, and an overall literacy rate should not be inferred from it.

Crossan's crude use of anthropological research into 'peasants' in different cultures is even worse. After quoting from Bar-Ilan's article, he continues, 'Jesus was a peasant from a peasant village. Therefore, for me, Jesus was illiterate until the opposite is proven.'[42] Turning Jesus from a major Jewish religious leader into a vague Mediterranean peasant flies in the face of basic evidence about Judaism and about Jesus. I consider this next.

One of the most important differences between Judaism and the Gentile world was that Judaism was centred on the Torah. The Torah was a major collection of written works. Written scrolls of the Torah were kept, and they were read by adult Jewish males at Jewish meetings every sabbath and on other occasions. Moreover, Josephus is quite specific in saying that the Law (*nomos*, the standard Greek translation of the Hebrew *Torah*) orders children to learn 'letters', so as to understand the laws and the deeds of the ancestors (*Apion* II, 204). Philo, while not specific on learning letters, confirms that Jewish people were devoted from childhood to the laws as God-given oracles (*Leg. ad Gaium*, 210–11).

Some later traditions should not be applied literally to Galilee at the time of Jesus, but should nonetheless be taken seriously as providing insights into his Jewish culture. For example, Simeon ben Shetah is said to have laid down that children should attend *beth ha-sepher*, literally 'the house of the book' (y. Ket. 32c). It does not follow that there was any such institution in Nazareth, but the tradition does fit with the view of children knowing the Torah as we have seen it in Josephus and Philo. A later saying attributed to Rab Judah looks back to our period:

> Rab Judah said in the name of Rabbi . . . at first, whoever had a father was taught the Torah by him; whoever had none, did not learn the Torah . . . Afterwards, it was ordained that teachers of boys should be appointed in Jerusalem . . . Joshua ben Gamla came and decreed that teachers be appointed in every province and every town, and children of six or seven years be brought to them.
>
> (b. B.B. 21a)

Joshua ben Gamla was high priest c. 63–64 CE. Again, this passage should not lead us to exaggerate, and Nazareth was too small to be considered a town in the sense assumed by this passage. What should be regarded as culturally inconceivable is that Joseph and Miriam produced *two major Jewish religious leaders*, Jesus himself and his brother Jacob, without Joseph ever making it to the first stage indicated in this passage and teaching the boys Torah at home. Many passages of the above kind show that this was culturally normal in Israel

---

42   Crossan, *Birth of Christianity*, p. 235.

at the time of Jesus. When they grew up, Jesus and Jacob will have become, like Joseph, adult male Israelites who read from the Torah in Hebrew on the sabbath and at major festivals.

All this is the cultural context within which we should interpret the evidence specific to Jesus himself. The most general features of his ministry are those of a man steeped in the scriptures. He drew on the wellsprings of the prophetic tradition. John the Baptist had however been the only major prophet for centuries, and Jesus was familiar with the works of the prophets themselves. The two major abstract concepts in his teaching, the kingship and fatherhood of God, are both biblical.[43] Up to a point, such things might be learnt orally in an observant home, helped by listening orally to the exposition of the scriptures at Jewish meetings on the sabbath and on other occasions. A decisive argument is accordingly to be found in Jesus' detailed reliance on scripture to establish major points, especially significant matters of halakhah.

For example, when challenged by Pharisees because his disciples were plucking grain on the sabbath, Jesus cited in their defence the example of David in 1 Samuel and the purpose of the sabbath at the creation (Mk 2.23-28).[44] The terms with which he began his first argument are especially relevant at this point: 'Have you not *read* what David did . . .'. These are not the words of an illiterate peasant! These are the words of a major religious leader arguing with Pharisees whom he could rely on to be learned in the same Hebrew scriptures. Jesus had an unusual exegesis of the end of Malachi 3, according to which the prophecy of Elijah coming again before the day of the Lord had been fulfilled in John the Baptist. His exposition of this (Mk 9.11-13) can only be understood in the light of his understanding of other passages, including Isaiah 40 and Job 14.[45] This innovative exegesis of several passages together could only be carried through by a person learned in the scriptures. Jesus' unusual and possibly unique prohibition of divorce was justified by his appeal to texts from the creation narrative of Genesis (Mk 10.2-9, citing Gen. 1.27; 2.24). His innovative exegesis of these fundamental scriptural texts was preceded by this explanation of Deut. 24.1, which gives scriptural permission for divorce: 'because of the hardness of your hearts [Moses] *wrote* this commandment for you' (Mk 10.5). This shows his awareness of the *written* text which he interpreted.

When Jesus carried through the major prophetic act known to us as the Cleansing of the Temple, his control of the halakhah in the court of the Gentiles was made possible by his charismatic preaching on biblical texts which included Isaiah 56 and Jeremiah 7.[46] The terms in which he introduced two quotations in the brief fragment of his speech handed down to us are again significant: 'Is it not *written* that "my house shall be called a house of prayer . . ."' (Mk 11.17, quoting Isa. 56.7) He concluded a parable in which he foretold his final triumph

---

43 See pp. 204–26.

44 On the historicity and interpretation of this passage see pp. 321–23.

45 See further pp. 178–80, 367–68, and for detailed discussion, Casey, *Aramaic Sources of Mark's Gospel*, pp. 111–37.

46 On the historicity and interpretation of this incident see pp. 412–15.

over the chief priests with a quotation from one of the *Hallel* psalms: 'And have
you not *read* this scripture, "A stone which the builders rejected has become the
head of a corner . . ."' (Mk 12.10, quoting Ps. 118.22).[47] Why 'have you not *read*'
when quoting a scripture well enough known to be sung, necessarily by heart,
probably in Aramaic, after the Passover meal?[48] Because this was an attack on
the chief priests by a major religious leader, not an illiterate peasant!

Another example is found when some Sadducees, the group to which most
of the chief priests belonged and who did not believe in the resurrection of the
dead, came to challenge this belief.[49] Jesus employed vigorous exegesis of the
revelatory text of Exod. 3.6 as if it were a decisive argument which established
belief in the resurrection of the dead (Mk 12.26-27). The terms in which he did
so are again important, and include a reference to the biblical text natural in a
culture in which no copies of the Torah had anything like the chapter and verse
divisions which make it so much easier for us to refer to particular passages:
'And concerning the dead, that they are raised, have you not *read* in the scroll of
Moses at The Bush how God spoke to him, saying "I (am) the God of Abraham
and the God of Isaac and the God of Jacob"' (Mk 11.26, quoting Exod. 3.6).
Jesus also relied upon the scriptures, including Psalm 41 and the *Hallel* psalms,
for predictions of his betrayal, death and resurrection.[50]

All this is part of the evidence of Jesus' detailed knowledge of the Hebrew
scriptures, his complete trust in the truth of the scriptures, and his absolute
confidence in his own innovative exegesis. It is clear from this that he knew the
written text itself. In first-century Israel only the original Hebrew text (with
Aramaic in Ezra and Daniel) was sufficiently sacred for him to have relied on it
like this, and it is the only version to which he could have referred with 'have you
not *read*'. The evidence that Jesus knew the scriptures in the original Hebrew is
accordingly overwhelming.

Finally, in order to establish this important point, I have not relied on passages
unique to Luke, whose evidence is however of interest. At Lk. 2.41-51, Jesus is
taken to Jerusalem at the age of 12 for the major feast of Passover, and is left in
the Temple where he debates with teachers. At Lk. 4.16-30, Luke has a much
longer account of Jesus' return to Nazareth than either Matthew or Mark, and in
it Jesus stands up and reads from a scroll of Isaiah. Neither of these points from
Luke's stories is impossible, but Luke was a wondrous storyteller; the first story
has much in common with other stories of child prodigies, and the second is a
longer version of Mk 6.1-6. It is therefore important that we have unshakeable
evidence from Mark of Jesus' detailed knowledge of the scriptures in Hebrew.
We should not try to override it with minimalist guesses about the general rate
of literacy in the Galilaean countryside, which are not relevant to the knowledge
of the scriptures displayed by a major Jewish religious leader.

In addition to his religious life, Jesus also had a trade, on which his family

---

47   For discussion of this parable see pp. 417–22.
48   On the singing of the *Hallel* psalms, cf. pp. 429, 432, 435.
49   See further pp. 423–24.
50   See pp. 421, 430–32.

depended for their livelihood. He was a carpenter. The Greek word is *tektōn* (Mk 6.3, cf. Mt. 13.55), a translation of the Aramaic *naggārā*. Both words could be used of people who worked in stone, as well as wood, though they are usually used of carpenters. In either case, it is possible that Jesus had to work for people outside Nazareth. Nazareth was a small village, and it is possible that it was not sufficient to maintain the family business.[51] Some scholars who have been involved in or concerned with the excavations of the nearby city of Sepphoris imagine him working there, and speaking Greek for this purpose.[52] This is entirely possible, and absolutely uncertain. We know from the evidence of the Gospels that the historic ministry was not conducted in the major cities of Galilee. The only major city in which Jesus is known to have preached is Jerusalem. His avoidance of other cities may however not have been due to ignorance. For all we know, Jesus may have worked in Sepphoris when he was a young man. There he may have been appalled by Jews whose prayers on the street corners were no better than play-acting in the theatre (cf. Mt. 6.5), which he may have known only too well.

Sepphoris is now known to have been a very Jewish city,[53] so Jesus is not very likely to have encountered Gentiles there, and if Joseph and he worked there, they may have been able to conduct all their necessary business in Aramaic. Greek was certainly needed only at the court of Herod Antipas, though it was used more widely than that. For example, a lead market weight of the first century CE has a Greek inscription, 'under the market inspection of Simon son of Aianos son of Justus'.[54] Whether these men, with Jewish names in a Greek inscription on a weight with a Roman measure, were bilingual and fluent in Aramaic, we do not know. This weight illustrates beautifully the fusion of cultural influences which could take place in a Jewish city without undermining its Jewishness. The same is true of Greek influence in its architecture.

Jesus may also have visited other cities, where he may have been to the theatre and may have been appalled by what he saw as mindless Gentile prayer (cf. Mt. 6.7). The main point is that we do not know things of this kind. The Hidden Years are hidden to us, and all we can infer with certainty is that Jesus spent these years as a carpenter and as an observant Jew, a profoundly religious man who spoke Aramaic and studied the scriptures in Hebrew.

Nazareth, where Jesus was brought up and lived for some considerable time, was a small Jewish town, or rather village. Its population may have been no more than 300–400 people. It was somewhat less than 4 miles to the south-east of the city of Sepphoris, about 20 miles east of the Mediterranean and 15 miles

---

51 On Nazareth see further pp. 163–64.

52 E.g. R. A. Batey, *Jesus and the Forgotten City: New Light on Sepphoris and the Urban World of Jesus* (Grand Rapids: Baker, 1991).

53 See further pp. 166–67. Pagan mosaics, including the famous 'Mona Lisa of the Galilee', are much later in date. For pictures of this and others see e.g. http://gervatoshav.blogspot.com/2009/07/israel-trip-2d-april-30-sepphoris.html. I am grateful to Dr Jim West for this reference.

54 Details of this weight are given by Reed, *Archaeology and the Galilean Jesus*, pp. 121–22.

from the sea, or rather lake, of Galilee. It has been difficult to excavate because later building has destroyed most of what was there.[55] Finds of an appropriate date include a winepress, stone-walled terraces and three stone towers, all apparently part of a vineyard. Other finds include simple locally made pottery, and no luxury items. There are also fragments of stone vessels, necessary to keep the purity laws. The Jewishness of Nazareth is in no doubt. We must therefore infer normal Jewish activities in it. Here people believed in the one God, and there were no signs of paganism. While there is no precise information about the level of observance, a completely Jewish environment means that male children were circumcised on the eighth day, and non-kosher food was not available. There were Jewish meetings every sabbath, at which people prayed to God and an adult male Israelite read from the scriptures. It is extremely probable that this man read from the scriptures in the original Hebrew, that someone translated the reading into Aramaic, and someone expounded the scriptures in Aramaic. Joseph and his sons *Yēshua'*, Jacob, Joseph, Judah and Simeon will have performed these tasks at one time or another. At least some people observed the purity laws and major festivals. How many people went to Jerusalem, and how often, we have no idea. The uncertainties over some of these points must not be allowed to conceal the main point: Jesus' native environment was completely Jewish.

4. *Galilee and the Surrounding Areas*[56]

The area surrounding Nazareth was fertile countryside. Most of the Galilaean countryside was cultivated because of its fertility. Major crops included olives, so that olive oil was a significant export. The large variety of trees grown included vines and fig trees, grain was grown for bread, and some land was pasture on which sheep, goats and cattle were kept. The people who worked this land may reasonably be described as peasants. They produced a surplus, some of which went in tithes, and a significant part of which went in taxes collected on behalf of the local ruler, Herod Antipas, the tetrarch of Galilee, who in turn paid taxes to Rome. Some of the land was owned by rich people rather than by the peasants themselves, and they had retainers who managed it for them. In either case,

---

55 For brief accounts of Nazareth, and of what has and has not been found there see Rousseau and Arav, *Jesus and His World*, pp. 214–16; Crossan and Reed, *Excavating Jesus*, pp. 49–60, 65–73; Reed, *Archaeology and the Galilean Jesus*, pp. 131–32; Charlesworth, *Jesus and Archaeology*, pp. 38–39; Reed, *Visual Guide to the New Testament*, pp. 54–77 passim, 151–53.

56 For further information on Galilee see especially S. Freyne, *Galilee, Jesus and the Gospels: Literary Approaches and Historical investigations* (Dublin: Gill and Macmillan, 1988); R. A. Horsley, *Galilee: History, Politics, People* (Valley Forge: Trinity Press International, 1995); R. A. Horsley, *Archaeology, History, and Society in Galilee: The Social Context of Jesus and the Rabbis* (Harrisburg: Trinity Press International, 1996); Reed, *Archaeology and the Galilean Jesus*; Charlesworth, *Jesus and Archaeology*, pp. 15–22, 38–42, 49–55; Reed, *Visual Guide to the New Testament*, pp. 54–77.

the peasants are not likely to have wanted to spend their lives living in a state of purity. Jesus did not himself belong to this group, but his teaching is full of imagery drawn from the countryside and its agriculture. This is natural in a person from a country village.

Galilee was dotted about with other towns and villages of varying size. Josephus claims that there were no less than 204 of them (*Life*, 235), though there is good reason to suspect Josephus of exaggeration.[57] Some of these towns and villages were beside the Galilean lake. This freshwater lake was also very fertile, and produced a massive quantity of edible fish. There was accordingly an important export trade in dried, salted and pickled fish. Bethsaida, an important centre of the ministry, and said to have been the original home of three members of the Twelve, Peter, Andrew and Philip (Jn 1.44), means literally 'House of Fishing'.[58] In one of its houses, archaeologists found weights for fishing nets, anchors, needles and fishhooks. Herodian coins have also been found there, and a coin of Pontius Pilate dated 29 CE. There are also coins of its ruler, Herod Philip the tetrarch, dated 30 CE, when he made it a 'city', renamed it 'Julias' in honour of the emperor Tiberius' mother and built a temple, perhaps to her. Limestone vessels, essential for purity, testify to the Jewishness of at least the majority of the population.

Magdala, on the western shore of the lake and the home town of Mary Magdalene, was later known in Greek as Taricheae, 'Salted Fish', and in Aramaic as *Migdal Nunya*, 'Tower of Fish'.[59] A first-century mosaic found there shows a boat with one mast, a square sail and three oars on each side. An actual boat found on the north-western shore of the lake was in use at the time of Jesus.[60] It is 27 feet long, had a shallow draft and sat low in the water, so it would be easy to pull nets full of fish into it, but it could fill quickly with water in a storm. Fishing people might be hired labourers like those employed by Zebedee, or they might be like Zebedee, having both his sons Jacob and John and the hired labourers in his business (Mk 1.19-20//Mt. 4.21-22). A fisherman like Zebedee might be a relatively prosperous householder and businessman. He would not however have anything like the wealth of rich people in large cities.

Capernaum, apparently the major centre of the ministry, where Peter, Andrew and their family had their home (Mk 1.21, 29–30), was another small town, with perhaps some 2,000 inhabitants, on the north-western shore of the lake.[61] Its

---

57 Cf. e.g. Reed, *Archaeology and the Galilean Jesus*, pp. 69–70.

58 On Bethsaida see Rousseau and Arav, *Jesus and His World*, pp. 19–24; Charlesworth, *Jesus and Archaeology*, pp. 40–42, 533–38; R. Arav, 'Bethsaida', in Charlesworth, *Jesus and Archaeology*, pp. 145–66.

59 On Magdala see briefly Rousseau and Arav, *Jesus and His World*, pp. 189–90; and at greater length, J. Schaberg, *The Resurrection of Mary Magdalene: Legends, Apocrypha, and the Christian Testament* (London/New York: Continuum, 2002), pp. 47–64; J. Schaberg, with M. Johnson-Debaufre, *Mary Magdalene Understood* (London/New York: Continuum, 2006), pp. 17–31.

60 For a brief discussion including both boats see Rousseau and Arav, *Jesus and His World*, pp. 25–30.

61 On Capernaum see Rousseau and Arav, *Jesus and His World*, pp. 39–46; Reed, *Archaeology*

houses were built round small courtyards, where archaeologists have found parts of ovens, fishhooks, and implements such as grinding stones, presses and loom weights. There is also ordinary pottery, much of it from the village of Kephar Ḥananya in Galilee, and undecorated Herodian lamps. Herodian stone vessels, necessary for purity, have also been found. There are no luxury objects, and no major public buildings. The streets were narrow.

The walls of the houses were generally constructed with pieces of black basalt held together with clay, and these were not strong enough to stand the weight of a second storey. Roofs were normally made from wooden beams, placed at intervals, covered with branches or reeds which were plastered with clay. A lot of attention has been focused on one particular house, which some people have identified as Simeon Peter's house. This identification is not certain, but it is a typical house of the period. Finds in it include Herodian coins and lamps, and fish hooks. These show that it was occupied as early as the first century BCE. Excavators have also reported a first-century BCE structure under the later synagogue, but we do not know whether this was a synagogue building or not.

Towns of any size needed products made by artisans – clothing, pottery, glassware, housing, furniture and so on. This is where Jesus and his father Joseph fit in, certainly as carpenters who worked in wood, and possibly also people who worked with stone. The artisans themselves needed to sell goods at a profit, over and above the cost of raw materials and the wages of any people whom they employed. For this purpose they might use markets in towns or cities of any size, make items on a small scale for single individuals, or on a larger scale for rich individuals or official projects. The largest cities in the area were Sepphoris and Tiberias.[62] After its destruction in 4 BCE, when it was sacked by the Romans because of a revolt under Judah son of the brigand Ezekiah, Sepphoris was rebuilt by Herod Antipas, and he made it his principal residence until he built Tiberias on the western shore of the lake. Tiberias was founded in 18 or 19 CE. Antipas called it after the emperor Tiberius, and soon made it the capital of Galilee. These big cities were the most likely places in Galilee to find Greek and even Roman influence. For example, at some time, probably many years after the time of Jesus, Sepphoris had a theatre and an aqueduct. Sepphoris and Tiberias are just the sort of places where Joseph, Jesus and his brothers might or might not have worked. Equally, the family business might have been the original reason for Jesus' move to Capernaum. In the absence of direct and detailed information, we do not know such things.

The building of these two cities will have had a serious economic impact on the countryside. We do not know how early this became significant enough to be considered an important possible cause of Jesus' ministry and his popular following, as well as of the action which Herod Antipas took against John the Baptist

    and the Galilean Jesus, pp. 139–69; Reed, *Visual Guide to the New Testament*, esp.
    pp. 10–12, 74–75.
62 For discussion of these cities see Rousseau and Arav, *Jesus and His World*, pp. 248–51,
    316–18; Reed, *Archaeology and the Galilean Jesus*, pp. 77–138.

and sought to take against Jesus.[63] By the time of the outbreak of the Roman war in 66 CE, rural Galilaeans vigorously attacked Sepphoris, and would have been happy to sack both Sepphoris and Tiberias and kill all their inhabitants. Jesus' teaching is full of preferring the poor to the rich, but sayings attacking cities are confined to the relatively small towns which were centres of the ministry. People attacked include Herod Antipas and people in a marketplace, together with behaviour such as praying ostentatiously on street corners. There are however no sayings which mention Sepphoris or Tiberias. This is probably because Jesus opposed the oppression of the poor by the rich wherever it happened, and the ministry was not conducted in Sepphoris or Tiberias.

The massive gap between the urban rich and the rural poor sometimes led to outbreaks of brigandage. One of the first things that Herod the Great did after being appointed king late in 40 BCE was to put down brigands in Galilee, a process which he had begun years earlier when he killed the brigand leader Ezekiah, whose son Judah later led the revolt which resulted in the sacking of Sepphoris in 4 BCE. At that time, Judah plundered the palace at Sepphoris, and according to Josephus he sought kingly rank (*Ant.* XVII, 271–72). In response, Varus, governor of Syria, brought his legions down, sacked Sepphoris, and sold the population into slavery. Varus took his legions into Judaea as well, because of unrest and brigandage there. Jesus was crucified between two brigands (Mk 15.27//Mt. 27.38), and when Pilate crucified him as 'king of the Jews' (Mk 15.26//Mt. 27.37//Lk. 23.38), he will have thought that he was in effect another brigand. The general situation, with a permanently massive gap between rich and poor leading at times to unrest and brigandage, is culturally important in understanding how Pilate could be persuaded to crucify a major prophet who led the Jesus movement and cleansed the Temple.

To the south of Galilee was Samaria, a basically Jewish province whose inhabitants however had serious differences from other Jews.[64] The Samaritans worshipped the one God, and adhered to other basic Jewish customs, such as circumcision of boys on the eighth day, and keeping the sabbath and major festivals. Major differences included the fact that they had had their own Temple on Mount Gerizim, where they still worshipped, and their scriptures were simply the Pentateuch, with some readings different from other versions. There was serious hostility between Samaritans and other Jews.

Samaria was also partly Gentile, and there is significant evidence of Greek influence, including the settlement there of some of the veterans of Alexander the Great more than three centuries previously. Herod the Great began major construction work in the city of Samaria itself in 30 BCE. He renamed it Sebaste,

---

63   The best discussion which I have seen of this extremely difficult topic is J. G. Crossley, *Why Christianity Happened: A Sociohistorical Account of Christian Origins (26–50 CE)* (Louisville: Westminster John Knox, 2006), pp. 35–74. I am grateful to Dr Crossley for giving me a copy of this book, and for discussing all the main issues with me at length.

64   For further discussion see e.g. E. Schürer, rev. and ed. G. Vermes, F. Millar, M. Goodman *et al.*, *The History of the Jewish People in the Age of Jesus Christ* (3 vols. Edinburgh: T&T Clark, 1973–87), esp. vol. II, pp. 15–20, 160–64.

after *Sebastos*, the Greek translation of Augustus, the emperor's name. As well as a theatre, Sebaste had a temple of Augustus, so Graeco-Roman influence was pagan as well as cultural. When Herod's son Herod Archelaus was deposed in 6 CE, the province was brought under the direct rule of the Roman governor of Judaea, who was in due course Pontius Pilatus (26–37 CE).

In other directions, Galilee was surrounded by Gentile areas, many of whose inhabitants were seriously influenced by Graeco-Roman culture. To the north and west was the territory of Phoenicia, part of the Roman province of Syria. Here were the two major cities of Tyre and Sidon.[65] Both were ancient Semitic cities: Tyrian shekels, used in the Jerusalem Temple because of their relatively pure silver content, each bore the image of the ancient Semitic deity Melkart. By the time of Jesus, the area had undergone significant Hellenization, and Melkart had been identified with Hercules. Hence the Syrophoenician woman whose daughter Jesus is reported to have exorcized at a distance is described as 'Greek' (Mk 7.26).

To the north and east of Galilee was the area ruled at the time of Jesus by Herod Philip, another tetrarch. This area included the ancient city of Caesarea Philippi, which was by this time very Hellenized as well as being largely pagan.[66] Herod the Great built a temple of Augustus there, and it was a centre of the worship of Pan. Herod Philip made it into a significant city, and called it Caesarea in honour of Augustus.

To the south of Philip's tetrarchy, and thus to the east and south-east of Galilee, was the Decapolis, supposedly an area of ten cities, though lists of them vary and do not always number ten.[67] On the west of the Jordan, just south of Galilee, was Scythopolis: the others were on the east of the Jordan, except for Hippos, on a hill just to the east of the lake of Galilee itself. In general these cities were very Hellenized, with theatres, amphitheatres and temples to Graeco-Roman deities. Gadara, some 6 miles south-east of the lake of Galilee, was a notable cultural centre, being the home town of the poet Meleager and of the cynic philosopher Menippus.

Trade between these places required the carriage of various goods. While the notable Roman roads of Galilee are all of much later date, there were established routes between some places. The major place to which observant Jews in Galilee are known to have travelled is Jerusalem. There was however nothing to stop Jewish people from travelling to the two major cities in Galilee, or to the more Gentile areas around.

It is important that these general points should not be used to distort the environment of Jesus' ministry. Roads across Galilee do not entail cynic philosophers at the crossroads. The major Galilaean city of Sepphoris was a Jewish city, as Tiberias probably was too. Josephus is extremely critical of the foundation of Tiberias, alleging that it was founded on a site of destroyed tombs (*Ant.* XVIII, 36–38). The story has stuck, but it has not been adequately verified. The main

---

65   On Tyre and Sidon see Rousseau and Arav, *Jesus and His World*, pp. 326–28.
66   Schürer *et al.*, *History of the Jewish People*, vol. II, pp. 169–71.
67   Schürer *et al.*, *History of the Jewish People*, vol. II, pp. 36–40, 125–27, 132–36, 142–45.

function of this story at the time may have been to keep Pharisees and their ilk away, and Antipas will not have minded that.[68]

Gentile cities in the area roundabout had Jewish communities in them. We should moreover note the evidence of Josephus that Pharisees were especially well thought of in cities (*Ant.* XVIII, 15).[69] The proximity of Gentiles to Jews could produce every imaginable Jewish reaction, from assimilation by Jews who did not observe the Torah to determined defence of visible Jewish identity with an expanded version of Jewish laws and customs. So, for example, at the beginning of the Roman war, the Jewish inhabitants of the Gentile city of Caesarea Philippi paid very high prices to obtain Jewish olive oil rather than use that produced by Gentiles (Jos. *Life*, 74–76). Accordingly, when Mark says that in addition to his normal audience from Galilee, people from Judaea, Jerusalem, Idumaea, Peraea and round about Tyre and Sidon came to hear Jesus (Mk 3.7-8), we should not regard this as a description of Jews followed by Gentiles. The people from Peraea and round about Tyre and Sidon will have been primarily Jewish, perhaps with some assimilating people of shifting and changing identities and an occasional Gentile. When Gentiles were important, we are told so, as with the Syrophoenician woman (Mk 7.24-30).

5. *Conclusions*

Jesus emerged from his native environment as an observant Jew. He was born into an observant Jewish family. The Gospel stories of his birth, however, while his mother Miriam was still a virgin, are not literally true. Nor are modern conjectures that his birth was illegitimate, or that he was treated as a *mamzer*. His father was Joseph, the husband of Miriam. Jesus was circumcised on the eighth day, and called after Joshua, the major figure of Jewish history. He had four brothers, Jacob, Judah, Joseph and Simeon, and some sisters too. Like everyone in his environment, he spoke Aramaic. He also learned to read the Bible in Hebrew, part of his education in an observant family. He was brought up in an observant Jewish environment in a completely Jewish place, the small town, or village, of Nazareth. This means that he kept the sabbath and dietary laws, and observed the major festivals, and that non-kosher food was not available.

By trade, Jesus was a carpenter. Whether this involved working elsewhere, and whether he learnt any significant amount of Greek, we do not know. We do however know that the nearest city, Sepphoris, was a Jewish city which was not seriously Hellenized, so he may not have needed to learn Greek if he did work there. Rural Galilee was generally a very fertile area, in which agriculture was a major occupation. The lake of Galilee was very fertile too, so that fishing was

---

68   Cf. M. H. Jensen, *Herod Antipas in Galilee* (WUNT 2, 115. Tübingen: Mohr Siebeck, 2006), esp. pp. 91–99, 135–46, and on Antipas, cf. pp. 338–44.
69   See further pp. 315–19.

a major occupation. Both the rural areas, and small towns such as Capernaum, the major centre of the ministry, were completely Jewish.

By the time of the historic ministry, Jesus had not merely learnt to read the Bible in Hebrew, he was soaked in the Hebrew scriptures and able to quote from them in learned debate with scribes and Pharisees. More than that, Jesus *belonged* to the prophetic tradition. He was baptized by the most important prophet in Israel in the preceding years, John the Baptist. I consider this in the next chapter.

CHAPTER 5

John the Baptist, Call and Ministry

1. *Introduction*

Jesus' ministry is often thought to have begun with a sort of call vision on the occasion of his baptism by John the Baptist. This view is based on genuine material at the beginning of the Gospel of Mark, and it is sufficiently reasonable to require discussion. In my view, however, it is related to our complete ignorance of the length of Jesus' ministry. The ministry is often thought to have lasted less than a year, and this view is often attributed to Matthew, Mark and Luke. None of them however says any such thing. The whole idea of such a short ministry has resulted from overliteral interpretation of the fact that all three synoptic evangelists record a ministry in Galilee followed by only one visit to Jerusalem. This was in reality Jesus' last visit, which was of exceptional importance because of the major events which took place during that visit, including the Cleansing of the Temple and his crucifixion. The Gospel of John, however, implies that the ministry lasted over two years, and this is inherently so much more reasonable than less than one year that many scholars believe it. John does not however say this. This view also results from counting up Jesus' visits to Jerusalem, which John increased for reasons of his own. I therefore discuss the question of the length of the ministry in some detail.

Moreover, whatever view is taken of Jesus' vision at his baptism in relation to the chronology of his ministry, his baptism by John the Baptist was an event of major importance. I therefore discuss this in detail too. For this purpose, I consider first of all the prophetic tradition which was inherited by both John the Baptist and Jesus, since this is essential for understanding the ministry of each of these men, and for understanding why Jesus was attracted to John in the first place.

2. *The Prophetic Tradition*

A major aspect of the prophetic tradition was the words of the prophets in scripture. They were read and expounded at Jewish meetings on the sabbath, and we have seen that Jesus was soaked in these Jewish scriptures. As well as the prophetic books, there were scriptural stories about other prophets, most notably Elijah and Elisha. The two major aspects of these traditional prophecies were announcing the word of God, and acting upon it. For example, the word came to Jeremiah from YHWH to stand in the gate of the Temple and announce God's judgement on sinful Jews, with a threat to destroy the Temple and lay waste the land (Jeremiah 7). At the end of the ministry, during the incident generally known as the Cleansing of the Temple, we shall see Jesus reapplying this word of the Lord to Jeremiah to the current situation in the Temple.[1] He will also have been familiar from childhood with the story of Elijah reviving a woman's son when he seemed to be dead, including the woman's response: 'Now this I know, that you are a man of God, and the word of YHWH in your mouth is truth' (1 Kgs 17.24). Thus the two central aspects of Jesus' ministry, preaching and healing, were both part of the prophetic tradition.

It is sometimes thought that prophecy had died out in Israel, but this can be misleading. When Jesus was young, it was obvious to everyone that there was no one like Elijah or Isaiah in Israel, and some people naturally regretted this. Very few people, however, if any, thought this meant that God would not raise up another prophet if and when it seemed good to him. There is ample evidence that some people hoped that he would, and from time to time some people believed that he had. For example, God's promise to Moses that he would raise up a prophet like him (Deut. 18.18-19) was collected into a group of scriptures preserved in one of the Dead Sea Scrolls (4Q175), and the Community Rule laid down how people were to live 'until there comes a prophet and the anointed ones/ Messiahs of Aaron and Israel' (1QS IX, 11). By the time of Jesus, the community believed that these last times were overdue, so a prophet was certainly expected, together with a righteous high priest and a king of David's line.

Josephus relates that, before the time of Jesus, the Jewish king John Hyrcanus had the gift of prophecy (*B.J.* I, 68–69//*Ant.* XIII, 299–300). Somewhat after the time of Jesus, there arose a prophet called Theudas. Josephus' account of him is extremely biased, but the advent of a powerful figure can be seen in spite of this:

> When Fadus was procurator of Judaea, a certain impostor, Theudas by name, persuaded a very great crowd to take up their possessions and follow him to the river Jordan. For he said he was a prophet, and that he would part the river by his command and provide an easy passage for them. With these words he deceived many people. Fadus, however, did not allow them to benefit from their foolishness, but sent out a troop of cavalry against them, which fell on

---

1   See pp. 411–15.

them unexpectedly and killed many, and took many alive. They captured Theudas himself, cut off his head and took it to Jerusalem.

(*Ant.* XX, 97–98)

It is evident even from this hostile report that Theudas had a significant popular following. Many people believed that he was a prophet sent by God, who would repeat ancient miracles by parting the waters of the Jordan and settling them on the other side of it. The Roman action too can be explained only if this were a significant popular movement. They would only have sent cavalry to kill members of the movement if they felt it was dangerous, and taking Theudas' head to Jerusalem means that they felt it necessary to prove to the inhabitants that Theudas was dead. They must therefore have believed that stories about him might lead to further disturbances, unless this clear proof of his death were provided. It follows that Theudas was a powerful prophet in his time.

Jesus accordingly lived at a time when a prophet was hoped for, and might be well received. This is the cultural context both of his own ministry, and of that of the great prophet who preceded him, John the Baptist.

3. *John the Baptist*

John was born in Judaea c.4 BCE, the son of Zechariah, a priest of the course of Abijah who served in the Temple. His mother was Elizabeth, who was also of priestly descent (Lk. 1.5, 8). John was circumcised on the eighth day, and he received a profoundly Jewish upbringing in an observant priestly home. Luke reports that he lived in the wilderness before the beginning of his ministry (Lk. 1.80). Luke also made a great effort to relate the beginning of John's ministry to secular history (Lk. 3.1-2). He dates it in 28–29 CE, and provided that he is allowed some margin of error, this should be regarded as approximately correct. Mark portrays John as an ascetic figure, clothed in camel's hair and eating locusts and wild honey, kosher food which was available in the wilderness (Mk 1.6). His disciples fasted when disciples of the Pharisees fasted, and Jesus' disciples did not fast (Mk 2.18).

The centre of John's prophetic ministry was the symbolic act of baptism, which symbolized repentance. The Aramaic word for repentance (*tethūbhā*) meant not simply being sorry for wrong one had done, but more profoundly *returning* to God, and Jews believed that God always forgave repentant Jews their sins.[2] Ritual washing was widespread in the Judaism of this period, and prophets and psalmists had long ago used the act of washing as an image of the removal of sin. For example, Isaiah preached to the people of Israel when he called upon them to stop sinning and return to YHWH:

2   On repentance see further pp. 200, 219, 231, 282–84, 292.

> Wash yourselves, make yourselves clean, remove the evil of your doings from before my eyes. Cease to do evil, learn to do good. Seek justice, correct the oppressor, vindicate the orphan, plead for the widow.
>
> (Isa. 1.16-17)

This is a very clear example of washing as a symbol of corporate repentance, the return of people to YHWH, which involves ceasing to sin and doing good works instead. Washing was also used as a symbol of individual repentance:

> Show favour to me, O God, according to your lovingkindness. According to the abundance of your compassion, blot out my transgressions. Wash me thoroughly from my iniquity, and cleanse me from my sin.
>
> (Ps. 51.1-2)

Here the psalmist portrays a person approaching God for forgiveness, and uses washing as a symbol of the way in which God will effectively change a repentant individual.

In the wilderness, washing played a part in the process of admitting people to the Qumran community. The discussion of this makes especially clear the symbolic nature of the washing, and the need for the person washed to be absolutely genuine.

> And by the spirit of holiness uniting him to His truth he shall be purified from all his iniquities, and by the spirit of uprightness and humility his sin shall be atoned for. And by the humble submission of his soul to all the precepts of God, his flesh shall be purified in being sprinkled with waters of (removing) impurity and sanctified by cleansing water.
>
> (1QS III, 7–9)

We can see from these examples that washing was a central Jewish symbol of repentance.

It is this symbol which John transformed to create his central prophetic act. By doing it in the Jordan, he used another major symbol of Jewish history. Naturally, he preached the word of God to accompany it. Mark's account briefly delineates a successful popular ministry:

> John was baptizing in the wilderness and preaching a baptism of repentance for the forgiveness of sins. And there came out to him the whole country of Judaea and all the people of Jerusalem, and they were baptized by him in the river Jordan, confessing their sins.
>
> (Mk 1.4-5)

While there is some exaggeration here, such large movements of people were more characteristic of their society than of ours. Mark says later that 'everyone', that is, people in general as opposed to chief priests, scribes and elders, 'held that John was truly a prophet' (Mk 11.32), and that is entirely coherent with his practical account. The opening 'Q' account of John's ministry also contained John's warning to those baptized by him that they should 'do fruit worthy of repentance' (Mt. 3.8//Lk. 3.8). This is confirmed by the brief account of Josephus, who notes that John's highly effective preaching required people to exercise 'righteousness towards each other' (*Ant.* XVIII, 117). Luke transmits some detailed ethical instructions (Lk. 3.11-14). Prophets were expected to be more generally active in the societies in which they lived, and Mark notes John's condemnation of Herod Antipas' marriage to Herodias (Mk 6.18).

Prophets were also expected to make predictions. Christian belief that Jesus fulfilled one of John's predictions led to it being recorded in both Mark and in 'Q' material. The prediction must be authentic, because the 'Q' material records John's own uncertainty as to whether Jesus fulfilled this prediction.[3] It may be reconstructed as follows, reproducing in English one of the overliteral renderings of the Aramaic source:

> One stronger than I is coming after me, of whom I am not worthy/sufficient to bend down to undo the latchet of the sandals of him. I baptize you in/ with water, and he will baptize you in/with holy spirit and fire, whose winnowing shovel is in his hand, and he will cleanse his threshing floor, and he will gather his wheat into the storehouse, but the chaff he will burn with unquenchable fire.
>
> (Mk 1.7, continued at Mt. 3.11-12//Lk. 3.16-17)

John evidently felt that he was not God's final messenger to Israel, and the reason for this was not the presence of anyone else in Israel at the time. He may simply have felt that his own ministry, centred on a baptism of repentance and thus on bringing Jews back to God, did not measure up to Jewish expectations of the last days. He is also likely to have been influenced by particular passages of scripture. These surely included Malachi 3. In the first verse of this chapter, God promises to send his messenger, and it is reasonable to suppose that it is this figure who is described as 'the Lord' (*hā'ādhōn*), a term in normal use for superior human beings. It would therefore be reasonable for John to describe him as 'One stronger than I'. Malachi also says of this figure 'is coming'. Mal. 4.1 (3.19 in the Hebrew text) also uses the image of the wicked as stubble who will be burnt up, just the kind of image to inspire the rest of John's prediction. This is more generally reminiscent of other Jewish pictures of judgement. For example, at Hos. 13.3, idolatrous Israelites will be like chaff from the threshing floor. Thus John's threat to the wicked is clear: the winnowing shovel and burning of the chaff mean perdition for them. It is evident that conventional Jewish leaders were among the wicked (cf. Mk 6.18; 11.31-32; Mt. 21.32), and the implication of John's preaching as a whole is that they would not be alone.

Equally, the gathering of the wheat into the storehouse, or barn, implies the salvation of many of the crowds who flocked to John's baptism. This is also

---

3 For more detailed discussion see pp. 181–83.

an essential part of traditional Jewish expectation. For example, at Isa. 27.12 YHWH will thresh and the people of Israel will be gathered, and at Mic. 2.12 God will gather Jacob, and the remnant of Israel. The dominant context in the Hebrew Bible is one of return from exile, and John's imagery of gathering wheat into the barn has transmuted this beautifully for people who lived in Israel.

Thus John framed his expectation of another figure who was still to come from within standard Jewish traditions. Within the varied expectations characteristic of the Judaism of this period, the precise form of his expectation was unique, and he did not give this figure a title. He had no need to do so. In particular, however important and final this figure was to be, there was no need for John to call him 'the Messiah'. The reason for this is that the term *m^eshīhā*, the Aramaic for 'anointed', had not yet crystallized out as a title, 'the Messiah', meaning a/ the final redemptive figure.[4]

4. *Jesus' Baptism and Call*

We can now see what attracted Jesus to John. John exercised a large-scale and highly successful prophetic ministry of repentance to Israel. He called upon the whole of Israel to return to the Lord, and he backed this up with ethical teaching. He offered salvation and predicted judgement in terms which recreated the Judaism of the prophetic tradition. This explains why Jesus underwent John's baptism (Mk 1.9-11//Mt. 3.13-17//Lk. 3.21-22). Jesus thereby joined this vigorous renewal of prophetic Judaism. Unlike later sources, Mark shows no concern that this implied repentance.[5] Nor should he have done so. As a faithful Jew, Jesus will have repented of his sins. This does not mean that he had previously been a liar or a thief. All great religious figures have a sense of their own imperfections compared with the holiness of God, and it is this feeling which Jesus will have shared, as he joined in the corporate experience of mass baptism. As he put it later, when an observant Jew who admired him greatly addressed him as 'Good Rabbi', rather than the conventional 'rabbi': 'Why do you call me good? None is good except the one God' (Mk 10.18). Unlike later Christian tradition, which has been quite incapable of coming to terms with this authentic comment, Jesus meant *exactly* what he said. God alone is perfectly good, and no man can be compared with him.

On the occasion of his baptism, Jesus had a visionary experience. Matthew and Luke edited this to make it an objective event, but Mark believed in the accuracy of his Aramaic source, though his word 'immediately' may well represent a translator's solution to a difficult problem, as I suggest here with 'in it in the hour', a literal translation of the Aramaic *bāh b^esha'thā*:

---

4   See pp. 392–99.
5   On the embarrassment shown by later sources see p. 105.

> And in it in the hour he went up from the water and saw the heavens splitting open and the Spirit descending on him like a dove.
>
> (Mk 1.10)

In the Judaism of this period, the spirit was God in action, not a person of a Trinity. This means that Jesus had a symbolic vision of God inspiring him. The image is quite violent, as anyone who has experienced a flapping pigeon descending on them will be unable to forget. The way it is put cannot be due to the early church, and must be accepted into the historical record. The violent imagery is continued in v. 12:

> And immediately the Spirit drove him into the wilderness. And he was in the wilderness for forty days being tried by Satan, and he was with the wild animals, and (the) angels served him.
>
> (Mk 1.12-13)

This too is the record of real experience which the early church had no reason to produce.

All three Gospel writers seek to take us further. Mark has Jesus hear a voice from heaven, when he saw the heavens splitting open immediately after his baptism, and the voice proclaims Jesus as 'my son, the beloved' (Mk 1.11). There is one small indication that the story was transmitted in Aramaic, the last word of the speech by the heavenly voice. In Greek, this is in the aorist tense *eudokēsa*, literally 'I was well pleased', a natural translation of an Aramaic perfect, which we might translate 'I am well pleased'. Moreover, 'my son the beloved' in first-century Judaism means that Jesus was a faithful Jew chosen by God to do for Israel something that mattered.[6] While fiction could be written in Aramaic as much as in English, most of the story is obviously true, for it makes excellent sense as an event in the life of Jesus, and none at all as an invention of the early church. It is therefore probable that the auditory part of the vision is as genuine as the event itself.

The 'Q' material in Matthew and Luke (Mt. 4.3-10//Lk. 4.3-12) has actual temptations in conversations between Jesus and the devil, in which Jesus' use of scripture is a prominent feature. This is an imaginative midrash with a large scriptural element, so this should be attributed to an early Christian storyteller.

It is therefore doubly important that the basic information found in Mark is unquestionably accurate. Jesus had a vision at his baptism, and spent a period of solitude in the wilderness afterwards, during which he felt tempted by Satan. This vision was in the tradition of the call visions of the prophets.

6   See further pp. 388–91.

5. *Jesus, John and the Length of the Historic Ministry*

How long Jesus stayed with John the Baptist we do not know, because we have no direct evidence bearing on this. The Fourth Gospel has Jesus conduct a ministry of baptism overlapping with that of John, before John was imprisoned by Herod Antipas. This is so unlikely that one of its own authors corrected it, announcing that Jesus did not baptize, but his disciples did (Jn 4.2 seeking to correct Jn 3.22; 4.1). We should not believe this. The synoptic Gospels have no trace of Jesus or his disciples baptizing, and they had no reason to omit it, because it would have been so easy and fruitful to see this as the origin of Christian baptism. We must infer that this is another example of historically inaccurate creativity in the Johannine community. The whole passage (Jn 3.22–4.3) is a quite overblown attempt to portray John the Baptist's inferiority to Jesus, and it will have been partly inspired by the reality of Christian baptism. At the same time, it contains the correct view that some of Jesus' ministry took place 'when John had not yet been thrown into prison' (Jn 3.24), and that might be due to tradition rather than incidentally correct invention.

There is one small indication in the 'Q' material that Jesus remained in the wilderness for some time following his baptism, and a second piece of evidence, beginning the same passage of 'Q', that John was still alive during the first part of the ministry of Jesus.[7] The first indication is at Lk. 7.24-26, where Jesus asks the crowds three times what they have come out into the wilderness to see, concludes 'a prophet . . . more than a prophet' and makes further references to John. Whereas the Matthaean version (Mt. 11.7-9) uses aorist tenses, which indicate that Matthew thought Jesus was referring to a single past event, most manuscripts of Luke (7.24-26) use perfect tenses, which ought to mean that the crowds had come out into the wilderness and were still there when Jesus spoke to them, and that therefore John was still in the wilderness at the time. Moreover, Luke must be repeating this from 'Q', because he had no reason to change aorists to perfects, whereas Matthew was concerned to make clear that John was in prison at the time, so he had good reason to alter 'Q' perfects to aorists. The original Aramaic perfects could be interpreted either way, so it is the behaviour of the 'Q' translator which is of the greatest interest. He chose to use perfect tenses when he could have used simple past tenses, as he must often have done to translate Aramaic perfects. The 'Q' translator must therefore have believed that Jesus was in the wilderness when he delivered this speech, and consequently the crowds and John were there too. Moreover, this 'Q' translator was in touch with this early and accurate tradition, which may well have been written down by Matthew the tax-collector on one of his wax tablets.[8] We should therefore believe him.

The whole passage is also of great interest because Jesus told the crowds what he thought of John. I translate a reconstructed 'Q' version, adding some words in brackets, to bring out the meaning, particularly of the Greek perfect tenses.

---

7 For detailed discussion see Casey, *Aramaic Approach to Q*, pp. 105–29.
8 Cf. pp. 86–88.

What have you come out (and are still here) to see? A reed shaken by a wind? But what have you come out (and are still here) to see? A man dressed in soft clothing? Ha! those who wear soft clothing (are to be found) in kings' palaces. But what have you come out (and are still here) to see? A prophet? Yes, I tell you, and more than a prophet. This is he of whom it is written, 'Behold! I am sending my messenger before my face, who will prepare your way before you' (cf. Mal. 3.1)

The passage begins with two rhetorical contrasts. A 'reed shaken by a wind' was a very common sight in the wilderness beside the Jordan, by the lake of Galilee and elsewhere, so it is comically obvious that this is not what they came out to see. The wilderness is quite the wrong place for 'a man dressed in soft clothing', a contrast with the dress of John the Baptist who was 'clothed in camel's hair' (Mk 1.6). Galilaean members of Jesus' audience may have thought of Herod Antipas. He was dressed in soft clothing, lived in a palace, was known as a king, and issued coins portraying reeds.[9]

Jesus' dismissal of these two ridiculous notions leads to the first serious point. The normal verdict of Jews who went out into the wilderness to be baptized by John was right: John was a prophet. Jesus then went further, identifying him as God's messenger predicted at Mal. 3.1, somewhat adapted to the current situation in which John came to prepare the way for Jesus. Matthew has another saying which further clarifies Jesus' view of John:

And if you are willing to receive (him/it), he is Elijah who is going to come.
(Mt. 11.14)

This refers to the prophecy at the end of the book of Malachi:

Behold, I will send you Elijah the prophet before the great and aweful day of YHWH comes.

(Mal. 4.5)

After John's death, Jesus had no doubt that John was Elijah. During his Galilaean ministry, Jesus' disciples asked him why the scribes said that Elijah must come 'first', so making another reference to Mal. 4.5. Jesus responded by saying that 'Elijah has come', referring to John's death and his own as well (Mk 9.11-13). This can only be a reference to John as Elijah.[10] Accordingly, Mt. 11.14 must come from early in the ministry, and makes excellent sense in the same setting as Jesus' adapted reference to Mal. 3.1. Luke does not have it, either because it was not in his collection of 'Q' material, or because he omitted it. As an educated Greek, he would not like the identification of one person as another, and he omitted Mk 9.11-13 too. He put his own version of Jesus' view, suitably modified for Greek audiences, in his story of John's birth. Here an angel of the Lord appears

9   On Antipas see further pp. 388–94.
10   See further pp. 355–56, 367–68.

to John's father Zachariah and, with an indirect reference to Mal. 4.5-6, predicts that John will come 'in the spirit and power of Elijah' (Lk. 1.17). This shows that Luke inherited the traditions which are transmitted elsewhere in Matthew and Mark. They have a perfect setting in the teaching of Jesus, and the early church had no reason to invent them. We must therefore believe them.

Two conclusions follow. First, Jesus taught in the wilderness when John the Baptist was conducting his ministry of baptism and repentance there. Secondly, Jesus had an extraordinarily high view of John, whose ministry was of such importance that God inspired Isaiah and Malachi to write about it. These two points cohere very well together, and they build into a coherent picture with Jesus' decision to undergo John's baptism, and with his vigorous spiritual experiences at and immediately after his baptism.

How long Jesus taught in the wilderness we do not know. Nor do we know to what extent he preached, taught and healed before he went into the wilderness and was baptized. Both these points must be borne in mind in assessing an authentic tradition which looks at first sight as if it is intended to recount the beginning of Jesus' ministry.

> After John was handed over, Jesus came into Galilee preaching the Gospel (*euangelion*) of God and saying, 'The time is fulfilled and the kingdom of God is at hand. Repent and believe in the good news (*euangelion*).'
>
> (Mk 1.14-15)

It was well known in the ancient church that Mark was not present during the historic ministry, and did not write his account of it in order.[11] Mark does not say that this was the beginning of the ministry, nor that Jesus did not preach, teach and heal before he went into the wilderness for his baptism. These impressions are simply the result of the way in which Mark ordered his material. Given that Mark did not receive his material in logical or chronological order, the order which he chose is perfectly reasonable. He put Jesus' forerunner before him, and he put Jesus' call vision at the beginning. This provided his story with the essentials of an ancient narrative plot: beginning, middle and end. We should not expect more of Marcus, a not very well-educated bilingual, struggling with the translation of Aramaic sources as he composed the First Gospel in Greek.

The tradition which Mark inherited intended to say something amazing, which is liable to be overlooked because we have become so familiar with it. To see this, it helps to ask an unusual question. What would a normal person in Jesus' position have done, when Herod Antipas arrested and imprisoned John? One obvious possibility would have been to move to the relatively safe territory of Philip the tetrarch, out of reach of Herod Antipas. Another would have been to flee further north and then perhaps east, in the Aramaic-speaking Jewish diaspora, much safer still. Jesus did not do any such thing! He did the amazing and dangerous thing, he headed straight back into Galilee, the kingdom ruled

---

11 See pp. 65–69.

by Herod Antipas, and openly and publicly preached the good news, that God would soon establish his kingdom. In due course, some Pharisees brought him the news which any sane person would have known was inevitable: 'Herod wants to kill you' (Lk. 13.31). Jesus did not respond by refusing to die: he undertook to continue his ministry, and to die in Jerusalem (Lk. 13.32-33).[12]

This is why we do not know the length of Jesus' ministry. It may not have had a sufficiently clear beginning, and the major eyewitnesses on whom we ultimately depend for the transmission of information to the three evangelists are not likely to have been present when Jesus first taught and healed. Consequently, Mark did not have, and Luke could not find, clear information about the opening of the ministry. Mark did his best by putting his material in a logical order, with a clearly defined beginning and end, and the substance of the ministry in the middle. Matthew and Luke had little option other than to follow him. None of them will have thought that the ministry lasted only one year, and all three will have taken it for granted that Jesus made several visits to Jerusalem. Important material about previous visits did not however reach them as such, perhaps because nothing which was felt to be important happened on many such occasions, and in any case chronology was not what was important to the people who transmitted traditions about Jesus in brief notes on wax tablets, single sheets of papyrus and the like.

The second indication that there was some overlap between the ministry of John the Baptist and Jesus is found in the immediately preceding passage of 'Q' material, which may be reconstructed from Mt. 11.2-6//Lk. 7.18-23. Matthew and Luke both edited the beginning quite heavily, but John's question to Jesus and Jesus' answer are certainly authentic. I translate my reconstruction of an original Aramaic source.[13]

> And John sent by the hand of his disciples and said to him, 'Are you him coming, or shall we wait for another?' And he answered and said to them, 'Go inform John of what (people) see and hear: blind (people) see and lame (people) walk, people-with-skin-diseases are cleansed and deaf (people) hear, and dead (people) are raised and poor (people) have good news preached to them. And blessed is whoever does not stumble over me.'

John's question only makes sense when John was still alive, and cannot possibly have been made up by the early church, which believed that Jesus fulfilled the prediction referred to in John's question. This is phrased in terms of John's own prediction, not in terms of Jewish expectation in general. I have discussed this prediction previously.[14] I noted that it was inspired by passages of the prophetic scriptures, and they included Malachi 3, so that John expected a figure other than himself to fulfil Mal. 3.1, whereas Jesus believed that the prophecies of Malachi 3–4 were fulfilled in John himself. John's prediction indicates that this figure would

---

12   See further pp. 96–97, 324–25, 342–43, 403–4.
13   For detailed discussion see Casey, *Aramaic Approach to Q*, pp. 105–15.
14   See pp. 175–76.

bring a lot of judgement. Jesus was an obvious candidate for the strong one coming, for he had been baptized by John and was conducting a dramatic ministry to the people of Israel. At the same time, he had so far brought more repentance and less judgement than John had expected from this figure. Accordingly, John's question has an excellent setting towards the end of John's ministry, and when Jesus' ministry was sufficiently well established for its nature to be clear.

Jesus' reply also has an excellent setting when his ministry was well established, so that he could refer to major aspects of it. I discuss his healing ministry in Chapter 7, which shows that the events alluded to in Jesus' response to John were indeed of central importance. Jesus' summary is strongly reminiscent of prophetic passages of scripture, especially Isa. 29.18-19; 35.5-6; 61.1. Jesus seems to have claimed in this indirect way to be fulfilling the hopeful parts of these prophecies, but not the prophecies of judgement in the very same passages. At Isa. 29.18-19, 'And the deaf shall hear on that day . . . the eyes of the blind shall see', and there are references to the joy of the poor and needy. At Isa. 35.5-6, 'Then the eyes of the blind shall be opened, and the ears of the deaf shall be opened, then the lame shall leap like a ram . . .'. Isa. 61.1 includes the bringing of good news to the poor, as well as reference to the spirit of the Lord YHWH being 'upon me', which John would recall taking place at Jesus' baptism. This is so extensive that it was evidently deliberate, and John the Baptist, being also learned in the prophetic scriptures, could reasonably be expected to pick it up. Jesus' reply accordingly means that he is the expected figure, and that he was bringing more salvation and less judgement than John had expected. This is the point of the allusions to scripture in which Jesus saw his ministry foretold by God through the prophet Isaiah. His reply ends with a beatitude which should be seen as a reference to another passage of the prophet Isaiah. At Isa. 8.14-15 there will be 'a rock of stumbling' and similar obstacles, 'And many among them shall stumble and fall . . .'. Those who do not stumble and fall like this are blessed by Jesus, and this general statement in prophetic terms is obviously applied particularly to John.

Matthew edited or inserted an introduction to this passage: 'Now John, having heard in prison the deeds of the Christ . . .' (Mt. 11.2). Luke's more elaborate introduction (Lk. 7.18-19) makes no reference to John's imprisonment. The order of Luke's narrative entails that John was in prison, for Luke narrates John's imprisonment by Herod the tetrarch at Lk. 3.19-20. The compiler of this part of the 'Q' material did not think this, as we know from the perfect tenses at Lk. 7.24-26. We should follow the 'Q' translator. Neither Matthew's editorial introduction nor Luke's order of events can be relied on. Moreover, Josephus reports that Herod Antipas imprisoned John in the fortress of Machaerus, miles away not just on the far side of the Jordan, but so far south as to be east of the Dead Sea (*Ant.* XVIII, 116–19). It is not probable that John could send disciples from there to question Jesus, with any reasonable hope of them being allowed back to tell him Jesus' answer. We should infer that Jesus' ministry was well under way, but that John's ministry was still active, and he was not yet in prison.

We must draw two conclusions of different kinds. One is that John was a fundamental influence on Jesus. He was the first major prophet in Israel for centuries. Jesus was brought up in the prophetic tradition as a major part of traditional Judaism. In John, he found his own forerunner. He believed that John fulfilled the prophecy of Malachi that God would send Elijah before the great and aweful day of the Lord. He believed this because John was the visible incarnation of the prophetic tradition, a fearless and original prophet whose ministry of baptism and repentance brought many Jews back to God. Jesus underwent John's baptism, and experienced a call vision in the tradition of major prophets. He continued to exercise his ministry in the wilderness, where he preached and taught that John was sent by God to restore Israel. He believed that he himself was the final messenger to Israel predicted by John. His major ministry was conducted in Galilee. When it was in full swing, John sent messengers to ask Jesus whether he was the figure whom he had predicted. Jesus answered in the affirmative, citing his ministry of teaching and healing, and alluding to passages of the prophet Isaiah which he was fulfilling.

The other major conclusion is that we possess nothing remotely like a chronological outline of Jesus' ministry, and we have no idea of how long it lasted. We must not be misled by the position of Mk 1.14-15, the content of which is true and important. When John was arrested by Herod Antipas, Jesus immediately went back into Galilee and preached that people should return to God, who was about to finally establish his kingdom. This was not however the beginning of the historic ministry, it was the beginning of its final phase. Mark put it at the beginning because he inherited information about the ministry in pieces, with no chronological outline, and it makes a narratively satisfying start. It follows that we do not know how much of the rest of the story had already taken place.

In a sense, Luke's evidence is even more important than that of Mark, because Luke was such an excellent historian by normal ancient standards. Hence he made a real effort to date the beginning of John the Baptist's ministry, following Mark in putting Jesus' baptism by John just before the apparent beginning of Jesus' ministry:

> In the fifteenth year of the reign of Tiberius Caesar, when Pontius Pilatus was governor of Judaea, and Herod was Tetrarch of Galilee, but Philip his brother was Tetrarch of the region of Ituraea and Trachonitis, and Lysanias was Tetrarch of Abilene, in the highpriesthood of Annas and Caiaphas, the word of God came to John the son of Zachariah in the wilderness.
>
> (Lk. 3.1-2)

After Jesus' baptism, Luke also took the trouble to tell us that, at the beginning of his ministry, Jesus was about 30 years old (Lk. 3.23). Nonetheless, Luke did not improve on Mark's lack of a genuine chronological outline of the ministry. He could also be taken to believe that the ministry lasted only a year, though he too never says this, so we should not attribute such an opinion to him either. Of especial interest in this connection is the extraordinarily static journey to Jerusalem at Lk. 9.51–18.14. Here Luke leaves the outline of Mark's Gospel, which he normally follows, and inserts a massive amount of 'Q' and special Lukan material. He evidently did not know at what particular points in the ministry the events and teaching of this section took place, and was not concerned to invent a particular narrative framework for them. Thus, despite the many differences between Mark and Luke, including Luke's addition of the birth narratives at the beginning of his Gospel, he has the same essentials of an ancient narrative plot: beginning, middle and end.

To understand this, we must first consider the ancient genre to which the four canonical Gospels belong. Early twentieth-century scholars argued that they were not biographies. Bultmann was conspicuous and influential. He commented for example, 'There is no historical-biographical interest in the Gospels, and that is why they have nothing to say about Jesus' human personality, his appearance and character, his origin, education and development . . .'.[15] All this shows, however, is that the Gospels are not biographies in the modern sense. More recent scholarship has however considered them in the light of ancient lives (*Bioi*, or *vitae*) of people, and the complete appropriateness of this has been established by the outstanding work of Richard Burridge.[16]

Burridge has shown that all four canonical Gospels fit within the rather broad parameters of ancient lives of people. For example, Mark's Gospel is of similar length to the average length of the lives written by Plutarch, one of the greatest and most prolific ancient writers of lives, while Matthew and Luke are comparable to his longest lives, such as *Alexander* or *Antonius*. Again, Jesus is the subject of about a quarter of the verbs in the Gospel of Mark, a normal proportion for an ancient life. Furthermore, some lives have an extended discussion of the subject's death, or of an especially important event in the subject's life, such as the Battle of Mons Graupius in Tacitus' *Agricola*. This means that the lengthy treatment of Jesus' Passion and death, one of the most important events in his life, puts the Gospels within the parameters of ancient lives, not outside them.[17] These are only examples of main points. The great value of Burridge's work is to show that, for many reasons such as these, the Gospels are normal documents written within the range of the ways that other ancient authors wrote lives of important people.

Burridge also comments that the Gospels have a *basic* chronological structure not dissimilar from those in ancient lives.[18] For example, Suetonius begins his *Deified Augustus* (*Divus Augustus*) with an account of his family, birth, and a few chronological details, followed by his actions at the time of the death of his uncle Julius Caesar. He then comments in a single sentence on his holding supreme power with Antonius and Lepidus at first, then with Antonius for nearly 12 years, and finally by himself for 44 years (*Divus Augustus*, I–VIII). He ends with an account of his death, very precisely dated, funeral and will. In between, however, his account is in topical rather than chronological order, with

---

15 Bultmann, *History of the Synoptic Tradition*, p. 372.
16 R. Burridge, *What Are the Gospels? A Comparison with Graeco-Roman Biography* (SNTSMS 70. Cambridge: CUP, 1992. 2nd edn, Grand Rapids: Eerdmans, 2004). I am grateful to Prof. Burridge for many illuminating discussions, and for giving me a copy of his book.
17 Burridge, *What Are the Gospels?*, esp. pp. 199–200, 196, 197–99.
18 Burridge, *What Are the Gospels?*, esp. pp. 139–41, 200–2.

only occasional chronological references. Plutarch's *Cicero* also has a beginning, middle and end, but with few indications of chronology. For example, it begins with his family, birth, schooldays and time in Athens, but it does not date any of these events. It ends with his death. In between, it does deal with his life with one event happening after another, but these events are not dated.

All this indicates that ancient authors did not share our ideas of time. Douglas Estes has offered an extremely learned and complex discussion of this with reference to the Fourth Gospel.[19] The most important point is that we must not read back into the ancient world our ideas of absolute linear time, foreshadowed by Aristotle, and dependent above all on Newton. Of course they knew that one event happened after another, but they did not necessarily relate events in chronological order, as a modern historian would, because that was not what necessarily interested them. The Fourth Gospel is the most obvious example, because it is structured round sacred, symbolic time. For example, it has the Cleansing of the Temple, which literally took place at the end of the ministry (Mk 11.15-18), at the beginning (Jn 2.13-22), to symbolize the replacement of Judaism with Christianity. Again, it passes seamlessly from Tabernacles to Hanukkah, literally some two months later, because Hanukkah was regarded as Second Tabernacles, and the symbolism of Jesus' discourses throughout John 7–10 is controlled by the symbolism of these feasts.[20] The synoptic Gospels are not controlled by theological symbolism in this way, but they have the same lack of concern for detailed chronology, like many ancient lives. This is the profound reason why Mark was content to begin his Gospel with John the Baptist and Jesus' call vision, followed by Jesus' dramatic return to Galilee after John the Baptist's death (Mk 1.1-15). This makes a highly effective opening, the Passion narrative makes a historically accurate ending, and everything else is in the middle. Even more dramatically, Luke, having opened with birth narratives, follows Mark with John the Baptist and Jesus' arrival in Galilee, ends Jesus' life with the Passion, and puts masses of material in the extraordinarily static journey from Galilee to Jerusalem.

We must therefore be content without a chronological outline of the ministry, and without knowing how long it lasted. I therefore discuss most aspects of Jesus' historic ministry in chapters 6–10, and pick up the story in Chapter 11 at the point where there is a genuine narrative, when Jesus headed deliberately for his death in Jerusalem. One major event not too late in the ministry was the calling of the Twelve, so I discuss that next, before undertaking a more systematic treatment of the main points of the ministry.

---

19 D. Estes, *The Temporal Mechanics of the Fourth Gospel: A Theory of Hermeneutical Relativity in the Gospel of John* (Leiden: Brill, 2008). This originated as a doctoral thesis done under the supervision of Prof. Richard Bell at the University of Nottingham. I am grateful to Dr Estes for a very fruitful discussion of his fascinating thesis at his *viva voce* examination, and for giving me a copy of his book. I am also grateful to Prof. Bell for fruitful discussions of the issues raised. I make no claim to understand the scientific knowledge of these scholars, who have shared with me their quite exceptional breadth of learning.

20 See pp. 511-25, and for more detailed discussion, Casey, *Is John's Gospel True?*, esp. pp. 4–14, 25–29, 134–36.

6. *The Call of the Twelve*

We do not have much information about the Twelve, especially when we consider that what we do have establishes their fundamental importance. It is a reasonable inference that what is missing was not of positive interest to the early church, or rather perhaps to Gentile churches. This is understandable, because only the central group of three played any significant role in the church for any considerable time after Jesus' death. Mark puts the call of four of the Twelve at the beginning of his account (Mk 1.16-20): Simon (later Peter), Jacob and John, so the inner circle of three, together with Simon's brother Andrew, one of only two of the Twelve to have a Greek rather than an Aramaic name. Somewhat later, Mark tells us that Jesus 'made Twelve so that they might be with him, and so that he might send them out to preach and to have power to cast out demons' (Mk 3.14-15). This corresponds to the two central points of his ministry. Jesus' preaching and teaching ministry was directed at Israel as a whole, so it is logical that he should send his closest followers out to carry on that ministry. That there should be 12 of them corresponds symbolically to the twelve tribes of Israel. Exorcism and healing were central to his ministry, and of all kinds of healing, exorcism is most obviously a healing which enables people classified as socially unacceptable to return to the community.

The account of the Twelve during the ministry bears out this summary. They turn up with him at various points, including his final Passover (Mk 14.17, 20). They are sent out, which might have made them 'apostles', for the Greek word *apostoloi*, from which we get our English word 'apostles', simply means 'sent', as does the underlying Aramaic *sheliḥīn*. However, this was surely not the term normally used, since it is rare in the earliest sources. Mark uses it only at 6.30, which is very logical, because this is when they return after being sent out: there are no examples in the 'Q' material. Moreover, it is conspicuously added by Matthew and Luke (Mt. 10.2; Lk. 6.13, cf. 11.49; 17.5; 22.14; 24.10), and, unlike 'the Twelve', the term 'apostle' has an obvious setting in the early church. We must infer that the inner group were known as the Twelve, the term used by Mark when they are sent out (Mk 6.7) and in an old tradition about the Resurrection, when they were surely 11 (1 Cor. 15.5). They were 11 because one of the Twelve had betrayed Jesus, a desperately memorable fact which the early church cannot have invented. The Markan account of their sending out mentions unclean spirits, or demons, twice (Mk 6.7, 13), and adds the preaching of repentance and healing the sick by anointing with oil (Mk 6.12-13). Thus the earliest source material is entirely coherent, and has an excellent setting in first-century Judaism, but not in the early church, for whom the Twelve were not of continuing importance for long after the election of Matthias (Acts 1.12-26). The authenticity of this material should therefore be accepted.

Further information may be gleaned from the 'Q' saying, Mt. 19.28// Lk. 22.30. Some of the opening part of it has been removed through the editing of the evangelists. Matthew has the Son of man sitting on the throne of his glory, surely a redactional presentation of the last times, so he was not satisfied with the way something was put in his source (cf. Mt. 16.28; 25.31).

Luke has equally redactional references to 'my Father' (Lk. 22.29) and 'my kingdom'. We must infer that Jesus said something eschatological which was not satisfactory for either Matthew or Luke, and which we consequently have no hope of recovering. Luke's version also contains the words 'you will eat and drink at my table'. Luke had little reason to edit this in. If Jesus really said something longer on these lines, Matthew and Luke might both have reason to replace it with what we now read. It would also make an excellent occasion for the Twelve to sit on 12 thrones, and for all of them to drink new wine. What Jesus said must therefore have included this: '. . . you will eat and drink at my table . . . you will sit on thrones judging the twelve tribes of Israel.' This is quite extraordinary: the Twelve will judge Israel. Not Abel, not Abraham, not Moses, but the Twelve. Abraham, Isaac, Jacob and much of the Jewish diaspora would be there, reclining as at feasts (Mt. 8.11-12//Lk. 13.28-29), but not judging Israel. This puts in its proper perspective Jacob and John's request to sit on Jesus' right and left in his glory (Mk 10.37). They merely ask for seats of honour when every man of the Twelve will judge the twelve tribes of Israel. As always in his teaching, the position of Jesus himself is implied rather than stated. It is evidently central, as Jacob and John understood when they referred to his glory.

A little more can be gleaned from the names of the Twelve. The Gospels transmit the original name of their leader as 'Simon'. This is a normal Greek name, but in an Aramaic (or Hebrew) environment it would represent *Shim'on*, for which the normal English is Simeon. Jesus called Simeon *Kēphā*, which means 'Rock': this was transliterated into Greek as *Kēphas*, and from Greek into English as 'Cephas'. This is the name by which he is referred to in a piece of tradition about Resurrection appearances, quoted by Paul. According to this, the risen Jesus 'appeared to Cephas, then to the Twelve' (1 Cor. 15.5). Cephas is also the name by which Paul usually refers to him (e.g. Gal. 1.18; 2.9, 11,14), so his Aramaic nickname caught on in Greek-speaking churches. *Kēphā* was also translated into Greek as *Petros*, from which we get 'Peter', the name by which he is usually known in English. Paul refers to him like this once (Gal. 2.7-8), and all four Gospels and Acts do so abundantly. In the garden of Gethsemane, Jesus called him 'Simeon' (cf. Mk 14.37), as Jesus' brother Jacob did in a major speech (Acts 15.14). Thus at major points in their lives, both Jesus and Jacob his brother referred to him with his original name *Shim'on*, rather than his nickname. I therefore call him 'Simeon the Rock', treating 'Simeon' as his name and *Kēphā* as his epithet.

Matthew has a speech in which Jesus hails Simeon the Rock as the founder of the church, but it seems to be a mixture of primary and secondary traditions. Matthew's Greek may reasonably be translated as follows:

Blessed are you, Simon Bar Jona, because flesh and blood did not reveal (this) to you, but my Father who (is) in the heavens. And I tell you that you are Peter (*Petros*), and on this rock (*petra*) I will build my church (*ekklēsia*), and (the) gates of Hades will not prevail against it. I will give you the keys of the kingdom of the heavens, and whatever you bind on the earth will be bound in the heavens, and whatever you release on the earth will be released in the heavens.

(Mt. 16.17-19)

It has been very difficult for scholars to sort this out. As so often, the most important obstacles are in the later world. This passage was used by Catholics to legitimate authoritarian and often corrupt popes. This was naturally objected to by Protestants, and it has given some Protestant scholars an undue sense of certainty that Jesus cannot have said any of it.

It has frequently been argued that Jesus' expectation of the coming of the kingdom in the near future is well attested and excludes the founding of the church. This is true, as we shall see in Chapter 6, but as an objection to the authenticity of this passage it presupposes conventional Greek and modern translations, from which we get 'church' or the like. Aspects of the Matthaean tradition imply an Aramaic background. Jesus addresses him as 'Simon Bar Iōna', a Greek version of the Semitic 'Simeon' followed by the Aramaic for 'son of Jonah'. 'Flesh and blood' is a Semitic expression, though it is one which was known to Greek-speaking Jews. More important is the Aramaic original for the central declaration. In Matthew's Greek, there is a pun between Peter (*Petros*), and the rock (*petra*). We have however seen that in Aramaic Jesus called him *Kēphā*, which means 'rock'. Thus the pun works perfectly well in Aramaic too, and that is not likely to be a coincidence. Moreover, Jesus must have meant something, and since Simeon really was the leader of the Twelve, and thus the leader of the Jesus movement second only to Jesus himself, this is the obvious thing for Jesus to have meant. The question therefore should be whether there is an Aramaic word which Jesus could have used to refer to his movement, and which would cause a reasonable translator to put Matthew's *ekklēsia*, which is normally translated here as 'church', though it meant any kind of assembly, and it is regularly so translated when it occurs in other Greek texts. Much the best answer is the Aramaic *qehal*. In the Septuagint, *ekklēsia* almost always translates the Hebrew *qahal*, and this normal word for 'assembly', 'congregation', 'community', is found in Aramaic too. It was therefore an entirely reasonable term for Jesus to have used for the movement which he founded, and Matthew's *ekklēsia* is a perfectly reasonable translation of it.

So far, then, this could be a saying of Jesus. Equally, however, some aspects of Jesus' speech appear to be secondary. The first is its connection with 'Peter's confession', as it is usually called, in the immediately preceding verse (Mt. 16.16). In Mark, this is 'You are the Christ' (Mk 8.29). In Greek, as in English, this is a sound Christian confession, but any possible underlying Aramaic would mean only 'You are (a/the) anointed', a possible thing to say, but not enough to be a major confession.[21] It is therefore secondary, a product of the early Christian church, and perhaps written by Mark himself. Matthew has elaborated it into 'You are the Christ, the Son of the living God' (Mt. 16.16). This is accordingly

---

21 See pp. 392–99.

secondary too. It follows that most of Mt. 16.17 is secondary, and the end of it is indeed very typically Matthaean: 'flesh and blood did not reveal (this) to you, but my Father who (is) in the heavens.' Jesus also had no reason to add Mt. 16.19, giving Simeon the keys of the kingdom of heaven, and power to bind and loose. The saying as a whole has on the other hand an excellent setting in the Jerusalem church in the early years after Jesus' death, when Simeon the Rock was in charge of that church, so we should infer that this passage was rewritten there.

Accordingly, Jesus' original saying had nothing to do with 'Peter's confession'. It was what Jesus said when he gave Simeon the epithet *Kēphā*, and it included this:

> Blessed are you, Simeon son of Jonah, and I tell you that you are (a/the) Rock (*Kēphā*), and on this rock (*kēphā*) I shall build me a/the community (*qehalā*).

This provides a proper and historically appropriate reason why Jesus should give Simeon this epithet, an epithet which he fully justified in his leadership of the community, both during Jesus' life and afterwards in his leadership of the Jerusalem church, when Jesus' saying was rewritten and updated. Its present position is the responsibility of Matthew the Evangelist, but he may have been given (secondary) reasons to put it where he did.

The other two members of the inner three, Jacob and John the sons of Zebedee, were also given an epithet, 'the sons of thunder' (Mk 3.17). It is unfortunate that the Aramaic *benē re'em*, 'sons of thunder', was transliterated into Greek so badly as to give us the English 'Boanerges', directly from Mark's *Boanē rges* printed with no gaps between the words, and this has caused scholars no end of trouble. As Collins put it mildly in the most recent enormous commentary on Mark, 'the original is difficult to reconstruct . . . Neither Matthew nor Luke includes the surname of the sons of Zebedee in the parallel passages, perhaps because it was not intelligible to their respective authors.'[22] We must start from *benē re'em*, and see what went wrong with the process of transliterating *benē re'em* into Greek letters.[23] Many bilinguals are not very good at transliterating, especially between languages which have such different alphabets as Aramaic and Hebrew, on the one hand, and Greek on the other. Mark's first problem was a *shewa*, a short noise in Aramaic and Hebrew, represented by the raised *e* in both *benē* and *re'em*. In Greek, this might be represented by a, e, or o, all short vowels. Mark must have asked someone what to do, and misunderstood their answer, because either a or o would have been all right, but oa is ridiculous. He can't have been very happy with what he put either, because when he got to the *shewa* in *re'em*, he left it out. His next problem was the Aramaic *'ayin*, in the middle of *re'em*. This is a guttural noise made at the back of the throat, which has no equivalent in Greek. It was however quite often represented with the Greek gamma, the equivalent of our 'g', and Mark followed this normal habit. He then misread the final Aramaic

---

22   A. Y. Collins, *Mark: A Commentary* (Hermeneia. Minneapolis: Fortress, 2007), p. 219.
23   Cf. Casey, *Aramaic Sources of Mark's Gospel* pp. 197–98.

'm' as an 's', a natural mistake if he was used to letters being written as they are in the Dead Sea Scrolls, natural that is if he did not recognize the Aramaic word for 'thunder'. That is also natural in a bilingual, for most bilinguals are not fully competent in both their languages, so Mark may not have recognized the Aramaic *r^e'em*, because he always called thunder *brontē* in Greek.

Two conclusions follow. First, we do know exactly what Jesus called Jacob and John. He called them *b^{e}nē r^e'em*, the normal Aramaic for 'sons of thunder'. Secondly, this is further evidence that Mark was a normal and fallible bilingual, and that he did not finish his Gospel. I have noted other evidence that it not merely lacks the ending which he intended to write, it is unrevised all the way through.[24]

It remains difficult to see *why* Jesus called Jacob and John 'sons of thunder'. We know that they saw fit to ask to sit on Jesus' right and left in his glory (Mk 10.37) and that in pursuit of this position they declared their willingness to die with him (Mk 10.38-39). John also prevented an outsider from exorcizing in Jesus' name (Mk 9.38).[25] It may be more important that they both proposed to call fire down from heaven on a Samaritan village which did not welcome them (Lk. 9.52-56). The original connotation remains however a mystery, and I have not encountered a plausible suggestion.

At his call, Simeon the Rock was fishing with Andrew his brother (Mk 1.16), and they had their own house in the small lakeside town of Capernaum (Mk 1.29-30), whether or not it was the one known as 'Peter's house'.[26] It follows that they were not peasants, but townspeople who had a successful fishing business. Like Simeon the Rock and his brother Andrew, Jacob and John were fishermen, and at their call they left their father and hired labourers (Mk 1.19-20). We must infer that they too were not peasants on the breadline, but members of a successful fishing business.

Less is known about the next two men in Mark's list of the Twelve. Philip, the second of the Twelve to have a Greek name, is also said to have come from Bethsaida (Jn 1.44; 12.21). Bartholomew represents the Aramaic 'son of Talmai', but we know nothing further about him. Thanks to a combination of 'Matthew' the Evangelist and the traditions inherited and transmitted by the early Church Father, Papias of Hierapolis, we know a lot more about Matthew, or Mattai, the next of the Twelve in Mark's list. I discussed him in Chapter 2.[27] He was a tax-collector, not a peasant on the breadline, and consequently accustomed to writing information down, legibly and accurately, on wax tablets. He made good use of his skill by writing down traditions about Jesus, mostly sayings, in Aramaic. Some of this was what we now know as 'Q' material, and it is entirely probable that some of it has survived in Greek as material special to Matthew, Mark or Luke. Since other people had to translate this material into Greek, with varied

---

24 See further pp. 74–78, 477–78.
25 See p. 253.
26 On this house, cf. Rousseau and Arav, *Jesus and his World*, pp. 40–42; Crossan and Reed, *Excavating Jesus*, pp. 129–35; on Capernaum see pp. 165–66.
27 See pp. 86–89.

results, it must be inferred that Matthew spoke only Aramaic. This may have been an important reason for him not to have left Galilee and played any other important role in the early church. This may have been true of other members of the Twelve as well, though this leaves us wondering why they did not spread the Gospel in the Aramaic-speaking diaspora. It is probable that they expected God to finally establish his kingdom at once, but such beliefs did not normally stop anyone from spreading such good news.

We know less about the next men in Mark's list too. Thomas was a Greek name. It represents the Aramaic *thōmā*, 'the twin', a description, not a name, and hence he turns up in the Fourth Gospel as 'Thomas, called Didymus' (Jn. 11.16; 20.24; 21.2), 'Didymus' being the Greek word for 'twin', as well as a name. In the Syriac-speaking church he was known as 'Judas Thomas', so Judah the twin, and this could possibly be right, even though the Syrian story that he was Jesus' own twin brother is a piece of later creative interpretation.[28] The next man in Mark's list is Jacob the son of Alphaeus. He was presumably the brother of Levi son of Alphaeus, the tax-collector who was called at Mk 2.14 but who is not listed here among the Twelve. This is another man who was not a peasant on the breadline, and both brothers are possible candidates for writing down traditions about Jesus during the historic ministry.

The next man in Mark's list is called Thaddaeus, and we know nothing else about him. One major manuscript, with some ancient support, has Lebbaeus instead, but we know nothing about that either. Luke leaves him out, and has Judah son of Jacob instead (Lk. 6.16), as at Acts 1.13, and this may well reflect a change of personnel during the ministry. Luke also has the story of Peter leading about 120 brethren in the replacement of Judas Iscariot with Matthias, quoting Ps. 109.8 (Acts 1.15-26). This shows a perceived need to maintain the fixed group of the Twelve, the choice of whom was originally made by Jesus. It is inherent in having a fixed group of Twelve that dead or renegade members must be replaced, so it may well be that Jesus was in charge of the replacement of Thaddaeus by Judah, son of Jacob, during the historic ministry, and Simeon the Rock later followed his example in organizing the replacement of Judas with Matthias. Be that as it may, nothing further is known about him either. The eleventh man in Mark's list is Simeon 'the Cananean', which represents the Aramaic *qanānā*, correctly translated by Luke as 'zealot' (Lk. 6.15; Acts 1.13). This distinguished him readily from Simeon the Rock, and from Jesus' brother Simeon. It means that he was an exceptionally keen Jew, but not necessarily violent or in any way connected with what was later a particular Zealot movement. We know nothing further about him either.

The last man in Mark's list is Judas Iscariot (*Iskariōth*, with some variations among the ancient manuscripts). This means that his name was Judah. His epithet represents the Hebrew (not Aramaic) *'īsh Keriōth*, 'man of Kerioth'. This locates him as man from a village in the very south of Judaea, and thus the only one of the Twelve known to have been from Judaea rather than Galilee. It is accordingly

---

28 Cf. Meier, *Marginal Jew*, vol. III, pp. 203–5, 255–56.

probable that he could speak and read Hebrew as well as Aramaic. His origins may have been fundamental to his decision to hand Jesus over to the chief priests, for he may have been more committed to the conventional running of the Temple than the Galilaean members of the Twelve.[29]

It is remarkable how little information we have about most of these men. Late legends more than made up for this with extensive stories. For example, as noted above, Judas Thomas was known in the Syrian churches as the twin brother of Jesus, a creative interpretation of his name *Thōmā*, the Aramaic for 'twin'. He was believed to have founded the churches of the East, especially that in the major Syriac centre of Edessa. Indian Christians told further stories about his role in the spread of the Gospel to their regions.[30] Eusebius also says that Pantaenus, who taught Clement of Alexandria (c.150–215 CE), 'is said to have gone to India, and the story goes that he found his arrival anticipated by the Gospel according to Matthew among some who knew Christ, for Bartholomew, one of the apostles, had preached to them and left them the writing of Matthew in Hebrew letters, which was preserved until the time indicated' (Eus. *H.E.* V, 10, 3). None of these stories are literally true, so they are of no further concern to this book. From our meagre information, we must infer that most of the Twelve were not major leaders in the Jerusalem church, and did not participate significantly in the Gentile mission which gradually turned the Jesus movement into what we now know as Christianity. They will have continued to live in the form of Judaism which Jesus had so vigorously recreated, and we shall see that some of them did not believe in his Resurrection (cf. Mt. 28.17).[31]

The call of the Twelve illustrates graphically the nature of Jesus' ministry: he felt called to restore Israel, to prepare the chosen people for God's final establishment of his kingdom.

7. *Women in the Historic Ministry*

It is notable that all the Twelve were men. This reflects the male-dominated society in which Jesus lived. It is doubly remarkable that Luke has a summary of his migratory ministry which continues by specifying these people with him:

> and the Twelve with him, and some women who had been healed from evil spirits and illnesses, Mary called Magdalene from whom seven devils had gone out, and Joanna wife of Chouza, Herod's steward, and Susanna and many others, who supported them from their private resources.
>
> (Lk. 8.1-3)

---

29 Cf. pp. 425–27, 439.
30 Relatively early material is summarized in Bentley Layton, *The Gnostic Scriptures* (London SCM, 1987), pp. 359–75.
31 See pp. 479–81, 495.

This indicates that these women were very important during the historic ministry. Mary Magdalene must have been very distressed for such an extreme exorcism to have been carried out, and that experience would have made her dependent on Jesus. The same must to some extent have been true of the other women whom he healed.

Mary's epithet, 'Magdalene', is at one level simple – it means that she came from Magdala, a fishing town on the western shore of the lake of Galilee.[32] Given however that this town was on the shore of the lake of Galilee, we have to ask why she was called after it, since many relatively local people came from there. Of course, since 'Mary' was the commonest woman's name in Israel, some means of distinguishing different women called Mary was necessary. Given, however, that, as we shall see, she must have been relatively wealthy, that something quite different from poverty had caused her great distress, and that she played a major role in organizing Jesus' ministry in Galilee, it is a reasonable inference that she was a locally famous woman from Magdala.

The practical support of all these women must have been extremely welcome, and fundamental to the conduct of the ministry. The description of them, providing support 'from their private resources', means that these women possessed private wealth, which they used to finance Jesus' ministry in Galilee. How far this means that they had rich husbands and/or fathers who were very supportive of the ministry too, whether some of them had inherited wealth or were rich widows, we have no idea, except in the case of Joanna.[33] The description of her husband as 'Herod's steward' means that he was a rich and important figure at Herod's court in Tiberias. Joanna herself was Jewish, as her Jewish name (spelt e.g. *Yōḥanna*) indicates. Her husband was almost certainly Nabatean, because his name, Chouza, is almost certainly Nabatean (originally therefore *Khūza*). Nabataea was a large kingdom which was partly to the east of Israel, and which stretched much further to the south. Its inhabitants were Arabs who originally spoke Aramaic, and who were significantly Hellenized by the time of Jesus. Herod Antipas' grandmother, and his wife, the daughter of the Nabatean king Aretas IV, whom he divorced to marry Herodias, and some members of his court, were all Nabatean. *Khūza* will have had to convert to Judaism when he became such an important figure in Galilee, and married a Jewish wife. He would already have been circumcised, as well as bilingual in Nabatean Aramaic and Greek.[34]

This brief report of Joanna is also important at a different level: the early church would not have been motivated to make it up. Moreover, the clear implication is that the otherwise unknown Susanna, and the much maligned Mary

---

32 On Magdala (briefly) see p. 165.

33 For the variety of ways in which ancient Jewish women could have moderate or large amounts of disposable income, without being directly dependent on support from their husbands or fathers see the fine and unprejudiced discussion of R. Bauckham, *Gospel Women: Studies of the Named Women in the Gospels* (Grand Rapids/London: Eerdmans/T&T Clark, 2002), pp. 121–35.

34 For a brief account of the Nabateans see Schürer *et al.*, *History of the Jewish People*, pp. 574–86. The view of Joanna and Chouza taken above should be regarded as established by the detailed discussion of Bauckham, *Gospel Women*, pp. 135–61.

Magdalene, were conspicuous among the women who gave massive practical support to the ministry. Neither of them played any known role in the early church either, another clear indication that Luke's tradition is accurate. Both of them must have been relatively wealthy. It is also important that there were 'many others'. These women may not have been individually as rich as Mary, Joanna and Susanna, but the cumulative effect of their various donations and work was evidently important to the practical organization of the final stages of Jesus' migratory ministry in Galilee.

The importance of some women is confirmed by the equally important report of Mark, which is placed at the crucifixion, but which refers back to their support of the ministry in Galilee:

> Now there were also women watching from afar, among whom (were) Mary Magdalene, and Mary the wife of Jacob the little and mother of Joses, and Salome, who, when he was in Galilee, used to follow him and support him, and many others who had come up with him to Jerusalem.
>
> (Mk 15.40-41)

Apart from watching the crucifixion at a distance, which itself indicates strong commitment to Jesus, most of this report reflects the same situation as that reported at Lk. 8.1-3. Mary Magdalene is again the first to be mentioned, which underlines once more her importance during the historic ministry. We know nothing about the other Mary and Salome beyond what we are told here. It means that they too not only followed Jesus, but also gave financial and other practical support to Jesus for his Galilaean ministry.

It should not be held against the authenticity of this report and Lk. 8.1-3 that they do not altogether agree as to which women they name. There are separate reasons for believing in the authenticity of each passage, as we have seen for Lk. 8.1-3. That Mark gives this information only at this point means that his information was transmitted to him by androcentric men who were not interested in narrating separately the role of women in supporting the ministry. This is probably the reason why even Mary Magdalene is not mentioned until this point in Mark's Gospel. The tradition is transmitted at this point because of the notoriously unavoidable fact that all Jesus' male disciples had fled.[35] At this point, therefore, the transmitters of Jesus traditions did need to say that the crucifixion was witnessed by Jesus' female supporters, who watched at a distance because of the obvious fact that it was too dangerous to approach any nearer. Since they had not been mentioned in the stories about the historic ministry, some explanation of who they were and what they had been doing was now necessary. That Mark and Luke, in completely independent reports, both put Mary Magdalene first, shows what a central figure she was. That they selected two different women for special mention as well merely indicates that, as both reports say, there were several of these women giving practical support to Jesus'

---

35 See pp. 439–40.

ministry in Galilee, and independent reporters might be struck by different ones. It may also be that Mary, wife of Jacob the little and mother of Joses, and Salome were selected by Mark because they watched the crucifixion, whereas Joanna and Susanna did not. Likewise, it may be that Joanna and Susanna were selected by Luke because he was especially interested in women who had been healed by Jesus, whereas Mary, wife of Jacob the little and mother of Joses, and Salome were healthy women who did not need to be healed. Be that as it may, this is a case where two independent reports may be harmonized, because both seem to be perfectly reliable.

Among the women who watched Jesus' crucifixion from a safe distance, Mark adds 'many others who had come up with him to Jerusalem' (Mk 15.41). This is also important, because it shows that Jesus had a large number of female followers, a fact of regrettably little interest to the men who transmitted the Gospel traditions. At this level, when our earliest sources say for example that 'everyone' in the synagogue was amazed at Jesus' teaching and exorcisms (Mk 1.27), or that Jesus 'began to speak to the crowds' (Mt. 11.7//Lk. 7.24), we should not imagine that only men were present.

All this evidence indicates that Jesus was emotionally and administratively more dependent on a small group of women than the Gospels tell us. It should be obvious that they were his disciples, in the normal sense of being his followers, and it should not matter that the men who wrote the Gospels do not use the word 'disciple' with specific reference to women in their very brief comments on them. A high proportion of Gospel references to 'disciples' are editorial (e.g. Mk 4.34; Mt. 12.49, inserted into Mk 3.34; Lk. 6.13, editing Mk 3.13; Jn 4.1-2), and some of those which are genuine are not obviously gender-specific (e.g. Mk 2.23). It follows that so few Gospel references to 'disciples' are genuine references to male followers of Jesus (e.g. Mk 14.12-13, 16) that genuine traditions transmitted to the Gospel writers rarely used the term 'disciple' of Jesus' male followers. Moreover, Jesus himself is reliably recorded to have used the term 'disciple' of his followers only once, in a message designed to conceal his identity, to help ensure that he could celebrate his final Passover before his arrest. Two disciples were instructed to say to a householder, 'The rabbi says, "Where (is) the place of my-spending-the-night, where I will eat the Passover with my disciples?"' (Mk 14.14).[36] Even this one example was not in practice gender-specific, though Jesus may well have deliberately used this term so that his two male disciples, arriving with the Passover victim, looked and sounded like disciples of a conventional rabbi. Normally, he did not use the term, perhaps because the Aramaic *talmīdhīn* already referred to men sitting at the feet of an orthodox rabbi learning his teaching, and was therefore not a helpful term for the followers of a prophet who was a teacher from a prophetic perspective. The Greek *mathētai*, freely used by the Gospel writers themselves, did not carry such connotations. The use of the word 'disciple' of Jesus' followers should therefore not be regarded as historically important. It was and should remain important

36   See pp. 429–30.

that lots of people followed Jesus, and that many women did so, just as much as men.

It is regrettable that the position of some of these women has been drastically exaggerated, both in the ancient world and in modern scholarship and modern fiction. The one to suffer most from posthumous fiction has been Mary Magdalene.[37] In ancient orthodox churches, she was identified with Mary of Bethany (Jn 11.1-2; 12.3-8) and the sinful woman of Lk. 7.36-50, and turned into a prostitute, who reformed when Jesus cast seven demons out of her. Among the Gnostics, she became a major revelatory figure. In the mediaeval period, there were massively varied developments in storytelling. Some developed her as a reformed prostitute, some have her as the apostle to the apostles who was a vigorous and successful evangelist after the Resurrection, whereas others portray her as having sex with Jesus, some of them presenting her as his concubine. In Dan Brown's *Da Vinci Code*, Jesus was married to her and fathered her child, Sarah.[38] Jane Schaberg argues that she was Jesus' successor. She suggests that the story of Mary's prophetic empowerment was based on 2 Kings 2 and that it is still visible in John 20, in which however it has been effectively suppressed by men. Her important position later emerged in Gnostic documents such as the Gospel of Mary.[39]

None of this is true to the memory of a remarkable woman, who was genuinely devoted to Jesus, and an important figure during his historic ministry in Galilee.

A different kind of exaggeration is found in the kind of mainstream comments by Christian scholars represented by Witherington in his standard work on women in the ministry of Jesus:

> For a Jewish woman to leave home and travel with a rabbi was not only unheard of, it was scandalous. Even more scandalous was the fact that women, both respectable and not, were among Jesus' travelling companions.[40]

This is seriously misleading. It reads back into first-century Galilee late rabbinical comments, which should not be applied to a first-century prophet who lived and moved among the ordinary people of the land. We do not know many details of Jesus' travel arrangements, especially not that women who were not

---

37 On Mary Magdalene in history and fiction, including early legends see especially B. D. Ehrman, *Peter, Paul, and Mary Magdalene: The Followers of Jesus in History and Legend* (Oxford: OUP, 2006), pp. 179–256; for more extensive discussion of secondary material see Schaberg, *Resurrection of Mary Magdalene*, summarized for the general reader in Schaberg with Johnson-Debaufre, *Mary Magdalene Understood*. On the Gospel of Mary see pp. 535–37.

38 For brief discussion of this novel see pp. 25–26.

39 Schaberg, *Resurrection of Mary Magdalene*, ch. 7: 'Mary Magdalene as Successor to Jesus'; Schaberg with Johnson-Debaufre, *Mary Magdalene Understood*, ch. 5: 'Mary Magdalene as Successor to Jesus'.

40 B. Witherington, *Women in the Ministry of Jesus: A Study of Jesus' Attitudes to Women and their Roles as Reflected in His Earthly Life* (SNTSMS 51. Cambridge: CUP, 1984), p. 117.

'respectable' were his travelling companions. We do however know that he had vigorous orthodox opponents, whose criticisms of him are transmitted by the Gospel writers, together with Jesus' answers. There is not however any evidence that women attached to him caused any scandal, nor is any kind of comment on such a matter attributed to Jesus.

Putting aside fiction and exaggeration, I conclude that Jesus' female followers were numerous and important to him. Mary Magdalene was particularly important, and other rich women were instrumental in providing for financing and other practical aspects of the organization of the ministry in Galilee. A large crowd of female followers also went up with him on his final visit to Jerusalem, and they were sufficiently committed to watch the crucifixion from a safe distance, together with Mary Magdalene, Mary the wife of Jacob the little and mother of Joses, and Salome.

8. Conclusions

The following conclusions may therefore be drawn. Jesus belonged to the Jewish prophetic tradition. This was a tradition of vigorous innovative people who preached the word of God, acted on it, and made important predictions. Some of them were involved in healing too. Much the most important prophet in recent centuries was John the Baptist, whose ministry of baptism and repentance began c.28–29 CE. This prophetic ministry is what attracted Jesus to him, and he was so impressed that he underwent John's baptism. He hailed John as a major prophet, as well as the fulfilment of Malachi's prophecy of the coming of Elijah before the day of the Lord, and of other important prophecies too. He saw himself as fulfilling John's prediction of one who would come after him. John was uncertain as to whether Jesus fulfilled this prophecy because his dramatic ministry to Israel involved more salvation and less judgement than he had expected. When he sent messengers to ask Jesus about this, Jesus responded by referring to his healing and preaching ministry, and to scriptural passages which he believed that his ministry fulfilled.

Jesus continued in the wilderness after his baptism. After John was arrested by Herod Antipas, Jesus went straight back into Galilee, Herod's territory. It is unfortunate that Mark placed his perfectly correct report of this important fact at the beginning of his account of Jesus' ministry. Partly as a result of this, and partly for lack of information available to all three evangelists, we do not know how long Jesus stayed with John, nor how long the historic ministry lasted, nor how much of it took place before that final phase.

Early in the ministry, Jesus called the Twelve, a group of followers led by Simeon the Rock. They were 12 to symbolize the restoration of the twelve tribes of Israel. They accompanied Jesus during the ministry, and he also sent them out on a migratory ministry of preaching, exorcism and healing, in Galilee. The ministry was also supported by an important group of women, who were sufficiently well off to give practical financial and organizational support to the ministry in

Galilee. The most important was Mary of Magdala. Other important named women were Joanna, wife of Herod's steward Chouza, Mary the wife of Jacob the little and mother of Joses, Salome and Susanna. These women were very important to Jesus. He also had many other followers, both male and female.

Since we do not have a chronological account of the ministry, I deal with its main points systematically in chapters 6–10, and pick up the storyline in Chapter 11, when Jesus headed for Jerusalem expecting to die an atoning death in accordance with the will of God, his heavenly Father. God was central to the whole of his life, and it is to his view of God that I turn next.

CHAPTER 6

God

1. *Introduction*

Jesus' life was centred in God. He had a vigorous prayer life, and he experienced God in action in his ministry of exorcism and healing. He expounded his view of God in his preaching with two major metaphors, the Fatherhood and kingdom, or kingship, of God. I consider these two metaphors in some detail. First, I discuss his experience of God, to put these metaphors in the context of his life. After discussing this, and his two major metaphors, I offer an Aramaic reconstruction and discussion of the Lord's Prayer. This has iconic status in Christian churches, for the very good reason that Jesus presented it as a model prayer for his disciples. I also discuss his other comments on how to pray.

2. *Jesus' Spiritual Life*

In addition to his public ministry among his fellow Jews, Jesus is reported to have gone out on his own to pray. For example, Mark reports the following, at the beginning of a narrative which fits perfectly into the migratory ministry of Jesus and which contains nothing which the early church would need to produce:

> And very early in the morning, while it was still dark, he got up and went out and went away to a deserted place, and there he prayed.
>
> (Mk 1.35)

Silent prayer was not a known custom at that time. Nonetheless, Jesus' action in leaving Simeon and Andrew's house and going out early simply to communicate with God himself all on his own is part of the evidence that he had a vigorous spiritual life which included this personal level of communication.

We have also seen that Jesus had a visionary experience when he was baptized

199

by John the Baptist.[1] This seems to have been the equivalent of the kind of call vision experienced by the major prophets. In accordance with this tradition, Jesus had vigorous spiritual experience of being inspired by God. Immediately afterwards the Spirit drove him into the wilderness, where he remained for some time being tried by Satan (Mk 1.12-13). This also reflects a major experience which presaged a main point of Jesus' ministry. He himself experienced God, and he experienced a conflict with the devil which he saw at the heart of his ministry of exorcism and healing.

Calling on people to return to God was at the centre of Jesus' public ministry, as it had been for John the Baptist. It is first mentioned at the beginning of Mark's account of the ministry. We have seen that this is not in chronological order, but that the tradition, including this summary of Jesus' preaching, is perfectly accurate:[2]

> The time is fulfilled and the kingdom of God is at hand. Repent/return and believe the good news.
>
> (Mk 1.15)

Here the Greek word translated 'repent' represents the Aramaic word *tūbh*, which also means 'return'. Jesus was not just calling on people to regret wrongs which they had done, he was calling on the people of Israel to return to God before God finally established his kingdom. The same message is presented in other ways, as for example in what is usually called the parable of the prodigal son, which might rather be called a parable of the Father's love (Lk. 15.11-32). Here the son who left home to live a dissolute life is welcomed back by his father, who forgives him and celebrates his return. This portrays in story mode the return of repentant sinners and God's forgiveness of them. This theme in Jesus' message underlines the centrality of God for him.

Exorcism and other forms of healing were central to Jesus' public ministry, so much so that I devote Chapter 7 to a detailed discussion of them. The exorcisms are a particularly dramatic example of the way in which Jesus saw God working through him. He commented:

> If I cast out demons by the finger of God, the kingship of God has come upon you.
>
> (Lk. 11.20//Mt. 12.28)

This is a direct claim to be inspired by God to successfully overcome the work of the devil.[3] A similar view is expressed with reference to other healings:

> This daughter of Abraham, whom Satan bound, look!, for *eighteen years*,

---

1   See pp. 176–77.
2   See pp. 180–81.
3   See further pp. 253–54.

(is/was) it not fitting that she should be released from this bond on the day of the sabbath?

(Lk. 13.16)

The importance of these comments lies partly in the fact that they are not *only* teaching. When Jesus performed exorcisms and other healings, he *experienced* the power of God working through him and overcoming evil. During the public ministry, these experiences were central to his life. This built on the spiritual experiences of his earlier years, when such dramatic events were not part of his life.

So strong was the hold of God's presence on Jesus' life that he sacrificed his life because he believed that this was God's will for the redemption of Israel. On the first occasion that he mentioned this, Simeon the Rock naturally tried to dissuade him. Jesus' reaction was very sharp and quite revealing:

He turned and seeing his disciples, he rebuked Peter and said, 'Get behind me, Satan, for you are not considering the (will) of God but the (affairs) of men'

(Mk 8.33)

This is not just a little unfair to Simeon. It also reveals the strength of Jesus' feelings. His forthcoming death was the will of God. Opposition to it was accordingly the work of Satan, even when it was expressed by the leader of the Twelve.

I examine the events leading up to Jesus' death in Chapter 11. We shall see that he deliberately went to Jerusalem in order to die. He deliberately cleansed the Temple, an act which was bound to lead to serious action against him. Subsequently, he deliberately waited in the Garden of Gethsemane so that he could be arrested, when he could have escaped. There he prayed to God to deliver him from his fate. The inner group of disciples transmitted the main points to the tradition, and Mark transliterated *Abba* as well as translating it:

Abba, Father, all things are possible for you. Take this cup away from me. But not what I will, but what you (will).

(Mk 14.36)

Jesus also told Simeon, Jacob and John, the inner group of disciples who were with him, that the spirit was willing but the flesh was weak (Mk 14.38). We must infer that he felt the normal fear of dying, but that his certainty that this was the Father's will led him to make the supreme sacrifice of his own life.

Jesus also saw aspects of his ministry, including his death and Resurrection, written in the scriptures. These included Ps. 41, which he referred to at the Last Supper (Mk 14.18, 21), and the second set of *Hallel* psalms, those which were set for singing at Passover (as referred to at Mk 14.26). It follows that he regarded his death as so important to God that He had inspired David to write about it in the psalms centuries previously. This is the God whom Jesus experienced as the driving force of his ministry. It follows that his experience of God drove his interpretation of these scriptures.

All this explains Jesus' response when a scribe asked him, 'Which commandment is first of all?', that is to say, the most important of all. He responded with the opening of the *Shema'*, the commandment written at Deut. 6.4-5, and said by faithful Jews every day:

> Hear, Israel, the LORD our God, the LORD is One. And you shall love the LORD your God with all your heart and with all your being and with all your might.
>
> (Deut. 6.4-5, cf. Mk 12.29-30)

The scribe completely agreed with Jesus, which reflects the centrality of God in the Judaism of the period.[4]

Similarly, when a man addressed him as 'Good rabbi', rather than just as 'Rabbi', Jesus responded: 'Why do you call me good? None is good, except the one God' (Mk 10.17-18). This again reflects the uniqueness of God to him, and in saying it Jesus was not only offering some teaching, but reflecting the goodness of God as he had perceived it working through him against Satan in his ministry of exorcism.

With all this in mind, Jesus produced a prayer especially for his disciples, which I discuss in detail at the end of this chapter. It begins with God, using Jesus' two favourite metaphors, Fatherhood and kingship, and the Lukan version implies that he began with his favourite word for God, the Aramaic *Abba*.[5]

> Father (*Abba*),
> May your name be kept holy.
> May your kingdom come (cf. Mt. 6.9-10a//Lk. 11.2)

This prayer begins with an address which assumes that God is readily approachable, and continues with words which indicate his position as infinitely the supreme being in the universe, followed by hope for the final establishment of his kingdom. This is an extraordinarily concentrated presentation of main points. Jesus' view of the movement which he sought to create within Judaism was such that he once referred to those around him as his mother and brothers, explaining,

> Whoever does the will of God, s/he is my brother and sister and mother.
>
> (Mk 3.35)

This further intensifies the centrality of God to him.

As a faithful Jew, Jesus observed the major festivals. This was so unremarkable

---

4　See further pp. 424–25.

5　On *Abba* see further pp. 204–12; and on the Lord 's Prayer, pp. 226–33, where I explain all my divergences from Matthew and/or Luke.

that we have specific and reliable information only about his final Passover. I discuss this event in Chapter 11. The feast itself celebrated God's mighty act in delivering Israel from Egypt. We shall see that Jesus took steps to ensure that he celebrated the actual Passover meal before his arrest. He then interpreted some of the main elements of the meal in terms of his forthcoming death. This again shows the combination of a free and open prophetic relationship with God together with a vigorous concept of his mighty power.

Two of Jesus' parables appear to be directed entirely at presenting the fundamental importance of the kingdom, or kingship, of God. To see what Jesus said, we must turn Matthew's editorial 'kingdom of heaven' back into 'kingdom of God':[6]

> The kingdom of God is like a treasure hidden in a/the field. When a man found it, he hid it, and out of joy he went away and sold all that he had and bought that field.
>
> (Mt. 13.44, cf. Mt. 13.45-46)

This is so concerned to make the main point that the kingdom of God is more valuable than anything else that it does not even pause to clarify the morality of the man's action. The Greek definite article with 'field' represents an Aramaic definite state, and the early church does not seem to have been interested in creating parables like this. We must infer that the parable is genuine teaching of Jesus. This presentation of the importance of God's kingship further underlines the centrality of God himself.

The centrality and power of God are further illustrated by Jesus' reasons for believing in resurrection. He accused some Sadducees, who had asked him an awkward question because they did not believe in the resurrection, of not knowing the scriptures or the power of God (Mk 12.18-27). His single argument was based on God's scriptural declaration, 'I am the God of Abraham and the God of Isaac and the God of Jacob' (Exod. 3.6 at Mk 12.26). Jesus himself glossed this, 'He is not God of the dead but of the living' (Mk 12.27). For Jesus, that was sufficient. His conviction that God was the God of the living was so strong that it showed that Abraham, Isaac and Jacob were alive in heaven, and this was sufficient indication that people in general would survive death.[7]

It follows that Jesus had an exceptionally intense spiritual life, in which he believed that God worked powerfully through him, both doing positive good and defeating the devil. It is natural therefore that people who believed themselves to be possessed of demons should have recoiled from the presence of God in him. They referred to him as 'the holy one of God' (Mk 1.24, in a narrative) and perhaps as 'the son of God' (Mk 3.11, in a Markan summary). In first-century Judaism, these two terms were similar in meaning: 'son of God' meant generally that God approved of him and that he was fulfilling his vocation as a faithful Jew

---

6 On the reasons for this change see pp. 213–14.
7 On this incident see further pp. 423–24.

in obedience to God.[8] Both terms accordingly indicate external descriptions of him by people who felt his power, power based on his own experience of God.

We must therefore conclude that Jesus' view of God was a central facet of his life experience, not only a matter of his teaching. As a major prophet, he taught extensively about God as well. For this purpose he used two major images or metaphors, the Fatherhood and Kingdom, or Kingship, of God. Both these images have been distorted by later Christian belief in his position as the incarnate Son of God, the second person of the Trinity, and by Christian belief in the reality of the kingdom, usually seen in the church, and in the infallibility of Jesus. I propose to set aside later tradition, and see Jesus' use of these two images in the context of first century Judaism.

3. *The Fatherhood of God*

It is usually accepted that the Fatherhood of God was central to the teaching of Jesus. It has recently become controversial, on account of two quite different approaches to it. These two approaches have in common that they are based on people's existential situations in the modern world, and consequently both have produced serious distortions of the teaching of Jesus.

The first of these approaches was, and remains, a traditional Christian concern to show that Christianity is superior to Judaism. In his still standard 1933 article on *Abba*, the Aramaic word for Father used by Jesus to address God at Mk 14.36, the Nazi Christian scholar Gerhard Kittel put this succinctly:

> He applies to God a term which must have sounded familiar and disrespectful to His contemporaries because used in the everyday life of the family . . . Jewish usage shows how this Father-child relationship to God far surpasses any possibilities of intimacy assumed in Judaism, introducing indeed something which is wholly new.[9]

This approach was carried further by the influential research of Jeremias, which was centred on the Aramaic word *Abba*.[10] Jeremias became so overexcited at the time that he was later constrained to withdraw what became one of his most famous contentions, popularized in a form which he himself never used, that *Abba* was the equivalent of 'Daddy'. He commented on 'the mistaken assumption that Jesus adopted the language of a tiny child', admitting 'even I believed this earlier.'[11] James Barr later became famous for the title as well as the contents of

8   See further pp. 388–92.
9   G. Kittel, 'ἀββᾶ', *Theological Dictionary of the New Testament*, vol. 1 (1933. Trans. G. W. Bromiley. Grand Rapids: Eerdmans, 1964), p. 6.
10 J. Jeremias, *The Prayers of Jesus* (1966. Trans. J. Bowden. London: SCM, 1967), pp. 11–65.
11 J. Jeremias, *New Testament Theology*, vol. 1, *The Proclamation of Jesus* (Trans. J. Bowden. London: SCM, 1971), p. 67.

his decisive article '*Abba* isn't "Daddy"'.[12] Jeremias himself, despite admitting that he had gone too far, nonetheless continued to maintain on the very same page:

> It would have seemed disrespectful, indeed unthinkable, to the sensibilities of Jesus' contemporaries to address God with this familiar word. Jesus dared to use '*Abba* as a form of address to God.

This comment continues the very sharp distinction between addressing God and talking about him which neither Jeremias nor anyone else ever justified. Nonetheless, his research was not only influential in itself, it was also used to justify traditional Christian belief that Jesus was the Son of God in a special sense. For example, Dunn commented in 1991:

> . . . in scholarly circles there is a widespread agreement that *Jesus probably did indeed see himself as God's son, or understood himself in relationship to God as son.* In terms of historical critical analysis the point is most securely based on the tradition of Jesus' prayer to God using the Aramaic form of address 'Abba' ('Father').[13]

The second ideologically conditioned approach is that of feminism. It is entirely natural that vigorous intellectual women should be dismayed by the male domination characteristic of Christian churches. Some have left Christianity altogether, or proposed very serious modifications to it. For example, in 1990 Daphne Hampson made the following comments:

> The question which feminism poses for Christianity is . . . whether Christianity is ethical. That is to say, is it not the case that a religion in which the Godhead is represented as male, or central to which is a male human being, necessarily acts as an ideology which is biased against half of humanity? Is it not the case that such religion is by its very nature harmful to the cause of human equality? That is a serious charge against Christianity . . .[14]

Such comments are entirely proper, and do not entail, or even necessarily encourage, distortions of the teaching of Jesus.

Problems can however arise when feminists need to present Jesus as on their side. This is the point at which they may share the major fault of the quest of the historical Jesus, that of distorting the teaching of Jesus in the direction of one's own social subgroup. For example, reacting to the traditional concerns of the male scholars illustrated above, Mary d'Angelo declared that '*Abba* cannot be shown to have been unique to Jesus, characteristic of Jesus, or even to have been

---

12 J. Barr, '*Abba* isn't "Daddy"', JThS NS 39 (1988), pp. 28–47.
13 J. D. G. Dunn, *The Partings of the Ways Between Christianity and Judaism and their Significance for the Character of Christianity* (London: SCM, 1991), pp. 169–70.
14 D. Hampson, *Theology and Feminism* (Oxford: Blackwell, 1990), p. 53.

used by Jesus'. Again, she argued that '"father" as an address to God cannot be shown to originate with Jesus, to be particularly important to his teaching, or even to have been used by him. If indeed "father" was used by Jesus, the context is less likely to be familial intimacy than resistance to the Roman imperial order.'[15]

The way in which both these approaches have treated the teaching of Jesus may be considered to involve an overliteral view of theological language. As we approach Jesus' teaching about the Fatherhood of God, we should look for *his understanding of God* in the light of *Jewish* tradition about *God*: we should not look for his view of fatherhood, or more general Jewish views of fatherhood, let alone our own views of fatherhood, and assume we can apply any of that to Jesus' view of God.

The Fatherhood of God was a well-established image in the Hebrew Bible. For example, when David was already anointed king over Israel, Nathan the prophet announced in God's name that David's successor would build God's house, commenting,

> I will establish the throne of his kingdom forever. I will be a father to him, and he will be a son to me.
>
> (2 Sam 7.13-14)

This declares the Fatherhood of God and the sonship of the king as simply as possible. The sonship of Israel as a whole is declared equally straightforwardly. The prophet Jeremiah looked forward to the return of a remnant of Israel, attributing to God the words:

> I have become father to Israel, and Ephraim is my firstborn.
>
> (Jer. 31.9)

Another major prophet, known to us only as 'Second Isaiah', associated the Fatherhood of God directly with the redemption of Israel:

> You, YHWH, our Father, our Redeemer from of old your name.
>
> (Isa. 63.16)

At the time of Jesus, passages such as these were part of the sacred text of the Jewish people.

The image of the Fatherhood of God was also a live one, which Jewish people continued to use. A fine example of metaphor and simile is to be found in the Dead Sea Scrolls:

> And your just/righteous rebuke (is) with my [faults],
> and your safeguarding peace delivers my soul.

---

15 M. R. D'Angelo, '*Abba* and "Father": Imperial Theology and the Jesus Traditions', *JBL* 111 (1992), pp. 611–30 (616, 630).

And with my steps (is) abundance of forgiveness,
and a multitude of [comp]assion (is) in your judgement of me.
And until old age you will care for me,
for my father did not know me,
and my mother abandoned me to you.
For you (are) Father to all [the sons] of your truth,
and you rejoice over them
like her who loves her baby,
and as a foster-parent with a child in their lap,
you care for all your creatures.

(1QH XVII (=IX), 33–36)

This is a complex picture in which God is compared to a mother and a foster parent, with the words 'like' and 'as'. The metaphor of fatherhood was however so much better established that the author uses the blunter 'you (are) Father to all [the sons] of your truth', effectively portraying God as the father of all faithful Jews.

This usage continued in Judaism after the time of Jesus. One later source has it in the particular context of the intentions of faithful Jews in prayer:

The pious ones (*ḥasīdīm*) of old used to spend an hour before praying to direct their heart to the Father who (is) in heaven.

(m. Ber V, 1)

It follows from evidence of this kind that 'Father' was a normal term for first-century Jews to use when they talked to, and about, God.

'My Father' could also be used as an address to God, without any suggestion that the person so addressing God was more closely attached to him than other faithful Jews were:

My Father and my God, do not abandon me into the hands of the gentiles; do me justice so that the poor and the afflicted may not perish. You do not need any nation or people for any help; [your fin]ger is greater and stronger than anything in the world.

Prayer of Joseph (4Q 372, frg 1, 16–18)

It was therefore natural that Jesus should use this image too. It is commoner in teaching attributed to him than in non-Christian Jewish sources. His very success in recreating this image has however left a problem for the historian. Some of his followers responded to it so well that they used it themselves, with the result that many examples are secondary, especially in Matthew. For example, Jesus told Jacob and John that they would share his fate of a martyr's death, but that he could not grant their request to sit on his right and left in his glory. Mark puts this in rather unsatisfactory Greek because he was translating literally an Aramaic source which may reasonably be translated into English as follows:

but to sit on my right or left is not mine to give, except to those for whom it
has been prepared (cf. Mk 10.40).

Here it would be culturally obvious that these places were prepared by God.[16]
Matthew felt he had better say so, and added his favourite image to give 'but
for whom it has been prepared by my Father' (Mt. 20.23). For such reasons, a
number of examples of the Fatherhood of God must be attributed to the evangelists, and these probably include all examples of 'my Father'.

Genuine sayings of Jesus portray a supreme being who watches carefully over
people, expects to be obeyed and forgives those who repent. One saying tries
to direct people's attention away from the cares of life to the centrality of God,
using the term 'kingdom' as well as 'Father'.

> Do not worry, saying 'What are we to eat?', or 'What are we to drink?', or
> 'What are we to wear?', for all these things the nations seek. For your Father
> knows that you need these things. But seek his kingdom, and these things
> will be added to you.
>
> (Mt. 6.31-32//Lk. 12.29-31)

Here the contrast with the Gentiles reflects God's perceived position as especially
the Father of Israel. As such, he will see to their basic needs, while they should
seek him. Another saying in Matthew rejects Gentile prayer habits, and again
makes it clear that God the Father watches over Israel:

> When you pray, do not babble like the Gentiles, for they think that they will
> be heard through speaking lots of words. Do not be like them, for your Father
> knows what you need before you ask him.
>
> (Mt. 6.7-8)

Another saying argues by analogy from human fatherhood to divine care. The
Matthaean version shows fewer signs of secondary editing, except in the omission of Luke's v. 12:

> Which man of you, whom his son asks for bread, will give him a stone? Or
> he asks for a fish, will give him a snake? If you, being evil, know how to give
> good gifts to your children, how much more will your Father in heaven give
> good things to those who ask him.
>
> (Mt. 7.9-11, cf. Lk. 11.11-13)

A Markan saying uses the Fatherhood of God to assure repentant sinners that
their sins are forgiven, with the underlying assumption that we should imitate
God.

16   For discussion of the whole passage see pp. 404–5.

And when you stand praying, forgive, if you have anything against anyone, so that your Father who is in heaven may forgive your transgressions.

(Mk 11.25)

I have noted the parable of the prodigal son (Lk. 15.11-32). Here the central character is really the Father, who welcomes back his dissolute son when he returns, a portrayal of the Aramaic word *tūbh*, which means to repent as well as to return. God as Father is thus presented consistently as caring for his people and forgiving them, in material of very different kinds.

It is natural that in these circumstances Jesus should overtly urge people to take upon themselves some of the qualities of God. The Lukan version of one saying has a parallel in Jewish sources (e.g. Tg. Ps-J Lev. 22.28), and this is most likely to be what Jesus said:

Be merciful, as your Father is merciful.

(Lk. 6.36, cf. Mt. 5.48)

What Jesus urged upon repentant sinners, he also used in direct and indirect attacks upon his opponents. One such passage concerns almsgiving. Jesus was in favour of almsgiving in itself, but opposed to the outward display with which it was done by rich people. His comments use the Greek term *hupokritēs* in its original Greek sense of 'actor' rather than 'hypocrite', and make fun of customs not fully known to us, perhaps blowing trumpets for fast days (already Joel 2.15) and giving alms in response to this.

Take care not to do your righteousness before people so as to be seen by them – otherwise, you have no reward with your Father who (is) in heaven. When you do almsgiving, do not sound a trumpet before you as the actors (*hupocritai*) do in the synagogues and in the streets, so that they may be glorified by people: amen I'm telling you, they have their reward. But you, when you do almsgiving, do not let your left hand know what your right hand is doing, so that your almsgiving (may be) in secret, and your Father who sees in secret will reward you.

(Mt. 6.1-4)

Jesus' use of the term 'Father' as an image of God was accordingly substantial and extensive. We have seen that his use of the Aramaic form *Abba* has been thought to be especially important, but that both this claim and its significance are now controversial.[17] The Aramaic word *Abba* is preserved, transliterated into Greek letters, in the Greek text of Mk 14.36; Rom. 8.15; Gal. 4.6, so in three documents written in Greek for Greek-speaking churches. It follows that the term *Abba* was very important to the churches in the earliest period, and this can only be because Christians believed it to be a significant link between Jesus'

17 See pp. 204–6.

prayer life and their own. This should be regarded as enough to establish the fact that Jesus' use of *Abba* was important during the historic ministry, and that he expected his disciples to use it as he did. It is therefore appropriate that it should have been the first word in the Lord's Prayer. This must be inferred from Luke's version, which begins with the simple term 'Father' (Lk. 11.2), for which *Abba* is the only Aramaic term that can reasonably be reconstructed. Matthew's 'Our Father in heaven' is a natural expansion in accordance with Jewish custom. It has been thought important that 'Father', and therefore 'Abba', is the only way in which Jesus is recorded to have addressed God (except Mk 15.34//Mt. 27.46, where he is quoting scripture).[18] It must however be doubtful whether any further examples in the Gospels are genuine sayings of Jesus, and he is bound to have addressed God with expressions such as 'Our Father, our King', when he took part in prayers in the synagogue. There are no sayings in which he offers any criticism of conventional Jewish ways of addressing God, and his vigorous and outspoken opponents are never recorded as criticizing his use of *Abba*. In his parable of the Pharisee and the tax-collector, *both* characters begin their prayer with the simple address 'God' (Lk. 18.11, 13). We must therefore consider Jesus' use of *Abba* as part of his experience of God and teaching about God, and cease to regard the way he addressed God as more important than other aspects of his view of God.

In Jewish Aramaic, *Abba* was a normal term for 'father'. While it may once have been used as an onomatopoeic word by small children, an approximate equivalent of the English 'daddy', any such origins had long since been left behind. While it was used by children, it was so used because it was everyone's normal term for 'father'. So, for example, Esau, when grown-up, is represented in one of the Aramaic translations of Genesis as using *Abba* in respectful address to his father, Isaac:

> Let father (*Abba*) arise and eat from his son's game, so that your soul may bless me.
>
> (Targum Neof I, at Gen. 27.31)

Consequently, *Abba* is found in later rabbinical literature not only as a term for one's natural father, but also as a term of respect for other elderly men. One such man was Abba Hilkiah, grandson of Honi the Circle-drawer, and an approximate contemporary of Jesus. Jesus objected to this usage, in a saying which barely makes sense except in the original Aramaic, and which cannot be satisfactorily reconstructed in Aramaic except by putting *Abba* for the Matthew's first use of 'father' (*patera*). The best I can do to translate a reasonable Aramaic reconstruction into English is this:

---

18   E.g. Jeremias, *Proclamation of Jesus*, p. 66, followed with slight qualification e.g. by J. D. G. Dunn, *Jesus and the Spirit: A Study of the Religious and Charismatic Experience of Jesus and the First Christians as Reflected in the New Testament* (London: SCM, 1975), pp. 22–24.

And *Abba* do not call for you (anyone) on earth, for your Father in heaven is one.

> (Mt. 23.9)

This saying was addressed to grown-up disciples, so that the use of this term by children to address their natural fathers will not have been brought to mind. Jesus was rather criticizing the use of *Abba* as a term of respect for older men, and in this he did diverge from normal Jewish usage.

Other Jewish use of *Abba* as a term for God is rare enough to confirm that Jesus' usage was unusual, but its very existence shows that he recreated the Fatherhood of God from a prophetic perspective, he did not invent an understanding proper only to the second person of the Trinity:

> When the world needed rain, the rabbis used to send school-children to him [Hanan], and they seized the train of his cloak and said to him, 'Abba, Abba, give us rain'. He said to the Holy One, Blessed be He, 'Master of the universe, do this for those who do not distinguish between *Abba* who gives rain and *Abba* who does not give rain'.
>
> (b. *Ta'anith* 23b)

The central character in this passage is another charismatic figure, Hanan, another grandson of Honi the Circle-drawer, described by Josephus as 'a righteous man and dear to God' (*Ant.* XIV, 22). In the first place, the passage establishes the use of *Abba* as an address to an older man by children, at about the time of Jesus, and probably in Galilee. Secondly, confronted with nothing more devastating than children calling him *Abba*, Hanan, having like Jesus inherited the tradition of using Fatherhood as an image of God, could simply refer to him as '*Abba* who gives rain'. This is not the same as the usage of Jesus, but it indicates that this was a possible development for an original and charismatic figure to make.

We have seen that Jesus addressed God as Father, with the Aramaic word *Abba*, at the major crisis of his life, when he waited in the Garden of Gethsemane to be arrested:

> *Abba*, all things are possible for you. Take this cup away from me. But not what I will, but what you (will) (cf. Mk 14.36)

This confirms the intensity of Jesus' religious life, and the importance of the image of Fatherhood in the relationship with God which is reflected in his teaching.

All this sets Jesus firmly inside Judaism, a culture in which the Fatherhood of God was already a central image. At the same time, his appreciation and teaching of the Fatherhood of God was part of his vigorous recreation of Jewish identity, which inspired the tradition to inherit, recreate and expand this material. The use of '*Abba*, Father' in the Pauline churches (Rom. 8.15; Gal. 4.6) shows how important Jesus' use of the image of the Fatherhood of God was to the churches in the earliest period of the Gentile mission. Matthew especially extended the use of the Fatherhood of God for Greek-speaking churches. Like Luke, however, he dropped *Abba* from Mk 14.36 (Mt. 26.39//Lk. 22.42). This dropping of a particular word, combined with the expansion of Jesus' teaching, shows how profoundly Matthew recreated the teaching of Jesus for his own Greek-speaking community. We are accordingly fortunate that sufficient evidence has survived for us to recover the teaching of Jesus himself, and see that it was in fact he who refashioned this image of God as he sought to recreate Judaism from his prophetic perspective.

4. *The Kingdom of God*

The other major term which Jesus used of God was his kingdom, or kingship. The Hebrew and Aramaic word *malkūth* means both a kingdom, a land ruled by a king, and abstract kingship, the power of a ruler. Some of Jesus' parables seem concerned to say only that the kingdom of God was of central importance. I have noted Mt.13.44 (again replacing Matthew's 'kingdom of heaven' with Jesus' normal expression 'kingdom of God'):[19]

> The kingdom of God is like a treasure hidden in a/the field. A man found it and hid it, and out of his joy he went away and sold all he had and bought that field.

Since this term permeates the teaching of Jesus, and since it is so much commoner in his teaching than in other surviving Jewish texts, it is remarkable that Jesus never explains what he means by the kingdom/kingship of God. This can only mean that, however unusual his teaching about it may have been, his concept of the kingdom/kingship of God was conventional. I therefore begin with Jewish sources, which tell us what was so obvious to Jesus' audiences that he did not need to say it, and/or the Gospel writers did not need to transmit it.

In Jewish texts, the kingship of God indicates the divine status of superiority, and divine functions of power and rule. In the Hebrew Bible, it is generally referred to with the term 'king' rather than 'kingdom' or 'kingship', but this seems to make no difference, as in the following passage:

> For YHWH the Most High is awesome, a great king over all the earth. He subdues peoples under us, and nations under our feet.
>
> (Ps. 47.2-3)

The kingship of God could be perceived in particular events of the present time. There is a striking biblical example of this in the behaviour of the Babylonian king Nebuchadnezzar, who was healed of a serious mental illness. He is portrayed as recalling his reaction at the time:

---

19   On the reasons for this change see pp. 213–14.

And I blessed the Most High, and praised and honoured the One who lives for ever. His sovereignty is eternal sovereignty, and his kingdom/kingship (*malkūth*) from generation to generation . . . Now I Nebuchadnezzar praise and extol and honour the King of Heaven. All his deeds are truth, and his ways justice, and he can bring low those who walk in pride.

(Dan. 4.34, 37)

Several points are worth noting here. First, both 'kingdom/kingship (*malkūth*)' and 'king' are used in the same passage with reference to God's status, power and action. Secondly, what is celebrated is God's eternal position as King, which he always has had, has now, and always will have. Thirdly, he can be referred to as 'King of Heaven', a realm where he is always adored and obeyed. Fourthly, God's kingship is here celebrated because of his recent action in healing a person on earth in the present time.

Such personal appropriation of the kingship of God is further developed in rabbinical literature. This literature was written after the time of Jesus, but this way of using this metaphor was probably available much earlier:

From where (do we know that) a man shall not say, 'I do not want garments of mixed fabric, I do not want to eat pig's flesh, I do not want incestuous sex', but 'I want (these things), and my Father who is in heaven has forbidden them to me'? Thus Scripture teaches, 'and I have separated you from the nations, to be mine' (Lev. 20.26). He is found keeping away from transgression, and taking upon himself the kingdom/kingship (*mlkūth*) of heaven.

(Siphra, 93d)

This passage also uses the Fatherhood of God, as Jesus did. It uses 'kingdom/ kingship of heaven' rather than 'of God', as Matthew usually does. The term is used with reference to the faithful Jew's complete submission to his Father in heaven, because of which he obeys his commandments.

There is no significant difference in meaning between 'kingdom of heaven' and 'kingdom of God'. Matthew will have usually altered 'kingdom of God' to 'kingdom of heaven' because 'kingdom of heaven' was the term most used in his environment. It is often supposed that the reason for the use of 'heaven' rather than 'God' in passages like this, and in Matthew's Gospel, is that Jews avoided the name of God out of reverence. In a regrettably influential discussion, Dalman argued that Jesus himself used 'kingdom of heaven'. He suggested that 'Mark and Luke, out of regard to heathen readers, avoided the specifically Jewish expression' [i.e. kingdom of heaven], whereas 'Jesus will have preferred the popular expression [i.e. kingdom of heaven] because He also readily abstained from the use of the divine name.'[20] This is a serious mistake, which scholars should stop repeating.[21] God's name was YHWH, which most scholars believe was pronounced as

20   G. Dalman, *The Words of Jesus, Considered in the Light of Post-biblical Jewish Writings and the Aramaic Language* (1898. Trans. D. M. Kay. Edinburgh: T&T Clark, 1902), pp. 93–94.

21   Among fine scholars who do not repeat this are Davies and Allison, who conclude correctly,

'Yahweh'. Jews did avoid this divine name. It was supposed to be pronounced only by the high priest on Yom Kippur, when he quoted Lev. 16.30:

> 'For on this day atonement shall be made for you to cleanse you. From all your sins, before YAHWEH you shall be clean.' And the priests and the people who were standing in the Temple Court, when they heard the pronounced Name come out of the mouth of the High Priest, used to kneel and bow down and fall on their faces and say, 'Blessed be the name of the glory of his kingdom for ever and ever.'
>
> (m. Yoma 6, 2)

That this should be narrated in a collection of regulations, written down more than a century after the destruction of the Temple, shows how awesomely God's name was kept holy.

After the destruction of the Temple, no one was supposed to pronounce the name of God, and it is found only in magical papyri where people used it because they believed in its power. This has nothing to do with the word 'God' itself, which is a description of the supreme being, not his name, and which continued in normal use. Hence for example, the book of Daniel refers to 'the God of heaven' (e.g. Dan. 2.36), and Jesus himself is always represented in our earliest and most accurate sources as saying 'kingdom/kingship of God'.

When heaven is described, terms such as 'kingdom' may be used to describe God's rule/realm up there, as in the following example:

> These are the chiefs of those wondrously clothed for service, the chiefs of the kingdom/realm (*mmlkūth*), the kingdom (*mmlkūth*) of the holy ones of the King of holiness in all the heights of the sanctuaries of the kingdom (*mlkūth*) of his glory.
>
> (*Songs for the Holocaust of the Sabbath*, 4Q405 23 ii.10–12)

The chiefs described here are the senior angels, clothed for the service of God. Here the term 'kingdom' refers to the heavenly realm, where God is always king. The particular occasion for celebrating it is the service of God on the sabbath, which also makes it obvious that he exercises his kingship in the present time.

On earth, however, God's kingship did not always appear to hold sway. At the time of Jesus, this was especially obvious in Roman control over Israel. Israel being ruled by polytheistic pagans was not consistent with the kingship of God on earth. Many Jews also believed that some people were possessed by demons, the servants of Satan, and this was not consistent with the kingship of God over everyone's lives. Many Jews hoped that God would finally establish his kingdom on earth soon. This hope could be seen in the biblical text, which could readily

---

'All this leads us to think of "kingdom of heaven" as nothing more than a stylistic variant of "kingdom of God"' (*Matthew*, vol. 1, p. 392).

be updated from its original reference to Greek rulers to the Romans who ruled Israel at the time of Jesus.

> And in the days of those kings the God of Heaven will set up a kingdom (*malkū*) which (is) for ever. It shall never be destroyed, and the kingdom (*malkūthāh*) will not be released to another people. It will crush and bring to an end all these kingdoms, and it will stand for ever.
>
> (Dan. 2.44)

Here the kingdom of God which is to be set up is also the kingdom of the Jewish people, which is the point of the statement 'the kingdom will not be released to another people'. This is all the clearer in Daniel 7, where 'the people of the holy ones of the Most High' can only be the people of Israel:

> And the kingship (*malkūthāh*) and the dominion and the greatness of the kingdoms under all the heavens shall be given to the people of the holy ones of the Most High. His/its/their kingdom (*malkūthēh*) (is/shall be) an eternal kingdom (*malkūth*), and all dominions will serve and obey Him/them.
>
> (Dan. 7.27)

If this was reapplied to the time of Jesus, as the scriptures generally were at the time, it was bound to mean that the Romans would be driven out of Israel and made subject to the Jewish people. Nothing like this is ever explicitly stated in the teaching of Jesus. If however he made quite simple statements such as 'the kingdom of God is at hand' (cf. Mk 1.15), he is not likely to have imagined that the Romans would be left in charge of Israel. Moreover, whatever he himself actually meant, and however much he believed in the action of God rather than armies, hostile opponents would have no difficulty persuading the Roman governor that he was preaching the downfall of the Roman empire.

A notable Jewish prayer for deliverance is the *Qaddish*. It is certainly an Aramaic prayer from the ancient period, and its rather close parallel to the opening petitions of the Lord's Prayer, which it cannot possibly be based upon, shows that an ancient version of it was older than the time of Jesus, and known to him:

> May his great name be exalted and kept holy in the world which he created according to his will. May he let his kingdom (*mlkūthēh*) rule in your lifetime and in your days and in the lifetime of the whole house of Israel, speedily and in the near time. Amen.[22]

This is an unambiguous prayer for the final establishment of God's kingdom.

---

22 It is regrettable that the texts of such documents are not more readily available. This one may be found in the useful collection of material in C. A. Evans, *Jesus and His Contemporaries: Comparative Studies* (AGJU XXV. Leiden: Brill, 1995), ch. VI: 'Jesus and Rabbinic Parables, Proverbs and Prayers', pp. 283–84.

The repeated temporal indications are especially important: 'in your lifetime and in your days', 'speedily and in the near time'. This means that a dramatic event was hoped for in the near future.

These expectations arose from the very unsatisfactory situation in which Israel was oppressed by foreign nations, and from faith in God, who was accordingly expected to deliver Israel. In Daniel 7, before the prophecy of the final establishment of God's kingdom, the author(s) provided details of a hostile king known to us as Antiochus Epiphanes, but not named in the text. He would among other things 'speak words against the Most High, and wear out the holy ones of the Most High.' They knew that much from their own experience, and they predicted that they 'will be given into his hand for a time and two times and half a time' (Dan. 7.25), by which they meant 3½ years. The author(s) expressed themselves differently at the beginning of Daniel 12. Here they predicted that 'at that time' Michael who 'stands up for the sons of your people' would arise, and 'there will be a time of distress such as there shall not be from the time when there was a nation until that time' (Dan. 12.1). Then the people would be delivered, 'and many who sleep in a land of earth shall awake, some to eternal life, and others to reproach, to abhorrence for ever' (Dan. 12.2). The time of distress in Chapter 12 fits perfectly well with the predictions of the persecution of Antiochus Epiphanes in Chapter 7. Both were present events to the real authors, so a consistent description was not difficult. The final authors, however, made no attempt to achieve consistency in their significantly different predictions, one of which has the kingdom 'given to the people of the holy ones of the Most High', while the other has the resurrection of many of the dead.

The problem with predictions of this kind is that life may not turn out as predicted. What happened in this case was the Maccabaean victory. The armed forces of Israel, led by Judas Maccabaeus, defeated the Greek forces of Antiochus Epiphanes, drove them out of Israel and rededicated the Temple. This was after three, not three and a half years, and there was no resurrection of the dead. Between them, Jewish interpreters of Daniel had two different approaches to this situation. One was to suppose that the prophecies were fulfilled in the Maccabaean victory, an interpretation which later became dominant in the Syriac-speaking churches.[23] The prophecies of Dan. 7 were not difficult to interpret in this way. For example, part of St Ephraem's comment on Dan. 7.26-27 reads:

> To destroy and slay Antiochus . . . who oppressed and persecuted them, the zealots of the house of Maccabees. He removed him from life because of his wickedness, and to them he gave dominion and greatness.

Resurrection in Dan. 12 might be expected to be more difficult, but interpreters of prophecies in which they believe perform wondrous feats of interpretation.

---

23 On this see P. M. Casey, *Son of Man: The Interpretation and Influence of Daniel 7* (SPCK, 1980), ch. 3, 'The Syrian Tradition'. This includes details of where to find the texts, some of which are difficult to obtain in the original languages, and not available in any English translation.

For example, the Church Father Polychronius comments on Michael arising at Dan. 12.1:

> The angel's help was shown above all in the battles in which Judas Maccabaeus was victorious in the struggle against the generals of Antiochus.

At Dan. 12.2, Isho'dad of Merw comments on those who sleep in the dust:

> Those who lie prostrate with misfortunes, laid low by adversities, that is, the Maccabees.

On the two groups who would rise from the dead, he comments:

> Because of their endurance and righteousness they will enjoy life in both worlds, and in all generations the living will honour them with excellent memory . . . The wicked priests who led people astray will be put to death because of their wickedness, and they will have an evil and shameful reputation among their fellows for ever.

A different approach was to suppose that the sacred text predicted different events still in the future. By the time of Jesus, this approach had already affected people in Israel and the West, where it became the dominant tradition.[24] This involved updating the prophecies of Dan. 7 completely. For example, whereas the fourth kingdom was the Greek, and its most hostile king the unnamed Antiochus Epiphanes, Jerome comments on these:

> The fourth, which now rules over the world, is the empire of the Romans . . . . This concerns Antichrist, that is, the little horn which spoke great things, for his kingdom is to be destroyed for ever.
>
> (Jerome, *On Daniel*, at 7.7, 26)

There was no need to alter the 3½ years, and 'the holy ones of the Most High' could include Christians as well as ancient Jews, who would triumph at the time of the final judgement:

> For 'the time has come' means that the whole of time was fulfilled 'and the saints will receive the kingdom', when the Judge of Judges and King of Kings shall come from heaven, remove all the dominion and power of the Adversary and punish all the wicked by burning them up with eternal fire, but to his servants, prophets, martyrs and all those who fear him, he will give eternal sovereignty.
>
> (Hippolytus, *On Daniel* IV, 14, 3)

---

24 See P. M. Casey, *Son of Man: The Interpretation and Influence of Daniel 7*, ch. 4: 'The Western Tradition'. This also includes details of where to find the texts.

In Dan. 12, this approach had to alter the time originally intended by 'at that time' in Dan. 12.1, and could then continue with the resurrection of the dead in the future. For example, Jerome interprets the beginning of Dan. 12.1 'at the time of Antichrist', and then paraphrases the text on the resurrection of the dead.

Sometimes, people realized that what they expected had not happened, and continued to expect it, without any change to what they expected. A classic example of this faithful Jewish reaction is found in the Qumran commentary on the book of Habakkuk:

> 'For yet a vision for the appointed time. It will tell of the End and it will not lie' (Hab. 2.3a). Its interpretation is that the final age will be prolonged and exceed all that the prophets have said, for the mysteries of God are wonderful. 'If it tarries, wait for it, for it will surely come and not delay' (Hab. 2.3b). Its interpretation concerns the men of truth who do the Law, whose hand will not slacken in the service of truth when the final age is prolonged upon them. For all the ages of God reach their appointed end as He has determined for them in the mysteries of his prudence.
>
> (1QpHab VII, 5–14)

These are three different ways in which faithful Jews responded to situations in which their predictions were not fulfilled, and all were inherited by early Christians. They have in common continued faith in God, because that is what the predictions were based on in the first place.

People have found some of this material paradoxical, and most scholarship which has tried to understand Jesus' teaching in the light of it has failed to understand some part of it. It should however be regarded as perfectly consistent when understood in terms of ancient Jewish culture, rather than later tradition. Jews at the time of Jesus believed that God is permanently king of the whole universe. He reigns in his kingdom in heaven now, as always. At times, he may manifest his kingship in his intervention on earth, whether in subduing nations (e.g. Ps. 47.2-3 and the Maccabaean victory), or in punishing and helping individuals (e.g. Nebuchadnezzar, Dan. 4). His final intervention, when he will set up his kingdom on earth, is to be hoped for in the near future. Faith in God, combined with the distressing situation of Israel, caused people to predict the End when it did not come. Faithful Jews responded with fresh interpretation of the predictions, and/or adoration of the mysteries of God, not by blaming people, let alone God, for making mistakes.

All these points were so widespread that, because Jesus shared them, he could use the term 'kingdom', or 'kingship' (*malkūth*) without explaining what he meant. We must accordingly infer that Jesus shared normal Jewish concepts of what the kingdom/kingship of God was, of its permanent validity and future establishment.

A number of sayings of different kinds show that Jesus shared the hope of the future establishment of God's kingdom, and predicted that the kingdom would come soon. Mark begins his account of Jesus' teaching with a summary statement including this:

The time is fulfilled and the kingdom of God is at hand. Repent/return, and believe in the good news!

(Mk 1.15)

In the Jewish culture in which Jesus taught, this saying was unambiguous. It meant that God will finally establish his kingdom on earth soon. The time is fulfilled because Israel had been waiting for this event for such a long time. The call to repent is a call to return (*tūbh*) to God, and be on his side when this event occurs.[25] Those who return to God will enjoy the kingdom which he will establish, and hence Jesus' description of his announcement as 'good news'.

The same message was part of the instructions which Jesus gave to the Twelve when he sent them out on mission. The Matthaean version, with 'God' restored in place of Matthew's 'heaven', is probably nearest to what Jesus said, which may reasonably be reconstructed as follows:

Do not go away towarsds Gentiles and do not enter a city of Samaritans. Go rather to the lost sheep of the house of Israel. Go and preach and say 'the kingdom of God is at hand' (cf. Mt. 10.5-7, Lk. 9.2; 10.9, 11)

This includes a classic definition of the object of Jesus' ministry, those Jewish people who had fallen away from God. The imminence of the kingdom was a central point for the mission. The very short Markan account of this incident says that the Twelve preached that people should repent (Mk 6.12). This again reflects the use of the Aramaic word *tūbh*, which means 'return', and which was especially appropriate when the lost sheep of the house of Israel repented, that is, returned to the Lord. The preaching of the kingdom of God was part of the central rationale of this return to God.

This hope for the coming of God's kingdom was so important to Jesus that it is prominent in the Lord's Prayer. The second petition is as simple as possible:

tēthē malkhūthākh

May your kingdom come.

(Mt. 6.10//Lk. 11.2)

This has been faithfully repeated by many Christians who have thought of the establishment of the church, or of patient waiting for over 1,900 years until God finally establishes his kingdom someday. Neither of these interpretations was possible for the disciples who originally prayed this petition. In its first-century Jewish context, this petition could refer only to the final establishment of God's rule, and could only be a prayer for him to do so soon.

Two other sayings provide straightforward evidence of this expectation.

---

25   On the Aramaic *tūbh* see pp. 200, 209, and pp. 282–84.

Amen I'm telling you that there are some of those standing here who will not taste death until they see the kingdom of God come in power.

(Mk 9.1)

Given the Jewish evidence which I have surveyed, the expression 'the kingdom of God come *in power*' and not in the present, but rather in the near future, can only mean the final establishment of God's kingdom. When it was said, we do not know. Although it follows a collection of sayings, Mark introduces it with 'And he said to them', presumably because he found it in a separate source. He also caused endless trouble to subsequent interpreters by following it with the narrative of the Transfiguration (Mk 9.2-8). We have seen that Luke tried to maintain that this was the real reference of the saying (Lk. 9.27, editing Mk 9.1), so that his Gentile Christian audiences could believe that Jesus' prediction was fulfilled at once in the experience of the Transfiguration by Peter, Jacob and John (Lk. 9.28-36).[26] For this purpose, Luke removed the words 'in power' from Mk 9.1: he could see that the kingdom did not come *in power* in a single event witnessed by three people. He also altered the introduction to the Transfiguration to read 'Now it came to pass about eight days after these words' (Lk. 9.28). This might persuade a Gentile audience, who were not familiar with Jewish expectation of the final establishment of God's kingdom in the near future, that Jesus' prediction was fulfilled in the Transfiguration.

Matthew, however, was still part of first-century Jewish culture. When he wrote, Jesus had been dead for some time, and his return had been imagined for some time and found in the scriptures. In one of the early speeches of Acts, Jewish expectation of a future redeemer figure is shifted onto him, incorporating the new fact that he had already lived an earthly life:

. . . so that times of refreshment may come from the face of the Lord and he may send the Christ who was appointed for you, Jesus, whom heaven must receive until the times of the restoration of all things, of which God spoke through the mouth of his holy prophets from the beginning.

(Acts 3.20-21)

When Mark wrote, the scriptures had been searched and the coming of Jesus on the clouds of heaven was predicted in terms which can only derive from Dan. 7.13, from which the term 'Son of man' was taken (Mk 8.38; 13.26; 14.62).[27] Paul produced an even more imaginative picture, according to which the Lord will descend, those dead in Christ will be raised first and living survivors will be caught up and meet the Lord in the air (1 Thess. 4.15-17). Matthew therefore altered Mk 9.1 to include Jesus, adding in the term 'the Son of man' which Mark used in the previous verse (Mk 8.38, much edited at Mt. 16.27):

26   See p. 96.
27   See further pp. 374–77.

> Amen I'm telling you that there are some of those standing here who will not taste death until they see the Son of man coming in his kingdom.
>
> (Mt. 16.28)

All this editing should underline the main point. In its original cultural context, Jesus' prediction could only refer to the final establishment of God's kingdom. In a world where early death was a normal occurrence, it was a hyperbolic way of saying that the final establishment of God's kingdom would take place in the very near future.

The editorial work of both Matthew and Luke falls within the parameters of the reactions of faithful Jews outlined above, for Matthew belonged to first-century Jewish culture and Luke inherited it. Consequently, Matthew clarified Jesus' prediction, expecting that God would fulfil it soon, and Luke saw it fulfilled in an event which took place at the time. Both maintained the unshakeable faith in God which inspired Jesus' original prediction. Neither of them was disappointed, or considered Jesus to be mistaken. Accurate history, however, demands that we take a different view from them. Jesus was mistaken, and the kingdom did not come as he predicted. At the same time, from a historian's point of view, this was not a serious mistake. It was a normal part of Jewish culture at the time, and Jesus' profound experience of God during the historic ministry made him more likely to make such a mistake, not less.

Jesus also looked forward to the coming of the kingdom when he celebrated his final Passover with his disciples.[28] When he had interpreted the bread and wine of his body and blood, thereby looking forward to his sacrificial death, he made a prediction which shows several signs of the Aramaic which he spoke, and which requires careful reconstruction. I translate my reconstruction as follows:[29]

> Amen I'm telling you that we will not drink again [literally, we will not add to drink] from the fruit of the vine until that day on which I drink it and it (will be) new in the kingdom of God (cf. Mk 14.25).

Again, in a first-century Jewish context, this can only refer to the final establishment of God's kingdom. Moreover, given the evidence already surveyed, it must mean that Jesus and the disciples will drink wine again soon. It is also more likely to be intended literally than figuratively. We have seen that the normal expectation was that God would set his kingdom up finally on earth, and that Jesus shared this view. Further evidence is provided in a saying the opening of which has undergone obvious alterations by both Matthew and Luke, leaving only a partial glimpse of what Jesus really said:

> . . . that you may eat and drink at my table . . . and you will sit on thrones judging the twelve tribes of Israel.
>
> (Lk. 22.30, cf. Mt. 19.28)[30]

28 See pp. 429–37.
29 For detailed discussion see Casey, *Aramaic Sources of Mark's Gospel*, pp. 242–47.
30 See further pp. 186–87, 420–21.

Abraham, Isaac, Jacob and much of the diaspora would be there, reclining as at feasts, but not judging Israel. Some of this is explicit in another saying where the Lukan version appears to be more original, and fired at Jesus' opponents:

> There will be weeping there, and gnashing of teeth, when you see Abraham and Isaac and Jacob and all the prophets in the kingdom of God, and you (will be) thrown out. And they will come from east and west and . . . recline in the kingdom of God.
>
> (Lk. 13.28-29, cf. Mt. 8.11-12)

This is evidently the same occasion. People, who would be mostly Jews from outside Israel but including any Gentiles who turn to the Lord, would recline to eat and drink, so this is when the Twelve will all be at Jesus' table, as on the next occasion when they would drink new wine with him.

This is the proper context for Jacob and John's request:

> Let us sit one on your right and one on your left in your glory.
>
> (Mk 10.37)

This would make no sense on a purely spiritual plane, in which there is no right, left or sense of place. It makes perfect sense in the kingdom of God set up on earth. This is Jesus' 'glory', in which his position would be supreme: Matthew changed it to 'in your kingdom' (Mt. 20.21), which is more conventional and consequently clearer. Jesus responded to Jacob and John's request by asking in metaphorical terms whether they could share in his death. Their immediate agreement shows that they had learnt from Jesus' rebuke of Simeon the Rock, when the leader of the Twelve objected to Jesus' plans to die (Mk 8.31-33). Jesus accepted their undertaking to die with him. His next response has proved somewhat difficult to understand in Greek, because of Mark's very literal translation of the final words. This however means that Jesus' original Aramaic can easily be recovered, and this may be translated as follows:

> . . . to sit on my right or my left is not mine to give, except to those for whom it has been prepared (cf. Mk 10.40).

Jesus evidently did not know the identity of the people who would be on his right and his left. The passive, 'it has been prepared', means 'prepared by God', a conventional use of the passive to speak indirectly of God's action. We can only conjecture the identity of two very important people. Abraham, Moses and Peter should be among those who come to our minds. Moreover, Jacob and John have not been excluded. Our unresolvable conjectures have one useful function: they should remind us of how important this future occasion would be. Since, moreover, at least Jesus, Jacob and John were to die first, at least they would have to rise from the dead. Whether Jesus expected the general resurrection to take place at this point is more difficult to determine, and we must not systematize isolated sayings too much. It would however make excellent sense if this were so.

Since the coming of the kingdom was so important, it is natural that Jesus should have presented it in other ways, without necessarily using the actual term. One conspicuous feature of the evidence is the parables of watching. While we cannot confirm the authenticity of their details, let alone the verbatim accuracy of stories which were meant to be told and retold, the basic picture fits into the ministry of Jesus, who told far more parables than we find in the rest of the literature which stems from the early church. Mark retold this one, perhaps adding the introduction (and v. 37 as a conclusion):

> Watch, be alert, for you do not know when the time is. As when a man away from home left his house and gave authority to his slaves, to each one his task, and commanded the doorkeeper to watch. So watch! For you do not know when the Lord of the house is coming, whether in the evening, or in the middle of the night, or at cockcrow or early, lest he should come suddenly and find you asleep.
>
> (Mk 13.33-36)

Here there is a constant shift between the parable and the reality. The message should not however be difficult to see: God will come suddenly. This is what is portrayed elsewhere as the final establishment of his kingdom. Even Jesus' favourite image was not indispensable to a central aspect of his teaching.

Jesus also saw the kingship of God displayed during his ministry. We have seen that God's kingship was an overarching metaphor, referring to God's sovereignty in the here and now as well as in the future. I noted especially the evidence of the book of Daniel. This book is full of apocalyptic hopes for the final establishment of God's kingdom. Nonetheless, without any perceived inconsistency, this book also celebrates God's eternal kingship at the point when Nebuchadnezzar is healed.[31] The situation is similar in the case of Jesus. We have seen ample evidence that the coming of the kingdom in the near future was a significant part of his preaching during the public ministry. At the same time, Jesus used the image of God's kingship when his ministry of exorcism came under verbal attack, and he responded by saying that the kingship of God was displayed in them:

> But if I cast out demons by the finger of God, the kingship of God has come upon you.
>
> (Lk. 11.20, with 'finger' replaced by 'spirit' at Mt. 12.28)

Here both the 'finger' and the 'kingship' of God are ways of talking about God's powerful action.

The temporal aspect of the kingdom is not prominent in several sayings which primarily convey teaching about other matters. This too should not be surprising, in view of the overarching nature of kingship as a metaphor of God's power. For example, Mark tells the story of a scribe who asked Jesus which were the two

---

31 See pp. 212–13.

most important commandments. When Jesus responded with the commandments to love the one God, and one's neighbour as oneself, the scribe approved vigorously. Jesus responded, 'You are not far from the kingdom of God' (Mk 12.34). This is strongly reminiscent of rabbinical sayings about taking the yoke of the kingdom upon oneself. Jesus' approval means that the scribe's attitude towards the centre of the Torah was close to acceptance of God's complete control over his life.[32]

Another saying refers to sins caused by what people look at, in the hyperbolic manner characteristic of Jesus' jokes:

> And if your eye offends you, pluck it out! It is good that you should go one-eyed into the kingdom of God, rather than have two eyes and be thrown into Gehenna.
>
> (Mk 9.47)

Here the contrast with 'Gehenna', the Jewish term for hell, and the parallel with 'life' in vv. 43 and 45, show that the eschatological aspect of the kingdom of God is in view. This implies that God's kingdom will be eternal, and that the final judgement will take place when it is set up.

A strand of Jesus' teaching favours the poor over against the rich. The metaphor of kingship is used to declare this bluntly in one of the beatitudes:

> Blessed are the poor, for yours is the kingdom of God.
>
> (Lk. 6.20, cf. Mt. 5.3)

Jesus gave similar teaching when a rich man declined to sell his goods, give the proceeds to the poor, and join the Jesus movement:

> How hard it is for those who have wealth to enter the kingdom of God . . .
> It is easier for a camel to go through the eye of a/the needle than for a rich man to enter the kingdom of God.
>
> (Mk 10.23, 25)

At one level, this is another of Jesus' hyperbolic jokes, but as always he had a serious point to make. It is evident from the context that in Jesus' view riches prevented people from putting God first in their lives. God's fatherly care, however, would always look after the poor.

Jesus also used his favourite image when his disciples tried to stop people from bringing their children for him to touch them. He was annoyed, and expressed himself forcibly:

> Let the children come to me, do not stop them, for of such is the kingdom of

32   On this passage see further pp. 424–25.

God. Amen I say to you, whoever does not receive the kingdom of God like a child will certainly not enter it.

(Mk 10.14-15)

If the kingdom is treated as an abstract concept, this comparison can be difficult to understand, and it is better to recognize a simple and memorable incident in the life of Jesus. People brought their children to him, and disciples who expected him to preach the Gospel to grown-ups, and who may have feared something magical in the need for touching, tried to stop them. That is why Jesus was annoyed; he used his favourite image to ensure that children were allowed to come to him, and he was entirely happy for them to touch him. He obviously understood that this was good for everyone!

Jesus' frequent use of such an overarching metaphor extended also to direct and indirect attacks on his opponents. One saying was intended to make people stop and think about themselves, but it also implies that there was something seriously wrong with Jesus' orthodox opponents (I have again restored 'God' for Matthew's 'heaven'):

I tell you that unless your righteousness exceeds that of scribes and Pharisees, you will not enter the kingdom of God.

(Mt. 5.20)

We shall see that the scribes and Pharisees had a view of righteousness which Jesus considered seriously defective, in that they observed many small details of the Torah, but failed to observe its main points.[33] Other sayings make this clear – this one was intended to cause people to think about this central matter. Another was a more general attack on Jesus' opponents (I have removed Matthew's stylized 'hypocrites' as well as restored 'God' for 'heaven'):

Woe to you, scribes and Pharisees, for you shut up the kingdom of God from before men, for you do not enter it nor do you let those who are entering it go in.

(Mt. 23.13)

This effectively accuses scribes and Pharisees of such a defective view of God's will that their behaviour positively damages the religious lives of other people. We shall see in Chapter 9 that this is consistent with Jesus' other polemic.

As well as these different ways of using his overarching metaphor of kingdom/ kingship, Jesus told pretty stories about the kingdom of God. These parables of the kingdom are difficult to interpret, because we no longer have the context, or contexts, in which they were delivered, and we do not always understand the aspect of God's kingship which they were intended to illustrate. The evangelists had similar trouble – the famous parable of the sower is given a secondary

---

33   See pp. 320–38.

interpretation already in the oldest Gospel (Mk 4.3-20). Some parables seem concerned to stress the importance of the kingdom, and its mighty power when it is finally established, and we should perhaps not push some of them much further than this (cf. e.g. Mk 4.26-29, 30–32).

I therefore conclude that in the teaching of Jesus, as in Second Temple Judaism, the kingship/kingdom of God is an overarching metaphor, referring to God's sovereignty both in the present and in the future. It was a central image in his teaching, where it is much commoner than in other surviving sources of the same date. It was especially important to Jesus that God would finally establish his kingdom on earth in the near future. This was at the centre of Jesus' preaching, and part of the basis on which he called upon people to repent, that is, to return to God. In a sense, his predictions were mistaken, in that what he predicted did not come to pass. From a cultural point of view, however, this was a normal mistake, and one which his profound experience of God made him more likely to make, not less. Consequently, his followers were able to adjust to it, as faithful Jews of the period always did, because they shared the faith on the basis of which these predictions were made. This locates Jesus as a first-century Jew, not as someone who was *seriously* mistaken.

Jesus also made use of the rest of the range of meaning of this image, notably seeing the kingship of God displayed in his exorcisms. This illustrates the fact that his appreciation of God included both the intimacy of genuine personal experience of God as Father, and recognition of God's awesome nature as King of the universe. We should appreciate the appropriateness of Jesus' use of both these metaphors together in the opening of the Lord's Prayer.

5. *Teaching Others to Pray*

Jesus taught his disciples to approach the one God of Israel with what is generally known as the Lord's Prayer. It survives in two different forms (Mt. 6.9-13// Lk. 11.2-4), a reflection of its use by different people to approach God. Many scholars have argued that Luke's shorter form is the original one. The main reasons for this view were clearly expressed in the influential work of Jeremias:

> the decisive observation . . . is the following: the shorter form of Luke is completely contained in the longer form of Matthew. This makes it very probable that the Matthaean form is an expanded one, for according to all we know about the tendency of liturgical texts to conform to certain laws in their transmission, in a case where the shorter version is contained in the longer one, the shorter text is to be regarded as original. No-one would have dared to shorten a sacred text like the Lord's Prayer and to leave out two petitions if they had formed part of the original tradition.[34]

---

34   J. Jeremias, *The Prayers of Jesus* (London: SCM, 1967), ch. III (Trans. J. Reumann), 'The Lord's Prayer in the Light of Recent Research', pp. 89–90.

This is remote from the cultural environment of Jesus, his disciples and the author of Matthew's Gospel. It has one point right – it would be natural for Jesus' disciples to expand an original prayer, so it is right to be on the lookout for this, and I follow scholars who believe that Matthew expanded the opening address. None of Jeremias' other comments should be accepted. The Gospels of Matthew and Luke were written too early for this prayer to be regarded as part of a fixed liturgy. The notion that Luke, an outstanding Gospel writer committed to transmitting selected teachings of Jesus for Gentile Christian audiences, would not have dared shorten what he inherited, presupposes that the Lord's Prayer had a degree of fixed sanctity characteristic of later Christian tradition, and it is remote from the authorial habits of ancient writers in general and Luke in particular. We know from Luke's rewriting of Mark and his editing of the 'Q' material that he omitted points which he found unhelpful. Moreover, in accordance with Jewish customs and his own ministry, Jesus will have expected his disciples to use this prayer, not necessarily to repeat it verbatim, though there would be nothing wrong in doing that either.

It is possible that Jesus himself gave more than one version of this prayer, but there is good reason to believe that the two versions in Matthew and Luke were derived from a single Greek translation of an Aramaic original. This is the very high degree of verbal identity in those parts of the prayer which are found in both Matthew and Luke. One word is of crucial importance, the Greek word *epiousion*, which qualifies 'bread'. This word is conventionally translated 'daily', so that we ask for 'our daily bread'. However, it does not occur elsewhere, and this has made the whole petition difficult to understand. Moreover, the search for an Aramaic word underlying the Greek *epiousion* did not go well. Ironically, however, modern scholarship has found the right answer by going back to the Church Father Jerome. When Jerome wrote his commentary on Matthew, he got stuck too, but in those days he had a resource which has not survived into modern times, a Gospel which he called 'According to the Hebrews'. He comments:

> In a Gospel which is called 'According to the Hebrews' . . . I found 'mahar', which means 'tomorrow's', so that the meaning is 'Give us to-day our bread "for tomorrow"', that is, 'for the future'.

The Aramaic word *maḥar* means 'tomorrow', and these Jewish Christians are more likely to have preserved the Lord's Prayer in Aramaic than to have translated it from Greek, because they will have said it in Aramaic themselves. We should therefore accept the originality of this word, and the interpretation passed on by Jerome. Moreover, while it is understandable that *one* translator, faced with the task of rendering the Aramaic *maḥar* into Greek, should form the new adjective *epiousios* from the common Greek expression *tē epiousē*, 'on the next (day)', the chances of *two* translators doing so independently are negligible. It follows that both Matthew and Luke are dependent on a single Greek translation. It is therefore much more probable that they are both dependent on a written Greek source than that they have taken the prayer from the worship of their own churches.

Several attempts to discuss the Lord's Prayer in the light of Aramaic reconstructions have already been made.[35] This is a remarkable testimony to its iconic
status, especially as most New Testament scholars cannot and will not do this
with most of his other sayings. In the light of all this work, I propose the following Aramaic reconstruction as a reasonable approximation to what Jesus
originally said:

Abbā
yithqaddash sh^emākh
tēthē malkhūthākh
tehwē re'ūthāk bish^emayīn ūbhear'ā
habh lanā yōmā dēn laḥmanā d^elimḥar
ūsh^ebhaq lanā ḥōbhaynā k^edhī '^anaḥnā sh^ebhaqnā leḥayyābhaynā
w^elā ta'ēlinnanā l^enisyōn lāḥēn shēzibhnā min b'īshā.

Father,
May your name be kept holy.
May your kingdom come.
May your will come to pass in heaven and on the earth.
Give us to-day our bread for to-morrow.
And forgive us our sins (lit. debts) as we forgive those who sin against us
(lit. our debtors),
And do not lead us into trial, but deliver us from evil.

This begins with the particular term *Abba*. This was central to Jesus' recreation
of the traditional image of the Fatherhood of God. Luke's shorter opening with
the simple term 'Father' must therefore be right. Matthew, who furthered the
recreation of the image of the Fatherhood of God but who was not especially
concerned with the actual word *Abba*, expanded the address in a conventional
Jewish way to 'Our Father who is in heaven'. This should not be seen as in any
way unfaithful to the teaching of Jesus. The different versions of this prayer in
Matthew and Luke, and some interference in the textual tradition, show that
verbatim repetition was not a recognized requirement of Jesus' followers or the
earliest churches, just as it was not a requirement for the Jewish prayers to which
Matthew had always been accustomed. It follows nonetheless that Luke was not
copying Matthew, since he would have no reason to alter 'Our Father, who is in
heaven', if that had been what he read.

The approachability of God was central to addressing God as *Abba*, and this
makes it doubly important that it be combined with, not dissociated from, the
opening petitions.

---

35 The main ones accompanied by discussions in English are the following: C. F. Burney, *The
    Poetry of Our Lord* (Oxford: Clarendon, 1925), pp. 112–13; E. Lohmeyer, *The Lord's Prayer*
    (1946. Trans. J. Bowden. London: Collins, 1965); Jeremias, *Prayers*, pp. 82–107; B. Chilton,
    Jesus' Prayer and Jesus' Eucharist: His Personal Practice of Spirituality (Valley Forge: Trinity
    Press International, 1997), pp. 24–51.

The first prayerful hope, 'May your name be kept holy', is a conventional recognition of the unique awesomeness of God, reminiscent of the *Qaddish*, which began 'May his great name be exalted and kept holy'. The name of God, quite unlike the name of any other being, was so sacred that it was not supposed to be pronounced except by the high priest on Yom Kippur. We have seen how important that was to Jewish people at the time of Jesus, and that it was sufficiently well kept for there to be some uncertainty as to exactly how YHWH was pronounced.[36] The opening of Jesus' prayer accordingly makes clear that the being who may be approached as *Abba* is the unique creator and ruler of the universe, whose awesome name is to be venerated in accordance with conventional Jewish tradition. It is essential to keep both these points together. Jesus' vigorous prophetic renewal of the standard Jewish view of the Fatherhood of God was not somehow opposed to the veneration of the awesomeness of the ruler of the universe; it was part of it.

The sheer awesomeness of the creator of the universe is carried on in the second petition, 'May your kingdom come', which uses Jesus' other central image of God, his kingship. We have seen that this is a prayer for God's final establishment of his kingdom in the near future. Its position in this prayer reflects the importance of this hope to Jesus and his followers.

The next petition is found only in Matthew, but it should be accepted as a genuine part of Jesus' prayer. From a cultural point of view, it says something of what the second petition meant:

tehwē re'ūthāk bish^emayīn ūbh^ear'ā

May your will come to pass in heaven and on the earth.

(Mt. 6.10)

Here I have followed Codex Bezae in omitting the conventional Greek *hōs*, 'as'. Codex Bezae is an important ancient manuscript which preserves many original readings, especially those which reflect Jesus' original Aramaic, and here, as often, it has some other ancient support. This shorter reading makes it much easier to reconstruct a feasible Aramaic source, which a normal translator might well translate to produce Matthew's third petition. The word which I have translated 'and' is the conventional Greek *kai*, which normally means 'and'. It can be used following the Greek *hōs*, which means 'as', and this makes Matthew's Greek mean literally 'May your will come to pass, as in heaven, so on earth.' Conventional translations change this, to make more fluent English. The trouble with this is the Greek word *kai*, which must here be translated 'so'. Any feasible Aramaic, such as *kēn*, which is often the equivalent of English words such as 'so', 'thus', would naturally be translated into Greek with the word *houtōs*, which also means 'so, 'thus', rather than with *kai*. The conventional longer reading is within the range of normal Greek. The addition of *hōs*, 'as', was accordingly a

---

36 See pp. 213–14.

very simple way for early scribes to avoid the unwanted implication that God's will might not be done in heaven.

Jesus' original plea, however, makes excellent sense in his prayer. It was well known in first-century Judaism that God's will had not always been done in heaven. The most notorious example was the story of the sons of God, who descended from heaven to mate with the daughters of men. This biblical story (Gen. 6.1-4) was retold with much development in the Judaism of our period (e.g. 1 Enoch 6–16). At Zech. 3.1, Satan's traditional role as the accuser does not seem to be in accordance with the will of God, since he is rebuked for his intention to accuse the high priest Joshua (Zech. 3.2). At 2 Enoch 29.4-5, Satanail (i.e. Satan) is thrown down from heaven, having turned away with a complete order of angels. In the War Scroll from Qumran, Belial (another name for Satan) and his host are to be defeated in the last days when the rule of Michael will be established. In 11Q Melchizedek, the final victory will be carried out by Melchizedek, and it is a reasonable interpretation of this fragmentary piece that he at least will be in heaven when he defeats Belial and his hosts. At Rev. 12.7-9, Satan is finally defeated and thrown out of heaven. Jesus could not have known this last text, but it comes from the same culture, and the very idea that Satan could still rise up against God in heaven illustrates graphically what Jesus prayed might *not* happen. Luke, or one of his predecessors, left out what they could not imagine, and copyists of Matthew edited it.

All this is closely related to Jesus' battle with Satan in his ministry of exorcism. We shall see in the next chapter that Jesus believed that he was fighting a winning but serious battle against Satan and his demons. When the disciples returned from a successful mission which included exorcism, Jesus commented:

I saw Satan fall like lightning from heaven.

(Lk. 10.18)

This brief report indicates that Jesus had another important vision.[37] This vision is the vital link between Jesus' prayer and the fragmentary Jewish material. Satan was so powerful on earth that an assault on heaven could not be excluded, nor could the defection of more angels as in the old stories of 1 Enoch. Jesus' prayer amplifies the final establishment of God's kingdom, which would mean his will being done in heaven as well as on earth. When his will was done, neither Satan nor the Romans would survive with their powers. During the successful mission of the disciples, Jesus saw another significant step forward in the battle between God and Satan which was conducted throughout the historic ministry.

It follows that this petition has an excellent setting in the life and teaching of Jesus. It should therefore not be attributed to Matthew's inventiveness, for which he would have little reason. Luke left it out because he did not share the apocalyptic orientation which would contemplate a battle in heaven. This petition is accordingly closely related to the hope that God would finally establish

---

37   See further p. 250.

his kingdom soon. These two petitions, like the prayer that God's name be kept holy, presuppose the absolute power of the awesome creator of the universe.

The next two petitions move from God to people. We have seen that the difficult word *epiousion* represents the Aramaic *mahar*, which means 'to-morrow's', so that the petition means, 'Give us to-day our bread for to-morrow'. We should not make this another eschatological petition. Jesus lived in a society where some people lived on the breadline and having a reasonable surplus of food was a constant concern. Bread was such a basic commodity that the Aramaic and Hebrew words for 'bread' were used to mean 'food', and we should interpret Jesus' prayer in accordance with this. Famines occurred, and they were major disasters. Jesus' teaching also shows a particular concern for the poor. This petition is accordingly as practical as the next one. It effectively asks God to guarantee a proper food supply, which he could do for example by sending appropriate weather and not sending plagues of locusts. Matthew's version is a natural translation of the original Aramaic, which Luke has slightly altered to make clear that we ask for to-morrow's food every day, not just once, which is in accordance with what Jesus meant.

The next petition asks God to do something important, in which his followers undertake to imitate him. It asks for the forgiveness of our sins. God's forgiveness of repentant sinners was a normal part of ancient Judaism. For example, in a Palestinian recension of the 18 benedictions, the fifth and sixth benedictions read as follows:

> Cause us to return, LORD, to you, and let us return anew in our days as before. Blessed art thou, LORD, who delights in repentance [*teshūbhāh*, lit. 'return'].

> Forgive us, our Father, for we have sinned against you. Wipe out our transgressions from before your eyes. Blessed art thou, LORD, who abundantly forgives.[38]

In response to God's forgiveness of them, repentant sinners were expected to love God and keep the precepts of the Torah. People's forgiveness of each other was a central part of the teaching of Jesus. Hence the two kinds of forgiveness are associated here. As they ask God to forgive their sins, the disciples undertake to forgive other people. This was also part of traditional Judaism: 'forgive your neighbour the wrong he has done, and then, when you pray, your sins will be forgiven' (Sir. 28.2). The Matthaean version of this petition has two straightforward Aramaisms, which enable us to reconstruct the exact words for 'sins' and 'sin against' used by Jesus. In Aramaic, the words for 'debt', 'be in debt' and 'debtor' were used metaphorically for sin, as they were not in Hebrew or Greek, so Matthew's use of such words in Greek will be due to overliteral translation of Jesus' original Aramaic. Luke sensibly used the ordinary Greek word for 'sins',

---

38 A complete text and English translation is provided by Evans, *Jesus and His Contemporaries*, pp. 277–80.

though he used the metaphorical 'everyone in debt to us', which again shows Aramaic influence.

The final petition has often been thought to be about normal daily life too, but it is more probable that it refers to events before God's final establishment of his kingdom. Forgiveness of sins has already been asked for, so it is perhaps unlikely to be followed, rather than preceded, by a petition not to be tempted to commit minor sins. Moreover, God does not lead people into temptation to commit sins, this is rather the work of the devil. Jesus' brother Jacob, perhaps aware of some misunderstanding, put this bluntly, in accordance with normative Judaism and the teaching of Jesus:

> Let no-one, being tempted, say 'I am tempted of God'. For God cannot be tempted with evil, and he himself tempts no-one.
>
> (Jas 1.13)

A dreadful time of trial was however to be expected immediately before God finally established his kingdom. We have seen this at Dan. 12.1, where immediately before the final events with the resurrection of many of the dead, 'there will be a time of distress such as there shall not be from the time when there was a nation until that time' (cf. Mk 13.19-20//Mt. 24.21-22). No one could possibly know how bad this time of distress would be, how long it would last, or who would be subjected to it. This is therefore best seen as a prayer by the disciples not to be subjected to this. Jesus referred to it in the Garden of Gethsemane, when he told the inner group of three, 'Watch and pray that you may not enter into trial' (Mk 14.38//Mt. 26.41//Lk. 22.46).

Only Matthew has the second half of this petition, 'but deliver us from evil'. It is difficult to be sure whether Matthew expanded the original or Luke abbreviated it, but fortunately this does not matter much because it simply expands the meaning of the first part. In its context, the evil from which we pray to be delivered is primarily the time of trial before God's final establishment of his kingdom. It may be that Luke knew this interpretation, and felt that his shorter version was a clearer prayer to be delivered from ordinary temptation, which he would have preferred to Jesus' eschatologically oriented prayer.

Christians are accustomed to a doxology at the end of this prayer, but there is none in Luke nor in some of the oldest and best manuscripts of Matthew, so it was not transmitted as part of this prayer. This however matters less than one might think. The prayer condenses Jesus' most important teaching in its assistance to his followers in approaching God. As normal Jews, they will have added conventional praise at the end of it as and when they liked, much as Matthew expanded the opening to 'Our Father who is in heaven'. When they said it as a group rather than individually, they are also likely to have added 'Amen'.

The prayer has not survived in normative Judaism, because of the split between Judaism and Christianity. The high regard in which it has for centuries been held by Christians illustrates its effectiveness as a brief prayer from within the perspective of the teaching of Jesus, and this despite some changes in meaning imposed by the passage of time and some shift in culture. Seen in its original cultural context, this prayer offers a way of approaching God in the context of a summary of the main points of Jesus' teaching.

Jesus' teaching contains very few other instructions about prayer. This is natural, for prayer was an established feature of Judaism, and Jesus' followers were faithful Jews, whether they were his followers for this reason, or whether they had returned to God because of his ministry. Jews prayed to God both formally and informally. The most basic of fixed prayers was known as the *Shemaʻ*, its first word in Hebrew, though later sources permit it to be said in any language, and this is likely to have been an ancient custom:

> Hear, Israel, the LORD our God, the LORD (is) One, and you shall love the LORD your God with all your heart and with all your being and with all your might.
>
> (Deut 6.4-5)

There follows an injunction, 'And you shall speak in them . . . when you lie down and when you rise up' (Deut 6.7). This was taken up into a custom of praying twice a day, and the complete *Shemaʻ* was held to be Deut. 6.4-9, 11.13-21 and *Num.* 15.37-41. Josephus interpreted Moses as follows:

> Twice each day, when it begins, and when it is time to turn to sleep, (people should) bear witness to God for the gifts which he granted them after releasing them from the land of the Egyptians . . .
>
> (*Ant.* IV, 212)

There was also a custom of praying three times a day, the other time being at 3 p.m, the time when the continual offering (the *Tamid*) was sacrificed in the Temple. This is reflected in Luke's report that Peter and John went up to the Temple 'at the hour of prayer, the ninth' (Acts 3.1). The book of Daniel already records Daniel praying to God three times a day, as a fixed custom of his (Dan. 6.10). Hence also a major prayer of repentance by Ezra is set 'at the evening sacrifice' (Ezra 9.5), and while Daniel was making another major prayer of repentance, 'Gabriel . . . reached me at the time of the evening sacrifice' (Dan. 9.21). Accordingly, we should not doubt that Jesus and his disciples said the *Shemaʻ* and observed the three fixed times for prayer.

There were other known prayers as well, though there is no reason to believe that they were fixed in form, and some reason to believe otherwise. I have quoted the *Qaddish*, which was said in Aramaic.[39] Another known prayer was the 18 benedictions. They were not however set in order until the rabbis met at Javneh, after the destruction of the Temple in 70 CE (b. Ber. 28b; b. Meg. 17b). Moreover, the destruction of the Temple is presupposed in surviving texts of benedictions 14 and 16, and even at a late date, the rabbis allowed people to say an 'abbreviated 18' (e.g. b. Ber. 29a). It follows that the text of this prayer was

---

39   See pp. 215–16.

not fixed at the time of Jesus, and we do not know to what extent it was recited, either in the synagogues or by individuals.

As well as fixed prayers, Jews might pray informally at any time. Ps 116.1-4, part of the sacred text and one of the *Hallel* psalms sung at Passover and at other times, records the psalmist praying to the Lord when he was in distress. Prayer when in a place of danger is still recommended by R. Joshua (m. Ber. 4.4). Honi the Circle-drawer prayed for rain when asked during a time of drought, not at a fixed time of day (m. Ta'an 3.8). We have seen how important prayer was to the life of Jesus himself. We should not doubt that spontaneous and informal prayer was part of the life of his followers as well. This custom was naturally continued in the early church. So, for example, Luke says that Peter went up to the roof to pray at midday (Acts 10.9), and we are left to assume that he did so because prayer was a natural part of his life. When Paul and Silvanus were flung into prison, Luke has them praying and singing hymns in the middle of the night (Acts 16.25).

This is the context in which we should understand the other instructions about prayer in the teaching of Jesus. Matthew precedes the Lord's Prayer with Jesus' criticism of orthodox Jews who pray ostentatiously, and Gentiles who babble at length when they pray (Mt. 6.5-8). Both instructions distance Jesus' followers from alien groups. Jesus' reason for not praying like Gentiles was more central to his ministry: 'your Father knows what you need before you ask him' (Mt. 6.8). This takes for granted the Fatherhood of God, and informal petitionary prayer, which is hereby controlled, not rejected. Other sayings emphasize the need for forgiving other people, and relate this to God's forgiveness of people, as in the Lord's Prayer itself (Mt. 6.14-15, Mk 11.25, cf. Mt. 5.23-24).

All this forms the cultural background against which we can appreciate the nature and importance of the Lord's Prayer.

6. *Conclusions*

God was central to the Jewish tradition which Jesus recreated. This recreation was profoundly informed by Jesus' own spiritual experience. He used to pray on his own, as well as taking part in public prayers. During the public ministry, his exorcisms and other healings were especially important, for they were perceived by him as direct experience of God working through him and defeating the devil. He went willingly to his death, because he believed that this was the will of God, which he saw written in the scriptures. The *Shema'*, the daily prayer requiring Israel to love and obey the one God, was isolated by him as the most important commandment.

In expounding God in his teaching, Jesus made particular use of two images or metaphors, the Fatherhood and kingdom/kingship of God. Both are used in the first part of the Lord's Prayer, which he taught his disciples. They are both traditional Jewish metaphors, which Jesus vigorously recreated. His teaching portrays a supreme being who watches carefully over people, expects to be obeyed and forgives those who repent. Jesus addressed God as *Abba*, the normal Aramaic word which people used of their natural fathers.

The importance of the Lord's Prayer illustrates further the centrality of God in the teaching of Jesus. God was central to Jesus' own experience, as well as to his teaching. Of especial importance was the effect of his experience of God on others in his ministry of exorcism and other healings. I consider this in detail in the next chapter.

CHAPTER 7

Exorcism and Healing

1. Introduction

The study of Jesus' healing ministry has traditionally been dominated by the Christian agenda of miracle. Many scholars coming in from a Christian perspective have believed many or all of the Gospel stories, and have treated them as miracle stories. They have traditionally regarded even stories of exorcism as miraculous.[1] Moreover, many such discussions have taken for granted the kind of committed definition of a miracle given by the Christian philosopher Richard Swinburne:

> an event of an extraordinary kind, brought about by a god and of religious significance.[2]

Only a theist can accept the reality of miracles so defined.

Some definitions are more specific to the Judaeo-Christian definition, and make reference to the traditional concept of the laws of nature. For example:

> Acc. to the traditional view, a miracle is a sensible fact (*opus sensibile*) produced by the special intervention of God for a religious end, transcending the normal order of things usually termed the Law of Nature.[3]

Only a member of the Judaeo-Christian tradition can accept the reality of miracles defined like this.

---

1 For recent defence of this tradition, G. H. Twelftree, *Jesus the Miracle Worker* (Illinois: IVP, 1999). For the history of the discussion of miracles, C. Brown, *Miracles and the Critical Mind* (Exeter/Grand Rapids: Paternoster/Eerdmans, 1984. Repr. pb. Pasadena: Fuller Seminary, 2006).
2 R. Swinburne, *The Concept of Miracle* (London: Macmillan, 1970), p. 1.
3 F. L. Cross (ed.), *The Oxford Dictionary of the Christian Church* (Oxford: OUP. Rev. 3rd. edn, ed. E. A. Livingstone, 2005), p. 1098.

In response to this agenda, more critical students of the New Testament have been sceptical about the literal truth of many Gospel stories. For example, Lüdemann comments on Jesus' healing of a paralytic at Mk 2.1-12: 'The healing of the paralysed man cannot be called historical. It belongs to the phase of primitive Christian propaganda in which the figure of Jesus drew every possible miracle to him like a magnet.' He comments equally bluntly on the healing at Mk 3.1-6: 'Because of the parallelism with 1 Kings 13.4-6, the miracle story about the spontaneous healing of the withered hand is similarly secondary, quite apart from the fact that it would break the laws of nature.'[4] In spite of comments like this, the attestation of Jesus' ministry of exorcism and healing is so strong that the majority of New Testament scholars have argued that the tradition had a historical kernel. Bultmann, the doyen of radical Christian critics, concluded, 'there can be no doubt that Jesus did the kind of deeds which were miracles to his mind and to the minds of his contemporaries, that is, deeds which were attributed to a supernatural, divine cause; undoubtedly he healed the sick and cast out demons.'[5]

Very few scholars have attempted a historical investigation in which the issue of miracle is not of primary concern. Vermes is perhaps the best of these. He offered a discussion of Jesus' exorcisms against the fruitful background of other Jewish evidence of exorcism. He also sought to bring to bear other Jewish evidence of healing, as part of the background to Jesus' more general healing ministry.[6] His work was properly used in the outstanding critical discussion of E. P. Sanders.[7]

Underlying both of the conventionally extreme approaches to the Gospel stories is one of the major cultural problems for the vast majority of investigators. Many of the kinds of events related in the Gospels do not occur in our daily lives. For example, I have never seen an exorcism, or the healing of a paralytic, nor have I knowingly met anyone who has. Consequently, it is natural that committed Christians should believe that Jesus' successful ministry of exorcism and healing must be due to divine intervention, because such things do not happen otherwise. It is equally natural that atheists should believe that such stories are not literally true, because such things never happen, and lots of people love telling stories in which the impossible happens. Recent scholarship has however provided two major resources which we can increasingly use to try to determine which of the Gospel stories are literally true, without necessarily first deciding in what sense they are miraculous: some aspects of modern medicine, especially psychosomatics, and the anthropology of medicine. Both fields of study contain many carefully documented instances of events which do not occur in the daily lives of most people in our culture, including exorcisms, and the healing of paralytics.

The application of such knowledge to the Gospels is however extremely difficult. It requires extensive learning outside the field of New Testament Studies,

---

4   Lüdemann, *Jesus after 2000 Years*, pp. 15, 21.
5   R. K. Bultmann, *Jesus and the Word* (1926. Trans. L. P. Smith and E. H. Lantero. New York: Scribners, 1934. Pb. Collins: Fontana, 1958), p. 124.
6   Vermes, *Jesus the Jew*, ch. 3.
7   Sanders, *Historical Figure*, ch. 10.

and the traditional problems of a variety of dogmatic commitments, and the nature of the source material, will not go away. Perhaps the best attempt to grapple with all this material is *Disease and Healing in the New Testament* by Keir Howard.[8] Keir Howard was 'a practising specialist physician, and also an ordained Anglican priest'[9] when he wrote the doctoral thesis on which this book is based. It is a vigorous attempt to advance knowledge by seeing Jesus' healing ministry in the light of Western biomedicine, taking into account also the cross-cultural study of healing. The purpose of this chapter is accordingly to take as much as possible of this work into account, building on the work which I have previously done on a very small number of Gospel narratives.[10] In the light of all this I offer a discussion devoted particularly to the oldest sources about Jesus seen especially against the background of primarily Jewish source material.

I also propose another definition of a miracle, because I regard it as a fruitful definition for specifically *historical* research:

A miracle is a remarkable deed performed by an unusual person believed by their followers to be in close touch with a deity.[11]

The main reason why this definition can be fruitfully used is that it allows for more than one perspective on miracles *by the eyewitnesses of the deeds themselves*. This is important in dealing with the miracles of Jesus, because there is clear evidence that some people who saw them were not convinced of their validity. Moreover, at least some of these people, and probably the vast majority, were faithful Jews who genuinely believed that God performed miracles. This facet of the evidence is not fully appreciated in traditional scholarship. Conservative Christian scholars tend to use it as evidence of the historicity of the miracle stories, which indeed it is, but they also exaggerate how much of the tradition it vindicates, and do not take it seriously as evidence of the ambiguity of the actual events. More radical critics tend to ignore it. I argue that it is of central impor-

---

8   J. Keir Howard, *Disease and Healing in the New Testament: an Analysis and Interpretation* (Lanham: University Press of America, 2001). I am grateful to Dr Justin Meggitt for reading two outstanding papers, at Sheffield University and to the Jesus seminar of BNTC, for fruitful discussions, and for sending me an advance copy of his essay 'The Psycho-Social Context of Jesus' Miracles', in F. Watts (ed.), *Jesus and Healing* (Cambridge: CUP, forthcoming). For other notable attempts, each however dominated by a particular perspective see S. L. Davies, *Jesus the Healer: Possession, Trance and the Origins of Christianity* (London: SCM, 1995); J. Wilkinson, BD, MD, FRCP, *The Bible and Healing: A Medical and Theological Commentary* (Edinburgh: Handsel, 1998); J. J. Pilch, *Healing in the New Testament: Insights from Medical and Mediterranean Anthropology* (Minneapolis: Fortress, 2000).

9   Keir Howard, *Disease and Healing*, p. vii.

10 Casey, *Aramaic Sources of Mark's Gospel*, pp. 138–39, 173–92, on Mk 3.1-6; *Aramaic Approach to Q*, pp. 146–84, on the Beelzeboul controversy; *Solution to the 'Son of Man' Problem*, pp. 144–67, on Mk 2.1-12.

11 I proposed this in M. F. Bird and J. G. Crossley, *How Did Christianity Begin? A Believer and Non-believer Examine the Evidence* (London/Peabody: SPCK/Hendrickson, 2008), p. 186, with brief discussion (pp. 186–91).

tance in understanding the nature of Jesus' miracles. When they are defined like this, there should be no doubt that they were central to his ministry.

2. *Secondary Development*

The miracle agenda was not set by modern scholarship. It is already to be found in the Gospels. I consider this next, to see what kind of evidence of secondary development of the miraculous is present in our oldest sources.

The most obvious examples of deliberately written miracle stories are in the Fourth Gospel.[12] At Jn 5.2-9, Jesus heals a man who was apparently paralytic, so this is similar to some stories in the synoptic Gospels. It has two unsynoptic features. One is the information that the man had been ill for 38 years. This makes sure that the story is miraculous in the strictest sense, an event which cannot take place in the real world except by divine intervention. Jesus also tells the healed man to carry his pallet, when it was the sabbath. This is precisely what the synoptic Jesus does not do, for it is contrary to the written Law (Jer. 17.21-22, 24). Moreover, Jesus defends himself as working like his Father, and this implies his deity (Jn 5.17-18). This leads 'the Jews' to seek to kill him, 'because he not only abrogated the sabbath, but also called God his own Father, making himself equal to God' (Jn 5.18). A lengthy and quite unsynoptic discourse follows. All this shows that the story has been written up in a cultural context of mostly Gentile Christianity at the end of the first century.

The most dramatic miracle of all is the raising of Lazarus, a character who does not even appear in the synoptic Gospels. People who are thought to be dead occasionally revive, which led to the ancient Jewish ruling that the bereaved could visit the grave for up to three days (b. Sem. 8, 1). Lazarus is accordingly said to have been dead for four days (Jn 11.39), so that, here again, Jesus is deliberately portrayed as achieving the impossible. Moreover, this story too is shot through with secondary Johannine features, including its extraordinarily high Christology. 'The Jews' are mentioned five times in 11.1-44, and at 11.45, 54, 55. John 11.8 is as external and hostile as possible: 'The disciples said to him, "Rabbi, the Jews were now seeking to stone you . . ."'. This has the drastic division between 'the disciples' and 'the Jews' which reflects the situation in Ephesus after 70 CE. John 11.25-26 offers a classic summary of specifically Johannine features:

> I am the Resurrection and the Life. He who believes in me will live even if he dies, and everyone who lives and believes in me will not die for ever.

The miracle is presented as the immediate cause of the final action against Jesus (Jn 11.45-53). This context is secondary, for we know from Mark that the real trigger of the Passion was the Cleansing of the Temple.[13]

---

12   P. M. Casey, *Is John's Gospel True?* (London: Routledge, 1996), pp. 51–57.
13   See pp. 411–22, 513–14.

We must therefore infer that the authors of the Fourth Gospel deliberately produced miraculous events as part of the process of rewriting Jesus traditions to meet the needs of their largely Gentile community in Ephesus at the end of the first century.

There are also signs of the tradition being rewritten in the way that Matthew and Luke rewrite Mark and 'Q'. I have already noted non-miraculous examples of this. I have also argued that the miracle of Jesus' virgin birth was produced by the writing of stories which are not literally true.[14] The 'Q' account of the dispute between Jesus and others about how he cast out demons is introduced by an account of an exorcism (Mt. 12.22-3//Lk. 11.14, cf. Mt. 9.32-33). In Lk. 11.14, the demon is dumb, and the simple opening is the kind of description that one might expect from an Aramaic source: 'And (he) was casting out a demon, and it was dumb'. In the closely parallel story at Mt. 9.32-33, the demoniac is dumb too. At Mt. 12.22-23, however, a generally similar story in its 'Q' position at the start of the dispute, the demoniac is blind as well as dumb. There are also purely linguistic signs that Matthew is rewriting the story in Greek, such as the opening word 'then' (*tote*), which he uses no less than 90 times, and it ends with the crowds saying 'Is not this the Son of David?' Matthew has this term 'Son of David' eight times, whereas it is rare in the rest of the synoptic tradition. We should infer that this is the same kind of rewriting here in Matthew as we have seen more pervasive in John. He has intensified the exorcism to be more miraculous than it was in his source.

There are several other examples of Matthew's rewriting in this vein. When he took over Mark's story generally known as 'the Gadarene swine' (Mt. 8.28-34, editing Mk 5.1-20), he produced *two* men with demons, rather than Mark's single 'man with an unclean spirit'. Similarly, whereas Mark tells the story of Jesus healing 'the son of Timaeus, Bartimaeus, a blind beggar' (Mk 10.46-52), Matthew has 'two blind men', who speak in unison throughout his version of the story (Mt. 20.29-34). Again, Matthew took over Mark's dramatic and accurate story of the Cleansing of the Temple, an important event not connected to Jesus' healing ministry (Mt. 21.12-17, editing Mk 11.15-19). Matthew's substantial rewriting includes this assertion: 'And blind and lame (people) came to him in the Temple, and he healed them' (Mt. 21.14). This effortless healing of lots of people is not part of the oldest tradition. All this is part of Matthew's general rewriting of the tradition to meet the needs of the Christian communities for whom he wrote his Gospel.

Luke rewrote the tradition in a generally similar manner. For example, Mk 1.40-45 tells the story of Jesus healing a man with a skin disease, literally *lepros*, which represents a variety of skin diseases, not what is technically known as Hansen's disease, which we call 'leprosy'.[15] People who were classified like this had to be declared clean, and the man duly asked Jesus to cleanse him, rather than heal him. What is not altogether clear from Mark's account is whether the man had already recovered from his skin disease, and whether anyone looking

14   See pp. 62–65, 145–51.
15   See pp. 266–68.

at him, fully clothed, would notice any signs of a skin disease. Luke altered the description of the man to 'a man full of leprosy' (Lk. 5.12). This has the effect of ensuring that the man looked terrible, and Jesus' cleansing was a miraculous cure in the strictest sense.

When Jesus was arrested in the Garden of Gethsemane, Mark, followed by Matthew, records that someone drew his sword, struck the high priest's slave and cut off his ear (Mk 14.47//Mt. 26.51, cf. Jn 18.10-11). Luke, who evidently had at least one more source for at least parts of the Passion narrative, is the only one of the evangelists to record the following:

> But Jesus answered and said, 'No more of this!' And he touched his ear and healed him/it.
>
> (Lk. 22.51)

The addition of this by Luke is a sufficient indication that it is not part of the historical record. He has inserted a miracle, an event normally as impossible as the raising of Lazarus. In real life, the slave will have had access to a doctor, who will have staunched the flow of blood and dressed the wound.

I have discussed Jesus' summary of his healing ministry in his reply to a question from John the Baptist, who wanted to know whether Jesus was the person whose coming John had felt inspired to prophesy (Mt. 11.2-6//Lk. 7.18-23).[16] The Matthaean version correctly has John's question followed by Jesus' answer. Luke, however, has an additional report in between the question and the answer, and it shows some signs of specifically Lukan Greek style (e.g. 'granted', _echarisato_):

> And in that hour he healed many people from diseases and scourges and evil spirits, and he granted sight to many blind (people).
>
> (Lk. 7.21)

The healing of these masses of people all at once is surely due to Luke's summary rewriting.

It follows that rewriting the tradition to make it more miraculous is a feature of the editing of both Matthew and Luke. All the Gospel writers also tell stories which are not literally true. I have discussed in detail a conspicuous example, the stories of the virgin birth in Matthew and Luke.[17] An equally conspicuous example in Mark is usually known as 'the Gadarene swine' (Mk 5.1-20//Mt. 8.28-34//Lk. 8.26-39). This is set in the Gentile area of the Decapolis. The man himself is an extreme case: 'no-one could bind him with a chain any more, for he had often been bound with fetters and chains, and the chains had been torn apart by him and the fetters smashed, and no-one had the strength to control him' (Mk 5.3b-5). In a detailed discussion, Aus has shown that such aspects of the story have been inspired by stories of Samson.[18] The first aspect of the

---

16 See pp. 181–83, and pp. 272–73.
17 See pp. 145–51.
18 R. D. Aus, _My Name is 'Legion': Palestinian Judaic Traditions in Mark 5.1–20 and Other Gospel Texts_ (Lanham: University Press of America, 2003), pp. 1–99.

story that is untypical of Jesus, but widespread in stories of exorcism, is that, even after making an effort to order the unclean spirit out of the man (Mk 5.8), Jesus has to ask it its name (Mk 5.9). This is narratively convenient so that the storyteller can tell us its name is 'Legion, for we are many', the first indication that the storyteller was disenchanted with Roman legions. The second feature untypical of Jesus, but widespread in stories of exorcism, is that Jesus sends the demons out in such a way that they visibly enter something else, so they can be seen to have gone out. What they are sent into is a 'large herd of pigs'; indeed somewhat belatedly the storyteller entertains us with the information that there were about 2,000 of them! (Mk 5.11-13). Pigs were notoriously unclean animals, because Gentiles kept them and ate pork, as Jews did not. From a Jewish perspective, therefore, pigs were especially suitable animals for unclean spirits to be sent into. The existence of a herd of 2,000 pigs, though not strictly miraculous, is not something that would ever happen in real life; it is part of a story told to entertain people, and enable them to marvel at Jesus' ability to defeat the powers of evil with the power of God.

At this point, we can be more precise about the 'Legion'. The author had in mind the tenth legion, Legio Decem Fretensis, which had a boar as one of its symbols. It was stationed in the province of Syria, firstly at Cyrrhus, so it was the northernmost of the Syrian legions, and then from 18 CE onwards in the client kingdom of Commagene, which was annexed to Syria.[19] The otherwise powerless storyteller has made great fun of a legion. The effect of Jesus sending the demons into 2,000 pigs is equally entertaining: 'the herd rushed down the steep bank into the sea . . . and drowned in the sea' (Mk 5.13). This effectively gets the demons back into the underworld where they belong, for the story assumes they go down to the Abyss. It also dumps a legion where many Jews would have loved to see the Roman legions go. But the storyteller, a Jewish Christian entertaining Christians miles away, where he knew about Decem Fretensis, was regrettably unconcerned about the geography of the Decapolis. Whether this took place in the country of the Gerasenes (the original text of Mark) or the Gadarenes (some manuscripts which were influenced by Matthew) is the difference between whether the pigs had to run 33 miles, or just 6 miles, to get to the lake of Galilee! The storyteller was not concerned either to think about pigs which can swim.

This is a wonderful tale, which should not be taken literally. That it is a tale, not an accurate account of an amazing exorcism, in no way casts any doubt on the genuine effectiveness of the historical Jesus' ministry of exorcism. Indeed, its serious message that the power of God worked through him when he defeated evil through exorcisms is fully in accordance with his historic ministry. It is nonetheless a warning to us that, as we assess the historicity of miracle stories in the Gospels, we must be wary of the wiles of storytellers.

We must now leave all this creative writing, and restart at the bottom end of the tradition, to see how far it is possible to see right back to the role of the historical Jesus in exorcism and other types of healing. First however, I consider

---

19   See J. H. Farnum, *The Positioning of the Roman Imperial Legions* (BAR International Series 1458. Oxford: Archaeopress, 2005).

briefly the cross-cultural study of healing, and healing among Jewish people at about the time of Jesus.

3. *Healing*

In general, cross-cultural work on healers shows a massive variety of phenomena.[20] Many cultures have healers to whom people go when they are ill, and who perform, or instruct them or their relatives to perform, many different rituals, including prayers and taking potions. The intellectual structures surrounding these events are also varied, and include the placation or intervention of a wide variety of deities and spirits. The perception that someone is ill may depend on the person themselves, and/or on the social group to which they belong. The perception that they are better always includes a change in the classification of the person, and may or may not include a change in symptoms.

There were healers in Second Temple Judaism. For example, Josephus says of the whole sect of Essenes:

> They are extraordinarily interested in the treatises of the ancients, singling out most of all those concerned with the welfare of soul and body. Hence, with a view to the healing of sufferings, they investigate effective roots and the properties of stones.
>
> (*War* II, 136)

---

20   There is a very large bibliography, much of it written by specimens rather than analysts. I have found the following especially helpful or interesting: J. D. Frank and J. B. Frank, *Persuasion and Healing: A Comparative Study of Psychotherapy* (Oxford: OUP, 1961. Baltimore: John Hopkins,[3]1991); E. M. Pattison, N. A. Lapins and H. A. Doerr, 'Faith Healing: A Study of Personality and Function', *Journal of Nervous and Mental Disease* 157 (1973), pp. 397–409; D. Landy, *Culture, Disease and Healing: Studies in Medical Anthropology* (London/New York: Macmillan, 1977); A. Kleinman, *Patients and Healers in the Context of Culture: An Exploration of the Borderland between Anthropology, Medicine and Psychiatry* (Berkeley/LA: Univ. of California, 1980); M. J. Christie and P. G. Mellett, *Foundations of Psychosomatics* (Chichester: Wiley, 1981); L. Eisenberg and A. Kleinman (eds), *The Relevance of Social Science for Medicine* (Dordrecht: Reidel, 1981); A. J. Marsella and G. M. White (eds), *Cultural Concepts of Mental Health and Therapy* (Dordrecht: Reidel, 1982); D. C. Glik, 'Psychosocial wellness among spiritual healing participants', *Social Science and Medicine* 22 (1986), pp. 579–86; M. Stacey, *The Sociology of Health and Healing* (London: Unwin Hyman, 1988); M.-J. D. Good, B. J. Good and M. J. Fischer (eds), *Emotion, Illness and Healing in Middle Eastern Societies* (*Culture, Medicine and Psychiatry* 12, 1, 1988); C. Bass (ed.), *Somatization: Physical Symptoms and Psychological Illness* (Oxford: Blackwell, 1990): I. E. Wickramasekera, 'Somatization: Concepts, Data, and Predictions from the High Risk Model of Threat Perception', *Journal of Nervous and Mental Disease* 183 (1995), pp. 15–23; I. Pilowsky, *Abnormal Illness Behaviour* (Chichester: Wiley, 1997); L. K. Hsu and M. F. Folstein, 'Somatoform Disorders in Caucasian and Chinese Americans', *Journal of Nervous and Mental Disease* 185 (1997), pp. 382–87; Y. Ono *et al.* (eds), *Somatoform Disorders: A Worldwide Perspective* (Tokyo: Springer, 1999).

Philo presents healing as a feature of the Therapeutae (*Vit. Cont.* 2), who may or may not have been a branch of the Essenes. He says they cured not only bodies, but also souls oppressed with various things, including 'sorrows and fears'. Both these reports indicate serious and prolonged interest in healing both diseases of the body, and what is known in our culture as psychosomatic illness.

Prayer is central in stories about the Galilaean charismatic Ḥanina ben Dosa, who seems to have lived only a few years later than the time of Jesus. The story goes that the son of Gamaliel was suffering from a mortal fever (y. Ber. 5, 6/2(9d)//b. Ber. 34b). Gamaliel sent two of his disciples to tell Ḥanina this. Ḥanina went and prayed, and came back to tell the two men to return home, because the fever had left the boy. Gamaliel later confirmed that the fever had indeed left his son at this time. In the version of the story found in the Babylonian Talmud, the two messengers respond to the announcement of the healing by asking Ḥanina whether he was a prophet. This is an interesting reflection on a category into which Ḥanina might have been put because of such a healing, because it is the same category into which Jesus was in fact put. Ḥanina's response was negative. His response is amplified by a quotation from the earlier tradition of m. Ber. 5, 6. This earlier tradition begins with a general statement according to which Ḥanina used to pray for the sick and could tell who would live and who would die. He explained:

> If my prayer is fluent in my mouth, I know that it is accepted: if not, I know that it is rejected.

This tradition is especially interesting because it shows both that Ḥanina performed other healings by means of prayer, and that this process was not always successful. Moreover, the relatively early tradition of m. Ber. 5, 6 is not the kind of thing that the Mishnah would produce of itself – it may be explained only as old tradition the general historicity of which should be regarded as unshakeable.

From this perspective, Jesus should be put in the general category of being a healer, even though an equivalent noun is not actually used of him in the Gospels. His position as a traditional healer is especially well shown in a visit to Nazareth, where he could do very little healing because of his traditional role as a craftsman (Mk 6.1-6).[21]

A major feature of traditional healing is the cure of somatized illness behaviour, when people with psychological problems behave as people with physical illnesses. Kleinman comments on his extensive field work in Taiwan:

> Somatized illness behaviour is an important adaptive mechanism . . . It also seems for many to be personally adaptive as well . . . for some patients the illness behaviour is quite clearly maladaptive . . . Certain culture-bound disorders seem to be constructed in the same way: they represent loculated somatic delusions involving culturally specific Explanatory Models that shape a universal disease into a culturally specific illness.[22]

---

21   See further pp. 143–44.
22   Kleinman, *Patients and Healers*, pp. 158, 163.

An example of somatized illness behaviour is the phenomenon of hysterical paralysis in late nineteenth- and early twentieth-century Europe. Hysteria was a fashionable illness at the time, so it was a natural choice for people who needed to be patients but who had nothing else wrong with them. Equally, hypnotism was a culturally acceptable form of manipulating people. Consequently, there are a number of accounts of hysterical paralysis, some cases of which were curable under hypnosis. The culturally determined nature of these cases is especially well illustrated by those who could move their limbs under hypnosis, but could no more do so afterwards than they had done before. At this stage, the majority of cases were Victorian women, and the work of J.-M. Charcot was especially important in the classification and popularity of this illness.[23] Consequently, hysterical paralysis was the illness suffered by many men who could not cope with being soldiers in the First World War. After that war, instances of hysterical paralysis soon underwent a drastic decline, with Charcot's particular form of hysteria disappearing within a decade of his death. This further clarifies the culturally oriented nature of this illness. It is important that it is only the extent and classification of this illness that are culture-specific to the late nineteenth and early twentieth century. Paralysis itself is much more widely attested.

A classic investigation of a different kind is worthy of mention here. Pattison and his associates asked a group of Americans who had been through a healing event what had previously been wrong with them. Some of them did not know. They were also asked whether they were still taking medicines. It was found that some of them did indeed take medicines for remaining symptoms, even though they believed themselves to have been healed.[24] These findings underline the nature of healing events. They are events in which people who are regarded as ill are cared for, following which they may declare themselves healed, regardless of whether there is any change in their symptomatology. When the event is successful, the person is reclassified as no longer ill. The effects of this are not necessarily permanent.

Jesus' healings generally fall within the parameters of what is perceived to be possible by traditional healers who operate within communities of people who accept their powers. He does not heal broken limbs, prevent illness or grant immortality. He enables people who have been classified as ill to return to normal life. There is very little information as to how long his healings were effective. Exorcisms are especially prominent in the bottom layer of the tradition.

Exorcisms are abundantly attested in many parts of the world as well as in past history, with many variations on the basic theme.[25] Exorcism permits an exceptionally sharp characterization of the role of a traditional healer. It presupposes that a person has been possessed by a demon. This is a particularly clear example of a person being labelled with a role. This role may be caused by their behaviour, their behaviour may be cited as evidence of it, and they may behave

---

23 A. R. G. Owen, *Hysteria, Hypnosis and Healing: The Work of J.-M. Charcot* (London: Dobson, 1971).

24 Pattison, Lapins and Doerr, 'Faith Healing'.

25 See G. H. Twelftree, *Jesus the Exorcist* (WUNT 2, 54. Tübingen: Mohr Siebeck, 1993).

in ways which indicate that they have labelled themselves as possessed. The demon is then cast out in a visible event. As a result of a successful exorcism, the person must be reclassified as a former demoniac from whom a demon has been cast out, and to some extent, depending on what they have been doing, they must alter their behaviour. For this purpose, they must be reintegrated into the social group.

There is no doubt that exorcism was practised in Second Temple Judaism. Josephus recounts one effect of Solomon's wisdom:

> Now God granted him understanding of the skill used against demons for the help and healing of people. He also composed incantations by which diseases are alleviated, and he left methods of exorcisms by which those who are entangled drive out demons so that they never return.
>
> (*Ant.* VIII, 45)

This is immediately followed by an account of successful exorcism by Eleazar, witnessed by Josephus himself. We have seen that this is a perfect example of social memory, in that the biblical account of Solomon has been expanded to make it directly relevant to events of Josephus' own day.[26]

It follows that Jesus' behaviour as an exorcist fits into the culture of his time. At the same time, we shall see reason to believe that he was exceptionally able as an exorcist.

4. *Exorcism in the Ministry of Jesus*

The first exorcism reported by Mark took place in a synagogue in Capernaum one Sabbath:

> And immediately there was in their synagogue a man with an unclean spirit. And he cried out and said, 'What have we to do with you, Jesus the Nazarene? You have come to destroy us! I know you, who you are, the Holy One of God.' And Jesus rebuked him, saying, 'Be muzzled and come out of him!' And the unclean spirit tore him and cried out with a loud voice and came out of him. And everyone was amazed, so that they discussed it with each other, saying 'What's this? New teaching with power! And he commands the unclean spirits, and they obey him!'
>
> (Mk 1.23-27)

This dramatic story has several signs of being a fairly literal translation of an Aramaic source, beginning with Mark's chronically frequent 'immediately' (*euthūs*, 41 times), probably here an attempt to translate an Aramaic expression

---

26 See pp. 133–34.

which may be rendered more literally 'in it in the hour' (*bāh besha'thā*). There are also several indications of authentic tradition, and the story contains nothing which the early church might have needed to invent. The presence of a demoniac in the synagogue on the sabbath could probably not be avoided, unless people took violent measures to keep out anyone so classified, and in any case most of the people present may not have known that he was thought to be possessed until his outburst. How far the man's presence shows some willingness to be overpowered into a more normal state of being is difficult to determine. The story follows an account of Jesus' teaching, however, and this suggests that the man's outburst may have been a convoluted cry for help.

The description 'unclean spirit' is normal in Aramaic (or Hebrew), rather than in Greek. The man's reference to himself in the plural ('we', 'us'), as well as the singular ('I know'), is evidence of a drastically disturbed state of being. His description of Jesus as 'the holy one of God' is the recoil of someone who has accepted the classification of himself as a man with an unclean spirit, and who will also have accepted that Jesus was a prophetic figure inspired by God. He will have accepted also, therefore, that Jesus could cast out his demon. If the early church had produced this speech, it would surely have produced a Christological title. From a technical point of view, the man's naming of Jesus and declaration of his identity is an attempt by the demon to control the potential exorcist. Paradoxically, however, this is consistent with the man's willingness to be exorcized, for his speech told Jesus what he believed was the matter with him. Shouting out loud is another aspect of the man's disturbed behaviour. Jesus seems to have needed to shout louder to restrain these people. The Greek word usually translated 'rebuke' (*epetimēsen*) can only represent an Aramaic word *ge'ar*, which also means 'shout', and even 'roar'. The semantic area of *ge'ar*, including 'shout' and 'rebuke', is natural in a culture where people were rebuked by shouting at them.

Jesus' vigorous order 'Be muzzled' (Greek *phimōthēti*, representing Jesus' Aramaic *ithhasam*) is often toned down by translators, but it is significantly different from the ordinary Greek word for 'be silent'(*siōpō*). There are parallels to it in the magical papyri, where it belongs to efforts to control evil spirits, the same basic situation as here. In response to Jesus' command, Mark says that the spirit 'tore him', 'cried out with a loud voice' and came out of the man. This looks very much like what we would call a convulsion. Unfortunately, Mark does not provide any description of the man's behaviour after the unclean spirit was thought to have come out of him. He must have ceased to shout, have convulsions, and refer to himself in the plural as if he knew he was possessed. As always, there is no follow-up either. We do not know whether the man joined the Jesus movement, or relapsed into demonic behaviour at a later date, or anything of this kind.

Mark relates the kind of follow-up that was convenient for Jesus' followers: everyone was amazed, both at his authoritative teaching and at his control of unclean spirits. This should be accepted into the historical record: Jesus was exceptional, both as a teacher and as an exorcist. One other aspect of people's reaction is important: no one objected to the exorcism on the ground that it was work on the sabbath. We shall see objections of this kind from the extreme orthodox wing of Jesus' opponents. When he first performed an exorcism on the sabbath in a Capernaum synagogue, however, people were impressed, and perhaps relieved, that he controlled a disruptive demoniac at their meeting. It will not have occurred to them, any more than it did to him, that removing a denizen of the devil by the power of God was work. Work was ploughing, carpentry and the like, and people were glad to rest from it on the sabbath.

This is one narrative of exorcism which betrays many signs of being literally true, and which has no features characteristic of the early church. As well as other narratives, our earliest sources have other kinds of evidence of Jesus' ministry of exorcism. Mark has this summary:

> And unclean spirits, whenever they saw him, used to fall down before him and shout out, saying 'You are the son of God'. And he rebuked them much, so that they should not make him known.
>
> (Mk 3.11-12)

This is a reasonable summary written up in the light of Mark's major concerns, and we cannot tell with certainty where the borderline between source material and rewriting lies. That demoniacs fell down before him and shrieked abominably is confirmed by all our narratives, as well as being a standard part of the behaviour of disturbed human beings. The cry 'You are the son of God' looks at first sight like the work of the early church. This may be the case, for the sonship of Jesus was important in the early church, and clear signs of this are already found in this Gospel (Mk 1.11; 9.7; 14.61-62; 15.39). Moreover, 'son of the Most High God' is the term used to address Jesus in the only one of Mark's exorcism narratives that is the creation of a storyteller (Mk 5.7).[27] At the same time, however, in Second Temple Judaism 'son of God' meant a faithful Jew, not the second person of the Christian Trinity. Accordingly, like 'holy one of God', the term used by a demoniac to address Jesus at Mk 1.24, the use of the term 'son of God' may belong to genuine exorcisms, in which it could have been part of a cry for help by these demented people. When Jesus was so hailed, it may have encouraged him to proceed to exorcize a demon from a person who had indicated that s/he would prefer to be on Jesus' side.

Jesus' rebuke again reflects his behaviour in out-shouting these people, as indicated by the Aramaic *geʿar*. The end of Mark's summary is likely to be his own work. Mark was concerned at the absence of evidence that Jesus presented himself as Christ and Son of God. He therefore imagined Jesus not making such matters generally known during the ministry (cf. Mk 4.10-12, 33–34; 8.30; 9.9; 11.33). It is therefore probable that Mark misinterpreted the way in which Jesus silenced demoniacs in accordance with one of Mark's own major concerns. Nonetheless, this summary is valuable because it means that, in addition to the narratives which he passes on, Mark had sufficient evidence of many exorcisms to produce a summary too.

---

27 See pp. 242–43.

Another significant piece of evidence is a parable from the 'Q' material. It has to be decoded, but the situation which it represents should not admit of doubt.

When a/the unclean spirit goes out from a/the man, it goes through waterless places seeking rest, and does not find any. It says, 'I will return to my house from which I came out.' And it goes and finds (it) swept and decorated. Then it goes and brings along seven other spirits worse than itself, and they go in and live there. And the last state of that man becomes worse than the first.

(Mt. 12.43-45//Lk. 11.24-26)

This parable deals with the fate of demoniacs who are not looked after when they have been exorcized. It begins with an exorcism. The demon's subsequent return to its house must mean going back to possess the man from whom it had been driven out. Matthew added 'empty' to 'swept and decorated', entering into the story-mode description of a former demoniac who has not returned to God and filled himself with the spirit. This would necessarily happen to a man who had been a demoniac, and who was not welcomed back into a worshipping community afterwards. The reference to seven demons is properly decoded at the end, with the statement that the last state of that man becomes worse than the first. This shows Jesus' clear awareness that the effect of exorcism is not necessarily permanent. We must infer that the effect of his exorcisms was not always permanent.

The importance of exorcism in Jesus' ministry is further shown by its importance in the work of his disciples. When the Twelve were chosen, Mark gives as one reason that they should be with him, the deliberate choice of an inner group to symbolize the twelve tribes of Israel; and as a second reason, 'so that he might send them out to preach and to have power to cast out (the) demons'(Mk 3.14-15).[28] In the story of them being sent out in twos, Mark duly records that 'he gave them power over (the) evil spirits', and that 'they cast out many demons' (Mk 6.7, 13). Luke found an additional saying of Jesus, which refers to an associated vision which Jesus had, and which has nothing about it characteristic of the early church:

I saw Satan falling like lightning from heaven.

(Lk. 10.18)

This again illustrates the kind of battle in which Jesus thought that he and his disciples were involved.

At the same time, Jesus was the most outstanding exorcist of all. Mark illustrates this with an account of a particularly difficult exorcism. This was a dumb boy who tore himself, ground his teeth and foamed at the mouth. His father took him to Jesus' disciples, who could not cast the demon out (Mk 9.17-18). Jesus commented,

28 See further p. 186.

O faithless generation, how long will I be with you? How long shall I endure you?

This testifies to Jesus' awareness of the centrality of faith in exorcism. When the demoniac put on a performance, falling to the ground, rolling around, and foaming at the mouth, Jesus asked the boy's father how long he had been like this. The father said he had been like this from childhood, and used to throw himself into fire and into water. He also asked Jesus to have pity on them and help them. He thus went further in his attempt to co-operate with Jesus in producing a successful exorcism. Moreover, he did so in the presence of his son, who must by this stage have been aware that if he altered his behaviour by co-operating in the exorcism, his father would no longer treat him as possessed. Jesus then proceeded to further stress the need for faith, which led the father to cry out, 'I believe: help my lack of faith' (Mk 9.24).

Then Jesus 'rebuked the unclean spirit and said to it, "Dumb and deaf spirit, I command you, come out of him and do not go back into him again"' (Mk 9.25). This is notable because of the explicit order to the unclean spirit not to return: this is in effect also an order to the boy not to resume his anti-social behaviour. It is entirely coherent that Jesus should feel a need to give this unusually explicit order to a particularly difficult case. Mark recounts the effect of Jesus' order. The boy shouted and went into convulsions, and then from the perspective of the observers the demon went out, for the boy became like a corpse. Jesus took him by the hand and pulled him to his feet. As usual, we have no information about the later behaviour of the boy.

There is however some further discussion. The disciples ask why they could not cast the demon out. This is partly because Jesus did so, but it also implies that their ministry of exorcism was normally successful. Jesus' response is equally fascinating:

This kind cannot go out except by prayer and fasting.

(Mk 9.29)

There is only one other reference in the synoptic tradition to Jesus fasting (Mt. 4.2, when Jesus was in the wilderness, being tempted by Satan in a lengthy midrash, and ministered to by angels). This one is omitted by two or three major Alexandrian manuscripts, with very little other support, while neither Matthew nor Luke saw fit to keep the verse at all. This reference should however be regarded as inalienable. The early church had no reason to produce it, and copyists did not generally insert it into manuscripts of the New Testament. We have already seen that, for the exorcism to be successful, faith was required from the father, who would have to treat the boy as a former demoniac, and co-operation was needed from the boy. We now have a little insight into the sort of person that Jesus felt he was, as a successful exorcist. He was a person in touch with God through prayer, and fasting was part of his spiritual life. He will have felt that this was essential to a successful ministry of exorcism, and he will have seen this as fundamental to his practical ability to obtain the social co-operation necessary in these events. It is not mentioned much in the synoptic tradition because in normal circumstances it was unremarkable, and it was not normally connected to specific incidents. Indeed, when Jesus' disciples were not fasting at a time when both the disciples of John and the disciples of the Pharisees were fasting, some people thought it worth coming to ask him why his disciples were not fasting (Mk 2.18). Fasting is referred to at Mk 9.29 because Jesus mentioned it in *memorable circumstances*, when he performed a particularly difficult exorcism.

The boy in this story is usually thought to have been epileptic, because his severe symptoms are consistent with this. Epilepsy was well known in the ancient world, and was described in detail by the Greek medical writer Hippocrates (460–355 BCE), and/or his followers, in his/their treatise 'On the Sacred Disease'. Hippocrates denied that epilepsy is a sacred disease due to divine visitation, as was commonly thought. There are Jewish and other parallels to the view that it was specifically caused by demonic possession. Matthew seems to have thought that the boy was epileptic, for he describes him as 'moonstruck' (*selēniadzetai*, Mt. 17.15, not in Mark or Luke). Wilkinson, a qualified doctor coming in from an exceptionally conservative Christian perspective, concludes that he was suffering from '*idiopathic epilepsy*, which means epilepsy for which no organic physical cause can be found'.[29] He declares there is no cure known to modern medicine, so this comes out as a miracle due to direct divine intervention. Wilkinson also considers that this diagnosis is consistent with the boy's illness being due to demon possession.

For this he is interestingly rebuked by his fellow Christian physician Keir Howard, who comments, 'Such an approach is irresponsible and capable of causing immense suffering to innocent patients.'[30] Keir Howard also casts doubt on the diagnosis of epilepsy, suggesting that some aspects of the boy's symptoms point to 'a diagnosis of conversion disorder, rather than true epilepsy, and as such it would have been very amenable to the forms of treatment used by Jesus.'[31] All this underlines the extreme difficulty, and consequently limited value, of trying to make a diagnosis in Western biomedical terms on the basis of a story of exorcism, even when the story gives a comparatively full account of the demoniac's symptoms.

Another difficult exorcism did result in a cure which lasted at least as long as the ministry of Jesus. One of Jesus' faithful and important female followers was Mary of Magdala.[32] Luke lists her among healed women who supported the ministry, and describes her as 'called Magdalene, from whom seven demons had gone out' (Lk. 8.2). To be classified as having had seven demons, she must have been a very bad case, and the process of exorcism must have been difficult.

---

29 Wilkinson, *Bible and Healing*, p. 130.
30 Keir Howard, *Disease and Healing*, pp. 133–34 n. 208, referring to the earlier work of J. Wilkinson, *Health and Healing: Studies in New Testament Principles and Practice* (Edinburgh: Handsel, 1980), p. 62; J. Wilkinson, 'The epileptic boy', *ExpT* 79 (1967), pp. 39–42.
31 Keir Howard, *Disease and Healing*, p. 114.
32 See pp. 192–97.

There is evidence of yet another kind that Jesus was exceptionally famous as an exorcist. Mark reports that his disciples found a man exorcizing in Jesus' name, even though he was not a member of the Jesus movement (Mk 9.38). The disciples stopped him, but Jesus told them to let him continue. Jesus must have been an exceptionally effective exorcist himself for an exorcist who did not belong to his group to exorcize in his name. Jesus' own attitude is also noteworthy: he accepted the validity of this man's exorcisms. We shall see other evidence that he accepted the validity of exorcisms done outside his movement. This underlines the strength of his conviction that exorcism took place because the power of God worked through the exorcist to defeat Satan.

This highly successful ministry of exorcism ran into a great deal of opposition, some of it very fierce. Jesus was accused of casting out demons by the power of the devil himself. This is one of the best-attested aspects of the ministry, for it occurs in sayings of different kinds in both Mark and in the 'Q' material (Mk 3.22-29; Mt. 12.22-32//Lk. 11.14-23; 12.10).[33] There is moreover no way that the early church would have produced this dispute, because the accusation itself is too uncomplimentary to Jesus, and casts doubt on the validity of his mission even at a point where it appeared to be a great success. The best-known opponents who made this accusation are 'scribes who came down from Jerusalem' (Mk 3.22). It seems likely however that 'Q' reported this as coming from other people too (Lk. 11.15). The involvement of both groups makes excellent sense of Jesus' reported responses. These include homely analogies suitable for ordinary Jews, as well as the accusation that his opponents were guilty of an unforgivable sin, which fits well into his criticisms of scribes and Pharisees. The more homely analogies concern the declaration that a kingdom divided against itself cannot stand. This indicates Jesus' general view that Satan did indeed have a kingdom, a mode of control over the demonic world, and this is what Jesus and others fought against.

The Markan version of the dispute has Jesus' response begin with the programmatic question, 'How can Satan cast out Satan?' (Mk 3.23). This is a matter of experience rather than logic. Jesus had experienced the power of God casting out Satan in the exorcisms which he had performed. This is why he could not imagine Satan amassing such overwhelming power against his own minions. Hence Mark was quite right to put this question at the head of the analogies which flow from it. I have discussed a 'Q' saying in which Jesus used his favourite metaphor of the kingship of God to celebrate his triumph over the forces of evil in his exorcisms:

And if I cast out demons by the finger of God, the kingship of God has come upon you.

(Lk. 11.20, with 'finger' replaced by 'spirit' at Mt. 12.28)

Here both the 'finger' and the 'kingship' of God are ways of talking about God's

---

33   See Casey, *Aramaic Approach to Q*, pp. 146–84.

powerful action.[34] Jesus had no doubt that this is what was taking place through him.

As we have already seen, Jesus also accepted the exorcizing ministry of other Jews. This is entailed in an *argumentum ad hominem* from the present dispute. In this saying, *Ba'al zeboul* is probably an old Hebrew term for the devil:

> And if I cast out (the) demons by *Ba'al zeboul*, by whom do your sons cast them out? Therefore they will be your judges!
>
> (Mt.12.27//Lk. 11.19)

Here Jesus aligns himself with other Jewish exorcists. He knew that the evidence, successful exorcisms, was basically similar in several cases. This gave him a very useful argument. If people inferred from his successful exorcisms that he was in league with the devil, they ought to make the same inference in the case of other people of whom they approved. This is another argument by down-to-earth yet entirely reasonable analogy. Jesus' absolute confidence that other Jewish exorcists would vindicate him is further testimony to his absolute confidence in the power of God working in the experience of exorcism. He knew from his own experience that other successful exorcists could not possibly confuse the power apparent in his successful exorcisms with the power of the devil.

At the same time, Jesus had no doubts about the seriousness of the opposition to him. This is especially clear in a saying which has never been clearly understood because it does not make proper sense in Greek, as it does in Aramaic. Consequently, only a minority of Greek manuscripts preserve the original Greek reading, which is a literal translation of an Aramaic saying of Jesus which may reasonably be translated into English as follows:

> Whoever is not with me is against me, and whoever does not gather with me scatters me.
>
> (Mt. 12.30//Lk. 11.23)[35]

In Greek, as in English, one cannot scatter a person, and it is this which created problems for both copyists and interpreters. In Aramaic, however (and similarly in Hebrew), the same word (*baddar*) is used of separating one creature from a group as is used for scattering a whole group. Hence the image of Israel as 'a scattered sheep' (Jer. 50.17), a similar kind of image to the one which we need for understanding this saying of Jesus. His whole ministry could reasonably be described as gathering in the lost sheep of the house of Israel (cf. Mt. 10.6; 18.12-14//Lk. 15.4-7). Scribes and Pharisees who were opposed to him were not merely refusing to gather with him. The accusation that he cast out demons by *Ba'al zeboul* was so serious that it amounted to an attempt to isolate him from Israel altogether. This is the serious and precise sense of 'whoever does not gather with me scatters me'.

---

34   Cf. further pp. 200–1.
35   See Casey, *Aramaic Approach to Q*, pp. 148–49, 176–77.

The final argument transmitted from this dispute accused Jesus' opponents of an unforgivable sin. Its exact form is difficult to reconstruct because Jesus used an Aramaic idiom which has no literal Greek equivalent, and the content of the saying was not altogether congenial to some of the Christians who transmitted it. Bearing in mind that the Aramaic term *bar* (*e*)*nāsh*(*ā*), literally 'son of man', was used in general statements which referred particularly to the speaker, I translate a reconstructed original Aramaic literally into English like this:

> And whoever speaks a word against a/the son of man, it will be forgiven him. But whoever speaks a word against the spirit of holiness, it will not be forgiven him for ever (cf. Mk 3.28-29; Mt. 12.32; Lk. 12.10).[36]

The first part of this saying is a general statement decreeing forgiveness to people who oppose or even slander other people, the kind of view to be expected in the teaching of Jesus. The use of the term 'son of man', however, is the particular idiom whereby the statement refers particularly to Jesus himself. The saying therefore appears at first sight to grant forgiveness to Jesus' opponents. The sting is in the second half. The spirit of holiness, or holy spirit, is a metaphor for God in action. Nowhere is the action of God to be seen more vigorously and obviously than in Jesus' exorcisms. The accusation that he cast out demons by *Ba'al zeboul* is accordingly an unforgiveable sin. What Jesus seems to concede in the first part of the saying is thus quite removed in the second part. This polemic, like the content of the saying, accordingly has an excellent setting in this dispute over Jesus' exorcisms. The 'son of man' idiom is also specifically Aramaic. Once again, this is certainly a genuine word of Jesus.

This dispute provides further evidence that Jesus' ministry of exorcism was truly remarkable. It is a much more natural event than a survey of the success of Jesus' ministry of exorcism might suggest. We shall see in Chapter 9 that Jesus had serious opponents whose teaching on the observance of the Torah he did not accept. Indeed, he rejected some of it very vigorously. What then could they make of his ministry of exorcism? In their culture, they had only two alternatives. It was either the power of God, or the deceitful menace of the devil. Moreover, if they did not say or do something, many people would obviously accept Jesus' view that it was the power of God working through him. In that case, they would accept the rest of his teaching too, and the authority of scribes and Pharisees would be hopelessly undermined. Hence the accusation by scribes who came down from Jerusalem (Mk 3.22).

The accusation by unnamed people in 'Q', correctly represented at Lk. 11.15, is on a somewhat different level. Two kinds of people were liable to react against Jesus' ministry of exorcism. Some people had maltreated the demoniacs and thereby helped to cause their wild and peculiar behaviour. These must necessarily have included some of those closest to demoniacs, who are liable to have been present at exorcisms. Some of them may not have been pleased. Other opponents

---

36   Cf. pp. 366–67: Casey, *Aramaic Approach to Q*, pp. 148–49, 177–82.

could be faithful Jews who had other reasons to disapprove of the Jesus movement, such as because it was not halakhically strict enough, or undermined the authority of scribes and Pharisees. They too would find it difficult to see the power of God working in the exorcisms, and they might follow the lead of powerful scribes and see the power of the devil instead.

This opposition, however, could not possibly be created by an occasional event of an ambiguous kind. It makes sense only as opposition to a vigorous and successful ministry of exorcism. Accordingly, this dispute may be added to the other kinds of evidence which I have surveyed to give us one absolutely certain fact about Jesus: he conducted an extensive, vigorous and successful ministry of exorcism.

5. Healing Other Illnesses

Jesus performed a variety of other healings which fall within the parameters of what traditional healers can achieve. Immediately after he exorcized the demoniac in the synagogue at Capernaum, Jesus went to the house of Simeon the Rock and his brother Andrew, with Jacob and John, the sons of Zebedee. They told him that Simeon's mother-in-law was lying down with a fever. Mark says that he went and took her by the hand and raised her up. The result was that 'the fever left her, and she served them' (Mk 1.29-31). Fevers were normal in the ancient world, and in this part of Israel, they could be associated with malaria, which was endemic. A sudden healing might be possible, depending on details which Mark does not supply. Keir Howard comments, 'Perhaps she was in the post-febrile stage of her illness with its concomitant depression and lassitude and this was overcome by the charismatic authority of Jesus.'[37] It follows that this healing was a normally possible event, even if the illness was not a minor fever. The incidental details might well be repeated by an eyewitness, and the story contains nothing that the early church would want to create. The common conjecture that this was an eyewitness account by Simeon the Rock himself is entirely reasonable.[38]

Jesus is also reported to have cured paralysis. The narrative at Mk 2.1-12 (subsequently rewritten at Mt. 9.1-8; Lk. 5.17-26) has suffered some expansion. I have argued elsewhere for the following reconstruction, which includes all the main points which I discuss.[39]

> And he entered Capernaum again after some days. And it was heard that he was at home. [2]And many (people) gathered together, and he was giving them a speech. [3]And they came to him bringing a paralytic, and four (people) were carrying him. [4]And they were not able to approach him because of the

---

37   Keir Howard, *Disease and Healing*, p. 65.
38   So Taylor, *Mark*, p. 178, citing Weiss, Branscomb, 'and many others'.
39   Casey, *Solution to the 'Son of Man' Problem*, pp. 144–67.

gathering. And they took off the roofing where he was and dug it out. And they lowered the mattress on which the paralytic was lying.[5]And Jesus saw their faith and said to the paralytic, 'Child, your sins have been forgiven/undone/released'. [6]And some of the scribes were sitting there. [8]And he said to them, 'Why are you considering these things in your hearts? [9]Which is light, to say "Your sins have been forgiven/undone/released", or to say "Get up and take up your mattress and walk"? [10]And so that you may know that a/the son of man on earth has power/authority to forgive/undo/release sins, [11]"Get up, I tell you, take up your mattress and go to your house."' [12]And he got up, and at once he took up his mattress and went out in front of all of them. And everyone was amazed and glorified God. And (they were) saying, 'We have not seen (anything) like this.'

The story is set in a house in Capernaum. The common conjecture that this would be the house of Simeon the Rock and Andrew his brother is possible, but cannot be verified. The healing incident begins with the arrival of four people carrying a man described as 'paralytic'. It is evident that he could not or would not walk. What was wrong with him?

In general, some kinds of paralysis come within the realm of illnesses which have psychological causes and may be subject to spontaneous remission and/or therapy. Hence this is within the area of illnesses which people in the ancient world might think were curable by deities and/or healers. So for example Jablensky includes 'problems with movement, paralysis' among the World Health Authority's classification of 'narrowly defined somatoform symptoms'.[40] Murphy likewise includes 'paralysis' as one of the examples of 'conversion disorder' which 'suggests neurological disease'. He notes that 'an episode of conversion is usually of short duration with sudden onset and resolution'.[41] In discussing paralysis among 'disorders of hysterical conversion', Toone notes that hysterical weakness 'involves principally the extremities, and the legs more than the arms'. It is 'usually a paralysis of movement rather than a weakness of individual muscles'; in these cases, strength is retained in the muscles.[42]

Shorter has written a history of psychosomatic illnesses in the modern world. In his chapter on 'Motor Hysteria' he notes that recorded instances of paralysis increased greatly after 1800, and he gives many useful examples. In particular, what was known as hysterical paralysis increased as the century passed. It could be very difficult for conventional doctors to cure, and it was susceptible to other kinds of treatment. Shorter quotes Osler declaring in 1892, 'Perhaps no single affection has brought more discredit upon the profession, for the cases are very refractory, and finally fall into the hands of a charlatan or faith-healer, under

---

40 A. Jablensky, 'The Concept of Somatoform Disorders: A Comment on the Mind-Body Problem in Psychiatry', in Ono *et al.* (eds), *Somatoform Disorders*, pp. 3–10 (7).

41 M. R. Murphy, 'Classification of the Somatoform Disorders', in Bass (ed.), *Somatization*, pp. 10–39 (25).

42 B. K. Toone, 'Disorders of Hysterical Conversion', in Bass (ed.), *Somatization*, pp. 207–33 (217).

whose touch the disease may disappear at once.'[43] At this stage, the majority of cases were Victorian women, and I have noted the importance of the work of J.-M. Charcot in the classification and popularity of this illness.[44] Consequently, hysterical paralysis was the illness suffered by many men who could not cope with being soldiers in the First World War.

This was part of a massive increase in psychosomatic illnesses during that war. This led to a lot of study. In the light of this, Micklem wrote a classic work in which he suggested that the paralytic in Mk 2.1-12 suffered from hysterical paralysis, which Jesus was able to cure.[45] As I pointed out above, instances of hysterical paralysis underwent a drastic decline soon after the First World War, with Charcot's particular form of hysteria disappearing within a decade of his death.[46] The importance of this is that it further clarifies the culturally oriented nature of this illness, an observation which must be held together with the fact that paralysis itself is much more widely attested. Shorter has an example of psychogenic paralysis from 1682.[47] A detailed report on several cases studied together was published in 1987: it includes one paralyzed man who responded to the injunction 'get up'.[48] This is a particularly good parallel to Jesus' ability to cure some people with a word of command.

Paralysis is a well-attested illness in the ancient Graeco-Roman world, and the cure of limbs is attested in votive offerings. At Epidaurus, for example, Hermodikas of Lampsacus is said to have been paralyzed of body. He was healed in his sleep, and is said to have carried a large stone into the sanctuary the following morning. Kleimenes of Argos was also paralyzed. He was cured after a night in which he had a vision of Asclepius.[49]

There are also passages in Jewish sources which indicate knowledge that paralysis might result from fear. For example, in Jeremiah 6, God threatens to bring a merciless people against Zion because so much wrong has been done in the city. The people's reaction to this news includes paralysis of the hands resulting from fear among sinful people (Jer. 6.24). In the opening chapter of *3 Maccabees*, Antiochus is on the verge of the obviously sinful act of entering the sanctuary.

---

43   E. Shorter, *From Paralysis to Fatigue: A History of Psychosomatic Illness in the Modern Era* (New York: Free Press, 1992), esp. ch. 5: 'Motor Hysteria' (p. 125 has the above quotation from W. Osler, *The Principles and Practice of Medicine* (New York: Appleton, 1892), p. 974).

44   See p. 246.

45   E. R. Micklem, *Miracles and the New Psychology: A Study in the Healing Miracles of the New Testament* (London: OUP, 1922), esp. pp. 85–91.

46   See p. 246.

47   Shorter, *From Paralysis to Fatigue*, p. 7.

48   J. H. Baker and J. R. Silver, 'Hysterical paraplegia', *Journal of Neurology, Neurosurgery and Psychiatry* 50 (1987), pp. 357–82.

49   E. J. Edelstein and L. Edelstein, *Asclepius: A Collection and Interpretation of the Testimonies* (2 vols. Baltimore: Hopkins, 1945), pp. 224, 228, no. 423 (=IG IV,1, nos 121–22) XV and XXXVII. These texts may be more readily available in L. R. LiDonnici, *The Epidaurian Miracle Inscriptions: Text, Translation and Commentary* (Atlanta: Scholars, 1995), pp. 96–97 (A15), 112–13 (B37).

In response to prayers led by Simon the high priest, he is struck down by God, with the result that he ends up helpless on the ground, with paralyzed limbs and unable to speak. He was taken away by friends and bodyguards, and in due course recovered, being no longer in danger of committing this particular sinful act.

All this is sufficient to indicate that paralysis might be included among illnesses which could result from sin, and that it might be thought of as temporary. This is accordingly the first part of the Explanatory Model according to which the paralysis of the man in Mark's story might be thought of as caused by sin, and as something from which he could recover, provided that his sins were forgiven.

The remarkable but realistic setting has four men dig through the roof of the overcrowded house and lower the paralytic down to Jesus on a mattress. This shows that the five men had a very strong investment in the success of the healing event. They must have been absolutely determined to get the paralytic healed, and he must have been ready to be healed. The narrator tells us that Jesus saw their faith. The paralytic's faith was essential for the healing to take place, and the support of his friends would be very helpful, for they could subsequently support him as a healed person, just as they had previously treated him as a paralytic.

Jesus responded in accordance with the first part of the Explanatory Model of this man's illness, by announcing that the man's sins were forgiven. The Explanatory Model which attributes illness to sin is attested in the Hebrew Bible. For example, Psalm 32 has a man who was ill when he did not confess his sins to God, and who recovered when he did. This model is further attested in later sources. A saying of R.Alexandri in the name of R.Ḥiyya bar Abba puts it bluntly: 'A sick person does not arise from his sickness until they forgive him all his sins' (b. Ned. 41a). The first part of the Explanatory Model is accordingly clear. The man's illness has been attributed to his sins. Jesus therefore began the healing process by reassuring him that his sins have been forgiven. The passive, 'your sins are forgiven/undone/released' presupposes that his sins have been forgiven by God. It is repeated at v. 9.

The opening of v. 9 has caused problems to interpreters, because Mark reports Jesus as saying, 'Which is easier, to say to the paralytic "Your sins have been forgiven", or to say "Get up and take up your mattress and walk"?' Commentators therefore discuss which of these is easier, and the majority view is still represented by Taylor: 'Superficially, it is easier to declare sins forgiven; for to say "Arise, etc." is to expose oneself to the test of success or failure, while to say "Thy sins are forgiven" is to declare what cannot be verified.'[50] However, Jesus cannot have said 'Which is easier' because there is no comparative word 'easier' in Aramaic. Mark's 'easier' (*eukopōteron*) is however a natural translation of the Aramaic *qallīl*.

The Aramaic word *qallīl* means 'light', in weight. Like its opposite *ḥōmēr*, 'heavy', *qallīl* was used metaphorically with regard to commandments, or legal judgements. It meant that they were comparatively of lesser importance. The semantic area of *qallīl* extends further to 'lenient', 'insignificant'. Its legal usage

---

50 Taylor, *Mark*, p. 197.

is of particular interest here, partly because it makes excellent sense of Jesus' comments, and partly because it makes excellent sense in the presence of scribes. Jesus used a conventional legal term to ask which of his proposed actions, pronouncing the forgiveness of sins or telling the man to get up and walk, was 'light', that is to say, a matter of no great significance. It will be noted that at the present stage the forgiveness of sins is still in the passive. This is important, because the passive shows that Jesus was pronouncing the forgiveness of sins by God. The answer to his question was, from his perspective, 'neither'. The pronouncement of the forgiveness of sins by God was a matter of the greatest importance because it enabled the cure to go ahead in accordance with the will of God. The cure itself was of central importance, because the healing ministry was at the centre of Jesus' ministry as a whole.

The translation of 'Which is light . . . ?' from Aramaic into Greek was difficult, because terminology of this significance was not available in Greek. The permanent comparison between 'light' and 'heavy' might however lead a translator to use a comparative. Moreover, 'light' commandments are by their nature easier to observe than heavier ones. Hence Mark went for *eukopōteron*, 'easier'. He will have agreed with Jesus that neither matter was a light one.

Thus v. 9 told everyone that Jesus was about to tell the man to get up, take up his mattress and walk. This prepared the man for the centre of the healing event, when he would actually do so. The pressure on the man to do as he was told was now extremely strong. Jesus' assurance that God had forgiven his sins, which is effectively repeated in this verse, will have taken the necessary weight off his mind. The 'Son of man' saying tells him this *for the third time*. This, in a drastically short narrative, underlines the profundity of Jesus' belief in the Explanatory Model noted above: he perceived that this man was paralyzed because he was overburdened by his sins.

The way that Jesus put it this third time has caused interpreters endless trouble, centred on the term 'Son of man', generally treated as a title of Jesus alone. This has often been read back into the passive declarations of the forgiveness of the man's sins in vv. 5 and 9. For example, in the very sentence in which he shows knowledge of the passive to indicate the action of God, Marcus seeks to undermine it here:

> But 'are forgiven' is probably not just a divine passive in the Markan context . . . the scribes interpret 'your sins are forgiven' as a claim that Jesus himself has the power of absolution, and angrily reject this claim . . . The Markan Jesus does not draw back from the implication of near-divinity that gives rise to this objection.[51]

The use of the Son of man concept has the further problem that Jewish documents which use the term 'Son of man' of an exalted figure do not mention his forgiving sins. Scholars have frequently sought to meet this difficulty by referring

---

51   Marcus, *Mark 1–8*, pp. 216, 222.

to Dan. 7.13.[52] But in this text 'one like a son of man' is given authority as a symbol of God granting victory to the Jewish people and power over their enemies. There is nothing in it to cause Jesus to use the term 'son of man' in respect of the forgiveness of sins. If he had been so peculiar, no one would have caught the reference, but as usual there is no sign of puzzlement as to what he said.[53]

Such problems arise from studying this verse in Greek, in the light of Christian tradition. From these habits comes the whole idea that 'Son of man' is a messianic title in this verse, and refers to Jesus alone. To recover what Jesus originally meant, we must set Christian tradition aside, and consider what the saying might have meant in Aramaic:

> [10]And so that you may know that a/the son of man on earth has power/ authority to forgive/undo/release sins, [11]Get up, I tell you, take up your mattress and go to your house.

The saying ends with Jesus' orders to the man to get up, take up his mattress and go home. It follows that there is a sense in which v. 10 refers to the power of Jesus in particular. At the same time, the idiomatic use of *bar* (*e*)*nāsh*(*ā*), 'son of man', also has a general level of meaning. This can be very general, but many examples of this idiom are primarily about the speaker, or about other people made clear by the context. This example is primarily about Jesus, as his healing of the man demonstrates. It also includes a restricted group of people who may also pronounce the forgiveness of sins. In the nature of the case, these people are not defined. They must include prophets, and healers must also be included, for only so could they perform healings for which this was the appropriate Explanatory Model.

At this point, the semantic areas of Mark's Greek word *aphienai*, usually translated 'forgive', and the underlying Aramaic *shebhaq*, are crucial, for both have large semantic areas, and neither is primarily an equivalent of the English word 'forgive'. The Aramaic *shebhaq* approximates to English words such as 'allow', 'abandon', 'set free', and within this broad context it can mean to remit a debt, and it is used twice in the Dead Sea Scrolls of the forgiveness of sins (4Q 242; 11Q10 XXXVIII.2 (Job 42.10)). The next question is this: how could a healer heal someone suffering from paralysis of psychosomatic origin? Only by doing something to relieve the psychosomatic cause of this illness. What then if the Explanatory Model discussed above was the appropriate one, and the man was overburdened with a consciousness of sin? Somehow or other, that burden had to be lifted. Jesus has already attempted this twice, using the passive: 'your sins have been forgiven/undone/ released'. The 'son of man' saying is a third attempt to express God's activity, with the idiomatic use of *bar* (*e*)*nāshā*. The reason for putting it this way was Jesus' central role in the healing event, which he was about to demonstrate. It gave very powerful reassurance to the man that he had done the right thing in coming to Jesus personally, since Jesus had the power to undo

---

52 E.g. Marcus, *Mark 1–8*, pp. 222–23.
53 On the term 'son of man' see further pp. 358–88.

his sins himself, as he and the man must now demonstrate. The term *shebhaq* facilitates this way of putting it, because of its broad semantic area. It also permits the general level of meaning which is an essential facet of this idiom.

This general level of meaning assumes that more people than Jesus had the ability to undo the effects of sin in the case of psychosomatic illnesses for which the Explanatory Model used here was appropriate. This must have been the case, because both Essenes and Therapeutae were involved in the healing of what we would call psychosomatic illness, and the Explanatory Model according to which illness was caused by the sick person's sins was a biblical and well-known model. How well aware Jesus was of the detailed behaviour of other healers we do not know. He may have been generalizing from his own experience. In that case, the aggressive way he expressed himself was due to his abilities being denied by his opponents, and perhaps not generally accepted by other people. We have seen that he accepted the ability of other exorcists, even though he was the most able exorcist of his time known to us.[54] He may well have deliberately sought to demonstrate that God enabled people to undo the effects of sin upon illness to a much greater degree than people realized. This is explicit in the editorial work of Matthew, who has the crowds glorify God because he had given such power to men (Mt. 9.8). However secondary this editing was at a literary level, it is culturally accurate in recognizing the general level of meaning implied by Mk 2.10. The power of healers to pronounce the forgiveness of sins is also implicit in Jesus' sending the disciples out on a healing ministry (Mk 6.7, 13, 30), since cases of illness for which the same Explanatory Model was appropriate are likely to have been encountered.

The word of command is then given to the man at v. 11. It requires him to use all his main limbs, since he has to walk and carry something. This is the point of getting him to go home, rather than to sit and join the crowd. The crowd reacts in a standard Jewish way to a healing event, by being amazed and glorifying God. This implies that events of this kind had not been taking place in Capernaum much in recent times, which is reasonable enough.

There should therefore be no doubt that Jesus cured this paralyzed man. I have however omitted as a secondary gloss Mark's comment that the scribes 'were questioning in their hearts, "why is this man speaking like this. He is blaspheming! Who can forgive sins except God alone?"' (Mk 2.6b-7). This must be secondary because, even according to Mark, the scribes say nothing. Moreover, the accusation of blasphemy is inappropriate, because Jesus' announcement of the forgiveness of the man's sins presupposes that it is God who has forgiven him. This comment presupposes the extreme hostility to Jesus' ministry which we have already seen in the accusation that he cast out demons by the power of the devil himself. The same hostility is explicit in Mark's other account of Jesus healing a paralytic, in this case a man who could not use his arm (Mk 3.1-6).[55]

This is the second of two sabbath disputes: some Pharisees, who had already

---

54   See pp. 253–54.

55   For detailed discussion, including a reconstruction of Mark's Aramaic source see Casey, *Aramaic Sources of Mark's Gospel*, pp. 138–39, 173–92.

objected to Jesus' disciples plucking grain on the sabbath, watched at a meeting in the synagogue to see whether Jesus would also heal on the sabbath. While this is not against the written Law, Pharisees who were vigorously opposed to Jesus were also involved in expanding the Law to apply it to the whole of life. It is they who decided that healing was work. Their attitude is revealing. In the first place, they were watching to see whether he would heal *on the sabbath*, to accuse him of breaking the sabbath – they had no doubt that he could carry out the healing. Secondly, when the healing was performed, they did not have second thoughts, as faithful Jews would have when presented with an unambiguously mighty act of God. They took counsel to destroy him, because from their perspective he had violated the sabbath by doing work on it, not by doing the impossible on it. This is reinforced by the fact that the narrator does not report any kind of amazement from the onlookers, though the healing was done in the full sight of everyone at a public meeting.

Mark describes the man as having his hand or arm 'dried up'. When Jesus carried out the healing, he told the man to stretch his arm out (Mk 3.5). We must infer that the man had not been using his hand/arm properly, and had not been stretching it out. When Jesus healed him, we usually read that 'his hand was restored' (e.g. NRSV), because this is a sound translation of Mark's Greek *apekatestathē*. In the Septuagint, however, this verb usually translates the Hebrew *shūbh*, because these two words overlap so much in meaning, and the equivalent Aramaic *tūbh* is the only word which it could have been used to translate here. Consequently, the underlying Aramaic can only mean something slightly different from Mark's Greek:

ūphᵉshat wᵉtūbh lēh yᵉdhā.

And the hand/arm stretched out and returned to him.

This gives a graphic picture of the man using his arm again, stretching it out and bringing it back to himself, so using the muscles of his wrist and/or elbow as one should be able to. This effect can surely not be accidental: this adds to an argument of cumulative weight for the transmission of this story in an Aramaic version which has been literally translated.

The nearest parallel in ancient Judaism is the story of Jeroboam in 1 Kings 13. When he ordered a prophet to be seized, 'the hand which he stretched out against him withered/dried up, and he could not draw it back to himself' (1 Kgs 13.4). Here the trouble is caused by direct divine intervention, and Jeroboam's hand was stuck out in the position in which he had used it to order the prophet to be seized. When he asked the man to pray for his cure, he asked for a specific effect, 'pray for me, that my hand may come back to me' (1 Kgs 13.6). It is possible that the author of Mark's source had the Jeroboam incident deliberately in mind, but we cannot verify this. In any case, the Jeroboam story shows that this story is at home in Jewish culture. A man who could not stretch out his arm was a possible phenomenon, and a prophet who had access to God could restore him to normality.

Jesus' first order to the man was 'Get up (and come out) into the middle' (Mk 3.3). He then asked an important question, which may be reconstructed as follows:

> And he said to them, 'Is it permitted on the sabbath to do what is good, or to do evil, to save life/a person (*n*ᵉ*phash*) or to kill (him)?' And they were silent (cf. Mk 3.4).

The centre of Jesus' argument is the expression 'to save a life/person'. Whereas the Greek *psychē* is often translated 'soul', the Aramaic *n*ᵉ*phash* means both 'person' and 'life', and this range of meaning is essential to understanding Jesus' argument. Later rabbis wrote down the principle that saving life overrides the sabbath. Jesus' argument makes sense only if we suppose that this principle was already accepted by the Pharisees.

It had become a problem in serious form almost two centuries earlier, when some orthodox Jews died rather than defend themselves on the sabbath (1 Macc. 2.29-38). They expanded God's commandment not to work on the sabbath to include a ban on fighting even in self-defence, as in the written law of *Jub.* 50.12. Mattathias and his followers then agreed that they would fight on the sabbath, to prevent the destruction of the Jewish community. This was in accordance with all previous Jewish practice and with the main points of God's covenant with Israel, which was intended to bring Israel life, not genocide. It is therefore appropriate that Mattathias and his followers were immediately joined by a significant group of people labelled 'the pious' (*hasidhīm*), who offered themselves freely for the Law (1 Macc. 2.42). These 'pious' were the group from whom the Pharisees were descended, and Jewish armies have invariably adhered to the principle that saving life overrides the sabbath ever since. Consequently, Pharisees at the time of Jesus could be relied on to believe that saving life overrides the sabbath, a principle transmitted orally and a Jewish assumption which could be taken for granted, and which the rabbis wrote down in later texts.

That the halakhic judgement was in this form is further shown by the sharp contrast with 'to kill him'. The penalty for sabbath-breaking was officially death, and there is good reason to believe that the Pharisees will have warned Jesus about this, and that our text could take this for granted. The combination of this fact with the normal ruling that saving *life* overrides the sabbath explains this sharp contrast. We might suppose, and these Pharisees surely will have supposed, that Jesus was not saving the man's life, and that therefore his action was not covered by the halakhic agreement that saving life overrides the sabbath.

To understand Jesus' point of view, we must examine his argument in justification of another sabbath healing, that of a sick woman who could not stand up straight, though her condition was not serious enough to prevent her from attending synagogue (Lk. 13.10-17). Jesus healed her by the laying on of hands, as well as with a word of command. When challenged by the ruler of the synagogue, part of the story that shows signs of Lukan composition, he responded with a halakhic argument, the second part of which is as follows:

This daughter of Abraham, whom Satan bound, look!, for eighteen years, (is/was) it not fitting that she should be released from this bond on the day of the sabbath?

Jesus clearly took the view that this woman could not use her limbs properly because she had been bound by Satan. It is this view which explains the strength of his commitment to healing on the sabbath, and his description of it as 'to save a life/person'. He believed that he was saving people from the devil.

Keir Howard argues plausibly that this was a case of adult scoliosis. He comments,

> Non-structural forms of this condition are well recognized, including those due to psychological causes, such as conversion/somatization disorders. Chronic back pain itself, with no evidence of pathology, may induce a functional curvature of the spine, adopted by the patient in an attempt to avoid muscle spasm, and this may become a persistent feature of the person's gait, a feature frequently seen in the writer's own specialist medical practice.[56]

Jesus, however, thought her condition was caused by Satan. This is a different Explanatory Model from Mk 2.1-12, where the man's paralysis was caused by his sins. It should not be confused with demon possession, which Jesus dealt with by means of exorcism. It helps to explain Jesus' halakhic argument in Mk 3.1-6.

What Jesus did in his argument with the Pharisees was to expand the meaning of 'to save life/a person', which they agreed could be done on the sabbath, from stopping someone from dying to saving a person from Satan. He did this in a proposition containing words with which the Pharisees were bound to agree.

We can now reconsider the sharpness of 'to kill'. The Pharisees must have warned Jesus about breaking the sabbath, and the official penalty for sabbath-breaking was death. They would shortly take counsel with the Herodians to bring this about. This is what Jesus is contrasting with his own action – he is saving a person, whereas they are bringing about death. Not only therefore is he innocent – they are guilty, and guilty of breaking the Law just when they think they are observing it. It is this which explains the lead-in to this argument:

Is it permitted on the sabbath to do what is good, or to do evil . . .

Jesus considered that he was doing good by saving the man from the bond of Satan. The Pharisees, however, have every intention of doing evil on the sabbath, and do so when they take counsel with the Herodians to destroy Jesus.

In response to Jesus' halakhic argument, the Pharisees were silent. This further testifies to their determination to take action against Jesus. It is reminiscent of the silence of the scribes in Mk 2.1-12. The Pharisees could have had a halakhic argument with him. They preferred to be silent because, as Mark says in v. 2, they were waiting to accuse him. Jesus was angry that the Pharisees would not

---

56   Keir Howard, *Disease and Healing*, p. 159.

let him be the vehicle of divine action on the sabbath, and the narrator describes
this as their hardness of heart. We should accept this as a correct insight into the
views of the incident taken by the main participants.

The healing incident follows. The man has already chosen to be on the side of
Jesus rather than the Pharisees by obeying his order to come out into the middle.
Jesus must have had the ability to perceive when people were able to come out
of illness situations and be restored to normal life. He next issued the word of
command, 'Stretch out the hand/arm'. The man was able to obey this command
by stretching his arm out. His arm did not then become like that of Jeroboam,
stuck out in that position, but also returned to him. The man has accepted that
he is cured, and has made use of the muscles in his hand/arm. From an immediate perspective, therefore, he was cured. Jesus has now performed a healing on
the sabbath, and action against him by the Pharisees follows in the next verse.
These faithful Jews cannot have regarded the incident as a miraculous display
of the power of God.

I have discussed two healings in which the illness was attributed to the work
of Satan, though neither person was possessed, and Jesus performed healings,
rather than exorcisms. A story which sounds rather like an exorcism at times is
the cleansing of a man with skin disease at Mk 1.40-45, already discussed above.
Mark introduces it with a summary, which also concludes the preceding story:

> And he was preaching in their synagogues in the whole of Galilee, and cast-
> ing out demons.
>
> (Mk 1.39)

It follows that Mark saw nothing incongruous in this story following a summary
which made specific reference to exorcism.

> And there came to him a man with skin disease, who appealed to him and
> went down on his knees and said to him, 'If you wish, you can cleanse me'.
>
> (Mk 1.40)

The Greek word for 'a man with skin disease' is *lepros*. It is often translated 'a
leper', but this can be misleading. What we call 'leprosy' is technically known as
Hansen's disease, a very serious disease which was probably very rare in Israel
at the time of Jesus. The word *lepros*, however, like words from the underlying
Hebrew and Aramaic root *ṣera'*, has a wide range of meaning. It covers a wide
range of skin diseases in human beings, as well as, for example, fungal growths
in houses. None of the biblical descriptions of these conditions are specifically
reminiscent of Hansen's disease. Some skin diseases can be of psychosomatic
origin, and are within the range of what can be dealt with by traditional healers.
Moreover, relevant diseases such as psoriasis are subject to spontaneous remission, though not to instant cure. This is why it is important that the leper asked
to be 'cleansed', rather than healed. People suffering from such conditions were
regarded as unclean, and were not supposed to enter walled cities. Hence the
setting of the story during Jesus' migratory ministry around Galilee.

The man's comment shows a profound need to be cleansed. He will have been aware that Elisha the prophet had 'cleansed' a 'leper' who wanted him to 'remove' his 'leprosy' (2 Kings 5), and he will have known Jesus' reputation as a prophet and healer. Jesus' response, as we have it in Mark, is problematic, as we have seen,[57] so much so that most manuscripts have changed it:

> And being angry, he stretched out his hand and touched him and said to him, 'I am willing, be cleansed'.
>
> (Mk 1.41)

Here the problematic word is 'being angry', omitted by Matthew and Luke and altered in most manuscripts of Mark to 'having compassion'. It must be a translation of the Aramaic *r^egaz*, which has a somewhat wider range of meaning. It indicates profound emotional disturbance, to be expected of a man who outshouted demoniacs and felt the power of God working through him to defeat Satan. It is the process of confrontation with perceived evil which disturbed Jesus: we do not need to wonder what it was about the man that made him angry. The action of stretching out his hand and touching the man was part of the healing process. It was a very strong form of acceptance of a leprous person. Touching the man was not contrary to the Torah, and Jesus would consider himself unclean only if the man was not cleansed, whereas in fact he was. In any case, Jesus was probably unclean already.

The next verse has another difficult word at the beginning, perhaps another attempt to translate the Aramaic *g^e'ar*.

> And he censured/snorted at him, and immediately sent/drove him/it away/out, and said to him, 'See that you say nothing to anyone, but go, show yourself to the priest, and bring for your cleansing what Moses commanded, for a witness to them'.
>
> (Mk 1.43-44)

Here the snorting, or whatever it may have been, and the sending/driving out, are reminiscent of exorcism. The offering for the cleansing is not. It shows how completely Jesus stood within Judaism, not least because the man would have to go to the Temple in Jerusalem to offer the prescribed offerings (Lev. 14.1-32). The final verse has proved difficult to interpret, not least because the subject of each comment is not indicated, as often happens in Aramaic narratives. Since however the person preaches and spreads the word, and in the following verse it is obviously Jesus who goes to Capernaum, we should probably interpret all of it of Jesus:

> Now he went out and began to preach a lot and to spread the word, so that he could no longer go openly into a city, but was outside in deserted places. And (people) came to him from everywhere.
>
> (Mk 1.45)

---

57   See pp. 63–64.

This is indicative of the success of the migratory ministry which Jesus proposed at Mk 1.38.

As well as healing narratives, Mark offers a summary which has some primitive features, though Mark appears to have written up the end of it in accordance with his theory of a messianic secret.

> Now when evening came, when the sun had set, (they) brought to him all those who were ill and the demoniacs, and the whole city was gathered at the door. And he healed many who were ill with a variety of diseases, and he cast out many demons, and he did not let the demons speak, because they knew him.
>
> (Mk 1.32-4)

The opening phrases are very careful. The day had been a sabbath (Mk 1.21). Jesus had already performed an exorcism and a healing on the sabbath without anyone objecting (Mk 1.23-31). This was not against the written Law, and Jesus believed that this was the power of God operating through him, not that he was violating the commandment against working on the sabbath. Carrying burdens was however against the written Law (Jer. 17.21-22), and anyone who has tried to carry a sick person should understand that the person is so heavy and difficult to carry that bringing this under the prohibition of carrying burdens is almost inevitable. This is why Mark's note of time is so careful. The sabbath ended when darkness fell. 'When evening came' might not be clear enough: 'when the sun had set' settles it – we should now all know that people carried other people only when the sabbath was over, so as not to violate the written Law. This report cannot be the work of the early church: it must go back to a real report transmitted during the historic ministry, when this observance of the written Law mattered, and everyone took this so much for granted that the careful note of time was sufficient to bring it to mind. Mark, however, has clearly edited it, especially at the end.

A different kind of evidence for the historicity of healing narratives lies in Aramaic words, believed to be exactly the words which Jesus spoke. Two such words are found in the story of the raising of the daughter of one of the leaders of a synagogue, who was probably called Yā'īr, usually known in English as Jairus. He believed that she was near to death, but that Jesus could save her through the laying on of hands, so that she would live (Mk 5.23). It is regrettable that Mark's translation of Yā'īr's words for what was wrong with his daughter is such idiomatic Greek that an Aramaic reconstruction is difficult: he has *eschatōs echei*, literally 'has finally', rather like the idiomatic English 'is on her last legs'. It is reasonable to suppose that Mark read something like *nphlah lbhūsh bīsh*, 'has fallen into an evil evilness', which could not be translated literally, and meant that she was seriously ill. Others, however, came and said that she had died, which led Jesus to urge Yā'īr to continue to have faith (Mk 5.35-36).

Jesus took with him into the house only the inner circle of three, Simeon the Rock, and Jacob and John the sons of Zebedee, so one of them is likely to be the ultimate source of the story. He is then reported to have said, 'The child did not die, but is sleeping' (Mk 5.39). It is difficult to decode this, from another culture centuries later. It should however be taken more seriously than it has sometimes been taken in the Christian tradition. It must mean that Jesus was aware that the child was not dead, and being asleep is a metaphor for a state of being from which Jesus knew that he could arouse her. He was evidently more impressed by the words which Yā'īr spoke and Mark does not repeat (cf. Mk 5.23), than by the unhelpful comments of members of his household, who preferred to believe she was dead (5.35). These people were hostile enough to laugh at Jesus, and he threw them all out (5.40), a task in which Yā'īr must have supported him.

Jesus went to the girl with his three disciples, Yā'īr and Yā'īr's wife, the girl's mother. To rouse her, Jesus grasped her hand and said, '*Talitha koum*' (Mk 5.41). This is the Aramaic for 'Girl, get up', as transliterated into Greek letters. Mark expanded it in translation, as translators often do: 'Girl, I say to you, get up.' The decision as to whether to give significant words in their original languages is frequently rather arbitrary, but Mark did it elsewhere.[58] These two words are useful to us because they are right, and take us back to the Aramaic stage of the tradition. Moreover, we have seen that the majority of manuscripts read the technically correct written feminine form *koumi*, but that the feminine ending '*i*' was not pronounced. It follows that *Talitha qūm* (restoring the original Aramaic *q* from the Greek transliteration) is *exactly* what Jesus said.[59]

The girl then got up and walked. The girl's parents are said to have been amazed, and Jesus told them not to let anyone know, but to give her something to eat. He evidently felt that some members of the household were liable to continue being very unhelpful, and that the girl needed nourishment and practical care, which Yā'īr and her mother could be relied upon to give her, while Yā'īr ensured that everyone else was kept away from her.

In this story, Jesus was expected to lay hands upon the girl, and in fact grasped her hand. I have also noted him touch a man with skin disease, lay his hands on a woman who could not stand up straight, and grasp Peter's mother-in-law's hand and pull her up, as he did to a difficult demoniac. Occasionally, Jesus is reported to have done something more elaborate. In the healing of a deaf man who could not speak properly, Jesus was first urged to lay his hand upon him (Mk 7.32). He presumably did so when he took the man away from the crowd (Mk 7.33). Then he put his fingers in the man's ears, spat and touched his tongue (Mk 7.33). Then he looked up to heaven, groaned and gave another word of command which is transmitted in Aramaic, *Ephphatha*, which means 'be opened', as Mark correctly translates it (Mk 7.34).[60] Keir Howard suggests that the man was suffering from a conversion/somatiform disorder. He comments,

Deafness and mutism as well as speech defects are well-documented features

---

58　See pp. 189–90, and p. 277.
59　See p. 109.
60　For technical details see Casey, *Aramaic Sources of Mark's Gospel*, p. 55, referring to M. Wilcox, 'Semitisms in the New Testament', *ANRW* II.25.2 (1984), pp. 978–1029 (998–99).

of these conditions and it seems likely from the method of healing that this man represents a further case of such an illness . . . The method of healing, clearly very dramatic, suggests the sort of abreactive technique that would produce an effect in such cases, a point that was made by Micklem many years ago.[61]

The healing of a blind man at Bethsaida is similarly complex. Here too, people urged Jesus to touch the man (Mk 8.22). Jesus took the man by the hand, and led him out of the town. There Jesus first spat in his eyes, and laid his hands on him, specifically on his eyes, as we must infer from the next part of the story. Jesus then asked if he could see anything. 'And having regained sight, he said, "I see men, whom I see like trees walking"' (Mk 8.24, slightly altered to take account of the original Aramaic). In an extensive discussion, based on the work of professional ophthalmologists, Keir Howard has shown that this means firstly that this man's blindness was acquired, not congenital.[62] Acquired blindness was common in the Middle East, and most cases were caused by eye infections, together with cataracts. Jesus' use of saliva will have encouraged the man, who will have heard and felt Jesus spitting in his eyes, and who will also been aware of the healing properties ascribed to saliva. The saliva will also have removed dirt and dried secretions from the eyelids. The pressure of Jesus' fingers on the eyes caused the displacement of the lens into the vitreous chamber of the eye. This is why the man saw men as large as trees, and suffered from blurred vision. He remembered what men and trees looked like, because they were familiar sights before he suffered from cataracts.

The next stage of the healing followed: 'Then again he put his hands on his eyes, and he saw clearly and was restored and saw everything clearly' (Mk 8.25). Keir Howard explains that he will have been someone whose 'eyes are excessive in length and excessively distendable. The vitreous body is extremely fluid and the cataracts are eminently couchable. Further, traditional healers are often able to recognize those sufferers who will benefit most from their ministrations. After the cataract has been removed, such people tend to see much more sharply and clearly than the normal cataract patient.'[63]

In addition to healings by Jesus himself, his disciples are said to have anointed many sick people with oil and cured them (Mk 6.13). It is not probable that their methods were completely different from his. It follows from all the evidence surveyed above that Jesus did not heal only by a word of command. Moreover, we cannot tell whether some true healing stories have been abbreviated, and various actions omitted. It may be that the impression sometimes obtained that Jesus healed only by a word of command is also partly due to the prevalence of exorcisms in the earliest level of the tradition.

---

61 Keir Howard, *Disease and Healing*, p. 105, referring to Micklem, *Miracles and the New Psychology*, pp. 114–20.
62 Keir Howard, *Disease and Healing*, pp. 106–12.
63 Keir Howard, *Disease and Healing*, p. 111.

6. *The Mighty Works of a Prophet*

I have surveyed a good selection of the historical evidence for Jesus' ministry of healing. It is extensive, and includes the healing of several different illnesses. Healing was central to Jesus' ministry, and exorcism was an important part of the healing ministry. Two questions follow: why is Jesus never called a healer or an exorcist? Secondly, is he ever referred to in a culturally appropriate way for a man who performed these healings and exorcisms? The answer to both these questions is that he was regarded as a prophet, and that he was so central to the Jesus movement that his followers naturally gave him the title 'Christ', or 'Messiah', when that term became generally available, sometime after his death.

The commonest traditional person involved in healing in the Hebrew Bible is a prophet, for whom the term 'man of God' may be used.[64] In Genesis 20, God appears to Abimelech in a dream, and tells him to return Sarah to Abraham. His life and the ability of his wife and female slaves to have children are said to be dependent on Abraham praying for them, and God explains this by calling Abraham a prophet (Gen. 20.7). In 1 Kings 17, Elijah prays to God and the son of the widow of Zarephath is brought back to life. This causes the widow to say that she now knows that he is a 'man of God'. In 2 Kings 4, the Shunnamite woman goes for Elisha when her son dies, calling him 'the man of God'. He comes and revives him. In 2 Kings 5, Naaman is cured of his skin disease when he follows the procedure laid down by Elisha. He is said to have done so because he was advised by a Jewish captive who thought the prophet would remove his skin disease. Elisha also calls himself a prophet, and the narrative calls him 'the man of God'. The story clearly implies that Elisha had greater powers to cure people than the number of stories in the Bible would suggest. In 2 Kings 20//Isaiah 38, the prophet Isaiah is involved in the healing of Hezekiah, when Hezekiah has prayed to God. At the time of Jesus, all these stories were part of the sacred text. It follows that a prophet was an appropriate person to be involved in healing events.

The expanded version of the story of the Pharaoh taking Abram's wife illustrates the overlap between exorcism and other kinds of healing (Gen. 12.10-20, expanded at 1QapGen XIX–XX). It has Pharaoh and his household afflicted by an evil spirit. It lists the Egyptians who could not cure them as healers, magicians and wise men (1QapGen XX, 20). Abram expels the evil spirit by prayer, and by the laying on of hands on Pharaoh himself. In the surviving part of the text, this does not cause the narrator to give Abram any special label to indicate his role, but we have seen that, in the similar story at Genesis 20, God calls Abraham a prophet.

We have already seen that Jesus belonged to the prophetic tradition, and I shall argue that this was a broad enough term to be used for his ministry as a whole. This is the reason why the stories of Jesus' healing ministry do not lead

---

64   For more detailed discussion see H. Avalos, *Illness and Health Care in the Ancient near East: The Role of the Temple in Greece, Mesopotamia and Israel* (HSM 54. Atlanta: Scholars, 1995), pp. 260–77.

people to give him a special label such as 'healer' or 'exorcist'. This was rather subsumed under the general term 'prophet', to which was added 'teacher', a term denoting his other major role.[65] In short, even though he was the most successful healer and exorcist of his day, he was a much greater figure than that.

It is this whole healing ministry which explains Jesus' response to the question sent through messengers by John the Baptist (Mt. 11.2-6//Lk. 7.18-23). I have discussed major aspects of this already.[66] John had predicted that one mightier than he would come after him, and Jesus' reply indicated that he was that figure, bringing more repentance and less judgement than John had expected:

> Go inform John of what (people) see and hear: blind (people) see and lame (people) walk, people-with-skin-diseases are cleansed and deaf (people) hear, and dead (people) are raised and poor (people) have good news preached to them. And blessed is whoever does not stumble over me.

We have seen that this is strongly reminiscent of certain prophetic passages, notably Isa. 29.18-19; 35.5-6; 61.1. Jesus seems to have claimed indirectly to be fulfilling the hopeful parts of these prophecies, but not the prophecies of judgement in the very same passages.

There is now also a fragmentary piece from Qumran which predicts an anointed figure, or Messiah, and a ministry of healing:

> [For the heav]ens and the earth will listen to his anointed one/Messiah . . . For the Lord will seek out the pious (*ḥasīdīm*) and call the righteous by name, and his spirit will hover over the poor and he will renew the faithful with his strength. For he will glorify the pious on the throne of an eternal kingdom (*mlkūth*), liberating captives, restoring sight to the blind, straightening the be[nt] . . . And the Lord will do glorious things which have never been as . . . he will heal the wounded and give life to the dead, he will bring good news to the poor.
>
> (4Q521, frg. 2, col. II, extracts)

The fragmentary nature of this piece makes aspects of its interpretation difficult. Two points are particularly relevant. At first sight, it might seem that the author considered that the expression 'his anointed one/messiah (*mshīḥō*)' was sufficient to identify this figure, but this is simply a function of this expression being found in the first line of fragment 2 to survive. There is no other sign of the future Davidic king, and several scholars have suggested that the reference is to an eschatological prophet.[67] Prophets are called 'anointed' elsewhere at

---

65   On these terms see further pp. 172–76, and pp. 354–58.
66   See pp. 181–83.
67   E.g. J. J. Collins, *The Scepter and the Star: The Messiahs of the Dead Sea Scrolls and Other Ancient Literature* (ABRL. New York: Doubleday, 1995), pp. 117–22.

Qumran (CD II, 12; VI, 1; 1QM XI, 7), and an eschatological prophet was expected (1QS IX, 11). At Isa. 61.1, one of the passages to which Jesus referred in his reply to John the Baptist, the spirit of the Lord YHWH is upon the prophet because YHWH has anointed (*māshaḥ*) him to bring good news to the poor and to proclaim liberty to the captives. The suggestion that the figure in this passage is an eschatological prophet is therefore entirely reasonable.

A possible difficulty with this interpretation is that the Lord, referred to as *Adonai*, so unambiguously God himself, is clearly the subject of some sentences. From a purely literary point of view, despite some damage to the fragment, the Lord appears to be the subject of the crucial prediction of healing, including 'he will heal the wounded and give life to the dead, he will bring good news to the poor.' On the other hand, it is surprising that God himself should 'bring good news to the poor', a more natural task for an eschatological prophet, through whom God could also do the other remarkable deeds mentioned in this passage. It may well be that the Lord is literally the subject of these sentences because the author was consciously using Ps. 146.7-8, where there is no anointed one, and the Lord (YHWH) liberates prisoners, gives sight to the blind, and straightens the bent. The author will have assumed that the Lord would act through the eschatological prophet, and this might have been clearer if the whole text had survived. In that case, this would be a very close parallel to God acting through Jesus.

Be that as it may, this passage certainly has healing, raising the dead and evangelizing the poor all together. Moreover, raising the dead was something which Elijah and Elisha were both believed to have done, so something which it was appropriate for an eschatological prophet to do. We should infer that raising the dead is in an appropriate place among those aspects of Jesus' description of his ministry which were designed to persuade John to accept him. His description was deliberately focused on John's question, and selected references to prophecies interpreted in the same tradition as in 4Q521. Despite its selective nature, therefore, it confirms the other evidence of Jesus' successful healing ministry.

Moreover, Jesus' summary reply is generally coherent with the other accounts of Jesus' ministry, a selection of which I have discussed. So we have seen him heal a blind man (Mk 8.22-26), and a paralytic who was then able to walk (Mk 2.1-12). He 'cleansed' a man with skin disease (Mk 1.40-44), and healed a deaf man (Mk 7.32-37). It has been generally possible to see how an outstanding traditional healer might do all these things. Further narratives, and relatively early summaries by the evangelists, are sufficient to show that such healings were a central part of Jesus' ministry.

The notion that Jesus raised the dead has naturally been more controversial than these central features. Given that Jesus' reply has passages of Isaiah in mind, he may have intended a reference to Isa. 26.19, 'your dead will live', again ignoring the threat of God's wrath in the context. I have discussed the story in which he raised the daughter of a synagogue leader (Mk 5.22-24, 35–43). This story is true, but Jesus did not believe that the girl was dead. I have also discussed the raising of Lazarus (Jn 11.1-46). This story makes a point of ensuring that we know Lazarus was certainly dead (Jn 11.14, 17, 32, 37, 39), but the story is not literally true.[68]

There is only one other Gospel story in which Jesus appears to raise the dead, the raising of a widow's son at Nain, which is recorded only by Luke (Lk. 7.11-17). In this story, Jesus and his disciples meet the funeral procession, and Luke says that the widow's only son was dead (Lk. 7.12). When Jesus tells him to get up, 'the dead man sat up and began to speak' (Lk. 7.15). There is therefore no doubt that the man was dead. As so often, however, there are reasons to be suspicious about the accuracy of a story told by Luke alone. It fits excellently into the whole context, being placed conveniently before the story of the messengers coming from John the Baptist. Luke has not yet had any stories of Jesus raising the dead, so it was reasonable of him to put one here, and leave the raising of Jairus' daughter in its Markan position (Lk. 8.41-42, 49–56), amplified with the clear information that Jairus told Jesus that his only daughter was dead (Lk. 8.41-42), whereas in Mark he asks Jesus to come and save her because she is so ill (Mk 5.23). This means that Luke has one story of Jesus raising the dead before the messengers come, and another one soon afterwards. This is also coherent with his addition to the story of the messengers coming, in which Jesus performs a lot of healings 'in that hour' (Lk. 7.21). There are specifically Lukan stylistic features in the introduction (Lk. 7.11), in the description of Jesus as 'the Lord' (Lk. 7.13), and in the crowd's declaration that 'God has visited his people' (Lk. 7.16). The information that when the man sat up and began to speak, Jesus 'gave him to his mother' (Lk. 7.15), is verbally identical with LXX 1 Kgs 17.23, where Elijah gave back to his mother the widow's son whom he had just raised from the dead. Jesus' comment to the widow, 'Do not weep' (Lk. 7.13), is the singular of his comment to the mourners over Jairus' dead daughter, 'Do not weep' (Lk. 8.52, different from Mk 5.39). Jesus' words, 'Young man, I say to you, get up' (Lk. 7.14), is very similar to the Greek translation of Jesus' words at Mk 5.41, 'Girl, I say to you, get up'. There are parallels to this story elsewhere, notably in a story about Apollonius of Tyana.

All this forms a compelling argument of cumulative weight: we should not believe the story at Lk. 7.11-17. This leaves us with no true stories of Jesus raising the dead, and that is puzzling, for if it were the whole truth, the early church had insufficient reason to attribute to him such a claim, for his true claims were quite dramatic enough already. It is possible that Jesus revived people who were taken to be dead more often than in the perfectly true story about the raising of the daughter of the synagogue leader (Mk 5.22-24, 35–43). We now know from the careful collection of evidence by Derrett that many people who have been taken to be dead have revived.[69] In ancient Judaism, the survival of people believed to be dead led to the ruling that people could visit the grave for up to three days after a person was buried (b. Sem. VIII, 1).[70] This was due to the recognition,

---

68   For discussion see pp. 240–41, 268–69.

69   J. D. M. Derrett, *The Anastasis: The Resurrection of Jesus as an Historical Event* (Shipston-on-Stour: Drinkwater, 1982), ch. V.

70   Cf. further pp. 471–72.

widespread in different cultures, that death does not necessarily occur when a person first appears to be dead. This recognition lies behind the storyteller who declared that Lazarus had been dead for four days (Jn 11.17, 39), which was meant to tell everyone that he was certainly dead before Jesus raised him. In the light of such evidence, we should probably infer from Mk 5.22-24, 35–43, and from Jesus' response to John the Baptist's message, that he was able to perceive when he could cause an apparently dead person to live. From his point of view, this will have been a particularly good example of the power of God working through him, and therefore very suitable for isolating in his response to John the Baptist.

It would be wrong to end this section on a note of doubt. There should be no doubt at all that Jesus carried though a dramatic and successful ministry of exorcism and healing. He and his followers were completely convinced that this successful ministry was due to the power of God working through him, and this was a major feature in his ability to attract such a significant following. These were the mighty works of a great prophet, who was also an outstanding teacher. This is why he was known as a prophet and teacher, rather than as an exorcist and healer. Important as his ministry of exorcism and healing was, it was part of a larger ministry in which he called upon the lost sheep of the house of Israel to repent and prepare for the coming of the kingdom of God.

7. Jesus Was Not a Magician

In the ancient world, opponents of Christianity sometimes accused Jesus of performing magic. This accusation has been renewed in the modern world, most notoriously by Morton Smith in *Jesus the Magician*.[71] Jesus' ministry of exorcism and healing has usually been at the centre of these allegations, and the case has generally been made by drawing parallels between certain aspects of Jesus' behaviour and that of magicians in the ancient world. In the ancient world, it is understandable that opponents of Christianity were struck by the similarities between people whom they rejected. For modern scholars, however, there is no excuse for such misrepresentation of Jesus' Jewish life-world.

The classic ancient accusation is in the Babylonian Talmud. Here it is said that when Jesus the Nazarene was hanged, a herald went before him announcing, 'Jeshu the Nazarene is going out to be stoned because he has practiced sorcery and incited and led astray Israel' (b. San. 43a). It should be obvious that this is due to extreme hostility to Christianity, not to independent historical reporting. It is part of a vigorous attempt to claim that Jesus was justly put to death by a properly constituted Jewish court because of his grievous sins against God and

---

71 Morton Smith, *Jesus the Magician* (New York: Harper & Row, 1978. Pb. Wellingborough: Aquarius, 1985). Cf. also J. M. Hull, *Hellenistic Magic and the Synoptic Tradition* (SBT 2nd series, 28. London: SCM, 1974).

Israel.[72] This is why he is said to have been stoned, the proper rabbinical penalty for blasphemy, sorcery and leading Israel into idolatry. Its only connection with genuinely early tradition is that sorcery, or magic, is a natural accusation coming from people who were vigorously hostile to the tradition that Jesus performed miracles, including exorcisms. This is because magicians were generally believed to be able to do otherwise impossible deeds by magical means, and there were many stories to that effect.

Much earlier is the evidence of Celsus. It is evident from Origen's discussion in his tractate against Celsus (I, 38) that this very vigorous opponent of Christianity accused Jesus of performing miracles by magical means (*mageias*), having learnt such things in Egypt. Celsus wrote c.180 CE. His allegation too is not due to independent early tradition, but to hostile rejection of the Christian religion. In this context, as in the Babylonian Talmud, this is a natural accusation, and for the same reason, that in the Graeco-Roman world also, magicians were generally believed to be able to do otherwise impossible deeds by magical means, and there were many stories to that effect.

There are similar accusations scattered over second- and third-century sources. For example, in the pseudo-Clementine Recognitions (I, 42), it is reported that some of the guards at Jesus' tomb, or some of the wicked of the people, said that Jesus was a magician (*magum/ḥarāshā'*), when he could not be prevented from rising from the dead, while others said that the body was stolen.[73] This is clearly an elaboration of the reports at Mt. 27.62-66; 28.11-15, which are themselves an early mixture of Christian storytelling and anti-Christian Jewish polemic.[74]

These accusations of magic come from a different cultural environment from the Gospels, which should not be understood in the light of them.

Smith's argument has three major mistakes. First, he predates later sources, and reads earlier sources in the light of them. For example, he considers Justin's refutation of the second-century Jewish accusation that Jesus was a magician (*magon*), the earliest source to contain this accusation (Justin, *Dialogue with Trypho*, 69, 7). He then translates part of Matthew's story of chief priests and Pharisees trying to persuade Pilate to have Jesus' tomb guarded thus: 'That magician said, while <he was> yet alive, "After three days I shall rise".'[75] But

---

72 For detailed discussion see Schäfer, *Jesus in the Talmud*, esp. pp. 64–74. The original text is difficult to find, because it was censored. This and other texts were made readily available by R. Travers Herford, *Christianity in Talmud and Midrash* (London: Williams & Norgate, 1903. Repr. New York: Ktav, 1975).

73 There is no doubt about the main accusation of being a sorcerer, but other details of the text are uncertain because it has not survived. Scholars can find the Latin translation of Rufinus in B. Rehm (ed.), *Die Pseudoklementinen. 1. Homilien* (GCS 51. 3rd edn, ed. G. Strecker. Berlin: Akademie, 1992) and the Syriac translation, with a proposed reconstruction of the original Greek from the Syriac, in W. Frankenberg, *Die syrischen Clementinen mit griechischem Paralleltext; eine Vorarbeit zu dem literargeschichtlichen Problem der Sammlung* (TU 48, 3. Leipzig: Hinrichs, 1937).

74 See pp. 478–79.

75 Mt. 27.63, as translated by Smith, *Magician*, p. 54, apparently with Justin, *Dialogue* 69 and 108 in mind.

Mt. 27.63 has 'deceiver' (*planos*), not 'magician'. This is a serious accusation, which genuinely reflects early Jewish hostility to Jesus. It has a perfectly good setting in early first-century Judaism, and should not be confused with later accusations that Jesus was a magician.

Secondly, Smith interprets genuine aspects of Jesus' ministry as evidence of magic, by means of imaginative comments which are not properly based in Jesus' first-century Jewish culture. For example, as we have seen, when Jesus raised the daughter of a synagogue leader who was said by some of the leader's household to be dead, he said in Aramaic *talitha qūm*, 'Girl, get up'. Mark transliterated this into Greek letters as well as can be done, and translated it somewhat explicitatively, but perfectly accurately: '*talitha koum*, which is, when translated, "Girl, I say to you, get up"' (Mk 5.41).[76] Smith claims that this was translated by Mark 'as the Greek magical papyri sometimes translate Coptic expressions.'[77] This selection of translations from Coptic in the Greek magical papyri is a completely biased selection of evidence. Translators all the world over retain and translate occasional words from the texts which they translate. For example, at Gen. 22.13, Abraham found a ram caught in a 'thicket' (*sbk*). The Septuagint, the standard translation of the Hebrew Bible into Greek, simply translated most of the text, but both translated and transliterated this one word, the equivalent of writing in English, 'And Abraham looked up and saw with his eyes, and behold! a ram, held in a thicket sabek by its horns . . .' No one has suggested that this is due to magic! It is something which some translators do some of the time, and one cannot always see why. Mark does the same thing elsewhere. For example, at Mk 15.34, he recounts Jesus' final cry from the cross in Aramaic, before translating it into Greek:

> And at the ninth hour Jesus cried with a loud voice, '*Elōi, Elōi, lema sabachthani*', which is, when translated, 'My God, my God, why have you forsaken me?'

This is not magic either. Smith's suggestion is quite arbitrary, and again belongs to the wrong cultural context.

Smith further asserts that *talitha koum* 'circulated without translation as a magical formula', citing the story of Peter raising of Tabitha from the dead at Acts 9.36f. He regards this as evidence of 'continuing magical interest in the Christian communities which produced the Gospels.'[78] This argument consists of mistakes. The name of the woman supposedly brought back to life by Peter, was Tabitha (Acts 9.36). Tabitha was not, as Smith alleges, 'a mispronunciation of *talitha*'. It was a normal Aramaic name, meaning 'gazelle', correctly translated by Luke into Greek as Dorcas, a normal Greek name which also means 'gazelle'. Jesus' words *talitha koum* (Mk 5.41) are not found in the story of Peter raising Tabitha. When Peter raises her with the words 'Tabitha, get up',

---

76 See further pp. 268–69.
77 Smith, *Magician*, p. 95.
78 Smith, *Magician*, p. 95.

Luke has the Greek *anastēthi* for 'get up' (Acts 9.40, cf. 9.34). It follows from all this that *talitha qūm* were two words spoken by Jesus, they were not 'a magical formula', and there is no evidence that they 'circulated without translation'. Accordingly, this is not evidence of 'magical interest in the Christian communities which produced the Gospels', and provides no support for any notion that magic is an appropriate term for understanding the Gospels, or traditions about Jesus.

Thirdly, Smith adduces a variety of items which are not part of Jesus' ministry of exorcism and healing. For example, in the accounts of Jesus' baptism, he suggests that various rituals and formulae have been deleted, a suggestion which is based on no evidence at all. He then proposes that the story of the coming of the spirit is surprising because the event it describes is 'just the sort of thing that was thought to happen to a magician.' This again belongs to quite the wrong cultural context. Smith further notes that Luke and Matthew identify the spirit as 'holy' and 'of God', and comments 'surely to refute the charge of magic'.[79] But there is no sign of an accusation of magic in Matthew or Luke. Smith further suggests that the idea that this 'made him a "son of God" resembles nothing so much as an account of a magical rite of deification.'[80] This is the wrong culture again. When Jewish people described someone as a son of God, they meant a faithful Jew.[81]

We must conclude that Smith has completely misrepresented the cultural worlds of Jesus and of the synoptic Gospels. His accusation that Jesus was a magician appears to be due to malicious hostility to Christianity. His misinterpretation of the primary sources is so gross as to be virtually fraudulent. This should be borne in mind when considering the *Secret Gospel of Mark*, a document which he claimed to have discovered, and which he has been accused of forging.[82]

8. Conclusions

Exorcism and healing were central to Jesus' ministry. Jesus believed that in exorcism and in some other kinds of healing, he released people from the power of the devil. He thus felt the power of God working through him in this ministry. His ability was exceptional, but not altogether unique. He sent out his disciples to exorcize and heal too, and he accepted the divine inspiration of successful Jewish exorcists who did not belong to the Jesus movement.

Jesus himself was the most successful exorcist and healer of his time. There was however more than that to his ministry. This is why he is never labelled 'exorcist' or 'healer' in the Gospels, either by his followers or by his opponents. The term 'prophet' is in this respect the most important term to be used during

---

79   Smith, *Magician*, pp. 96–97.
80   Smith, *Magician*, p. 104.
81   See pp. 388–92.
82   See pp. 539–43.

the historic ministry, because it encompasses someone who was an exorcist and healer because he not only proclaimed the word of God, but also acted on it. Jesus' teaching was also central to his ministry, and he is still most famous to some people as a teacher of ethics. It is to this aspect of his ministry that I turn next.

CHAPTER 8

Jesus' Ethical Teaching

1. *Introduction*

Jesus is most famous to some people as a teacher of ethics. For example, the Jewish scholar Klausner commented, 'The main strength of Jesus lay in his ethical teaching. If we . . . preserved only the moral precepts and parables, the Gospels would count as one of the most wonderful collections of ethical teaching in the world.'[1] Verdicts of this kind have been quite common, yet the teaching of Jesus, as transmitted to us, does not expound an organized ethical system. The real reason for this has been somewhat obscured by a traditional Christian sense of superiority. Traditional Christianity, reflected in the work of traditional Christian scholars, has shown a profound need to maintain that the teaching of Jesus was superior to Judaism. For example, in his standard work on New Testament ethics, Schrage comments, 'the ethics of Jesus cannot be derived from the Torah . . . Jesus engaged in de facto polemic against the Torah itself . . . Jesus denied the Torah the central position it had for Judaism.'[2]

Other scholars have seen that the Torah was much more important to Jesus than that. For example, Theissen and Merx conclude, 'Jesus' ethic is a Jewish ethic . . . The centre of its content lies in the Torah, interpreted freely . . . The Torah is its basis.'[3] I argue that Jesus' ethical teaching presupposes its centre, and that its centre was indeed the Torah. The truth about the apparent difference between Jesus' teaching and Judaism is that in his teaching, unlike that of his Jewish opponents, the Torah was interpreted from a prophetic perspective. Moreover, Jesus taught from a prophetic perspective early in the first century

---

1 J. Klausner, *Jesus of Nazareth: His Life, Times and Teaching* (trans. H. Danby. London/New York: Allen and Unwin/Macmillan, 1925), p. 381.

2 W. Schrage, *The Ethics of the New Testament* (1982. Trans. D. E. Green. Minneapolis/Edinburgh: Fortress/T&T Clark, 1988), pp. 52, 67.

3 G. Theissen and A. Merx, *The Historical Jesus: A Comprehensive Guide* (1996. Trans. J. Bowden. London: SCM, 1998), p. 394.

CE, a major difference from rabbis who contributed to the ethical teachings of Judaism from a rabbinical perspective at a later date.

2. *Repentance*

I have noted the importance of repentance in the teaching of Jesus when discussing his preaching of the kingdom, or kingship, of God.[4] The actual words 'repent' and 'repentance' do not however occur very often in either Mark or Matthew, and this has led some scholars, most notably E. P. Sanders, to suppose that repentance was not a significant theme in the teaching of the historical Jesus.[5] The keys to the importance of repentance for the ethical teaching of Jesus, to the infrequent occurrence of the words 'repent' and 'repentance' in Mark and Matthew, and to the apparently unsystematic nature of Jesus' ethical teaching, all lie in the *Aramaic* word *tūbh*.

As we have seen, the Aramaic word for 'repent', *tūbh*, is not a specialized word for being sorry when one has done wrong: it is the word for 'return'. Consequently, this is the word which Jesus used when he called upon Jewish people to return to God and join the Jesus movement. It was not something which he kept urging his followers to do, for they had already taken this essential step. In the light of both these points, it can be seen that Jesus' call to repentance is multiply attested by source and form. Mark first mentions it in a summary of Jesus' preaching at the beginning of his account of the ministry. Like Matthew and Luke, however, he always translates it with the Greek word for 'repent' (*metanoeō*), because this is what the Gospel writers understandably thought Jesus meant, whereas Greek words for 'return' (e.g. *epistrephō*) are normally used for going back to places, and do not mean 'repent'. I shall therefore put 'repent/return' in my translation of such Gospel passages.[6]

> The time is fulfilled and the kingdom of God is at hand. Repent/return and believe the good news.
>
> (Mk 1.15)

As I argued above, Mark inherited a correct tradition that this is what Jesus did and said immediately after John the Baptist was arrested (though he wrongly placed it at the beginning of Jesus' ministry).[7] This was a deliberate continuation of the preaching of John the Baptist, whose ministry of baptism was centred on

---

4 See especially pp. 200, 218–19.
5 Sanders, *Jesus and Judaism*, pp. 106–13; *Historical Figure of Jesus*, pp. 230–35.
6 Detailed technical discussion of the translation process has been provided by J. G. Crossley, 'The Semitic Background to Repentance in the Teaching of John the Baptist and Jesus', *JSHJ* 2 (2004), pp. 138–57; and, more generally, Crossley, *Why Christianity Happened*, ch. 3: 'Jesus and the Sinners'.
7 See pp. 180–81.

calling people to return to God. This is why Jesus went back to Galilee straight after John's arrest by Herod Antipas, when most people would have found it prudent to lie low.

Mark also reports that one reason why Jesus appointed the Twelve was to send them out to preach (Mk 3.14), and that when he did send them out two by two, 'they preached that (people) should repent/return' (Mk 6.7, 12). This is the same call as in the ministries of John the Baptist and of Jesus himself, the call to people to return to God, without which they could not be given other ethical instructions.

I have noted the same message in the parable of the prodigal son (Lk. 15.11-32).[8] It does not matter that this parable is found only in Luke: the reason for this is that Mark is not long enough for lengthy parables, and Luke has more than Matthew. The parable does not contain the *word* 'repent' because it presents the repentance and forgiveness of the prodigal son in story mode, with the son representing a sinner who repents, the father representing God, and the other son who did not leave his father representing the righteous, who do not turn away from God, and who consequently do not need to turn back to him. So when the prodigal son decides to give up his dissolute life, it is enough for him to say 'I will get up and go to my father' (Lk. 15.18), from which it is obvious that he will return to his father. He decides to tell, and tells, his father, 'Father, I have sinned before heaven and before you' (Lk. 15.18, 21), which makes it obvious that he repents in the sense that he is sorry for the wrong he has done. It is also enough for the father to say 'This my son was dead and has come to life, he was lost and has been found' (Lk. 15.24, cf. 32). This presents the *theme* of repentance in a quite different way from the preaching of Jesus and Mark's report of the preaching of the Twelve, but it is the same theme.

The same theme is found in the 'Q' parable of the lost sheep. The two versions (Mt. 18.10-14//Lk. 15.3-7) have some differences because parables are stories which can be told and retold in different ways. It is accordingly important that the *theme* of repentance is quite clear in the Matthaean version which does not have the *words* 'repent' and 'repentance', both of which are used by Luke in his concluding summary (Lk. 15.7). Both versions have the story in which a man who has 100 sheep leaves 99 of them to search for one which is lost, and rejoices when he finds it. The Matthaean conclusion, with its 'will before' reflecting the idiomatic Aramaic *ra^a'wā min qedham*, must be nearest to what Jesus said:

So it is not (the) will before your Father in heaven that one of these little ones should be lost.

(Mt. 18.14)

This represents in another story mode God's search for sinners who have fallen away from him, a search which was being carried out in practice by Jesus and his followers. The metaphor is one of those used by the father of the prodigal

---

8   See pp. 200, 209.

son when his son returned to him, as sinners returned when God found them again.

We can now see that the theme of repentance is well attested in the teaching of Jesus. It does not appear to be pervasive because it refers to the beginning of the life of sinners in the Jesus movement, the point at which they responded to the preaching of Jesus by returning to God. After this, they did not need continual urging to return to God; they needed ethical instruction. They did not however need systematic instruction in a new system of ethics, because God's instructions were already available to them, written in the Torah. How this should be interpreted was not however always clear, and Jesus' ethical teaching was delivered at points, some of them controversial, at which he considered interpretation or additional teaching to be necessary. Before considering his detailed comments, I therefore consider first his major comments on the Torah in general.

3. *The Torah*

The two main points of the Torah may be thought of as love of God, and love of one's neighbour. Jesus' presentation of these two main points is especially clear in a classic incident which took place when he was teaching in the Temple. The story is told in our oldest source, Mk 12.28-34. The story must be true, because it has such an excellent setting in the life of Jesus, in the life of the scribe who began this particular conversation, and in the Temple, whereas the early church had no interest in inventing this kind of discussion.

The setting is in the massive outer court of the Temple, where many debates and disputes took place. Mark tells us a little about the scribe. He had been listening to Jesus debating with other people, and he was impressed: he might well be, hearing Jesus' teaching about the Torah from the perspective of a major prophet rather than a scribe. The Torah is large, and contains a great diversity of material. In the previous two centuries, the regulations found in the Torah had been massively expanded by orthodox Jews. The sabbath was a matter of particular concern. The Torah tells you not to work on the sabbath (Exod. 20.8-11// Deut. 5.12-15), and says especially that you must not light a fire on the sabbath (Exod. 35.2-3). Jeremiah said that you must not carry a burden out of your house on the sabbath (Jer. 17.22). Already by c.165 BCE, the orthodox authors of the book of Jubilees compiled a considerable list of things you must not do on the sabbath, and attributed them all to the revelation of the Torah to Moses on Mount Sinai. Its list of prohibitions includes lighting a fire, carrying a burden out of the house, going on a journey, having sex with your wife and making war (*Jub.* 50.7-13). In these circumstances, the scribe's question was an existential matter for any Jewish teacher who needed to see through these regulations and have a secure grasp of what he most needed to teach to the average Jew: 'He asked him, "Which commandment is the most important of all?"' (Mk 12.28).

Jesus' answer went straight to the centre of the Torah. He began with the opening of the *Shema'*, the confession of God's oneness which marked off the chosen people from all other peoples, and which goes on to witness to Israel's love of God. It is written at Deut. 6.4-5, and faithful Jews said it, and still say it, every day:

> Hear Israel, the Lord our God, the Lord is One. And you shall love the Lord your God with all your heart and with all your being and with all your might.

With the love of the one God firmly stated as the first duty of faithful Jews, Jesus went to Lev. 19.18 for another central commandment:

> You shall love your neighbour as yourself.

As is indicated by the scribe's need to ask the question in the first place, Jesus will have selected these commandments himself, not drawn upon tradition to quote them. Nonetheless, similar comments are found elsewhere. In Alexandria, an outstanding Jewish philosopher offered a basically similar summary:

> So on the seventh days there stand open in every city thousands of schools of understanding and prudence and courage and justice/righteousness and the other virtues . . . Among the vast number of particular principles and beliefs there stand out as it were two main heads above the others: one of duty to God through piety and holiness, one of duty to people through kindliness and justice/righteousness . . .
>
> (Philo, *On the Special Laws* II, 62–63 [extracts])

In some ways, Philo was a very different Jew from Jesus. He observed and believed a form of Judaism profoundly influenced by Greek philosophy rather than by the recreation of the prophetic tradition of Judaism itself. Two such different Jewish teachers could nonetheless produce similar summaries because it is a reasonable perception of Torah that these are its main points.

For the same reason, the scribe in the Temple greatly approved of Jesus' selection of two central commandments. He began with a summary quotation which picks up Deut. 6.4 and continues in terms reminiscent of Deut. 4.35 and Isa. 45.21:

> For good, rabbi, you have truly said that 'He is one and there is none beside him'.
>
> (Mark 12.32)

From a cultural point of view, this is the most perfectly Jewish response that one can imagine. The scribe continued with the transcending importance of these two commandments even over against the cultic centre in which he and Jesus stood together, a few days before they would faithfully observe the major feast of Passover:

> And to love Him with all one's heart and all one's mind and all one's strength,

and to love one's neighbour as oneself, is more than all the burnt offerings
and sacrifices.

(Mark 12.33)

This should not be interpreted as any kind of criticism of the sacrificial cult. It is
rather a question of how first-century Jewish people got their priorities straight.
For these two faithful and vigorous Jews, this meant that love of God and of
one's neighbour were the centre of Judaism. Jesus expressed his approval with
one of his favourite terms:

You are not far from the kingship of God.

(Mark 12.34)

Given that the scribe was a *scribe*, and not a member of the Jesus movement, this
is very strong approval. As we have seen, the kingship of God could be used as
a metaphor for God's control over one's life. Jesus' approval accordingly means
that in his view the scribe's attitude towards the centre of the Torah meant that
he had almost accepted God's complete control over his life.

In another memorable incident, Jesus put forward main points of the Torah as
the conditions for gaining eternal life. A rich man came to Jesus and knelt before
him and asked, 'Good rabbi, what shall I do to inherit eternal life?' (Mk 10.17).
The man is so famous for not accepting Jesus' *second* suggestion, that he sell
all his goods, give to the poor and follow him, that Jesus' first reactions have
become quite liable to be overlooked. His first reaction was to object to being
called 'good'. For this he gave a reason, straightforward in his own culture, but
so alien to later Christianity that the Church Fathers generally contradicted it and
conventional scholarship has found it difficult to come to terms with:

Why do you call me good? None is good, except the one God.

(Mk 10.18)

This makes two points, of which the second was much the more important at the
time. The first point is that this must mean that Jesus did not feel he was perfectly
good. This is a normal characteristic of great religious figures. We have seen that
it is also implied by his undergoing John's baptism of repentance.[9] It does not
mean that Jesus was really a liar or a thief: it simply means that faced with the
One God himself, Jesus did not feel *perfectly* good. And it is coming face to face
with the One God which is the main point. This is what Christian commentators
have been unable to cope with, because of their belief in Jesus' sinlessness. Some
of the Church Fathers argued that Jesus was leading the man to a perception of
his divinity. For example, Ambrose commented 'What he does not believe, Christ
adds, that he may believe in the Son of God, not as a good master, but as the good
God' (*De Fide*, II, 1). This is contrary to the text, and attributes to Jesus a later

9   See p. 176.

Christian belief unknown to him. More recently, Craig Evans comments, 'Jesus is not implying that he is somehow imperfect or less than good, but only that the focus must be on God'.[10] If that is what Jesus meant, he could have said it. *Jesus did not feel he was perfectly good*, and it is long past time that his sinful modern followers noticed that. In a profound sense, it does not mean much more than that Jesus was beginning at the same place as he did when he quoted the *Shema'* to the scribe in the Temple: with devotion to the one God.

With the main point established, Jesus could then refer to God's commandments. Coming in from the prophetic stream of tradition, he referred to major commandments, which the man would know, and which it was not beyond the power of faithful Jews to keep, whether they were rich or poor. Most of them are taken from what Gentile Christians know as 'the Ten Commandments':

> Do not murder, do not commit adultery, do not steal, do not bear false witness, do not defraud, honour your father and mother.
> (Mk 10.19, using Exod. 20.12-16//Deut. 5.16-20)

Compared with the standard texts of the Ten Commandments, 'do not defraud' has been added especially for a rich man who could get richer if he were less than honest, and the order has been changed. This is entirely within a reasonable interpretation of major commandments. From a cultural point of view, Jesus was under no obligation to quote the text literally, and he was entitled to select what he saw as main points. This is especially so since he could not quote the scriptures in Hebrew to Aramaic-speaking people. He would therefore be the more liable to explain rather than merely quote, as people often did when they explained the Hebrew scriptures in Aramaic.

Obediently dropping the term 'good', the man responded as a faithful Jew might well respond when faced with such basic points of Torah: 'Rabbi, I have kept all these from my youth' (Mk 10.20). Jesus' extreme response, that he should sell his goods, give everything to the poor and follow him, indicates how naturally the central group of commandments came to him as commandments which faithful Jews could keep. His subsequent debate with the disciples (Mk 10.23-30) shows that he was perfectly well aware of the extreme nature of his suggestion to the rich man. It also shows the centrality of the Jesus movement to Jesus' own view of salvation, in the sense that he was so confident that his movement represented the will of the one God that he genuinely believed that faithful Jews ought to join it, and that its opponents were opposing God. This throws into ever sharper relief Jesus' selection of major commandments in his first response to the rich man. However extreme Jesus' demands on his followers, they were a prophetic interpretation of the Torah for the Jews of his time and place, not something opposed to the Torah.

Jesus is recorded as offering two other summaries of the Torah. One specifies major points as 'justice, mercy and faith', over against the stringent interpretation

---

10   C. A. Evans, *Mark 8.27–16.20* (Word Biblical Commentary, 34B. Nashville: Nelson, 2001), p. 96.

of details, such as tithing of mint, dill and cumin (Mt. 23.23//Lk. 11.42).[11] This is fully in accordance with the prophetic tradition. When Isaiah criticized people who prayed and sacrificed to the Lord, and observed the sabbath and the major festivals, he urged them 'learn to do good seek justice', and he specified 'rescue the oppressed, judge/defend the orphan, plead for the widow' (Isa. 1.17). A closer parallel is provided by Micah, who summarized how God wanted people to behave: 'that you should do justice, love lovingkindness/mercy, and walk humbly with your God' (Mic. 6.8). Habakkuk also criticized some Jewish people, and contrasted 'the righteous', who 'shall live by his faithfulness' (Hab. 2.4). The main point here is not the closeness of Jesus' summary to any given text, but rather that he offered a summary of people's duties to God under the Torah. The first two points in this, 'justice' and 'mercy', refer to people's duties to each other. The third, which may be translated as 'faith' or 'faithfulness' in Jesus' summary as in the text quoted from Habakkuk, embraces both people's faithfulness to each other and their trust/faith in God. It follows that when we have spelt out the full meaning of this summary by viewing it against its cultural background, we can see more clearly that it recreates prophetic tradition and corresponds to the other two summaries which I have already considered.

Jesus is also said to have summarized the Torah with the 'golden rule': 'whatever you want people to do to you, do likewise to them' (Mt. 7.12//Lk. 6.31). The Matthaean version, but not the Lukan, ends 'for this is the Law and the prophets'. This is probably a Matthaean addition, but it is in accordance with the spirit of Jesus' teaching. Apart from this Matthaean addition, there are many parallels to the saying from many different cultures, for it is so basic a human sentiment. The culturally nearest are Tob. 4.15: 'And what you hate, do not do to anyone': and a saying attributed to Jesus' elder contemporary Hillel, who said to a Gentile who asked him to teach him the Torah while he stood on one foot: 'What is hateful to you, do not do to your neighbour: that is the whole Torah, and the rest is its commentary. Go learn!' (b. Shab 31a). Both these are negative in form, whereas that of Jesus is positive, but we do not know whether that is because Jesus developed this sentiment positively or because we have so little first-century Jewish evidence. What should not be uncertain is that he regarded doing good to others as a primary human duty, in accordance with the will of God revealed in the Torah.

4. *Particular Ethical Instructions*

Within this general framework of obedience to the will of God found in the Torah, Jesus offered detailed ethical instructions, all of which can be seen, as Matthew saw them, as intensification of the Torah. Many of these recommendations are

---

11 For interpretation of the whole context see pp. 331–38.

ways of telling people not to overreact to other people's misbehaviour, and forgiveness is a main theme. Matthew put one group of sayings under the heading
of Lev. 19.18. The setting is probably secondary, because none of the antitheses
occurs in Luke, who repeats a high proportion of the teaching which Matthew
arranges like this.

> You heard that it was said, 'You shall love your neighbour [Lev. 19.18] and
> hate your enemy'. But I say to you: love your enemies and pray for those who
> persecute you, so that you may become sons of your Father in heaven, for
> he makes his sun shine on wicked and good (people) and makes it rain on
> righteous and unrighteous (people). For if you love those who love you, what
> reward do you have? Do not the tax-collectors do the same? And if you greet
> only your brethren, what are you doing that is remarkable? Do not even the
> Gentiles do the same?
>
> (Mt. 5.43-47)

The injunction to hate one's enemy is not part of the biblical text. It is however
a perfectly reasonable interpretation of the context as a whole. The immediate context prohibits hating 'your brother' (Lev. 19.17) and taking vengeance
against 'the sons of your people' (Lev. 19.18). The broader context makes it
clear that God drove out Israel's enemies before them because they did various
things here prohibited to Israel (e.g. Lev. 20.22-26, cf. e.g. Deut. 7.1-6). Hatred
was also advocated by orthodox Jews at Qumran, where the members of the
community were to 'love all sons of light' and 'hate all sons of darkness' (1QS I,
9–10). Jesus' genuine injunction 'love your enemies' is accordingly a very strong
prophetic intensification of the biblical injunction to love one's neighbour. It is
moreover confirmed by the Lukan parallel (Lk. 6.27), which also has 'bless those
who curse you' (6.28).

The famous injunction to turn the other cheek (Mt. 5.39//Lk. 6.29) is in

We must take these various injunctions quite seriously when we seek to understand what Jesus really meant by 'love your enemies'. Taken together, they have
the same two aspects as we have already seen to be controlling principles in Jesus'
ethical teaching. Several of them are detailed injunctions to defuse rather than
intensify conflict with people whom we meet. These are Jesus' interpretation of
loving one's neighbour as oneself. Equally important is the assertion that people
will thus become 'sons of the Most High' (Lk. 6.35), expressed by Matthew as
'sons of your Father in heaven' (Mt. 5.45). The centrality of God is thus once
again seen to be quite inalienable.

The famous injunction to turn the other cheek (Mt. 5.39//Lk. 6.29) is in
this same category of defusing personal animosities, even if it be possible that it
should not be taken literally. A prophetic interpreter of the scriptures will not
have been uninfluenced by the kind of sentiment found at Lam. 3.30: 'let him give
a cheek to the smiter, and have a surfeit of reproach' (cf. Prov. 24.29; Isa. 50.6).
One of the underlying cultural assumptions is found even in the much stricter
environment of Qumran:

> I will not repay a man with an evil reward: I will pursue man with goodness.

For judgement of every living being (is) with God, and He will pay man his reward.

(1 QS X, 17–18)

The detailed injunction to give away more and more of one's clothing (Mt. 5.40// Lk. 6.29) is also in this category of defusing personal animosities, and again it may be that it should not be taken literally. Lk. 6.30 is in this same category: 'Give to everyone who asks you, and do not demand your things back from the person who takes them.' The parallel Mt. 5.42 is different in detail, to the point where it is evident that some secondary editing has taken place: 'Give to the person who asks, and do not turn away from the person who wishes to borrow from you.' Both versions of this saying commend kindness to others in quite hyperbolic terms. The instruction to go the second mile should be seen in the same way: 'And whoever presses you into service for one mile, go with him for two' (Mt. 5.41). This is labour forced upon people by officials, perhaps armed soldiers, of Herod Antipas. Impressing people into labour was a Roman custom, best known in the Gospels from the occasion when Jesus was too weak to carry the beam of his cross, and Simon of Cyrene was pressed into service to carry it (Mk 15.21). Jesus will not however have had Roman soldiers in mind, since there were none in Galilee at the time. The soldiers and officials of Herod Antipas are likely to have been primarily Jewish, and in any case Herod was in direct charge of Galilee, whatever proportion of Gentiles he may or may not have employed. Accordingly, Jesus was really dealing with potentially difficult relationships within the Jewish community, as John the Baptist did when he urged soldiers not to resort to extortion or blackmail (Lk. 3.14).

Some of these injunctions seem realistic but difficult, others hardly seem realistic at all. Our feeling that some of them should not be taken literally is confirmed by what appear to be three jokes solemnly collected together. Jesus' teaching contains a number of these striking hyperboles, but the Gospels never tell us that anyone laughed. This is probably because of the way the teaching was collected, by disciples interested primarily in getting sayings of Jesus written down in a short space, such as on a wax tablet, rather than in the more comical side of audience reaction. The Markan version has some signs of translation from the original Aramaic, particularly in its use of the word 'good', where English, like Greek, would naturally say 'better', as well as the loanword 'Gehenna', the ancient Jewish name for hell:

> And if your hand offends you, cut it off! It is good for you to go crippled into Life, rather than to go away two-handed into Gehenna, into the unquench-able fire. And if your foot offends you, cut it off! It is good that you should go lame into Life, rather than to have two feet and be thrown into Gehenna. And if your eye offends you, pluck it out! It is good that you should go one-eyed into the kingdom of God, rather than have two eyes and be thrown into Gehenna, where the worm does not die and the fire is not put out.
>
> (Mk 9.43-48, edited at Mt. 18.8-9 and paralleled
at Mt. 5.29-30)

Here the threat of eternal punishment is used to reinforce Jesus' message. The hyperbolic mode of expression, however, makes the original message less than clear 2,000 years later. When editing material for the Sermon on the Mount, Matthew already felt a need to illustrate how a man's eye could be offensive:

> You heard that it was said, 'Do not commit adultery' (Exod. 20.14// Deut. 5.18). But I say to you that everyone who looks at a woman to desire her has already committed adultery with her in his heart. But if your right eye offends you, pluck it out and cast it away from you, for it is to your advantage that one of your members should be destroyed and that your whole body should not be cast into Gehenna . . .
>
> (Mt. 5.27-29)

If this teaching were accepted and taken literally, there would be a lot of one-eyed people! We should accept Matthew's association, even if it is secondary, and we should be confident that we are dealing with a hyperbole, not with teaching which is to be taken literally.

Gehenna is similarly used, following on from the earthly judiciary, to ram home the message that people should not be angry with each other nor be rude to each other:

> Everyone who is angry with his brother is liable to judgement, and whoever says to his brother 'empty-head' (*raka*) is liable to the council, and whoever says 'fool' is liable to the Gehenna of fire.
>
> (Mt. 5.22)

The use of the word 'brother' of the other person again helps to make it clear that the whole of this ethical teaching was originally directed at relationships within the Jewish community, as does Matthew's preservation of the original Aramaic *reqā*, transliterated as *raka* in his Greek text.

Another threatening use of the earthly judiciary occurs in the command to be reconciled with one's legal opponent:

> Make friends with your accuser quickly while you are on the way with him, so that your accuser does not hand you over to the judge and the judge to the official and you are thrown into prison. Amen I say to you, you will not get out from there until you have paid the last penny.
>
> (Mt. 5.25-26//Lk. 12.58-59)

This must also be seen as an attempt to calm down relationships within the Jewish community.

The same applies to the illustration set in the Temple (Mt. 5.23-24). Here a person who is offering sacrifice, and who remembers that his brother has something against him, is exhorted to leave the sacrifice, be reconciled to his brother, and then offer his sacrifice. This is not very practical if taken literally either, especially if his brother happened to be in Galilee. Nonetheless, the message of reconciliation is absolutely clear. So also is the unquestionable assumption of the validity of the sacrificial system commanded by God in the Torah.

These many detailed instructions about people's behaviour towards each other are complemented by instructions to forgive others. The most famous is in the Lord's prayer (Mt. 6.12//Lk. 11.4), where the Matthaean version reflects most clearly Jesus' use of the Aramaic word *ḥōbh*, which means 'debt' as well as 'sin':

> And forgive us our debts/sins,
> As we forgive our debtors/those who sin against us.

This is another example where Jesus draws a clear analogy between the behaviour required of people and the behaviour known as that of God. It was universally accepted in Judaism that God forgave repentant sinners.[12] In this prayer, the disciples must indicate that they do the same to people who sin against them. Another saying carries the analogy further:

> And when you stand praying, forgive if you have anything against anyone, so that your Father in heaven may forgive you your transgressions
>
> (Mk 11.25)

Both these injunctions should be taken literally as well as seriously. The same applies to another one, which makes use of the double meaning of the Aramaic word *tūbh*, meaning 'return', 'turn back', as well as repent:

> And if your brother sins, rebuke him, and if he repents/turns back, forgive him.
>
> (Lk. 17.3)

The following saying makes more extensive use of the double meaning of *tūbh*, and one hopes that it should be regarded as a hyperbole:

> And if he sins against you seven times a day and returns to you seven times, saying 'I repent/return', you will forgive him.
>
> (Lk. 17.4, cf. Mt. 18.21-22)

Jesus' teaching about oaths should also be seen in the context of his attempts to improve the way in which human beings were treating each other. This teaching is transmitted by Matthew alone, in another passage of the Sermon on the Mount which begins with an antithesis (Mt. 5.33-37). We have seen that the authenticity of the antithesis form should not be accepted, because much of the teaching gathered together under these antitheses is found also in Luke, who never has this form of the antithesis. He had however no reason to drop this form, for it

---

12 See pp. 231–32.

underlines the authority of Jesus, and a Gentile Christian might well be happy to interpret some of Jesus' comments in the antitheses as criticism of the Jewish Law itself. As well as his authoritative 'but I say to you', Matthew's introduction has the word 'at all', which cannot be satisfactorily reconstructed in Aramaic. This Matthaean editing should also be removed. There are problems also at the end of the passage, where it is difficult to see how far Matthew has edited or even produced the conclusion. I have therefore put the conclusion in brackets. In either case, Jesus' teaching is entirely coherent and easy to fit into his teaching as a whole:

> Do not swear, either by heaven, for it is the throne of God, nor by the earth, for it is the footstool of his feet, nor by Jerusalem, for it is [a/the] city of the Great King, and do not swear by your head, for you cannot make one hair white or black. (But let your word be 'Yes, yes', 'No, no'. More than this is of/from (the) evil (one)) (cf. Mt. 5.34-37).

To help us understand this radical prohibition in a culture in which oaths were common, we must also take account of Jesus' severe criticism of scribes who attempted to regulate oaths in a manner which he regarded as ludicrous:

> Woe to you, blind guides who say, 'Whoever swears by the Sanctuary, it is nothing, but whoever swears by the gold of the Sanctuary, is liable.' Fools and blind (people), for which is greater, the gold or the Sanctuary which sanctifies the gold? And, 'Whoever swears by the altar, it is nothing, but whoever swears by the gift on it, is liable.' Blind (people), for which is greater, the gift or the altar which sanctifies the gift? So he who swears by the altar swears by it and by everything which is on it. And he who swears by the Sanctuary swears by it and by Him who dwells in it, and he who swears by heaven swears by the throne of God and by Him who sits on it.
>
> (Mt. 23.16-22)

Leaving aside for the time being Jesus' rejection of scribal casuistry, the reasoning which drew these detailed distinctions, we should be able to see that *all* Jesus' examples are of the same kind. In every single case, a man is swearing by an object. This is the common element between swearing by one's head, swearing by an obviously sacred object such as the altar, and swearing by heaven or earth, which Jesus objected to as sacred to God as well. This links the swearing which he criticized to the objections to excessive swearing common to Jewish and Graeco-Roman sources. For example, Philo says that it is best not to swear oaths, declaring that the oath casts doubt on the trustworthiness of the man. He was also concerned at the involvement of God in oaths. Hence, in objecting to people who have an evil habit of swearing incessantly, he declares that 'from much swearing grows false swearing and impiety' (Philo, *Dec.* 84, 86, 90–91, 92). Josephus records similar concerns among the Essenes:

> Everything said by them (is) stronger than an oath, but they avoid swearing,

regarding it as worse that swearing falsely, for they say that anyone who is not believed without an appeal to God has already been condemned.

(*War* II, 135)

Jesus was similarly concerned to prevent people from maltreating each other by swearing by objects all the time. This habit is always liable to lead people to deceive others by swearing an emphatic oath which they do not keep – hence Matthew began his antithesis by reminding his audiences of the traditional rejection of swearing falsely (Mt. 5.33). Equally, if people keep swearing extravagant oaths, others may not trust them even when they are sincere. As always, Jesus' solution to these problems was simple and radical – he prohibited these oaths altogether. He also integrated his expanded teaching of how people should love their neighbours as themselves with his respect for God, which is reflected in all his detailed criticisms of the examples mentioned.

Jesus' teaching is repeated in similar but much briefer form in the letter attributed to his brother Jacob:

Now above all, my brothers, do not swear either by heaven or by earth nor with any other oath, but let your 'yes' be 'yes' and your 'no' be 'no', that you may not fall under judgement.

(Jas 5.12)

A lot of trouble has been caused to both Christian tradition and modern scholarship by taking too literally, and generalizing, Matthew's injunction not to swear 'at all', and Jacob's 'nor with any other oath' (Mt. 5.34; Jas 5.12). Jesus' prohibition has then been seen as contrary to the Torah, which prescribes for example an oath by the Lord, when a man's animal kept by a neighbour dies or is hurt or is driven away without anyone seeing it (Exod. 22.10-11), and as prohibiting all oaths in courts of Law, which has caused severe practical problems.[13] None of this should be accepted. Jesus prohibited the kind of oaths which had a serious negative effect on the way people treated each other. The Torah did not legislate for this situation, so Jesus gave additional ethical teaching in accordance with the basic principle of loving one's neighbour as oneself. Given some of the oaths which men used, he reinforced this message with respect for the one God.

Jesus' teaching about oaths was therefore fully in accordance with the Torah, and with the central principles which governed all his ethical teaching. The resulting prohibitions, radical though they may seem at first sight, are not difficult to observe, when they are correctly understood.

---

13   In recent scholarship, this view has been vigorously propounded by Meier, *Marginal Jew*, vol. IV, ch. 33, on which see p. 58.

5. *Divorce and the Family*

Jesus' teaching on divorce is quite remarkable, for he prohibited it altogether. Divorce of women by men was a normal Jewish custom. It is permitted in the Torah, which seeks to regulate it a little (Deut. 24.1-4). It requires a man to write a proper certificate of divorce, and describes the possible reason as 'she does not find favour in his eyes because he finds something objectionable in her' (Deut. 24.1). While rabbinical authorities debated exactly what this might mean, it could obviously be taken to give a lot of latitude to the man. When Josephus recounts his divorce of his second wife, he says simply that he was not pleased with her habits (*Life*, 426). This recalls Deut. 24.1, and Josephus evidently thought he had sufficiently explained his divorce of his second wife. He proceeded to report his third marriage, his divorce of his second wife apparently being the obvious reason for him to marry again.

There are however signs of trouble over this at Qumran. One passage, which is difficult to understand and consequently to translate, prohibits something, probably marriage to a second wife while the first is alive.

> The builders of the wall (Ezek. 13.10) who walk after 'Precept' – 'The Precept', he (is/was) a preacher of whom it says, 'preaching they shall preach' (Mic. 2.6) – shall be caught in fornication twice by taking two wives while they are alive, and the foundation of the creation is 'male and female He created them' (Gen. 1.27), and those who went into the ark, 'Two by two they went in . . . to the ark' (Gen. 7.9).
>
> CD (Damascus Document) IV, 19-V, 1

At first sight, this does not look like the same as a prohibition of divorce, since in theory a man might divorce his wife and remain unmarried. As far as we know, however, men divorced their wives and married others. This passage would therefore upset the normal arrangements quite dramatically. Equally, it might seem to be a prohibition of bigamy, which would have led to criticism of people like Herod the Great. But bigamy does not seem to have been very common, and if this is all the author meant, he is surely likely to have been more precise. We should infer that the point is the prohibition of remarriage during the lifetime of a man's wife, which would effectively damage a major function of divorce. The way the author argues is particularly significant. He uses two passages of the Pentateuch to show that marriage between two people was God's intention at the creation of humankind, revealed also when he made arrangements for some beings to survive the Flood.

This is very close to Jesus' teaching as it is preserved in one verse at Lk. 16.18:

> Everyone who divorces his wife and marries commits adultery, and he who marries a woman divorced from her husband commits adultery.

The long version at Mark 10.2-9 is however unique. This version, founded on vigorous interpretation of the Torah from a prophetic perspective, must be

authentic teaching of Jesus, as it fits into his innovative ministry, and its origins
cannot otherwise be explained. It recounts an incident when a question was put
to him by people who must have known that he had unusual teaching to give
on this subject:

> And they asked him whether it is permissible for a man to divorce his wife,
> testing him. And he answered and said to them, 'What did Moses command
> you?' And they said, 'Moses allowed him to write a certificate of divorce and
> divorce (her).' And Jesus answered and said to them, 'For your hardness of
> heart he wrote you this commandment. But from the beginning of creation
> "He made them male and female" (Gen. 1.27): "For this reason a man shall
> leave his father and mother and the two shall become one flesh" (Gen. 2.24).
> So they are no longer two, but one flesh. Therefore what God has joined
> together, let not a man separate.'

Jesus' argument, like that of the Qumran author noted above, is firmly based on
the will of God revealed in the Torah. It follows that, whatever we may think of
Deut. 24.1, Jesus believed that he was interpreting the Torah, not that he was
contradicting it. His scriptural reasons for his judgement are very similar to those
in the Qumran passage. The man and woman becoming one flesh is repeated, so
Jesus evidently felt that this was a main point.

Jesus may also have been influenced by a passage from the prophetic tradition, depending on what text was available to him and how he interpreted it.
The Hebrew of Mal. 2.14-16 is very difficult: Jesus may have understood some
of it like this:

> Because the LORD was a witness between you and the wife of your youth
> . . . and did He not make one? . . . For I hate divorce, says the LORD, the
> God of Israel.

This would have been a very clear prophetic tradition for Jesus to have followed,
but we cannot be sure that the text was read and understood like this. To maintain his position, Jesus had in any case to give some account of Deut. 24.1, and
his account casts further light on the relationship of this judgement to the other
ethical teaching we have just been considering: 'For your hardness of heart he [i.e.
Moses] wrote you this commandment'. This can only mean that Jesus ascribed
divorce to man's hardness of heart. This aligns his judgement on divorce with
all his other instructions to people to forgive one another and to respond peace-
ably to oppressive behaviour. It is also entirely reasonable to see it as a defence
of women. In the case of divorce, the woman had to leave the man's home, a
fact so well known that some women can hardly have felt their home was their
own. Their welfare would depend on their having somewhere to go, presumably
most often their father's house. If followed, Jesus' teaching would guarantee their
welfare, and support efforts by husbands to be kind and caring. He may also have
believed that keeping parents together would benefit their children.

This teaching was however found problematical from a very early date. This is evident in the editing of Matthew, who introduced a major exception, so famous as to be called 'the exceptive clause'. Where Mark added further interpretation explaining that remarriage was a form of adultery against the first wife, Matthew edited Mark's addition to produce this:

> But I say to you that whoever divorces his wife except for unchastity and marries another, commits adultery.
>
> (Mt. 19.9)

This same exception is found in the summary of Jesus' teaching in the Sermon on the Mount (Mt. 5.31-32). Matthew also edited the Markan debate quite considerably, altering the order of the arguments, attributing the question to Pharisees and changing it to the one debated by contemporary rabbis: 'Is it permissable to divorce one's wife for any reason?' (Mt. 19.3). Thus a wife having sex with a man other than her husband becomes the reason, and the only reason, for divorce.

Matthew did not however alter Jesus' central arguments. He must therefore have regarded his view as *interpretation* of Jesus' teaching, not as changing it, much as Jesus thought he was interpreting the Torah, not changing it. This is perfectly logical, though it was not the view of Jesus. Jesus argued that the man and his wife become one flesh, in accordance with God's will at creation. Matthew accepted that, but he believed that this relationship was broken if the wife had sex with another man. Accordingly, the wife broke the relationship before her affair came to light, so that the man divorcing her could not be said to be breaking it. To achieve this understanding, Matthew will have gone back to Deut. 24.1 for his interpretation of the difficult words *'rwth dbr*, translated above 'something objectionable'. Like the school of Shammai, with whose judgements he will have been familiar, he took these words to mean unchastity on the part of the woman during marriage. In Matthew's view, therefore, divorce was permissible if, but only if, the woman had already broken the divine ordinance.

The situation known to Matthew in the real world was however a great deal further from the teaching of Jesus than that, so he added some comments which go much further than interpretation:

> The disciples said to him, 'If that's the situation of a man with a wife, it's not worth getting married.' But he said to them, 'Everyone does not accept this word, but those for whom it is given'.
>
> (Mt. 19.10-11)

In the Matthaean text, this forms a link to a saying about people who don't have sex, figuratively described as 'eunuchs':

> For there are eunuchs who were born like that from their mother's womb, and there are eunuchs who were made eunuchs by men, and there are eunuchs who have made themselves eunuchs because of the kingdom of heaven. He who can accept, let him accept.
>
> (Mt. 19.12)

Leaving aside Matthew's editorial work, this is likely to be a genuine saying. The language is very colourful, as often in genuine sayings of Jesus, and the saying itself has an excellent setting in the ministry of Jesus. Both he and John the Baptist were deliberately unmarried so as to carry out their work as major prophets. This was unusual, and could be colourfully described as making themselves eunuchs for the sake of the kingdom of God, a central concept in Jesus' teaching. Matthew will have received this saying separately, whether orally, or in a written collection of sayings, one of which he decided to use here. Matthew's editing of the passage as a whole is obviously secondary, and reveals a situation in which Jesus' teaching on marriage has been known, then reinterpreted, and finally not observed.

The disciples' comment (Mt. 19.10) may remind us of a passage from the book of Sirach, a text which Matthew and many Jewish Christians will have known:

> I would rather live with a lion and a dragon than live with an evil woman . . . Her husband sits among the neighbours, and he cannot help sighing bitterly . . . A bad wife is a chafing yoke: taking hold of her is like grasping a scorpion . . . A headstrong wife will be considered as a bitch . . . do not grant outspokenness to an evil wife – if she does not walk according to your will, cut her away from your flesh.
>
> (Sir. 25.16, 18; 26.7, 25; 25.25b-26)

In a culture where this was the trouble, and you could always marry another wife, Jesus' teaching did not always go down too well. There should however be no doubt as to what it was. The witness of Mark is absolutely clear, and confirmed at 1 Cor. 7.10-11 by St Paul, who was unmarried like Jesus himself. Their influence in our own society, where average lives are much longer than was the case in the first century, has been a perfect menace to human happiness. That, however, was not their doing. At the time, Jesus' teaching could be fitted into an overall framework of caring for other people. This is where it belonged in his teaching of his disciples, with all his other detailed injunctions which were designed to govern the way that his followers in the Jewish community treated each other.

Jesus' comments on family relationships have sometimes been considered to be in tension not only with his comments on divorce, but also with his basic understanding of the commandment to love one's neighbour as oneself. His comments should however be considered carefully within the context of the historic ministry. His prophetic ministry caused conflict with the orthodox wing of Judaism, and with the authoritative chief priests, as we shall see in Chapter 9, and this was bound to cause conflict within families. The ministry was also to some extent migratory, and this was bound to have a temporary effect on family life. In both cases, his comments should be seen as in some degree relativizing family relationships in face of the will of God for the redemption of Israel, not as permanently disruptive of normal human relationships.

One passage (Mt. 10.34-36//Lk. 12.51-53) predicts some effects of the ministry.

The two versions show significant variation in detail, and it is difficult to be sure how far one or both represents quite what Jesus said. The Matthaean version is as follows:

> Do not think that I came to bring peace on earth – I did not come to bring peace but a sword. For I came to set a man against his father, and a daughter against her mother, and a bride against her mother-in-law, and (the) enemies of a man (will be) his household.

This should be seen as a prediction of the effect of the ministry, presented as its purpose, in accordance with the teleological mode of thought characteristic of Judaism, which presents the effects of the will of God as if they were his purposes. The opening statement is very vigorously expressed. For 'sword', Luke has 'division', and we should accept that as decoding Jesus' original metaphor. The detailed comments are strongly reminiscent of Mic. 7.6, which is similarly used in other Jewish sources to predict conflict in the last days. In the following verse the prophet looks for the Lord, commenting 'I will wait for the God of my salvation', and an ancient exegete would have no difficulty in seeing a prediction of Jesus' death and resurrection at Mic. 7.8: 'when I fall, I shall rise'. We should accordingly see Jesus' comments as a prophetic prediction of the effects of his prophetic ministry, not as instructions to quarrel.

The next two sayings in Matthew are also from 'Q' material (Mt. 10.37-38// Lk. 14.26-27), followed by a saying which is independently attested in Mark (Mt. 10.39; Mk 8.35//Mt. 16.25//Lk. 9.24). It was reasonable of Matthew to take them all together, because they form a cultural whole:

> He who loves (his) father or mother more than me is not worthy of me, and he who loves (his) son or daughter more than me is not worthy of me. And he who does not take up his cross and follow after me is not worthy of me. He who finds his soul/self will destroy it, and he who destroys his soul/self for my sake will find it.

All these sayings should be seen in the cultural context created by Jesus' historic ministry, which called for decision at the approach of salvation and judgement, when the kingdom of God was about to come. In the first saying, Luke has 'If anyone comes to me and does not hate his father . . .'. The word 'hate' is simply a literal translation of the Aramaic *senā*, of which Matthew's 'love . . . less' is an interpretation which should be accepted. The following sayings make clear that the first saying indicates the sacrifices which must be made for disciples in the historic ministry: it does not consist of instructions to devalue family relationships in themselves. Luke added 'wife' to the relations to be 'hated'. We should not accept the authenticity of that. Jesus' teaching on divorce indicates that it was much too dangerous a thing to say – it might have been taken literally, which could have been disastrous.

A separate passage of Mark results from the same situation in the historic ministry. I have discussed Jesus' exceptional instructions to a rich man to sell all his property, give it to the poor, and follow Jesus.[14] Simeon the Rock responded by saying, 'Look, we left everything and have followed you' (Mk 10.28). This should be taken quite literally. Simeon and the others had *left* everything. He was not rich, and he had not sold his house in Capernaum leaving his wife and mother-in-law starving and penniless. He had left everything in Capernaum to lead the Twelve in the migratory phase of the ministry. This was a temporary arrangement, and in later life, when the kingdom of God had not come as expected, he took his wife with him, far from their original home (1 Cor. 9.5). At the time, Jesus replied as follows:

> Amen I'm telling you, there is no-one who left house or brothers or sisters or mother or father or children or fields for my sake and for the sake of the good news who should not receive a hundredfold now in the present time houses and brothers and sisters and mothers and children and fields, with persecutions, and in the coming age eternal life.
>
> (Mk 10.29-30)

The first part of this, introduced with Jesus' emphatic 'Amen', is simply explicit in amplifying what Simeon had just said. The second part effectively presents the Jesus movement as a fictive kinship group. There is no mention of wives. We know that some women went with him some of the time, and accompanied him on his final journey to Jerusalem (cf. Mk 15.40-41; Lk. 8.1-3), and the presence of women in the Jesus movement is implicit in the presence of sisters and mothers in the fictive kinship group.[15] It is not probable that many disciples took their wives with them, since this would be unusual enough to be mentioned. Wives would be the wrong people to put into the fictive kinship group, since this would create quite the wrong impression, and could lead to new partnerships, followed by divorce and suchlike chaos.

All these comments should be borne in mind in considering Jesus' comments on his own family. As we have seen, there was some kind of dispute when some of them came out to seize him.[16] Mark connects this with the accusation that he cast out demons by means of the devil (Mk 3.20-35), and this connection is probably right, so the dispute was serious at the time. Mark also connects this with an occasion when Jesus' mother and brothers sent to him and called him, when a crowd was sitting around him. It is very difficult to be sure whether this connection is historical. Be that as it may, Jesus' reaction was to put himself in a fictive kinship group similar to the one which he described in response to Simeon the Rock. He looked at the crowd sitting around him and said:

> Behold my mother and my brothers! Whoever does the will of God, this (person) is my brother and sister and mother.
>
> (Mk 3.34-35)

14 See pp. 286–87.
15 See further pp. 192–97.
16 See p. 144.

We should not take this description of a fictive kinship group too literally. We do not know how long Jesus' dispute with some members of his family lasted, but there is no evidence that it was permanent, and his brother Jacob became in due course the leader of the Jerusalem church, and probably the author of the epistle attributed to him. Jesus' saying means that the fictive kinship group formed in the Jesus movement was of great importance. There was nothing to stop members of his own or anyone else's natural family from joining it.

We must therefore be very cautious about turning any of Jesus' comments on family relationships into instructions to damage family relationships. He foresaw that the historic ministry would produce conflict in some families, but he did not instruct people to quarrel.

6. *The Good Samaritan*

The parable of the Good Samaritan (Lk. 10.30-37) is normally thought important for understanding Jesus' view of how people should treat each other. It is, but a complete understanding of it requires us to take account of the issues of Jewish purity Law which underlie it. Luke's introduction to it (Lk. 10.25-29) may be due to secondary editing, as obviously in his use of 'lawyer' (Lk. 10.25) to refer to what our sources usually call a 'scribe', but it correctly indicates the original cultural context to which the parable speaks, in that it explains in story mode how some fundamental aspects of the Torah should be observed.

In the introduction, the scribe produces as the basic requirements in the Torah for the inheritance of eternal life Deut. 6.5, part of the *Shema* requiring love of God, and Lev. 19.18: 'You shall love your neighbour as yourself'. Jesus naturally approves of this combination.

> But he, wishing to justify himself, said to Jesus, 'And who is my neighbour?'
>
> (Lk. 10.29)

We have seen that the context of Lev. 19.18 could readily be interpreted to mean that one's neighbour was one's fellow Israelite, and I have noted a Qumran text which advocated loving the 'sons of light' and hating the 'sons of darkness'. When we consider Jesus' conflict with his opponents, we shall find that they expected him not even to associate with some of his fellow Jews.[17] It was accordingly essential for a scribe, who would be responsible for teaching other Jews, to know to whom the teaching of Lev. 19.18 really referred.

> And Jesus said in reply: A man went down from Jerusalem to Jericho and fell among brigands, who stripped him and beat him and went away leaving him

---

17   See further p. 289, and pp. 320–21.

half-dead. Now by chance a priest went down on that road, and seeing him
he passed by on the opposite side.

(Lk. 10.30-31)

The parable opens with a desperate situation characteristic of societies where
brigands flourish beyond official control. The description 'half-dead' is very deliberate: anyone seeing him at any distance would not know whether he was alive or
dead. Consequently, a man coming down the same road from Jerusalem to Jericho
would not know whether he would incur corpse uncleanness if he approached
the man. Priests are forbidden in the Torah to incur corpse uncleanness:

And YHWH said to Moses: Speak to the priests, the sons of Aaron, and say
to them: No-one shall defile himself for a dead person among his people,
except for his nearest relatives . . .

(Lev. 21.1-2)

It might be thought to follow that a priest should not incur corpse uncleanness for
anyone outside his family. The priest in Jesus' parable was accordingly determined
to avoid corpse uncleanness. Moreover corpse uncleanness was believed to travel
upwards, so that the priest would have incurred corpse uncleanness by bending
over a corpse, a view natural to anyone who has bent over a rotting corpse. The
view of the priest in the story was not that of Jesus, who told this parable deliberately in order to suggest that Lev. 19.18 should override Lev. 21.1-2.

Jesus' view is not otherwise attested, but it is by no means without analogy.
The duty to bury the untended dead is taken for granted in the book of Tobit
(Tob. 1.17-18; 2.3-7; 12.11-15), where there is no clash with the duties of priests.
A clash does occur in the debates of later rabbis, who take for granted that a
priest should bury an untended corpse. The most notable example is a disagreement between R.Eliezer ben Hyrcanus and the Sages as to who should bury an
untended corpse if it should be found by the high priest and a Nazirite (m. Naz
7.1). The Nazirite was a Jew who had taken some specific vows (*Num.* 6.1-21),
with the result that, like the high priest, he was subject to stricter purity regulations than an ordinary priest, and that is what caused the rabbinical discussion.
It follows that Jesus knew that he was dealing with a potential clash of different
instructions in the Torah, and that he told a story which entails a definite decision:
the basic principle of Lev. 19.18, 'You shall love your neighbour as yourself',
overrides the detailed instructions of Lev. 21.1-4, which require a priest not to
incur corpse uncleanness in normal circumstances, except for a close relative.

It is that decision which is unique in extant documents. It presupposes opponents who were very concerned to remain in a state of purity, a view which we
shall find abundantly among Jesus' orthodox opponents. This is especially the
case because the priest did not know that the man was dead. Accordingly, in
circumstances where he should, if necessary, have incurred corpse uncleanness to
bury the dead, he refused to risk the possibility of incurring corpse uncleanness
when he could have saved a life. Saving life was a sacred duty. In later rabbinical documents it is a principle, and examples show that it was taken for granted

much earlier, not least by Jesus himself.[18] Jesus' story of the behaviour of the priest deliberately portrays the extreme commitment to remaining in a state of purity characteristic of his orthodox opponents.

This is even clearer in the behaviour of the next character.

> Likewise also a Levite, coming to the place and seeing, passed by on the other side.
>
> (Lk. 10.32)

The Levites were regarded as inferior to the priests, and could not for example offer the sacrifices on the altar. They had however many duties in the Temple. They provided for example the Temple police, and they were responsible for the music at Temple services. Consequently, the Levite in Jesus' parable, going down from Jerusalem to Jericho, was, like the priest, in a state of purity for the right and proper reason that he had been serving in the Temple. Levites were *not* however subject to the restrictions placed on the behaviour of priests at Lev. 21.1-4. There was therefore no doubt as to what the Levite in this parable should do: he should save life if the man were alive, and he should bury an untended corpse if he were dead. Like the priest, however, the Levite passed by on the other side because he wanted to avoid corpse uncleanness, and he declined to see whether he could save a wounded person in case he might be dead. That is why this is a more dramatic example than the previous one. At the same time, however, the Levite's behaviour was not however *randomly* peculiar. Like the priest, he has been set within the parameters of Jesus' orthodox opponents, who were extending purity laws to ordinary people, let alone Levites, and applying them to the whole of life. Jesus' parable is partly about how much harm this could do. The unique feature of Jesus' judgement is the biblical text with which this incident has been fronted: it is further evidence that Lev. 19.18 was a crucial text for him.

> Now a Samaritan who was travelling came to him and when he saw, he was moved with pity. And he came up to him and bound up his wounds, pouring on them olive oil and wine. And he loaded him on his own animal and took him to an inn and looked after him. And the next day he took out two denarii and gave them to the innkeeper and said, 'Look after him, and I will give you whatever you are owed when I return'.
>
> (Lk. 10.33-35)

This lays it on thick in story mode rather than by overtly giving a halakhic decision, but there should be no doubt about the halakhic point. From Jesus' totally God-centred perspective, the Samaritan was Jewish enough.[19] He worshipped the one God, he held the Torah in the Pentateuch sacred, and in obedience to God's will revealed in the Torah he was circumcised, and he kept the sabbath, the major festivals and purity and dietary laws. He could reasonably be assumed

---

18   See pp. 264–65.
19   For a brief account of Samaria see pp. 167–68.

to keep the main points of the Torah, loving the one God with all his being and practising justice, mercy and truth, and so here portrayed as loving his neighbour as himself.

From a conventional Jewish perspective, however, giving the favourable role to a Samaritan was a shocking thing to do. There was a massive degree of hostility between Jews and Samaritans. From a conventional Jewish perspective the Samaritans were ethnically not fully Jewish. They worshipped God in the wrong place, having had a temple on Mount Gerizim in Samaria, which they still held sacred and where they still worshipped, instead of at the Temple in Jerusalem. They did not venerate the whole of the scriptures, for their scriptures were simply the Pentateuch, with some readings different from other versions. In the parable, the Samaritan was simply 'travelling' (Lk. 10.33). Jesus' audience would know he was not coming from the Temple in Jerusalem, and would not imagine that he was in a state of purity. Nonetheless, he obeyed the will of God written at Lev. 19.18, and demonstrated by his practical action that he loved his neighbour as himself. Another point of purity law lies behind this. As a layman, the Samaritan was not subject to the restrictions of Lev. 21.1-4. But neither was the Levite. The Samaritans did not observe the expanded purity laws characteristic of Jesus' opponents, and this fact was crucial in enabling the Samaritan to observe Lev. 19.18. The parable thus illustrates how menacing too much devotion to expanded purity laws could be.

The concluding conversation takes us back to interpretation of Lev. 19.18.

'Which of these three do you think had become neighbour of the one who fell among the brigands?' And he said, 'He who did mercy with him'. And Jesus said to him, 'You too go and do likewise'.

(Lk. 10.36-37)

As well as Jesus' careful reference back to Lev. 19.18, this has a notable shift from the scribe's request for a *definition* to the *instruction* to obey it in the broadest possible sense. These major features have an excellent setting in the teaching of Jesus. Careful study of this parable is very instructive for our understanding of the real basis of Jesus' ethical teaching. The major command of Lev. 19.18 was elevated by Jesus to the status of a principle which overrode detailed commandments of the Torah whenever there was an apparent clash. This is a culturally Jewish step to take, as we know from the general analogies which I have considered. At the same time, there is no precise parallel to it: it is the kind of step which a vigorous Jewish prophet was more likely than anyone else to take. Moreover, the way in which the story becomes more meaningful as it is seen in the Jewish context which was of no interest to Luke is a decisive argument for its authenticity. When this is taken together with its uniqueness and its perfect coherence with the other teaching of Jesus, we have more than one decisive argument for its authenticity.

This brings us full circle to the summaries considered earlier in this chapter. All the details of Jesus' ethical teaching fit within a framework constituted by the two commandments, Deut. 6.4-5 and Lev. 19.18. They are detailed instructions to love one's neighbour as oneself, because in this way we love God, imitate him and obey his commandments. Jesus' ethical teaching should therefore be seen as a vigorous recreation of Jewish morals from a prophetic perspective.

7. *Poverty and Riches*

Jesus' teaching clearly favours the poor over against the rich, but how that should be fitted into his ethical teaching as a whole has been less than obvious. Two points about the cultural background are of crucial importance. One is the extraordinary gap between rich and poor, and especially the extraordinary poverty of the poor. There was no established social security system for poor people. This is why almsgiving was such an important custom – it was all the poor had to depend on. Consequently, poor people might end up naked, and starve for lack of food. Since Western biomedicine had not yet been developed, disease was rife, and life was short. The plight of orphans and widows was notorious. Secondly, and as a result of this, the prophets launched apparently simple attacks on rich people, and urged everyone to contribute to the welfare of the poor, the widow and the orphan. Jesus could see this massive gap between rich and poor, and he belonged to the prophetic tradition.

For example, Isaiah has God enter into judgement with 'the elders of his people and its princes', complaining that 'the spoil of the poor (is) in your houses', and 'you grind the face of the poor' (Isa. 3.14-15). Criticizing the same people as 'rulers of Sodom' and 'people of Gomorrah' (Isa. 1.10), he has God refuse to accept their prayers and sacrifices, and urge them, 'learn to do good seek justice', specifying 'rescue the oppressed, defend the orphan, plead for the widow' (Isa. 1.17). The people whom Isaiah criticized were not just relatively well off, they were very powerful, stinking rich and grossly oppressive. This tradition was taken up in later documents. For example, in the first half of the second century BCE, one writer in the Enoch tradition wrote this:

> Woe to you rich, for you have trusted in your wealth. However, you will have to depart from your wealth since in the days of your wealth you did not remember the Most High. You have committed blasphemy and iniquity . . .
> (1 En. 94.8-9)

Jesus was faced with a similar social situation, and he inherited the traditions critical of it in the name of God.

Jesus' parable of the rich man and Lazar (Lk. 16.19-31) describes the massive gap between the two main characters. Lazar, usually found in English as Lazarus, is short for Eleazar, which means 'God helps', a name so appropriate to this parable that it is probably the reason why Jesus gave him a name, as he did not give names to the rich man or to most characters in his parables.

[19]There was a rich man, and he used to dress in purple and fine linen, and celebrated sumptuously every day. [20]But a poor man by name Lazar was

thrown at his gate covered with sores [21]and craving to be filled from what fell from the rich man's table . . .

The first thing wrong with the rich man is found in vv. 20–21. Verse 19 shows that the rich man could have looked after the poor man, housed and fed him, and vv. 20–21 show that the fact that he did not do so is one thing wrong with his riches. The second thing emerges at the end of the parable. Lazar is in Abraham's bosom, not because he was good – the parable does not even say that he loved God! – but because he was poor and grossly oppressed during his earthly life. The rich man, in the fires of hell as punishment for his sins, asks Abraham that Lazar be sent to his five brothers to warn them, so that they do not end up in his place of torment. Abraham refuses, because they already have Moses and the prophets, and the parable ends with him reinforcing this message:

> If they do not listen to Moses and the prophets, they will not be obedient if someone rises from the dead.

This is the second thing wrong with the rich man, his brothers and their riches. The will of God that they should look after the poor and not oppress them is written abundantly in the scriptures, and if they loved God they would have obeyed his will which was so clearly given to them. This presents in another form one of the central points which Jesus recreated from the prophetic tradition: loving your neighbour as yourself (Lev. 19.18) is central to loving God.

This is the correct background against which to understand Jesus' simpler statements about the rich and poor. For example:

> Blessed are the poor, for yours is the kingdom of God.
>
> (Lk. 6.20)

This says nothing about how the poor should love God, pray to him, or the like. It is a presentation of Jesus' profound belief that God would look after the poor, in the next life if the sins of the rich prevented him from doing so in this. This is amplified in a famous collection of sayings found in 'Q' material, in which people are advised to trust in God for such basic things that they are evidently very poor:

> So I tell you, do not worry yourself about what you may eat, nor what you will wear on your body. A person is more important than food, and their body more important than clothing. Consider the ravens, that they do not sow or reap, they do not have a storeroom or barn, and God feeds them. You are more important than birds! . . . And do not worry and say, 'What shall we eat?', or 'What shall we drink?', or 'What shall we wear?' The Gentiles seek these things, but your Father knows that you need them. But seek his kingdom, and these things will be added to you (cf. Mt. 6.25-26, 31–33// Lk. 12.22-24, 29–31).

This advice is clearly directed at very poor people, who are liable to be worried about the basic necessities of life. Jesus attempts to get them to turn to God, and to reassure them that they will have basic necessities in this life, and they could expect God to establish his kingdom in the near future.

Jesus' simpler comments on the rich must be seen in a similar light. For example:

> It is easier for a camel to go through the eye of a/the needle than for a rich (person) to enter the kingdom of God.
>
> (Mk 10.25)

> No slave can serve two masters . . . You cannot serve God and mammon.
>
> (Mt. 6.24//Lk. 16.13)

In the second of these two passages, 'mammon' is Jesus' native Aramaic for wealth and property. He clearly has in mind people who are so obsessed with their wealth that they cannot serve God. They are accordingly the stinking rich and powerful who do not use their wealth to look after the poor, hungry and naked. I have already discussed Mk 10.25 in its context, part of a discussion which Jesus had with his disciples after he had told a rich man to sell all his property, give the proceeds to the poor and follow Jesus (Mk 10.17-31).[20] This is the only occasion on which he is said to have made any such suggestion. The man, who claimed to have observed the basic commandments which Jesus put to him, together with 'do not defraud', asked what he should do so that *he* could inherit eternal life, and we are told that he 'had many possessions' (Mk 10.22). It follows that Jesus knowingly made an extreme demand to an excessively rich man, who was not using his wealth to care for the poor and hungry.

In general, Jesus did not demand that his followers give up all their possessions, and as always in considering his ethics we should take account of his behaviour, as well as of those parts of his teaching that have been transmitted to us. I have noted the latter part of this Markan passage, in which Simeon the Rock declared, 'Look, we left everything and have followed you' (Mk 10.28).[21] Simeon and the others had indeed *left* everything. He was not rich, and he had not sold his house in Capernaum, leaving his wife and mother-in-law starving and penniless. He and his wife and family did however put their house to good use in supporting Jesus and his ministry when they were in Capernaum (cf. Mk 1.29-34; 2.1-12; 3.20-35; 9.28-29; 9.33-40).

It is equally significant that Jesus enjoyed the company of some relatively well-off people, whom he is not known to have criticized. The most important were the central group of women, including Mary Magdalene and Joanna, wife of Herod's steward Chouza, 'who supported them from their private resources' (Lk. 8.1-3).[22] These women used their resources properly; they did not give them

---

20   See pp. 286–87, 299–300.
21   See pp. 299–300.
22   See pp. 192–97.

all away. The man who provided the large upper room for Jesus' final Passover with his disciples in Jerusalem was evidently fairly well-off too, as was Simon the leper who put on a dinner which Jesus attended in Bethany, when a woman well enough off to have expensive ointment poured it over his head (Mk 14.3-8). Whereas some guests said she should have sold it and given the money to the poor, Jesus defended her for having done a 'good work' (14.6).

Jesus attended other posh dinners too, often enough for his malicious opponents to accuse him of being 'a man "glutton and drunkard" an associate of tax-collectors and sinners' (cf. Mt.11.19//Lk. 7.34).[23] At one such dinner, Jesus is recorded as being somewhat critical of some people present, in that he responded to criticism of himself by commenting:

> It's not the healthy who need a doctor but those who are sick. I did not come to call righteous (people) but sinners.
> (Mk 2.17, edited at Mt. 9.12-13, Lk. 5.31-32)

This recognizes that there was something wrong with people at that sort of dinner, which is not surprising, given that tax-collectors were notorious for exploiting people. We know what Jesus did about such people. He called upon them to repent, knowing that God always forgives repentant sinners. He was at this dinner because it was thrown in his honour by a tax-collector who repented. There is no record that Jesus expected him to dispose of all his wealth, or even to stop being a tax-collector. If Jesus had stopped people being tax-collectors, he would have been famous for that too, and the Gospels would not have failed to mention such an achievement. He will however have expected converted tax-collectors to be honest, not to oppress the poor, and to put their talents to good use. Matthew the tax-collector is a good example, because he became one of the Twelve, and transmitted some of the teaching of Jesus on wax tablets or the like, which he was already accustomed to using.[24]

The following conclusions may therefore be drawn. In a society where there was a massive gap between the rich and the poor, and the poor were shockingly poor and grievously oppressed, Jesus was opposed to grossly rich people who ignored God's commandments to look after the poor. He believed that this showed that they did not love God, and he expected them to end up in Gehenna. He believed that God favoured the poor without demanding anything of them, and that God would always care for them, in the next life if the rich prevented Him from doing so in this. He was not ascetic, and did not demand that relatively well-off people should give up their land, money and property. He thought they should use their wealth properly, which meant caring for the poor, and included supporting the Jesus movement.

---

23 For detailed discussion, Casey, *Aramaic Approach to Q*, pp. 105–7, 132–42.
24 See pp. 86–89.

8. *Two Problems*

I have left two detailed topics to the end, because in each case Jesus' teaching is considered by some scholars to be contrary to Jewish Law, and it is the rest of his teaching that renders this view so improbable that we should consider each topic very carefully.

The first is a 'Q' passage, which has been slightly altered by both Matthew and Luke (Mt. 8.21-22//Lk. 9.59-60). The situation was that of a disciple who wanted to perform a normal act of Jewish piety, that of burying his father, before joining Jesus' migratory ministry. With unavoidable uncertainty about some small details, the following reconstruction may be offered:

> Another said to him, 'Let me first go back and bury my father'. He said to him, 'Follow me, and leave the dead to bury their dead.'

The most influential discussion of this incident in modern scholarship has been that of Martin Hengel.[25] Hengel interprets the first occurrence of the term 'dead' to mean spiritually dead, 'those who do not allow themselves to be affected by Jesus' message or by the nearness of the Kingdom.'[26] This is reasonable, and should be accepted. More controversially, Hengel sees the saying as contrary to the fifth commandment: 'Honour your father and your mother . . .' (Exod. 20.12//Deut. 5.16). It attacked the heart of Jewish piety, where 'the last offices for the dead had gained primacy among all good works.' Even Sanders has accepted that in this case Jesus required the Torah to be disobeyed.[27] He concludes, 'At least once Jesus was willing to say that following him superseded requirements of piety and the Torah. This may show that Jesus was prepared, if necessary, to challenge the adequacy of the Mosaic dispensation'.[28]

Other scholars have challenged this approach to the interpretation of this saying.[29] The main point is that the man's father would not be left unburied. On the contrary, the man was to leave the (spiritually) dead to bury *their* dead, so the man's father will have had other members of the family to bury him, as would normally be the case. It follows that Jesus' decision should not be perceived as contrary to Torah. It rather belongs within the interpretation of Torah. Jesus' prophetic decision is that the man should join the mission to bring Jews back to God, and hence to the Torah, rather than being present at his father's funeral, which could be conducted by other people who did not realize the importance of Jesus' migratory mission. This is dramatic, and illustrates how urgent Jesus considered his prophetic ministry to be. The second point is that there is no

---

25 M. Hengel, *The Charismatic Leader and his Followers* (1968. Trans. J. C. G. Greig. Edinburgh/New York: T&T Clark/Crossroad, 1981), pp. 3–15.
26 Hengel, *Charismatic Leader*, p. 8, with n. 18.
27 Sanders, *Jesus and Judaism*, pp. 252–55; *Historical Figure of Jesus*, pp. 225–56.
28 Sanders, *Jesus and Judaism*, p. 255.
29 See especially Vermes, *Religion of Jesus the Jew*, pp. 27–29; Crossley, *Date of Mark's Gospel*, pp. 105–7.

sign in the primary sources of Jesus being accused of setting aside the Torah. As we have already seen, the sources do record serious accusations against him by vitriolic opponents. In the next chapter, we shall see that these included many complaints that he did not observe the Law in the ways that some other Jews thought he should. If he had set aside the fifth commandment, his opponents would not have failed to condemn him for doing so.

The second point arises from the fact that some people find it very important that some of Jesus' ethical teaching is concerned with people's inner beings rather than external Law. For example, at the beginning of Mark 7, scribes and Pharisees who had come down from Jerusalem ask why his disciples are eating without having washed their hands first.[30] In the days when no one had heard of germs, this was a matter of purity Law, not of hygiene. Washing one's hands before meals was not a biblical regulation, but part of the expanded purity law of strict orthodox Jews. Accordingly, the scribes and Pharisees asked why the disciples did not walk according to the tradition of the elders (Mk 7.5). The term 'walk' is not a normal Greek term in these circumstances, but the Hebrew and Aramaic *halakh* which is the origin of the Jewish term *halakhah*, which was used for a single detailed commandment, and is still used as a term for all the detailed commandments taken together. Jesus responded with a slashing attack on the scribes and Pharisees for abandoning the commandment of God when they keep the tradition of men. He followed this by suggesting that what goes into a person does not make their insides unclean, and he is said to have listed various moral defects which emerge from a person and do defile them, such as adultery, theft, murder and blasphemy.

We can see here the point of classifying this ethical teaching as concerned with people's inner beings rather than external Law. At the same time, however, this does not seem to have been a significant part of Jesus' usual ethical teaching directed at the crowds or at his disciples. It emerged for serious discussion when Jesus was confronted with his orthodox opponents, because he believed that they had lost sight of the main points of the Torah in observing its details, and he was very concerned that they should not make other Jews do the same. I therefore discuss it in more detail in Chapter 9, where I consider Jesus' conflicts with his opponents. I conclude that Jesus rejected recent and non-biblical developments of purity Law. His comments should not be generalized and turned into criticism of the careful observance of external regulations which are written in the Torah.[31]

9. *Observing Jesus' Ethical Teaching*

A major problem often found with Jesus' ethical teaching is that some of his recommendations have proved very difficult to keep, none more so than the injunction to love one's enemies (Mt. 5.44//Lk. 6.27). The history of Christian

30   For detailed discussion see pp. 326–31.
31   See pp. 320–38.

anti-Semitism is an especially poignant reminder of the hatred exercised by some of Jesus' followers towards the people to whom he belonged. This is however by no means the only problem, and a much more general problem was already perceived in the ancient church. In the second century, the Didache opined, 'If you can bear the whole yoke of the Lord, you will be perfect. But if you cannot, observe what you can' (Did. 6, 2).

Christian tradition contains notable attempts to deal with the difficulty of observing Jesus' ethical teaching, but these belong to church history, and lie beyond the scope of this book. There has been one major scholarly attempt to solve this perceived problem. Schweitzer began a scholarly tradition which suggested that Jesus' teaching was 'interim ethics', a sort of temporary measure while waiting for the kingdom.[32] There is however no sign of this in the primary sources. We have seen that Jesus really did expect God to establish his kingdom soon, as many Jews have expected before and since. At no point, however, is any connection made between this expectation and his ethical teaching. Nowhere does he urge supposedly difficult ethical teaching on the grounds that the kingdom was at hand.

A more fruitful scholarly suggestion is that Jesus' treatment of his opponents shows that he did not really love his enemies. For example, the Jewish scholar Montefiore, having in mind the polemic which I consider in detail in Chapter 9, notes the absence from 'the life-story of Jesus . . . [of] one single incident in which Jesus actually performed a loving deed to one of his Rabbinic antagonists or enemies'.[33] We have also seen, for example, that Jesus accused some of his opponents of blasphemy against the Holy Spirit, and he declared this to be an unforgivable sin (Mk 3.28-29, Mt. 12.31-32, Lk. 12.10). What he had in mind was their opposition to his ministry of exorcism, and particularly their accusation that he cast out demons by the power of the devil.[34] It is his description of this sin as unforgivable which appears at first sight difficult to reconcile with his instructions to love your enemies and forgive everyone. He also accused them in more figurative terms of being like whitewashed tombs, beautiful on the outside but advertising their uncleanness within (Mt. 23.27).

These apparent tensions should lead us to consider Jesus' teaching in its original setting. It belonged originally to a vigorous attempt to recreate Jewish identity from a prophetic perspective. It was not a set of systematic propositions, to be taken literally and observed literally at all times and in all places. It was a deliberate attempt to move people's behaviour in certain directions. It is thus perfectly consistent with vigorous criticism of the stinking rich, and of those people who sought to impose the orthodox form of identity on other Jews. It was also consistent with Jesus' vigorous action and with cleansing the Temple, an action which was bound to upset the chief priests and scribes who ran it, especially as

---

32   For discussion of this tradition see especially R. H. Hiers, *Jesus and Ethics. Four Interpretations* (Philadelphia: Westminster, 1968), ch. II.

33   C. G. Montefiore, *Rabbinic Literature and Gospel Teachings* (London: Macmillan, 1930), p. 104; see further pp. 320–38.

34   For detailed discussion see p. 255.

he taught daily in the Temple, controlled the halakhah in the outermost court, and condemned them in terms which made quite clear that they would end up in Gehenna as punishment for the damage they did to Israel.[35]

It is here that it is of fundamental importance to consider who Jesus was preaching to. His ministry was directed at normal Jews who had fallen away from God, and whom Jesus called upon to return to Him. In the process it is evident that he accepted tax-collectors and sinners. His standard of judgement is especially well presented at Mt. 21.31-32, where tax-collectors and prostitutes will go before his opponents into the kingdom of God because they believed John the Baptist. Forgiveness was moreover central to his ethical teaching. Jesus' teaching is fundamentally different from what it would be if it had been a collection of rules formulated in some of the same words as we have. Gentile Christians have found it difficult to observe partly because they have deified Jesus, and hence imagine that every word of his teaching is literally true, so they have in effect treated it as if it were an organized corpus of eternal truths valid for all human behaviour everywhere.

10. *Conclusions*

The success of the Jesus movement as a renewal movement within Judaism shows that Jesus' ethical teaching was an effective contribution to the society in which he lived. It was ideally adapted to its original setting. Jesus encouraged people to return to God and to treat each other as God himself would wish and did command. Hence the centrality of the two major commandments, Deut. 6.4-5 and Lev. 19.18. Jesus' treatment of Torah from a prophetic perspective was accordingly quite different from the way it was treated by many scribes and Pharisees, who approached life from an orthodox perspective. I consider next the conflict between Jesus and his opponents.

---

35 See pp. 411–25.

CHAPTER 9

Jesus' Conflicts with His Opponents

1. *Introduction*

In the last four chapters, I have discussed the vigorous and successful ministry which Jesus carried out in first-century Israel. From time to time, however, I have noted that some Jews were opposed to his ministry, and some of them were extremely hostile. In this chapter, I examine this opposition, to see how far we can understand Jesus' opponents, and explain their rejection of basic aspects of his ministry. The synoptic Gospels label some of them 'scribes', sometimes 'scribes from Jerusalem', and they label some of the others 'Pharisees'. I therefore begin by describing these two groups.

2. *Scribes*

Scribes were people whose functions included writing documents. At least some scribes within Judaism at the time of Jesus had the important function of interpreting and teaching the Torah. Scribes did not form any kind of sect, and their status and social functions were quite varied, so they did not form a social class.[1]

For centuries before the time of Jesus, people called 'scribes' were administrators throughout the ancient Near East. They could read and write in societies in which the majority of people were illiterate. They were accordingly responsible for all kinds of records. The most prestigious were senior imperial administrators.

When some Jews returned from exile in Babylon, this was the situation in the Persian empire, which had conquered the Babylonian empire and included

---

1 A thorough scholarly discussion is provided by C. Schams, *Jewish Scribes in the Second-Temple Period* (JSOTSup 291. Sheffield: Sheffield Academic, 1998).

Israel in its large province 'Beyond the River'. The most important Jewish scribe during this period was Ezra, whose return to Jerusalem, probably in 458 BCE, is described in the books of Ezra and Nehemiah. In a commissioning letter attributed to the Persian king, he is described as 'Ezra the priest, the scribe (*sepher*) of the Law of the God of Heaven' (Ezra 7.12). This description does not indicate the position of an average scribe, but a senior religious official within Judaism, appointed to an important post by the Persian administration. In this capacity, Ezra read the Law (Torah) of Moses publicly to the people, and it was translated into Aramaic and explained by a number of people, some of whom are described as Levites (cf. Neh. 7.73–8.18). Other eminent scribes included Zadok, one of the men whom Nehemiah appointed over the storerooms (Neh. 13.13). More ordinary scribes were employed in the middle and lower levels of the Persian administration, where they dealt with financial matters, and were responsible for all kinds of records.

When Israel was conquered by the Greeks, Greek kings continued to run it in a basically similar way. In the early second century BCE, a letter from king Antiochus III granted privileges to people including 'scribes of the Temple', who are mentioned separately from 'priests' and 'temple-singers' (Jos. *Ant.* XII, 142). The 'scribes of the Temple' were an important group of people. In addition to keeping necessary records, and copying and keeping Torah scrolls, they would be responsible for advising priests on the observance of the Law in the running of the Temple. What proportion of them were themselves priests or Levites we do not know. They should be kept in mind when the Gospels associate scribes with chief priests, or have them coming down from Jerusalem to Galilee.

In the early second century BCE, a rather idealized but informative account of the work of a distinguished scribe was written by *Yeshua‘* son of Eleazar son of Sira, generally known as Jesus son of Sirach.[2] He begins by saying that the wisdom of the scribe (*sōphēr*) depends on the opportunity of leisure (Sir. 38.24), contrasting the busy lives of ordinary working people. His scribe is devoted to the study of the Law of the Most High (Sir. 38.34), the distinctive feature of specifically Jewish scribes. He seeks out the wisdom of the ancients, and understands prophecies, proverbs and parables (Sir. 39.1-3). His distinguished status is indicated by the fact that he serves among the great and appears before rulers, in contrast with artisans, who do not sit as judges or attain eminence in the public assembly (Sir. 38.32-33; 39.4). Such are the kind of scribes who will have taken counsel with chief priests and elders to have Jesus put to death. They should also be kept in mind when the Gospels mention scribes coming down from Jerusalem to Galilee.

By the time of Herod the Great, there is also clear evidence of village scribes, who had probably been working in Israel for at least two centuries previously. These were people of much lower status. They kept records, wrote documents such as bills of divorce, and instructed ordinary people, many of whom could not read, in what the Law said and how it should be observed. They therefore

---

2 Cf. p. 124.

had a significant amount of power in their local communities. They should be kept in mind for example when Mark records that some scribes were present in Capernaum at the healing of a paralytic (Mk 2.6), and when ordinary people in Capernaum were amazed at Jesus' teaching because he taught with authority and 'not like the scribes' (Mk 1.22).

The position of scribes as teachers of the Law appears especially clearly in later rabbinical literature. Here, in addition to the written Torah, and the halakhah, some of it recorded as Oral Torah, some judgements are described as 'words of the scribes'. These did not have the same authority as the written Torah, but they belonged to debates about how the Law should be observed and applied to the whole of daily life.

Scribes might therefore be Pharisees, though we do not know how many scribes were in fact Pharisees. There is accordingly nothing strange in Mark's reference to 'the scribes of the Pharisees' (Mk 2.16), unusual though that description is. It is equally natural that the two groups should frequently be associated. Sometimes the scribes are especially associated with the interpretation of scripture (e.g. Mk 9.11). Scribes and Pharisees are also mentioned together as interpreters of 'the traditions of the elders' (Mk 7.5), and as authoritative interpreters of the Law (Mt. 23.2-4). This is natural because both groups were involved in the interpretation of the Torah and its application to the whole of life.

3. *Pharisees*

The Pharisees were a religious sect. Josephus claims that when he returned to normal city life in Jerusalem at the age of 19, after a period of ascetic living with a hermit in the wilderness, he began 'following the sect of the Pharisees' (*Life*, 12), though he evidently did not join them. He was in a good position to know what they were like, and some of the information which he provides is important. He describes them as a sect (*hairesis*), as does Luke (Acts 15.5), who attributes this view to Paul (Acts 26.5), who had been a Pharisee (Phil. 3.5; Acts 23.6; 26.5), and whom Luke accompanied on some of his journeys.[3] This shows that the Pharisees were a quite distinct group, who to some degree kept themselves separate from other people. This is also implied by their name, which is derived from the Hebrew *perūshim*, which means 'separated' (the English 'Pharisees' is derived directly from the Greek *Pharisaioi*, which is derived from the Aramaic, rather than Hebrew, *Pharisayā*). This is probably because to a significant degree they kept themselves separate from other people, at least partly so that they could live in a greater state of purity than the average Jew. Josephus says that during the time of Herod the Great they numbered more than 6,000 men (*Ant.* XVII, 42). These men will have been mostly heads of households, but 6,000 is still a relatively small number, indicating again that they formed a minority religious movement.

3   Cf. pp. 94–95.

Josephus says repeatedly that the Pharisees handed on to the people regulations (*nomima*) from the fathers which are not to be found in the Law of Moses, and he says that this was at the centre of their disputes with the Sadducees (*Ant.* XIII, 297). He declares that they followed what was handed on to them, and deferred to their elders (*Ant.* XVIII, 12), which is consistent with this view of their traditions. This is also consistent with the evidence of the Gospels. For example, Pharisees and some scribes from Jerusalem (Mk 7.1) asked Jesus why his disciples did not 'walk according to the tradition of the elders' (Mk 7.5). This is explicit recognition that their habit of washing their hands before meals was a tradition handed on to them, not found in the Law of Moses. Paul says that during his previous life within Judaism, which is when he was a Pharisee, he was extremely zealous for the traditions of his forefathers (Gal. 1.13-14), another reflection of the Pharisees' view of their traditions.

All this is supported by the evidence of judgements attributed to Pharisees in general and to known Pharisees. For example, it is said that the clothes of one of the 'people of the land' convey 'touch uncleanness' to Pharisees (m. Hag 2.7), which means that mere contact with an ordinary Jew would make a Pharisee unclean. This is evidently a tradition followed by Pharisees who were trying to live as far as possible in a state of purity, a view not to be found in the Hebrew Bible. Perhaps the most famous individual Pharisee is Gamaliel I, described by Luke as a Pharisee and a teacher of the Law honoured by all the people (Acts 5.34). He was the father of Simeon son of Gamaliel, who is described by Josephus as a Pharisee (*Life*, 191), and who was himself the father of Gamaliel II. Paul was taught by Gamaliel I in Jerusalem (Acts 22.3). He is described as Rabban Gamaliel the Elder in rabbinical sources, to distinguish him from his grandson. It was said that 'When Rabban Gamaliel the Elder died . . . purity and abstinence/separateness (*perīshūth*) died' (m. Sot. 9, 15).

Josephus also says that the Pharisees are considered to interpret the regulations (*nomima*) 'with accuracy' (*War* II, 162, cf. *Life*, 191). Luke similarly reports Paul saying that he was educated at the feet of Gamaliel 'accurately' in the Law (Acts 22.3), and that as a Pharisee he lived according to 'the most accurate sect' (Acts 26.5). These perceptions also reflect the vigorous way in which the Pharisees tried to observe the Law accurately and apply it to the whole of life.

There is also some evidence about the Pharisees in a small number of Qumran scrolls. In these, members of a group whom most scholars rightly identify as Pharisees are not called by the name 'Pharisee', but by terms such as *dōreshē halaqōth*, which means literally 'seekers of smooth things'. This is a pun on *dōreshē halakōth*, which means 'seekers of legal judgements', judgements which together make up the halakhah. This reflects the position of the Pharisees as a distinct group who had their own legal judgements with which the sectarian authors of some Dead Sea Scrolls did not agree.

The scrolls also locate the 'seekers of smooth things' in Jerusalem, which was the main centre of the Pharisees. One passage (4QpNah I, 6–8) refers to a notorious incident during the reign of King Alexander Jannaeus (103–76 BCE), who had some 800 of his opponents crucified and their families slaughtered while he and his concubines feasted and watched (Jos. *Ant.* XIII, 380). Many of the victims were probably Pharisees, and the Pharisees took their revenge during the reign of Alexandra Salome (76–67 BCE). This was the only period when they exercised political power in government, and Josephus records that Queen Alexandra restored the regulations (*nomima*) which the Pharisees had previously introduced in accordance with the traditions of their fathers (*Ant.* XIII, 408–9).

After this, they no longer had the power to impose their traditions, but they continued to observe them and pass them on to others. When Herod the Great was king with Roman support (effectively 37–4 BCE), the Pharisees had no political power as a group. Indeed, Herod imposed a fine on them when they refused to take an oath of loyalty to the emperor and the king's government, putting to death some who predicted his demise, while exempting Pollio and Samaias and some of their disciples (*Ant.* XV, 370; XVII, 41–4). During the ministry of Jesus, they still had no political power as a group. Judaea was officially ruled by the Roman governor Pontius Pilate (26–37 CE), who in practice left the running of the province to the chief priests, led by the high priest Joseph Caiaphas (18–36 CE). Galilee was ruled directly by Herod Antipas, who was a client king of Rome. We do not know whether any Pharisees lived in cities such as Sepphoris, or in smaller places such as Capernaum: if so, they too had no political power as a group.

Individual Pharisees might however hold powerful positions. We know that Gamaliel I was such a person. Among other things, he wrote to Jews everywhere decreeing the intercalation of a month because the lambs were too young and the birds so small (t. San. 2.6//y. San. 1, 2/17 (18d)//b. San. 11b). This postponed the major pilgrim festival of Passover, as Gamaliel could only have done if he had been given an important official position. On the whole, the extent of the power of the Pharisees depended on how far people were prepared to listen to them.

Josephus also says that the Pharisees were especially influential among the townspeople, and that the way that they conducted worship in accordance with Pharisaic views showed how the cities bore witness to their excellence (*Ant.* XVIII, 15). This is also consistent with other evidence, since it was more possible to follow their concerns for purity in cities than in the countryside. In cities, there was less need to become unclean, and it was easier to use stone vessels, immerse in appropriate pools (*miqwaōth*) and follow other purity customs.

Moreover, the Pharisees emerged as a sect in the second century BCE, as a result of a crisis in which the centre of Judaism suffered badly from Greek influence. A gymnasium was built in Jerusalem, and some Jews were so assimilated that they removed the marks of circumcision. A persecution was instituted by the Greek king Antiochus IV Epiphanes, in which his statue was erected on the altar in the Temple, the sacrifice of pigs was required, and observance of the Law was prohibited. This situation led to the torture and death of many martyrs. An immediate result was the Maccabaean revolt, which was successful, and led to the rededication of the Temple in 164 BCE, an event celebrated at the festival of Hanukkah every year (1 Macc. 1–4).[4] Another result was the emergence of pious Jews who reinforced Jewish identity by means of careful observance of the Law. It

---

4   On all this see further p. 140, and pp. 406–7; Schürer-Vermes-Millar, pp. 137–63.

is from this group that the Pharisees came, devoted to the observance of the Law and to expanding the regulations to cover the whole of life. This is how Pharisees at the time of Jesus came to be devoted to the traditions of the elders.[5]

New cities at the time of Jesus included Sepphoris, rebuilt by Herod Antipas when Jesus was a child, and Tiberias, which he founded in 19–20 CE.[6] There was a massive amount of visible Greek influence in these cities, though both were Jewish. New inhabitants of these cities accordingly had decisions to make. Would they assimilate and become more Greek? Would they feel their traditional Jewish identity threatened, and seek to reinforce it with attendance at synagogue and careful observance of the Torah? In this situation, a sect deliberately devoted to the reinforcement of Jewish identity by means of careful observance of the Torah was naturally influential among faithful Jews who did not go as far as joining the sect, perhaps because for practical reasons they could not do so. A similar situation recurred in well-established but predominantly Greek cities, such as Scythopolis just to the south of Galilee. Such cities had Jewish minorities. In that situation, some Jews assimilated into the Greek world. Others, however, reinforced their Jewish identity with attendance at synagogue and careful observance of the Torah. They too would naturally admire the Pharisees and observe some of their teaching, without necessarily joining the sect. All this explains why the Pharisees were especially influential among Jewish townspeople, even though they themselves remained a sect, a minority religious group.

Josephus records other points which distinguished the Pharisees from other groups. One is their belief in the resurrection of the dead, in terms which suggest that they believed in what we would call the immortality of the soul rather than the resurrection of the body (*Ant.* XVIII, 14).[7] Luke, who was in Jerusalem when Paul was examined by a Sanhedrin, relates how Paul caused dissension at that meeting by appealing to Pharisees who believed in resurrection, over against Sadducees who did not (Acts 23.6-10).

Another point is the relative leniency of the Pharisees in judgement (*Ant.* XIII, 294), in contrast to the severity of the Sadducees (*Ant.* XX, 199). Two incidents are often cited to illustrate this. At Acts 5.17-42, Luke relates how the high priest and others, all being members of the sect of the Sadducees, arrested the apostles and brought them before their Sanhedrin, and when they examined them, they were proposing to put them to death (Acts 5.33). Gamaliel I, being both a Pharisee and a member of that Sanhedrin, a fact which reflects his outstandingly distinguished position, urged them to be cautious on the ground that if the movement was merely human it would fail, and if it was of God they could not and should not oppose it (Acts 5.34-39). They therefore had the apostles beaten, cautioned and set free (Acts 5.39-41).

Secondly, Josephus actually says that the Sadducees were more savage than other Jews concerning punishment when he relates how Ananus son of Ananus,

---

5 See e.g. A. I. Baumgarten, *The Flourishing of Jewish Sects in the Maccabean Era* (Atlanta: Society of Biblical Literature, 1997).

6 See further pp. 338–39.

7 See further pp. 466–69.

better known as Annas, the father-in-law of Joseph Caiaphas (Jn 18.13), had Jesus' brother Jacob stoned to death, an event which took place in 62 CE. Josephus records objections from 'those who were considered most fair-minded of those in the city and accurate concerning the laws' (*Ant.* XX, 201). They objected to the Roman procurator Albinus, who had not yet arrived in Israel, and to King Agrippa II, who replaced the high priest. Josephus' description entails that these objectors included Pharisees, though the fact he does not mention them entails that other orthodox Jews were involved as well.

All these points taken together make a coherent whole. The Pharisees were a distinct, and distinctive, minority religious movement. The majority of scholars are therefore right to call them a sect. The Pharisees were nonetheless very influential, especially in the cities.

4. *Orthodoxy in Second Temple Judaism*

In a previous book, I suggested using the modern term 'orthodox' as an analytical tool to assist with the analysis of scribes, Pharisees and other Jews who observed additional regulations as they sought to observe the Torah and apply it to the whole of life. This can only be done if a careful definition of the term 'orthodox' is offered, which brings out the main point of their lives and does not read back features of modern orthodox Judaism into the ancient period. This is the definition which I offered:

> Orthodox Jews accepted as divinely inspired the accounts of the history and halakhah of the Jewish people recorded in the written and oral Laws, and codified in sacred books such as the Pentateuch. In the face of threats of assimilation, they stood firm as guardians of the Law seeking to ensure that it was observed and applied to the whole of life. This led them to discuss and codify additional enactments, both orally and in written collections such as the Zadokite document and the book of Jubilees. This was a central concern of their lives, and in this way they embodied and defended Jewish identity. Orthodox Jews thus included both Pharisees and Essenes. A significant proportion of Jews did not observe the additional enactments of the orthodox, and some Jews did not obey the halakhah at all. The difficulties which this caused for the orthodox world-view are evident in works such as Daniel 9 and 4 Ezra.[8]

My discussion was criticized by some scholars, who maintained the traditional view that there was no orthodoxy in Second Temple Judaism.[9] In so doing,

---

8   P. M. Casey, *From Jewish Prophet to Gentile God: The Origins and Development of New Testament Christology* (The Cadbury Lectures at the University of Birmingham, 1985–86. Cambridge/Louisville: James Clarke/WJK, 1991), pp. 17–18, with discussion at pp. 18–20.

9   See especially J. D. G. Dunn, 'The Making of Christology – Evolution or Unfolding?', in J. B.

however, they used Christian assumptions about what orthodoxy should be, that is, a group of people who agreed with each other and who were in some sense normative. The above definition is not of this kind. It is based on the embodiment and defence of Jewish identity by applying the Law to the whole of life, a process which has always involved the expansion of detailed enactments. I did not suggest that orthodox Jews thought and/or acted the same as each other, since that would be patently false, in the ancient and modern worlds alike. On the contrary, I explicitly included in my definition both Pharisees and Essenes, who were different sects, and I did not confine my discussion of orthodox opposition to Jesus to Pharisees.[10] Equally, I did not suggest that these people were in any real sense normative. The use of Jewish categories for the analysis of Second Temple Judaism is an especially obvious ploy, and one which should be judged on its own terms, not by imposing Christian assumptions on it. I therefore continue to use the term 'orthodox' in explicating the nature of some of Jesus' most serious opponents.

5. Jesus' Conflicts with Scribes and Pharisees

The first dispute recorded in Mark's Gospel shows the irreconcilable nature of the difference between Jesus and his orthodox opponents. There was a large party when the tax-collector Levi, son of Alphaeus, decided to follow Jesus. Jesus would naturally use the Aramaic word for 'healer' where Mark has 'doctor', an inevitable change in the translation of the account from Aramaic into Greek. This reveals Jesus' analogical argument more closely tied to his own ministry, for he was a healer ('āsē) himself. The original source must have run somewhat as follows:

> And he was reclining in his house. And many tax-collectors and sinners reclined with Jesus and his disciples, for they were many and they were attached to him. And scribes of the Pharisees saw that he was eating with sinners and tax-collectors, and they said to his disciples, 'Why does he eat with tax-collectors and sinners?' And Jesus heard and said to them, 'It's not healthy (people) who need a healer but the afflicted. I did not come to call righteous (people), but sinners'.
>
> (cf. Mark 2.15-17)

By Old Testament Law, Jesus had done nothing wrong. He might become unclean, if he was not unclean already; but the Torah does not object to people

---

Green and M. Turner (eds), *Jesus of Nazareth: Lord and Christ: Essays in Honour of Prof. I. H. Marshall* (Carlisle/Grand Rapids: Paternoster/Eerdmans, 1994), pp. 437–52, at p. 441, and my comments in Casey, *Aramaic Approach to Q*, pp. 65–70.

10   Casey, *From Jewish Prophet to Gentile God*, pp. 17 and e.g. 61–65. I am grateful to Rabbi Prof. Seth Kunin for a very helpful discussion, in which we tried without success to find a different term.

becoming unclean in such ways, it tells them how to become clean again, a matter which became of central importance only when they needed to enter the Temple. As we have seen, however, the Pharisees had been active in the orthodox expansion of purity legislation. They sought to maintain their Jewish identity by keeping themselves in a state of purity whenever possible, a process which served to separate them from ordinary observant Jews, as well as those who were not properly observant. This can be seen most clearly in later orthodox sources. I noted for example that the clothes of one of the 'people of the land' convey touch uncleanness to Pharisees (m. Hag. 2.7), so that mere contact with an ordinary Jew would make a Pharisee unclean. Again, it is characteristic of an 'Associate' that he undertakes not to make ready his ritually prepared food with one of the 'people of the land', and to eat ordinary food in a state of purity (t. Dem. 2.2).

All this was perceived to be obedience to the Law of God himself, revealed to Moses on Mount Sinai, and since Jesus had a reputation as a religious teacher, Pharisaic scribes asked why he was not following their expanded purity regulations. Neither tax-collectors nor the more vaguely defined 'sinners' were fully observant, and they were most unlikely to be in a state of purity.[11] We can however see from the story of Levi that these purity laws were contrary to the centre of Jesus' mission. Their very function in separating some people from others was contrary to the prophetic tradition, which called upon the whole of Israel to return to the Lord.

Quite early in Mark, the dispute is already a matter of life and death. This emerges from two disputes about sabbath halakhah, the details of how to observe God's commandment not to work on the sabbath (Exod. 20.10//Deut. 5.14). Mark's account (Mk 2.23–3.6) begins with a mistake which can only have arisen from slightly misreading and translating a written Aramaic source.[12] Mark says 'his disciples began to *make* a path', an improbable and illegal action which is not mentioned in the subsequent dispute. In Aramaic, however, 'make' is *'bhar*, only one letter different from 'go along' (*'bhadh*), with 'dh' (ד) rather than 'r' (ר) as the final letter, and 'go along' is just what the context requires to set up the following dispute. Moreover, these two letters, very similar in the square script which I have printed here, were often virtually indistinguishable in an ancient written text. Mark's Aramaic source may be accordingly reconstructed and translated as follows, with the somewhat redundant 'began', another sign of an Aramaic source, and the singular 'sabbath', where Mark has the Greek plural, because the Aramaic singular in the definite state[13] (*shabbatā*) looks like the basic Greek plural (*sabbata*), with the result that all forms of the Greek plural (here *sabbasin*) were conventionally used in Jewish Greek to refer to a single sabbath:

---

11 On 'sinners' see further pp. 282–84, 363–64.

12 For detailed discussion of Mark 2.23–3.6, including a reconstruction of Mark's Aramaic source see Casey, *Aramaic Sources of Mark's Gospel*, pp. 138–92.

13 The definite and indefinite states in Aramaic have been very difficult for New Testament scholars to understand: I have tried to explain them as simply as possible on pp. 360–61.

And he was, on the sabbath, going through the cornfields, and his disciples began to go along a path and to pluck the ears of corn.

(Mk 2.23)

This gave first-century Jews a great deal more information than may now be seen on the surface of the text. In that environment, everyone knew that the only circumstance in which people went along a path plucking grain from other people's fields was when they were taking *Peah*, the grain left at the edges of fields for poor people. The basic regulations for *Peah* are biblical:

When you reap the harvest of your land, you shall not complete the border (*Peah*) of your field, and you shall not gather the gleaning of your harvest. And you shall not glean your vineyard and you shall not gather the fallen grapes of your vineyard: you shall leave them for the poor and for the sojourner.

(Lev. 19.9-10)

It follows also that the disciples were poor and consequently hungry. Jesus, however, did not take *Peah* because he was a craftsman who was not that poor.

Pharisees were also allowed to walk on paths through fields within the sabbath limit, about half a mile from the edge of Capernaum. They are more likely to have been there on purpose than by mistake. They asked Jesus why the disciples were doing something which was not allowed (Mk 2.24). Taking *Peah* on the sabbath is not against the written Law. Orthodox Jews had however been active in expanding the sabbath halakhah to prohibit everything they felt should not be done. Some had already written down the following:

A man shall eat on the sabbath day only what has been prepared, and from what is decaying in the fields.

(CD X, 22–23)

This restricts people to prepared food, and fruit which must have fallen off the day before, so the opposite of what needs to be plucked. We should infer that the Pharisees took a similar view. It was however a strict expansion of the Law from an orthodox perspective. Hence it was not accepted by the ordinary Jews who were Jesus' disciples, nor by Jesus himself.

Mark records two arguments put forward by Jesus in defence of his poor and hungry disciples. The first argument uses the example of David, who obtained loaves of the shewbread from the priest to feed his men 'when he had need and was hungry, he and those with him' (Mk 2.25 see 1 Sam. 21.1-6). Jesus and the Pharisees alike would assume that the incident took place on the sabbath, because the shewbread was the only bread which the priest had (1 Sam. 21.4), and it was changed on the sabbath (Lev. 24.8-8; Jos. *Ant.* III, 255–56). Thus the sabbath was the day when the shewbread would be the only bread available to the priest. This is a Jewish assumption which is not explicitly mentioned, so this is further evidence that Mark's narrative is dependent on a very early Jewish source. The argument then makes perfect sense – if David used the shewbread to feed the hungry on the sabbath, it was in accordance with God's will that Jesus' poor and hungry disciples should take advantage of the Torah's provision of taking *Peah*, grain deliberately left for them, on the sabbath.

On the face of the text, Jesus seems to have dated the incident under the wrong high priest, Ahimelech rather than Abiathar. This is another mistake which arose when Mark's Aramaic source was translated into Greek. The original Aramaic simply means that Abiathar was a great/important chief/high priest (*kāhēn rabh*), and from a cultural point of view he was conspicuously not Zadok, the founding father of the Sadducees. The Pharisees could be expected to agree that the Law was correctly observed under King David before Solomon replaced Abiathar with Zadok. Abiathar was therefore a significant part of Jesus' original argument. Mark simply failed to notice that in rendering literally *kāhēn rabh* 'great/chief priest', with the Greek word *archiereōs* in the singular without any article, he could naturally be taken to mean that Abiathar was the high priest at the time. Once again, a mistake leads us to an Aramaic original just at a point where the argument was significant for Jesus, but would not have interested the early church.

Jesus' second argument began from God's purpose in creating the sabbath for the benefit of people:

> The sabbath was made for man, and not man for the sabbath.[28]Surely, then, a/the (son of) man is master even of the sabbath.

This uses a general statement containing the term 'son of man' which refers especially to Jesus himself, an Aramaic idiom which provides further evidence that Mark's text is a literal translation of an Aramaic source.[14] It is another feature of the text which the early church would have no interest in producing. This argument also makes excellent sense. Since God made the sabbath for people, they may feed themselves on the sabbath, and people in general may decide this. The idiomatic reference to Jesus himself means that he in particular was entitled to make decisions about sabbath halakhah, as he was doing on behalf of his disciples.

These two arguments of different kinds are both based on scripture. They will have convinced Jesus' disciples, but not the Pharisees.

We are not told what the Pharisees said, but we are told what they did. In a meeting at the synagogue, presumably later that day, they watched to see whether Jesus would perform a healing, so that they could accuse him (Mk 3.2). I have already discussed the healing itself,[15] so I concentrate now on the dispute. Why were the Pharisees looking for a second violation of the sabbath? Their behaviour is comprehensible only on the basis of an assumption characteristic of later Jewish source material – a person cannot be prosecuted for one sabbath violation, but must be warned, and can only be prosecuted if they do it again (m. San. 7, 8;

14   For the idiomatic use of the term 'son of man' see pp. 358–68.
15   See pp. 262–66.

y. San. 7, 14/1 (25c)). This is a sensible custom. The Jewish community can flourish if people are encouraged to observe the Torah, sabbath included. The biblical
penalty for breaking the sabbath is, officially, death (Exod. 31.14; 35.2). If this
were normally carried out without warning, it would wreck the Jewish community as disastrously as a major persecution. Hence we do not know of a single
case from the whole of the ancient period, nor have I heard of any instances in
the modern world. Warning people, however, is normally a mode of encourag-
ing observance.

On what basis did the Pharisees consider that healing on the sabbath was
violating it? It is not against the written law. We have however seen that taking
Peah was not against the written law either, and that Pharisees belonged to the
orthodox wing of Judaism. They were expanding the written law as they applied
it to the whole of life, and just as they were shocked at the disciples plucking
grain on the sabbath, so they were shocked that Jesus should heal on the sabbath.
Later sources show concern that things connected with healing should not be
done on the sabbath (m. Shab. 14, 3f), with the major exception that saving life
overrules the sabbath. We have seen that Jesus used this exception as the basis
for his major argument in favour of healing on the sabbath. He believed that in
healing the man he was saving a person.[16]

The serious nature of this dispute is presented in the final verse. Mark's Greek
is again troublesome because he suffered from interference as he translated from
an Aramaic source. He says the Pharisees gave 'council' (*sumboulion*) against
Jesus when he meant that they gave 'counsel' (*sumboulian*). The Aramaic *'ētsā*
means both, and the two Greek words differ by only one letter, so this is another
natural mistake in the work of a bilingual translator. The reconstructed source
may accordingly be translated as follows:

> And the Pharisees went out in that hour with the Herodians and gave counsel
> against/concerning him how they might destroy him.

The Herodians were supporters of Herod Antipas, who was tetrarch of Galilee.[17]
He had recently had John the Baptist put to death (Mk 6.17-29; Jos. *Ant.* XVIII,
116–19). This is the reason for Pharisees to contact the Herodians and co-operate
with them. The aftermath of this event is found at Lk. 13.31-33. Luke had an
Aramaic source for this tradition. It had idiomatic and metaphorical uses of time
intervals, and 'be perfected' as a metaphor for death, as in Aramaic but not in
Greek. Once again, a Gospel passage has clear signs of translation from an Aramaic
source just at the point where the traditions in it must be authentic because they
have a perfect setting in the life of Jesus, and contain nothing that the early church
would want to make up. Luke's source may be translated as follows:

> [31]In that hour Pharisees went and said to him, 'Get out and go away from
> here, because Herod wants to kill you'. [32]And he said to them, 'Go tell that

16   See pp. 264–65.
17   On Herod Antipas, and the Herodians see pp. 338–44.

jackal, Look! I am casting out demons and performing healings to-day and tomorrow, and on the third day I am perfected. [33]But I am going to proceed to-day and day after day, for it would not be fitting for a prophet to perish outside Jerusalem.'[18]

This shows the strains and stresses of the temporary alliance between Pharisees and Herodians. If Herod thought John the Baptist was a threat to the Herodian state (Jos. *Ant.* XVIII, 116–19), he was likely to take the same view of Jesus. The alliance between Pharisees and Herodians, however, not only supplied him with a reason for killing Jesus, but also alienated some of the Pharisees. Pharisees were basically orthodox Jews. If some felt so strongly that taking *Peah* and healing on the sabbath were, or should be, against the Law and that this should be enforced with the death penalty, others, whether generally inclined to leniency or not, are likely to have felt that their view of how the Law should be observed should not be imposed on everyone, especially not on a prophetic teacher who brought so many Jews back to basic observances. Indeed, they may have believed that killing such a person for such a reason was a straightforward violation of the sixth commandment, which prohibits murder. They therefore came and warned Jesus. At the same time, they did not blame their fellow Pharisees, who did not have enough power to destroy Jesus unless they co-operated with the secular authorities. They blamed Herod, who had already killed John the Baptist, action which they may well have regarded as a murder already committed.

Jesus' response reflects the same aspects of his ministry as the incident of Mk 3.1-6. He refers directly to his ministry of exorcism and healing, and to his forthcoming death. The opposition to his ministry was so serious that he was planning to die in Jerusalem.

I have noted the serious nature of the opposition to Jesus' ministry of exorcism.[19] We have seen that Jesus was accused of casting out demons by the power of the devil himself. Some of the opponents who made this accusation were 'scribes who came down from Jerusalem' (Mk 3.22). To have gone to this trouble, this group must have been led by seriously distinguished scribes who were experts in the interpretation of the Torah. How many of them were orthodox we cannot tell. They are likely to have been mixed from that perspective, for the chief priests will have been as concerned as the Pharisees about what was going on in Galilee, and at least the majority of the chief priests were Sadducees. Moreover, this dispute has nothing about it that suggests the opponents were orthodox.

The accusation is as serious as possible, and so was Jesus' reply. It is an extraordinary saying in that it has been translated no less than three times in the Gospels: the following translation is based on the Aramaic saying of Jesus which lies behind all three passages cited:[20]

---

18 See further pp. 96–97, 114–15, and pp. 342–43, 403–4. For the Aramaic reconstruction, with discussion see Casey, *Aramaic Sources of Mark's Gospel*, pp. 188–89.

19 See pp. 253–56.

20 See further pp. 311–12, and for detailed discussion, Casey, *Aramaic Approach to Q*, pp. 148–49, 177–82; *Solution to the 'Son of Man' Problem*, pp. 140–43.

And whoever speaks a word against a/the son of man, it will be forgiven him. But whoever speaks a word against the Holy Spirit, it will not be forgiven him for ever (cf. Mk 3.28-29; Mt. 12.32; Lk. 12.10).

We have seen that the first part of this saying decrees forgiveness to people who oppose or even slander other people. The use of the term 'son of man' (bar (ᵉ)nāsh(ā)), however, is the particular idiom whereby the statement refers especially to Jesus himself. The saying therefore appears at first sight to grant forgiveness to Jesus' opponents. The sting is in the second half. The Holy Spirit is a metaphor for God in action. Nowhere is the action of God to be seen more vigorously and obviously than in Jesus' exorcisms. The accusation that he cast out demons by the power of the devil is accordingly an unforgivable sin. What Jesus seems to concede in the first part of the saying is thus quite removed in the second part. Here too the dispute between Jesus and his scribal opponents was as serious as possible.

Mark reports another serious dispute with 'Pharisees and some of the scribes who came from Jerusalem' (Mk 7.1), and here it is obvious that the opponents are orthodox because of the nature of their question. This evidently used the culturally key term halakh, 'walk', which is the origin of the Jewish term halakhah:

Why do your disciples not walk according to the tradition of the elders, but eat bread with profane hands?

(Mk 7.5)

Mark has already made it clear that this means that they did not wash their hands before meals (Mk 7.2). This is a typical orthodox expansion of purity law, and in calling it 'the tradition of the elders' these orthodox Jews openly recognized that this is not a biblical regulation.

The nature of this orthodox view has been very difficult to understand, because many of our sources are of later date, and orthodox views were never altogether uniform and changed over time. However, recent scholarly work, especially that of Crossley and Furstenburg, has enabled us to see more clearly the point of the dispute.[21] There are two main points. First, in a society in which people ate with their hands rather than with cutlery, liquids could convey impurity to the hands which would then convey impurity to a mix of solid food and liquids (cf. m. Tebul-Yom 2.2). This is the impurity which could be removed by handwashing before touching the food.

In the second place, there was a significant new development. This was to suppose that the consumption of food, which had been made unclean through contact with a person's hands, made the person eating it unclean. This is assumed, for example, in a debate between R.Eliezer and R.Joshua, who lived in the second half of the first century CE (m. Toh. 2, 2). Moreover, m. Toh. 4, 11, like m.

---

21 Crossley, *Date of Mark's Gospel*, pp. 183–205, 'Dating Mark Legally (II): Mark 7.1-23';
    Y. Furstenburg, 'Defilement Penetrating the Body: A New Understanding of Contamination
    in Mark 7.15', *NTS* 54 (2008), pp. 176–200, both with bibliography.

Zab. 5, 12, defines the impurity caused by the consumption of contaminated foods as 'words of the scribes', which means that it was known to be an addition to scripture. This is reinforced at b. Yoma 80b, where the question is raised as to whether this judgement might be scriptural, and the conclusion is drawn that it is rabbinical. This is the reason why scribes and Pharisees asked why Jesus' disciples did not walk 'according to the tradition of the elders': they knew perfectly well that the disciples were not violating a biblical law. Furstenburg has an especially clear declaration of this from the great mediaeval commentator Rashi: 'According to the Torah food does not contaminate the person eating it.'[22] Jesus shared this uniform perception that the view that food touched by unclean hands was not a biblical regulation. This is why he believed that kosher food touched by unclean hands did not make a person unclean. Consequently, he rejected the whole idea of handwashing before meals. Food forbidden in the Torah has no relevance to this dispute: that is why neither Jesus nor his opponents discuss it.

Jesus' reply to the orthodox question was quite explosive. He let fly with a quotation of Isa. 29.13, and proceeded to accuse these orthodox Jews of *replacing* the commandment of God with their own tradition:

[6]. . . Isaiah rightly prophesied about you actors, as it is written, 'This people honours me with their lips, but their heart is far from me. [7]In vain they worship me, teaching commandments of men as teachings' (Isa. 29.13). [8]Abandoning the commandment of God, you hold fast to the tradition of men!

[9]And he said to them: You do well set aside the commandment of God to uphold your tradition.[10]For Moses said, 'Honour your father and your mother' (Exod. 20.12//Deut. 5.16), and 'He who reviles his father or mother shall be put to death' (Exod. 21.17//Lev. 20.9).[11]But you say, 'If a man says to his father or mother, "Korban (which means 'gift') be whatever you are owed from me"' –[12]you no longer allow him to do anything for his father or mother,[13]making void the word of God through your tradition which you have transmitted. And you do many other such things.

(Mk 7.6-13)

This is a massive attack on the oral traditions of orthodox Jews. We shall find some cases in which Jesus accepts the expanded oral halakhah of orthodox Jews, provided that they retain the central points of the Law, love of God and of one's neighbour. Here, however, he clearly argues that they make void the word of God in observing their own traditions. Moreover, the example given is a very serious one, for the commandment to honour one's father and mother could be cited as the 'heavy of heavies', the most important commandment of all.[23]

Jewish sources written in Aramaic confirm that *qorbān* means 'gift', and

---

22   Furstenburg, 'Defilement Penetrating the Body', p. 182, quoting Rashi on b. Shab. 13b, with a parallel at b. Yoma 80b.
23   See pp. 332–33.

that it was used when people gave gifts to the Temple.[24] This is further evidence of the Aramaic origin of these traditions at another point where the content of the argument has a proper setting in the ministry of Jesus, not in the disputes of the early church. Jewish sources do not however confirm this abuse of the custom, according to which people gave gifts to the Temple and did not look after their parents. It may be that Jesus and his opponents took a different view of the same situation, in which some people gifted things to the Temple which Jesus thought should be spent on their parents. Alternatively, it may be that our Jewish sources are simply too meagre to give us clear evidence of this abuse. The latter is suggested by a passage of the Damascus Document, fragments of which survive among the Dead Sea Scrolls: this criticizes people who rob the poor in circumstances which strongly imply that they did so by means of 'legitimate' offerings in the Temple:

> And all who have been brought into the covenant are not to enter the sanctuary to light His altar in vain . . . They shall take care to . . . separate from the sons of the Pit, and to abstain from the wicked wealth which defiles acquired by vow or anathema and from the treasure of the sanctuary, and from robbing the poor of His people, from making widows their spoil and murdering orphans.
>
> (CD VI, 11–17, extracts)

Jesus' criticism of these orthodox Jews provides further evidence of an extreme state of hostility. That he suggests they did other things of the same kind further indicates his drastic rejection of their basic ideas of how to observe the Torah. He evidently believed, what he says more clearly elsewhere, that their additional regulations were not part of the faithful observance of God's Law, and that in observing them his orthodox opponents were failing to observe its main points.

This vitriolic rejection of current orthodox praxis was more important to Jesus than a literal answer to their question. This follows next, with a saying which has proved difficult to interpret. Christians have loved to follow the gloss 'cleansing all foods' at Mk 7.19, and imagine that Jesus dropped Jewish food laws. The chances of him doing any such thing were however negligible. The ministry was conducted almost entirely among Jews, and in places like Capernaum non-kosher food will not have been available. Jesus therefore had no motivation for dropping the food laws. Secondly, the basic food laws are biblical, so Jesus had a decisive reason for keeping them. It follows, thirdly, that if Jesus had dropped the food laws, he would have had unusual and important reasons which he could not have failed to give, and that there would be an explicit dispute about it more ferocious

24   J. A. Fitzmyer, 'The Aramaic *qorbān* Inscription from Jabel Ḥallet eṭ Ṭûri and Mk 7.11/Matt 15.5', *JBL* 78 (1959), pp. 60–65; rev. edn., *Essays on the Semitic Background of the New Testament* (London: Chapman, 1971; repr. Missoula: Scholars, 1974), pp. 93–100; repr. *The Semitic Background of the New Testament* (Grand Rapids/Livonia: Eerdmans/Dove, 1997), pp. 93–100.

than that about small details of sabbath observance. Fourthly, Simeon the Rock would not have needed a vision to persuade him to eat Gentile food, and Luke would not have presented him as making the significant point that he not previously eaten anything common or unclean (Acts 10.9-16, esp. 10.14).

It follows that the words 'cleansing all foods' (Mk 7.19) are the centre of Mark's rewriting of the tradition. From a grammatical point of view, they are an obvious gloss on words attributed to Jesus. Moreover, this comment satisfies an important need of the early church, which really did need to drop Jewish food laws, because of the success of the Gentile mission. The actual saying which is interpreted like this is Mk 7.15:

> There is nothing outside a man going into him which can make him unclean, but the (things which) come out of a man are what make the man unclean.

Mark has Jesus explain this saying to the disciples 'in the house away from the crowd' in response to their asking him about 'the parable' (Mk 7.17). Jesus' explanation consists of a lengthy list of sins including adultery, theft and deceit, which come out of a man and defile him (Mk 7.18-23). If Jesus intended Mk 7.15 to mean that, he would surely not have called the crowd together in order to say Mk 7.15 to them without any such explanation, for they would not have had a hope of understanding him. He would rather have taught the crowd in terms which they could understand, a task for which vv. 21–23, with the extensive list of sins, are perfectly well adapted, provided only that this is what Jesus really meant. We must therefore infer that, like the obvious gloss in 7.19, 'cleansing all foods', the explanation of Mk 7.15 with a list of sins is part of Mark's rewriting for the early church. Jesus' criticism of the disciples' lack of understanding in needing an explanation (Mk 7.18) should also be interpreted as part of Mark's rejection of Jewish food and purity laws, when the successful Gentile mission needed them to be rejected. This fits well with Mark's criticisms of the disciples elsewhere.

At the same time, given that Mark believed his own explanation of what Mk 7.15 meant, he is most unlikely to have invented it as a single saying directed at the crowd. We must infer that Mk 7.15 was transmitted to him as part of Jesus' public teaching. Moreover, the repetition of the two halves of the verse at the end of 7.18 and in 7.20 is very like 7.15 but with some variation at a verbal level:

> . . . everything from outside going into a man cannot make him unclean (7.18)
> . . . what comes out from a man, that makes the man unclean (7.20)

The version in Mk 7.18 has the particularly idiomatic Aramaic (or Hebrew) negative, 'everything . . . not', rather than 'nothing'. We must infer that Mark used, or more probably made, two translations of the same Aramaic original, that in Mk 7.15 being slightly more idiomatic Greek.

For the original interpretation of Jesus' saying, we must turn to Jewish purity law. From this perspective, the second half of the saying is the easier to interpret:

> . . . what comes out of a man, that makes the man unclean
>
> (Mk 7.20)

From the perspective of Jewish purity law, things coming out of people do make them unclean: the Bible specifies bodily discharge (Lev. 15.2-15), semen (Lev. 15.16-18), menstrual blood (Lev. 15.19-24), and any other discharge of blood from a woman (Lev. 15.25-30). Jesus is bound to have believed this, because these commands are biblical and unambiguous.

The first part of the saying makes perfect sense in the original context of the first part of this dispute, referring to the unnecessary nature of washing to remove uncleanness from people's hands:

> . . . everything from outside going into a man cannot make him unclean.
>
> (Mk 7.18)

This is one reason why we should infer that unclean food was so remote from Jesus' environment that he did not have it in mind. Matthew's editing shows that he thought that handwashing was one main point, for he concludes his account of this dispute:

> but eating with unwashed hands does not defile the man.
>
> (Mt. 15.20)

In this respect, Matthew was right.

The next major point is that the term 'man' does not mean everyone, particularly not absent Gentiles. Its real reference is to observant Jews, as so often with Hebrew words for 'man' in Jewish legal regulations. The following is a typical example:

> Clothes vendors who go out on the sabbath with cloaks folded (and) lying on their shoulders are liable to a sin-offering. And they [sc. the sages] said this not of clothes vendors alone but of every man (*kol Ādām*), but that it is in the nature of merchants to go out like that.
>
> (b. Shab. 147a)

The term 'every man' has nothing to do with the behaviour of Gentiles. Rather, the cultural context makes it so obvious that observant Jews are referred to that the description 'every man' can safely be used of them without confusion. Similar uses of terms for man are found already before the time of Jesus, as in the following passage:

> And on the sabbath day a man ('*īsh*) shall not speak a foolish or idle word.
>
> (CD X, 17–18)

This passage, from a document found among the Dead Sea Scrolls, was not trying to regulate the behaviour of Gentiles who do not observe the sabbath, but only of Jews whom its authors wanted to be observant in the same way as they were themselves.

It follows that, to approximate in English to the original meaning of Mk 7.15 in Aramaic, we must use an English paraphrase which replaces the term 'man', which we interpret too generally, with 'observant Jew':

> There is nothing outside an observant Jew which goes into him which can make him unclean, but the things which come out of an observant Jew are what make the observant Jew unclean.

This is obviously true in its original cultural context. Nothing going into an observant Jew can defile him, for he would not dream of eating anything that could defile him, whereas substances such as semen (Lev. 15.16-18) and menstrual blood (Lev. 15.19-24) come out of observant Jews and do defile them. Moreover, the saying is now perfectly relevant to the dispute which began with the question from scribes and Pharisees. It is a vigorous rejection of the view of scribes and Pharisees that for reasons of purity observant Jews should wash their hands before meals, thereby preventing visible dirt and less visible uncleanness from entering them. This notion is quite unbiblical, and Jesus therefore rejected it.

An important aspect of this dispute is its extraordinary ferocity, like the disputes between Jesus and his opponents over sabbath observance and exorcism. It is evident that the basic dispute between Jesus and his Jewish opponents was extremely severe, at least some time before the end of the historic ministry.

I have noted another passage (Mt. 6.1-4) in which Jesus appears to have used the Greek term *hupokritēs* in its original Greek sense of 'actor', and to have made fun of customs not fully known to us, perhaps blowing trumpets for fast days and giving alms in response to this.[25] Here too the contrast is between open display and genuine adherence to the will of God expressed in the Torah.

All this must be borne in mind as we seek to understand the ferocity of the polemic gathered together in Matthew 23, with several parallels in Luke 11. These sayings show many signs of transmission in Aramaic, which Luke misread more than once and thoroughly re-edited for his Gentile congregations. I translate the reconstructed source of Mt. 23.23-28//Lk. 11.39-44, following the order of Matthew because it was the order of this part of the 'Q' material:

> Woe to you, scribes and Pharisees, who tithe mint and dill and cumin, and transgress/pass over the 'heavy' (things), which (are) justice and mercy and trust. These, surely, (one) was liable to do, and (one was liable) not to pass over them (i.e. the others). Blind guides, who strain out the gnat and swallow the camel!
>
> (Mt. 23.23-24//Lk. 11.42)[26]

---

25 See p. 92.
26 For more detailed discussion see Casey, *Aramaic Approach to Q*, pp. 64–65, 72–77.

The Aramaic words *'sar*, 'tithe', *'ebhar*, 'pass over', or 'transgress', and *'ebhadh*, 'do', form a series of puns. Moreover, that on *'ebhar* and *'ebhadh* is so basic that it cannot have been unintentional. The tithing of herbs is not explicitly commanded in the biblical text. For example, Deut. 14.23 specifies tithing corn, wine and oil, that is to say, basic food and drink. Tithing provided for priests and Levites, for Jerusalem and for the poor. Tithing basic food and drink would ensure the survival of priests, Levites and the poor, all of whom received tithes directly in kind. At the same time, the tithing of herbs is a natural interpretation of biblical Law from an orthodox perspective. For example, Lev. 27.30 specifies tithing of 'the seed of the earth' and 'the fruit of the tree'. Such general expressions would encourage people who applied the Law to all the details of life to provide herbs with everything else. They might reason for example that the priests and Levites deserved some dill with their fish, and/or their cucumbers needed pickling, so dill should be included in general expressions such as those of Lev. 27.30. Hence later orthodox sources provide for dill and cumin to be tithed (m. Dem. 2.1, cumin; m. Maas. 4.5, dill). The tithing of mint, not registered in rabbinical sources, reflects the same approach to life. Scribes and Pharisees will have seen it commanded in the general statements of scripture, to provide priests and Levites with mint, which perhaps they might eat with their lamb or goat, or use to make mint tea. A general principle was written down later:

> They stated a general principle concerning tithes: everything which is eaten
> and kept and which they grow from the earth is liable for tithes.
>
> (m. Maas. 1.1)

This is what is summarized by 'mint, dill and cumin'. Jesus evidently believed that orthodox Jews were failing to observe the main points of the Law, and that this was combined with commitment to observing these details. His concern has an excellent setting in his ministry, and does not have one in the early church, which was not concerned about the details of tithing. The historicity of this saying should therefore be accepted. The general situation is confirmed by t. Men 13.22, which looks back on the Second Temple period in trying to explain the fall of the Temple, and says that people laboured over the Torah and were careful about tithes.

The Aramaic term *hōmerayā*, literally 'heavy', did require definition, when neither it, nor Matthew's Greek word *barutera*, had acquired the meaning 'weighty'. From our perspective, it had two meanings, which we generally represent by two different words in English, perhaps 'weighty' or 'important' for one meaning, and 'stringent' for the other. So 'the heavy of heavies' may be 'Honour thy father and mother' (Abba bar Kahana at y. Qid I, 7/22(61b)), or the commandment isolated as 'the heavy' may be 'Thou shalt not take the name of the Lord thy God in vain' (b. Shevu. 39a). These are obviously very important commandments, and the Jewish community would suffer very badly if they were not kept. The opposite of 'heavy' was 'light'. So the 'light of lights' is said to be the prohibition of taking a mother bird at the same time as her young or eggs (Deut. 22.6-7, Abba bar Kahana at y. Qid. I, 7/22(61b) again). Most people are not tempted to do this, and the Jewish community would not suffer serious damage if some people did.

The other aspect of 'heavy' is illustrated by the judgement that Rabban Gamaliel's house were 'heavy', or rather 'stringent' with themselves, and 'light', or rather 'lenient', towards Israel. This was because they let Jews in general bake large loaves on festival days, the ruling of the house of Hillel, while they themselves baked only thin cakes, the ruling of the house of Shammai (m. Bes. 2.6//m. Ed. 3.10). 'Heavy' in this case is approximately equivalent to the English 'stringent', rather than 'important' or 'weighty', and the Jewish community would have come to no harm if they had all followed the ruling of the house of Hillel by baking large loaves on festival days. It follows that orthodox Jews will have thought they *were* 'doing the stringent things (*hōmerayā*)' when they tithed mint, dill and cumin, because they were applying the instructions in the Torah to all the details of life. From their perspective, people who overlooked (*ᶜebhar*) mint dill and cumin transgressed (*ᶜebhar* again) the stringent things (*hōmerayā*) of the Law.

This clarifies the point of Jesus' definition. It defines central aspects of the Law as 'justice and mercy and trust' in accordance with the main thrust of the prophetic tradition, over against people who were expanding it with detailed regulations. This definition has its proper setting in the ministry of Jesus, for whom this was a central concern. It does not have a proper setting in the early church, which dropped such things as tithing altogether, and consequently was not concerned about this kind of contrast. This applies particularly to 'to pass over (*ᶜebhar*)', at the end of Mt. 23.23//Lk. 11.42:

These, surely, (one) was liable to do, and (one was liable) not to pass over them [i.e. the others].

Jesus had no reason to prevent the tithing of herbs. He will have known people who were devoted to justice, mercy and trust, and who automatically tithed their herbs with everything else, people like his brother Jacob rather than those scribes and Pharisees to whom he objected.

The joke with which this attack ends is an extraordinary hyperbole, and it presumably made people laugh:

Blind guides, who strain out the gnat and swallow the camel!

(Mt. 23.24 only)

Guides were necessary for the blind, and for camels. Blind people cannot strain gnats out of liquids. Camels are unclean, as food (Lev. 11.4). Gnats are not mentioned explicitly in biblical dietary laws. Some people will have thought they were forbidden as swarming things which fly (Lev. 11.20; Deut. 14.19). We should infer that scribes and Pharisees strained liquids such as water and wine to ensure that they did not eat insects. Hatching larvae may have been considered a significant danger. Later orthodox sources record the practice of straining wine (m. Shab. XX, 2). At b. Hul. 67a, small insects may or may not be removed by this process. A Qumran document interprets Levitical texts to prohibit the eating of creeping things, from the larvae of bees to every living thing which creeps in water:

A man shall not defile himself with any living creature or creeping thing by eating them, from the larvae of bees to any living creature which creeps in water.

(CD XII, 11–13, cf. Lev. 11.10, 44, 46)

This is the right culture at an earlier date than Jesus, and shows the mind-set of his opponents already established. This passage carefully applies Levitical texts (Lev. 11.10, 44, 46) not only by amalgamating them, but by specifying the larvae of bees, which would require people to strain honey. This is an exceptionally strict judgement, like the following requirement to drain the blood from fish. Orthodox Jews will have strained water and wine also to remove the larvae themselves, even before they became swarming things which fly. Jesus' picture of blind guides, trying to strain gnats out of wine or the like, and swallowing an unclean animal larger than themselves, is as ludicrous as possible, and presented with extraordinary economy. It has an excellent setting in the teaching of Jesus, where it indicates the profundity of his rejection of his most legalistic opponents, who sought to guide others in the interpretation of the Torah. The saying does not have a proper setting in the early church, which was not concerned about which form of Judaism to have, and whose Gospels do not notice jokes when they pass them on. This one was too Jewish for Luke, who simply left it out!

The next saying shows equally profound rejection of orthodox opponents. It takes off from circumstances in which scribes and Pharisees might cleanse the outside of vessels. I translate my Aramaic reconstruction, using the Aramaic *brīthā'* for 'outside'. There was another Aramaic word *brīthā'* which meant 'creation' and 'creature', so I give some different possible translations of it in the final saying, because this explains how Luke could produce 'everything is clean'. He had also misread *dakkau*, 'cleanse', as *zakkau*, 'give alms', one of his concerns, so he ended up with a saying suitable for his Gentiles audiences:

But give alms inwardly, and look! everything is clean for you.

(Lk. 11.41)

Almsgiving and inward disposition were Luke's concerns, and 'everything is clean for you' also fits these concerns, and has nothing to do with Jewish concerns about the purity of vessels. To recover Jesus' original saying, and what it meant, we must leave Luke's editing behind and consider my translation of my reconstruction of the Aramaic source of both Matthew and Luke.

Woe to you, scribes and Pharisees, who cleanse the outside of the cup and dish, and the inside is full from robbery and excess. Fools! (lit. Empties!) He who made the outside, did he not make the inside too? So cleanse the inside, and look! the outside/person/everything is clean.

(cf. Mt. 23.25-26//Lk. 11.39-41)[27]

---

27   For more detailed discussion see Casey, *Aramaic Approach to Q*, pp. 64–65, 77–83.

Later orthodox sources do have a distinction between the inside and outside of vessels. One passage contemplates liquids falling on certain parts of vessels such as the handles, in which case you wipe them and they are clean:

> The bases of vessels and their rims and their hangers, and the handles of vessels which have a receptacle, if unclean liquids fall on them, they dry them and they are clean . . . Vessels whose outsides are unclean from unclean liquids, their outsides are unclean, their insides and rims and hangers and handles are clean.
>
> (m. Kel. 25.6)

We should infer that Jesus knew orthodox Jews who in certain circumstances wiped only the outside of cups and bowls, and thereby removed limited impurity. The insides were not considered ritually unclean. His accusation involves extortion, for the shift from the ritual concern of cleansing the outside of the cup and dish to the accusation that the vessels are full from robbery and excess points to this kind of moral wickedness. It fits most easily into a temple context, as does *Ass. Mos.* 7.3-10. In this passage, men who will rule over Israel are described as impious, but are said to proclaim themselves righteous. Their faults include devouring the possessions of others and extravagant banquets, at which they eat and drink. They are said to have their hands and minds on impurities, while they tell other people not to touch them, in case other people make them unclean. Like some of Jesus' opponents, and like priests, they thought they lived in a state of ritual purity, which they were determined to maintain. The author(s) of the *Assumption of Moses* thought they were wicked, in much the same way as Jesus viewed the people whom he criticized.

The priestly context of the Q passage follows from careful study of some of its details. Of course, some of the scribes may have been priests, and priests could be Pharisees too. But priests are not isolated for particular mention by this text, so corruption in the priesthood alone cannot be the main point. We must therefore ask a more difficult question. What would orthodox Jews support, as righteous observance of the Law, that Jesus of Nazareth might describe as filling cups and dishes from robbery and excess? And the answer to that, surely, is the halakhah to tithing, which had the effect of enabling rich priests to extract produce from the poor.

Josephus writes as if the extraction of tithes was a morally debatable business. He presents himself as not taking tithes to which he was due (*Life* 80), while his fellow priests took lots (*Life*, 63). Shortly before the Roman war, he also records the forcible extraction of tithes (*Ant.* XX, 181, 206–7). T. Men. 13.21 records woes against important families, attributed to Abba Saul ben Bitnith, a shopkeeper in Jerusalem before its fall, and Abba Yose ben Yohanan, who lived in the city at the same time. Among the families condemned are that of Annas, on account of their whispering. These woes conclude:

> For they are chief priests, and their sons treasurers, and their sons-in-laws supervisors, and their servants come and beat us with staves.

This can only refer to the extortion of tithes on behalf of rich priests, and its setting is certainly before the destruction of the Temple. The passage goes on to suggest that the Second Temple could not have been destroyed like the first, because people laboured over the Torah and were careful about tithes.

It should also be noted that the second tithe was to be spent in Jerusalem. This was a tithe of produce which was not given to the priests and Levites, but was consumed by the producers themselves. Anyone who lived far away from Jerusalem was to convert it into money, which they should spend in Jerusalem on food, wine and the like for celebrating in Jerusalem (Deut. 14.22-26), so this tithe was for the support of Jerusalem. At the time of Jesus, there was a massive influx of people from the diaspora for the major festivals. High prices for food and wine would necessarily follow, and this would make some people richer. They would be Jerusalem traders rather than priests, and orthodox Jews would necessarily support the spending of the second tithe in Jerusalem because this is ordained in the Torah (Deut. 14.22-26).

We now have the full cultural context for Mt. 23.25-26//Lk. 11.39-41. Jesus objected to orthodox Jews who supported the extraction of tithes, and who participated in consuming the results. This did indeed involve robbery and excess. This also tells us what is wrong with tithing mint, dill and cumin. At one level, nothing; there is no need to pass over them. But failure to exercise justice, mercy and trust could mean guiding people, including poor people, into the belief that they should tithe ever more strictly for the benefit of rich priests and traders, and supporting violent collection of the tithes deemed to be due, in accordance with a stringent interpretation of the Law.

Thus there is a connection between Mt. 23.23-24//Lk. 11.42 and Mt. 23.25-26 //Lk. 11.39-41 which is absent from the surface meaning of the text, and obvious when the Jewish assumptions of the second saying have been uncovered. The next argument is a blunt declaration of the unity of vessels, over against people who were separating them into different parts and cleansing the outside:

> He who made the outside, did he not make the inside too?
>
> (Lk. 11.40)

The rest of the passage carries further the moral criticism begun with the accusation of extortion. At one level, Jesus affirms the normal Jewish view that vessels are uniform in matters of purity. At another level, God made people's inner beings, or whatever we may call them, not just their visible bodies. The view which Jesus was rejecting evidently regarded different parts of these vessels as independent from the perspective of purity Law. The end of the passage was obviously true as a matter of purity Law:

> So cleanse the inside, and look! the outside/person/everything is clean.

To cleanse the inside, you must immerse the vessel in a *miqveh*, and that cleanses the outside. Secondly, if scribes and Pharisees stopped supporting robbery and excess, their vessels would no longer be associated with the moral uncleanness that Jesus was attacking. At a different level, if they repented and became pure in heart, cleansing the insides of themselves, scribes and Pharisees would be wholly pure as people, fulfilling the intentions of their creator. Once again, Jesus has used the extreme halakhic habits of his opponents to launch a severe attack on their way of life as a whole.

This is carried even further at Mt. 23.27, which is so metaphorical that the Gentile Luke misread and misinterpreted his Aramaic source, and the Jewish Matthew felt it necessary to decode it at Mt. 23.28. The original source may be reconstructed as follows:

> Woe to you, scribes and Pharisees, who are like whitewashed tombs, which (are) beautiful on the outside and inside are full of dead people's bones and of all uncleanness.[28]

There is ample later evidence that graves were marked with whitewash in time for Passover. One passage comments,

> 'And of graves, with lime', the mark (being) of white, like bones. 'And one dissolves and pours', to make it more white.
>
> (b. BQ 69a)

This implies that they marked the graves, rather than whitewashing them all over. This is right, since the point was to enable people to avoid them, and a clear whitewashed mark would do this, without the extraordinary labour involved in whitewashing the lot. Many tombs in Jerusalem were splendid marble monuments, highly ornamented and much venerated. They were accordingly considered beautiful all the time. They would remain beautiful if they were merely marked with whitewash, a process deliberately intended to draw attention to the uncleanness inside of them, to enable people to avoid unnecessarily incurring corpse uncleanness. Such monuments would not have been beautified by the wholly unnecessary process of *covering* them in whitewash!

We should also infer that some scribes and Pharisees wore mostly white garments. This is a symbol of purity all the world over. Josephus notes that one group of orthodox Jews, the Essenes, made a point of wearing white clothing (*War* II, 123). It is difficult to see why they should do this except as a symbol of purity. They are not likely to have been unique in this, because other orthodox Jews shared their concern for purity (cf. also Rev. 3.4), and obtaining white garments was not difficult. Some cultic references to linen seem likely to have assumed it was white, as with the garment of the high priest on the Day of Atonement (cf. Lev. 16.4; b. Yoma 35a), and probably the linen robes which the Levitical singers in the Temple were later to wear on equal terms with priests (Jos. *Ant.* XX, 216). We can thus see the real sharpness of 'whitewashed tombs'. Scribes and Pharisees were drawing attention to their distinguished status as exceptionally

---

28 For Aramaic reconstruction and more detailed discussion see Casey, *Aramaic Approach to Q*, pp. 64–65, 89–92.

observant Jews, but in Jesus' view they symbolized their unsatisfactory way of life, their insides being equivalent to dead people's bones in tombs.

Scholars have had great difficulty with the logic of Jesus' polemic. In an influential comment, T. W. Manson argued that 'the comparison breaks down at the vital point. For in this verse the outward appearance of righteousness is assumed in order to *conceal* the evil condition within; whereas the whitewashing of the tombs *advertises* the fact that they are full of corruption.'[29] This underestimates the severity of Jesus' polemic. Scribes and Pharisees did indeed think that they had the outward appearance of righteousness. Jesus thought otherwise. He effectively declared that their white garments advertised the uncleanness within them. He completely rejected their concern with purity, which made them appear decent but in fact, to anyone who knew their whole way of life, drew attention to their sins. Matthew's explanation is accordingly right:

> So you on the outside seem to people (to be) righteous, but inside you are full of hypocrisy and lawlessness.
>
> (Mt. 23.28)

Jesus' condemnation of his orthodox opponents was accordingly very severe. We have seen that their condemnation of him was equally severe – they accused him of casting out demons by means of the devil himself. A quarrel as serious as this was liable to be terminal. To understand what eventually happened, we must consider more briefly other opposition to Jesus.

6. *Herod Antipas*

Herod Antipas was the tetrarch of Galilee and of Peraea, an area to the east of the river Jordan, from 4 BCE until after Jesus' death.[30] He and his brother Herod Archelaus were sons of Herod the Great by his Samaritan wife Malthace. They were brought up in Rome, where they lived with 'a certain Jew' (Jos. *Ant.* XVII, 20).

Antipas was appointed tetrarch of Galilee and Peraea by the emperor Augustus after the death of Herod the Great in 4 BCE. He built or rebuilt three significant cities. The first was Sepphoris in Galilee, just some 4 miles from Nazareth. This was his capital for some time. He renamed it Autocratoris, the Greek for 'Imperator', which by this time meant 'Emperor', in honour of the emperor Augustus. The second was Betharamphtha in Peraea, which he renamed Livias,

---

29 T. W. Manson, *The Sayings of Jesus* (London: Nicholson & Watson, 1937, as Part II of *The Mission and Message of Jesus* ed. H. D. A. Major *et al*. Reprinted separately, London: SCM, 1949), p. 237.

30 For a general account see M. H. Jensen, *Herod Antipas in Galilee* (WUNT 2, 115. Tübingen: Mohr Siebeck, 2006), where full justification of the following comments on Herod Antipas may be found.

in honour of Augustus' powerful wife Livia, and subsequently Julias when she became Julia Augusta in accordance with Augustus' will. The third was Tiberias, which he founded in 19–20 CE, and named after the emperor Tiberius. It replaced Sepphoris as the capital of Galilee. These were all Jewish cities, though Tiberias was organized like a Greek city with a Greek constitution.

As the names of these cities indicate, Antipas was very favourable to the Romans under whose general jurisdiction he ruled. He was on good terms with Augustus, and with his successor Tiberius. All the coins which he minted have their inscriptions in Greek. For example, the coins minted in his 24th regnal year in connection with the foundation of Tiberias have the name of Tiberias in Greek letters on the reverse, and 'Herod the Tetrarch' in Greek letters, with a reed plant, on the obverse (the front of the coin). He was personally very Hellenized, and very Romanized, and the main language spoken at his court is likely to have been Greek. This is shown further by inscriptions in honour of 'Herod the Tetrarch son of King Herod' from the Greek islands of Cos and Delos, which indicate also that he took part in Graeco-Roman cults when away from Israel, as Herod the Great had done. At home, he made considerable efforts to accommodate Judaism. His coins have no images of people or animals on them, because these would have been offensive to observant Jews, and he went to Jerusalem for major festivals at least some of the time. Nonetheless, he was not the sort of ruler to stand too much trouble from vigorous Jewish prophets.

Antipas is most notorious for putting John the Baptist to death. A brief but true account of this is given by Josephus. He begins with a brief and accurate account of John's successful popular ministry, based on preaching and baptism. He continues:

> And when others gathered together, and were quite carried away when they heard his words, Herod became alarmed that eloquence which had such an effect on people might lead to revolt, for it seemed that they would be guided by his counsel in what they did. He considered it was much better to act first and do away with him, rather than regret falling into a difficult situation when an upheaval took place. And because of Herod's suspicions, John was sent in chains to Machaerus . . . and there put to death.
>
> (*Ant.* XVIII, 118–19)

This account is perfectly coherent, and perfectly in character for a ruthless Romanized ruler, and for a son of Herod the Great. Machaerus was Herod Antipas' fortress in Peraea, so a very suitable place to have John taken to and safely executed.

Mark's story is so entertaining that it has given rise to much wonderful literature and music, but it is not literally true, as Aus and Crossley have shown.[31] Its main inspirations were Jewish stories elaborating on those in the book of Esther,

---

31 R. Aus, *Water into Wine and the Beheading of John the Baptist: Early Jewish-Christian Interpretation of Esther 1 in John 2.1–11 and Mark 6.17–29* (Brown Judaic Studies, 150. Atlanta: Scholars, 1988), pp. 1–7, 39–74; J. G. Crossley, 'History from the Margins:

and attributing the responsibility for John's death to the wiles of naughty women. Major improbabilities include the following. First, Herod was 'afraid of John, knowing that he was a righteous and holy man' (Mk 6.20). Antipas was not the sort of man to be afraid of John 'because he was a righteous and holy man'. In the first Targum to Est. 5.3, however, the Persian king Ahasuerus was afraid of the Jews in case they should rebel against him, and the real Herod Antipas was afraid that John the Baptist's ministry might lead to a revolt (*Ant.* XVIII, 118, quoted above). A second improbability is that Herod should have John put to death at a birthday banquet for 'his magnates and chiliarchs and the chief men of Galilee' (Mk 6.21), which any normal reader would naturally assume took place at his palace in his capital Tiberias, not four days' journey away in Machaerus. Ahasuerus' banquet was naturally in his palace in his capital Susa (Est. 1.2-3), and later Jewish elaboration of Est. 1.3 put it on Ahasuerus' birthday, so this was suitable inspiration for a story of Herod's birthday banquet.

Thirdly, it is almost unthinkable that an aristocratic Jewish woman's daughter would dance for the men at a banquet, a task normally reserved for courtesans and prostitutes. In a late Jewish tradition, however, it is said that the kings of Media, when they were eating and drinking, used to get their women to come and dance naked before them. When Ahasuerus had been drinking wine at his banquet, he wanted his queen Vashti to do so. She refused because she was the daughter of a king, so he had her executed. Moreover, in Esther 2, young girls of marriageable age gave even more pleasure to king Ahasuerus. They went in one at a time for a night with him alone, and Esther delighted the king so much that he made her queen in place of Vashti. Fourthly, Herod promises Herodias' daughter anything up to half his kingdom (Mk 6.23), which he was in no position to do because of his relationship with the Romans, whereas Ahasuerus promised Esther anything up to half his kingdom (Est. 5.3, 6; 7.2), and could have given it to her. Fifthly, it is not probable that Antipas would have John the Baptist's head brought in on a platter normally used for food, whereas this is exactly what happened to Vashti's head in stories about Esther.

Accordingly, the only certain truth in Mark's entertaining tale is what we know from Josephus, that Herod had John put to death. It is also entirely plausible that John said that it was unlawful for Herod to marry his brother's wife (cf. Mk 6.18), which would have made Herod want to put John to death, not be afraid of him (cf. Mk 6.19).

Bearing in mind Josephus' true story of Herod putting John to death because he was genuinely alarmed that his successful ministry might lead to political trouble, it was likely that he would sooner or later take the same view of Jesus. I have already considered the straightforward evidence that Herod did in fact intend to kill Jesus (Lk. 13.31).[32] The first indication that something like this

The Death of John the Baptist', in J. G. Crossley and C. Karner (eds), *Writing History, Constructing Religion* (Aldershot: Ashgate, 2005), pp. 147–61.

32 See pp. 114, 324–25.

might happen is found at the end of the dispute with some Pharisees recorded at Mk 2.23–3.6:[33]

> And the Pharisees went out in that hour with the Herodians and gave counsel against/concerning him how they might destroy him.
>
> (Mk 3.6)

We have seen that the Herodians were supporters of Herod Antipas. Mark's word 'Herodians' does not occur elsewhere, except at Mk 12.13//Mt. 22.16. In form it is a Latinism, on the analogy of Caesariani, which meant 'followers of Caesar', and 'Tiberiani' which meant 'followers of Tiberius'. The most famous word of this kind is the later Christiani, our word 'Christian'. This was coined in the Latin-speaking business community of Antioch to mean 'followers of Christ' (cf. Acts 11.26). The Latin Herodiani accordingly meant 'followers of Herod', the same people referred to by Josephus with more normal Greek expressions (*War* I, 319; *Ant.* XIV, 450//*War* I, 326). The word will not have changed since the days of Antipas' father, Herod the Great. It will have been used in Mark's Aramaic source because this was what they were actually called, and there was no straightforward Aramaic alternative. Mark therefore simply took it over into his Greek translation.

We have also seen that Herod the Great and Herod Antipas both had strong Roman connections.[34] Herod the Great's buildings with Graeco-Roman names included the fortress of Antonia in the Temple complex at Jerusalem, called after Mark Antony, and the city of Caesarea. He also renamed the rebuilt Samaria as Sebaste, after the Greek form of Augustus, and he named two fortresses Herodium, after himself. This is just the sort of person who would produce Herodiani on the analogy of Caesariani. We have also seen that Herod the Great sent his son Antipas to be educated in Rome for several of his teenage years. When Herod Archelaus died, Antipas took over the dynastic name of Herod, and used it on coins and inscriptions. We have also seen that his Greek cities with Roman names included Tiberias, his new capital, after the emperor Tiberius, and Livias, later Julias, after Augustus's wife. This is just the sort of person to maintain the description of his supporters as Herodiani. This is precisely the situation required for speakers of Aramaic to use the Latin term Herodiani.

Many scholars have refused to believe that the Pharisees co-operated with the Herodians, on the ground that these two groups were not natural allies. This has sometimes been given as one reason for regarding Mk 3.6 as the redactional work of Mark. In particular, it has been suggested that it originated a few years later, when Pharisees were on much better terms with Herod Agrippa II.[35] It is true that these groups were not natural allies, but we have seen that our primary source material enables us to explain this unusual alliance up to a point. This is precisely

---

33 On this dispute see further pp. 321–25.
34 See pp. 167–68, 338–39.
35 B. W. Bacon, 'Pharisees and Herodians in Mark', *JBL* 39 (1920), pp. 102–12 continues to be regrettably influential.

because Herod Antipas was the secular authority in the area, and he had recently had John the Baptist put to death. This is the obvious reason for Pharisees to contact the Herodians at that time, and to co-operate with them. What we do *not* know is whether Antipas was already considering taking equally violent action against Jesus. This is because the Gospels do not provide sufficiently detailed chronological information. If the ministry had been very effective for some considerable time, some action by Herod Antipas would be almost inevitable, given what we do know of him, and it would obviously have given the Pharisees more reason than ever to take counsel with the Herodians.

I have also argued that the aftermath of this event is to be seen at Lk. 13.31-33.[36] I reconstructed Luke's Aramaic source as follows:

> [31]And in that hour Pharisees went and said to him, 'Get out and go away from here, because Herod wants to kill you'. [32]And he said to them, 'Go tell that jackal, Look! I am casting out demons and performing healings to-day and tomorrow, and on the third day I am perfected.[33]But I am going to proceed to-day and day after day, for it would not be fitting for a prophet to perish outside Jerusalem.'

By this stage, Herod Antipas, having already had John the Baptist put to death, clearly had decided to take similar action against Jesus. Pharisees who were naturally unhappy about a prophetic figure being killed, probably because they saw such action as a violation of the prohibition of murder in the sixth commandment, therefore came and warned Jesus.

Jesus' response refers directly to his ministry of exorcism and healing, and to his forthcoming death. He is usually thought to have referred to Herod Antipas as a fox, because this is the word (Greek *alōpēx*) which Luke uses. Scholars then describe Antipas as cunning, for foxes were commonly thought of in the Greek world as cunning.[37] This does not however make very good sense, since Herod Antipas is not otherwise known to have been particularly cunning. Moreover, Jesus' Aramaic word can only have been *ta'alā*, which also means 'jackal' (*canis aureus*), and there seem to have been more jackals than foxes in Israel. Luke's translation of *ta'alā* with *alōpēx* was virtually inevitable, because *ta'alā* does mean 'fox', and there were lots of Greek fables about foxes, whereas there was no standard Greek word for 'jackal', because there were no jackals in Greece.[38] We must therefore conclude that Jesus described Herod as 'that jackal'.

This makes perfect polemical sense! The jackal was a noisy, unclean nuisance of an animal, a predator which hunted in packs. This is a beautiful description of one member of the pack of Herods. They were not genuinely observant Jews, and some of them were ruthless rulers who worked with packs of supporters to hunt down their opponents and kill them, as Antipas had hunted down and

---

36   See pp. 324–25.
37   E.g. Jensen, *Herod Antipas*, pp. 116–17, not mentioning the Aramaic reconstruction and discussion of Lk. 13.31-33 in Casey, *Aramaic Sources of Mark's Gospel*, pp. 188–89.
38   See further pp. 114–15, pp. 362–63.

killed John the Baptist and was now hunting down Jesus himself. Moreover, the behaviour of Herod the Great, and of Antipas' brother Herod Archelaus, was very well known, like that of Antipas himself, so Jesus' sharp polemic will have been readily understood. The references to Jesus' death are indirect, like all those before the final sequence of events. The first prophecy uses 'be perfected', a possible Aramaic metaphor for death, and shown to be so here by the context. The second one uses a more straightforward word, 'to perish'. In this saying, however, Jesus does not speak directly of himself, but uses a general statement about prophets. The stories about the deaths of prophets in Jerusalem were so extensive by this time as to make this a perfectly plausible general statement. Jesus used it to say that he would not let himself be caught by Herod – he would die his divinely ordained death in Jerusalem.

This means that Galilee was no longer a safe place for Jesus to be, and shows his clear awareness that the political opposition to him would be fatal. There is just one more reference to Herod during the ministry in Galilee. This is when Jesus warns his disciples to beware of the leaven of the Pharisees and the leaven of Herod (Mk 8.15). The terms in which this is expressed are likely to be genuine, because 'leaven' is the kind of metaphor which Jesus might well use (cf. Mt. 13.33// Lk. 13.20-21), whereas neither Mark nor the early church had any reason to produce it. The context however shows every sign of Markan creativity, including severe criticism of the disciples for not seeing what Jesus meant (Mk 8.16-21). We are not in a much better position than the disciples! The most we can say is that this warning reflects Jesus' awareness of two major sources of opposition to him, as we know much better from more straightforward source material.

The accounts of Jesus' final visit to Jerusalem have one more mention of the Herodians, who come with Pharisees to ask Jesus whether it is lawful to pay tribute to the emperor or not (Mk 12.13-17//Mt. 22.15-22; Lk. 20.20-26 replaces the Pharisees and Herodians with 'spies'). This is the same alliance as at Mk 3.6, and it shows that some Pharisees were still working with followers of Herod Antipas to bring about Jesus' demise, as they would do by co-operating with the chief priests and with Pontius Pilate.[39]

Luke alone relates a remarkable episode during the final events of Jesus' life. According to him, when Pilate found out that Jesus was from Galilee, he sent him to Herod, who was in Jerusalem at the time (Lk. 23.6-15). Herod examined him without much success, so he mocked him and sent him back to Pilate. The account shows signs of having been written up by Luke himself, but there may have been a real event of this kind. We shall see in Chapter 11 that Mark's account of the final events is very patchy, brief but reliable when the events took place very publicly or in the presence of some of Jesus' disciples, but created by Mark to fill in gaps when neither the disciples nor lots of people were there. Luke alone reports that Joanna, the wife of Herod's steward Chuza, was one of the women who supported Jesus' ministry in Galilee (Lk. 8.3). I have argued that this report should be accepted.[40] It is possible that Joanna got to know the basic

39 See further pp. 347–48, 422–23.
40 See pp. 192–95.

information that Pilate sent Jesus to Herod Antipas, and that Herod sent him back again, and that she was the ultimate source of a basic report which reached Luke, who wrote it up somewhat creatively. Luke also reports a prayer of the disciples in the early chapters of Acts, which has Herod and Pontius Pilate among those who gathered together against Jesus 'in this city' (Acts 4.27). This too could be based on a genuine source. In the absence of clearly reliable information, it is difficult to be sure about this.

Despite some uncertainties, the main points about opposition to Jesus from Herod Antipas are clear. In the final stages of Jesus' ministry in Galilee, this opposition was extremely serious, and potentially fatal. Jesus however succeeded in his aim of avoiding capture by Antipas' men in Galilee, and went to Jerusalem, where he fully intended to die. Herod's supporters played some role in these events, and Herod himself may possibly have been involved too, but the major role was played by the chief priests, elders and scribes, who persuaded Pontius Pilate that Jesus posed the sort of threat that Antipas imagined.

7. Chief Priests, Elders and Scribes

The opposition to Jesus in Mark's account of his last days in Jerusalem is mostly described as 'chief priests and scribes' (e.g. Mk 11.18), or 'chief priests and scribes and elders' (e.g. Mk 11.27). This is significantly different from the opposition during the rest of the historic ministry, which consists largely of 'scribes' and 'Pharisees', according to the uniform witness of our earliest sources. The connections between 'scribes and Pharisees', and 'chief priests and scribes and elders' are much closer than scholars have often realized, and one purpose of this section is to explain this.

At the time of Jesus, the chief priests were effectively the administrative rulers of Judaea. Valerius Gratus was the Roman governor (*praefectus*) 15–26 CE, followed by Pontius Pilatus, 26–37 CE. The *praefectus* was in overall charge of the province, and came to Jerusalem on major occasions such as Passover every year. He also made major decisions, such as to use Temple funds to build an aqueduct for Jerusalem (Jos. *War* II, 175–77). Most of the time, however, he stayed with his soldiers and staff in Caesarea on the coast, and left the day-to-day running of the province to the chief priests. The chief priests were led by the high priest. At the time of Jesus' ministry, the high priest was Joseph Caiaphas (18–36 CE). Like Herod the Great before them, the Romans changed the high priest when they wanted to. For example, when Vitellius, governor (*legatus Augusti pro praetore*) of Syria, had sent Pilate to Rome in 36 CE to give an account of his conduct in an affair at the end of which he executed several Samaritans, he also replaced Joseph Caiaphas as high priest (*Ant.* XVIII, 88–89, 95). For most of the time from Herod the Great until the outbreak of the Roman war (37 BCE–66 CE), the high priest was in office for a very short time – there were no less than 27 of them during that period. Two of the three longest-serving were Annas, 6–15 CE, and his son-in-law Joseph Caiaphas, 18–36 CE. This means that Annas and Caiaphas both worked closely and very successfully in harmony with the Roman administration.

In addition to being important political figures, Annas and Caiaphas were awesome religious figures. This is illustrated by the high priest's special vestments, of which there are two accounts by Josephus, who personally served as a priest in the Temple before the fall of Jerusalem (*War* V, 230–36; *Ant.* III, 159–87). The high priest wore an extraordinary robe of blue, woven in one piece, with decorations including real bells and imitation pomegranates hanging like fringes from the bottom to symbolize thunder and lightning. The robe was also decorated with precious stones including two very large sardonyxes on the shoulders, on which were written the names of the sons of Jacob, after whom the 12 tribes were called: these were believed to symbolize the sun and the moon (*Jos. Ant.* III, 165–66, 185). The high priest's headdress was very ornate, including a gold crown on which was written YHWH, the name of God, in the old Hebrew script (*Ant.* III, 178//*War* V, 235).

Herod the Great had these garments locked up in the fortress Antonia, from which they were released for the high priest to wear on the only occasions when the high priest had to conduct sacrifices personally, the three major pilgrim festivals of Passover, Pentecost and Tabernacles, and Yom Kippur (he usually officiated without them on sabbaths and new moons). The Romans did the same, but do not seem to have dreamt of touching them. When Vitellius in 36 CE wished to show favour to the Jewish people by granting their request that the high priest's vestments be returned to the custody of the priests, he did so only after he had written to the emperor Tiberius, and obtained his personal authorization to do so.

When he entered the Holy of Holies on Yom Kippur, the high priest had changed from his blue robe into a special white robe made of the most expensive linen, and still wore his special headdress. He emerged, with YHWH written on the gold crown of his headdress, and blessed the people, expressly pronouncing God's name aloud, the only time anyone could legitimately do so. Then he would see the people kneel and bow down and fall on their faces and say, 'Blessed be the name of the glory of his kingdom for ever and ever.'[41] Sira's grandson wrote an emotional eyewitness account of a service conducted by Simeon the righteous, high priest 219–196 BCE (Sir. 50.1, 5–21).

> How glorious he was . . . as he came from the house of the curtain, like a star shining among the clouds, like the full moon at the festal season, like the sun shining on the Temple of the King . . . When he put on his splendid robes and clothed himself in perfect splendour, when he went up to the glorious altar, he made the court of the sanctuary glorious . . .
>
> (Sir. 50.5-7, 11)

Josephus records a tradition that in those days the sardonyx on the high priest's right shoulder shone when God himself personally attended the sacred rites (*Ant.* III, 214–16).

---

41   See further pp. 213–14.

All this gives a glimpse of the awesome authority of the high priest, who alone entered the innermost sanctuary where God dwelt with his people on earth.

The identity of the 'chief priests' used to be controversial, but now seems clear. Part of the problem is that in English and other modern languages there is a different word for the 'high' priest and the 'chief' priests, whereas in Hebrew, Aramaic, and Greek the expressions for 'high priest' (Hebrew *hakōhēn hagādhōl*, Aramaic *kahanā rabbā*, Greek *archiereus*) were used in the plural for the whole inner circle of 'chief priests' (Hebrew *hakōhanīm hagedhōlīm*, Aramaic *kahanīn rabbīn*, Greek *archiereis*). The chief priests included senior members of an inner group of families from whom the high priest was usually chosen. They included any former high priests, such as Annas during the ministry of Jesus, and the holders of major offices, such as the *sagān*, the high priest's deputy, who was directly responsible for security in the Temple, the chief priests in charge of the Treasury, the chief priest in charge of bird offerings, and the like.

Luke mentions several of these. At Lk. 3.2, he has John the Baptist's ministry begin 'in the high priesthood of Annas and Caiaphas'. This is not quite accurate, but it reflects the continued power and influence of Annas years after he had technically been replaced as high priest by Ishmael son of Phiabi I, and, after two more men who also served very briefly (Eleazar son of Annas, and Simeon son of Qimḥīth), by Annas' own son-in-law Joseph Caiaphas. At Acts 4.5-6, Luke has a gathering of 'the rulers and the elders and the scribes in Jerusalem, and Annas the high/chief priest (*archereus*) and Caiaphas and John and Alexander and whoever was of the high priestly family', and at Acts 5.17 he mentions 'the high priest and all those with him, being the sect of the Sadducees'. This correctly reflects the fact that most of the chief priests were Sadducees, a largely aristocratic and priestly sect. At Acts 4.1-3, Peter and John are arrested by 'the priests and the Captain of the Temple and the Sadducees' who were upset 'because they were teaching the people and preaching in Jesus the resurrection of the dead.' The person described by Luke as 'the Captain of the Temple' was the *sagān*, who was in charge of security in the Temple, so it is entirely reasonable that he should be in charge of the arrest of Peter and John. The Sadducees did not believe in the resurrection of the dead, so this aspect of Luke's report is coherent too.

Given this basic information, it is obvious that the chief priests, led by the high priest Joseph Caiaphas, would be in charge of the final Jewish action against Jesus. It is equally obvious that they would liaise with Pontius Pilate, the Roman governor, who was in Jerusalem at Passover with armed troops in case of any kind of disturbance of the peace, as Pilate and the chief priests might see it.

The chief priests would also be aware of what had been going on in Galilee. At this point, the crucial group are 'the scribes'. Mark describes two separate incidents of conflict between Jesus and 'scribes who came down from Jerusalem'. These are the *same* people as were involved with the chief priests in the final Jewish action against Jesus. At Mk 7.1-15, they are with Pharisees, and they ask what seems at first sight to be an orthodox question, since they want to know why Jesus' disciples did not follow 'the traditions of the elders', which Pharisees observed and Sadducees did not observe.[42] At the same time, the question involved washing hands before meals, so priests who had to be in a state of purity when officiating in the Temple, and had to make sure that their hands did not convey uncleanness to their food, may have been more interested in this question than one might expect.

The more important conflict is that in which Jesus was accused of being possessed by the devil, and of casting out demons by means of his power (Mk 3.22-30).[43] Mark attributes this accusation to 'the scribes who came down from Jerusalem' (Mk 3.22). Their accusation is in no way particularly orthodox. Moreover, we know that the Jerusalem authorities did not accept the prophetic ministry of John the Baptist either, and they are therefore the obvious candidates for the anonymous accusation that he had a demon (Mt. 11.18 //Lk. 7.33).[44] This group of scribes must have been associated with the chief priests and elders, and they can hardly have failed to return to Jerusalem, and there report to the chief priests, to other scribes, and to elders. It follows that chief priests, scribes and elders were seriously opposed to Jesus long before his final visit to Jerusalem.

We can now see why the third element in the group of people who took the final action against Jesus are described as 'elders' rather than 'Pharisees'. The Pharisees were not involved as a definable group because they were split. We have already seen this in a conflict over sabbath halakhah in Galilee (Mk 2.23–3.6).[45] At the end of the second dispute, some Pharisees took counsel with the Herodians to destroy Jesus. The aftermath of this is found at Lk. 13.31-33, where, still in Galilee, some Pharisees came to warn Jesus that Herod was seeking to kill him. In response, Jesus indicated his determination to die in Jerusalem.[46] Affairs in Jerusalem show continued signs of this split. One of the arguments in the Temple occurred when 'some of the Pharisees and Herodians' came to ask Jesus the politically hot question 'Is it lawful to give tribute to Caesar or not?' (Mk 12.13-17). That only *some* of the Pharisees were involved indicates that the Pharisees as a whole were still split. That some of them were still creating trouble with Herodians shows that the alliance formed in Galilee was alive and well. There is later evidence of Pharisees on both sides too. I have noted Acts 5.17-42, where the high priest and others arrested the apostles and were proposing to put them to death (Acts 5.33). Gamaliel I, the most distinguished Pharisee present, urged them to be cautious, with the result that they had the apostles beaten, cautioned and set free (Acts 5.39-41). Paul his pupil, however, as a Pharisee, proceeded to persecute the followers of Jesus. Some years later, Luke nonetheless records the presence of Pharisees among the followers of Jesus (Acts 15.5).

All this evidence is entirely coherent. As a definable sect, the Pharisees were not involved in taking the final action against Jesus because they were split. Some of them had however been involved for some time in trying to bring about Jesus'

---

42 See further pp. 326–31.
43 See pp. 253–56.
44 See pp. 363–64.
45 See pp. 321–24.
46 See pp. 324–25.

demise, and they were involved in the final events. They are described with others by means of the more general term 'elders'. This was a traditional term for senior and respected Jews. In Mark's account of the final events, it refers to senior and respected Jews who were neither 'chief priests' nor 'scribes' (Mk 11.27; 14.43, 53; 15.1). This is where 'Herodians' should be found as well. They had also been involved for some time in trying to take action against Jesus, and Mk 12.13-17 shows that they were still involved. In Galilee, they were followers of Herod Antipas. In Jerusalem, they will still have included followers of Herod Antipas, but they will also have included old men who had been followers of Herod the Great, and their sons, some of whom may have been enthusiastic supporters of Herod Archelaus as well. Which other senior and respected Jews were involved we do not know, but they must have been senior and respected, or they would not be described as 'elders'. They may have included Joseph of Arimathea, since the best Mark could do was to describe him as 'a distinguished counsellor, who was also expecting the kingdom of God' (Mk 15.43). That is enough to make him an 'elder', and since he asked Pilate for Jesus' body and led the burial party (Mk 15.43, 45–46), he was almost certainly co-operating closely with the chief priests.[47]

We now have a clear idea of the group of 'chief priests, scribes and elders' who were responsible for taking the final action against Jesus. There is also evidence of Jesus' forthcoming conflict with authorities in Jerusalem in a 'Q' saying (Mt. 23.37-39//Lk. 13.34-35). I reconstruct the following from the slightly divergent versions in Matthew and Luke:

> [37]Jerusalem, Jerusalem, who kills (the) prophets and stones those sent to you, how often/much I have wanted to gather your sons/children as a bird gathers her young under her wings, and you were not willing.[38]Behold! Your house is left to you![39]I'm telling you, you will not see me until you say, 'Blessed is he who comes in the name of the Lord' (Ps 118.26).

This saying is correctly set by Matthew in Jerusalem, but on Jesus' final visit, which does not make sense because Jesus intended to die on that visit, and in this saying he is threatening to return. Luke sets it in his extraordinarily static journey from Galilee to Jerusalem, in which he put masses of non-Markan material, the original location of which he evidently did not know. This is not historically accurate either, for the saying only makes sense as addressed to Jerusalem, and makes much the best sense as a threat issued by Jesus when he was there. We have moreover seen that the Gospel writers did not know the length of Jesus' ministry, which cannot possibly have lasted for only part of a single year.[48] Jesus must have been to Jerusalem on previous occasions, for faithful Jews in Galilee frequently went to Jerusalem for major festivals, and a religious leader of his commitment and importance cannot possibly have gone only once. We must infer that this saying was spoken on the visit before his last one.

---

47   See further pp. 448–53.
48   See pp. 178–85.

When Jesus was arrested on his final visit, he said he had been teaching every day in the Temple (Mk 14.49). He will have done so on previous visits too. The saying must accordingly have been spoken when he was about to return to Galilee, leaving the Temple to its inhabitants, who would not have to endure his outspoken prophetic preaching for the time being. Many translations of it include the word 'desolate', which has helped many scholars to interpret it as a prediction of the fall of Jerusalem, with the quotation from Ps. 118.26 taken as a prediction of Jesus' second coming on the clouds of heaven.[49] We should not do this. The word 'desolate' is absent from Luke and from important manuscripts of Matthew, so it belongs to later interpretation, not to a saying of the historical Jesus. The word for 'is left', both in the Greek of the evangelists and in Jesus' Aramaic (*shebhīq*), is a very general word, which makes excellent sense in its present context of the Temple being left by Jesus to its inhabitants ('to you') for the time being. Psalm 118.26 is never used in the New Testament with reference to Jesus' second coming. It was an important verse for Jesus to quote because it comes from one of the Hallel psalms which were set for singing at Passover.

Thus the final sentence of this saying, with this quotation, looks forward to Jesus' next Passover visit, when the crowd at the triumphal entry duly shouted it out (Mk 11.9), and all the inhabitants of Jerusalem said it, and sang it, during the Passover celebrations. On that visit, Jesus would cleanse the Temple, control the halakhah in the court of the Gentiles, and once more preach every day, as he already intended to do. These are the words of a charismatic prophet, fully in control of his prophetic warning, which he would act on in accordance with the will of God, as he understood it.

8. *Division*

With such serious opposition from scribes, Pharisees, Herod Antipas and Herodians, chief priests and elders, Jesus was bound to encounter opposition from ordinary Jews who were not important enough to be specifically mentioned in the Gospels. Two kinds of sayings recognize this. I have discussed sayings which predict that the ministry would cause conflict within families (Mt. 10.34-36//Lk. 12.51-53), and which call for people to love Jesus more than the members of their families (Mt. 10.37//Lk. 14.26).[50] Given the vigorous nature of Jesus' prophetic ministry, and the extent of the opposition to him which I have discussed in this chapter, such splits within families were virtually inevitable.

Sayings which condemn his whole generation reflect a similar split, and those which condemn whole cities likewise reflect the fact that Jesus did not persuade everyone even in those places where the ministry was most successful. Jesus'

---

49 Cf. e.g. Davies and Allison, *Matthew*, vol. III, pp. 321–24; Hagner, *Matthew 14–28*, pp. 678–81; Fitzmyer, *Luke*, pp. 1033–37.
50 See pp. 298–301.

disillusionment with his generation shows for example in a difficult exorcism. When his disciples could not perform it, he commented:

> O faithless generation, how long will I be with you? How long will I endure you?
>
> (Mk 9.19)

As with the whole of the biblical use of the term 'generation', this does not refer to everyone on earth. Nonetheless, these comments indicate disillusionment with many people, and strongly imply that Jesus was expecting his death in the near future.

Jesus also looked forward to the last judgement in this light:

> The men of Nineveh will stand up with this generation in the judgement and condemn it. For they repented at the preaching of Jonah, and look! more than Jonah is here.
>
> (Mt. 12.41//Lk. 11.32)

This implies that there is something seriously wrong with this generation, and that this includes the fact that they had not repented, as Jesus had called upon them to do. This makes sense only if a lot of people had not accepted the preaching of Jesus. It is clearly stated that they will be condemned at the final judgement.

Finally, there is Jesus' judgement on Bethsaida, Chorazin and Capernaum. Capernaum was the centre of the Jesus movement when it was at its most successful. Yet it comes at the climax of this judgement on cities which did not accept his mission. His genuine comments have been somewhat edited by the evangelists, but cannot have been seriously different from this:

> Woe to you, Chorazin, woe to you, Bethsaida: for if the mighty works which took place in you had happened in Tyre and Sidon, they would have repented long ago in sackcloth and ashes. But I say to you, it will be more tolerable for Tyre and Sidon in the day of judgement than for you. And you, Capernaum, were you exalted to heaven? You shall be cast down to Gehenna. For if the mighty works which took place in you had happened in Sodom, it would have remained until this day. But I tell you that it will be more tolerable for the land of Sodom in the day of judgement than for you.
>
> (Mt. 11.21-24//Lk. 10.12-15)

There is a lot of valuable information here, some of it rather extraordinary. We must infer that Jesus' ministry of exorcism and other healing had been successful in Chorazin, a small town 2 miles from Capernaum, and in Bethsaida, a town at the north-eastern tip of the lake of Galilee. We would not otherwise have known this, since Chorazin is not mentioned again in the Gospels, and there is only one other reference to Bethsaida which is likely to be authentic (Mk 8.22, cf. also Jn 1.44; 12.21). This underlines the lack of accurate geographical and chronological information in the traditions which have come down to us. By the time this saying was spoken, these towns as a whole had not repented as Jesus understood that term, so he had not succeeded in converting them as a whole to his view of Judaism. The comparison with Tyre and Sidon is a severe judgement. Both were important pagan cities on the Mediterranean coast. Both are vigorously denounced and threatened with judgement in Isaiah 23 and Ezekiel 28. A number of other passages denounce them more briefly (e.g. Zech. 9.2-4). This means that Jesus contemplated the divine destruction of cities in which he had worked.

The situation of Capernaum is if anything even worse, since it is presented in our earliest sources as the centre of the most successful phase of Jesus' ministry. Its exaltation to heaven is presumably a figurative way of recalling this, as is more plainly the mention of the mighty works done there. It was notorious that Sodom was destroyed by God on account of the wickedness of its inhabitants (Gen. 18.16–19.29, often taken up proverbially, as e.g. at Jer. 50.40). Jesus must therefore have felt that, however successful he had been in some aspects of his ministry there, he had not converted most of the inhabitants. He therefore declared divine judgement on the city as a whole, in devastatingly destructive form, even though this condemnation obviously did not include those who did follow him.

These sayings make sense only towards the end of the historic ministry. At this time, Jesus clearly believed that his ministry had not been sufficiently successful in bringing the people of Israel back to God. This was an important element in his overwhelming conviction that God called upon him to die an atoning death for the redemption of his people.

9. Conclusions

We can now survey the vigorous and large-scale opposition to Jesus' ministry, in the context of which he was to meet his death. He encountered serious opposition from the orthodox wing of Judaism. Some of these people were Pharisees, who were so dedicated to maintaining an expanded sabbath halakhah that they combined with Herodians to try to get Jesus put to death. Jesus accused his orthodox opponents of replacing the commandments of God with their own traditions. He believed that they had lost the main points of the Law altogether in their attachment to small details. This polemic represents a fatal conflict, on account of which there were scribes and elders among the people involved in bringing Jesus to his death. Moreover, the accounts of the disputes between Jesus and his orthodox opponents show clear signs of being transmitted in Aramaic, the language in which these sayings were originally spoken. These indications of Aramaic uniformly occur in accounts of incidents which have an excellent setting in the life of Jesus, but which do not belong to the environment of the early church as we know it from the epistles and from Acts. We must infer that, whether at the time, or following the crucifixion, some of Jesus' disciples found it important to write down accounts of these disputes. These are found in both

Mark and in the 'Q' material. The top layer of rewriting, mostly in the Gentile writer Luke and to a lesser extent in Matthew, is in general quite easy to remove. We must infer that my reconstructions of these traditions represent absolutely bedrock traditions, brief but accurate accounts of conflicts which certainly took place.

Jesus also provoked fatal opposition from chief priests, scribes and elders, who took the final actions necessary to bring about his execution by the Roman governor. This opposition was formed long before his final visit to Jerusalem. The 'scribes' were the same people as those who came down to observe the ministry in Galilee. The 'chief priests' were effectively in charge of the running of Jerusalem and Judaea. They had previously rejected the ministry of John the Baptist, and they were in constant touch with 'scribes' who had observed the ministry in Galilee. They had endured Jesus' prophetic preaching in the Temple on previous visits, and the final straw for them was the Cleansing of the Temple on his final visit. The 'elders' included two significant groups who had been opposed to Jesus' ministry in Galilee. Some were Pharisees. They are not mentioned as a group in the accounts of Jesus' last days because Pharisees as a whole were split. The second group were 'Herodians'. These were supporters of Herod Antipas, and in Jerusalem surviving supporters of Herod the Great and Herod Archelaus as well. Herod Antipas had put John the Baptist to death, and was seeking to kill Jesus too. Jesus avoided him, however, and was determined to die in Jerusalem. This opposition accordingly dates from the final phase of Jesus' ministry in Galilee. The 'Herodians' are not mentioned as a specific group because they were not influential enough at this stage. Hence they are also concealed under the term 'elders'. The 'elders' included other senior and respected Jews, who will have been opposed to the ministry for the same reasons as Jesus' other opponents.

There is also evidence of Jesus' ministry splitting families. This is natural when there was a serious dispute between the orthodox and prophetic wings of Judaism. By the end of the ministry, Jesus expressed disillusionment with cities which he had not converted to his prophetic form of Judaism. These included Capernaum and other towns at the centre of his ministry, which at one stage seemed to be so successful. They also included Jerusalem. This will have increased his feeling that it was God's will that he should die, for the redemption of Israel. On his last visit to Jerusalem, he cleansed the Temple, thereby precipitating the final and fatal opposition to him from the chief priests who controlled it. They were able to use aspects of his life and teaching to claim before the Roman governor that Jesus was guilty of sedition. I discuss these final events in Chapter 11. First, however, I consider what kinds of terms were felt appropriate for the figure of Jesus during the historic ministry.

CHAPTER 10

Christological Terms

1. *Introduction*

The terms and titles used of Jesus changed and developed as the Jesus movement changed and developed after his death and gradually became a more and more Gentile religion, known in due course as Christianity. I have noted that Jesus accepted the terms 'prophet' and 'rabbi', or 'teacher', which were applied to him during the historic ministry, and used them of himself on a small number of occasions when he needed to speak of himself indirectly.[1] I have discussed some genuine sayings in which Jesus used the Aramaic term *bar* (*e*)*nāsh*(*ā*), 'son of man', of himself in a particular Aramaic idiom, in which a speaker used a somewhat general statement to refer to himself, or himself and other people.[2] I have also argued that he believed he was addressed as 'my Son' by a heavenly voice at his baptism, and may possibly have been addressed as 'son of God' by some demoniacs.[3]

   The purpose of this chapter is to offer a more complete discussion of the terms 'prophet' and 'teacher' as applied to Jesus during his ministry, and to discuss the three major Christological titles in the synoptic Gospels, Son of Man, Son of God, and Christ. All three titles were very important to each of the Gospel writers, and they have been of central importance throughout Christian history. I propose to clarify how far each of them goes back to the historic ministry, and how far they were part of the developing Christology of the early church, and the editorial work of the Gospel writers. I also explain what they meant, for their meaning has developed throughout Christian history as well. For the sake of clarity I include some brief comments on the Fourth Gospel, because the same three titles were of major importance to the Johannine community, and the Fourth Gospel was also influential in their subsequent development.

---

1   See pp. 195, 271–72.
2   See pp. 115–16, 255.
3   See pp. 176–77, 249.

2. Prophet

I argued in Chapter 5 that the prophetic tradition was central to Jesus' life. It was a live tradition of vigorous innovative people who preached the word of God, acted on it, and made important predictions. Some of them were involved in healing too. The most important prophet in recent centuries was John the Baptist. His prophetic ministry was what attracted Jesus to him, and he was so impressed that he underwent John's baptism. He hailed John as a major prophet, as well as the fulfilment of Malachi's prophecy of the coming of Elijah before the day of the Lord, and of other important prophecies too. He saw himself as fulfilling John's prediction of one who would come after him.

I have also noted two occasions on which Jesus described himself as a prophet.[4] One was during a rather unsuccessful visit to his home town of Nazareth, where he was not accepted as a religious leader because he was regarded as an ordinary person, a carpenter whose family were still there. Jesus responded:

> A prophet is not without honour except in his home town and among his kinsfolk and in his house
>
> (Mk 6.4)

Here, faced with an embarrassing situation, Jesus used a general statement in which the term 'prophet' applies particularly to him. This makes no sense unless he believed that he was a prophet, and this belief was shared by people who accepted him.

The other example is of a similar kind. Jesus was warned that Herod Antipas sought to kill him. He responded by accepting that he would soon die, but that this would be in Jerusalem, and he used another general statement to say this:

> But I am going to proceed to-day and day after day, for it would not be fitting for a prophet to perish outside Jerusalem
>
> (Lk. 13.33)

This presupposes current thoughts about the deaths of the prophets.[5] It follows from this passage that Jesus not only regarded himself as a prophet, but that he expected this description to be acceptable both to his followers and to those Pharisees who were sufficiently favourably disposed towards him to have come and warned him about Herod's intentions.

Similar verdicts are recorded from other people too. The most amazing is attributed to Herod Antipas after John the Baptist's death, but the report is particularly interesting because it records the verdicts of other people too. The context is that of Antipas himself hearing reports of Jesus, and the passage proceeds, as Aramaic narratives often do, with an unmarked change of subject:

---

4 See pp. 144–45, 324–25.
5 See pp. 404, 418.

. . . and (people) were saying, 'John the baptizer has been raised from the dead, and because of this the mighty works are being done through him'. And others said, 'It is Elijah'. And others said, 'A prophet like one of the prophets'. But when he heard, Herod said, 'John whom I beheaded, he has been raised'.

(Mk 6.14-16)

To us, the sanest verdict is 'A prophet like one of the prophets'. This was an entirely reasonable view to take of Jesus, very like the view which he took of himself. He spent the whole of his ministry preaching the word of God and acting on it. His ministry was dramatically effective, sufficient to put him in the same category as prophets like Isaiah.

The verdict that he was Elijah is in fact very similar, strange though it may seem to us. It picks up the prophecy of Malachi:

Behold! I am sending you Elijah the prophet before the great and aweful day of the Lord comes. And he will turn back the heart of the fathers to the children and the heart of the children to their fathers . . .

(Mal. 4.5-6)

Aramaic-speaking Jews who said that Jesus was Elijah believed that Jesus was a great prophet who fulfilled this prophecy. I have noted the similar way in which Jesus identified John the Baptist as Elijah.[6] Luke's Greek and Gentile perspective was more like ours. He did not repeat this, even though it was the verdict of the historical Jesus himself. Instead, he has an angel of the Lord tell Zechariah that John will come 'in the spirit and power of Elijah to turn the hearts of fathers to children' (Lk. 1.17). This is a proper explanation for Greek-speaking Gentile Christians of what Jesus meant when he identified John as Elijah. It is also very similar to what Aramaic-speaking Jews meant when they said that Jesus was Elijah. Accordingly, their view is very similar to that of those Jews who believed that he was 'A prophet like one of the prophets'.

The most extraordinary view is that attributed to Herod Antipas: 'John whom I beheaded, he has been raised'. Mark surely intended his audiences to interpret this as the verdict of a guilty man, frightened of God, the same man of whom Mark says, 'he feared John, knowing that he was a righteous and holy man' (Mk 6.20). These are not however the opinions of the historical Herod Antipas, who had John the Baptist put to death, and who subsequently pursued Jesus with the same intention.[7] This makes the more popular opinion with which the passage begins all the more interesting: 'John the baptizer has been raised from the dead, and because of this the mighty works are being done through him' (Mk 6.16). This indicates the importance of Jesus' successful ministry of exorcism and healing. It is likely to be a verdict on the basis of hearsay, rather than

6 See further pp. 179–80.
7 See pp. 339–44, pp. 422–23.

real knowledge of the two men, but a genuine opinion of Jews who had heard about both of them.

The other passage which quotes people's views of Jesus is also a mixture of authentic tradition and Mark's rewriting. The verdicts belong to ancient tradition:

'John the Baptist', and others (say) 'Elijah', and others 'one of the prophets'.

(Mk 8.28)

Here the description 'Elijah' is the same as at Mk 6.15. The verdict 'John the Baptist' is likely to be a summary of the verdict which I have noted from the same passage. Both Matthew and Luke interpreted 'one of the prophets' to mean one of the ancient prophets (Mt. 16.14; Lk. 9.19). This is not impossible, but it is perhaps more likely that this too meant 'A prophet like one of the prophets'. In any case, all these verdicts are of the same general type. The category of prophet was flexible enough to denote a vigorous, original and authoritative figure who led a renewal movement for Israel.

This category could also be used in a hostile manner. When Jesus allowed a sinful woman to anoint, kiss and wipe his feet and the like, Luke represents Simon the Pharisee as saying to himself, 'If he were a prophet, he would know who and what sort of a woman is touching him, that she is a sinner' (Lk. 7.39). This presupposes that the category of prophet was generally available. More evil use was made of it when Jesus was beaten up after his arrest. Mark has his Jewish captors taunt him with the cry 'Prophesy!' (Mk 14.65). Matthew and Luke both had access to a different account, which continued with a malicious require-ment that a prophet tell them something: 'Who is it that hit you?' (Mt. 26.68// Lk. 22.64). Attestation by both Mark and 'Q' material is very strong, so it is likely that this part of the story is literally true. It shows that Jesus was very well known as a prophet.

It is thus appropriate that, despite his own much higher Christology, Luke put into the mouth of Cleopas and another disciple the description of Jesus as 'a prophet mighty in word and deed before God and the whole people' (Lk. 24.19). That is exactly how Jesus was perceived.

Thus many people regarded Jesus as a prophet, and Jesus used the term 'prophet' of himself. Moreover, the reasons for the use of the term prophet are very straightforward. It follows that this category should be taken very seriously in any historical assessment of his ministry.

3. Teacher

Jesus' ministry was also a ministry of teaching and preaching, and this led to the other term which we know was generally used of him. Mark has ten examples of Jesus being addressed as 'teacher', plus four which preserve the Aramaic 'rabbi' (Mk 9.5; 11.21; 14.45), or the longer form of the same word, 'Rabbouni' (Mk 10.51). These are the only plausible Aramaic terms for 'teacher', so this is what Jesus was originally called.

People who addressed Jesus as 'Rabbi' included his followers. For example, this term was used by John, one of the inner three of the Twelve, when reporting to him on an outsider who was casting out demons in his name (Mk 9.38). It was likewise used by Judah of Kerioth, who addressed Jesus as 'Rabbi' when he betrayed him in Gethsemane (Mk 14.45). This term was also used by outsiders, both favourably, as by the scribe who thought Jesus had answered a fundamental question very well (Mk 12.32), and by a hostile group of Pharisees and Herodians who asked him an awkward question (Mk 12.13-14).

We must infer that 'rabbi' was already in use as a form of address to a Jewish teacher, despite the fact that it is not attested in our meagre Jewish sources until a later date. At the time of Jesus, however, it meant only 'teacher', as it is correctly translated in the Gospels. It did not mean that, like St Paul, Jesus had sat at the feet of someone like Gamaliel for any kind of formal rabbinical training, or that he had undergone any kind of official ordination. It also follows from the evidence which I have briefly surveyed that Jesus was normally addressed as 'Rabbi'.

It is accordingly natural that Jesus should have referred to himself as a teacher when he gave two disciples a password, arranging to celebrate his final Passover with his disciples before his arrest:

> And where you go in, say to the owner of the house, 'The rabbi says, "Where (is) the place-of-my-spending-the-night, where I will eat the Passover with my disciples?"'

> (Mk 14.14)

This makes sense only if Jesus was well known as a rabbi, and accepted this description of himself.

The term 'disciple' is also relevant, because it reflects Jesus' function as a teacher. It is frequent throughout the synoptic Gospels, being used no less than 43 times in Mark alone. However, as we have seen, the majority of examples in the Gospels are due to the editorial work of the evangelists themselves, because the Greek term *mathētai*, 'disciples', was a natural term for Jesus' adherents. The Aramaic *talmīdhīn*, 'disciples', however, may have already referred to men sitting at the feet of an orthodox rabbi learning his teaching, and this may be why Jesus did not normally use it.

The term *talmīdhīn* was used by outsiders. For example, Pharisees and scribes from Jerusalem are recorded as asking Jesus:

> Why do your disciples not walk according to the tradition of the elders, but eat bread with profane hands?

> (Mk 7.5)

This reflects the fact that Jesus was well known as a teacher, who had adherents who listened to him, followed his teaching, and presumably repeated it too. It is entirely probable that Matthew was already writing some of it down on wax tablets, and others may have done the same.[8]

All this evidence is accordingly unambiguous. During the historic ministry, everyone thought Jesus was a teacher, for he taught extensively and had his own followers.

4a. *Son of Man: Introduction*[9]

As the synoptic Gospels now stand, the Greek term 'the Son of man' (*ho huios tou anthrōpou*) is much the commonest title of Jesus, and it is the term which he characteristically uses to refer to himself. Scholars have however found it exceptionally difficult to understand, and there is no agreement as to which 'Son of man' sayings Jesus said, nor as to what he meant, if he said it.

In the synoptic Gospels, the Greek term 'the Son of man' occurs no less than 69 times. The oldest Gospel, Mark, has 14 examples in the teaching of Jesus, and when all parallels are discounted, the three synoptic Gospels still contain 38 independent sayings. At least some of them must go back to Jesus, for the following reasons: the term occurs very frequently: it is found in all Gospel sources – Mark, the 'Q' material, the separate traditions of both Matthew and Luke, as well as the Fourth Gospel and some non-canonical traditions; the early sources attribute it almost exclusively to Jesus himself; it is not normal Greek, a fact which can be explained only if it originated as a translation of the Aramaic expression *bar* (*ᵉ*)*nāsh*(*ā*); the early church did not use it in any of its confessions; and it does not occur in any of the New Testament epistles, all of which were written in Greek. This combination of reasons should be regarded as decisive: Jesus certainly used the term 'son of man'.

In Aramaic, however, the term *bar* (*ᵉ*)*nāsh*(*ā*) was an ordinary everyday term for 'man', or 'human being', and it never lost this general level of meaning. For example, the author of the Genesis Apocryphon wanted to reproduce in Aramaic God's promise to Abraham that he would multiply his descendants (Gen. 13.16), so he put this:

> And I will multiply your seed like the dust of the earth which no son of man can count . . .
>
> (1QapGen. XXI, 13)

Here the fact that 'son of man' (*bar ᵉnōsh*) was used to translate the simple Hebrew *'īsh* (man) must mean that it was felt to be especially suitable for a general statement.

---

8   See pp. 86–89.
9   For full discussion see P. M. Casey, *The Solution to the 'Son of Man' Problem* (LNTS 343. London: T&T Clark International, 2007).

For the same reason, the term *bar* (*ᵉ)nāsh(ā)* was used in tractates about humankind, and in the most general references to human beings and the variety of our life experiences. The following example is taken from the oldest general discussion of humankind to survive in Aramaic sources, attributed to the Christian writer Bardaisan of Edessa and probably to be dated in the early third century CE:

> This is the nature of the son of man, that he should be born and grow up and reach his peak and reproduce and grow old, while eating and drinking and sleeping and waking, and that he should die.
>
> (Bardaisan, *The Book of the Laws of the Countries*,
> p. 559 lines 11–14)

Here the term 'son of man' (*barnāshā*) refers to human beings in general, and this account of the son of man's basic human experiences naturally includes death.

Such comments on humankind in general are of limited value in trying to understand 'Son of man' sayings in the Gospels, because the Gospel sayings appear to concern Jesus alone. The key to genuine sayings of Jesus lies in a particular Aramaic idiom, in which rather general statements can be used because the speaker wants to make a point about himself, or himself and a group of other people made obvious by the context. This idiom is first attested centuries before the time of Jesus in the following passage:

> And if you think of killing me and you put forward such a plan, and if your son's son thinks of killing my son's son and puts forward such a plan, or if your descendants think of killing my descendants and put forward such a plan, and if the kings of Arpad think of it, in any case that a son of man dies, you have been false to all the gods of the treaty which is in this inscription.
>
> (Sefire III, 14–17)

This example is taken from an Aramaic inscription written c.750 BCE in the name of Barga'yah, king of Kittik, in a treaty with the king of Arpad, all in what is now the north of Syria. It uses *barᵉnāsh* in a general statement. In view of its cultural context, it is most unlikely that it was intended to refer to the death of anyone other than people on the side of the king of Kittik, and it probably refers only to the king and his descendants. Precise description is not part of this idiom, the effectiveness of which depends on the plausibility of the general level of meaning. When this passage is taken together with many later passages, it becomes clear that dying is a universal characteristic of *bar* (*ᵉ)nāsh(ā)*, and that this was already so long before the time of Jesus.

The same idiom is attested much later too. One example is attributed to R.Simeon ben Yohai, a Galilean rabbi who hid in a cave for 13 years after the unsuccessful revolt against Rome in 132–35 CE. When he was wondering whether it was safe to come out, he saw birds being hunted. Some were captured, others escaped, and he declared:

A bird is not caught without heaven; how much more the soul (*nphsh*) of a son of man.

(Gen.R. 79, 6)

When he had said this, R.Simeon emerged from the cave. It follows that he intended to apply the statement to himself. At the same time, the first sentence, 'A bird is not caught without heaven', is quite clearly a general statement: the concluding comment must be interpreted in the same way, because 'son of man' (*br nsh*) was a general term for 'man', and this ensures that 'how much more the soul of a son of man' balances and follows from the general statement about birds. The general statement may be used to refer to more people than the speaker. In this version of the story, R.Simeon has his son with him, and since they both emerge from the cave, the general statement is clearly intended to refer to them both.

It is clear from these examples that this idiom was in use for centuries before and after the time of Jesus. This is natural, because Aramaic was a very stable language. The idiom is moreover a natural one, for it consists of a simple application of general statements to fulfil a normal human need, that of speaking indirectly about oneself. If therefore sayings of Jesus emerge as examples of this idiom when straightforwardly reconstructed in their original Aramaic, they should be accepted as examples of it.

There is another complicating factor in attempts to recover genuine Aramaic examples of this idiom from Gospel examples which have been translated into Greek with two Greek definite articles, the *approximate* equivalent of the English definite article 'the'. This is doubly so if we have in mind English translations which always use the English definite article 'the' for the first of the two definite articles in the Greek expression *ho huios tou anthrōpou*, and capitalize at least 'Son', so we are accustomed to 'the Son of man' being a title of one person, Jesus. In these circumstances, the generic use of the English article never occurs to us, however familiar we may be with sentences such as 'The beaver builds dams'. In a sentence of this kind, the word 'the' obviously refers to beavers in general, not to a particular beaver. The Greek definite article is used generically more often than the English article, so much so that translators of the New Testament into English never represent in English the most obvious example in the New Testament, the generic article before 'man' in this very expression *ho huios tou anthrōpou*, which could be rendered word for word 'the son of the man', which would not make proper sense. It is for this same reason, the normality of the generic use of the definite article in Greek, that bilingual translators, faced with the difficult task of rendering into Greek an Aramaic idiom which has no Greek equivalent, used the article before the word 'son', where it can be either generic or specific.

From a bilingual translator's point of view, there were in any case inherent problems in translating into Greek Aramaic nouns which were in the definite or indefinite state. Every Aramaic noun must be in either the definite state (e.g. *barnāshā*), or the indefinite state, otherwise known as the absolute state (e.g. *barnāsh*). These states are sometimes said to be the approximate equivalent of the English definite and indefinite articles.[10] This would make *barnāshā* the equivalent of '*the* Son of man', '*the* man', and *barnāsh* the equivalent of 'a man', 'a person'. This is quite wrong, because the definite state was always used more often than the English definite article. In particular, it was quite normal in generic expressions of all kinds, where it was always completely optional.[11] Moreover, it eventually lost its force altogether. For the same reasons, the Aramaic definite and indefinite (or absolute) states overlap with the presence and absence of the Greek definite article, and with the Greek particle *tis*, which means approximately 'a', 'a certain', but Aramaic and Greek usage are by no means the same.

In the difficult situation of this being important in translating into Greek an Aramaic idiom which has no Greek equivalent, the translators came up with a strategy. Translators often employ strategies when they are repeatedly faced with the task of translating an expression in the text in front of them which has no literal equivalent in the target language. The strategy of the Gospel translators was this: when the term 'son of man' in this idiom referred to Jesus, they would translate it into Greek with two articles, so *ho huios tou anthrōpou*, overliterally 'the son of the man', only both articles may be generic rather than specific. The rest of the time, when the term referred to anyone else or was used in the plural, they would use other words for 'man', excluding altogether the word 'son'.

Accordingly, as we try to recover the original force of sayings of Jesus which used this idiom, we must reverse the translation process. We must go back to the term 'son of man' being *bar* (*e*)*nāsh*(*ā*), an ordinary Aramaic term for 'man', used in an idiomatic way in a general statement which refers particularly to the speaker with or without other people. I shall use 'a/the' in the following translations into English to represent this. It is not normal English, but I hope that, unlike more conventional translations, it will not mislead anyone.

4b. *Son of Man: Genuine Sayings of Jesus*

This Aramaic idiom accounts for about a dozen sayings in the synoptic Gospels. One of the more straightforward examples is Mk 2.28, which concludes a dispute between Jesus and some Pharisees.[12] Some of Jesus' followers had been going along a path through the fields, plucking the grains of corn, an action to be expected of poor and hungry people taking *Peah*, the corn left for poor people at the edges of fields. Jesus' disciples were however doing this on the sabbath, and for this reason the Pharisees objected. Jesus rejected the Pharisees' criticism with two arguments, the second of which may be rendered as follows:

---

10 E.g. F. Rosenthal, *A Grammar of Biblical Aramaic* (Wiesbaden: Otto Harrassowitz, 2nd edn, 1963), p. 24 § 46: 'Use of the abs.st. and the det.st. agrees by and large with the non-use or use of the definite article in English.'

11 Casey, 'Aramaic idiom and the Son of Man Problem', *JSNT* 25 (2002), pp. 3–32 (12–18).

12 See pp. 321–23.

²⁷The sabbath was created for man, and not man for the sabbath. ²⁸Surely, then, a/the son of man is master even of the sabbath!

The general nature of Mk 2.28 is guaranteed by the general statement of Mk 2.27. This idiom, in which a general statement is deliberately used to refer indirectly to the speaker, is the only use of 'a/the son of man' which makes proper sense of both sentences in Aramaic. The declaration of Mk 2.27 looks back to God's purpose at creation, when he made man effectively lord of the creation, provided that he remains obedient to God (cf. Gen. 1.26, 28; Ps. 8.6-9; 2 Esd. 6.54; *2 Bar.* 14.18). Thus the general statement of Mk 2.28 includes the disciples, who as masters of the sabbath were entitled to take *Peah* on it. It is an indirect way of making clear that Jesus had the authority to take the halakhic decision that they were entitled to take *Peah* on the sabbath.

Jesus' general statement is a dramatic one, but no more dramatic than that of R.Aqiba, who settled another small point of sabbath law with the declaration, 'Make your sabbath profane, and don't depend on people' (b. Shab. 118a//b. Pes. 112a). This really meant that a man entirely dependent on charity for all his meals should eat two rather than three meals on the sabbath, as he did on other days. If the saying is taken out of its cultural context and interpreted literally, it can easily be given a quite inappropriate meaning. Similarly, at Mk 2.28 Jesus declared his right to fend off unwanted sabbath halakhah, indirectly claiming his prophetic ability to interpret the will of God, but not using any Christological title.

One of the examples of this idiom in the 'Q' material has suffered especially badly from mistranslation:

> Jackals/foxes have holes, and the birds of heaven/the sky have roosts, but a/ the son of man has nowhere to lay his head.
>
> (Mt. 8.20//Lk. 9.58)

This saying[13] belongs to the migratory phase of Jesus' ministry, when he moved through the towns and villages of Galilee. It was spoken in response to a disciple, probably a scribe (so Mt. 8.19), who undertook to follow Jesus wherever he went. It contrasts the divine provision of natural haunts for animals with the lack of such provision for people, who have to build houses to live in.

It is therefore important that the birds have 'roosts', not the traditional 'nests', which nature does not provide. Neither Matthew nor Luke has 'nests' (for which the straightforward Greek word would be *nossias*). Both have a general word for dwelling-places (*kataskēnōseis*), so Jesus will have used an equally general Aramaic word (e.g. *mishkenīn*). At this point, the behavioural patterns of birds in Israel are important. Palestine was a major flyway for centuries before and after the time of Jesus. Most of the birds seen there were migratory – they stopped on their way over to roost, not to build nests and rear their young. Moreover,

---

13   See further Casey, *Solution to the 'Son of Man' Problem*, pp. 168–78.

among the many species native to Israel, Cansdale noted the Lesser Kestrel, which 'travels in large flocks and roosts in hundreds, in such conspicuous places as the trees round Capernaum.'[14] Thus the places which the birds had to stay for as long as they needed were provided for them by God in the ordinary course of nature, and they were provided for them as they moved about the countryside.

Equally, 'holes' are places where both foxes and jackals lay up in the daytime, they are not 'dens' which they may or may not have to dig out to rear their young (both animals take over existing holes even for this purpose, sometimes made by other animals, when these are available). Both Matthew and Luke have 'foxes' (Greek *alōpekes*) rather than 'jackals', but Jesus can only have used the Aramaic *ta'alāyā*. Tristram commented on the related Hebrew *shū'al*:

> The Hebrew word undoubtedly includes the jackal (*Canis aureus*) as well as the fox (*Vulpes vulgaris*). Indeed, in most of the passages where it occurs, the jackal rather than the fox is intended, as may be seen from the context. The Hebrew *shu'al*, Arabic *jakal*, the Persian *shagul*, and the English *jackal*, are all the same word . . . But the two animals are commonly confounded by the natives of Syria, though they are perfectly aware of their distinctness . . . The natives of the East discriminate very little between the two animals, or rather look on the fox as a small and inferior species of jackal. Indeed their appearance to a cursory observer is very similar, the jackal having its fur of paler colour, or yellowish rather than reddish in hue.[15]

This was probably true in the ancient period as well. Both Matthew and Luke virtually had to specify 'foxes' because the Greek 'foxes' (*alōpekes*) is a perfectly correct translation of the Aramaic *ta'alāyā*, and there was no normal Greek word for 'jackal' because there were no jackals in Greece.

We can now see the general level of meaning which cannot be avoided in the original Aramaic. The reference will have been in the first place to Jesus himself, for he had nowhere to go as he moved about, and he could not provide for his disciples. This would be a humiliating thing to say, and consequently Jesus used an indirect way of saying it. The general level of the saying also takes in his followers, especially the one who had just declared that he would follow Jesus wherever he went (Mt. 8.19//Lk. 9.57).

Another genuine saying of Jesus responds to criticism from opponents of both John the Baptist and Jesus. We have seen that Jesus regarded both John and himself as prophets sent by God, and he put criticism of them together here:

> John has come not eating and not drinking, and they say 'He has a demon'. A/the son of man comes/has come eating and drinking and they say, 'Look! A man 'glutton and drunkard', an associate of tax-collectors and sinners'
>
> (Mt. 11.18-19//Lk. 7.33-34)[16]

---

14 F. S. Cansdale, *Animals of Bible Lands* (Exeter: Paternoster, 1970), p. 140.

15 H. B. Tristram, *The Natural History of the Bible* (London: Christian Knowledge Society, 1867, 10th edn, 1911), pp. 85, 110.

16 Casey, *Solution to the 'Son of Man' Problem*, pp. 136–39.

The first sentence, which concerns John the Baptist, is quite straightforward. He had an ascetic lifestyle, hence he 'came not eating and not drinking'. He lived in the wilderness, away from cities, as demoniacs sometimes did too. He dressed and ate unconventionally, less than his opponents. The accusation that he had a demon will have come as naturally to his opponents as it did to 'scribes who came down from Jerusalem' and accused Jesus of casting out demons by the prince of demons.[17] Other evidence shows that opposition to John's prophetic ministry came from the same circles as were opposed to Jesus. The debate between Jesus and the chief priests, scribes and elders at Mk 11.27-33 shows that they did not accept John the Baptist's ministry.[18] The same groups are almost certainly the anonymous 'you' in Jesus' saying at Mt. 21.31-32:

> Amen I'm telling you that the tax-collectors and prostitutes are going ahead of you into the kingdom of God. For John came to you in a/the way of righteousness and you did not believe him, but the tax-collectors and prostitutes believed him. But you saw this and did not change your minds afterwards and believe him.

All this evidence is coherent. Authorities who could not deny the effectiveness of the prophetic ministries of John and Jesus accused each of them of working by means of power from the devil and his minions. The early church had no interest in making up material like this.

In response to criticism of himself, Jesus avoided both a direct claim to prophetic authority and the direct humiliation of saying how he had been criticized by using the generalizing expression 'a/the son of man'. The first part of this sentence is as general as possible. Everyone does come eating and drinking, otherwise they die! It should be clear that 'comes' or 'has come' has this very general level of meaning, as in the previous sentence about John the Baptist; it does not refer to Jesus' pre-existence, a piece of Christian doctrine which had not yet been invented.

This general statement leads into the more precise comments which follow. These reflect the criticism of Jesus made by his opponents. For its plausibility, the next part of the saying depends on there being other people who ate and drank among tax-collectors and people whom strict orthodox Jews would label 'sinners'. Against the general background of Jesus' ministry among normal rather than ascetic or orthodox Jews, the existence of more such people is blindingly obvious. It also depends on the condemnation of such people being normal. Against the background of intra-Jewish polemic in the Judaism of this period that is also obvious. The particular accusation against Jesus was of being a glutton and a drunkard. This is not only a reflection on his social habits, it is also a reference to the stubborn and rebellious son of Deut. 21.20. Jesus' sometimes difficult relationship with his mother and the rest of the family will also lie behind

17 Cf. pp. 253–54.
18 See pp. 415–17.

this.[19] The tradition of condemning people for being gluttons and drunkards is well known from Jewish literature, and must therefore have been a reality too. This general level of meaning enabled Jesus to reject criticism of himself as on the same level as criticism of John the Baptist.

Since this idiom is a way of speaking about oneself, with or without others, in circumstances where one might be humiliated, it was a useful idiom for Jesus to employ when talking about his forthcoming death. I have noted a general statement in which Jesus used the term 'prophet' (Lk. 13.33) when looking forward to his death, and his use of three very indirect metaphors of being 'baptised' (Mk 10.38-39; Lk. 12.50), drinking a cup (Mk 10.38-39) and of being 'perfected' (Lk. 13.32).[20] Deliberately putting himself in a position where he was likely to be put to death was naturally a very difficult thing for him to discuss, and hence the idiomatic use of 'a/the son of man' was a natural idiom for him to use. During his final Passover, he used it twice when predicting his betrayal (Mk 14.21):

> A/The son of man goes as it is written concerning him, and woe to that man by whose hand a/the son of man is betrayed/handed over: (it would be) good for him if that man had not been born.[21]

In the first general statement, 'a/the son of man goes as it is written concerning him', the word 'goes' is a normal Aramaic metaphor for 'dies' (*'azal*). The statement depends on the universal fact that people die, recorded in scriptural passages such as Gen. 3.19 and Isa. 40.6. At this general level, this 'son of man' statement would seem to be obviously true, because everyone knew that God's verdict on humankind, written in the scripture at Gen. 3.19, was that we should return to the ground and become dust again, a figurative pronouncement of the universality of the death of people. The function of this first 'son of man' statement being obviously true was to make it easier for his followers to accept the application of it to Jesus himself. At a second level, accordingly, the saying is a prediction of Jesus' forthcoming death, together with any of his closest followers who might die with him. There should be no doubt that Jesus did interpret scriptural passages of himself, including his forthcoming death.[22] Nonetheless, this example is on the most general level of the spectrum, in the sense that the general level of meaning is true of all people.

The first part of Mk 14.21 also helps to set up the indirect condemnation of Judah of Kerioth, which follows. This begins with the second 'son of man' saying: 'Woe to that man by whom a/the son of man is betrayed'. This can be understood as a general condemnation of traitors, a highly functional level of meaning because it would command almost universal assent. The application of this saying to Jesus himself will also have been perfectly clear. The verse ends with a quite indirect condemnation of Judah: '(it would be) good for him if that man

---

19 Cf. pp. 300–1.
20 See pp. 114–15, 404–5.
21 See further pp. 430–32.
22 See further pp. 430–39.

had not been born.' This is also perfectly comprehensible in the general terms of the previous sentence – it is generally accepted that traitors should come to a sticky end. Throughout this verse, the general level of meaning functions to enable the vigorous condemnation of Judah of Kerioth to be accepted without objection because the condemnation of traitors is so normal, and the references to Jesus' own death are made easier to deal with by means of the two idiomatic uses of the term 'a/the son of man'.

This idiom accounts for about a dozen 'Son of man' sayings in the synoptic Gospels. I discuss in more detail Mk 2.10; 10.45; Mt. 12.32//Lk. 12.10 (cf. Mk 3.28-29); and Lk. 22.48 elsewhere in this book, so I summarize my comments briefly here.

Mark 2.10 is part of the story of the healing of a paralytic (Mk 2.1-12).[23] Jesus used a 'son of man' saying as part of his comment to hostile scribes as well as to the paralytic, followed at once by his command to the man to get up, which would show that he was healed:

> [10]And so that you may know that a/the son of man on earth has power/authority to forgive/undo/release sins,[11]Get up, I tell you, take up your mattress and go to your house.

This example is primarily about Jesus, as his healing of the man demonstrates. The general level of meaning of the 'son of man' saying also includes a restricted group of people who may also pronounce the forgiveness of sins. In the nature of the case, these people are not defined. They must include prophets, and healers must also be included, for only so could they perform healings for which this was the appropriate Explanatory Model. In this example, the general level of meaning is as restricted as this idiom would tolerate.

The next saying has survived in no less than three translations. Mt. 12.32 and Mk 3.28-29 are in the versions of the Beelzeboul controversy in the 'Q' material and in Mark, the original context of the saying in the ministry of Jesus. Luke 12.10 has been collected separately with two other 'Son of man' sayings (Lk. 12.8-9). I translate a reconstructed original Aramaic literally into English like this:

> And whoever speaks a word against a/the son of man, it will be forgiven him. But whoever speaks a word against the holy spirit, it will not be forgiven him for ever (cf. Mk 3.28-29, Mt. 12.32, Lk. 12.10).[24]

The first part of this saying is a general statement decreeing forgiveness to people who oppose or even slander other people, the kind of view to be expected in the teaching of Jesus. The use of the term 'son of man', however, is the particular idiom whereby the statement refers particularly to Jesus himself. The saying therefore appears at first sight to grant forgiveness to Jesus' opponents. The

---

23 See pp. 258–62.
24 Cf. pp. 253–56, and pp. 372–73.

sting is in the second half. The spirit of holiness, or 'holy spirit', is a metaphor for God in action. Nowhere is the action of God to be seen more vigorously and obviously than in Jesus' exorcisms. The accusation that he cast out demons by *Ba'al zeboul* is accordingly an unforgiveable sin. What Jesus seems to concede in the first part of the saying is thus quite removed in the second part. This polemic, like the content of the saying, accordingly has an excellent setting in this dispute over Jesus' exorcisms.

Luke 22.48 is the only Gospel example of this idiom outside Mark and the 'Q' material.[25] Mark records how Judah of Kerioth betrayed Jesus by identifying him in the darkness of Gethsemane with a kiss. Jesus' words were transmitted by one of Luke's sources:

Judah, do you betray a/the son of man with a kiss?

As usual, the reference is primarily to Jesus himself, but this time the general level of meaning underlines the dastardly nature of Judah's actions. It presupposes the general human feeling that betraying people is wrong, and betraying someone with a kiss is even worse. At this level, it is comparable with Mk 14.21b.

The example at Mk 9.12 has been found exceptionally difficult, because the context implies that the term 'Son of man' applies to John the Baptist, whereas 'Son of man' sayings in the Gospels always refer to Jesus. Here too the answer lies with the Aramaic term *bar* (*e*)*nāsh*(*ā*), this time in a general statement used deliberately to refer to both John and Jesus. I translate my Aramaic reconstruction as follows:[26]

And (they were) asking him and saying, 'Why do (the) scribes say that Elijah is going to come first?'[12]And he said to them, 'Elijah comes first and turns back all, and how it is written of (a/the son of) man that he suffers much and is rejected![13]And I tell you that, moreover, Elijah has come, and they did in the case of him whom they desired according as it is written concerning him/it.'

Here the discussion presupposes the prophecy of Mal. 4.5: 'Behold, I will send you Elijah the prophet before the great and aweful day of YHWH comes.' Jesus identified the fulfillment of this prophecy in the ministry of John the Baptist.[27] John had however been put to death by Herod Antipas, and the prophecies of Malachi said nothing about that. Jesus therefore used an idiomatic general statement referring to more general scriptures, such as Isa. 40.6-8 on the transitoriness of human life and the suffering of man in Job 14. He also had in mind the rejection of people in Jeremiah 6–7. This is the suffering and rejection which John the Baptist experienced, and which Jesus was expecting to experience, together with any of the inner group of his followers who would die with him. This is

25 See further p. 439.
26 For an Aramaic reconstruction and discussion of the whole passage, Casey, *Solution to the Son of Man Problem*, pp. 125–31.
27 Cf. pp. 179–80.

not what was expected of Elijah, nor of anyone who would come to redeem Israel. Hence Jesus associated himself with John the Baptist in this 'son of man' saying.

Mark had even greater difficulty than usual in translating this saying into Greek. Since the death of Jesus was more important to him than that of John the Baptist or anyone else, he followed his strategy of using the Greek *ho huios tou anthrōpou*, which made the reference to Jesus clear. Unlike modern scholars, he was a bilingual who could also see the original Aramaic idiom in his Greek translation, and consequently the reference to both John the Baptist and to Jesus. He will have been content that he had done as well as possible by rendering the Aramaic *bar* (*e*)*nāsh*(*ā*) with the Greek *ho huios tou anthrōpou*, as he always did when there was a genuine reference to Jesus.

Finally, two or three genuine 'son of man' sayings lie behind Lk. 12.8-9// Mt. 10.32-33 and Mk 8.38, but it is difficult to recover them all with precision from the somewhat vigorous editing of the evangelists.[28] With some uncertainty about details, there should be no doubt that Jesus said something along the following lines:

> Everyone who confesses me before (the sons of) men,
> a/the son of man will confess him too before the angels of God.
> And whoever denies me before (the sons of) men,
> a/the son of man will deny him before the angels of God.

The two settings presupposed are Jesus' ministry and the final judgement. The angels form the heavenly court, and it is assumed that God is the judge. The court will hear witnesses, and this is why Jesus could use a general statement with 'son of man'. At the same time, just as people's witness for or against Jesus will be crucial to the court's verdict, so the use of the 'son of man' idiom is an indirect way of saying that he will be the most important witness. This reflects the centrality of Jesus as God's final messenger to Israel.

This means that all but one example of this idiom is found in the oldest Gospel sources, Mark and the 'Q' material, with Luke the historian picking up just one example (Lk. 22.48) from his special material. No examples can be reconstructed from the 'Son of man' sayings in the Fourth Gospel, nor from 'Son of man' sayings found only in non-canonical sources, because they are uniformly too remote from the historical Jesus to be based on Aramaic idiom. Accordingly, my solution to the 'Son of man' problem fits perfectly with everything already known about the relative historical worth of Gospel sources.

---

28   See Casey, *Solution to the Son of Man Problem*, pp. 179–94.

4c. *Son of Man: The Translation Process*

The translation process turned the Aramaic term *bar* (ᵉ)*nāsh*(*ā*) into a major Christological title. This process has however been very difficult for scholars to understand. In a famous and influential discussion in 1894, Wellhausen bluntly declared that the translators rendered the Aramaic *barnascha* 'quite wrongly' with the Greek *ho huios tou anthrōpou*. Other influential negative comments include the description in 1971 of the Greek title *ho huios tou anthrōpou* by Jeremias as 'a rather barbaric literal translation'. Similar comments have been so widespread that a survey of scholarship published in 1999 classified me with scholars who 'have to assume that the Aramaic has been *mistranslated*' [my emphasis], a well known view which I have never held.[29]

There are three main points. First, literal translation was perfectly normal, as it still is. Hence the Aramaic *bar*, 'son', would be translated with the Greek *huios*, 'son', unless there was a strong reason for a translator to do otherwise. Moreover, these two words are such close equivalents that bilingual translators would encounter and use them in the same way on a daily basis in their normal lives, not only when translating. The same applies to the Hebrew *ben*, 'son', which was an equally close equivalent. Consequently, the Greek *huios* and the Aramaic *bar* are used hundreds of times to translate the Hebrew *ben* in the singular and plural in the Greek and Aramaic translations of the Hebrew Bible. It is therefore natural that these words were also used as equivalents in the text and translations of the Hebrew Bible in figurative and metaphorical expressions. For example, in the expression 'son of death' at 1 Sam. 20.31, the Hebrew has *ben*, and the Greek and Aramaic translations have *huios* and *bar*, the natural equivalents and normal translations. It follows that the translation of the Aramaic *bar* in *bar* (ᵉ)*nāsh*(*ā*) with the normally equivalent Greek *huios* is what should be expected. It is literal, but it is not 'barbaric'.

The same applies to the translation of (ᵉ)*nāsh*(*ā*), 'man', with the Greek *anthrōpos*, the extremely common Greek equivalent for 'man' in general. These two words are also such close equivalents that bilingual translators would use them in the same way on a daily basis in their normal lives, not only when translating. They are also close equivalents of the Hebrew *ādhām*, which is therefore normally translated with *anthrōpos* in the Greek translations of the Old Testament, and with (ᵉ)*nāsh*(*ā*) or *bar* (ᵉ)*nāsh*(*ā*) in the Aramaic translations of the Old Testament.

Consequently, the Hebrew *ben ādhām*, literally 'son of man', is usually translated *huios anthrōpou*, 'son of man', in the Septuagint, despite the fact that *huios anthrōpou* was not a previously known expression in Greek. Similarly, the Aramaic translations usually use *bar* (ᵉ)*nāsh*(*ā*) (except in the book of Ezekiel). The translations of the Hebrew plural *benē ādhām*, literally 'sons of man', meaning people in general, show a similar pattern. The Greek translators usually use (*hoi*)

---

29   J. Wellhausen, *Israelitische und Jüdische Geschichte* (Berlin: Reimer, 1894), p. 312 n. 1 ('durchaus falsch'); Jeremias, *New Testament Theology*, p. 260; D. Burkett, *The Son of Man Debate: A History and Evaluation* (SNTSMS 107. Cambridge: CUP, 1999), p. 93.

huioi tōn anthrōpōn, literally '(the) sons of (the) men', with the invariable article before 'men' being generic, and using the Greek plural *anthrōpōn* for the collective Hebrew singular *ādhām*, which refers to humankind in general. The translator of the book of Ecclesiastes, being more literal than others, used *(hoi) huioi tou anthrōpou*, literally '(the) sons of (the) man', with the invariable article before 'man' again being generic, and using the Greek collective singular *anthrōpou* for the collective Hebrew singular *ādhām*. These two similar translations account for 43 of the 48 examples of the translation of the Hebrew *benē ādhām* into Greek in the Septuagint. It follows that the use of both Greek words, *huios*, 'son', and *anthrōpou*, 'man', in the Gospel translation of the Aramaic *bar (ᵉ)nāsh(ā)* with the Greek *ho huios tou anthrōpou*, is literal, but it is normal, not 'barbaric'.

The second main point concerns the articles in the Gospel term *ho huios tou anthrōpou*, for this Christological title has two articles, the first *(ho)* before 'son' and the other *(tou)* before 'man'. The first of these two articles turns this expression into a Christological title, the equivalent of the English 'the Son of Man'. This is because this is a normal use of the definite article, in Greek just as in English, and for monoglot speakers of Greek, the reference to Jesus in particular would be imposed by the context, for Jesus is the central character and almost all the sayings make perfect sense of him alone.

For technical linguistic reasons, the Aramaic word *bar*, in the expression *bar (ᵉ)nāsh(ā)*, in which it means literally 'son of', cannot of itself be in the definite state. The expression as a whole, however, can be in either the definite state, *bar (ᵉ)nāshā*, or the indefinite (or absolute) state, *bar (ᵉ)nāsh*. Moreover, as a matter of empirical fact, in this particular Aramaic idiom, in which a speaker uses a rather general statement to refer to himself, or himself and other people made obvious by the context, the expression *bar (ᵉ)nāsh(ā)* may be in either the definite state, *bar (ᵉ)nāsh(ā)*, or the indefinite state, *bar (ᵉ)nāsh*. This is because *bar (ᵉ)nāsh(ā)* is a generic expression, and in Aramaic generic expressions may be in either the definite or indefinite state.

Why then did the Gospel writers invariably use both articles? One reason for this is that the Greek article is often generic, more often than the English definite article 'the'. Consequently, *bilingual translators* could see the original Aramaic idiom in their Greek translations. Mark 2.27-28 is an especially clear example of this. In the following translation, I put the English 'the' for every Greek article, with the Greek article in brackets and in italics. It should also be remembered that all Mark's letters were the same size, the equivalent of our capital letters, for small letters had not been invented. Consequently, no word could be picked out with a capital letter, unlike in English, in which we can distinguish between 'son of man' and 'Son of man'.

[27]The *(to)* sabbath was made for the *(ton)* man and not the *(ho)* man for the *(to)* sabbath, [28]so that the *(ho)* son of the *(tou)* man is lord of the *(tou)* Sabbath too.

It should be clear from this translation that all three articles before 'man' must be interpreted as generic, because the references are to humankind in general, not to a particular man. All three articles before 'sabbath' should be interpreted as generic too, for the references are to the sabbath in general, not to any particular sabbath. It is in this cultural and linguistic context that *bilingual translators* could not fail to see the article before 'son' as generic as well, and thus see the generic force of the Aramaic *bar* (*ᵉ*)*nāsh*(*ā*) preserved in their translation.

They will however have realized that monoglot speakers of Greek, that is, most members of the Greek-speaking churches for whom the Gospels were written, would not be able to see an idiom of which they were unaware. Greek-speaking Christians would naturally interpret the article before 'son' as a reference to a single person, Jesus, who to them was the most important person who had ever lived on earth. This was the central point in the transition of 'son of man' from an ordinary term for man, the Aramaic *bar* (*ᵉ*)*nāsh*(*ā*), into the major Christological title, the Greek *ho huios tou anthrōpou*. This however could hardly be helped, and the other reason why the translators and Gospel writers would be perfectly happy about this is the third main point.

Translators often produce translations with the needs of the target culture primarily in mind. This is so common that it has given rise to a whole theory of translation, formerly known as the *skopos* theory of translation, now often known as 'functionalism'.[30] The main purpose of this theory is to draw attention to the ways in which translators make alterations to satisfy the needs of the target culture. Neubert expressed clearly one of the most general points about the translation process: 'In plain words, *translation recasts the original for different people*, after an unavoidable *time lag* and, as a rule, at a *different place*. It is displaced communication.'[31]

Changes are particularly obvious in the work of translators who translate freely. A good example is the translation of the *Testament of Ephraem* from Syriac into Greek, which is in general a very free translation. For example, for the Syriac *kol barnāsh*, literally 'every son of man', meaning 'everyone', the translator put 'the church of God' (*T.Ephraem*, line 944). This is a dramatic change in the interests of the Christians for whom the translation was made. Less extreme examples are found in the work of more literal translators. For example, both the translation of the Septuagint of the book of Numbers into Greek, and Targum Onkelos, which is a translation into Aramaic, are in general quite literal. Nonetheless, at *Num.* 24.17, where the Hebrew text has a prediction that 'a sceptre' (*shēbhet*) shall arise out of Israel, the Septuagint has a 'man' (*anthrōpos*), and Targum Onkelos has 'the Messiah' (*mᵉshīḥā*). Both these translations are deliberately interpretative, in the interests of the Jewish communities for whom they were written. The Septuagint has clarified the term 'sceptre' by referring to a man who would lead Israel when the people were delivered, and Onkelos, written later when expectation of Israel's deliverance had crystallized round a single figure called 'the Messiah', has deliberately referred to him.

---

30 For an introduction, C. Nord, *Translating as a Purposeful Activity: Functionalist Approaches Explained* (Manchester: St. Jerome, 1997).

31 A. Neubert, *Text and Translation* (Übersetzungswissenschaftliche Beiträge 8. Leipzig, Enzyklopädie, 1985), p. 8.

This is the pattern into which the Gospel translation of the Aramaic *bar* (ᵉ)*nāsh*(*ā*) (a/the son of man) with *ho huios tou anthrōpou* (the Son of man) must be fitted. It produced a major new Christological title, which clearly refers to Jesus alone. This was just what the church needed, as we know from the way it caught on, and from the increase in Christological titles in the editing of the Gospels and in the rest of the New Testament. Two other aspects of the strategy were essential to it. First, the translators did not use this term, not even without the articles, when the Aramaic *bar* (ᵉ)*nāsh*(*ā*) was used in their sources with reference to anyone else. There are no exceptions to this. Secondly, they did not use it in the plural. The only exception to this is at Mk 3.28. We have seen that, in response to criticism of his ministry of exorcism, Jesus said something very much like this:

> And whoever speaks a word against a/the son of man, it will be forgiven him. But whoever speaks a word against the Holy Spirit, it will not be forgiven him for ever (cf. Mk 3.28-29, Mt. 12.32, Lk. 12.10).[32]

Here Mark was evidently unhappy about the idea of a word against Jesus being forgiven, so he put 'son of man' in the plural, and edited the saying as well. Matthew and Luke were not happy with this, presumably because it did not fit the strategy which they had inherited, and produced an expression ('the sons of men') which they did not like. The chaotic results may be seen in the following table:

Amen I say to you that everything will be forgiven the sons of men, the sins and the blasphemies, whatever they blaspheme. But whoever blasphemes against the Holy Spirit does not have forgiveness forever, but is liable for an eternal sin. (Mk 3.28-29)	Because of this I say to you, every sin and blasphemy will be forgiven men, but the blasphemy of the Spirit will not be forgiven. And whoever speaks a word against the Son of man, it will be forgiven him. But whoever speaks against the Holy Spirit, it will not be forgiven him, neither in this Age nor in the coming (one). (Mt. 12.31-32)	And everyone who speaks a word against the Son of man, it will be forgiven him. But he who blasphemes against the Holy Spirit will not be forgiven. (Lk. 12.10)

Here Matthew has changed Mark's 'the sons of men' to 'men' and has otherwise shortened Mk 3.28 at Mt. 12.31. Secondly, he has added a more conventionally translated version of the saying from the 'Q' material at 12.32. Luke left the

---

32   Cf. pp. 253–56, 366–67.

Markan version of the saying out altogether, and has no equivalent of it in his version of the Beelzeboul controversy. Instead, he collected his version of the saying at Lk. 12.10, also from 'Q' material, but separately translated from Aramaic, not an edited version of what we find in Matthew. This illustrates the chaos which could have ensued if the translators had not had a strategy.

The three aspects of the translation strategy together, using *ho huios tou anthrōpou* when the Aramaic *bar* (ᵉ)*nāsh*(*ā*) referred to Jesus, not using it with reference to anyone else, and not using the plural, made sure that *ho huios tou anthrōpou* was *unique*, much like the English 'the Son of Man'. The first article was thus used in a context which ensured that it would be interpreted as a reference to Jesus himself. Some reference to Jesus is always clear from the context, and the Greek article was a normal way of making clear a reference to a particular, previously known person. There was therefore no chance that monoglot speakers of Greek would interpret the first article as generic, even as they were interpreting the second article as generic. This also ensured that what everyone regarded as the most important aspect of the original use of the idiom, the particular reference to Jesus himself, was preserved and seen by everyone.

I have just pointed out that Mk 2.27-28 is a passage where bilingual translators could see the original Aramaic idiom with particular ease. Nonetheless, Mk 2.28 is a sound example of a passage in which monoglot speakers of Greek would see a Christological title. I repeat the above translation:

²⁷The (*to*) sabbath was made for the (*ton*) man and not the (*ho*) man for the (*to*) sabbath, ²⁸so that the (*ho*) son of the (*tou*) man is lord of the (*tou*) sabbath too.

Here monoglot speakers of Greek could not see the original Aramaic idiom because they did not know it. Following normal Greek usage, they would treat all the articles before 'sabbath' and before 'man' as generic, because these are obvious references to the sabbath in general, not to any particular sabbath, and to humankind in general, not to a particular man. The article before 'son of man' is however different. The reference is obviously to a particular man, namely Jesus. He is in charge throughout the narrative, in which he defends his disciples with decisive arguments which show that he, not the Pharisees, is in charge of sabbath halakhah. From the point of view of Mark, and of his audiences in the early church, this is a perfect end to the story. It is an unambiguous declaration of Jesus' authority, just what the early church needed. Moreover, from their perspective, it follows on perfectly from Mk 2.27. This recalls the original creation of the sabbath, when God himself rested on the sabbath and made it holy (Gen. 2.3), together with the fourth commandment, which gives this as the reason why people, together with their guests and animals, should rest on the sabbath (Exod. 20.8-11) It therefore follows that the son of humankind, the most important person to be on earth, was in charge of interpreting the observance of the sabbath for his disciples.

It should therefore be concluded that the translation of *bar* (ᵉ)*nāsh*(*ā*) with *ho huios tou anthrōpou* was a brilliant creative achievement. It was rather literal, but it was not 'barbaric', and *bar* (*ᵉ*)*nāsh*(*ā*) was not translated 'quite wrongly', or 'mistranslated'. It retained the main point of Jesus' original sayings, that they referred particularly to himself, and it produced a major Christological title, which has served the needs of the churches ever since.

4d. *Son of Man: Daniel 7.13*

The next step was to find the term 'Son of man' in scripture. It was found by Mark, or by his predecessors, in what became a classic text, Dan. 7.13:

> I was looking in the visions of the night and behold! with the clouds of heaven one like a son of man was coming, and he came to the Ancient of Days, and they brought him before Him, and to him was given power and glory and kingship, and all the peoples, nations and languages shall serve him . . .
>
> (Dan. 7.13-14)

Originally, 'one like a son of man' was a symbol of the people of the saints of the Most High, as should be clear from the interpretative section of the vision (Dan. 7.18, 22, 27). In its cultural context, this meant the Jewish people who would shortly afterwards defeat the Greek armies and restore the Temple to the worship of the Lord, an interpretation which survived in Jewish sources and in the Syriac-speaking church. The figure of 'one like a son of man' was however reinterpreted of an individual who would overcome the Romans, in due course known as the Messiah, and the early church reinterpreted it of the figure of Jesus.[33] All the Gospel sayings which use Dan. 7.13 expect the Son of man to come, and by this they mean the future return of Jesus.

The first obvious example of the midrashic use of this text is found at Mk 13.26, at the climax of Mark's eschatological discourse. This discourse has a number of features which have a natural setting in the period of the early church, rather than in the ministry of Jesus. The most striking, in a context of predicted persecutions which took place during the period of the early church, is the prediction that the Gospel must first be preached to all the nations (Mk 13.10). The Gentile mission does not have any setting in the teaching of Jesus – he expected the kingdom to come too soon for it to take place.[34] Equally secondary are the predictions that people will report the presence of 'the Christ', and that 'false Christs' will arise (Mk 13.21-22). These predictions are dependent on the development of the title 'the Christ' in the earliest period of the church.[35] After this complex of secondary events, Mark presents scripturally based predictions of heavenly phenomena such as the darkening of the sun and moon, and the

---

33 For detailed discussion of the original interpretation, and of the two later traditions of exegesis see Casey, *Interpretation and Influence of Daniel 7*, chs 2–4.
34 See pp. 218–22.
35 See pp. 392–99.

falling of the stars (Mk 13.24-25). There follows the climactic moment of Jesus' second coming:

> And then they will see the Son of man coming in clouds with much power and glory.
>
> (Mk 13.26)

The dependence of this verse on Dan. 7.13 is almost universally recognized. It has the crucial terms 'Son of man' and 'come', the distinctive clouds, and the common elements of power and glory. The reference of the title 'the Son of man' to Jesus alone is simply assumed. It follows that this Greek title of Jesus has been perceived in Dan. 7.13, which has been interpreted as a prophecy of Jesus' second coming. Moreover, this is part of a midrash on several Old Testament passages. Some of the other ones are difficult to locate with precision, because this midrash utilizes passages creatively rather than quoting them. For example, the falling of the stars at Mk 13.25 may well be from Isa. 34.4, and the gathering at Mk 13.27 could be from Zech. 2.10 LXX. Since people on earth see the event of the Son of man coming, he must come from heaven to earth, as the man-like figure should be seen to do in the original text of Dan. 7.13.[36] The passage should be interpreted literally, in accordance with the normal beliefs of the early church. It is immediately followed by the gathering of the elect, as for example at Deut. 30.4.

This passage accordingly shows 'the Son of man' used as a title of Jesus in Greek (*ho huios tou anthrōpou*), and seen in scripture at Dan. 7.13 in a prediction of his return. This mirrors the belief in his second coming found abundantly outside the Gospels in the New Testament, as already in a speech of Peter at Acts 3.20, which expresses the hope that 'the Lord may send the Christ appointed for you, Jesus'. Mark 13.26 differs from this and other such New Testament passages precisely in its use of Dan. 7.13 and the title 'the Son of man'. This strongly suggests that the use of Dan. 7.13 in particular was due to the perception that the title 'the Son of man' was to be found in the authentic sayings of Jesus which form the majority of 'Son of man' sayings in Mark.

An equally obvious example of the midrashic use of Dan. 7.13 is found at Mk 14.62, which is also embedded in a secondary context. The high priest is said to have asked Jesus at his 'trial', 'Are you the Christ, the Son of the Blessed?' (Mk 14.61). This question cannot be authentic, since the term 'anointed', or 'Messiah', in Aramaic (*meshīḥā*), for which the Greek is 'Christ' (*Christos*), had not yet crystallized into a title like this.[37] Moreover, every faithful Jew was a son of God, the high priest himself conspicuously so, and while 'the Blessed' sounds like a circumlocution for God, it is not attested as such.[38] The question has however an excellent setting in the early church, for whom both 'Christ', the Greek translation of 'Messiah', and 'Son of God', were important titles of Jesus. The question is accordingly setting up the answer for the purpose of Mark's theology,

---

36 Casey, *Interpretation and Influence of Daniel 7*, pp. 18–19, 22, 24, 28–29.
37 See pp. 392–99.
38 See further pp. 401, 440–41.

and if Mark is responsible for the question, he must also be responsible for the first part of Jesus' answer:

> I am, and you will see the Son of Man sitting on the right of the Power and coming with the clouds of heaven.

(Mk 14.62)

After his affirmative answer to the secondary question, Jesus continues with the same midrashic use of Dan. 7.13 as in Mk 13.26. Once again Mark uses the crucial 'Son of man' and 'come', and this time also 'with the clouds of heaven', five words running identical to the Greek translation of Dan. 7.13 attributed to Theodotion (the sound Greek translation of Daniel which gradually replaced the original LXX translation, which those learned in the scriptures could see was frankly frightful).

In Mk 14.62, Dan. 7.13 is combined with at least one other Old Testament text, with 'sitting on the right hand of the Power' certainly dependent on Ps. 110.1, and 'you will see' probably from Zech. 12.10. Psalm 110 is the most frequently used Old Testament text in the New Testament. It was important to the earliest followers of Jesus when they came to believe in his Resurrection.[39] Jesus' second coming is logically secondary to the Christian belief that he had risen from the dead and sat at the right hand of God, and Dan. 7.13 did not catch on in the rest of the New Testament, as it surely would have done if Jesus had used it in this clear way at such a climactic moment. Jesus' response, 'I am', is equally important. It brings Mark's 'Messianic secret' to an end, for this is the only place in the Gospel where Jesus says he is the Christ, the category which was of such central importance in the early church. Thus this sentence declares Jesus' future vindication with all three of the major Christological titles used by Mark. It explains that Jesus was wickedly condemned because he said who he really was and how God would vindicate him, and it thereby condemns his judges. All these points fit perfectly into the theology of Mark, and served the needs of the early church.

One thing, however, this declaration does not do: it does not give grounds for conviction on the legal charge of blasphemy indicated at Mk 14.63-64. Here the high priest tears his raiment before any verdict is given, as he had to do only after a legally binding verdict of blasphemy. He then accuses Jesus of blasphemy for the first time, and everyone there finds him worthy of death. It is very doubtful whether the conviction for blasphemy is justified by what Jesus is supposed to have said, since he did not mention the name of God, let alone fail to keep it holy, and in any case we have seen that he did not say what Mark alleges he said. Moreover, this is not properly related to his crucifixion on the orders of Pilate, from whose point of view Mk 14.62 would be a foolish claim by a mad Jew, not evidence that Jesus was a dangerous bandit. We can safely infer that Mark did not have sufficient information about the proceedings before Joseph

---

39   See pp. 460, 497.

Caiaphas, and wrote in Greek a story which includes the main points needed by the early church.

There are two more general reasons for not believing in the historicity of Mk 13.26 and 14.62. In the synoptic Gospels, Jesus never refers to his second coming except by using Dan. 7.13 and referring to the Son of man coming (except for the parabolic 'Lord of the house' at Mk 13.35, edited into the non-parabolic 'your Lord' at Mt. 24.42). It was not characteristic of Jesus to deal with a topic only in such rigidly scriptural terms. Secondly, the Resurrection of the Son of man and his coming are never combined, even though they are alternative ways of presenting his vindication: this implies a separate origin for these two groups of sayings.

It follows that the midrashic use of Dan. 7.13 does not go back to the historical Jesus. It was used in the early church so that the term 'Son of man' could be found in the scriptures, and his second coming could be seen as already predicted by the prophet Daniel and by Jesus himself.

4e. *Son of Man: Jesus Predicts His Death and Resurrection*

We have seen that the Gospel writers could edit authentic sayings, just as they could transmit them accurately, and create new ones. The most outstanding examples of secondary editing of authentic sayings are the predictions of Jesus' Passion and Resurrection at Mk 8.31//Mt.16.21//Lk. 9.22; Mk 9.31//Mt.17.22-23//Lk. 9.44; and Mk 10.33-34//Mt. 20.18-19//Lk. 18.31-33 (cf. Mk 9.9; 14.41//Mt. 26.45; Mt. 26.2; Lk. 17.25; 24.7). I begin from Mk 8.31:

> And he began to teach them that the Son of man must suffer many things, and be rejected by the elders and the chief priests and the scribes, and be killed, and after three days rise.

Like the other sayings in this group, this cannot be a translation of a satisfactory Aramaic sentence as it stands. It contains the vital term 'Son of man', which could only represent the Aramaic *bar* (*ᵉ*)*nāsh*(*ā*). As we have seen, this was a general term for 'man', and while it could be used idiomatically to refer to Jesus in particular, such examples must also have *some* general level of meaning. Here the problem is that the saying makes precise reference to 'the elders and chief priests and scribes', that is, to the circumstances of Jesus' death so specific as to preclude any general level of meaning. Peter is nonetheless portrayed as understanding this saying very clearly, and reacting in an understandable way that the early church would have no reason to invent:

> And Peter took him on one side and began to rebuke him. But he turned and seeing his disciples, rebuked Peter and said, 'Get behind me, Satan, for your mind is not set on the (will) of God but on the (concerns) of men'.
>
> (Mk 8.32-33)

Neither Peter rebuking Jesus, nor this serious criticism of Peter would be found in Mark's Gospel if this did not represent approximately what happened. But if Jesus' rebuke is authentic, and Peter's reaction is authentic, Peter must have had something like Mk 8.31 to react to, including Jesus' unwelcome reference to his forthcoming death. There are therefore good reasons why something like Mk 8.31 must be authentic, and good reasons why it cannot be authentic in its present form.

The solution to this puzzle lies in repeated editing by all three evangelists of one or more genuine sayings of Jesus. This can be seen most clearly in Matthew and Luke. In the central group of Markan predictions, Jesus predicts his Resurrection 'after three days' (Mk 8.31; 9.31; 10.34). Every single time, both Matthew and Luke alter this to 'on the third day'. The reason for this is obvious: they have edited the predictions in the light of their stories of the Resurrection, in which Jesus rises 'on the third day', not literally 'after three days'. Luke even refers back to his version of Jesus' predicting his Resurrection 'on the third day' as part of his replacement of the earlier tradition of Resurrection appearances in Galilee with his tradition of Resurrection appearances in Jerusalem.[40] So his two angels 'remind' the women in the empty tomb how Jesus predicted his passion and Resurrection when he was in Galilee:

> Remember how he spoke to you while he was still in Galilee, saying that the Son of man must be handed over into the hands of sinful men and be crucified and rise on the third day.
>
> (Lk. 24.6-7)

Both Matthew and Luke also add details to the predictions of Jesus' death. For example, only Mt. 20.19 predicts crucifixion, which Matthew also referred to in his new prediction at Mt. 26.2, and Luke added to his heavily reworked 'reminder' at Lk. 24.7.

Thus both Matthew and Luke edited the predictions of Jesus' death and Resurrection which they inherited from Mark to make them seem more convincingly accurate because of their increasing details. It is in this light that the increasing details of the successive predictions in Mark must be considered. For example, only Mk 10.33-34 (followed by Mt. 20.19 and Lk. 18.32-33) predicts that Jesus will be handed over to the Gentiles and scourged. This should also be attributed to Mark rewriting a prediction in the light of what he knew of the actual story of Jesus, the beginning of the process more clearly visible in Matthew and Luke.

We must therefore go back to Mk 8.31, and see whether it is possible to remove detailed references to the story of Jesus' death and thereby uncover a prediction with some general level of meaning. We have seen that some prediction of Jesus' death must have been involved for Peter to have had something to react to. The words 'after three days' must also be retained, since they do not fit

---

40   See further pp. 463–64.

a literal reference to the story of Jesus' Resurrection, in which Jesus seems already to have risen by the third day in Mark's unfinished account, a point made clearer in Matthew and Luke's predictions that he would rise 'on the third day'. We shall see that 'after three days' should not be taken literally: resurrection 'after three days' could mean after a short interval, or after a person was known with certainty to be dead, and this is how Mark will have interpreted his predictions. We shall also see that the Aramaic word *qūm*, which means 'rise', need not refer to *bodily* resurrection, and that going straight to heaven was a normal way to visualize the immediate fate of the suffering righteous.[41] It is evident from the story of the rich man and Lazar (Lk. 16.19-31), in which angels take Lazar to Abraham's bosom when he dies, that Jesus shared this view. Equally, all men die, and it was believed that people would rise at the general resurrection, which Jesus believed would take place before long.[42] All this fits beautifully so far: Jesus predicted his death and his Resurrection after three days, with a general statement using the term *bar* (*e*)*nāsh*(*ā*), which took for granted the death of everyone and the general resurrection.

We have also seen that we must eliminate 'by the elders and the chief priests and the scribes', because this is too specific to the fate of Jesus and has no proper general level of meaning. The word 'must' has often been eliminated on the ground that it has no precise equivalent in the Aramaic of this period, but in this context it is a perfectly reasonable translation of the Aramaic *ḥayyābh*, which is approximately equivalent to the English 'liable to'. The next word, 'suffer', has often been eliminated too on the ground it has no precise Aramaic equivalent. However we now know from the Dead Sea Scrolls that *kāabh*, a Hebrew word for 'suffer', was already used, as *kᵉēbh*, in the Aramaic of Jesus' time. So this a good start to reconstructing Jesus' original prediction:

ḥayyābh bar (*e*)*nāsh*(*ā*) *lᵉmikēbh saggī'*

A/the son of man is liable to suffer much

What about 'be rejected'? It is tempting to eliminate this, because in the present form of Mk 8.31 it is closely associated with 'by the elders and the chief priests and the scribes'. The rejection of the son of man is however found also, linked with his suffering much, at Mk 9.12, and there it is said to be written in scripture. In a complex discussion which cannot be repeated here, I have traced this rejection back to Jer. 6.27-30; 7.29, references on either side of the passage on which Jesus preached in the Temple during his last days (Jer. 7.11 is quoted at Mk 11.17).[43] Rejection is mentioned as follows:

41 See further pp. 466–73.
42 See further pp. 471–73.
43 On this preaching see pp. 411–15, and for discussion of the scriptural passages presupposed at Mk 9.12 see briefly pp. 367–68 and, in detail, Casey, *Aramaic Sources of Mark's Gospel*, pp. 126–30.

Refining he refines in vain, and the wicked are not drawn off: they shall be
called rejected silver, for the LORD has rejected them.

(Jer. 6.29-30)

For the LORD has rejected and abandoned the generation of his fury

(Jer. 7.29)

The implication of the use of this material is that Jesus would be rejected by God
when he died, to represent the rejection of Israel, for whom his death would
atone. This was how he felt when he was crucified, and cried out from the first
of the 'psalms of the righteous sufferer':

My God, my God, why have you forsaken me?

(Ps. 22.1, at Mk 15.34)

Moreover, the Aramaic form of Jesus' prediction, in which a/the son of man was
liable to 'be rejected' was likely to be interpreted of rejection by God, because
the passive was commonly used to refer indirectly to the action of God. Hence
someone, probably Mark himself, added 'by the elders and the chief priests and
the scribes'. There was an obvious need for such an 'explicitative' translation, one
which explains what the translator takes the text to really mean. The resulting
saying shows that Jesus was rejected by the Jewish leaders who were responsible for his crucifixion, rather than by God himself, which Mark may have felt
could be drastically misunderstood, in a way that his later quotation of Ps. 22.1
(Mk 15.34) would not. We must therefore add the Aramaic *ūlᵉethbᵉsārāh*, 'and
be rejected', to Jesus' original prediction.

We have seen that the original prediction must have included Jesus' death,
as only this will explain Peter's reaction and Jesus' rebuke of him. In its present
form, however, Mk 8.31 in Greek has 'be killed', and this stretches the general
level of meaning too far. This too should be regarded as an explicitative translation. Jesus will have said *ūlimᵉmāth*, 'and die', and Mark, knowing the Passion
story, will have translated this 'and be killed'. We now have this:

ḥayyābh bar (ᵉ)nāsh(ā) lᵉmikēbh saggī' ūlᵉethbᵉsārāh ūlimᵉmāth

A/the son of man is liable to suffer much and be rejected and die.

This leaves resurrection after three days, and we have already seen that this part
of the prediction must be genuine. We will remember also that the Aramaic word
qūm has a very wide range of meaning, including any sort of rising or getting
up. In this context, therefore, it includes any kind of resurrection of the body or
immortality of the soul. It should be concluded that Jesus said something very
like this:

*ḥayyābh bar (ᵉ)nāsh(ā) lᵉmikēbh saggī' ūlᵉethbᵉsārāh ūlimᵉmāth ūlimᵉqām
bāthar tᵉlāthāh yōmīn*

A/the son of man is liable to suffer much and be rejected and die, and rise after three days.

Given the cultural background in the Jewish scriptures sketched above, this has a perfectly good general level of meaning. At the same time, the idiomatic use of the Aramaic *bar* (*ᵉ*)*nash*(*ā*), 'son of man', was so well established that Simeon the Rock and the other disciples will have been left in no doubt that Jesus intended to put himself in a position where he would be put to death.

One question remains: why did Mark keep repeating an increasingly edited version of this particular prediction? We should infer that Mark knew perfectly well that Jesus used a form of this prediction several times, as he taught the inner group of his disciples before his final days in Jerusalem. The above reconstruction cannot be regarded as Jesus' exact words, but it should be regarded as a close approximation to a prediction which was very important to him and to his closest disciples in the latter part of his ministry.

4f. *Son of Man: The Gospels of Mark, Matthew and Luke*

We are now in a position to see clearly the whole of Mark's use of the Christological title 'the Son of Man' (*ho huios tou anthrōpou*). The production of this title was a natural outcome of the translation of genuine sayings of Jesus from Aramaic into Greek. It would not have been caused in the same way by midrashic use of Dan. 7.13, because the midrashic use of biblical texts is too loose a process to necessitate this. We have seen this in the context of Mk 13.26, where other biblical texts have evidently been employed, but so loosely that we cannot be certain as to which ones. We should note also Rev. 1.7:

> Look! He is coming with the clouds, and every eye will see him, and those who pierced him, and all the tribes of the earth will mourn over him.

Here Dan. 7.13 has been used midrashically with Zech. 12.10-14, but the title 'the Son of man' is not used. If Mark did not know 'the Son of man' (*ho huios tou anthrōpou*) from the translation process, he would have had no reason to produce it at Mk 13.26 or 14.62. It follows that Mark regarded 'the Son of man' as an important Christological term used by Jesus himself in his teaching. This is how Mark came to see it in Dan. 7.13, and thus use it with reference to Jesus' second coming.

This also explains how the pattern according to which Jesus used 'the Son of man' with reference to himself, and without any explanation, came to be established. From Mark's point of view, this was already a feature of genuine sayings of Jesus, and the fact that 'the Son of man' referred to Jesus himself was too obvious for Mark to feel any need for a special explanation of it.

With all this in mind, we can see how natural it was for Mark to use 'the Son of man' in his development of Jesus' predictions of his death. Jesus discussed his forthcoming death in two genuine 'son of man' sayings at Mk 14.21, and we have seen that the prediction of his death in the 'son of man' saying at Mk 8.31 is largely genuine. We have also seen his death referred to, together with that of others, in genuine 'son of man' sayings at Mk 9.12 and 10.45, where the use of the major Christological title 'the Son of man' (*ho huios tou anthrōpou*) would be obvious to everyone, and the general level of meaning lost on uninstructed monoglot Greeks.[44] This means that Mark already knew the major Christological title 'the Son of man' as a feature of sayings in which Jesus looked forward to his atoning death predicted in the scriptures. This explains why Mark used 'the Son of man' in the major predictions at Mk 9.31 and 10.33-34. Both sayings were formed on the basis of existing traditions, creatively rewritten in the light of the events of the Passion. Mark had every reason to retain the Christological title 'the Son of man' as he rewrote these traditions. From his point of view it was both characteristic of bedrock tradition in the sayings of Jesus, and perfectly adapted to the needs of the church.

Similar comments apply to Mk 9.9 and Mk 14.41. Mark 9.9 follows not long after the major 'Son of man' prediction of Jesus' death and Resurrection at Mk 8.31. It is part of a Markan link from the Transfiguration to the genuine Mk 9.11-13, where Jesus comments on the death of John the Baptist, as well as on his own forthcoming death, again using the term 'Son of man' (Mk 9.12):[45]

And as they were going down from the mountain he [Jesus] ordered them [Peter, Jacob and John] not to describe to anyone what they had seen, except whenever the Son of man had risen from the dead.

(Mk 9.9)

The many historical improbabilities in this short piece include the fact that the 'Son of man' saying cannot be reconstructed in Aramaic. Mark clearly wrote it with predictions like Mk 8.31 in mind.

Mark 14.41 was even stranger, as it is fairly clear that Mark wrote something which all the copyists altered, so I can only offer my best guess as to what Mark may have been struggling with. Jesus speaks to the inner circle of his three closest followers, when he finds them asleep for the third time, as he waits to be arrested:

And he came for the third time and said to them, 'Sleep on and rest! (He/It) is far off. The hour has come. Behold! The Son of man is betrayed into the hands of sinners. Get up and let us be going. Behold! He who betrays me is at hand'.

(Mk 14.41-42)

While most of this speech was probably based on something genuine, the 'Son of man' saying cannot be reconstructed in Aramaic and must be regarded as part of Mark's attempt to clarify a source which was difficult to understand, a brave

44   See further pp. 365–69, and pp. 430–32.
45   Cf. pp. 161, 179.

attempt which cannot be regarded as altogether successful because the preceding words remain obscure. The 'Son of man' saying, which is perfectly clear, is directly dependent on Mk 9.31, where 'the Son of man is handed over/betrayed into the hands of men', and Mk 10.33-34, where 'the Son of man will be handed over/betrayed to the chief priests and scribes'. These are Mark's second and third rewritings of a prediction very like that which I have recovered from Mk 8.31, and he will have had Mk 14.21 in mind too.

Mark's handling of the tradition is accordingly quite clear. He inherited and/ or produced 'the Son of man' as a major Christological title in the Greek versions of sayings of Jesus. He therefore continued to use it when he needed to rewrite these traditions as he put together a whole Gospel. He also found it in scripture at Dan. 7.13, and used it in two midrashically composed passages which employ other scriptures as well. He also produced new sayings which were dependent on the sayings which he inherited, some of which he rewrote, and which were not dependent on Dan. 7.13. It is especially important to note that secondary uses of 'the Son of man' are to a large extent due to its use in the Greek translations of genuine sayings of Jesus. It follows that we must be very careful not to infer that most 'Son of man' sayings are genuine simply on the grounds that they are largely confined to sayings attributed to Jesus. The distribution of 'the Son of man' in Mark is partly due to genuine sayings of Jesus, but it is also due to his own secondary use of this term.

The patterns of the usage of 'the Son of man' (*ho huios tou anthrōpou*) established by Mark were inherited and continued by Matthew. He took over some genuine sayings with very little or no editorial changes (e.g. Mk 10.45 at Mt. 20.28; Mk 14.21 at Mt. 26.24). We have seen that he also took over the already rewritten predictions of Jesus' death and Resurrection, and rewrote them further. He also used them to create new sayings of his own when he thought he needed them. For example, Mt. 26.2 begins with Matthew's edited version of Mk 14.1a, now part of a speech by Jesus, and continues with a 'Son of man' saying freely written on the basis of the traditions in Mark:

You know that after two days it is Passover, and the Son of man is handed over to be crucified.

This follows Matthew's rewritten prediction at Mt. 20.19, when he rewrote Mk 10.33-34, putting 'crucify' in place of 'kill' to make the prediction closer to subsequent events.

Matthew also recognized the use of Dan. 7.13 at Mk 13.26, and developed the saying much further. This development included a second 'Son of man' saying, which made midrashic use of Isa. 11.12, as well as material from Zech. 12.10-14 (Mt. 24.30):

And then the sign of the Son of man will appear in heaven, and then all the tribes of the earth will mourn and they will see the Son of man coming on the clouds of heaven with power and much glory.

With the words 'on the clouds of heaven' Matthew has made his use of Dan. 7.13 more precise than that of Mark. This shows that he was very happy to find this Christological title in that text. His use of the title creatively in a new saying, with use of Isa. 11.12, shows that he was delighted with it.

So does the fact that he uses it no less than 30 times. He inherited some of his non-Markan sayings from 'Q' material. Three of these are genuine sayings of Jesus: I have discussed Mt. 8.20//Lk. 9.58 and Mt. 11.19//Lk. 7.34, and more briefly Mt. 12.32//Lk. 12.10 (cf. Mk 3.28-29).[46] Other Matthaean 'Son of man' sayings from 'Q' material are not genuine sayings of Jesus, and they have no general level of meaning. At least the majority of them originated in Greek.

For example, in two sayings from 'Q' material, a comparison is made between the days of Noah and the days (Luke) or parousia (Matthew) of the Son of man. The Matthaean version runs as follows:

> For like the days of Noah, so shall the parousia of the Son of man be. For as in the days before the Flood they were eating and drinking, marrying and giving in marriage, until the day Noah entered the ark, and they did not know until the Flood came and destroyed everyone, so shall the parousia of the Son of man be.
>
> (Mt. 24.37-39, cf. Lk. 17.26-27)

Here Matthew's Greek term *parousia* refers to the second coming of Jesus, which is evidently expected some time after the end of his historic ministry. This makes excellent sense in the Gospels as they now stand. In both of them, the term 'the Son of man' is a title of Jesus alone. They both hoped fervently for his second coming, which is anticipated here, and which was a major need of the early church, as we know from Acts and the Epistles. Both evangelists also wrote for churches which were small minorities between the Jewish and Gentile worlds, and consequently they were happy to contemplate judgement on the rest of the world, as in the days of the Flood. The saying therefore has an excellent setting in the Gospel tradition, and was naturally rewritten by both evangelists because it was existentially relevant to their current situation. A satisfactory Aramaic reconstruction cannot be made, because the Aramaic term *bar* (*e*)*nāsh(ā)* always has a general level of meaning, which cannot be found in an Aramaic reconstruction of this verse. There is no natural Aramaic equivalent of Matthew's *parousia* either. Moreover, the reference to Jesus' second coming has no setting in the teaching of Jesus, who hoped for the coming of the kingdom and did not look into the distant future for his own return.

In addition to sayings from Mark and from 'Q' material, some of which he rewrote, Matthew has a number of secondary sayings of his own, all with an eschatological setting. For example, he introduces the parable of the sheep and the goats like this:

---

46   See pp. 253–54, 362–65, and pp. 528–29.

When the Son of man comes in his glory and all the angels with him, then he will sit on the throne of his glory, and all the nations shall be gathered before him . . .

(Mt. 25.31-32a)

This is set at the second coming of Jesus, and goes on to depict the final judgement. 'The Son of man' is a title of Jesus, and the saying has no possible general level of meaning. Several details again recall Dan. 7.13-14. The use of 'the Son of man' with 'comes' is sufficient to indicate dependence on this text. The term 'glory' is used at Dan. 7.14, and in more general terms, the whole scene is quite glorious. There are plural 'thrones' at Dan. 7.9, and the accompanying angels may also be seen round the throne of God at Dan. 7.9-10, and bringing the Son of man at Dan. 7.13. 'All the nations' at Mt. 25.32 could also be taken from Dan. 7.14.

It follows from all this that 'the Son of man' (*ho huios tou anthrōpou*) was an important title for Matthew in Greek. He was happy to inherit what he took to be sayings of Jesus from both Mark and from 'Q', and he increased them greatly with enthusiastic stress on eschatological events, which he expected to take place soon.

The patterns of the usage of 'the Son of man' (*ho huios tou anthrōpou*) established by Mark were also inherited and continued by Luke, with some further developments which differ significantly from those of Matthew. Like Matthew, Luke took over two authentic sayings from Mark without significant change (Mk 2.10 at Lk. 5.24; Mk 2.28 at Lk. 6.5, though leaving out 2.27). He dropped two genuine sayings, when omitting whole passages which he did not like (Mk 9.12; 10.45). Luke rewrote the predictions of Jesus' death and Resurrection which Mark had already rewritten. He even had the angels in the empty tomb 'remind' the women of a prediction so rewritten as to help him change the tradition of Resurrection appearances in Galilee to his tradition of appearances in Jerusalem (Lk. 24.6-7).[47]

Luke was particularly concerned to ensure that Jesus be thought to have predicted his second coming only in Luke's own time, not earlier. So before editing the prediction of Jesus' second coming at Mk 13.26, he radically re-edited the eschatological discourse of Mark 13 to make clear reference to the fall of Jerusalem, some time before the second coming:

Now when you see Jerusalem surrounded by armies, then know that its desolation is at hand . . . and they will be imprisoned among all the nations, and Jerusalem will be trampled by nations, until the times of nations are fulfilled . . . and then they will see the Son of man coming in a cloud with power and much glory.

(Lk. 21.20, 24, 27)

We can still see the influence of Dan. 7.13 here, but whether Luke did so is

---

47   See p. 378, and further pp. 463–64.

uncertain. He has altered Mark's 'in clouds' to the singular 'in a cloud', to make clear reference to a literal interpretation of his ascension narrative, which he would publish in his second volume (Acts 1.9, 11, cf. Lk. 24.51).

Luke was more obviously unconcerned about referring to Dan. 7.13 when he removed the eschatological orientation of Mk 14.62, part of a radical re-editing of Jesus' 'trial' before Joseph Caiaphas, probably with the help of another source:

> But from now the Son of man will be seated on the right of the power of God.
>
> (Lk. 22.69)

Here Luke has omitted 'you will see', and with it the notion that his judges would see the Son of man, and he omitted the coming with the clouds of heaven, so the second coming has been removed altogether from this passage, and with it all trace of Dan. 7.13. In its place, Luke declares that *from now* the Son of man will be sitting on the right of the power of God. This replaces a supposedly future event which had not happened with an exalted present state which cannot be falsified. It is all the more remarkable that Luke has retained the title 'the Son of man'. He evidently considered it to be an important title of Jesus, and not one which should be especially associated with eschatological events which had not occurred. Nonetheless, just as he used it in eschatological contexts where he makes clear that the coming of the Son of man was never intended to take place as soon as it was expected, so he produced a new 'Son of man' saying with reference to the situation when all the final earthly events are completed (Lk. 21.36). Here the believer will finally stand 'before the Son of man'. Luke's continued use of this title shows how important it was to him.

Like Matthew, Luke inherited some of his non-Markan sayings from the 'Q' material. Some of these are genuine sayings of Jesus. I have discussed Mt. 8.20// Lk. 9.58 and Mt. 11.19//Lk. 7.34, and I have noted Mt. 12.32//Lk. 12.10 (cf. Mk 3.28-29), and Lk. 12.8-9//Mt. 10.32-33 (with Mk 8.38).[48] Like Matthew, Luke also transmits from 'Q' material other 'Son of man' sayings which are not genuine sayings of Jesus. I have discussed Mt. 24.37-39, which forms part of Matthew's eschatological discourse, in which Matthew re-edited Mark 13 to further intensify the church's expectation that the end was at hand, complete with Jesus' second coming.[49] Luke put his version of these 'Q' sayings in an earlier discourse. Jesus begins by making quite clear that the end was *not* at hand when these sayings were spoken, and Luke includes a 'Son of man' saying of his own, together with another rewritten version of Jesus' prediction of his passion:

> Now being asked by the Pharisees when the kingdom of God was coming, he answered them and said, 'The kingdom of God does not come with watch-ing, nor will they say "Look, here!", or "There", for look! The kingdom of

---

48   See pp. 253–54, 362–65, and pp. 470–71, 528–29.
49   See p. 384.

God is among you.' But he said to the disciples, 'The days will come when you will desire to see one of the days of the Son of man, and you will not see (it) . . . for as the flashing lightning shines from under the heaven to under the heaven, so will the Son of man be. But first he must suffer much and be rejected by this generation. And as it was in the days of Noah, so it will be in the days of the Son of man. They ate, drank, married, were given in marriage, until the day Noah entered the ark and the Flood came and destroyed everyone . . .'

(Lk. 17.20-22, 24–27)

This shows that Luke was very happy with the title 'the Son of man'. He transmitted genuine sayings of Jesus, and he freely edited them when he thought this was desirable, especially in making clear that the second coming of Jesus should not have been expected during or soon after the period of the historic ministry. In doing this, he created some new sayings as well.

Luke also has a few independent sayings of his own, though fewer than Matthew, and not necessarily with an eschatological setting. For example, at the end of the story of Zacchaeus, a chief tax-collector who repents and promises to make restitution, Luke has Jesus announce salvation for Zacchaeus' house. Jesus then concludes with a saying in which he explains his own function:

For the Son of man came to seek and save the lost.

(Lk. 19.10)

This cannot be an original saying in its present form, because it has no reasonable general level of meaning. The saying makes excellent sense in Greek, for by this time 'the Son of man' was an unambiguous title of Jesus. Moreover, it correctly represents a significant aspect of the ministry of the historical Jesus, and it has an excellent setting at the end of this story.

It follows from all this that Luke regarded 'the Son of man' (*ho huios tou anthrōpou*) as a wonderful title of Jesus. Consequently, he used it no less than 25 times. He transmitted sayings of Jesus which he inherited, and rewrote and edited them when he saw fit to do so, especially to remove any impression that Jesus' second coming should have taken place before his time. He also produced a few new sayings, some of which have no particular eschatological orientation.

We must therefore conclude that we read the work of the synoptic evangelists at the end of a complex process of development. The historical Jesus used the Aramaic term *bar* (*ᵉ*)*nāsh*(*ā*), 'son of man', in a number of sayings in which he presented significant aspects of his life and teaching. In these sayings, the term *bar* (*ᵉ*)*nāsh*(*ā*) was an ordinary Aramaic term for 'man', used in a particular idiom in which the speaker spoke of himself, or himself and other people made obvious by the context, in an indirect way. There was however no such idiom in Greek, so the translators of sayings of Jesus adopted a strategy. They used *ho huios tou anthrōpou*, 'the Son of man' in Greek when the original Aramaic term was *bar* (*ᵉ*)*nāsh*(*ā*), and it was this which first turned it into a Christological title. Mark was very pleased with this title. He found it in Dan. 7.13, and formed new sayings both with this term and in further developments of the original sayings which he rewrote.

Matthew and Luke enthusiastically continued this process. As well as inheriting a small number of genuine sayings of Jesus from the 'Q' material as well as from Mark, they continued to rewrite genuine sayings and to form new sayings of their own. The result of this process is that, when we read the synoptic Gospels, we encounter a major Christological title which was unknown to the historical Jesus, used in more secondary sayings than in genuine sayings of Jesus.

5. Son of God

Of all the Christological titles, it is 'the Son of God' in which Jesus' deity has most often been seen. In the Fourth Gospel, this is right. For example, after Jesus has healed a man on the sabbath, 'the Jews sought all the more to kill Jesus, because he not only abrogated the Sabbath, but also called God his own Father, making himself equal with God' (Jn 5.18). Whereas Jesus justifies his action in appearing to break the sabbath, he does not attempt to answer any charge that he called God his own Father, or made himself equal with God, and he refers to himself as 'the Son' no less than eight times in the immediately following verses (Jn 5.19-26). Similarly at Jn 10.33ff., when 'the Jews' threaten to stone Jesus for blasphemy, and on the ground that he makes himself God, Jesus does not deny the charge but justifies his position, asserting as he does so 'I am the Son of God', and 'the Father (is) in me and I (am) in the Father'. This document portrays Jesus as the Son of God because he is God incarnate.[50]

In the synoptic Gospels, however, the term 'son of God' can be found with its original meaning in Jesus' Jewish environment. To find it, secondary material must once more be set on one side. One major point is the rarity of the term in the earliest sources, a quite different situation from the use of the term 'Son of man'. Jesus refers to himself as 'the Son' only once in Mark (13.32), and three times in a single saying in the 'Q' material (Mt. 11.27//Lk. 10.22), compared with 23 occurrences attributed to Jesus in the Fourth Gospel. The synoptic evangelists have more examples than are found in the teaching of Jesus in Mark (one) and the 'Q' material (three), but fewer than John: taking each Gospel as a whole, Mark has 7 examples, Luke 12, Matthew 17 and John 28. These basic facts further clarify the tendency of the tradition to insert a title which Christians were using by the time that the Gospels were written. Matthew can be seen at work: four of his 17 examples are inserted into passages of Mark which he largely copied (Mt. 14.33; 16.16; 27.40, 43). Thus the observable tendency of the tradition confirms the evidence of the distribution of this term, and its known setting in the early church, to show that as a major Christological title it belongs to the early church rather than the Jesus of history.

---

50   See further pp. 516–19.

These overall factors must not be lost sight of in considering the two sayings which are attributed to Jesus at Mk 13.32 and Mt. 11.27//Lk. 10.22. Both use the term 'the Son' in an absolute sense as an exalted Christological title. If Jesus had held this belief and found this usage appropriate, he was bound to have used the term more often, and a church which can be shown to have increased such usage within the synoptic tradition would not have failed to transmit a larger number of genuine sayings. Moreover, both sayings have an excellent setting in the early church.

Mark 13.32 arose from the delay of Jesus' second coming:

But concerning that day or that hour no-one knows, neither the angels in heaven nor the Son, but only the Father.

In its present context this saying clearly refers to the time of the End, including Jesus' second coming (Mk 13.26),[51] and it is difficult to see how it could ever have referred to anything else. It is evident from the epistles that some Christians had been expecting the End to come immediately for some years. In this respect they continued the expectation of Jesus himself, and we have seen that this view arises naturally out of the dynamics of Jewish expectation of the establishment of the kingdom of God.[52] We have also seen that Jesus' sayings predicted the coming of the kingdom in the near future, without giving any precise date: the church was therefore bound to deduce that Jesus had not known the time, provided only that they could face this information. In those days, the Son's ignorance was much easier to face than the delay of his second coming. No one had yet produced the idea that the Son knew everything. The delay of his second coming, however, confronted the church inescapably. Mark 13.32 meets this as well as possible. The Son is mentioned after the angels as the highest possible figure, the use of the absolute term 'the Son' balancing, as well as could be, the assertion of his ignorance. Matthew, also expecting the second coming soon, but later than expected and without a definite date in the tradition, kept this saying in his eschatological discourse (Mt. 24.36). Luke, however, with the delay of the parousia a serious problem, and determined as he was to present earlier Christian expectation that it should have come previously as a mistake, dropped the saying altogether.

Matthew 11.27//Lk. 10.22 is also untypical of the teaching of Jesus. The Matthaean form may be translated as follows:

All things have been given to me by my Father, and no-one knows the Son except the Father, nor does anyone know the Father except the Son, and anyone to whom the Son wishes to reveal him.

Here too, the use of the absolute term 'the Son' shows that the saying originated in the early church. Some aspects of it are strongly reminiscent of the Fourth Gospel, especially the correlation of the Son with the Father, and the position of

51 See pp. 69–71, 374–75.
52 See pp. 214–23.

the Son as the unique and necessary revealer of the Father. Hence this saying has been known at least since 1876 as 'the thunderbolt from the Johannine sky'.[53] Its function is to declare that knowledge of God is impossible except through Jesus. This view does not have a satisfactory setting in the teaching of the historical Jesus, for it necessarily implies that Jews in the diaspora, and any other Jews who could not go and hear Jesus preach, did not know God. When the Gentile mission was successfully under way, however, members of the churches believed that Christians rather than Jews formed the covenant community, and that Jesus was essential for salvation. In that setting, this is what the saying expresses. Christians know the Son, and therefore also the Father, while Jews who do not know the Son do not know the Father either. Non-Christian Jews are therefore rejected. Thus the saying was a serious step towards the Johannine community's Christology, and towards their rejection of 'the Jews'.

Possibly genuine uses of similar terms may be reflected in a summary statement at Mk 3.11:

> And the unclean spirits, whenever they saw him, used to fall down before him and cry out, saying that 'you are the son of God'.

This corresponds to the use of terms such as 'son of God' for wise and righteous individuals. The logic of this description was well expressed some 200 years before the historic ministry:

> be like a father to orphans, and in place of a husband to widows; and God will call you 'son', and be gracious to you and save you from the Pit.
>
> (Sir. 4.10)

This is a clear presentation of the connection between being a faithful Jew and sonship of God.

A striking example is found in a later source, but it is likely to be much earlier in date even than the rabbis named. It concerns the charismatic Ḥanina ben Dosa, and it says nothing that could not have been said in Judaism at the time of Jesus:

> According to Rab Judah, Rab said: Every day a heavenly voice (*bath qol*) goes forth from Mt Ḥoreb and says, 'The whole world is sustained on account of Ḥaninah my son, and Ḥaninah my son is content with a kab of carobs from sabbath eve to sabbath eve.'
>
> (b. Berakoth 17b//Taanith 24b//Hullin 86a)

This may give some people the impression that Ḥanina was son of God in a special or even unique sense, but its cultural context dictates the interpretation that Ḥanina, being a son of God like many other people, is being singled out for especial praise, not ontological uniqueness.

---

53 This description is attributed to K. von Hase, *Geschichte Jesu: nach akademischen Vorlesungen* (Leipzig: Breitkopf und Härtel, 1876), p. 422 (n.v.).

Such evidence is sufficient to show that Jesus could have been called a son of God by anyone who thought that he was a particularly righteous person. Given his ability as an exorcist, people who believed themselves possessed by evil might well use the term of so obviously holy and effective a figure. This would also be consistent with the story of the demoniac who called Jesus 'a/the holy one of God' (Mk 1.24). On the other hand, a Christian storyteller had the Gadarene demoniac address Jesus as 'son of God Most High' (Mk 5.7), which Luke retained (Lk. 8.28), while Matthew, abbreviating the story considerably but doubling the number of demoniacs, has them address Jesus more briefly as 'Son of God' (Mt. 8.29). It is possible that the Markan summary statement at Mk 3.11, according to which 'the unclean spirits' used to cry out 'you are the Son of God', is also due to Mark or the early church, making up for the meagre quantity of primary tradition about Jesus' sonship by attributing this knowledge to supernatural beings who could not help making it known. This fits with other material which has been drawn into Mark's 'Messianic secret'.

The only genuine use of such a term by Jesus himself is in the third person at Mk 12.6. This is part of an important parable (Mk 12.1-11), which Jesus told during his final visit to Jerusalem.[54] This parable takes up from Isaiah 5 the imagery of Israel as a vineyard, and has the owner of the vineyard let it to tenants. In due course, the owner sends messengers to the tenants, who maltreat all of them (the messengers) and kill some of them. This is an image of God sending the prophets to the people of Israel, who had never heeded them, and whose leaders were believed to have killed several of them. The parable continues, 'He still had one (person), a beloved son. He sent him to them last. He said, "They will respect my son"' (Mk 12.6). The tenants put him to death. This is an image of Jesus, who was expecting to be put to death by the chief priests and their associates. It fits with all the evidence that Jesus regarded himself as God's final and most important messenger to Israel, and it is in this light that it should be understood. Jesus' parabolic description of himself as 'a beloved son' owes something to Jesus' vision at his baptism. During this vision, Jesus experienced God addressing him 'my son the beloved'.[55] In first-century Judaism this description meant that Jesus was a faithful Jew chosen by God to do for Israel something that mattered. This was of obvious importance to him, and that is why he took it up in an important parable.

I therefore conclude that Jesus' sonship of God was important to him during the historic ministry, when Jesus believed that he was God's final messenger to Israel, and of fundamental importance in this role. At that time, however, the term 'the Son', or 'the Son of God', was not in use as a major Christological title. It may possibly have been used by demoniacs in its more ordinary sense of a faithful Jew. It was developed as a major Christological title by Jesus' followers during the period of the early church. It was used by all four evangelists. In the Fourth Gospel, it is used to present Jesus' deity, the use which has been of central importance to Christians ever since.

---

54   See pp. 417–22.
55   See pp. 176–77.

6. *Messiah, or Christ*

'Christ' is the English form of the New Testament Greek title *Christos*. This was originally the Greek translation of the Hebrew and Aramaic words 'Messiah', or 'anointed', (*ham*)*māshīaḥ* in Hebrew, *meshīḥā* in Aramaic. This term *Christos*, or 'Christ', was virtually a name of Jesus already in the New Testament period. It is very common in the Pauline epistles, and it is used of Jesus in every New Testament document except 3 John. The Aramaic and Hebrew term, 'Messiah', moreover, is familiar to students of Jewish tradition. For centuries, many Jewish people have expected the Messiah. They have disputed with Christians because they suppose that Jesus was not the Messiah, but everyone has generally assumed that the expectation of the Messiah was there for him to fulfil. Our oldest Gospel sources, however, have a grave peculiarity. Mark's seven occurrences of 'Christ' do not include a single example of Jesus using the term with reference to himself, and the word 'Christ' does not occur in the 'Q' material at all. This strongly suggests that Jesus did not apply the term 'Messiah' to himself, even though the early church applied it to him abundantly.

Did Jesus then not believe that he was 'the Messiah'? Traditional Christian scholarship has affirmed that he did, and has used Mark's Gospel as the basis of an explanation of why he did not use the term itself. The confession of Peter has been fundamental to this view. In response to Jesus' question, 'Whom do *you* say that I am?', Peter is reported to have declared 'You are the Christ' (Mk 8.29). Mark does not record Jesus saying either 'I am' or 'I am not', but continues 'And he sternly charged them to tell no-one about him.' In 1976, a sound Christian commentator expressed briefly, though with caution, the essence of the traditional view:

> On the lips of Peter the title 'Christ' would have referred to the messianic Son of David . . . The coming of a Davidic Messiah, who would restore the political fortunes of Israel and establish her national supremacy over the world, was a widespread hope . . . The political implications of the title probably explain why Jesus does not appear to have appropriated it during his ministry . . .[56]

Many scholars have argued that the 'political implications' of 'the title' constituted the sole and sufficient reason for Jesus not to have used it. He did not want to be misunderstood, he did not want to cause a Zealot revolt. Therefore he did not openly accept the title until the time of his humiliation when he could safely and rightly claim it in front of those who would not believe him, let alone revolt for him. Hence the scene at his 'trial' before Joseph Caiaphas:[57]

> Again the high priest asked him and said to him, 'Are you the Christ, the Son of the Blessed?' But Jesus said, 'I am, and you will see the Son of man sitting

---

56   H. Anderson, *The Gospel of Mark* (New Century Bible. London: Oliphants, 1976), p. 214.
57   On this see further pp. 344–46, 440–43.

on the right of The Power and coming with the clouds of heaven.'

(Mk 14.61-62)

Even here, the acceptance of the title 'Messiah' or 'Christ' is at once modified by the use of the term 'Son of man'.

This view has often been challenged from a more radical perspective. In view of the absence of the term from the earliest sources of Jesus' teaching and the repeated injunctions to silence in Mark's Gospel, it has been argued that Jesus did not believe that he was the Messiah, and that the 'Messianic secret' was a device used by Mark to explain why Jesus was not recognized and confessed as Messiah during his ministry. This radical view, which stems from a ground-breaking book by Wilhelm Wrede in 1901, has never been able to explain why the church proclaimed Jesus as Messiah so soon, with a term which was clearly widespread.[58]

The whole subject has been transformed by the discovery and publication of the Dead Sea Scrolls, though it remains controversial because of the persistence of the traditional Christian view, that Jesus was 'the Messiah' and knew this, but did not publicize it. It should now be clear that 'the Messiah' was not a title in the Judaism of Jesus' time, and that the term 'Messiah' or 'anointed' *on its own* was *not specific enough* to refer to the Messianic son of David, nor indeed to any single individual.

Anointing was not confined to Davidic kings: priests and prophets could be anointed as well, and the term could be used metaphorically. For example, at 1 Kgs 19.16 Elijah is instructed by God to anoint Elisha as a prophet instead of himself; at Lev. 4.3, the high priest is called 'the anointed priest'; and at Isa. 45.1, the Persian king Cyrus is referred to as 'his anointed', that is, God's anointed.

Thus it is natural that both the future Davidic king and other figures could be referred to with the term 'Messiah', or 'anointed'. For example, the Qumran community expected an eschatological high priest as well as a king of David's line, and they could refer to them both together as 'anointed ones' (or 'Messiahs') 'of Aaron and Israel'(1 QS IX, 11). Old Testament prophets could be referred to as 'anointed ones' (1 QM XI, 7, cf. Ps. 105.15), while in 11Q Melchizedek a figure subordinate to Melchizedek is referred to as 'anointed'.

We must infer from this general usage that anyone who wanted to refer to the future Davidic king would have to do more than use the one word 'Messiah', or 'anointed' to make their meaning clear. A good example of this comes from a Dead Sea scroll which includes this comment on Gen. 49.10:

While Israel has sovereignty there shall [not] be cut off one who sits on the throne for David (Jer. 33.17). For the 'staff' is the covenant of the kingship,

---

58 W. Wrede, *The Messianic Secret* (1901. Trans. J. C. G. Greig. Cambridge: James Clarke, 1971). For a survey of the debate begun by Wrede see J. D. Kingsbury, *The Christology of Mark's Gospel* (Philadelphia: Fortress, 1983), ch. 2, and see further H. Räisänen, *The 'Messianic Secret' in Mark* (1976. Trans. C. Tuckett, Edinburgh: T&T Clark, 1990); C. Tuckett (ed.), *The Messianic Secret* (London/Philadelphia: SPCK/Fortress, 1983).

> [the thous]ands of Israel are the 'divisions', until there comes the Anointed/
> Messiah (*mshīḥ*) of Righteousness, the Branch of David. For to him and to
> his seed was granted the covenant of kingship of his people for everlasting
> generations
>
> (4Q252 V, 1–4)

Here, after setting up 'one who sits on the throne for David' with great clarity in
the context, the author still felt the need for a run of full four Hebrew words to
identify 'the Anointed/Messiah of Righteousness, the Branch of David'.

In the light of all this, we need to be very careful about the interpretation
of Qumran passages such as for example 1QSa II, 11–21, from which these are
some extracts:

> . . . when [God] begets the Messiah/Anointed (*hmshīḥ*) among them, [] shall
> come . . . [at] the head of all the congregation of Israel and all [his brethren,
> the sons of] Aaron the priests . . . And afterwards [the Mess]iah/[Anoin]ted
> of Israel shall [] . . . And [when] they gather for the community [tab]le . . .
> let [no] man [extend] his hand over the first-fruits of bread and [new wine]
> before the Priest . . . And afterwa[rds], the Messiah/Anointed (*mshīḥ*) of Israel
> shall [ext]end his hands over the bread . . .

At first sight, the first occurrence of 'Messiah/Anointed (*hmshīḥ*) appears to be
an example of the use of 'Messiah' on its own as a title. We must however be
careful not to generalize from this, partly for the reasons already given, and
partly because of the context. This was written within and for the Qumran community, who shared an expectation of two anointed figures, of whom the future
high priest was the more important. Moreover, the author(s) had already set up
a more specific context, including all this:

> This is the rule for all the congregation of Israel at the end of days, when they
> join [the community to wa]lk according to the law of the sons of Zadok the
> priests and of the men of their Covenant . . . All the wi[se] of the congrega-
> tion . . . the perfect of way and the men of might . . . these are the men of
> the Name, the members of the assembly called at an appointed time of those
> designated to the council of the community in Israel before the face of the
> sons of Zadok the priests . . . [This the ass]embly of the men of the Name
> [called] to assembly for the Council of the Community, when [God] begets
> the Messiah/Anointed (*hmshīḥ*) among them. [] shall come . . . [at] the head
> of all the congregation of Israel and all [his brethren, the sons of] Aaron the
> priests . . .
>
> (1QSa I, 1–2, 27–28; II, 1–3, 11–13)

This sets up a great eschatological occasion. Members of the Qumran sect would
hear it in accordance with their expectations, some of which are clear to modern
scholars. It is clear that the Messiah/Anointed of Israel is a very important person
at the End of Days, and it is equally clear that 'the Priest' is superior to him.

Moreover, this is natural for a community among whom 'the sons of Zadok the priests' were so important, and it fits perfectly with everything we know about the two expected anointed figures, of whom the Messiah/Anointed of Aaron is the superior, whenever a text provides sufficient information about their relative status.

What is less clear is exactly who is referred to with the words 'when [God] begets the Messiah/Anointed (*hmshīh*) among them' (1QSa II, 11–12). Some scholars think this is the Messiah of Israel, others that it is the priestly Messiah.[59] This further underlines the main point, that at this stage of the development of Messianic hopes in Judaism, more than the one word Messiah/Anointed is needed to make clear who is meant. Yet this is in the middle of a passage with a full context provided by the subculture of the Qumran community, and by the (somewhat fragmentary but nonetheless real) literary context of this document. This is all lacking in Peter's confession at Mk 8.29, and the context provided at Mk 14.61-62 is not adequate either.

In general, therefore, the term 'anointed' or 'Messiah' was not specific enough to refer to the Davidic king without further qualification. This situation changed after the destruction of Jerusalem in 70 CE, when Judaism no longer had any prophets nor any anointed high priests officiating in the Temple, and Jewish hopes of deliverance crystallized around the traditional expectation of a future Davidic king. After years of this, Jews did eventually call this figure who would deliver them 'King Messiah', or 'the Anointed King', or even simply 'the Messiah'.

This provides a straightforward historical explanation of the fact that Jesus did not apply the term 'Messiah' to himself. The term was not sufficiently meaningful on its own, and it was not necessary for a figure who was playing a fundamental role in the salvation of Israel to produce a longer formulation containing it. We must therefore accept the radical view that passages such as Mk 8.29-30 were produced by the early church. Peter cannot have said 'You are a/the Anointed/ Messiah' as a major confession of Jesus' position and role because the term 'a/the Anointed/ Messiah' was not specific enough to be used in such a confession. The confession has however an excellent setting in the early church. The Messianic secret in Mark's Gospel appears to solve the problem of why this central term is absent from Jesus' own teaching. Peter's confession corrects the authentic and favourable verdicts of outsiders that Jesus was Elijah or one of the prophets (Mk 8.28), and balances the account of Jesus' rebuke of Peter in the following verses.[60] We have seen that the same applies to the high priest's question and Jesus' answer at his 'trial'.[61] From Mark's point of view, Jesus' open and public acceptance that he was the Christ brought the Messianic secret to an end.

One question remains outstanding. If the radical view is right in this instance, so that Jesus did not believe that he was a figure called 'the Messiah', and Peter did not confess him as such, how do we explain the widespread and early

---

59 Respectively, e.g. J. A. Fitzmyer, *The One Who Is to Come* (Grand Rapids: Eerdmans, 2007), pp. 92–93; Vermes, *Complete Dead Sea Scrolls in English*, p. 161.

60 See further pp. 356, 377–78.

61 See pp. 375–77.

application of 'Christ' to Jesus? It is not sufficient to refer to Jesus' condemnation as 'king of the Jews' (cf. Mk 15.2ff., esp. 15.26).[62] This was the 'charge' fixed on his cross, and it represents a successful charge of sedition before the Roman governor, who effectively crucified Jesus as a bandit, together with two other bandits.[63] We should probably also accept the authenticity of Mk 15.32, where chief priests and scribes are said to have mocked him, calling him 'the Christ, the king of Israel'. This could easily be a translation of the Aramaic 'the anointed king of Israel' (*malkā mᵉshīḥā dīsrāēl*), a use of the Aramaic term 'anointed' (*mᵉshīḥā*) in a way that makes perfectly good sense. In their expression 'the anointed king of Israel', the words 'king of Israel' provide precisely that definition so conspicuously absent from passages such as Mk 8.29. This is not however sufficient to explain why the disciples should have taken up the term 'anointed' and used it so much after Jesus' death and Resurrection. On the contrary, only the general use of 'anointed' noted above prevents this from being a reason why they should have avoided it.

The earliest followers of Jesus can however be seen beginning to use this term in the early speeches of Acts. One significant factor was precisely its broad range, because of which it might be used by Jesus' followers at any time, *without* necessarily carrying connotations of Davidic kingship. This use of the verb 'to anoint' is found at Acts 10.38, where Peter introduces his summary of Jesus' ministry by saying that God 'anointed' (*echrisen*) Jesus with Holy Spirit and power. The term 'anointed', that is, 'Messiah', or 'Christ', was also available in the scriptures. Moreover, it did not have to be tied to a Davidic king, especially not with the very flexible methods of interpreting the Bible available at the time. The term is found for example in Ps. 2.1-2, quoted in a prayer at Acts 4.24-30:

> Master, you who made the heaven and the earth . . . who said through the Holy Spirit through the mouth of our father David your servant, 'Why did Gentiles rage, and peoples imagine vain things? The kings of the earth stood up and the rulers were gathered together against the Lord and against his Christ' (*Christou*, translating the Hebrew *mᵉshīḥō*). For there were truly gathered together in this city against your holy servant Jesus, whom you anointed (*echrisas*), Herod and Pontius Pilate . . .
>
> (Acts 4.24, 25–27)

Here the term 'Christ' has been taken from scripture, and interpreted of Jesus. While no particular moment is mentioned, the meaning is the metaphorical anointing of Jesus by God in preparation for his ministry as a whole, so this is consistent with Peter's use of the verb to 'anoint' to introduce his summary of Jesus' ministry at Acts 10.38.

At Acts 2.36, the Messiahship and Lordship of Jesus are dated from the Resurrection:

---

62   E.g. N. A. Dahl, 'The Crucified Messiah' (1960), rev. ET in N. A. Dahl, *The Crucified Messiah and Other Essays* (Minneapolis: Augsburg, 1974), pp. 10–36, esp. 23–28.
63   See pp. 443–53.

So let the whole house of Israel know with certainty that God has made him Lord and Christ (*Christon*), this Jesus whom you crucified.

The reference to 'the whole house of Israel' underlines the fact that, however much later this account was written down by Luke, it is nonetheless a basically accurate account of a movement which was still within Judaism. In its original context, the view that Jesus was made 'Christ/Messiah/Anointed' at his Resurrection was perfectly logical. Jesus could reasonably be perceived as becoming Lord when he was exalted to the right hand of God, anointed to rule and to come again soon for the final deliverance of his people. However, the term 'Christ' was more likely to crystallize eventually round the beginning of the earthly ministry, because of the importance of the earthly ministry for salvation history. Moreover, as Jesus became the Son of God in a special sense and rose towards deity, the pinpointing of the Resurrection as his point of entry into Lordship was bound to seem less appropriate. In the early speeches of Acts, when pre-existence, Sonship and deity had not yet been developed, we find formulations which refer to each possible point of reference correctly left unreconciled.

Taking account of the features of these early speeches which indicate their genuineness, we must follow Luke in seeing the use of the verb 'to anoint' and the use of the term 'Messiah', translated into Greek as *Christos*, as a term which referred particularly to Jesus, as a development which took place in the earliest period of the church. How far, and how early, the Aramaic noun *mᵉshīḥā* became a title, or the equivalent of a name, we can no longer tell, because our earliest source for the earliest period of the history of the churches, Luke's Acts, was written in fluent educated literary Greek half a century later. What we can say is that there was nothing to prevent this development from taking place, and that all but two of the factors visible in the later Greek-speaking church were already of fundamental importance long before Paul wrote his epistles.

The most important positive feature was the nature of the ministry of Jesus himself. Here I simply summarize the main points discussed at length throughout this book. Jesus believed that he was appointed by God as his final messenger to call upon Israel to return to God before he established his kingdom. At his baptism, he experienced a vision in which God effectively appointed him for this task, saying, 'You are my son, the beloved, in you I am well pleased' (Mk 1.11). He healed many people and cast out demons, which he saw as the power of God working through him to defeat the powers of Satan. He taught the people, in accordance with the will of God working through him. He saw his ministry, including his atoning death, prefigured by God in the scriptures.

The second positive feature is that many Jewish people were expecting an anointed figure to redeem them. When added to the first positive feature, this is sufficient. From the point of view of Jesus' followers, he was anointed by God, as soon as that particular vocabulary occurred to them. Moreover, they believed that Jesus' ministry was completely successful. At this point, the variety and flexibility of Jewish expectations is important. Jesus' followers would not be tempted to imagine he was a failure because he was not a successful military leader, or because he was crucified. He did not claim to be any kind of king or military leader, he predicted his death, he taught them how his death was foretold by God in the scriptures, and in cleansing the Temple he precipitated his death. Then he waited in Gethsemane to be betrayed. That was success in his chosen destiny, not failure.

The third positive feature was Jesus' Resurrection. The belief of Jesus' followers that he had risen from the dead *confirmed* what they *already knew* from the historic ministry. Apart from the question as to how it might be explained, Jesus' Resurrection could not have been enough on its own, because anointed figures were not otherwise expected to die and rise again. On the contrary, such belief was necessary in the case of Jesus alone, because he predicted his death and Resurrection during the historic ministry. Jesus' followers believed that he died in accordance with God's will *and* rose again (e.g. Acts 2.22-24). This made him quite different from any other anointed figure in whom Jewish people might believe.

Two negative factors were also important. In the light of Jesus' ministry, his followers were not expecting any other anointed figure to come. On the contrary, the standard expectation that God would send such a figure was shifted straight onto the risen Jesus to form the expectation that God would send him from heaven (e.g. Acts 4.20-26). In due course, this became the conventional Christian hope for his second coming. Moreover, whereas Joseph Caiaphas might be thought of as the anointed high priest, Jesus' opposition to the chief priests and to the way the Temple was run, now seen in the light of the way that Caiaphas had Jesus' arrested and handed over to Pilate, ensured that Jesus' followers would not take any such view seriously. This means that, as far as Jesus' followers were concerned, there was no other anointed figure either present or expected. Consequently, the Aramaic *m^eshīḥā* could now develop into a title, in much the same way as *ho Christos* did in Greek.

The second negative feature is that the historical Jesus was no longer present. During the historic ministry, he was convinced of the central importance of his role, but he sought no title of any kind. He used of himself the terms 'prophet', 'teacher' and 'son of man', all of which were used of other people too. He used 'beloved son' of himself only once, indirectly in a parable. After his death and Resurrection, however, those followers who continued the Jesus movement as it turned into Christianity did need titles, as the New Testament bears witness. What Jesus would have made of the initial stages of this, we do not know. Since however he was no longer present, he could not inhibit this process.

Taking all these three major features and the two negative factors together, we should conclude that Jesus' earliest followers had decisive reasons for developing the Aramaic *m^eshīḥā* into a major title, and that this is what they did. We must therefore conclude that the term 'Messiah' or 'Christ' does not belong to the historic ministry of Jesus. At the same time, this does not mean that Jesus' ministry was 'non-Messianic'. It simply means that this term was not available at the time, and that Jesus did not seek titles for himself. When the term 'Messiah' or 'Christ' did become available, his followers applied it to him, because it was an entirely reasonable term for describing his role during the historic ministry.

7. *Conclusions*

The task of determining which terms for Jesus were in use during the historic ministry is exceptionally complicated. This is because Jesus did not use elevated titles of himself. He did however believe that God had called him to play a central role in salvation history, to bring Israel back to God before he finally established his kingdom. At some stage, Jesus came to believe that this would require his atoning death. He would however be vindicated by resurrection. Later, he became a figure of such central importance to the Christian churches that they did need titles for him. Two of these, Son of man and Christ, already permeate the synoptic tradition, and Son of God is already quite common there. It is this developmental process, more extreme in the synoptic Gospels than the development of most aspects of his life and teaching, which makes it so difficult for the historian to sort out which terms were used during the historic ministry, and how.

I have concluded that, during the historic ministry, Jesus was known as 'prophet' and 'rabbi', which meant 'teacher', and used both terms of himself. Both these terms were important, and referred to central aspects of his ministry.

Jesus also used the term 'son of man' of himself, and he believed that he was a son of God, a term which he used in a parable (Mk 12.6), and which some other people may have used of him as well. These terms were not however references to his human and divine natures, as they were to be in later Christian theology. The term 'son of man' was used by him in idiomatic references to himself. Genuine son of man sayings say important things about him, and include major predictions of his death and Resurrection. This is because Jesus used the ordinary Aramaic term *bar* (*e*)*nāsh*(*ā*) in an idiom which people used to avoid speaking directly of themselves in humiliating circumstances, including their deaths, and in circumstances where they would be especially important, as when he forgave sins, and would be vindicated by resurrection. After his death and Resurrection, the term was translated into Greek and found in scripture in Dan. 7.13, where it referred to his second coming. The early church and the evangelists then produced secondary sayings.

The term 'son of God' meant that he was a faithful Jew. He believed that God used it of him because God chose him for a fundamental role in salvation history. This is why he used it indirectly of himself in a parable which set out aspects of this role of immediate relevance as he prepared to die. It is possible that some other people, including demoniacs, used it of him because he was conspicuously a faithful Jew and seemed to exercise the power of God in exorcisms.

Taking his ministry as a whole, it is evident that he saw himself as the kind of figure who was later to be hailed as 'the Messiah', though he did not use the term of himself, because it was not yet properly established. After his death and Resurrection, his followers did use the Aramaic *meshīḥā* of him. They needed titles for him, and *meshīḥā* was flexible enough for this purpose, because it was in use for a variety of real and expected figures. Moreover, he had played a fundamental role in salvation history, and he had believed that God had chosen him for that role. The church neither believed in nor expected any other anointed figure, so the title became unique. When Christianity spread to the Greek-speaking diaspora, the Aramaic *mᵉshīḥā* was translated into Greek as *ho Christos*, because the Greek *Christos* was already used for similar terms in the LXX. At this stage Jesus was more uniquely anointed than ever, and Christian leaders continued to study the scriptures. This is why the term 'Christ' became so common.

CHAPTER 11

Death in Jerusalem

1. Introduction

I have argued that the conflicts during Jesus' ministry were quite sufficient for him to have expected to die. More than that, when he left Galilee to celebrate his final Passover with his disciples, he fully *intended* to die in Jerusalem. He believed that his death would fulfil the will of God for the redemption of his people Israel. This was an event of such importance that he found it foretold in the scriptures.

The main purpose of this chapter is to reconstruct the events which led directly to Jesus' death in Jerusalem. This is a difficult task, because our oldest narrative source, Mk 11–15, is a mixture of accurate but very brief reports of what took place, and creative writing, most of which was produced to fill gaps in Mark's knowledge. Matthew and Luke add very little genuine material to this.

Moreover, as well as some very fine scholarship on which I have built, the historian has to contend with conservative scholars trying to believe as much of the Gospel stories as possible, and radical scholars trying to dismiss them. For example, in defending the historicity of Mark's account of Jesus' trial before Joseph Caiaphas, Gundry defends the historicity of the high priest's question to Jesus 'Are you the Christ, the son of the Blessed?' (Mk 14.61), and Jesus' answer, beginning 'I am' (Mk 14.62). He ignores all the problems of the absolute use of the term *mᵉshīḥā*, the Aramaic term for 'anointed' which would have been used by the high priest as a clear title if the story were literally true.[1] He defends the otherwise unattested use of 'the Blessed' as a circumlocution for God with the conjecture that it might be an abbreviation for the rabbinical expression 'the Holy One, blessed [is] he', and with reference to the late corrupt Ethiopic text of 1 En. 77.2, which he cannot read.[2] Such views are not consistent with any reasonable approach to evidence and argument.[3]

---

1 See pp. 392–96.
2 Gundry, *Mark*, pp. 886–87, 908–14.
3 See further pp. 440–42.

From the opposite end of the spectrum, Crossan is prominent among scholars from the American Jesus Seminar who have suggested that most of the Markan Passion narrative was created by Mark on the basis of scripture.[4] He proposes a category of 'prophecy historicised', and begins from the report of Mk 15.33// Mt. 27.45//Lk. 23.44//G.Pet. 5.15; 6.22, according to which, during Jesus' crucifixion, there was darkness over the whole land from the sixth to the ninth hour, approximately 12.00 noon until 3 p.m. He correctly sees that this story is not literally true, and that its author will have had in mind Amos 8.9-10, where God says:

> 'I will bring in the sun at noon and I will darken the land/earth on a clear day. And I will turn your feasts to mourning . . . I will make it like mourning for an only son . . .'

Crossan therefore proposes that 'learned Christians searching their Scriptures . . . created that *fictional* story about darkness at noon to assert that Jesus died in fulfillment of prophecy.'[5] And that is all. The problem with this is that it does not *explain* enough. We may contrast the work of Roger Aus, who has a more pro-found understanding of Jewish culture, and especially of Haggadah. Aus correctly associated the darkness with the rending of the Temple veil (Mk 15.38), and with the centurion's conclusion that Jesus was son of God (Mk 15.39), and correctly concluded that this is a story about God mourning for his son. Consequently, Aus was able to *explain why* some of Jesus' earliest followers made up this story, without supposing that they made up most of Mark's Passion narrative.[6]

Crossan, however, has a technique, not an explanation. He proceeds to apply his category of 'prophecy historicised' in a culturally inappropriate manner to much of Mark's Passion narrative. For example, he begins his discussion of the betrayal of Jesus by Judas at Mk 14.18-21 and Jn 13.18, 21–30 by quot-ing Ps. 41.9, italicizing *'who ate of my bread, has lifted my heel against me'* in Ps. 41.9, and *'one who is dipping bread into the bowl with me'* in Mk 14.20.[7] This is simply *not enough to explain* why Mark made the whole story up. On the contrary, we shall see that this part of the story is entirely plausible, and the only reasonable explanation is that it happened. This is why Mk 14.21 contains so many Aramaisms:

> 'A/The son of man goes as it is written concerning him, and woe to that man by whose hand a/the son of man is betrayed/handed over. (It would be) good for him if that man had not been born.'

Here there are two idiomatic 'son of man' sayings, correctly using the Aramaic *bar* (*e*)*nāsh*(*ā*). Jesus had good reason to state the prediction of his death in

4   See especially Crossan, *Who Killed Jesus?*
5   Crossan, *Who Killed Jesus?*, pp. 1–4.
6   See pp. 447–48.
7   Crossan, *Who Killed Jesus?*, pp. 69–70.

scripture, and the doom awaiting the traitor, by means of general statements, whereas the early church had no reason to put anything so indirectly, and the use of Psalm 41 gave no storyteller any reason to write *this*. The Aramaic word 'goes' (*ᵃzal*) was a normal metaphor for 'dies', as the Greek word for 'goes' was not, so this is further evidence that Mark was translating an Aramaic source, an aspect of the evidence which Crossan always leaves out.

It is the task of an independent historian to approach the Passion narrative without any assumptions that it must be literally true, or that most of it must have been made up. I begin by going back to the historic ministry, and consider the evidence that Jesus predicted, intended, and interpreted his sacrificial death before he 'set his face to go to Jerusalem' (Lk. 9.51).

2. *Preparing the Way*

In Chapter 9, I discussed two serious disputes between Jesus and some Pharisees about the observance of the sabbath. After the second one, the Pharisees took counsel with the Herodians how they might destroy him (Mk 3.6). Although this alliance was unusual, it was natural, because these Pharisees could not have persuaded a court to impose the death penalty, whereas Herod Antipas was the local ruler who had recently had John the Baptist put to death (Mk 6.17-29; Jos. *Ant.* XVIII, 116–19).[8] It was therefore reasonable for hostile Pharisees to hope that Herod might dispose of Jesus too.

I noted also the aftermath of this event at Lk. 13.31-33, a literal translation of an accurate Aramaic source which I translated as follows:

> [31]In that hour Pharisees went and said to him, 'Get out and go away from here, because Herod wants to kill you'. [32]And he said to them, 'Go tell that jackal, Look! I am casting out demons and performing healings to-day and tomorrow, and on the third day I am perfected.[33]But I am going to proceed to-day and day after day, for it would not be fitting for a prophet to perish outside Jerusalem.'[9]

This warning shows that the Pharisees as a group were split. Some of them are likely to have thought that Herod had violated the sixth commandment when he had John the Baptist put to death, and they warned Jesus with a view to avoiding the murder of another major prophet. The warning was very plausible, and Jesus was bound to take it seriously. His labelling of Herod as a 'jackal', a predator which hunts in packs, will have had this aspect of his behaviour in mind. The rest of Jesus' response refers to the same aspects of his ministry as were involved in the incident of Mk 3.1-6. He referred directly to his ministry of exorcism and healing, and continued 'on the third day I am perfected'. The expression 'on the third

8   See pp. 321–25, 340–43.
9   See further pp.114–15, 347.

day' was an idiomatic way of saying 'in a short time', and 'I am perfected' is an idiomatic reference to his death. Though naturally couched in idiomatic Aramaic, this was an unambiguous prediction of Jesus' death in the near future.

This is continued in v. 33. In this saying, Jesus did not speak directly about himself, but used a general statement about prophets. Stories about the deaths of prophets in Jerusalem were so widespread as to make this a perfectly plausible general statement. For example, it was popularly supposed that Isaiah was sawn in half in Jerusalem, a tale told in the *Martyrdom of Isaiah*. The murder of the priest Zechariah in the court of the priests in the Temple in Jerusalem is recounted at 2 Chron. 24.20-22. At the time of Jesus he was thought of as a prophet, and Jesus refers to his death elsewhere (Lk. 11.51, with some mistaken editing at Mt. 23.35). At Lk. 13.33 Jesus used a general statement about prophets to say that he would not be caught by Herod – he would die like other prophets in Jerusalem. This prophecy of his forthcoming death is quite unambiguous, and so is the place where he intended to die.

Jesus also gave some theological interpretation of the purpose of his death, while he was still in Galilee. When Jacob and John asked to sit on his right and left in his glory, Jesus at first responded with a question:

> Can you drink the cup which I will drink, or be immersed with the immersion with which I am immersed?
>
> (Mk 10.38)

This has two more metaphors for Jesus' forthcoming death. That of immersion, or baptism, is found in another reference to Jesus' forthcoming death (Lk. 12.50). The metaphor of 'cup' has clear cultural resonances. Jesus used it again in the Garden of Gethsemane, when he prayed to God his Father to take away 'this cup', evidently meaning his forthcoming suffering and death (Mk 14.36). His death is clearly in mind at Mk 10.38-39, for it is taken up more explicitly at Mk 10.45, where a/the son of man is to give his life as a ransom for many. There is enough Jewish material to explain Jesus' use of this metaphor. For example one of the Aramaic Targums has Moses say of people in general, 'who die and taste the cup of death'. (Neof I at Deut. 32.1). In the Hebrew Bible, the cup may refer to the wrath of God: especially striking is Isa. 51.17, 22, where this cup is drunk by Jerusalem. The metaphor of the cup is also used with reference to his forthcoming martyrdom by Isaiah at Mart.Isa. 5.14. Here Isaiah sends the other prophets away, saying 'God has mingled the cup for me only'.

At Mk 10.38, therefore, Jesus asked whether Jacob and John were prepared to die with him. They immediately answered 'We can'. It follows that they understood Jesus' figurative references to death, and that they accepted that they should die with him. Jesus accepted that they should die with him, though he left to God the question of who would be on his right and his left:

> And he said to them, 'You will drink the cup which I drink, and be immersed with the immersion with which I am immersed,[40]but to sit on my right or my left is not mine to give, except to those for whom it has been prepared'.
>
> (Mk 10.39-40)

The other members of the Twelve were none too pleased with Jacob and John, to the point that Jesus found it necessary to instruct them on the need for service rather than superiority. He concluded with a saying which also presupposed that others would die with him. As we have seen, genuine 'son of man' sayings had a general level of meaning which was lost in translation, and a reconstruction of this one enables it to be recovered:

> 'What is more, a/the son of man does not come to be served but to serve, and to give his life/soul/self as a ransom for many.'
>
> (Mk 10.45)

Here the general level of meaning pulls the whole incident together. It means that the purpose of the lives of the inner group of Twelve is not to be served but to serve, an interpretation of their function as messengers of healing and repentance to Israel in the last times. This is carried further with 'to give his life/soul/self', which entails the devotion of the whole of one's life to others. It is carried to the ultimate conclusion in the final phrase 'as a ransom for many', which takes this service to the point of death as an atoning sacrifice for the redemption of Israel. This links up with the proposed deaths of Jacob and John with Jesus.

In due course, this was to be carried even further in theory, but not in practice. After the last supper, Jesus predicted that everyone would stumble, and that Simeon the Rock would deny him. Mark reports the reaction not only of Peter, his Greek term for 'Rock', but of all those present:

> But he said vehemently, 'If it be necessary for me to die with you, I will not deny you'. And they all said likewise.
>
> (Mk 14.31)

This should be taken as seriously as the comments of Jacob and John. We are accustomed to the atoning death of Jesus alone, because Jesus was the only member of the Jesus movement to die on the cross at the time, and subsequent Christian tradition has regarded his death, and his death alone, as an atoning sacrifice for people's sins. This was not, however, the position during the historic ministry. At the time of the question put by Jacob and John, he and they contemplated other members of the inner group dying with him. The theology of the significance of their deaths may accordingly be seen in the light of the theology of martyrdom available at the time.

The main group of people concerned are the Maccabaean martyrs. When faithful Jews were put to death during the major persecution of 167–164 BCE, other faithful Jews needed to understand their deaths within the context of the purposes of God. This was done already in the book of Daniel. In Daniel 7, the last chapter of the original Aramaic group of stories and visions, this goes only so far as reassurance that God will end the persecution and give everlasting kingship to the people of the holy ones of the Most High. Towards the end of the massive Hebrew vision which concludes the book, two additional developments are found. The first refers again to these martyrs:

And some of the wise will stumble, to refine among them and to purify and
to make white, until the time of the End . . .

(Dan. 11.35)

This text evidently supposes that the deaths of the righteous will have a beneficial
effect. Exactly how this works could not be spelt out in detail, because this is the
first positive evaluation of their deaths from a perspective which sees them within
the purposes of God. The second development is their reward at Dan. 12.2-3,
where they will be among those who rise from the dead and shine like the stars
of heaven. This is close to the position which Jesus will occupy, 'in your glory',
as the sons of Zebedee put it. Both these main points, the positive evaluation of
the death of martyrs and their reward through resurrection were thus established
within semitic-speaking Judaism more than a century before the time of Jesus.

This was elaborated in subsequent literature. For example, the accounts of
martyrdoms in 2 Maccabees 6–7 contain several references to resurrection. The
last of seven brothers to be martyred prays that in him and his brothers the wrath
of God, justly brought upon the whole nation, may cease:

Now I, like my brothers, give up body and soul/life for the ancestral laws,
calling on God to have mercy soon on our people, and . . . through me and
my brothers to bring to an end the wrath of the Almighty which has justly
fallen on our whole nation.

(2 Macc. 7.37-38)

Here the death of the martyrs is instrumental in removing the wrath of God, who
is thereby able to deliver the people.

The fourth book of Maccabees shows further developments in the same
direction. The following passage expounds the atoning death of these martyrs
in a quite explicit way:

And these men, therefore, having sanctified themselves for God's sake, have
been honoured not only with this honour, but also in that through them the
enemy did not prevail over our people, and the tyrant suffered punishment,
and our country was purified, they having as it were become a ransom for
the nation's sin: and through the blood of those pious men and the propitia-
tion of their death, the divine Providence saved Israel, who had previously
been afflicted.

(*4 Macc.* 17.20-22)

This clearly portrays the sacrificial death of these martyrs as a ransom for Israel's
sins, a very close parallel to the way that Jesus regarded his own death, and would
have regarded the death of those who died with him, had they done so.

In addition to these literary sources, the Maccabaean victory and the rededication of the Temple were celebrated every year at the eight-day festival of
Ḥanukkah (Dedication). The second book of Maccabees begins in the form

of a letter from 'the Jews in Jerusalem and those in the land of Judaea' to 'the brethren the Jews in Egypt' (2 Macc. 1.1), recalling their previous letter, dated in 124 BCE, urging them to keep 'the days of the festival of Tabernacles in the month of Chaseleu' (i.e. Chislev, so during our December: 2 Macc. 1.9). This shows the eight-day festival of Ḥanukkah already well established in Israel long before the time of Jesus. Towards the end of the first century CE, Josephus calls it 'Lights' (*Ant.* XII, 325), in the context of his account of its origins (*Ant.* XII, 316–26). The Fourth Gospel refers to it as 'Renewal' (*Enkainia*, Jn 10.22), and retains the connection between Tabernacles and Second Tabernacles at a symbolic level. It also applies some of its symbolism to Jesus, so that he is sanctified (Jn 10.36) as the altar had been, and he lays down his life (10.17) as the martyrs had done. At the time of Jesus, the annual celebration of this festival will have kept alive the memory of the Maccabaean martyrs among all observant Jews, so that martyrdom theology was part of living Jewish culture.

The material on the significance of Jewish martyrs shows how effectively the saying at Mk 10.45 drew together the whole incident of Mk 10.35-45. It follows directly on from the immediately preceding teaching on service, for it carries the service required of leaders of the Jesus movement to the devotion of the whole of their lives and even to the point of death. This links up with Jesus' debate with Jacob and John. The general level of meaning of the term 'son of man' further reinforces Jesus' assertion that they will share his fate, and it is clear that death is included. The general level of meaning is also sufficiently loose to include the other members of the Twelve. At the same time, the saying idiomatically refers primarily to the speaker, whose leadership in the whole incident was decisive.

I have argued that there is an authentic prediction of Jesus' death and Resurrection behind Mk 8.31 and similar texts, despite evidence of later rewriting.[10] I suggested the following reconstruction:

ḥayyābh bar (ᵉ)nāsh(ā) lᵉmikēbh saggī' ūlᵉethbᵉsārāh ūlimᵉmāth ūlimᵉqām bāthar tᵉlāthāh yōmīn

A/the son of man is liable to suffer much and be rejected and die, and rise after three days.

This approximates to a prediction which Jesus made to the inner group of disciples on the first occasion when he made it clear that he would die. I have also argued that Mark was right in supposing that Jesus repeated something like this prediction as he taught the inner group of disciples before his final days in Jerusalem. It is important that this prediction includes Jesus' Resurrection as well as his death.

Jesus' expectation that he would die in Jerusalem should therefore be regarded as a certain fact. We have seen that it is multiply attested by source and form.

10 See pp. 377–81.

It is equally certain that he *intended* to die, and that he interpreted his death as an atoning sacrifice for the sins of Israel. While he was still in Galilee, he also accepted that some members of the Twelve might die with him. Had this been so, he would have accepted them as fellow martyrs. However, very little of the material includes anyone other than him, so we must also conclude that his main expectation was that he would die, and this is what he repeatedly foretold.

I have also argued that one saying, spoken at the end of a previous visit to Jerusalem, looked forward to his final visit:

> [37]Jerusalem, Jerusalem, who kills (the) prophets and stones those sent to you, how often/much I have wanted to gather your sons/children as a bird gathers her young under her wings, and you were not willing. [38]Behold! Your house is left to you! [39]I'm telling you, you will not see me until you say, 'Blessed is he who comes in the name of the Lord' [Ps. 118.26].

> (Mt. 23.37-39//Lk. 13.34-35)[11]

This saying, differently placed by Matthew and Luke because they had no proper outline of the historic ministry, makes sense only at the end of a previous visit. Then, as in his final visit, Jesus will have taught day by day in the Temple (cf. Mk 14.49). This is what he referred to, when he told the inhabitants of Jerusalem 'Your house is left to you!', for he now stopped and went back to Galilee. The final quotation from a crucial verse of one of the *Hallel* psalms (Ps. 118.26) looks forward to his final visit at Passover, when all Jerusalem said and sang the *Hallel* psalms set for Passover (Pss. 113–18). The chief priests would accordingly remember him only too well, and knowing whatever reports they will have received from scribes and Pharisees who went to observe him in Galilee, they, with scribes and elders, will have been prepared for trouble, though not perhaps for the following details.

3. *Entry into Jerusalem, and the Cleansing of the Temple*

Given his certainty about his forthcoming death, his conviction that it was God's will foretold in the scriptures, and his interpretation of it, it is natural that Jesus should have played a major role in bringing it about. His first significant act was to go to Jerusalem for the feast of Passover, and there to cleanse the Temple, the action which would lead directly to his death.

Jesus' entry into Jerusalem on a donkey was a considerable event in itself. He had evidently made arrangements for the donkey to be provided for the last 2 miles or so of his journey, and he instructed two of his followers to fetch it, which they did (Mk 11.1-7). They put clothing on the donkey for him, and many

---

11   See pp. 348–49.

people strewed both clothing and branches on the path before him (Mk 11.7-8). They cried out from one of the *Hallel* psalms, the psalms set for Passover. Mark transliterates the first word, 'Hosanna': the crowd will have known that they called out a word from the psalm, meaning 'Save, (we) pray' (Ps. 118.25). They continued:

.Blessed is he who comes in the name of the Lord.

(Ps. 118.26)

On its own, this might be no more than a ritual salute to any pilgrim. In Jesus' case, however, this was a fulfilment of his threatening prediction that the people of Jerusalem would not see him again until they said this very verse (cf. Mt. 23.37-39 //Lk. 13.34-35).[12] The crowd's next cry was potentially dangerous:

Blessed (be) the coming kingdom of our father David.

(Mk 11.10)

We have seen that the preaching of the kingdom of God was central to Jesus' ministry.[13] Passover was the celebration of the deliverance of Israel from Egypt, by the mighty hand of God. At this feast, at least the majority of people looked forward as well, to the final establishment of the kingdom of God, as Jesus had preached. The crowd crying this to Jesus could be valuable evidence for the chief priests to set before Pilate.

Jesus did nothing to prevent this display, in which people looked forward to what he himself predicted. Matthew and John both present his entry into Jerusalem on a donkey as a fulfilment of Zech. 9.9, which tells the daughter of Zion, '. . . your king is coming to you . . . riding on a donkey' (Mt. 21.4-5; Jn 12.14-15), and Luke adds the word 'king' to his quotation of Ps. 118.26 (Lk. 19.38). Many scholars have attributed this to Jesus' own intentions. For example, Wright comments on Jesus' actions, 'The allusion to Zechariah . . . is obvious.'[14] This has been 'obvious' to many Christian scholars because they belong to a tradition which has believed this for centuries. However, none of the Gospel writers attributes such belief to Jesus, and John even recalls that this interpretation of Zech. 9.9 was not known to the disciples until after Jesus' resurrection (Jn 12.16). Accordingly, we should not attribute this to Jesus. He preached the kingship *of God* with great vigour, but there is no sign in the primary sources of him using the term 'king' with reference to himself. Equally, we should not follow the view of the American Jesus Seminar that the story 'is a contrivance of the evangelist', 'conceived under the influence of Zech 9.9' and 'also influenced by Ps 118.25–26'.[15] This leaves too much unexplained, and reflects that seminar's destructive removal of Jesus from Judaism and from historical reality.

---

12 See pp. 348–49.
13 See pp. 212–26.
14 Wright, *Jesus and the Victory of God*, p. 490.
15 Funk *et al.*, *Five Gospels*, p. 97.

There is however one event which the Gospel writers do not mention, and which was such an obvious contrast with Jesus' entry into Jerusalem that everyone must have been aware of it, Jesus included. This was Pilate's triumphal entry into Jerusalem, riding on a horse rather than a donkey, with a force of troops drawn from his auxiliary cohorts and cavalry. He was greeted subserviently by chief priests, elders and scribes, and hailed by some sort of crowd. He took up residence in the former palace of Herod the Great, where the troops who accompanied him were quartered. He did this every year at Passover, in case of any disturbances. He did not come 'in the name of the Lord', and in contrast with his worldly pomp, and the subservience of powerful Jewish leaders, Jesus' entry on a donkey was that of a faithful Jewish prophet.

When Jesus arrived in Jerusalem, he entered the Temple, and then went quietly to Bethany, where he had arranged to stay with the Twelve for the duration of the feast. Mark's mild report of this is so straightforward that it must be right:

> And he went into Jerusalem into the Temple. And when he had looked around at everything, the hour being already late, he went out to Bethany with the Twelve.
>
> (Mk 11.11)

This was only sensible, after a 13-mile walk from Jericho and some 2 miles on a donkey with a crowd of disciples. Mark's comment that it was late is also natural after a 15-mile journey with people on foot. It is also likely that the merchants and moneychangers in the Temple had stopped their work for the day. Thus Jesus had good reason to postpone vigorous action and effective preaching until another day, and the omission of this delay by Matthew and Luke is historically unrealistic.

We do not know the exact date of Jesus' entry into Jerusalem. The traditional Christian date of Palm Sunday, the Sunday before Jesus was crucified, is certainly wrong, and is not entailed by any of the synoptic Gospels. Mark has a precise date at Mk 14.1, two days before Passover and Unleavened Bread, but he does not say how long it had been since Jesus' entry into Jerusalem or the Cleansing of the Temple. He naturally recounted everything which he thought Jesus said and did during his final visit to Jerusalem, but until Mk 14.1 his account is no more in chronological order than the main part of the historic ministry, and even the date of the anointing at Bethany is quite vague (Mk 14.3). Matthew and Luke put more material into their accounts of Jesus' final visit to Jerusalem. Some of it clearly does not belong there, and they made no attempt to be precise about the detailed chronology either. We must infer that the precise date of Jesus' entry into Jerusalem was not known to the synoptic writers.

We do know that pilgrims went up to Jerusalem for Passover in time to purify themselves before entering the inner courts of the Temple, where they took their Passover victims for slaughter. It was assumed that most people would have indirectly contracted corpse impurity, and everyone believed that Numbers 19 contains the regulations for purifying them. The high priest had to preside over the burning of a red heifer which was slaughtered in his sight outside the

Temple. A clean person had to gather its ashes and deposit them in a clean place outside the Temple, where they were used for preparing the water for cleansing (*Num.* 19.9). Pilgrims had to be sprinkled with this water on the third day and the seventh. Hence Philo describes the purification as a seven-day event (*Spec. Leg.* I, 261); Josephus records that in one particular year the people were assembling on 8th Xanthicus, the equivalent of 8th Nisan, giving them just seven days before 14th Nisan when the Passover victims should be sacrificed (*War* VI, 290); and John records that at an unspecified time, certainly more than six days before Passover, which was however 'near', 'many' went up to Jerusalem 'to purify themselves' (Jn 11.55, cf. 11.56, 12.1).

Jesus must have observed these customs. He had every reason to do so, because they were thought to be biblical, and he was observant. Had he failed to do so, he would have had an important reason, and he would have caused a major scandal. We have the kind of sources which would have reported his reasons and his response to the inevitable criticism, but which do not record his unremarkable observance of conventional biblical Law. In view of all this, it is natural that his entry into Jerusalem has been dated on Friday, 8th Nisan.[16] This is probably too early as well. He arrived in Jerusalem when the hour was already late (Mk 11.11), he and all the disciples with him would need enough time to be sprinkled on the seventh day, and we must be careful not to date the Cleansing of the Temple on the sabbath. It is therefore probable that they arrived in Jerusalem not later than Thursday, 7th Nisan. Given that he preached 'day by day' in the Temple without being arrested (Mk 14.49), arrival earlier that week is more probable.

The main action in the Temple took place soon afterwards. Mark places it 'on the following day' (Mk 11.12). This date must be a little uncertain because it is closely associated with the cursing of the fig tree, the strangest of the Markan sandwiches (Mk 11.12-14, 20–25), plausibly interpreted as originally a tale symbolizing doom. The date may nonetheless be original, as Jesus had no reason to delay the major action which he had come to perform, after which he would control the halakhah in the outermost court of the Temple and preach about it 'day by day'.

And they came to Jerusalem. And he went into the Temple, and began to throw out those who sold and those who bought in the Temple. And he overturned the tables of the moneychangers and the chairs of those who sold the doves.[16]And he did not allow anyone to carry a vessel through the Temple.[17]And he was teaching, and he said, 'Is it not written "My house shall be called a house of prayer for all the nations" [Isa 56.7]? And you have made it "a robbers' cave" [Jer. 7.11].'[18]And the chief priests and the scribes heard, and sought how they might destroy him.

(Mk 11.15-18)[17]

---

16   E.g. Sanders, *Historical Figure of Jesus*, p. 250, with p. 309 n. 11.
17   For more detailed discussion, including a reconstruction of Mark's Aramaic source,

This action was intended to make the whole extended Herodian Temple a house of prayer. The buying, selling and changing of money was done in what is often called the Court of the Gentiles, the outermost court, which 'it was permitted for all, even foreigners, to enter' (Jos. *Apion* II, 103). People did not have to be in a state of purity to enter this court. Hence crowds could throng this court to pray and to change money, and those who had come early enough to be clean already could buy doves for sacrifice too. Money had to be changed for payment of the Temple tax, as well as for the purchase of sacrifices and perhaps other things. Jesus clearly objected to the Temple being used for these purposes. It would be useful to know whether these things had traditionally been done there, or whether this was a recent innovation. In a sense, such arrangements were necessarily novel, because Herod the Great's massive rebuilding of the Temple so drastically increased the size of the outermost court. This rebuilding included the royal portico, the obvious place to put this trading because it was a covered area. Equally, however, it was now some 45 years since the portico had been completed, so the rebuilding programme is not sufficient to tell us how long this trading had been done in the Temple.

Jesus' prohibition of carrying through is entirely coherent with his removal of traders, in that it defends the sacred space of the house of God. Most Jews believed that God really dwelt in his Temple. The *Tamid*, the daily sacrifice of a lamb in the morning and a lamb in the evening, was seen as a special sign of this. Jesus shared such beliefs. As he said in another halakhic argument, put forward to stop people from swearing by the Temple, 'And he who swears by the Temple swears by it and by Him who lives in it' (Mt. 23.21). For the prevention of carrying through, we have the information from Josephus that no vessel could be carried into the inner sanctuary (*Apion* II, 106). It is this halakhic judgement which Jesus applied to the whole of the Temple area.

What Jesus prohibited was taking any vessel through/across the Temple. The direct practical effects of this decision will have been obvious at the time, but we have to conjecture them. It presumably prevented people from carrying birds, bought for sacrifice, in any kind of cage or container across the outermost court, through the Court of the Women and the Court of the Israelites to the parapet of the Court of the Priests, where the birds were given to the priests for the sacrifices to be performed. Consequently, poor people would not have to buy baskets or bowls when they bought pigeons or doves for sacrifices. This would not impede the sacrifices in any way, and would make it easier for poor people to fulfil the requirements of the Torah. Equally, Jesus' judgement prevented the use of 'vessels' to carry joints of larger animals, which had been sacrificed, back from the edge of the Court of the Priests through and out of the Temple, and it perhaps agrees with the later source m. Ber. 9, 5 in preventing people, whether moneychangers or pilgrims, from carrying money-belts. More directly, it would stop merchants and moneychangers from having any sort of container for carrying money, without which they could not do business in the Temple precincts.

P. M. Casey, 'Culture and Historicity: The Cleansing of the Temple', *CBQ* 59 (1997), pp. 306–32.

Even more dramatically, it would prevent priests from having containers for taking money out of the Court of the Women, where the trumpets for the shekel offerings were placed. If they could not be taken out in quantity, the chief priests would no longer want them taken in. This mattered, because the chief priests insisted on Tyrian shekels because of their relative purity. Each Tyrian shekel bore the image of the pagan god Melkart, so Jesus' judgement would have ensured that these idolatrous images would no longer be taken into God's house.

Jesus' action was very vigorous, and might be perceived as disrupting the arrangements for divine worship. Mark gives next the scriptural texts which he expounded, for two very good reasons. The Word of God in scripture in principle provided Jesus with the strongest sort of reason he could have had for taking action. Expounding the Word of God also gave him a powerful means of controlling the behaviour of observant Jews in the house of God. Isaiah 56 is *about* the acceptance of people who hold fast to the covenant. To make the point quite clear, the text includes even foreigners and eunuchs among them. Keeping the sabbath is particularly specified, so these are people who were, or were becoming, observant. Isa. 56.6-7 is concerned with foreigners, and Isa 56.7 is concerned entirely with their acceptance in the Temple:

> [6]And the foreigners who join themselves to YHWH to minister to him and to love the name of YHWH and to be his servants, everyone who keeps the sabbath from profanation and those who hold fast to my covenant,[7]I will bring them to my holy mountain and make them joyful in my house of prayer, their burnt offerings and their sacrifices shall be acceptable on my altar, for my house shall be called a house of prayer for all peoples.

At the time of Jesus, everyone knew that the only part of the Temple foreigners were allowed in was the outermost court. Hence if they are to be joyful 'in my house of prayer', and this is to be 'a house of prayer for all peoples', *prayer* must be what the outermost court was for, and hence not trade.

Praying in the Temple was a normal Jewish activity. Jesus made vivid use of this custom in the parable of the Pharisee and the tax-collector (Lk. 18.10-14). The setting is quite straightforward: 'Two men went up into the Temple to pray'. At this point, the conventional modern term 'Court of the Gentiles' may be misleading. Neither the Pharisee nor the tax-collector had to go into an inner court to pray, and the outer court, which Gentiles were *allowed* to enter, was normally used by Jews. The practical effect of clearing out traders and money-changers would be to permit the throngs of Jewish people present for Passover to pray anywhere in the Temple area. There was not room for all of them in the inner courts, and many of them would not yet be pure enough to enter the inner courts.

Another point from Isa. 56.7 is to be noted. As well as praying in the outer court, foreigners who joined themselves to the Lord would have their sacrifices accepted. Indeed, the biblical text makes a close connection between sacrifice and prayer, which is culturally appropriate to the central sanctuary. It follows that there should be no question of an attack on the sacrificial system as such.

The Isaiah passage goes on to complain about the leaders of Israel. At Isa. 56.11, her 'shepherds' have no understanding, they have turned each one to their own 'profit', and the Hebrew word (*betsa‘*) clearly implies that their profit has been unjustly and violently gained. This is one point of contact with Jeremiah 7.

The context of Jeremiah 7 is one of vigorous criticism of Jews who worship in the Temple, but who commit various sins, including theft, idolatry and murder. They would be allowed to dwell in the land if they repented, a process which would have to include not oppressing the alien and the widow, not shedding innocent blood, and not walking after other gods. Otherwise, 'I will do to the house over which my name is called, in which you trust, and to the place which I gave to you and to your fathers, as I did to Shiloh' (Jer. 7.14). Everyone believed that God had destroyed Shiloh (cf. Ps. 78. 59–64). Exposition of Jer. 7.14 could accordingly form just the kind of conditional threat to the Temple which could lead even genuine eyewitnesses to disagree about quite what Jesus said he would do, and quite what he predicted. It is in this context that Jeremiah refers to the Temple, 'this house over which my name is called', a central point of contact between the two texts expounded. He labels it 'a robbers' cave' (Jer. 7.11). Jesus' use of this expression is a highly picturesque application of scripture to the Royal Portico. It means a cave used by brigands, leaders of armed gangs who committed theft and murder. It was a cavernous place, so the image is a good one at that level. It was built by Herod the Great, whose first major achievement as governor of Galilee was the defeat of brigands (Jos. *War* I, 203//*Ant.* XIV, 158–62). Herod's son Archelaus prevented Passover from continuing in 4 BCE by sending his troops into the Temple, and shedding a lot of innocent blood (*War* II, 8–13, 30//*Ant.* XVII, 208–18, 230–31, 237). Another son, Herod Antipas, the tetrarch, had recently shed the innocent blood of John the Baptist (Mk 6.16-29; Jos. *Ant.* XVIII, 116–19), and sought to kill Jesus (Lk. 13.31).[18] The biblical metaphor would be memorable for these reasons too.

We must also infer that the merchants and moneychangers were taking money from the poor. They will have done this in accordance with the Law. Poor people had to pay the Temple tax, just like rich people, and moneychangers always sell money for more than its face value, to make a profit. Rich priests, however, did not pay the Temple tax, and a number of scribal decisions would increase the money which people had to pay, poor people included. The most dramatic decision was that the Temple tax should be paid every year, rather than once in a lifetime. This is not an inevitable interpretation of Exod. 30.11-16 with Neh. 10.32, and it is contradicted by one of the Dead Sea scrolls, which preserves the older halakhah:

> [Concer]ning [the ransom]: the money of valuation which a man gives as ransom for himself (will be) half [a shekel], only on[ce] will he give it all his days.
>
> (4Q159 1 6–7)

---

18 See pp. 324–25, 340–43.

The annual offering gave the Temple far more money than it might be thought to need, and at half a shekel per person it was a burden only to the poor. Pigeons, or doves, were sacrificed by poor people, sometimes when richer people would sacrifice a larger animal (e.g. Lev. 12.6-8). Consequently, it will have been obvious to everyone that doves were especially important for the sacrifices of poor people.

There is also evidence of the massive wealth of the Temple, and of the chief priests, who could legally extract tithes from the poor. For example, Josephus notes the gold plating which covered parts of the Temple, and its other magnificent adornments (*War* V, 201–36). Joseph Caiaphas, shortly to be responsible for taking Jesus to Pilate, was high priest 18–36 CE, sufficient testimony to his massive personal influence with the Roman governor, long before his bones were placed in their exceptionally ornate ossuary.[19] I have noted evidence of extortion by rich priests, especially through the collection of tithes.[20] All this gives another level of meaning to the use of the scriptural polemic, 'robbers' cave'. Robbers hoarded their spoils, which authorities regarded as ill-gotten, in their caves. The merchants and moneychangers were essential to a system for accepting such massive quantities of money that it could be used for further plating the Temple with gold. Finally, the Tyrian shekels were used because of their relative purity, so that images of Melkart were brought into the house of God for financial gain.

When all this is taken into account, we can see that Jesus' criticism of the financial and trading arrangements in the Temple was consistent with his rejection of oaths by the Temple, with his criticism of the Korban system, of tithing mint, dill and cumin, and of the observance of additional purity laws concerning vessels full from the proceeds of wealth acquired by the rich from the poor.

4. *The Next Few Days*

Jesus' action was an obvious challenge to the power of the chief priests and their scribes. It could also be seen as a violation of the Temple, since it upset the normal arrangements for the conduct of worship at a major feast, and for the payment of the Temple tax. Serious opposition from the chief priests and scribes was therefore to be expected. This is first mentioned immediately after the Cleansing of the Temple. Mark says that they sought to kill Jesus, but feared the crowd (Mk 11.18). From a practical point of view, it was difficult for them to take immediate action. The Captain of the Temple, the *sagān* in charge of security in the Temple, will not have forgotten what happened in 4 BCE, when Herod Archelaus was faced with a serious protest arising from an incident in Herod the Great's reign. Archelaus first of all sent the Captain of the Temple to persuade people to give up their protest, an event comparable with the party sent to question Jesus in the Temple (Mk 11.27-33). When the *sagān* was driven off by force

19 See pp. 344–46.
20 See pp. 331–37.

and not allowed to speak, Archelaus sent others to speak to them instead. When Passover came round and they got more and more support, Archelaus sent in a cohort led by a tribune, so some 500 soldiers: they were stoned by the crowd with such vigour that most of the cohort were killed. Then Archelaus sent in his army in force, an action which resulted in 3,000 dead Jews and the wreckage of the major festival (Jos. *War* II, 5–13//*Ant*. XVII, 206–8). The unsuccessful sending in of the cohort, and the carnage wrought by Archelaus' army, illustrates what the chief priests were avoiding in the case of Jesus.

Mark reports them quite precisely, just two days before Passover:

> And the chief priests and scribes were seeking how they might seize him by stealth, and kill him,[2]for they said, 'Not in the festival crowd, in case there is a riot of the people'.
>
> (Mk 14.1b-2)

Here I have translated Mark's *en tēi heortēi*, correctly representing the Aramaic *behaggā*, 'in the festival crowd', a normal meaning of these words in both languages, and more appropriate than conventional translations such as 'during the festival' (e.g. NRSV), which miss the point. They wanted Jesus out of the way by stealth without a riot as soon as possible, not after the end of an eight-day feast.

Meantime Jesus continued to cause opposition by his teaching in the Temple. A delegation of chief priests, scribes and elders came to ask him by what authority he was acting in the Temple (Mk 11.27-28). This delegation was presumably led by the *sagān*, and must have included the chief priest in charge of bird offerings and at least one of the chief priests in charge of the treasury, together with scribes who were responsible for interpreting the Law to give judgements on what should and should not be allowed in the Temple. Jesus responded to their question with another question:

> The baptism of John, was it from heaven or of men?
>
> (Mk 11.30)

They will not have wanted reminding of John the Baptist, and Mark records their difficulty over this question:

> And they discussed it with each other and said, 'What shall we say? If we say 'From heaven', he will say, 'Why did you not believe him?' But shall we say, 'Of men'?' They were afraid of the crowd, for everyone knew that John was truly a prophet.
>
> (Mk 11.31-32)

This provides the vital information that many people supported the prophetic ministry of John the Baptist, but that the chief priests, scribes and elders had not believed in him. This shows that the rift between the prophetic tradition and the institutional centre of Judaism was already serious before the ministry of Jesus.[21] Moreover, we should accept the full implications of the power of Jesus' charismatic action and preaching, and the present tense of this delegation's question: 'By what power *do* you do these things?' (Mk 11.28). We should infer that the moneychangers were changing money outside the Temple, that doves were being sold outside the Temple, and that no one was allowed to carry vessels through the Temple.

It follows that Jesus had massive popular support. Since he had no temporal power, this popular support was necessary for him to impose his view as to what should and should not be done in the outermost court of the Temple. This was also the reason why the chief priests could not yet take more effective action to stop him. Roman soldiers, overlooking the scene from the rooftops and the Antonia fortress, had no reason to take any action until the chief priests told Pilate that something had to be done, and every reason not to enter the Temple in force. Jesus' practical display of spiritual power subverted the authority of the *sagān* and went contrary to the judgements of the chief priests in charge of the bird offerings and the treasury, and their scribes. It is not surprising that they would not tolerate this!

Jesus' question was accordingly very difficult for them to answer, and Mark records them replying feebly, 'We do not know' (Mk 11.33). Jesus therefore refused to give them a direct answer to their question about his authority. Instead, he responded vigorously with a beautiful parable and a scriptural text (Mk 12.1-11).

The parable sets off from a traditional parable, the prophetic criticism of Israel in Isaiah 5.

> A man planted a vineyard and put a fence round it and dug a wine-press and built a tower, and handed it over to tenants and went away.

The vineyard was a normal image for Israel. Clear examples include the explicit identification interpreting the parable of Isaiah 5:

> The vineyard of the LORD of hosts (is) the house of Israel, and the man of Judah the planting of his delight.
>
> (Isa. 5.7)

In Jesus' parable too, the vineyard is Israel, and its owner is God. The fence, or hedge, is a purely realistic item in Jesus' story, as at Isa. 5.5. The winepress, or vat, and the tower, both from Isa. 5.2, are a different matter, like the vineyard itself. The sanctuary *was* a conspicuous tower, obviously visible from the outermost court, where Jesus was preaching, and from much further away. Large quantities of wine were poured out at the foot of the altar, and the wine was collected in a

---

21   See further pp. 363–65.

pit at the side of the altar. This would also be obvious to men who took animals
for sacrifice up to the parapet between the Court of the Israelites and the Court
of the Priests, as Jesus and many others would shortly do again on the eve of
Passover. Hence the sanctuary, the altar and the pit all feature in Jewish exegesis
of Isa. 5.2.[22] The tenants, and the landlord going away, are both new but realistic items of the story, and the tenants are the Jewish leaders to whom God had
entrusted his vineyard, Israel.

> [2]And in time he sent a servant to the tenants, so that he might take from the
> tenants some of the fruit of the vineyard.[3]And they seized him and beat him
> and sent him away empty-handed.[4]And again he sent to them another servant,
> and they brayed him and dishonoured him.[5]And he sent another, and him they
> killed, and many others, and some they beat and others they killed.

The servants are the prophets, and Jesus could rely on everyone to recognize that
God sent his servants the prophets. For example, in Isaiah's call vision, Isaiah
heard the voice of God saying 'Whom shall I send?', and he replied, 'Here am I,
send me!' (Isa. 6.8). God later refers to him as 'my servant Isaiah' (Isa. 20.3). In
Jeremiah 7, one of the passages on which Jesus had recently preached when he
cleansed the Temple, God instructs Jeremiah to tell the people of Judah in the
Temple, '. . . from the day that your fathers came out of the land of Egypt until
this day, I have persistently sent to you all my servants the prophets, day after
day' (Jer. 7.25).

By the time of Jesus, Jewish people believed that several, but not all, of the
prophets were put to death. I have noted that Isaiah was believed to have been
sawn in half by the wicked King Manasseh (Martyrdom of Isaiah 5.1-14). The
lesser-known prophet Uriah son of Shemaiah was also put to death: after preaching in terms similar to Jeremiah, Uriah was killed by the sword on the orders
of the king, and his body thrown into the burial place of the sons of the people
(Jer. 26.20-23). Jeremiah, however, was not put to death. He was threatened
with death by the priests and other prophets (Jeremiah 26), thrown into a cistern
where he sank in the mud (Jer. 38.6), hauled out, and imprisoned in the court of
the guard until Jerusalem was taken (Jer. 38.28). All this is part of the background
to Mk 12.2-5, which would therefore appear to Jesus' audience to be a perfectly
realistic account of God sending the prophets to Israel, and their fate.

At v. 4, I have translated Jesus' rare and colourful Aramaic *rāshīn*, which
means 'pound, bray', with the rare English word 'bray', so this is another word
for 'beat up'. Mark did not recognize it, but he did recognize the first three letters
(*r'sh*) as the normal Aramaic and Hebrew word for 'head'. He therefore formed
a new Greek word, from the common Greek word for 'head'. Translators often
behave like this when they get stuck, and common translations, such as 'beat
over the head' (NRSV), correctly represent what Mark meant. Once again, we

---

22   On the Jewish background to Mk 12.1-12 see especially R. Aus, *The Wicked Tenants and
     Gethsemane: Isaiah in the Wicked Tenants' Vineyard, and Moses and the High Priest in
     Gethsemane: Judaic Traditions in Mark 12.1-9 and 14.32-42* (Atlanta: Scholars, 1996).

have Jesus' exact words just at a point where we have his authentic teaching, and Mark's Greek is generally regarded as no better than strange.

> [6]He still had one (person), a beloved son. He sent him to them last. He said, 'They will respect my son'. [7]And those tenants said one to another, 'This is the heir! Come, let us kill him, and the inheritance will be ours!' [8]And they seized him and killed him, and threw him out of the vineyard.

Jesus' use of the term 'beloved son' was derived from his call vision on the occasion of his baptism by John the Baptist. We have seen that he heard God address him as 'my son, the beloved', and that this meant that Jesus was a faithful Jew chosen by God to do for Israel something important.[23] Jesus' story that the owner sent a beloved son to the tenants 'last' reflects his belief that he was God's final messenger to Israel before the establishment of God's kingdom.

The owner's words have intensified scholarly criticism that this verse is unrealistic in supposing that the owner would send his son after the maltreatment of his servants, especially if he had the power portrayed in v. 9 to come and destroy the tenants.[24] This criticism is inappropriate. The parable portrays the extraordinary behaviour of God, not the behaviour of a normal vineyard owner.

Verses 7–8 portray in story mode Jesus' expectation that the chief priests, scribes and elders would ensure that he was arrested, and would take steps to have him put to death, as they did. With him out of the way, they expected to have complete control of Israel, and not to have to put up any longer with his control of the halakhah in the outer court of the Temple, nor with what they will have regarded as his more generally subversive teaching.

The final verse of the parable portrays God's intervention for judgement, and begins Jesus' prediction of his vindication.

> [9]What will the owner of the vineyard do? He will come and destroy the tenants, and he will give the vineyard to others.

The day of the Lord was a universal part of Jewish eschatological expectation. Examples include Malachi 3, where God will send Elijah before the great and terrible day of the Lord comes, a prophecy which Jesus believed had already been fulfilled in the ministry of John the Baptist (Mk 9.11-13).[25] At Isa. 3.14, the Lord enters into judgement with the elders and princes of his people, declaring 'It is you who have destroyed the vineyard . . .' Hence it is the tenants whom God will come and destroy. We should envisage God destroying the chief priests, scribes and elders who were in effective control of the Temple, Jerusalem and Judaea, as well as Herod Antipas, who was in control of Galilee, and probably in Jerusalem at the time.

---

23 See pp. 176–77.
24 E.g. J. D. Crossan, *In Parables: The Challenge of the Historical Jesus* (New York: Harper and Row, 1973), p. 90.
25 See pp. 178–80, 367–68.

Then he will give the vineyard to 'others'. Christian tradition interpreted this of Gentile Christians, but this is foreign to the teaching of the historical Jesus. Jesus did not anticipate Gentile Christianity, and he had a different idea of what would happen when the kingdom came. He did not however give a detailed exposition of this in teaching which has been transmitted to us, so we have to piece together what we can from isolated sayings, and use the end of the parable to further our understanding of his expectation.

I have discussed Jacob and John's request to sit on Jesus' right and left in his glory, and Jesus' response.[26] This presupposes that Jesus will be in glory after his death, and says that God will decide who will sit on his right and his left. Neither Jacob and John's request, nor Jesus' response, makes sense if this is to be in a purely spiritual realm, for in such a realm the terms 'right' and 'left' would be meaningless. At the same time, Jesus would have to rise from the dead to be in glory, as would Jacob and John if they fulfilled their undertaking to die with him. This must be the same occasion as is referred to at Mt. 19.28//Lk. 22.29-30. Unfortunately, both Matthew and Luke rewrote the beginning of the saying, and I have suggested that we can be confident of only the following, and of an eschatological setting which both evangelists rewrote: '. . . that you may eat and drink at my table, and sit on (?twelve?) thrones judging the twelve tribes of Israel.'[27] The extraordinary role given here to the Twelve in judging the twelve tribes of Israel can only belong to the teaching of Jesus, because it fits with the role of the Twelve and the early church had no reason to make it up. The Twelve must therefore be among the 'others' to whom the vineyard will be given. That they should eat and drink at his table fits well with his 'glory', when God would decide who would sit on his right and left. It follows that Jesus himself would be in charge of the 'others' to whom the vineyard would be given.

Another saying (Mt. 8.11-12//Lk. 13.28-29) must refer to the same occasion. Luke has clearly edited his version, so I mostly follow the Matthaean version as being nearer to what Jesus said, but I restore Jesus' characteristic term, 'kingdom of God' for Matthew's characteristic 'kingdom of heaven', and I keep Luke's 'you' for Matthew's 'the sons of the kingdom':

> Many will come from east and west and recline with Abraham and Isaac and Jacob in the kingdom of God, but you will be cast into outer darkness: there will be weeping and gnashing of teeth.

This tells us where the chief priests, elders and scribes will end up: in Gehenna with Herod Antipas. In terms of the parable, this is what happens when the owner comes and destroys the tenants. The background to this saying is the normal Jewish expectation of the restoration of Israel in the last times. As Second Isaiah said in the name of the Lord,

---

26 See pp. 186–87, 221–22.
27 See pp. 186–87.

Do not fear, for I have redeemed you . . . I will bring your seed from the East, and from the West I will gather you.

(Isa. 43.1, 5)

Jesus' term 'many' (Mt. 8.11//Lk. 13.28) is deliberately vague, and makes room for Gentiles, 'foreigners who join themselves to the LORD', as it is put in Isaiah 56, on which Jesus had recently preached when he cleansed the Temple. As at Mk 14.25, when Jesus assumed that he would drink new wine in the kingdom of God,[28] and as at Mt. 19.28//Lk. 22.29-30, Jesus presupposes a great meal on this occasion, and Abraham, Isaac and Jacob are obvious possible candidates for sitting on his right and left. Those who came from the East would naturally include the lost ten tribes, so the Twelve would have all twelve tribes to judge when they sat on their thrones.

The destruction of the tenants, and the gift of the vineyard to 'others' (Mk 12.9), ends the actual parable, but Jesus continued to predict his vindication with a quotation from Ps. 118, the same *Hallel* psalm as the crowd quoted during his entry into Jerusalem:

[10]And have you not read this scripture? 'A stone which the builders rejected has become a head of a corner.[11]This was from the LORD, and it is amazing in our eyes.'

The building imagery in this quotation follows naturally from the imagery of 'and he built a tower', repeated from Isa. 5.2 by Jesus at the beginning of the parable, where it is a direct reference to the sanctuary at the centre of the Temple. The meaning of the psalm quotation is essential to understanding the parable. The builders are the chief priests, as Simeon the Rock was to say explicitly a few weeks later (Acts 4.11). The rebuilding of the Temple was begun by Herod the Great c.20 BCE (Jos. *Ant.* XV, 380). At the time of Jesus, although the most important work had long since been done, the Temple was still not finished (Jos. *Ant.* XX, 219). Moreover, there was no king of Judaea, so the chief priests, who were always in charge of running the Temple, were effectively in charge of the building works along with everything else. It was therefore appropriate to interpret them as the builders. The stone, which the builders rejected, is Jesus, whom the chief priests rejected, and whose death they would shortly bring about.

The expression often translated 'cornerstone' at Ps. 118.22, picked up by Jesus in his reference to 'the head of the corner', has caused a lot of debate. Apart from debatable details, however, the main point is clear. It was an important stone visible at the top of a building such as the Temple, and therefore suitable for metaphorical interpretation as a very important person.

How could the stone, interpreted as Jesus himself, become the head of the corner? Simeon the Rock expressed this very clearly when he used the same quotation in a speech addressing 'rulers of the people and elders' (Acts 4.8),

---

28   See p. 435.

when those present included 'Annas the chief priest and Caiaphas and John and Alexander and whoever was of the high-priestly family' (Acts 4.6). Simeon described Jesus as 'the stone, the one rejected by you the builders, who/which became a head of a corner', straight after he had said of Jesus, 'whom you cruci-fied, whom God raised from the dead' (Acts 4.10-11). Resurrection is exactly what Jesus was looking forward to. I have discussed his predictions of this, and other recoverable aspects of his expectation of events in the last times.[29] Jesus would become a head of a corner when he rose from the dead. He would lead the Twelve when the vineyard of the Lord of hosts, the people of Israel, includ-ing the ingathered diaspora, the lost ten tribes, and such Gentiles as joined themselves to the Lord, was given to them, the 'others' of the main body of the parable.

The next verse describes the effect of Jesus' parable:

[12]And they sought to seize him, and they feared the people, for they knew that he spoke the parable against/about them. And they left him and went away.

This verse has been thought to have one problem of detail, namely that the sub-ject is not always clear. Changes of subject in Aramaic narratives are frequently unmarked, and must be inferred from the context, and so it was here with Mark's Aramaic source, which he understood and translated literally. Those who 'sought to seize him' are the chief priests, scribes and elders, assumed from Mk 11.27. Naturally, they are also the subject of the next verb, for it was they who 'feared the people'. The subject of 'knew', however, is the people as a whole. It is because the people knew that Jesus spoke the parable against the chief priests, scribes and elders that the chief priests, scribes and elders were afraid of the people. From their point of view, Jesus' teaching was quite subversive. He was now controlling the detailed running of the outermost court of the Temple. His actions and teaching were leading to popular resentment against them, and might lead to further popular action against them. Then the subject changes again, for it was the chief priests, scribes and elders who left him and went away. They were still seeking to destroy Jesus, as Mark says in translating his Aramaic source at Mk 11.18, and the chief priests duly rejoiced when Judah of Kerioth offered to betray him (Mk 14.10-11), the next important event in the moves towards Jesus' execution.

In the meantime, Jesus continued to teach in the Temple, and Mark transmits some further information, beginning with two significant disputes. The first dis-pute (Mk 12.13-17) shows that the alliance between some of the Pharisees and the Herodians was active in Jerusalem. They came to ask him whether tribute should be paid to the Roman emperor or not (Mk 12.13-14). This was a hot political issue. If Jesus gave too submissively an affirmative answer, he might lose support from faithful Jews who believed in his preaching about the kingdom of God. If he said 'no', they might get him on a charge of sedition or the like before the Roman governor, a merely political offence which he had no interest

29 See pp. 377–81.

in committing. Hence he told them to bring him a denarius, a Roman coin which they possessed and he did not.

This is a much sharper point than it may appear at first sight. Roman denarii were not in general use in Israel at that time. The Herodians, however, were supporters of Herod Antipas, and/or other highly Romanized Herods, so Jesus could rely on them having some Roman denarii, even in the Temple.[30] Moreover, those Pharisees who were allied with the Herodians were at least prepared to co-operate with them, and they had already taken counsel with them to get Herod Antipas to put Jesus to death (Mk 3.6). Jesus got them to point out the image and inscription of the emperor on the denarius. It is almost certain that the Herodians would have the current denarii which were in widespread circulation in the Roman empire as a whole, the second set minted by the reigning emperor Tiberius, in very large numbers. On one side (the obverse), every such denarius had Tiberius' laurel-crowned head and the inscription 'TI CAESAR DIVI AVG F AVGVSTVS', 'Tiberius Caesar Augustus, son of the deified Augustus'. On the other side (the reverse) was a seated female figure, perhaps Livia as Pax (Peace), and the end of Tiberius' inscription, 'PONTIF[EX] MAXIM[VS]', the Roman version of 'High Priest', the religious position of the Roman emperor, much worse than Joseph Caiaphas, whatever one thought of him.[31]

This idolatrous coin violated Jewish Law, and these Pharisees and Herodians had brought it into the Temple. In response to them, Jesus gave his famous judgement: 'Give to Caesar what is Caesar's, and to God what is God's' (Mk 12.17). This is shockingly clever. They can go and give the emperor's coins back to him if they like, for at one level they belonged to an idolatrous empire, not to God's chosen people. It was however their responsibility not to forget that 'the earth is the LORD's, and its fullness' (Ps. 24.1), including the metal from which idolaters had made the images on the coins which Pharisees did not need to use, and which Herodians possessed because they were supporters of a client king of Rome.

The next incident recorded by Mark involved Sadducees (Mk 12.18-27). They were the party of the chief priests, and they did not believe in the resurrection of the dead. They are appropriately reported to have asked him what they thought was an awkward question about it. This presupposes that if a man marries and dies childless, his brother should marry the deceased man's wife and raise up children by her (Deut. 25.5-6, which they quote at Mk 12.19). They made up an entertaining story in which this caused no less than seven brothers to marry the same wife, and then they asked whose wife she would be at the Resurrection! This presupposes a very literal view of bodily resurrection, of which they were making fun. Jesus dismissed them with a vigorous statement of his convictions, according to which there would not be any marriage after the general resurrection. He further argued in favour of belief in the resurrection of the dead, arguing from the nature of God himself, and quoting scripture. God is so clearly

---

30   On Herod Antipas and the Herodians see further pp. 341, 347–48.

31   See especially H. St J. Hart, 'The Coin of "Render unto Caesar . . ." (A note on some aspects of Mark 12.13–17; Matt. 22.15–22; Luke 20.20–26)', in E. Bammel and C. F. D Moule (eds), *Jesus and the Politics of His Day* (Cambridge: CUP, 1984), pp. 241–48.

the God of the living that his declaration to Moses 'I (am) the God of Abraham and the God of Isaac and the God of Jacob' (Exod. 3.6) was held by Jesus to demonstrate the survival of Abraham, Isaac and Jacob, and thereby the raising of the dead (Mk 12.26-27).

Another major incident was more in support of Jesus. A scribe asked Jesus which was the most important commandment of all, and Jesus responded with a summary of love of God and love of one's neighbour (Mk 12.28-34). Since this is of central importance in understanding Jesus' view of the Torah, I have discussed it in detail in Chapter 8, so I summarize only the main points here.[32] Jesus began with the opening of the *Shema'*, written at Deut. 6.4-5:

> Hear Israel, the Lord our God, the Lord is One. And you shall love the Lord your God with all your heart and with all your being and with all your might.

With the love of the one God firmly stated as the first duty of faithful Jews, Jesus went to Lev. 19.18 for another central commandment:

> You shall love your neighbour as yourself.

The scribe greatly approved of Jesus' selection of two central commandments. He began with a summary quotation which picks up Deut. 6.4 and continues in terms reminiscent of Deut. 4.35 and Isa. 45.21:

> For good, rabbi, you have truly said that 'He is one and there is none beside him'.

From a cultural point of view, this is the most perfectly Jewish response that one can imagine. The scribe continued with the transcending importance of these two commandments even over against the cultic centre in which he and Jesus stood together, a few days before they would observe the feast of Passover:

> And to love Him with all one's heart and all one's mind and all one's strength, and to love one's neighbour as oneself, is more than all the burnt offerings and sacrifices.

This should not be interpreted as any kind of criticism of the sacrificial cult. It meant rather that love of God and of one's neighbour were the centre of Judaism. Jesus expressed his approval with one of his favourite terms:

> You are not far from the kingship of God

> (Mk 12.34)

32 See pp. 284–86.

This is very strong approval. As we have seen, the kingship of God could be used as a metaphor for God's control over one's life. Jesus' approval accordingly means that in his view the scribe's attitude towards the centre of the Torah meant that he had almost accepted God's complete control over his life.

Jesus offered further criticism of the conventional institutional authorities who normally controlled the centre of Judaism. Mark records some criticism of open display (Mk 12.38-40), and Matthew places at this point a large quantity of vitriolic criticism of Jesus' opponents, some of which may have been delivered at this time.[33]

All three synoptic writers also insert an eschatological discourse at this point (Mark 13//Matthew 24//Luke 21). It is clear that Mark collected material together for this discourse, and that Matthew and Luke edited it in accordance with their own needs. I have already argued that much of this does not go back to Jesus, but reflects rather the hopes and expectations of the early church.[34] Accordingly, I do not offer further discussion of it here.

The conflict between Jesus and the Jerusalem authorities was now so serious that his death was only a matter of time, place and method.

5. Betrayal

The practical difficulties in the way of arresting Jesus were solved by a man usually known as Judas Iscariot. We have seen that this term originally meant Judah, man of Kerioth, a small village in the far south of Judaea, and that Judah was probably called after his place of origin because he was the only one of the Twelve who did not come from Galilee.[35] Judah went to the chief priests of his own volition and offered to hand Jesus over to them (Mk 14.10-11).

> And Judah, a man of Kerioth, one of the Twelve, went to the chief priests, in order to hand him over to them. And when they heard, they rejoiced, and promised to give him money. And he sought how he might conveniently betray him.

In due course, Judah took an armed party to arrest Jesus in an olive grove at night (Mk 14.43-50), thereby solving the chief priests' problem of how to arrest him without provoking a riot in a crowded place (Mk 14.1-2).

Judah's motives have proved very difficult to understand, because of the influence of later Christian tradition. If we imagine that Judah became one of the Twelve because he realized the perfect goodness of his Incarnate Lord coming from heaven to redeem the world, and because Jesus perceived in him the personal qualities needed by an apostle who would spread this wonderful news;

---

33   See pp. 331–38.
34   See pp. 69–71, 374–76.
35   See pp. 191–92.

and if we imagine that Judah's betrayal of Jesus was a perfectly evil act, bringing about the work of the devil by betraying him to perfectly evil people, we get an overnight transition from goodness to evil which is indeed impossible to explain. We cannot get further than the simple comment of the least accurate and most theological of the Gospel writers:

> Then Satan entered into him.
>
> (Jn 13.27, cf. Lk. 22.3)

To understand Judah's motives, we must leave Christian tradition behind and understand him as a faithful Jew. He joined the Jesus movement because he saw in it a prophetic movement dedicated to the renewal of Israel. Jesus chose him because he was a faithful Jew, dedicated to God and to the renewal of Israel, and with the qualities necessary to take a leading role in a ministry of preaching and exorcism. Like other faithful Jews, he was troubled by Jesus' controversies with scribes and Pharisees during the historic ministry. Exactly what he objected to, we have no idea. Perhaps he tithed mint, dill and cumin, and felt the decorated monuments of the prophets were quite magnificent. Perhaps it was something else – it must have been something which did not seem contrary to the prophetic renewal of Israel. While such details are conjectural, the main point is surely secure – Judah was troubled by these controversies, and he did not undergo an overnight conversion.

Nonetheless, given the point at which he went to the chief priests and the seriousness of what he undertook to do, there should be no doubt as to which event was the final straw for him – the Cleansing of the Temple. From the perspective of a faithful member of normative Jewish tradition, the will of God laid down in the scriptures was that the house of God should be run by the priests. In charge were the chief priests, as God had appointed, with scribes who interpreted the scriptures so that everyone knew how the Temple was to be run. From Judah's point of view, it was accordingly quite wrong of Jesus to run the Court of the Gentiles, and upset the arrangements duly made by the chief priests and scribes for the payment of the Temple tax and the purchase of the offerings most used by the poor. Moreover, Judah was from Judaea. He will have worshipped in the Temple long before there was a Jesus movement for him to join. How he came to be in Galilee we have no idea. Equally, we have no idea as to whether he had long-standing contacts with the Temple hierarchy. He is likely to have been concerned at what Jesus said when preaching in the Temple on previous visits.

Thus there is a lot we don't know. The main point is that, from our point of view, Judah changed sides and betrayed his master. From Judah's point of view, however, he did nothing of the kind. He was a faithful Jew doing the will of God from beginning to end, and when a most regrettable conflict became unacceptable, his only master was God. Moreover, Mark assumed that he had provided enough information for his audiences to see this. Mark underlined the connection between Jesus' action in the Temple and the final action against him. He says that the chief priests and scribes 'sought how they might destroy him' in the verse after he related the Cleansing of the Temple (Mk 11.18). He relates their question about his authority (Mk 11.27-33), a question which was bound to trouble many faithful Jews. Straight after Jesus' parable criticizing them and warning of their destruction, Mark says that 'they sought to seize him' (Mk 12.12). He tells us again that they could not arrest him in the festival crowd (Mk 14.2). Then he relates how Judah went to the chief priests of his own volition to hand him over when he could. If there was any particular previous connection between Judah and the chief priests, Mark was not informed of it. He thought however that he had said enough for people to see what Jesus' opponents thought the problem was, and it was enough to cause one of the Twelve to change sides and betray his master.

Judah is etymologically closely related to the word 'Jew' itself, and Judas Iscariot has been portrayed in anti-Semitic outbursts as the quintessential Jew. It is appropriate that this kind of view should now be regarded as morally wrong as well as inaccurate, but it is regrettable that it has led some scholars not merely to cast doubt on the accuracy of the above story, but even to argue that Judah of Kerioth did not exist, so that the rest of the story of the betrayal is not true either. Among recent scholars, Hyam Maccoby is notable for trying to read this anti-Semitism back into the Gospels themselves.[36] Even in the Gospels, however, the hostility to Judas evident for example in the theological declaration that 'Satan entered into him' (Jn 13.27, cf. Lk. 22.3), and in the improbable stories of his death (Mt. 27.3-10; Acts 1.16-20), does nothing to undermine Mark's entirely practical story, which has a perfect setting in the life of Jesus and which neither the early church nor Mark had reason to create.

In addition to following a conventionally late date for Mark, Maccoby pushes the importance of the absence of the betrayal story from Paul.[37] We have seen that the supposed absence of Jesus himself from the Pauline epistles is characteristic of arguments that he too did not exist.[38] The argument is even less convincing in the case of Judas, because Paul had even less reason to mention him in epistles mostly written to deal with particular problems in the Pauline churches, or in his more systematic epistle to the Romans. The early tradition in 1 Cor. 11.23 may mean that Jesus was 'handed over' (by God) rather than betrayed (by Judas), since Paul certainly believed that (Rom. 8.32, cf. 4.25). This still gave Paul no reason to explicitly mention Judas as he wrote epistles, not Gospels. Maccoby then notes that Paul has a tradition of a Resurrection experience to 'the Twelve' (1 Cor. 15.5), and contrasts Gospel accounts of an appearance to the Eleven at Mt. 29.16-20 and the very late Mk 16.14, which he wrongly attributes to Mark, as well as the mention of the Eleven at Lk. 24.33. He infers that the Gospel writers were undermining the tradition of an appearance to the Twelve, and hence that 'no tradition of the betrayal and defection of Judas existed before 60 CE'.[39] We should not follow this, because 'the Twelve' had to be 'the Twelve' for as long

36   H. Maccoby, *Judas Iscariot and the Myth of Jewish Evil* (London: Halban, 1992).
37   Maccoby, *Judas Iscariot*, pp. 23–24.
38   See p. 38.
39   Maccoby, *Judas Iscariot*, pp. 24–25.

as the group existed, to symbolize the twelve tribes of Israel (cf. Acts 1.20-26).[40] The early Pauline tradition was not concerned to change 'the Twelve', whereas Matthew and Luke wrote stories when the remaining Eleven were narratively important to them. None of this is sufficient to undermine the accuracy of Mark's story, because this has such a perfect setting in the life of Jesus.

This leaves Maccoby needing to account for the origins of Mark's story. He has Judas chosen for the story because of his name which signifies 'Jew', and the story invented because of increasing anti-Semitism in the period leading up to the composition of the Gospels.[41] At no stage, however, does he provide an *explanation* of how it came about that Mark has the story which we now read. He simply fastens on small details which he finds unconvincing. For example, Judas appears at Mk 14.41 to hand Jesus over, 'although no indication has been given that he ever left the company of Jesus.' Maccoby suggests this may indicate that 'the betrayal theme has been superimposed on an earlier narrative in which there was no such betrayal'.[42] This is quite fanciful, whereas it is well known and ought to be obvious that Mark did his best to construct a coherent narrative from the traditions which reached him, which were incomplete. Once again, points of this kind do not *explain why* Mark constructed a narrative, parts of which have such a perfect setting in the life of Jesus.

I return to the events which led up to Jesus' death. I have put forward abundant evidence that Jesus expected to die, to the point where he might be expected to take further steps to bring this about. Jesus was however determined to celebrate Passover with his disciples before he died. Luke found a tradition in which he said so explicitly. It makes excellent sense of Jesus, and it is not the kind of thing that the early church would be motivated to produce. It also begins with an idiomatic expression which was originally Hebrew and which was used in the Aramaic of the time of Jesus, evident in English in the use of both 'desire' and 'desired', so this may be exactly what he said:

> With desire I have desired to eat this Passover with you before I suffer. For I tell you that I will not eat it again until it is fulfilled in the kingdom of God.
>
> (Lk. 22.15-16)

This looks forward to the final establishment of the kingdom in the very near future, when Passover was finished, and before there was another one.

---

40   On the Twelve during the historic ministry see pp. 186–92.
41   Maccoby, *Judas Iscariot*, p. 27.
42   Maccoby, *Judas Iscariot*, p. 36.

6. *Jesus' Final Passover*

Essential points from Jesus' arrangements for this final Passover are related at Mk 14.12-16. This account, and that of the meal itself, is based on an old Aramaic source which made Jewish assumptions, and these must be recovered so that the account can be properly understood.[43]

> And on the first day of unleavened bread, when they were sacrificing the Passover (victim), his disciples said to him, 'Where do you want us to go to, and prepare for you that you may eat the Passover?'
>
> (Mk 14.12)

It was the afternoon of Thursday, 14th Nisan. The phrase 'when they were sacrificing the Passover (victim)' conveys a massive amount of information to anyone familiar with Jewish customs of the time.[44] Jesus and some of his male followers had to bring a 1-year-old lamb or goat into the inner court of the Temple, to the parapet which divided the Court of the Israelites from the Court of the Priests, which only priests were allowed to enter. As the leader of his group, Jesus himself will have slit the throat of the victim, here referred to in the customary way as 'the Passover'. Mark has *pascha*, not a Greek word, but the specifically Aramaic (not Hebrew) form of a word which may refer to the feast or the victim, depending on the context. Jesus would then let the blood of the Passover victim drain into a gold or silver bowl held by a priest. The priest passed the bowl back to a priest who was beside the altar, where he dashed the blood against the base of the altar, further soaking the bottom of his once white robes. The air would stink of blood and of burning fat, somewhat covered by incense. The Levites, and perhaps many other people, sang the *Hallel* psalms (Pss. 113–18), as always, to the accompaniment of trumpets and other musical instruments. Then the animal had to be flayed.

After all this was done in the Temple, the Passover victim had to be taken to the place where it was to be eaten, and roasted and so on. Those of Jesus' male followers who accompanied him for the sacrifice of the victim had to ask where this was, because they did not know. Jesus' arrangements were secret, so that he could avoid arrest. Mark recorded what his source told him of the rest of this part of the story:

> [13]And he sent two of his disciples and said to them, 'Go into the city and a man will meet you, and he (will be) carrying a pitcher of water. Go after him,[14]and where he enters, say to the owner of the house, "The rabbi says, 'Where (is) the place-of my-spending-the-night, where I will eat the Passover

---

43 See Casey, *Aramaic Sources of Mark's Gospel*, ch. 6.

44 For a brief summary see e.g. Sanders, *Judaism: Practice and Belief*, pp. 132–38. The outstanding monograph, sorting out which customs mentioned in later sources were already normal at the time of Jesus, is still B. M. Bokser, *The Origins of the Seder: The Passover Rite and Early Rabbinic Judaism* (Berkeley: Univ. of California, 1984).

with my disciples?'[15]And he will show you a large upper room, set out ready. And there prepare for us.'[16]And his disciples went forth and came into the city. And they found according as he said to them. And they prepared the Passover.

The man will have been recognizable because waterpots were normally carried by women, an assumption which Mark's source took for granted. The man will have been looking out for them, and the nature of these arrangements indicates that they were a mode of escaping detection. Likewise, the use of 'rabbi', rather than any clear identification of Jesus, and the conventional description of his followers as 'disciples', ensured that the two men would be less likely to be arrested if they should be overheard.

There is an especially precious piece of information in v. 15. Why a *large* upper room? Not for 13 men to stretch their legs, not with Jerusalem bursting at the seams. The large upper room makes good sense only if there were to be lots of people there. This is confirmed at v. 17, where Jesus comes with the Twelve. With the two men already sent ahead with the lamb or goat, this makes 15 people actually mentioned by Mark. There is further confirmation at v. 20, where the definition of the traitor as one of the Twelve is not very sensible if only the Twelve were there. We must infer the presence of a sizeable group of Jesus' followers. Women are not mentioned because the presence of women at Passover was too obvious to be worthy of mention. Jesus was not likely to have excluded some of his most faithful followers from his final Passover, and had he really determined to celebrate his final Passover with only the Twelve, he would have had a remarkable reason, and Mark would have commented on his remarkable behaviour. It follows that we do not know how big the company was. If we imagine 30, we have a margin of error, but if we follow the conventional 13, we are simply wrong. It is possible, but quite uncertain, that there were children there too. In that case, one of them will have asked for, and received, an explanation of the feast.

That evening, Jesus went with the Twelve to join his other followers in the large upper room (Mk 14.17). They 'reclined' (Mk 14.18), as Jews did at Passover, so the 'large upper room' had been 'set out' (Mk 14.15) with couches for them to recline on. They were 'eating' (Mk 14.18), so they will have begun the meal by eating bitter herbs dipped in a source known as *haroseth*. The next important event was Jesus' prediction of his forthcoming betrayal to the authorities.

> Jesus said, 'Amen I'm telling you that one of you will hand me over, he who "eats" with "me".'[19]And they began to be sad and to say to him one by one, 'Certainly not I!'[20]And he said to them, 'One of the Twelve, he who dips with me into a dish.[21] For a/the son of man goes as it is written concerning him, and woe to that man by whose hand a/the son of man is betrayed/handed over. (It would be) good for him if that man had not been born'.

Mark's definition of the traitor as 'he who eats with me' looks odd at first sight, since several people were eating with Jesus, but the key to this expression lies in

Ps. 41.9. The unique person referred to is the person of the psalm, 'a man of my peace, in whom I trusted, who eats my bread, he has made great his heel against me.' That is a reasonable description of one of the Twelve betraying Jesus. The reference to bread has been altered, so it follows that the unleavened bread had not yet been started: they were still dipping the bitter herbs into a dish of *haroseth*, as indicated at v. 20. The betrayal of Jesus by Judah of Kerioth could be seen at Ps. 41.6: 'And if he comes to see me, his heart speaks falsehood, he gathers wickedness, he goes outside, he speaks of it.' This gets Judah to the chief priests and scribes, who may be seen at v. 7: 'All those who hate me whisper together against me, they devise evil against me.' Their intention is given in v. 8, together with their denial of Jesus' resurrection, a denial equally comprehensible in Sadducees who did not believe in the resurrection, and scribes and Pharisees who thought he was too wicked to go to heaven: 'A thing of Belial will constrain him, and when he lies down, he will not rise again.' Then Judah of Kerioth at v. 9: 'Yes, a man of my peace, in whom I trusted, who eats my bread, has made great his heel against me.' There follows a plea for resurrection in v. 10, 'And you, LORD, be gracious and raise me up.'

All this is too simple, and too extensive, to be unintentional. We must infer that everyone knew Psalm 41, and that the betrayal of Jesus was written in this scripture. No one suggested that they should prevent him from being betrayed. Simeon the Rock had remonstrated with him once, and earned a very severe rebuke (Mk 8.31-33). Subsequently, Jacob and John had accepted promptly the notion that they would die with him (Mk 10.39). Now they all knew that he intended to die his atoning death for the redemption of Israel, which was such an important part of God's will that it was foretold in the scriptures. The plea for resurrection, unlike the original form of his predictions, is a plea for him alone to be raised. Like them, it uses the verb *qūm*, which means to 'rise' in any sense, and consequently might be interpreted of what we would call the immortality of the soul, just as much as the resurrection of the body.[45] This is one of the scriptures which Jesus' followers could hardly avoid returning to after the crucifixion, when some of them came to believe that God had indeed raised him up, according to the scriptures.

Despite all this, a group of normal human beings began to be sad, and to say one at a time, 'Certainly not I!' The feebler form of denial familiar from Christian tradition is due to their use of the idiomatic Aramaic *en ʾᵃnāh*, which may be literally translated 'If I!' This has no literal equivalent in Greek, any more than in English. Mark did his best by translating it with a form of question which is technically said to 'expect the answer "no"', but even that sounds as if each of them thought s/he might betray him by mistake. We must be fair to Jesus' followers, and restore to the historical record their vigorous and unambiguous assertions that they would not betray him. As they began to affirm that they would not betray him, Jesus narrowed down the group from whom the traitor came to one of the Twelve. This makes no sense if only the Twelve were present. With a bigger

---

45   See further pp. 466–71.

group, 30 or more, possibly less, it makes excellent sense, defining the scriptural prediction, making the betrayal the more shocking, yet also reassuring faithful disciples that their affirmations were accepted. The narrowing down to the Twelve also explains the mention of dipping into 'a dish'. Mark has literally 'into the one dish', but 'the one' is a literal translation of the Aramaic $h^edh\bar{a}$, the word for 'one' functioning as an indefinite article in the definite state, the equivalent of the English 'a', which is what Mark and his source meant. Reading therefore 'he who dips with me into a dish', we should infer that at least some of the Twelve were dipping into the same dish as Jesus, which everyone present could not do for practical reasons. Jesus' words also lead us to a very important conclusion: Jesus must have known that Judah of Kerioth would betray him.

The reference to scripture is carried further at v. 21:

'A/The son of man goes as it is written concerning him, and woe to that man by whose hand a/the son of man is betrayed/handed over. (It would be) good for him if that man had not been born.'

Here the idiomatic Aramaic *bar* $(^e)n\bar{a}sh(\bar{a})$, literally 'son of man', cannot lose its level of generality, though this is not the main point of the saying.[46] Jesus was in no doubt that he was going to suffer a humiliating death, and that this was to have a fundamental redemptive function. He therefore had good reason to state the prediction of his death in scripture, and the doom awaiting the traitor, by means of general statements. The Aramaic word for 'go' (*'azal*) was a normal metaphor for 'die', as the Greek word for 'go' was not, so this is further evidence that Mark was translating an Aramaic source. Despite the general level of meaning, no one will have been left in doubt that Jesus' own death was primarily referred to. Psalm 41 is one scripture clearly in mind. Others must have included the second group of *Hallel* psalms, those set for singing at Passover. These include the clear general statement of Ps. 116.15: 'Glorious in the eyes of the Lord is the death of his pious ones.' Surely none of them could sing that verse without thinking of the importance of Jesus' death. They could also include themselves, in so far as they formed any intention to die with him. The doom pronounced on the traitor was also made by means of general statements. The first is at one level a condemnation of traitors, and hence universally acceptable. This made it reasonable for Jesus to proceed with his condemnation of the traitor. This is in accordance with scriptural passages which call on the Lord to deliver the psalmist and put his opponents to confusion (e.g. Pss. 40.13-16; 41.10; 118.7). This also makes it quite clear that it was Jesus himself who condemned Judah of Kerioth in quite unequivocal terms.

Mark then moves to some time during the meal. His source was written by an Aramaic-speaking Jew from Israel, who was writing for people who shared his cultural assumptions. He said this was a Passover meal in vv. 12–16. He expected everyone to know what a Passover meal was like. Therefore he did not

---

46   For this idiomatic usage see pp. 358–68.

write an account of the meal. Rather, he narrated those aspects of the meal which enabled his audience to understand how and why Jesus died. We must therefore reconstruct the basic elements of the Passover meal as the proper background for Mark's narrative.

This celebration included the story of the deliverance of Israel from Egypt, possibly recited from Exodus 12. According to m. Pes. 10, 5, Gamaliel laid down that to fulfil the Passover obligation, mention must be made of three things, the lamb or goat, the unleavened bread and the bitter herbs. This must be Gamaliel I, the prominent Pharisee, contemporary of Jesus and teacher of Paul. It is not probable that he gave this judgement if customs were already uniform. The same decision is explicit in the habit attributed to their now departed contemporary, and prominent Pharisaic rabbi, Hillel, of making a sandwich of the unleavened bread, lettuce and Passover offering (t. Pes. 2.22; b. Pes. 115a). This is not some strict Pharisaic halakhah. The victim itself and the unleavened bread were central features of this major pilgrim feast, and the bitter herbs are biblical: 'and they shall eat the flesh that night, roasted with fire; with unleavened bread and bitter herbs they shall eat it' (Exod. 12.8). We must infer that Jesus gave traditional interpretations of the lamb or goat, and of the bitter herbs, as part of his exposition of God's redemption of Israel from Egypt. Like Gamaliel, who will have been leading a Passover group elsewhere in Jerusalem, he will have said something to the effect that 'we eat bitter herbs because the Egyptians embittered the lives of our fathers in Egypt'. Similarly, over the Passover offering, he will have said something to the effect that 'this is the Passover, for our Father in heaven passed over the houses of our fathers in Egypt'. He may have quoted Exod. 12.27: 'It is the sacrifice of the Passover for the Lord, who passed over the houses of the children of Israel in Egypt, when he slew the Egyptians and spared our houses.'

This hermeneutical framework was essential if Jesus was to use the interpretation of bread and wine to predict and interpret his forthcoming death. He was surrounded by Jewish followers. They had come on pilgrimage to Jerusalem to celebrate this major feast, when all Israel looked back to their deliverance from Egypt, and many looked forward to their deliverance in the future. He was therefore bound to make reference back to their deliverance from Egypt by the mighty hand of God, on whom alone they could rely for their deliverance in the future. Mark had the sort of source which, for that reason, did not need to mention it, when it could take it for granted while it made the main points relevant to understanding Jesus' death. This is presented in two new pieces of interpretation:

> [22]And they (were) eating and he took bread, and said a blessing, and broke (the bread) and gave (it) to them and said, 'Take! This it/is my body.'[23]And he took a cup and said a blessing and gave (it) to them, and all of them drank in it.[24]And he said to them, 'This (is/was) my blood, it (is) of the covenant, shed for many.'

Thus Jesus 'took' the unleavened 'bread', and 'said a blessing', a blessing of God, not of the bread. He 'broke' it and started to share it out, with his interpretation of it. His actual words were something very like this:

n^esubhū! d^enāh hū' gishmī.

Take! This it/is body-my.

As other interpretations looked back to the redemption of Israel at the Exodus, so this one looks forward to Jesus' redemptive death. The Aramaic *n^esubhū* simply means 'take', and begins the process of sharing the bread – it is not seriously different in Aramaic, English and Greek. The instruction to take of the bread which Jesus had broken must indicate some kind of shared experience. This was always true of the unleavened bread, as well as the lamb or goat, and the bitter herbs. The whole feast of Passover was an experience of shared redemption in the past, often accompanied by the shared experience of looking forward to redemption in the future. In the Passover context, the identification of the unleavened bread as Jesus' body is necessarily symbolic. This is facilitated by the Aramaic word *hu'*, which is not part of the verb to be, and which I have consequently translated twice, with 'it' as well as with 'is'. The Aramaic *gishmī* means 'my body', it just has the words attached to each other in a different order from natural English. We may infer that Jesus deliberately symbolized his intention that his followers, who already knew that he intended to die, should share in the benefits of his redemptive death.

Jesus next took a large enough cup to be passed round the whole group. He blessed God again, and they all drank some of the wine before he interpreted it. Jesus then began the symbolic interpretation of the wine as his blood, probably using the Aramaic words *d^emī d^enāh*, literally 'blood-my this'. There is again no direct Aramaic equivalent for 'is'. The symbolic context is too strong for anyone to have seriously felt that they had drunk blood. At the same time, this was a potential problem, sensibly reduced by giving the interpretation *after* they had all drunk from the common cup. The imagery is necessarily sacrificial, looking forward to the redemptive significance of Jesus' forthcoming death, just as they looked backwards to the redemption from Egypt.

The second statement expands somewhat on the scope of Jesus' death: *dī q^ayāmā' hū'*, 'of the covenant it'. This indicates that Jesus' death is important in the relationship between God and his people, Israel. When the people of Israel took upon themselves the observance of the Law, Moses threw sacrificial blood over them and declared, 'Behold the blood of the covenant . . .' (Exod. 24.8). The blood shed at circumcision could be called the blood of the covenant, and the blood of the Passover sacrifice had been fundamental in the deliverance of Israel from Egypt. A later source was able to draw on this same complex of tradition and declare,

But the Holy One, Blessed be He, said, 'By the merit of the blood of the covenant of circumcision and of the blood of Passover I have redeemed you out of Egypt, and by their merit you will be redeemed at the end of the fourth kingdom'.

(*Sayings of Rabbi Eliezer*, Chapter 29)

Jesus' interpretation also looks back and forward. His death would be important in the relationship between God and Israel. This is pushed somewhat further with the rest of the sentence, *mith^eshēdh 'al saggī'īn*, 'shed for many'. The word *saggī'īn*, 'many', must be interpreted with care, as at Mk 10.45.[47] It is not a direct reference to Gentiles, nor is it a deliberate restriction of the covenant to ethnically Jewish people. Basically, however, the covenant was between God and Israel, and that is the context in which Jesus himself saw his redemptive death.

One further saying of Jesus is recorded:

> [25]Amen I'm telling you that we will not add to drink from the fruit of the vine until that day on which I drink it and it (will be) new in the kingdom of God.

Here, with the words 'we will not add to drink', I have translated the most difficult reading, that of ancient Greek manuscripts which have preserved the idiom of Jesus' original, and perfectly normal, Aramaic. He meant, 'we will not drink again'. Mark translated it literally. Most scribes, however, altered it because it is exactly as peculiar in Greek as it is in English, and that is why most manuscripts read normal Greek for 'I will not drink' or 'I will not drink again'. The saying has an eschatological reference, as I pointed out when discussing Jesus' teaching about the kingdom of God.[48] The death of Jesus, and the deaths of any disciples who would die with him, would enable God to redeem Israel. That would be the coming of the kingdom, with the resurrection of the dead and the judgement of the twelve tribes of Israel by Peter, Jacob, John and the other members of the Twelve. Jesus meant that it would happen very soon.

After Jesus' prediction, he and his disciples sang the *Hallel* psalms, which brought the Passover meal to a close. This is indicated at Mk 14.26, where translations such as 'when they had sung a hymn' (RSV) give an impression taken from the wrong culture. These were the second group of *Hallel* psalms, in which it is written that the son of man goes. This is why they are mentioned, and the singing of the first group (Pss. 113–14) is not: even the most creative of ancient exegetes could not find Jesus' death in Pss. 113–14! The second group includes the clear general statement of Ps. 116.15: 'Glorious in the eyes of the Lord is the death of his pious ones', and might be thought to include pleas for resurrection. The following narrative shows that Jesus could have escaped if he had wished to, and makes it evident that he did not wish to.

Jesus and some of his followers went to Gethsemane, on the Mount of Olives (Mk 14.26, 32). The word Gethsemane is not Greek. It is a Hebrew, or possibly Aramaic, name, and it means 'oil-press'. We should therefore imagine them in an olive orchard. This location enabled them to fulfil their Passover obligation to remain in greater Jerusalem, an obligation which could have been overridden by danger to life, had Jesus wished to escape.

At this point, a negative result is of some importance. Jesus did not institute

47 Cf. pp. 404–7.
48 See p. 221.

the Eucharist. He is usually thought to have done so, but in the oldest account of this occasion, there is no mention of it. Christian scholars usually read the institution of the Eucharist into Jesus' interpretation of the bread and wine, because his comments on the bread and wine are very like the words of institution at Christian Eucharists. The notion that the Eucharist was instituted on this occasion was invented by St Paul. Paul was faced with Corinthian Christians who gathered together as if they were at a Gentile banquet, so that, for example, some would be drunk when others were still hungry (1 Cor. 11.21). He roundly declared that when they gathered together, it was not to eat the 'Lord's Supper' (1 Cor. 11.20). This was the cause of Paul's rewriting: he does not mention Passover. Paul tried to control the Corinthians by getting them to eat the 'Lord's Supper', connecting it with 'the Lord Jesus' by means of his rewritten tradition. He begins by saying that he 'received' and 'handed on' to them the account, both words being normal terms for the transmission of traditions. He claims to have 'received' the tradition 'from the Lord', thereby naming the fountainhead of the tradition, in accordance with normal Jewish custom.[49] He locates the meal 'on the night in which he was handed over/betrayed' (1 Cor. 11.23), so there is no doubt that he refers to the same meal as that reported by Mark.

The first discrepancy is Paul's omission of 'and gave to them'. This is part of Mark's narrative report, and Paul did not need it. The next discrepancy is in the interpretation of the bread. In Mark's account this must be unleavened bread, because the sacrifice was dated on the first day of unleavened bread (Mk 14.12), and because the meal has been declared a Passover meal. Paul mentions neither, which facilitates the application of Jesus' rewritten words to Corinthian meals, at which the bread will have been leavened. Paul added 'Do this in remembrance of me'. This was essential, to persuade the Corinthians to treat regular church meals as an imitation of Jesus' last meal. It is another reason why he should omit the Passover context, as this would inhibit the application to anything other than an annual celebration at Passover time. It has no place at the original event, when Jesus expected God to establish his kingdom soon, not leave the disciples on earth celebrating memorial meals. The Twelve should have been judging the twelve tribes of Israel long before Paul got to Corinth!

The word over the cup has been equally rewritten. It is placed after the meal (1 Cor. 11.25), so that the Corinthians will not start to drink before they have finished eating. They will then be less likely to get drunk, and certainly will not do so while some are still hungry. There is no mention of all drinking the cup, another part of Mark's narrative report that Paul did not need, not least because the Corinthians will not have all drunk from the same cup. The interpretation of the cup has been completely altered. The identity statement 'This is my blood' (Mk 14.24//Mt.26.28) has been omitted. With the Passover context omitted, and the Eucharistic context not yet established, the identification of red wine with Jesus' blood could have been very unpleasant, for Gentiles just as much as for Jews. In place of 'of the covenant' Paul has 'the new covenant'. This provides the

---

49   I gathered together the results of recent work on the authorship of Jewish documents in 1996: Casey, *Is John's Gospel True?*, ch. 8.

comfortable 'This cup is the new covenant in my blood' (1 Cor. 11.25), just what Paul needed Gentile Christians to have. Paul has also removed 'shed for many', which belonged in the original context of God's covenant with Israel. The command to repeat the rite, 'Do this, as often as you drink (it), in remembrance of me' (1 Cor. 11.25), is even more carefully focused than before, since the words 'as often as you drink' push all fellowship meals into the Pauline frame of reference. This is pushed further in 11.26, which has these meals relate to the Lord's death 'until he comes'. Here hope for Jesus' second coming has replaced the historical Jesus' expectation of the kingdom, a standard shift from the teaching of Jesus to a central concern of the early church.

There should therefore be no doubt that Paul's version of this meal has been rewritten to meet the situation with which he was faced in Corinth. Paul rewrote the tradition in accordance with the normal ways in which first-century Jews rewrote traditions which they inherited. The result is another classic case of 'social memory'.[50]

Luke's account is also a result of rewriting tradition. The longer text of Lk. 22.19-20 was extensively influenced by the Pauline rewriting. It is attested by the vast majority of manuscripts. Moreover, Luke worked in the Pauline mission field for many years, and he was a companion of Paul for some considerable time.[51] It is therefore entirely reasonable that he should have inherited a version of the last supper which was influenced by the way in which Paul rewrote the tradition. We should therefore follow the majority of manuscripts, and suppose that Luke wrote it. Luke has important points in common with Mark. The most important is the narrative context, in which it is absolutely clear that this was a Passover meal. One central Pauline feature is the six words in common with 1 Cor. 11.24 straight after the interpretation of the bread: 'do this in remembrance of me' (Lk. 22.19//1 Cor. 11.24). In effect, this means that Luke was the only one of the Gospel writers to portray the Last Supper as an occasion on which Jesus instituted the Eucharist. Apart from the word 'is', which is not necessary in Greek as it is in English, Luke also has Paul's version of Jesus' interpretation of the cup: 'This cup (is) the new covenant in my blood . . .' (Lk. 22.20//1 Cor. 11.25). He does not however have the second command to repeat the occasion after the interpretation of the cup, perhaps because 'as often as you drink' was felt to be unsuitable for a narrative of the Last Supper.

All this rewriting by Paul, and subsequently by Luke, throws into relief the nature of Mark's source, and the literal and unelaborated translation of it which now stands in Mark's Gospel. It gives a literally accurate but abbreviated account of Jesus' final Passover, and shows no signs of rewriting in the interests of the early church in general, or of the community to which Mark belonged.

---

50   Cf. pp. 132–41.
51   See pp. 94–95.

7. Arrest

We have seen that, after his last Passover meal, Jesus went with some of his followers to Gethsemane on the Mount of Olives. Unfortunately, however, some details of the following narrative are historically dubious, and the narrative parts company with accurate history almost completely after Jesus' arrest, when most of his followers fled.

First, we must believe in the historicity of the undertaking given by some of Jesus' followers, led by Simeon the Rock, to die with him (Mk 14.29, 31). This follows from the theology of martyrdom which underpinned Jesus' view of his death, it corresponds to the undertaking given by the sons of Zebedee to die with him, and the early church had no motivation to invent it.

Equally true is the story of Jesus' agonized prayers in Gethsemane. The epistle to the Hebrews provides independent confirmation of the actual event:

> . . . in the days of his flesh, he offered prayers and supplications to Him who could save him from death, with loud crying and weeping.
>
> (Heb. 5.7)

Jesus took aside the inner group of three of the Twelve, Simeon the Rock, and Jacob and John the sons of Zebedee. He went just a short distance away and fell to the ground and prayed (Mk 14.35). Consequently, the inner group of three heard his loud crying, a normal way for a faithful Jew of that time to pray to God when in distress. They transmitted the main points to the tradition, and Mark transliterated the Aramaic *Abba* as well as translating it:

> *Abba*, Father, all things are possible for you. Take this cup away from me. But not what I will, but what you (will).
>
> (Mk 14.36)

This is a plea not to have to die, using the metaphor of 'cup' for death, as Jesus had done before.[52] He must have hoped that God would intervene and finally establish his kingdom there and then. This is of central importance, since it did not happen, and the prayer would certainly not have been invented by the early church. There should therefore be no doubt about its authenticity.

After a while, the three most important members of the Twelve went to sleep, as some of the others, further away, may have done too. They will not have been used to staying awake long after dark, and they had drunk more wine than usual because of Passover. Jesus remonstrated with the leader of the Twelve:

> Simeon, you're sleeping! Did you not have the strength to watch for one hour? Watch and pray, that you may not enter into trial. The spirit is willing but the flesh is weak.
>
> (Mk 14.37-38)

---

52 See pp. 404–5.

This brief request for prayer is quite similar to part of the Lord's prayer. As there, the word translated 'trial' can include any sort of temptation, but in this context it must refer to the major period of distress expected before the coming of the kingdom. Jesus told his three closest followers to pray to be spared this distress, just as he asked God to take away the cup from him.

The narrative of Jesus' arrest is also historically accurate. Judah of Kerioth came with people 'from the chief priests and scribes and elders' (Mk 14.43), who were armed with swords and clubs. He identified Jesus in the dark by addressing him as 'rabbi' and giving the prearranged signal of kissing him. Jesus was revolted, and his comment, omitted by Mark's brief source, was memorable enough to be transmitted to Luke:

> Judah, do you betray a/the son of man with a kiss?
>
> (Lk. 22.48)

At this moment, Jesus used the idiomatic Aramaic term 'son of man' in a general statement referring to himself. As usual, the reference is primarily to Jesus himself, but this time the general level of meaning underlines the dastardly nature of Judah's actions.

One of those present also had a sword, with which he cut off the ear of one of the high priest's slaves (Mk 14.47). Resistance was however very limited, and with Jesus in any case determined to let himself be arrested so that he would be put to death, his followers fled (Mk 14.50), though not before some of them heard what he said, as he let himself be arrested when he might have tried to flee too:

> As if against a bandit you have come out with swords and clubs to seize me! Day by day I was with you in the Temple teaching, and you did not seize me. But so that the scriptures may be fulfilled!
>
> (Mk 14.48-49)

Bandits could expect no mercy from authorities, and we shall see that Jesus was crucified as a bandit. He had nonetheless waited to be arrested, because this was God's will written in the scriptures. Even after his desperate prayer in Gethsemane, Jesus knew *exactly* what he was doing.

The last remaining eyewitness, except for Simeon the Rock, followed Jesus when he was arrested, and then fled in such desperate and humiliating circumstance that Mark thought it worth recording:

> And a certain young man was following him with a linen garment over his naked (body), and they seized him, but he left the linen garment and fled naked!
>
> (Mk 14.51-52)

This is more realistic than some scholars have realized.[53] It was quite normal to wear what to us would be a bit of linen rather like a sheet or blanket draped round the body with very little fastening, and not everyone wore underclothes, so that a violent attempt to seize the man by his garment could leave him able to flee, provided he regarded the obvious dangers as more serious than losing his modesty by fleeing naked in the dark. There are consequently several examples from the ancient world of men losing their outer garments in a variety of circumstances. In the classic article demonstrating the normality of this, Jackson's examples include the Greek orator Demosthenes losing his outer garment when speaking before a public assembly, because someone tugged at it (Dem. *Or.* 21, 217).[54] From Mark's point of view, the last of Jesus' followers fleeing naked completed the humiliation of their flight.

8. *Trial and Conviction*

The chief priests now had another problem. They had arrested Jesus, but he was not guilty of any crime under Jewish Law. Joseph Caiaphas (High Priest 18–36 CE) and his council therefore took him to Pontius Pilatus (*Praefectus Iudaeae* 26–37 CE), and successfully pressed a charge under Roman law.

Some details of our accounts of the Jewish 'trial' are improbable. For example, the high priest rends his garments because of Jesus' 'blasphemy', as a result of the following exchange:

> Again the high priest asked him and said to him, 'Are you the Christ, the Son of the Blessed?' But Jesus said, 'I am, and you will see the Son of man sitting on the right of The Power and coming with the clouds of heaven'.
>
> (Mk 14.61-62)

We have seen that the term 'Messiah' was not yet in use as a title like this, 'the Blessed' is not a known circumlocution for 'God', it is most unlikely that Jesus would refer to the Son of man coming on the clouds of heaven in Dan. 7.13, and, from a legal perspective, it would not have been blasphemous for him to do so.[55] Moreover, Jesus was not put to death for blasphemy. The scene however has an excellent setting in the early church in general and the theology of Mark in particular. Jesus' reply 'I am' has him claim both the Church's major titles for

---

53   This is one element in the large quantity of bizarre speculations built on this passage, which include further calumny of Jesus' disciples, importing references to Christian baptism, and the primacy of the *Secret Gospel of Mark*. Summaries of these are provided by Brown, *Death of the Messiah*, vol. 1, pp. 294–304; Collins, *Mark*, pp. 688–93.

54   H. M. Jackson, 'Why the Youth Shed His Cloak and Fled Naked: The Meaning and Purpose of Mark 14.51–52', *JBL* 116 (1997), pp. 273–89, with all manner of alternative suggestions catalogued in the footnotes.

55   See pp. 375–77, 392–99.

himself, thus bringing to an end Mark's 'Messianic secret' which characterizes his account of Jesus' ministry. The rest of Jesus' reply is a midrash created on the basis of Dan. 7.13, Ps. 110.1 and probably Zech. 12.10, just the sort of activity characteristic of the early church, who searched the scriptures for evidence of Jesus' speedy return.[56] Moreover, Jewish opponents of Christianity will have found Jesus' reply blasphemous in the popular sense of such terms in Aramaic, Hebrew, Greek and English alike.

Furthermore, the fact that the high priest rent his garments shows that Mark intended to describe a *formal trial*, at which Jesus was found guilty of the capital offence of blasphemy, for which the traditional penalty was stoning. Whether the Jewish authorities had the right to inflict capital punishment is uncertain. It is known that the proceedings are not in accordance with Jewish Law as it was written down later. According to m. San IV, 1, a verdict of guilty in a capital case required a second sitting of the court on the following day. Both sittings had to be in the daytime, and neither of them should be on the eve of a sabbath or a festival, let alone on a festival itself. It is also most improbable that a court would be convened in the high priest's house. It is possible that the chief priests were not bound by these laws in the early first century. It is however important that *all* these arguments can be circumvented by supposing that this was *not a formal trial*. Joseph Caiaphas was perfectly entitled to gather together a Sanhedrin in his own house late that evening, or past midnight, to take counsel as to what to do about Jesus. We may conclude that this is precisely what he did.

Finally, all the improbabilities in our surviving sources are related at points where none of the disciples were present. We should therefore infer that there was no reliable source for what took place at the meeting, and that Mark and/or his predecessors produced a narrative plausible to them. Jesus was not found guilty on a formal charge of blasphemy, and the high priest did not tear his garments. Even this part of the story was however written quite early. Mark's sources did not identify the high priest by name, probably because he was still high priest, as he had been for years, whereas Matthew, Luke (3.2) and John do identify him by name, because they were written long after Joseph Caiaphas had been high priest. Mark himself had no reason to add in his name, for when he wrote c.40 CE, everyone knew that Joseph Caiaphas, who was still alive and kicking, had been high priest at the time.

Reliable eyewitnesses, including Simeon the Rock, passed on to the tradition what really was known. There was a meeting of a Sanhedrin in Joseph Caiaphas' house very late on Thursday evening, when 15th Nisan had begun at dark, or very early on Friday morning, still 15th Nisan. Their decision was to take Jesus to Pilate. This was a very sensible decision, whether or not Caiaphas had arranged it with Pilate already, a matter into which we have no insight. Pilate had the authority to execute disruptive provincials – he was present in Jerusalem at Passover because of possible disturbances. Jesus was the leader of a popular movement, just what the Romans were concerned about. He had cleansed the Temple, an

56 See pp. 375–77.

action which the chief priests could reasonably present as disruptive. He had preached the imminent coming of the kingdom of God, in which the Romans would have no place, a fact which the chief priests could interpret for Pilate too. Moreover, Jesus' popular following meant that, if the chief priests took severe action against him, they would be unpopular with a lot of people. Roman rule over Judaea, however, was drastically unpopular already, and Pilate would be more concerned to be powerful, safe and successful, than popular.

Mark put his account of the meeting of the Sanhedrin, a mixture of basic fact with fictional details, as the filling of a Markan sandwich, the outside of which (Mk 14.53-54, 66–72) is largely accurate. His story of Peter's denial of Jesus must be largely historical, because the early church had no reason to make up a story so discreditable to the leader of the Twelve. When they took Jesus to the high priest, Simeon the Rock followed at a distance, not being recognized in the dark, and got right into the courtyard of the high priest's house. By normal standards, that was very brave of him. The courtyard was however lit up by a fire and by conventional torches, and one of the high priest's servant girls identified him by sight as one of Jesus' disciples. Simeon denied this and went out to the outer courtyard, where, after further comments by the servant girl, bystanders identified him as Galilaean, perhaps because of his accent (Mt. 26.73). Simeon denied again, swearing an oath as well. The story has been made more difficult by references to a cock crowing (e.g. Mk 14.30, 72). These references probably originated as a misunderstanding of the Roman name for the third watch of the night. It was called 'cockcrow', and lasted approximately from midnight to 3 a.m., the right time for these events. Be that as it may, the rest of the story is entirely plausible, and ends with Simeon weeping.

At this point, Mark has a mistranslation of an Aramaic source characteristic of bilingual translators suffering from interference.[57] He says 'throwing, he wept' (Mk 14.72). In Greek this is nonsense, but in Aramaic people could 'throw' (*shedhā*) threats and curses, much as in English people can 'hurl' abuse, and this is exactly what Simeon had just been doing. That is what Mark meant. He will however have misread the Aramaic *shr'*, 'began', as *shd'*, a difference of one letter, reading 'd' (ד) rather than 'r' (ר). The source read: 'And he began to weep'. It follows that Mark had a written Aramaic source for this event, and the original source of the true parts of this story was probably Simeon the Rock himself. Moreover, Matthew and Luke were so puzzled by 'throwing, he wept' that they consulted another source for the same event, or Matthew did so, and Luke copied Matthew. After copying Mark as usual, they have a run of five identical words instead of Mark's mistake: 'And going outside, he wept bitterly' (Mt. 26.75// Lk. 22.62). This means that the story of Peter's denial was multiply attested. Apart from chaos over the cock, there should be no doubt that it is true.

Simeon will have been very disappointed with himself and other followers of Jesus, as everyone knows. He had undertaken to die with Jesus, and so had some of the others, but they had all fled, and he, after bravely getting as far as the inner

---

57   See pp. 74–76.

court of the high priest's house, had denied that he knew Jesus at all. He may have been disappointed with Jesus and God as well. It was Simeon who had objected when Jesus first predicted his own death.[58] He may never have been altogether happy about Jesus' intentions, though he followed him faithfully all the same. He was within earshot when Jesus prayed in Gethsemane 'Take this cup away from me' (Mk 14.36). Jesus also instructed the inner circle of three 'Watch and pray, that you may not enter into trial' (Mk 14.38). Jesus had effectively prayed that God would deliver them by setting up his kingdom there and then. Simeon may well have thought that God should have done exactly that. Now he could only hope and pray for Jesus' Resurrection, and wonder whether he would ever sit on a throne judging the twelve tribes of Israel.

Early next morning, the chief priests convened a Sanhedrin with scribes and elders, had Jesus bound, and handed him over to Pilate (Mk 15.1). At this point, however, when none of Jesus' disciples was present, our sources have very improbable stories about the proceedings at what should have been a *cognitio extra ordinem*, a sort of investigation at which the Roman governor had such gross powers over a provincial that we would hardly regard the proceedings as legal proceedings at all. Among the unlikely features is the custom by which the Roman governor released one prisoner whom the people requested at Passover (Mk 15.6). This custom is otherwise unknown, and it is most improbable that Pilate, while seeking to please a Jewish crowd (Mk 15.15), would refer to a man whom he wanted to release by the external and hostile term 'the king of the Jews' (Mk 15.9, 12). If Pilate wanted to release Jesus, he merely had to order his release. It is also very strange that the full name of the released prisoner should be preserved as Jesus Barabbas (some manuscripts of Mt. 27.16-17), Aramaic for 'Jesus son of the Father', using '*Abba*', Jesus' central term when he recreated Jewish traditions about the Fatherhood of God. As with the 'trial' before a Sanhedrin, it seems that there was no reliable source for what happened at this meeting, and that Mark and/or his predecessors produced a narrative plausible to them. We must therefore work back from the evidence of the crucifixion to see on what grounds he was put to death.

Jesus was mocked by his Jewish opponents as a prophet (Mk 14.65) and probably as 'the anointed king of Israel' (Mk 15.32), Jewish rejection of a prophet who led a movement and preached the coming of the kingdom of God. He was mocked by auxiliary Roman legionaries and crucified, with two brigands, as 'king of the Jews' (Mk 15.16-27). Pilate, who was responsible for the inscription on the cross, was necessarily concerned about anyone who appeared to be a threat to Roman rule, and he had three men crucified together. Mark describes the other two as 'bandits', or 'brigands' (Mk 15.27), and there is ample evidence of the use of the term 'king' by insurgents:

> Then a shepherd also dared to lay claim to kingship. He was called Athronges and what recommended hope to him was strength of body and a soul

---

58   See pp. 201, 377–78.

contemptuous of death, and, in addition to these, four similar brothers. He put each of these in charge of an armed band and used them as generals and satraps for raids, but he himself, like a king, dealt with graver matters. So then he put on a diadem . . .

(Jos. *War* II, 60–62)

This is what Pilate meant by 'king'. Crucifixion was a fearsome form of punishment, and sedition, probably *maiestas*, is an entirely comprehensible charge as a basis for Jesus' crucifixion, together with two other people on a similar charge. Thus Roman involvement in Jesus' death was essential and purposeful, and resulted from perceiving him as a threat to the peace. The evidence given to Pilate by the chief priests (cf. Mk 15.3) will have been essential to his decision that Jesus was subversive enough to be crucified. The immediate cause will have been the Cleansing of the Temple seen in the context of Jesus' leadership of the Jesus movement as a whole. The chief priests were able to present to Pilate a picture of a man dangerous in the first place because of his leadership of a vigorous movement. We have seen that Jesus used his position to control the running of the Court of the Gentiles in the Temple. However the chief priests put it exactly, this effective leadership of a group which could subvert the running of the Temple will have weighed heavily with Pilate.

The second major point which the chief priests could use was Jesus' preaching of the kingdom of God. We have seen that this was an important feature of his leadership of the Jesus movement. Moreover, Jesus was at Passover hoping that God would finally establish his kingdom. Where would that leave the Romans? Not in the land of Israel, and perhaps not on the earth at all. The chief priests could push that at Pilate too.

It follows that Jesus was crucified on some kind of charge of sedition. Neither Pilate nor the chief priests had at this stage sufficient reason to take measures against his followers. Those at the scene of his arrest had run away, and all the authorities may well have hoped that the movement might now disintegrate.

We have further details of Jesus' gruesome death. After his Jewish examination, he was beaten up by his Jewish tormentors as a prophet, a piece of information culturally too precise not to be true. It is also attested by both Mark (14.65) and by another source (Mt. 26.68//Lk. 22.64), which preserved the malicious question put to Jesus by the unknown men who may have blindfolded him (Mk 14.65, Lk. 22.64, not Mt. 26.67-68), and had probably blinded him with punches and spit anyway:

Prophesy! Who is it that hit you?

This was nothing to the way Jesus was maltreated after Pilate had condemned him to death by crucifixion. Pilate first had him flogged (Mk 15.15), a very severe penalty in itself, so that Jesus would be in unbearable pain as well as suffering from loss of blood. The soldiers responsible for flogging and tormenting him then took him into the courtyard, into which they called the whole cohort. The cohort would be some 500 men, led by a tribune with six centurions under him, so this was a right royal mockery by a large and cruel crowd of brutish men. They dressed him in purple and put a crown of thorns on his head, and as well as beating him and spitting on him, they bowed down before him and hailed him as 'king of the Jews'. This external and hostile description in so maliciously appropriate a context is further evidence of the charge on which Jesus was crucified. It was as a rebellious bandit that he was condemned to the most severe and shameful death penalty imposed by the Roman imperial power.[59] Flogging was a normal procedure before crucifixion, and other torments were at the discretion of those in charge of a particular case.

9. *Crucifixion: A Bandit's Shameful Death*

One result of this maltreatment was that Jesus was so weak that, when he was taken out to be crucified, he could not carry his crossbeam. The Romans, auxiliary legionaries probably raised in Caesarea and Samaria, therefore impressed into service Simon of Cyrene, described by Mark as 'the father of Alexander and Rufus' (Mk 15.21). This part of the story was therefore presumably based on the account of an eyewitness whose children were known to Mark. Moreover, an ossuary naming Simon and Alexander of Cyrene, dated in the first century CE, has been found in Jerusalem,[60] so this looks like three members of the Jerusalem church.

> And they took him to the Golgotha place, which is in translation, place of 'Skull'.
>
> (Mk 15.22)

Who took him there? There has been no change of subject in Mark's narrative since the mockery by a whole cohort. This may well mean that the whole cohort attended the crucifixion of three men regarded by Pilate as dangerous leaders who might be rescued by armed followers. This puts the impressing of Simon of Cyrene into its context as a piece of gross Roman imperialism, regardless of the precise ethnicity of the soldiers. With some 500 tough Roman soldiers available, the crossbeam must be carried by an ordinary provincial!

At another moment when the story is certainly correct, there is also another Aramaic word, albeit oddly transliterated: an Aramaic word of the approximate form *gōlgōlthā* meant 'skull'. Christian tradition has interpreted this of a skull-shaped hill, but some aspects of Christian tradition are late pilgrim inventions, and this aspect of the tradition may not contain any truth at all. The rocky protuberance known as the 'Rock of Calvary', now in the Church of the Holy Sepulchre, could not have had three people crucified on top of it, and the notion that Jesus

---

59 For an accurate account of all the gruesome details, M. Hengel, *Crucifixion* (1976. Revised text trans. J. Bowden. London/Philadelphia: SCM/ Fortress, 1977).

60 See p. 126.

was crucified on a hill is not supported by the New Testament accounts. It remains possible that Jesus was crucified near the traditional site, perhaps some 200 metres to the south.[61] This was outside the city at that time, outside the Gennath Gate, near the main road which went west, and not far from a road going north, so it was possible for him to be mocked by people passing by (Mk 15.29).

The truth about 'the Golgotha place' is probably quite gruesome. The Romans generally left the bodies of crucified people on the cross when they died, to be food for dogs and vultures. This is reflected in a Jewish context in tractate *Great Mourning* (*Ēbhel Rabbāthī*, known euphemistically as *Sᵉmāḥōth, Rejoicings*). This says that the family of someone executed by the state (*mlkūth*), so the Romans, not Jewish authorities, should begin to count the days of mourning 'from when they give up hope of asking' successfully for the body of the executed person (b. Sem II, 9). More specifically, the wife, husband or child of a crucified person is instructed not to carry on living in the same city 'until the flesh has gone and the figure is not recognizable in the bones' (b. Sem. II, 11). This gives a graphic picture of families being unable to obtain the bodies of crucified people when they died, and the bodies being left on crosses until they were unrecognizable.

When the flesh rotted or was torn from the bones, the bones themselves would fall to the ground. Dogs love arm-bones and leg-bones, and are not averse to picking rib-cages, but they are not generally known to run off with skulls. So the tribune, his cohort, the three victims, and Simon of Cyrene probably arrived at a place strewn with skulls, and hence known as 'The Skull Place'.

The crucifixions took place at about 9 a.m. (Mk 15.25). The Romans considered Jesus so important that they fixed to his cross a description which is approximately a charge, 'The King of the Jews' (Mk 15.26). They let Jesus' opponents near enough to mock him in his agony. Chief priests and scribes are recorded mocking him in terms which suggest an Aramaic original best translated 'The Anointed King of Israel' (cf. Mk 15.32). This is again culturally too precise to be inaccurate, the Jewish equivalent of 'the King of the Jews', but a distinctively Jewish version.

At about 3 p.m., Jesus cried out the opening verse of a psalm especially appropriate for a faithful Jew in such gross distress. Mark gives this in transliterated Aramaic as well as in Greek, not the Hebrew of the original psalm:

Elōhi, Elōhi, lemā shebhaqthānī

My God, my God, why have you forsaken me?

(Ps. 22.1, at Mk 15.34)

Once again, we should believe Mark's report. This is the first of the 'psalms of the righteous sufferer'. It reflects Jesus' belief that he was experiencing God's

---

61 The best scholarly discussion I have seen is J. E. Taylor, 'Golgotha: A Reconsideration of the Evidence for the Sites of Jesus' Crucifixion and Burial', *NTS* 44 (1998), pp. 180–203, on which these comments are based.

rejection of Israel, as he died an excruciatingly painful but atoning death which would enable God to redeem Israel despite her sins. It should therefore be taken seriously as a profound cry, but not interpreted overliterally or in isolation from the rest of Jesus' relationship with God. Jesus will have known these psalms by heart. The latter part of this psalm includes a prayer for help, and the next psalm is Psalm 23, which many Jews and Christians have recited when they believed they were at the point of death, as Jesus knew he was.

Shortly afterwards, Mark records that Jesus died (Mk 15.37). With such good reasons to believe parts of this narrative, it is likely that some of it goes back to an eyewitness who was not yet a disciple of Jesus. The obvious candidate for the source is Simon of Cyrene.

At this point, however, Mark provides more creative writing, with his report that the curtain of the Temple was split in two from top to bottom (Mk 15.38). The outer curtain of the Temple was some 82 feet wide and 23 feet from top to bottom. It was made of Babylonian tapestry, with embroidery of blue, fine linen, scarlet and purple, and Josephus describes it as an image of the universe, portraying a panorama of the heavens (*War* V, 212–13). If it had suddenly split in two, Jewish sources could not have failed to mention this dramatic portent; it would have deeply affected both the chief priests and the mass of pilgrims in Jerusalem at the time; Jewish people who could not have failed to mention it include Gamaliel pleading for moderation in dealing with the movement after Jesus' death (Acts 5.34-39); and Christian sources which could not have uniformly omitted it include the whole narrative of Acts. There are however many stories of prodigies occurring to mark the deaths of important people. For example, it was said that when R.Samuel son of R. Isaac died, fire came down from heaven and there was thunder and lightning for three hours (y. AZ 3, 1/4(42c)). These stories were intended to be taken symbolically, and the nature of this one has been sorted out by Roger Aus: it presents God mourning for his son, when normal human mourning was not possible.[62]

One mourning custom was to put out the lights. God's greater light was the sun, so he put it out for three hours, making darkness over the whole land from midday till 3 p.m. (Mk 15.33). The original author will have had in mind Amos 8.9-10:

> And it shall come to pass on that day – oracle of the Lord YHWH – I will bring in the sun at noon and I will darken the land/earth on a clear day. And I will turn your feasts to mourning . . . I will make it like mourning for an only son . . .

Another mourning custom was to tear one's garment, from the top to a little way down. The Temple curtain was God's visible garment. In tearing it from top to bottom, God displayed extreme grief at the death of his son.

---

62 R. D. Aus, *Samuel, Saul and Jesus: Three Early Palestinian Jewish Christian Gospel Haggadoth* (Atlanta: Scholars, 1994), ch. 3, esp. pp. 134–57.

Now when the centurion who stood opposite it saw that he expired in this way, he said 'Truly this man was a son of God'.

(Mk 15.39)

The original author of this verse envisaged the crucifixion taking place somewhere such as the Mount of Olives, from where this centurion could see the outer curtain of the Temple torn in two. He is portrayed as drawing the correct conclusion from three hours' darkness and the tearing of God's garment: the dead man must be a son of God.

10. *A Bandit's Shameful Burial*

Mark's story of Jesus' burial (Mk 15.42-47) not only explains that Jesus was really dead, but also prepares the way for his story of the empty tomb, and in the next chapter I argue that this is not literally true. We therefore have the difficult historical task of trying to see which parts of Mark's account of Jesus' burial, and of the women at the tomb, are literally accurate, and where creative writing takes over. It has been suggested that the whole story of Jesus' burial is false. Among recent scholars, Crossan is especially notorious for suggesting not only that Joseph of Arimathea is 'a total Markan creation in name, in place and in function', but also more dramatically, Jesus' body was 'left on the cross or in a shallow grave barely covered with dirt and stones' and in either case 'the dogs were waiting'.[63]

These radical opinions have two major points in their favour. First, the Gospel stories about Joseph of Arimathea show a lot of secondary development. Secondly, as we have seen, the Romans normally left the bodies of crucified criminals to rot on crosses, to be devoured by vultures and dogs. There are however three reasons not to accept Crossan's view. First, the Romans did sometimes grant the bodies of dead crucified criminals for burial, so Mark's story of Pilate granting Jesus' body to Joseph of Arimathea is plausible. Secondly, Jewish people believed that dead bodies should not be left hanging on crosses overnight because this defiled the land (Deut. 21.22-23). This gave Joseph a good reason for burying Jesus before the beginning of the sabbath during Passover (cf. Mk 15.42). This was moreover a reason which Pilate might find it politically convenient to respect, especially as, from his point of view, the chief priests, scribes and elders, of whom Joseph was one, had deliberately handed this dangerous bandit over to him. Thirdly, and decisively, aspects of Mark's story are not consistent with the early church, or Mark, making up the whole story.

As Mark's story goes, Jesus' body was requested by Joseph from Arimathea, which should almost certainly be identified as Ramathaim (1 Sam. 1.1), some 20 miles north-west of Jerusalem. Mark describes him as 'a distinguished

---

63   Crossan, *Who Killed Jesus?*, p. 172; *Revolutionary Biography*, p. 154.

councillor, who was also expecting the kingdom of God' (Mk 15.43). This is surely right. The term 'distinguished councillor' means that Joseph of Arimathea was the kind of person who could be called upon by the high priest for the meeting of the Sanhedrin which decided to hand Jesus over to Pilate. Mark's description as a whole means that Joseph cannot have been a follower of Jesus, and makes it almost certain that he acted in collusion with the chief priests, perhaps partly because he was a member of that particular Sanhedrin. This makes excellent sense of his pious action in burying what would otherwise have been an untended corpse. The chief priests, scribes and elders will not only have believed that Jesus' dead body should not be left hanging on a cross overnight because this defiled the land (Deut. 21.22-23), they will also have felt responsible for doing something about it because it was they who handed Jesus over to Pilate.

This also explains why there is no sign of any co-operation between Joseph, on the one hand, and Mary Magdalene and Joses' Mary on the other. According to Mark's account, they were among the women who saw the crucifixion 'from afar' (Mk 15.40), and, when Joseph buried him, they 'saw where he was laid' (Mk 15.47). If Joseph were a disciple of Jesus, they would surely have co-operated with him, and could have anointed the body and prepared it for an honourable burial.

The later evangelists changed this. Matthew says Joseph was a disciple of Jesus (Mt. 27.57). Luke says that Joseph 'had not consented to their decision and action' (Lk. 23.51). The Fourth Gospel has 'Joseph from Arimathea, being a disciple of Jesus, but secretly, because of fear of the Jews' (Jn 19.38). All this is secondary rewriting. It is in striking contrast to Mark's description of him, which correctly went no further than claiming that Joseph was also expecting the kingdom of God, which identifies him as a faithful Jew sharing a common hope which was central to the teaching of Jesus.

The original account is confirmed by a tradition attributed to Paul (Acts 13.16, 29). 'The inhabitants of Jerusalem and their leaders' (Acts 13.27) are reported to have found no cause for death in Jesus, and to have asked Pilate to do away with him (Acts 13.28). It is said of them in v. 29, 'having taken him down from the cross, they put him in a tomb'. This means that he was officially buried, and it assumes the obvious fact that Joseph of Arimathea had a group of men to help him. He could not have acted alone, because the task of removing a corpse from a cross and burying it is too great for one man, and a 'distinguished councillor' would be accustomed to getting other men to help with such work.

The report of Acts 13.29 also fits very well with the view that Jesus was buried in a common criminals' tomb. The Mishnah says that the Court (*Beth Dīn*) kept graves for this purpose. It comments on the fate of executed criminals:

> And they did not bury them in the graves of their fathers, but two graves were arranged for the Court (*Beth Dīn*), one for (those) stoned and (those) burned, and one for (those) beheaded and (those) strangled.
>
> (m. San. VI, 11)

While this document is later than the time of Jesus, it is likely to represent old tradition, because no one would be motivated to make it up later. A special grave was not necessary for crucified people, since crucifixion was not an official Jewish penalty. We should probably infer that Joseph of Arimathea and his party buried Jesus in one of these graves.

According to Mark, Pilate was surprised that Jesus was already dead, and sent for 'the centurion', who confirmed that Jesus was indeed already dead (Mk 15.44-45). From Mark's point of view, Pilate and the centurion were the best witnesses that Jesus was dead, because they were the authoritative outsiders responsible for his death. Some people would therefore be motivated to produce this story. On the other hand, this story was not retained by either Matthew or Luke. Many people lasted much longer than six hours on a Roman cross, even after being scourged, and people were occasionally taken down and revived. Matthew and Luke may not have liked Pilate's surprise that Jesus was dead, as it might encourage people to believe that the centurion was wrong, and Jesus survived crucifixion for a time, rather than being raised from the dead. It is accordingly more probable that the story thus far is literally true.

Moreover, we have seen that Simon of Cyrene was pressed into service to carry Jesus' crossbeam (Mk 15.21). The traditional explanation of this unusual feature of a crucifixion, that Jesus was too weak to carry the crossbeam, is the only reasonable one. It is therefore entirely probable that Jesus died on the cross unusually quickly, in six hours. Pilate will have been concerned that Jesus should not survive, and he may not altogether have trusted Joseph of Arimathea because of his apparent haste. He may perhaps also have been aware of Joseph's traditional Jewish piety, 'expecting the kingdom of God', which had no place for the Roman empire in it. The centurion also coheres very well with supposing that a whole cohort attended the crucifixion of three men regarded by Pilate as dangerous leaders who might be rescued by armed followers. Hence Pilate felt it safe, as well as necessary, to send for the senior centurion personally: this would give him the opinion of a responsible experienced battle-hardened soldier who knew from much experience the difference between a wounded man and a corpse, and it would leave the victims guarded by an armed cohort, perhaps still led by a tribune assisted by five centurions. Hence also Mark's perfectly correct information that Mary Magdalene and some other women watched from a distance (Mk 15.40). They will not have been able to approach nearer, and had any of the men joined them, they would have been liable to suffer the same fate as Jesus, or to have been summarily, or slowly and cruelly, dispatched, as pleased their captors.

This also explains why there is no mention at this point of the two bandits crucified with Jesus. They were still alive, suffering horribly as crucified people were supposed to. The biblical text which says that the corpse of a hanged man should not be left on the tree at night, because it defiles the land (Deut. 21.22-23), says nothing about live men hanging on trees. The Romans deliberately left people hanging on crosses as a visible deterrent to anyone who might consider challenging Roman power. They will have done so in this case too.

Joseph of Arimathea, having been granted Jesus' body by Pilate, led a party who took Jesus' body down from his cross. At this point, it is important that Jewish criminals were supposed to receive a shameful and dishonourable burial. I have noted one aspect of this, that those condemned by the Court (*Beth Dīn*) were not buried in the graves of their fathers, but special common graves were kept for burying them. While Jesus was sentenced to crucifixion by the Roman governor, not by a Jewish court, he was handed over by a Sanhedrin convened by the high priest, so that a common criminals' grave was the obvious place for Joseph to have buried him. The normal rites of mourning were not followed for such people, either. The general situation was sufficient for Josephus to comment on the end of a biblical thief, 'And after being immediately put to death, he was given at night the dishonourable burial proper to the condemned' (Jos. *Ant.* V, 44). Somewhat similarly, he says of anyone who has been stoned to death for blaspheming God, 'let him be hung during the day, and let him be buried dishonourably and secretly' (Jos. *Ant.* IV, 202).

Aspects of Mark's account of Jesus' burial fit with this pattern. There is no mention of the body being washed, anointed and laid out for burial. The historicity of this should be accepted – Jesus received a shameful burial, as was normal for condemned criminals. Joseph of Arimathea led a party to bury him to prevent the land from being defiled, not out of any regard for Jesus, his followers or his family.

So much is clear. Unfortunately, there are problems with the rest of Mark's account. The first problem is at v. 46. Here Joseph, carrying out the task of burying an executed criminal in some haste because it was not long before the sabbath would begin, buys a cloth to wrap the body in. On the major feast of Passover, this was almost certainly against the Law, and it was quite unnecessary, since the body could be buried naked. Matthew and Luke both kept the cloth, Matthew adding that it was clean, but both omit Joseph buying it, probably because Matthew knew this was against the Law, and Luke knew Matthew and/ or received a similar tradition (Mt. 27.59, Lk. 23.53). We should probably infer that Mark's rewriting begins here. He has imagined Jesus buried in a shroud because this was more decent than being deposited naked in a common tomb.

Mark's rewriting probably continues with Jesus buried in a rock-hewn tomb with a stone covering the entrance. This prepares the way for the women to wonder how they could remove the stone, and find it miraculously removed (Mk 16.2, 4). On the other hand, this much could possibly be based on old tradition. Most tombs in Jerusalem were carved out of the soft *meleke* limestone, because that was what was there, and it is especially likely that the *Beth Dīn*, keeping graves especially for criminals, would have them carved out of limestone and sealed with a stone, as most tombs were.[64] Mark is certainly rewriting when he says that Joseph *rolled* a stone against the door of the tomb (Mk 15.46). This prepares the way for the 'very large' stone, which three women would need other

---

64 A detailed and unbiased account of tombs in Jerusalem is given by Rachel Hachlili, *Jewish Funerary Customs, Practices and Rites in the Second Temple Period* (JSJSup 94. Leiden, Brill, 2005).

beings to *roll* away (Mk 16.3-4). This is creative writing.[65] Most tombstones were square or rectangular. Very large round stones, which had to be rolled, have been found only in a small number of large tombs for the very rich and distinguished. Such for example was the tomb of Queen Helena of Adiabene and her family, which was built a little later, c.50 CE, and which was sealed by a rolling-stone, which was accessible through a depression in the floor of the porch, and moved by an unusual mechanism.[66]

This rewriting gives the impression that Jesus was not buried in a common criminals' tomb, or any ordinary tomb for that matter. Matthew and Luke made a similar point more carefully. Matthew says that Joseph buried Jesus 'in his new tomb' (Mt. 27.60), while Luke says that no one had yet been laid in the tomb (Lk. 23.53). John says that they put Jesus in a 'new tomb, in which no-one had ever been put' (Jn 19.41-42). We should not believe any of this rewriting.

Mark concludes this part of the story by saying that Mary Magdalene and Joses' Mary saw where he was put (Mk 15.47). We are now completely within the rewritten part of the story. This is to enable us to imagine that the women could not have gone to the wrong tomb. This rewriting continues in the story of the Resurrection (Mk 16.1-8), where the angel also shows that Jesus' remains had gone from the correct tomb. He points out the part of the tomb where Jesus was laid (Mk 16.6), so the women could not have failed to recognize a rotting body and imagined that he had gone from an empty space left for the next one. This reflects the natural assumption that more than one person was buried in the tomb, as was normal in rock-cut tombs in Jerusalem, not only the Court's tombs for criminals. Matthew and Luke excluded the possibility that the women misinterpreted an empty space more effectively with their claims that the tomb was new or that no one had been laid in it (Mt. 27.60; Lk. 23.53).

I argue in Chapter 12 that the story of the empty tomb is not literally true and did not originate in the very earliest period of the church. It follows that Jesus was probably buried in a common criminals' tomb. Mark's story of his burial, the first part of which is true, has been affected by early Christian belief in his Resurrection.

The only reason for some uncertainty about Jesus being buried in a common criminals' tomb is that we do not know where the tombs kept by the Jewish authorities for the burial of criminals were, and even the site of the crucifixion is less than 100 per cent certain. This is something of a problem, because Joseph did not have very long between Jesus' death and the beginning of the sabbath (Mk 15.42). We do not know how far his party had to carry the body, and we could not know what he would do if darkness fell and the sabbath began without a reliable source telling us, and it is a reasonable inference from the authentic parts of the Gospel tradition that our sources say nothing because they did not know, or because the story was too shameful for them to wish to tell it.

The traditional site of Jesus' tomb is in the church of the Holy Sepulchre.

---

65   See further pp. 461–62, 465, 474–75.
66   Hachlili, *Jewish Funerary Customs*, p. 36, citing M. Kon, *The Tombs of the Kings*, i.e. *Kivre ha-melakhim: nefesh bet ha-melakhim mi-Ḥadayev* (in Hebrew. Tel Aviv: Dvir, 1947. n.v.).

This is a feasible place, more than 50 cubits outside the city walls as they were at the time of Jesus. Moreover, there were tombs under it at the right time, as well as in the surrounding area. If Jesus was crucified some 200 metres further south, he could have been buried in this area, which is also a feasible place for tombs kept by the *Beth Dīn* for criminals. This site is however supported only by a late pilgrim tradition, which does not emerge until the fourth century, and the conjecture that the tradition was handed down from the first witnesses is extremely improbable, since no early source mentions it.

The other definite proposal is the Garden Tomb, or Gordon's Tomb. It is north of the Damascus Gate. It is in a feasible area for tombs. However, there is no clear evidence that it was used for tombs at anything like the right date, so this site, though favoured by some Christians, is correctly not supported by scholars.[67]

I conclude that we do not know exactly where Jesus was buried. It is probable that he was buried in a common criminals' tomb in the general area of the Church of the Holy Sepulchre.

11. *Conclusions*

It is sometimes difficult to distinguish accurate history from creative writing and rewriting. I hope the above account has done so as accurately as possible. Jesus was crucified as a bandit. The main reasons were that he led a major religious movement, and caused a major disturbance in the Temple, which he did deliberately because he believed that it was God's will that he should die an atoning death for the redemption of Israel. He not only threw out those who changed money and sold doves in the outermost court of the Temple, he continued to control the halakhah in the outermost court, and he continued to preach against the chief priests and the scribes every day in the Temple. When he had celebrated his final Passover with his disciples, he waited in Gethsemane to be arrested, knowing that he was being betrayed by Judah of Kerioth, one of the Twelve.

Jesus was not however guilty of any offence under Jewish Law. The chief priests therefore took him to Pilate, and successfully pressed a charge of sedition or the like. Pilate therefore had him crucified as a bandit, with two less important men found guilty on similar charges. He died exceptionally quickly. Joseph of Arimathea requested his body from Pilate, so that a dead body hanging on a cross would not defile the land, a situation for which neither he nor the chief priests would wish to be responsible. When Pilate granted this request, Joseph gave the body a shameful burial, probably in a common criminals' tomb.

With the disciples having fled, Jewish and Roman authorities alike will have hoped that the Jesus movement would now effectively cease to exist. It did not do so. On the contrary, some of Jesus' followers came to believe that he had risen from the dead. How this came about is the subject of the next chapter.

---

67 See Rousseau and Arav, *Jesus and His World*, pp. 104–9.

CHAPTER 12

Did Jesus Rise from the Dead?

1. *Introduction*

The belief that Jesus rose from the dead has been a central feature of Christianity from the earliest times. As Paul put it:

> But if Christ has not been raised, then our preaching is vain, and your faith is vain too
>
> (1 Cor. 15.14)

Scholars have however found the origins of Christian belief in Jesus' Resurrection very difficult to understand. Moreover, the subject is phenomenally controversial, because religious and anti-religious convictions about it are so strong. Conservative Christians believe not merely that Jesus rose from the dead, but that he rose *bodily* from the dead, leaving an empty tomb behind. This is in accordance with the witness of all four canonical Gospels. In recent years, there have been two outstanding scholarly defences of this tradition, the standard works of William Lane Craig, and of Bishop Tom Wright.[1]

Many educated Christians, on the other hand, believe that God raised Jesus from the dead, but *not bodily*. They follow what used to be a conventional view among critical scholars, that the disciples saw appearances of Jesus after his death, but that the stories of the empty tomb are not literally true. As Barnabas Lindars put it, 'so far from being the origin of belief in the Resurrection, the empty tomb stories arose from this belief.'[2]

On the whole, people from outside the Christian religion simply do not

---

1 W. L. Craig, *Assessing the New Testament Evidence for the Historicity of the Resurrection of Jesus* (Lewiston: Mellen, 1989); N. T. Wright, *The Resurrection of the Son of God* (London: SPCK, 2003).

2 B. Lindars, 'The Resurrection and the Empty Tomb', in P. Avis (ed.), *The Resurrection of Jesus Christ* (London: Darton, Longman and Todd, 1993), pp. 116–35 (118).

believe in the Resurrection at all. The most scholarly book by someone who has left the Christian faith is that of Lüdemann.[3]

I discuss this from a historical perspective. In my view, two significant results have emerged from the scholarly work done so far. First, the belief that Jesus had risen from the dead was held at a very early date. Secondly, this belief was based on appearances of Jesus seen by some of his earliest followers, on the tradition of Jesus' predictions, and on the scriptures. The earliest belief was not based on the empty tomb, nor on the stories of Resurrection appearances which are now found in the four Gospels. I therefore begin with the early belief that Jesus rose from the dead.

2. Early Experiences and Belief

The early date of the belief that Jesus had risen from the dead follows from its presence in the earliest sources. 1 Corinthians 15.3-8 provides direct Pauline testimony to the relatively early date of its list of appearances:

> For I handed on to you in the first place what I also received, that Christ died for our sins according to the scriptures, and that he was buried and that he was raised on the third day according to the scriptures, and that he appeared to Cephas, then to the Twelve: then he appeared to over 500 brethren at once, of whom the majority remain until now, but some have fallen asleep: then he appeared to Jacob, then to all the apostles: but last of all, as if to an aborted foetus, he appeared also to me.

This piece was written c.54 CE, some years after the events related. Paul claims that it is earlier tradition, and he uses the terms 'received' and 'handed on', which were characteristic terms for describing the transmission of Jewish traditions. The actual date of this tradition is however difficult to determine. Paul first visited Corinth c.50 CE, so this is the (not much earlier) date at which he handed it on to the Corinthians.[4] When he received it, and in what shape or form, is quite another matter. Conservative scholars suppose that Paul received it more or less as we have it at a very early date, but the arguments which they use are by no means decisive. For example, Craig argues that 'Paul probably received the formula mentioning the appearances to Peter and the Twelve in Damascus shortly after his conversion . . .'. Craig's reasons include 'he most likely received instruction in the faith during that time, and such a formula would be suitable

---

3   G. Lüdemann, *The Resurrection of Jesus: History, Experience, Theology* (1994. Trans. J. Bowden. London: SCM, 1994).

4   The best recent discussion of the relevant chronology known to me is R. Riesner, *Paul's Early Period: Chronology, Mission Strategy, Theology* (1994. Trans. D. Stott. Grand Rapids: Eerdmans, 1998).

for that purpose . . .'.[5] This is true, but it does not follow that this formula had already been produced. We must see how far analysis of the formula helps.

It has several remarkable features. First, Christ is said to have been raised 'according to the scriptures', before the mention of any experiences. This underlines the centrality of the scriptures, both as a fundamental source of revelation in Second Temple Judaism, and, consequently, as a central aspect of belief in Jesus' Resurrection from the earliest days. The non-Pauline phrase 'according to the scriptures' also indicates that Paul did not receive and hand on a formula literally translated from Aramaic, which does not have a sufficiently close equivalent to this expression.

Secondly, Paul says that 'Christ' died 'for our sins'. The term 'Christ' was applied to Jesus only after his death and Resurrection, and this use of 'Christ' on its own with no article is typically Pauline, and not a literal translation from an Aramaic tradition.[6] Moreover, the idea that 'Christ' died 'for our sins' is a product of the Gentile mission. This means that, however early Paul inherited this tradition, it has been rewritten. We have seen that Paul himself rewrote the tradition about the Last Supper, which he also inherited.[7] The forgiveness of sins was so important that Matthew rewrote Jesus' word over the cup, adding that Jesus' blood was shed 'for the forgiveness of sins' (Mt. 26.28, expanding Mk 14.24). It follows that we should not believe anything in 1 Cor. 15.3-8 simply because Paul tells us that he inherited the tradition which he handed on.

Thirdly, Paul equates his vision of Jesus on the Damascus Road with a Resurrection appearance. We know from the accounts in Acts that this was a vision which other people present at the time did not see or hear properly (Acts 9.3-8; 22.6-11; 26.12-18). Thus it stands within the visionary tradition characteristic of the Judaism of this period.[8]

Fourthly, most of these appearances were seen by the inner group around Jesus. The first in Paul's list was to Cephas, the Aramaic nickname of Simeon the Rock, the leader of the Twelve. He is otherwise known as a visionary, certainly from Acts (10.10-20; 11.5-10), perhaps also from the Transfiguration (Mk 9.2-8//Mt.17.1-8//Lk. 9.28-36), though the historicity of the latter is more doubtful. Another was to the Twelve, the traditional term for the inner group of disciples who currently numbered eleven, following the removal of Judah of Kerioth. Another was to Jacob. Most scholars believe this was Jacob brother of Jesus. This is probably right, because 'the Twelve' have already been mentioned, and this group included Jacob son of Zebedee. Jesus' brother was another person close to Jesus who had just been traumatically bereaved. Another appearance was to 'all the apostles', so a somewhat larger group of people sent out by Jesus during the historic ministry. It follows that, according to this tradition, the majority of appearances were seen by bereaved people who had been close to the historical Jesus.

5   Craig, *Resurrection of Jesus*, p. 16.
6   See pp. 392–99.
7   See pp. 435–37.
8   See pp. 488–90.

The fifth remarkable feature of the Pauline tradition is that one appearance was to 'over 500 brethren at once'. A corporate vision on this scale is much more remarkable than a vision experienced by a single person. Paul's comments are equally noteworthy: 'of whom the majority remain until now, but some have fallen asleep'. This means that Paul had information about several supposed eyewitnesses of the Resurrection, but it does not follow that he knew any of them. It also means that, after saying that he 'received' this tradition, he was quite happy to add something as he reminded the Corinthians of it, something which was obviously a secondary tradition. Once again, this is typical of the way in which Jews handed on their traditions. They could repeat them verbatim, rewrite them, or a combination of the two.

The sixth remarkable feature of this tradition is that the appearance to Paul ends the list. The extraordinary metaphor of 'aborted foetus' (*ektrōma*) caused endless trouble to commentators until Nickelsburg worked it out.[9] It presupposes that Paul was called like a prophet from his mother's womb (Gal. 1.15-16), and was as it were 'born' when he became the apostle to the Gentiles. Thus he was as it were 'an aborted foetus' when he was persecuting the church before his vocational 'birth'. As was well known, the appearance of Jesus to him on the Damascus Road marked the point at which he ceased to persecute the churches and began to fulfil his vocation as apostle to the Gentiles. Paul's description of this as the last of the Resurrection appearances indicates that all the other appearances took place within a relatively short space of time. This fits perfectly with most of them being seen by bereaved people. They were not considered to be a lasting feature of church life at the time, even though visions of Jesus have continued to be a feature of Christian experience ever since.[10]

The seventh remarkable feature of the Pauline tradition is that there is no mention of an empty tomb.

Some scholars have argued that the empty tomb is implied by the information 'he was buried' (1 Cor. 15.4). For example, Craig comments that 'in saying that Jesus died – was buried – was raised – appeared, one automatically implies that an empty grave has been left behind.'[11] This reflects Craig's own beliefs rather than those of Paul and other Second Temple Jews, and his supporting arguments are extraordinarily weak. For example, he tries to use the literal meaning of Paul's Greek word *egēgertai* (1 Cor. 15.4), which is usually translated into English with a past tense, 'was raised', and which is a perfect tense which effectively means that Jesus was raised – a single event 'on the third day' – and that he is still raised, so a present state, not a *mere* past event. Craig argues that, like the other major New Testament word for rising from the dead (*anistanai*), *egeirein* means 'awaken' from sleep. Further,

9   G. W. E. Nickelsburg, 'An *ektrōma*, Though Appointed from the Womb: Paul's Apostolic Self-Description in 1 Cor 15 and Gal 1', *HThR* 79 (1986), pp. 198–206.

10 Cf. P. H. Wiebe, Visions of Jesus: Direct Encounters from the New Testament to Today (Oxford/New York: OUP, 1997).

11 Craig, *Resurrection of Jesus*, p. 88.

... sleep is a euphemism for death; no doctrine of soul-sleep is implied. The picture is thus of a dead person's waking up again to life. Both verbs also mean 'to raise upright' or 'to erect'. This can only have reference to the body in the grave . . . the very words appear to imply resurrection of the body.[12]

All this involves taking language very literally at a time when beliefs were not sufficiently fixed for us to do so. Like Jesus' own Aramaic term *qum*,[13] these words could be used analogically to the degree that any author found fruitful to describe an incomprehensible act of God. Craig's arguments illustrate the extent to which he thinks logically only within his ideological convictions, and their function is to remove one of the most important pieces of evidence in the primary sources: neither the earliest kerygmatic formulation, nor Paul himself, mentions the empty tomb.

Moreover, the mention of Jesus' burial has an important but quite different significance. As we have seen, the Romans usually left the bodies of crucified people on the cross to rot and be eaten by dogs and vultures. This was shameful and contrary to Jewish custom, so the fact of Jesus' burial was important to the earliest Christians. Also, it was well known that people occasionally survived crucifixion, and Jesus was crucified for only six hours (cf. Mk 15.25, 33–34, 37, 44–45). That he was buried showed that he was dead. This makes the absence of any mention of the empty tomb more remarkable, not less.

Ironically, this is the most important piece of hard evidence that this tradition is early. It was not rewritten in the light of the first written effort to tell the story of the empty tomb, that of Mark c.40 CE. That Paul personally did not write the empty tomb into the tradition may mean that he did not personally believe in any such thing, which is one possible interpretation of the rest of his comments in 1 Corinthians 15.

Similar experiences and belief are implied by the speeches of the first apostles in the earliest chapters of Acts, though here there are even more signs of rewriting. For example, the qualifications laid down by Simeon the Rock for any replacement for Judah of Kerioth among the Twelve include being a witness of Jesus' Resurrection (Acts 1.22). Simeon also reported the limited number of witnesses to this event (Acts 10.40-41). This confirms the tradition of appearances to a limited number of people who had been close to the historical Jesus, until Paul saw Jesus in his vision on the Damascus Road. There is once again no mention of an empty tomb.

Some scholars have argued that the empty tomb is implied in Peter's speech at Pentecost (Acts 2.14-36). According to Luke, Peter used a scriptural proof of Jesus' Resurrection, which says that 'you will not abandon my soul to Hades, nor give your holy one to see corruption' (Ps. 16.10 at Acts 2.27). Peter interprets this of 'the resurrection of the Christ', commenting 'he was not abandoned to Hades, nor did his flesh see corruption' (Acts 2.31). At first sight, this looks inconsistent with Jesus' body rotting in a common criminals' tomb. Wright comments,

---

12   Craig, *Resurrection of Jesus*, pp. 89–90.
13   On this see pp. 377–81.

'the only reason for choosing Psalm 16 (LXX 15) as the key text to interpret the extraordinary events of Easter is that Luke at least believed, and the early sources he drew on seem to have believed, that the resurrection of Jesus involved not the corruption of his physical body in the tomb . . . but its incorruption.' Wright adds, 'It would thus be futile to make anything of the fact that the proclamation in Ac. 10.40f. does not mention the empty tomb. As in 1 Cor. 15.3f., it is clearly assumed.'[14]

The first of Wright's two points is a reasonable comment on Luke writing in Greek c.85 CE. Luke believed in the empty tomb, and he rewrote and created stories about it to encourage other Christians to believe the same.[15] He will therefore have been happy with Psalm 16, because he 'believed that the resurrection of Jesus involved not the corruption of his physical body in the tomb . . . but its incorruption.' This is not however a reasonable comment on 'the early sources he drew on', and certainly not on Simeon's original speech. Simeon's original speech will have been delivered in Aramaic, and Simeon knew the text of Psalm 16 in Hebrew. The text of Ps. 16.10 does not use the Greek term Hades, nor a word for 'corruption'. It has 'Sheol' and 'the Pit'. When Simeon quoted it, he will have quoted it saying 'For you will not abandon my soul (*naphshi*) to Sheol, you will not give your faithful/pious one to see the Pit.' The first Christians genuinely believed that God did not leave Jesus in Sheol, nor did he see 'the Pit'. On the contrary, God raised him from the dead, where he sat at the right hand of God, an event seen as foretold in Ps. 110.1 at Acts 2.34-35, before the end of this same speech. If therefore Luke has reproduced Simeon's original speech, it did not imply that Jesus' tomb was empty: that is an interpretation based on Luke's quotation of the *Greek* text of Ps. 16.10. Moreover, the early Christians' belief that God raised Jesus from the dead gave Simeon a perfect reason to quote Psalm 16 as well as Ps. 110.1.

Wright's second point is accordingly wrong too. It is very important that 'the proclamation in Ac. 10.40f. does not mention the empty tomb', and the rest of Acts does not do so either. It is no more 'clearly assumed' than it is in 1 Corinthians 15. Wright has made the same mistake as Craig. He has looked at the primary sources in the light of his own beliefs, and he has seen his belief in the empty tomb assumed when it is not there.

Moreover, Acts has ample narrative space. If Jesus had been raised bodily from the dead, leaving a literally empty tomb, not one occupied by anyone else's remains, this would have been a very remarkable event in itself. The site of the tomb would not have been forgotten, and the narrative of Acts would surely tell us of excited disciples visiting it, venerating it and praying there, just as other Jews did at tombs which were important to them, though hardly as important as this one would have been to people who believed that God raised Jesus bodily from it so that his earliest followers found it empty.[16] It would also

---

14 Wright, *Resurrection of the Son of God*, p. 455, with n. 13.
15 See pp. 481–85.
16 The classic work on Jewish tomb veneration is still J. Jeremias, *Heiligengräber in Jesu Umwelt (Mt. 23,29; Lk. 11,47): Eine Untersuchung zur Volksreligion der Zeit Jesu* (Göttingen:

have been as important to their preaching as it is in the narrative accounts of all four Gospels.

The attempts of conservative Christian apologists to circumvent this aspect of the primary sources are also remarkable. For example, Dunn, noting that there is no evidence of Jesus' tomb being venerated, and correctly finding this 'striking', also finds it 'obvious' that 'they did not believe any tomb contained his body. They could not venerate his remains because they did not think there were any remains to be venerated.'[17] Dunn does not however explain why they might venerate 'remains', but not celebrate the known site of the event at the centre of their faith, Jesus' Resurrection from the dead. As Barclay put it in an outstandingly clear essay about modern scholarship on the Resurrection, this argument 'completely backfires: the tomb would not have to contain Jesus' bones for it to be venerated (cf. the Holy Sepulchre) and, indeed, the lack of veneration might support the case that the whereabouts of Jesus' burial was simply unknown.'[18]

We should again infer that Jesus was probably buried in a common tomb for criminals. The earliest form of belief in his Resurrection was that God had vindicated him by taking him up to heaven, where he sat at God's right hand. This is why the site of his shameful tomb was irrelevant – it was probably an official tomb for criminals, and consequently unfit for veneration. The earliest Christians may in any case not have known the site of it, in which case they could not venerate it.

3. *Gospel Appearance Narratives*

The tradition that there were Resurrection appearances may at first sight seem to be supported by the fact that all four Gospels report some, and all three completed Gospels narrate some. Unfortunately, however, such an argument is of limited value. It has become clear from scholarly analysis that the Resurrection narratives in our Gospels are not reports of real facts. They do not coincide with each other, and they contain internal inconsistencies. Moreover, these are not the sort of minor disagreements which happen when important events are related by different people over a lengthy period of time: they are organically serious disagreements, which arose because of the needs of the independent Christian communities for whom the Resurrection stories were written and rewritten. This is another classic example of social memory.

Mark evidently intended to write an account of Jesus meeting the disciples in Galilee. Three women, Mary Magdalene, Jacob's Mary and Salome, go to Jesus' tomb to anoint his body (Mk 16.1). Finding the large stone covering the tomb

---

Vandenhoeck & Ruprecht, 1958). There is no English translation.

17 Dunn, *Jesus Remembered*, pp. 837–38. Likewise, e.g. Craig, *Resurrection of Jesus*, pp. 372–73.

18 J. M. G. Barclay, 'The Resurrection in Contemporary New Testament Scholarship', in G. D'Costa (ed.), *Resurrection Reconsidered* (Oxford: OneWorld, 1996), pp. 13–30 (23).

rolled away, they enter the tomb and see a 'young man . . . wearing a white robe' (Mk 16.5), a perfectly normal ancient description of the appearance of an angel. After telling them that Jesus has been raised, and pointing out the place where he had been laid, he instructs them:

> But go tell his disciples and Peter that he is going before you into Galilee. There you will see him, as he told you.
>
> (Mk 16.7)

This looks back to a prediction attributed to Jesus in one of the historically mixed parts of the Passion narrative, where Jesus says that after he has been raised, 'I will go before you into Galilee' (Mk 14.28). Mark cannot possibly have written these passages unless he intended to write an account of at least one Resurrection appearance of Jesus in Galilee.

Some scholars have tried to make sense of Mark's ending on the assumption that he intended it to end where it does, but such attempts have not been very successful.[19] This is the importance of the result presented briefly above, that the *whole* of Mark's Gospel is unfinished.[20] It is not *merely* lacking a proper ending. It is a first draft which cries out for revision at many points. This is why I inferred that Mark did not live to finish his Gospel, so we cannot know what his account of Jesus appearing in Galilee would have looked like.

Matthew agrees with Mark's tradition of an appearance in Galilee. He rewrote Mark's story of the empty tomb so that an angel of the Lord tells the women,

> . . . go quickly and tell his disciples that he has been raised from the dead, and look! he is going before you into Galilee, there you will see him. Look! I told you!
>
> (Mt. 28.7)

Matthew then has the women run to tell the disciples, replacing Mark's unsatisfactory ending that the women 'said nothing to anyone, for they were afraid' (Mk 16.8). He inserts a brief appearance to Mary Magdalene and Jacob's Mary in Jerusalem to reinforce the point. Here the risen Jesus tells the two women:

> Do not be afraid. Go tell my brethren to go away to Galilee, and there they will see me.
>
> (Mt. 28.9-10)

Matthew follows this with an appearance to the Eleven in Galilee (Mt. 28.16-20). It follows that, in rewriting Mark, Matthew inserted an appearance to the two

---

19   E.g. recently J. C. Fenton, 'The Ending of Mark's Gospel', in S. Barton and G. Stanton (eds), *Resurrection: Essays in Honour of Leslie Houlden* (London: SPCK, 1994), pp. 1–7. For further discussion of the ending see pp. 76–77, pp. 477–78.

20   See pp. 74–78.

women in Jerusalem only so that Jesus could tell them to tell other people to get to Galilee for the most important appearance. He was not anticipating the later tradition of appearances in Jerusalem. On the other hand, he saw nothing untoward in an appearance in Jerusalem as well, and that might be because he knew of a tradition of appearances in Jerusalem.

The evidence of our two oldest Gospels is however basically unanimous: this tradition put the major Resurrection appearances in Galilee.

Luke rewrote this tradition to put *all* the appearances in Jerusalem. He *replaced* Mark's prediction of Galilaean appearances (Mk 16.7) with a comment by two 'men in gleaming clothing' (Lk. 24.4), another perfectly normal ancient description of angels, as they are explicitly said to be later (Lk. 24.23). The two angels remind the women, apparently Mary Magdalene, Joanna, Jacob's Mary and others (cf. Lk. 23.55–24.1; 24.10), how Jesus predicted his Passion and Resurrection when he was in Galilee:

> Remember how he spoke to you while he was still in Galilee, saying that the Son of man must be handed over into the hands of sinful men and be crucified and rise on the third day.
>
> (Lk. 24.6-7)

This is *deliberate replacement of one tradition with another*. It is also dependent on Luke's rewriting of Jesus' predictions. It includes a prediction of resurrection 'on the third day', with which Luke replaced 'after three days' in the predictions placed in the body of his narrative to conform them more literally to the story of Jesus' Resurrection narrated here; and a specific prediction of crucifixion, a more secondary detail than Luke put into even his earlier rewritten predictions. Luke then tells us that the women 'remembered his words' (Lk. 24.8), rewritten as they have been. The women then announced all this to 'the Eleven and all the others', again replacing Mark's unsatisfactory ending that the women 'said nothing to anyone, for they were afraid' (Mk 16.8). There should therefore be no doubt that this is secondary rewriting by Luke.

Luke next narrates two appearances in the Jerusalem area, and reports an appearance to 'Simon' (Lk. 24.34). The story of the second appearance is followed by Jesus' Ascension (Lk. 24.50-52), which leaves no room for any appearance in Galilee. As well as being deliberate departure from Markan tradition, this is not literally consistent with the story of the Ascension in Acts 1.3-11. This reveals Luke's own awareness that he was expressing important religious truths in story mode. Apart from the location, the stories in Matthew and Luke do not contradict each other so much as give an impression of total disassociation, as if neither of them knew the traditions to which the other had access (apart from the story of the empty tomb, which both of them took from Mark).

Moreover, with Acts in front of us, we can see why. Luke changed the site of the major appearances to Jerusalem because it was the centre of the world, the place from which the Gentile mission set out. He anticipates this perfectly at the end of Jesus' final Resurrection appearance:

Thus it is written that the Christ suffers and rises from the dead on the third day, and repentance for the forgiveness of sins is preached in his name to all the nations, beginning from Jerusalem. You are witnesses of these things. And look! I am sending out the promise of my Father upon you. But you, stay in the city until you are clothed with power from on high.

(Lk. 24.46-49)

That really settles it! Luke not merely omitted the true story that all the disciples fled from Gethsemane (Mk 14.50), he has made sure that none of them fled to Galilee, and he has left no room for any Galilaean appearances at all. It follows that to try to believe all the synoptic evangelists is to create a harmonized picture contrary to the witness of Mark and Matthew, and which Luke was determined to exclude. On the other hand, Luke may have been able to utilize earlier traditions of appearances in Jerusalem.

The Fourth Gospel's narrative is different again. As in Luke, there is no command to go to Galilee, and the appearances in John 20 all take place in Jerusalem. The first, to Mary Magdalene (Jn 20.11-18), is not mentioned by Luke, and hardly overlaps with the appearance to Mary Magdalene and Jacob's Mary at Mt. 28.9-10. There follows an appearance to the disciples unknown to Matthew (Jn 20.19-23), barely overlapping with an appearance to the disciples at Lk. 24.36ff. Finally, the appearance to Doubting Thomas and other disciples (Jn 20.26-29) is unique, and has him bear witness to the specifically Johannine belief in Jesus' deity. The whole of John 20 is written as if its authors did not know the tradition of Galilaean appearances. Unlike Luke, however, the Fourth Gospel says nothing to exclude the possibility of Resurrection appearances in Galilee as well.

A lengthy appearance in Galilee was provided by the author(s) of the appendix to this Gospel. However, the story of the appearance in Jn 21.1-23 barely overlaps with anything in Matthew, and deals with later concerns. It gives Simon Peter a major role in church leadership, and predicts his death in terms which show that it had occurred before this part of the passage (Jn 21.15-19) was written. It also deals indirectly with the deaths of members of the community before Jesus' second coming. For this purpose it uses 'the disciple whom Jesus loved' as a cipher for community members.[21] It says that Jesus never predicted that he would not die, but that it should not matter to Jesus' followers whether they died or survived until the second coming (Jn 21.20-24).

It is clear from this survey that the Gospel appearances do not relate properly to the early tradition of Resurrection appearances found at 1 Cor. 15.3-8. This is another crucial piece of evidence that the early traditions have been extensively rewritten in the Gospels as they stand.

Moreover, in addition to the differences in the appearances which I have noted, including the change of venue from Galilee to Jerusalem, the Gospel narratives of the discovery of the empty tomb have many disagreements in detail.

---

21 On this see pp. 523–25.

For example, at Mk 16.1 Mary Magdalene, Jacob's Mary and Salome go to the tomb, taking spices with which to anoint Jesus' dead body. At Mt. 28.1, Salome is not mentioned, and the purpose is to see the tomb instead, for there is no mention of spices or anointing. Luke has Joanna in place of Salome, and as in Mark the women bring the spices which they had prepared (Lk. 24.1, 10). At Jn 20.1, only Mary Magdalene goes. She brings no spices, the body having already been anointed under the guidance of Nicodemus, who is not known to the synoptic writers (Jn 19.39-40). Thus, apart from Mary Magdalene, there is no agreement as to who went to the tomb, why they went or what they took.

In Mark's story, the three women on the way to the tomb ask each other who will roll away the stone from the entrance of the tomb (Mk 16.3), a major problem for it was 'very big' (Mk 16.4). At Mt. 28.2 'an angel of the Lord' descends from heaven with a great earthquake, rolls back the stone and sits on it. Moreover, Matthew had already created more drama by having the chief priests and the Pharisees make the tomb secure by sealing the large rolling-stone and posting a guard (Mt. 27.62-66, cf. 27.60). Accordingly, when an angel of the Lord descended from heaven, his appearance like lightning and his clothing white like snow, rolled away the large rolling-stone and sat on it, the guards 'shook with fear of him and became like dead men' (Mt. 28.4). Luke and John have no such story, and there are no signs of earthquakes at the time of Jesus' death in Acts or in Jewish sources.

At Mk 16.5-8, the women enter the tomb and see 'a young man sitting on the right wearing a white robe', so *one* angel *in* the tomb. The angel tells them that Jesus has risen, but they tell no one, 'for they were afraid' (Mk 16.8). In Matthew, 'an angel of the Lord' rolls back the stone and sits on it (Mt. 28.2), so this is *one* angel *outside* the tomb. This angel tells the women that Jesus has been raised (Mt. 28.6), so they do not need to enter the tomb, and they go and tell the disciples (as we must infer from Mt. 28.7-10, 16). In Luke the women do enter the tomb, and *two* 'men in gleaming clothing' appear, so this is *two* angels *in* the tomb. The angels tell them that Jesus has been raised (Lk. 24.3-6). The women therefore tell the Eleven and all the others, or the apostles, who do not believe them (Lk. 24.9-11).

In the Fourth Gospel, Mary Magdalene comes to the tomb and sees the stone taken away from the tomb (Jn 20.1). She runs to Simon Peter and 'the other disciple whom Jesus loved', and tells them 'they have taken the Lord from the tomb and we do not know where they have put him' (Jn 20.2). The two men have a race to get to the tomb (Jn 20.3-4). The 'other disciple' looks in and sees the grave clothes. Simon Peter goes in, and 'the other disciple' goes in after him and comes to faith before any appearances (Jn 20.5-8). Mary then goes to the tomb, and sees two angels when she looks in. Jesus appears to her, and the story of the appearance ends with him telling her to inform his brethren. She goes and tells the disciples that she has seen the Lord, and gives them his message.

These discrepancies are too great to have resulted from reporting perceptible events. Accordingly, we need to try to understand why these narratives have been written as they are. This might help us to establish how much genuinely early material they contain, from which we might be able to work out what really

happened, and what the beliefs of the earliest Christians were. Then we can hope
to see why the Gospel writers offer us stories which do not altogether match the
earliest reports handed on by Paul and found in the early speeches of Acts, and
which are so different from each other that all of them cannot be literally true.

For this purpose, I discuss contemporary Jewish beliefs in Resurrection, and
immediately relevant teaching of Jesus.

4. *Jewish Beliefs in Resurrection*

Jewish documents from about the time of Jesus put forward more than one view
of survival after death, and their comments appear to be related to the situation
which they consider, rather than to concepts held by them. They tend to put
forward something like a view of resurrection when they consider the general
resurrection at which Israel or the righteous will finally be vindicated. When
they consider the fate of individuals at death, however, they generally make comments which are more akin to our concept of immortality. The most important
point for present purposes is that the comments in the primary Jewish sources
are quite varied.

For example, Dan. 12.1-3 portrays the end of all things:

> And at that time, Michael, the great prince who stands over the sons of your
> people, will arise. And there will be a time of distress such as there shall not
> be from when there was a nation until that time. And at that time your peo-
> ple will be delivered, everyone who is found written in the book. And many
> who sleep in a land of earth shall awake, some to eternal life and others to
> reproach, to abhorrence for ever. And the wise shall shine like the brightness
> of the firmament, and those who cause the many to be righteous like the stars
> for ever and ever.

This portrays the final deliverance of Israel after the persecution which led to the
Maccabaean revolt.[22] It also envisages the resurrection of many people at a single
moment in time. The reference to their sleeping in a land of earth is often taken to
imply that their graves will be empty when they rise, though this is not explicitly
stated. It is quite clear that the resurrection of the righteous is a form of vindication. The particular mention of 'the wise' and of 'those who cause the many to
be righteous' highlights the faithful Jews who stood firm during the Maccabaean
persecution and some of whom were martyred. This event is placed in the future,
though in apocalyptic literature this means in the very near future.

Some later sources elaborate the nature of the resurrection as a resurrection of
recognizable bodies. For example, in the second book of Baruch, God describes
the resurrection like this:

---

22   On this see pp. 216, 405–7.

For the earth will surely give back the dead at that time; it receives them now in order to keep them, not changing anything in their form . . . And as I have delivered them to it, so also it will raise them. For then it is necessary to show those who live that the dead live again . . . And it will happen that when those who know each other now have recognised each other, then the judgement will prevail . . . the form of those who are found guilty will be changed, as also the glory of those who have been declared righteous. For the form of those who now act wickedly will be made more evil than it is . . . Also, the glory of those who have now been found righteous through my Law . . . their brightness will then be glorified by transformations, and the form of their faces will be changed into the light of their beauty.

(*2 Bar.* 50–51.3, extracts)

This passage, written c.100 CE, has a straightforwardly literal understanding of the resurrection of the body. People's bodies will be raised in recognizable form, and it follows that their tombs will be empty. Their bodies will be transformed *after* the final judgement. There is no serious doubt that this concept of resurrection was available to people in the early church. If applied to Jesus, it could easily be taken to mean that his tomb was empty, provided that he was assumed to have been raised in the same way that other people will be raised at the last day.

This is quite different from Josephus' account of the belief of the Pharisees, when he considers the fate of people at death:

It is their belief that souls have power to survive death, and under the earth there are rewards and punishments for those who have led lives of virtue or wickedness. Some receive eternal imprisonment, while others pass easily to live again.

(*Ant.* XVIII, 14)

Here there is no mention of the resurrection of the body. Rather, surviving death means the continued existence of souls. There is no indication of any kind of pause after death before a final judgement: the natural interpretation is that the soul goes to its eternal fate at once. The reference to rewards again means that the righteous will be vindicated after their deaths. These people would certainly not leave an empty tomb behind.

The vindication of martyrs is especially interesting. It is already implicit in the book of Daniel, since some of the wise clearly die for the benefit of others at Dan. 11.35, and we have seen that they not only rise at Dan. 12.2, but shine like the stars at Dan. 12.3. This was developed further. For example, at 2 Macc. 7.9, one of the martyrs says his final words to the king in charge of his torture:

You wretch, you release us from the present life, but the King of the Universe will raise us up to an eternal renewal of life, for we have died for his laws.

Here the theme of vindication is especially clear. So is eternal life, but there is no mention of *bodily* resurrection, nor of an empty tomb.

This is even clearer in another later work, which has been subjected to Greek influence, but is still thoroughly Jewish in its view of martyrs. Here the narrator comments on the fate of the Maccabaean martyrs:

> Now the tyrant himself and the whole council were amazed at their endurance, because of which they now stand beside the divine throne and live the blessed age. For Moses says, 'And all the sanctified are under your hands'.
>
> (*4 Macc.* 17.17-19, quoting Deut. 33.3 LXX)

Here the martyrs have been vindicated by being taken straight to heaven. There they already have eternal life, the life of the age to come. No empty tombs are involved in this process. The belief of the narrator is supported from scripture, and their presence beside the divine throne is quintessentially Jewish.

There is not much evidence in the Gospels of Jesus' view of resurrection and immortality in general, but what there is fits perfectly well into the attitudes characteristic of Jews who believed in survival after death. For example, we have seen that some Sadducees, who did not believe in resurrection, asked Jesus about a woman who had seven husbands successively on earth – whose wife would she be when they all rose from the dead?[23] In his reply, Jesus assumed that there will be an occasion when the dead rise:

> For when they rise from the dead they neither marry nor are given in marriage, but are like angels in the heavens.
>
> (Mk 12.25)

The natural assumption is that the dead rise on a particular occasion, and Jesus conspicuously fails to say that they will not have bodies at a point where such a conception would have been helpful to his argument. His comments entail a final resurrection, in which people have some kind of body, albeit one like the angels, so there is no particular need to imagine that their tombs would be empty.

On the other hand, the parable of the rich man and Lazar[24] (Lk. 16.19-31) pictures the fate of the righteous and the wicked at death. Consequently, there is no pause in time after Lazar's death before he is taken away by angels to Abraham's bosom. Equally, there is no lapse in time after the rich man is dead and buried before he is portrayed in hell. It would be contrary to the nature of this story to imagine that the rich man left an empty tomb behind, or that Lazar left an empty space in whichever common tomb some pious Jews threw his dead body to avoid a corpse remaining unburied. Jesus also portrays Abraham as already in the next world, with powers to send a messenger from the dead if he wished. This has nothing to do with his tomb being empty either. The actual process of Abraham sending a messenger, which he declines to do, is described as 'going from the dead' at Lk. 16.30 and 'rising from the dead' at Lk. 16.31. Thus Jesus envisages in story mode a person going to heaven after death without

---

23   See pp. 423–24.
24   On this name see p. 305.

leaving his tomb empty, being sent to five people, and this being described as 'rising from the dead'.

These beliefs are culturally central for understanding Jesus' Resurrection. The process of going to heaven after death has *no necessary connection* with a person's tomb being empty. This was a standard Jewish idea, which Jesus shared. It follows that his followers shared this view, and it would become fundamental after his death. It is reflected in Luke's (creative and improbable) story that Jesus told one of the men crucified with him, 'To-day you will be with me in paradise' (Lk. 23.43). This has both of them in heaven immediately after death, before even Luke supposed that Jesus' tomb was found empty. The strength of Jesus' own belief in survival after death is further illustrated by his supposedly crushing argument against the Sadducees. He argued from the nature of God himself. God is so clearly the God of the living (cf. Jer. 10.10) that his declaration to Moses 'I am the God of Abraham and the God of Isaac and the God of Jacob' (Exod. 3.6) is held to demonstrate the survival of Abraham, Isaac and Jacob, and thereby the raising of the dead (Mk 12.26-27).[25] There is however no suggestion that their elaborate and much venerated tombs were empty.

The fate of Moses is especially interesting at this point, as Aus has shown.[26] The end of the biblical account of his life is a little strange:

> And Moses, servant of YHWH, died there . . . on/according to the mouth/ authority of YHWH. And he buried him (?) . . . and no-one has known his grave to this day.
>
> (Deut. 34.5-6)

This led to abundant speculations of a most entertaining kind. One view was that he did not die. At first sight, the comments of Josephus about Moses' fate are ambiguous:

> . . . a cloud suddenly standing over him, he disappeared in a ravine. But he has written in the sacred books that he has died, fearing that because of his surpassing virtue they might dare to say that he had returned to the divine.
>
> (*Ant.* IV, 326)

Any doubts about what Josephus meant may be removed by comparing the similar language which he uses about the end of the lives of Enoch (*Ant.* I, 85) and Elijah (*Ant.* IX, 28), both of whom were believed not to have died (Gen. 5.24; 2 Kgs 2.11). Josephus believed that, like these two men, Moses did not die because God took him. Some rabbinical passages record this opinion:

---

25 See further pp. 423–24.
26 R. D. Aus, *The Death, Burial, and Resurrection of Jesus, and the Death, Burial and Translation of Moses in Judaic Tradition* (Lanham: Univ. Press of America, 2008), esp. pp. 208–30. I am grateful to Dr Aus for giving me a copy of this outstanding book.

> Others say: Moses did not die but stands and serves on high.
>
> (Siphre on Deuteronomy, Piska 357)

This means that Moses went straight to heaven and continues to minister up there.

Other Jewish sources take a different view. For example, at Deut.R. XI, 10 a heavenly voice tells Moses that the time of his death has come. When Moses asks not to be handed over to the Angel of Death, God reassures him that He will attend to his burial himself! God then comes down from the highest heavens to take Moses' soul (*nishmāthō*), accompanied by three angels of service, Michael, Gabriel and Zigzagel. When Moses' soul tries to remain in his body, God says:

> Soul, go! Do not delay, and I will raise you to the highest heavens, and I will settle you under the throne of my Glory beside Cherubim, Seraphim and troops (of angels).

This is not the *same* as sitting at the right hand of God, but it is a very clear example of an outstandingly faithful Jewish leader being taken to be with God in heaven, leaving his body in his grave.

All this illustrates the massive variety of beliefs which Jesus' followers could generate after Jesus' death. It is especially important that believing that God had taken someone straight to his throne after their death did not entail that an empty tomb was left behind on earth.

Most of Jesus' comments about his own fate are not very specific. Moreover, the relationship between his fate and the final establishment of the kingdom is not generally clear, because one or the other is generally the central focus. For example, at Mk 10.40, responding to a question from Jacob and John, Jesus accepted that people will sit on the right and left of him in his glory. This must be a fairly physical form of glory, since otherwise the terms 'left' and 'right' make no sense, but how this relates to Jesus' Resurrection remains obscure. There are a few other sayings which likewise imply that Jesus will have a central position in the kingdom, from which we must infer Jesus' survival. This is implied in passages such as Mk 9.1, where some of the disciples will not die before they see the kingdom of God come in power, and Mk 10.29-30, where those who have made sacrifices for Jesus' sake will receive rewards which include 'eternal life in the coming age'. Perhaps the most striking passage is Lk. 12.8-9 (cf. Mt. 10.32-3; Mk 8.38):

> Everyone who confesses me before men, a/the son of man will also confess him before the angels of God, and he who denies me before men will be denied before the angels of God.

This presupposes the standard Jewish model of the heavenly court in the last days. The 'son of man' saying has a general level of meaning which asserts that people who confess Jesus on this earth will find favourable witnesses to them in the final judgement.[27] At the same time, the saying refers idiomatically in the first place to Jesus himself, so it presupposes his position as the pre-eminent witness to his followers in the last times. The second saying has a passive which in this context implies the action of God himself. This means that those who deny Jesus in this life will find God himself witnessing against them at the final judgement. These sayings accordingly do more than presuppose Jesus' survival: they presuppose his pre-eminent position at the last day.

The one genuine saying which predicts instead of assumes Jesus' survival is that which lies behind Mk 8.31, 9.31 and 10.33-34. I have suggested that an original form of this prediction was on the following lines.

ḥayyābh bar (ᵉ)nāsh(ā) lᵉmikēbh saggī' ūlᵉethbᵉsārāh ūlimᵉmāth ūlimᵉqām bāthar tᵉlāthāh yōmīn

A/the son of man is liable to suffer much and be rejected and die, and rise after three days.[28]

I argued that, while some details of this prediction may be considered uncertain, the reference to Resurrection 'after three days' must have been an original part of it. The Aramaic word for 'rise' can only have been *qūm*. This is a very general word for 'rise', and could refer to what we might call either resurrection or immortality. An interpretation of 'after three days' may be deduced from midrashic sayings which declare that Israel, or the righteous, will not be left in distress for more than three days, a view supported with several passages of scripture (e.g. Jon. 2.1; Hos. 6.2). One such occasion is the last days, when deliverance will be by means of the resurrection. For example, Gen.R. LVI, 1 comments on Gen. 22.4, beginning with a quotation of Hos. 6.2, and with the following among its examples:

> . . . on the third day of Jonah, 'and Jonah was in the belly of the fish three days' (Jon. 2.1): on the third day of those returning from the exile, 'and we dwelt there for three days' (Ezra 8.32): on the third day of the resurrection of the dead, 'After two days he will revive us, on the third day he will raise us up and we shall live before him' (Hos. 6.2)

Similarly, Est.R. IX, 2 comments on Est. 5.1:

> Israel are never left in dire distress for more than three days . . . of Jonah it says 'And Jonah was in the belly of the fish three days and three nights' (Jon. 2.1). The dead also will come to life only after three days, as it says, 'On the third day he will raise us up, and we shall live before him' (Hos. 6.2)

If 'three days' is interpreted like this, Jesus' Resurrection could be expected 'after

---

27 See further p. 368.
28 See pp. 377–81.

three days'. It is to be noted that these passages do not seem to mind whether scripture says 'three days' or 'on the third day', which is natural if a short interval is what is really meant.

I have discussed two other sayings of Jesus, which are translated into Greek at Lk. 13.32, 33, and which use a three-day interval in a similar metaphorical sense to indicate a relatively short time.[29]

> And he said to them, 'Go tell that jackal, "Look! I am casting out demons and performing healings to-day and tomorrow, and on the third (day) I am perfected. But I am going to proceed to-day and tomorrow and on the following (day), for it would not be fitting for a prophet to perish outside Jerusalem"'(cf. Lk. 13.32, 33).

In the first of these sayings, Jesus used a more elaborate version of the three-day interval to look forward to his death on the third day. In the second saying, he used another more elaborate version of the three day interval, effectively to predict his death after three days. Both sayings show Jesus using a three-day interval metaphorically to indicate a relatively short period of time.

At a more literal level, three days was considered to be just long enough to ensure that a person was really dead. This is why Lazarus is said to have been dead for four days (Jn 11.39). This excludes the possibility that he had revived in the tomb, and ensures that Jesus' action in raising him is miraculous in the strictest sense. For the same reason, bereaved people were allowed to visit the graves of their relatives for three days (b. Sem. VIII, 1).[30] Thus 'after three days' could also signify, 'when I am certainly dead'. We may therefore conclude that, in the original saying, Jesus meant that he would be vindicated by resurrection soon after his death. The way he put it was however rather opaque, and was open to reinterpretation after his death.

I have moreover given reasons to believe that, as Jesus headed deliberately for his death in Jerusalem, he predicted his death and Resurrection more than once, with sayings on these lines.[31] What we can reconstruct as apparently a single saying is accordingly as important as a surface reading of the synoptic Gospels would suggest – as his last days approached, Jesus predicted his death and Resurrection repeatedly.

I have also noted that Jesus interpreted his death by means of psalms which call for resurrection.[32] I followed through Jesus' interpretation of Psalm 41, in which he saw his betrayal: at Ps. 41.10, the psalmist calls upon God to raise him up, using the Hebrew word *qūm*. More could be seen in Psalm 118, the last of the *Hallel* psalms set for Passover. The Hebrew text of part of v. 17 (v. 15 in English versions) could easily be read, 'I shall not die because I shall live' and that could be interpreted of resurrection. Verses 22 and 23 were memorably used by Jesus

---

29 See pp. 114–15, 403–4.
30 See further pp. 240, 274–75.
31 See pp. 377–81.
32 See pp. 430–32.

to end a parable, in which he portrayed the sending of the prophets by God to Israel, followed by his beloved son, whom the tenants put to death (Mk 12.1-12). When the disciples contemplated the stone rejected by the builders becoming the head of the corner, they were bound to fit it into the pattern of Jesus' vindication by survival after death.[33]

These predictions must also be seen within the overall context of Jesus' ministry. During the historic ministry, Jesus so recreated the prophetic stream of Judaism that from the perspective of his followers he effectively embodied Jewish identity itself.[34] The ministry of Jesus was consequently formative for the recreation of his followers' own Jewish identity. He renewed their view of God, using especially the images of Fatherhood and kingship. He carried out a highly effective ministry of exorcism and healing, which could be seen to show that God was on his side. Moreover, the tight social bonding of the Jesus movement means that his followers received constant confirmation that Jesus' view of Judaism was the right one. This included the participation of some of them in the ministry of exorcism and healing. This underlines the experiential nature of participating in the Jesus movement. Jesus' followers were not *merely* the recipients of some teaching: the inner group of his most committed followers had their whole lives transformed from a perspective which always remained within the Judaism in which they were brought up. The ministry was also very controversial, suffering vigorous opposition from the orthodox wing of Judaism. Jesus' followers could not now change sides in this dispute. This is the context in which Jesus predicted and interpreted his death, and predicted his Resurrection too. The unjust death of this righteous embodiment of Judaism could not cause his most committed followers to disbelieve his predictions and abandon their identity.

5. *The Gospel Narratives Again*

I now examine the Gospel narratives in detail with three purposes especially in mind. First, I propose to recover any literally accurate information that they contain, beyond the centrally important fact that some of Jesus' original followers had experiences which they interpreted as appearances of Jesus after his death. Secondly, I propose to see how far we can recover the reasons why each of these stories was written as they were. Thirdly, conservative Christian apologists have offered vigorous defences of the literal historicity of each of these stories. I propose to refute their most important arguments.

I begin with Mark's Gospel. I have argued that there is a great deal of truth in Mark's story of the burial of Jesus by Joseph of Arimathea.[35] Joseph was 'a distinguished councillor', not a disciple of Jesus. He buried Jesus as a pious

---

33 On this parable see pp. 417–22.

34 Detailed justification of this and the following comments depends on the whole of chapters 5–11.

35 See pp. 448–53.

duty, to prevent a corpse left hanging on a cross from polluting the land. It was a dishonourable burial, in which the body was not washed or anointed. Joseph probably buried the body in a common criminals' tomb. This would not have a large rolling-stone to cover it (Mk 15.46; 16.3-4), since these were very rare and found only in the family tombs of the very rich. It is accordingly extremely unlikely that Mary Magdalene and Joses' Mary saw where he was laid (Mk 15.47), especially as there is no further sign that the site of the tomb was known.

The story becomes more bizarre when these two women go to the tomb with Salome, taking spices to belatedly anoint Jesus' body (Mk 16.1-2). On the way to the tomb, the three women ask each other who will roll away the stone from the entrance of the tomb (Mk 16.3), a major problem for it was 'very big' (Mk 16.4). In real life, it would have been very silly of them to have gone to the tomb without thinking of that first. In Mark's story, however, this creates narrative tension, which is resolved when the women find the stone rolled away (Mk 16.4) and an angel tells them that Jesus has been raised (Mk 16.6). Moreover, the fact they are portrayed as asking such a question reflects the shameful historical fact that the male disciples had fled (Mk 14.50). Mark assumes that the men had fled so far that the women could not ask for their help.

Aus has discovered what inspired Mark's story of the enormous rolling-stone.[36] This is the stone which was 'rolled' from Jacob's well (Gen. 29.3, 8, 10). This stone was 'large' already at Gen. 29.2, and the shepherds explain that they cannot water their flocks until the stone is rolled away (Gen. 29.8). In later Jewish tradition, there are three shepherds (corresponding to the three flocks of Gen.29.2), who could not roll the stone away, whereas Jacob did so (e.g. Neof I on Gen. 29.8, 10). In story mode, it was thus perfectly reasonable for Mark to have three women who knew they could not roll away the stone, and wondered who would remove it. Jacob was a young man when he rolled away the stone from the well, and it is a natural interpretation of Mark's narrative that the stone had been removed from the tomb by the angel, who is described as a 'young man' (Mk 16.5).

In Jewish tradition, Jacob's well was the same as Abraham's well, Isaac's well and above all Miriam's well or Moses' well, which accompanied the Israelites in the wilderness. The well is described as 'like a rock' which 'rolled along' (e.g. Tanḥ. Bemidbar 2, 21, on *Num.* 1.1). Jewish tradition interpreted *Num.* 21.18-20 to mean that the well ended its journey 'at the top of Pisgah', where Moses died (Deut. 34.1-5). Pisgah is interpreted as *Ramatha*, 'height' (e.g. Tg. Ps-J. *Num.* 21.20 *rmth'*), and Joseph coming from Arimathea is sufficient to remind a storyteller of this. Pisgah is also interpreted in some passages of the LXX with terms which mean 'hewn from rock' (e.g. *Num.* 21.20), which could have caused a storyteller to say that Joseph placed Jesus in a tomb 'hewn from rock' (Mk 15.46), or a genuine tradition that Jesus was placed in a tomb for criminals

---

36 Aus, *Death, Burial and Resurrection*, pp. 139–97.

which was in fact 'hewn from rock' could have further helped a storyteller to make up his story about the big rolling-stone and the young man.

Defences of the historicity of the stories of the empty tomb usually depend heavily on the improbability of the first witnesses being presented as women, unless this part of the story is literally true. For example, Wright comments, 'women were simply not acceptable as legal witnesses.' He quotes Josephus: 'From women let no evidence be accepted, because of the levity and temerity of their sex' (*Ant.* IV, 219). Noting the absence of the women in this story from the early tradition in 1 Corinthians 15, Wright declares 'It is, frankly, impossible to imagine that they were inserted into the tradition after Paul's day.'[37]

There are several things wrong with this approach. First, the New Testament is not a law court. Accordingly, the position of women in court is irrelevant until John 20, which was written by people in open conflict with the Jewish community. Secondly, Josephus was biased. Thirdly, women were widely accepted in Judaism as Jewish heroines, especially as outstanding characters in stories. Fourthly, these particular women were genuine characters from the historic ministry, and they were notable among the female witnesses of the crucifixion (Mk 15.40-41), when the men had fled (Mk 14.50//Mt. 26.56).

Jewish heroines were so well thought of in Judaism that there are several in the Bible. For example, one of the judges was Deborah the prophetess (Judges 4–5). She summoned Barak, son of Abinoam, who brought 10,000 warriors to fight the Canaanite army under Sisera. Deborah told him: 'YHWH has given Sisera into your hand' (Judg. 4.14). Duly defeated, Sisera fled, and Jael, the wife of Heber, enticed him into her tent. When he slept, she killed him by hammering a tent-peg through his temple into the ground. So Deborah and Barak sang a song, celebrating how 'Deborah arose, mother in Israel', and praising Jael, 'of tent-dwelling women most blessed' (Judg. 5.7, 24). In addition to women being given significant roles at intervals throughout the Bible, women are the central characters in three whole books held sacred by the time of Jesus, the books of Ruth, Esther and Judith. This is the real cultural background for the role of women in the stories of the empty tomb: they are heroines, not witnesses in a court of Law.

The three women whom Mark presents in the story of the empty tomb are Mary Magdalene, Jacob's Mary and Salome (Mk 16.1), the same three as he picks out particularly as witnesses of the crucifixion, commenting that they 'followed him and served him when he was in Galilee' (Mk 15.40-41). The importance of Mary Magdalene and other women in the ministry of Jesus is confirmed by Luke (8.2-3), and the authenticity of both traditions should be accepted.[38] These three women were the only witnesses of the crucifixion named in the traditions which Mark inherited, except for Simon of Cyrene. Simon, however, was not yet a follower of Jesus, whereas the three women had participated in the historic

---

37 Wright, *Resurrection of the Son of God*, p. 607, with n. 55; likewise, e.g. Dunn, *Jesus Remembered*, pp. 832–34; Dale C. Allison, *Resurrecting Jesus: The Earliest Christian Tradition and its Interpreters* (London/New York: T&T Clark International, 2005), pp. 326–31.

38 See pp. 192–97.

ministry in Galilee. If Mark was to write a story of the discovery of the empty
tomb, therefore, they were the obvious candidates to find it. They had witnessed
the crucifixion. They could have followed Joseph of Arimathea at a distance and
seen where it was. This is why Mark says that two of them did so (Mk 15.47),
at a point where we have seen that he was already writing creatively.

But why should he write a story of an empty tomb at all? There are two main
points. The first is the variety of Jewish beliefs in resurrection, which I discussed
in Section 4 above. In understanding how the first disciples could believe that
God had raised Jesus from the dead, leaving his body in a common criminals'
tomb, it is important that God could raise the dead to his heavenly throne with
quite new spiritual bodies, according as pleased him. At this point, however, it is
important that many Jews believed in *bodily* resurrection. Moreover, Jesus had
predicted his own resurrection in terms which could naturally be taken to recall
the general resurrection at the End, when Jewish beliefs could be taken to imply
empty tombs even in passages such as Dan. 12.1-3, where the dead rise from a
land of earth. If this view of bodily resurrection were applied to the resurrection
of Jesus, it would follow that his tomb was left empty.

Secondly, not everyone sympathetic to the teaching of Jesus, and none of the
opponents of the early Christian movement, believed that Jesus had risen from
the dead. The advantage of the empty tomb story, complete with an angel declaring 'he has been raised, he is not here' (Mk 16.6), is that it reassures believers
that Jesus really had been raised from the dead.

The combination of these two reasons explains why Mark wrote the story.
He expressed himself in story mode, but in ancient terms that means he believed
his story was profoundly true, not that it was false. Hence he used characters
whom he knew could have been there, because his traditions told him that they
were important eyewitnesses of the crucifixion, whereas the men were not available, because they had fled.

It is regrettable that scholarly discussion of the fact that the male disciples
had fled has been sidetracked into a discussion of whether they fled immediately
all the way to Galilee, which we do not know. For example, this enables Craig
to follow von Campenhausen in dismissing 'any supposed flight of the disciples
to Galilee' as 'a fiction of the critics', citing also Weiss referring to it as a 'scholarly legend'.[39] Craig himself then declares that 'the story of the denial of Peter
indicates that all the gospels held the disciples to be in Jerusalem.'[40] This does
not follow at all. This story does not tell us where most of the disciples were on
the Sunday after they had fled from Gethsemane. The original tradition of their
flight, followed by Resurrection appearances in Galilee alone, is *consistent with*
most of them fleeing to Galilee at once, or with most of the Twelve heading back
to Bethany at once, and leaving for Galilee as soon as Simeon the Rock could

---

39 Craig, *Resurrection of Jesus*, p. 190, with n. 37, citing H. F. von Campenhausen, *Der Ablauf
    der Osterereignisse und das leere Grab* (Heidelberg: Winter, 3rd rev. edn, 1966), pp. 44–49,
    and quoting in English J. Weiss, *Der erste Korintherbrief* (KEKNT 5. Göttingen: Vandenhoeck
    & Ruprecht, 9th edn, 1910), p. 350.
40 Craig, *Resurrection of Jesus*, pp. 190–91.

get away from the high priest's courtyard and join them. At the same time, the evidence of our oldest sources, Mark and Matthew, does *not demand* such a conclusion. It demands only that the male disciples made themselves pretty scarce at once, did not watch the crucifixion even from a distance, escaped detection by the authorities, and headed back to Galilee after a while, there to see one or more Resurrection appearances.

Mark's story ends oddly. The angel's order to the women is only slightly peculiar, and has some logic:

> But go tell his disciples and Peter that he is going ahead of you into Galilee. There you will see him, as he told you.
>
> (Mk 16.7)

This confirms the Galilaean tradition of appearances, with no appearances in Jerusalem, so at this level Mark is simply being consistent. What is slightly odd is that the angel assumes that, after being unable to contact the men to help them move the enormous rolling-stone, the women can and need to tell the disciples and Peter to go to Galilee, when Jesus had already made this clear at Mk 14.28. However, this is not incomprehensible. Mark 14.28 is not historically probable, and Mark may have felt that it needed reinforcing. Secondly, Mark's story of the women buying spices and coming to the tomb so early makes sense only if the disciples had stayed in Jerusalem. He may simply have assumed that the Eleven were back at the house of Simon the leper in Bethany, so that the women would be able to walk out there and give them the angel's message.

Whatever we make of that, the end is even stranger:

> And going out, they fled from the tomb, for trembling and amazement held them. And they said nothing to anyone, for they were afraid.
>
> (Mk 16.8)

In the ancient world, this satisfied no one. As we have seen, Matthew and Luke replaced it with their own endings. Ancient copyists of Mark added two different endings. The Shorter Ending is very short, and poorly attested. It has the women go promptly and tell 'those around Peter' everything they had been commanded. This interprets Mark's 'they said nothing to anyone' to mean they said nothing to people in general, but told 'those around Peter'. This is very forced. It concludes with a very brief summary of the preaching of the Gospel from the East to the West. The Longer Ending is found in the majority of manuscripts, which shows how widespread was the feeling in the ancient churches that Mark needed a proper ending. It is an amalgam of traditions, beginning with an appearance to Mary Magdalene, with use of Luke's appearance to two disciples and of Matthew's appearance to the Eleven.

All this underlines the fact that Mark's Gospel is genuinely unfinished. As it stands, the silence of the women functions to explain why the story of the empty tomb had not been heard before. After the angel's explicit command, and the obvious fact that Mark intended to recount at least one appearance to the disciples in Galilee, this creates narrative tension, and we do not know what Mark intended to do with that, or what his appearance(s) would have been like.

The tradition of appearances in Galilee only was continued by Matthew. We have seen that he rewrote Mark's traditions of the burial and of the discovery of the empty tomb. He turned Joseph of Arimathea into a disciple of Jesus (Mt. 27.57), and has him bury Jesus 'in his new tomb' (Mt. 27.60), so Mary Magdalene and the other Mary, 'sitting opposite the tomb' (Mt. 27.61), obviously knew which honourable and respectable tomb this was. Matthew not only has an angel of the Lord descend from heaven and roll away the stone from the tomb, he has this accompanied by a 'great earthquake' (Mt. 28.2), an extraordinary event not found in the other Gospels, Acts or Jewish sources. Since he has already produced a story of guards at the tomb (Mt. 27.62-66), Matthew has to do something with them here, so he has a wondrously dramatic story of them shaking with fear and becoming like corpses (Mt. 28.4).

Matthew alone has the extraordinary account of a guard being placed at the tomb by the chief priests and Pharisees, after consultation with Pilate (Mt. 27.62-66). After the Resurrection, the guards are supposed to have told the chief priests the story of the Resurrection. The chief priests then bribed the guards to say that the disciples came and stole the body (Mt. 28.11-15). In its present place in Matthew, this story functions as an absolute proof that the tomb was empty. One item in the story is literally true – the information that a story of the disciples stealing Jesus' dead body was circulating 'among Jews' in Matthew's day (Mt. 28.15). Some Jews who heard the story of Jesus' bodily Resurrection from an empty tomb will have found the story absolutely unconvincing and they responded with a story of their own, one which reflects their absolute and understandable mistrust of Christians. We should not take this story literally either: it will have been made up far away from Israel some time after Jesus' death and burial, by people who knew that most Jews in Jerusalem at the time had never believed the story of Jesus' Resurrection.

Craig uses this story to argue in favour of the historicity of the empty tomb. He comments, 'From information unintentionally furnished by Matthew, we know that the Jewish opponents of the Christian Way did not deny that Jesus's tomb was empty. Instead they charged that the disciples had stolen Jesus's body.'[41] This shift from some Jewish opponents of Christianity in Matthew's day to '*the* Jewish opponents of the Christian Way' (my emphasis) is completely unjustified. This story does not tell us anything about what, for example, the high priest and his Sanhedrin thought about the empty tomb when they arrested Peter and the apostles, considered the death penalty, and were persuaded by the relative leniency of Gamaliel to have them beaten and released (Acts 5.17-41). It is however obvious they did not believe them.

Craig further argues that 'The fact that the Jewish polemic never denied that Jesus's tomb was empty, but only tried to explain it away is persuasive evidence

---

41 Craig, *Resurrection of Jesus*, p. 371.

that the tomb was in fact empty.'[42] There are two things wrong with this, both serious. First, Craig has made up the story that 'the Jewish polemic never denied that Jesus's tomb was empty'. We have no idea what Jewish polemic usually said, because we have no early non-Christian Jewish sources at all. What we do know is that the Christian story was rejected by most Jews who were in Jerusalem at the time, and has been rejected by most Jewish people ever since.

Secondly, Craig has quite misunderstood the nature of ancient polemic. What the Jewish community needed was to *reject Christian belief in Jesus' Resurrection*. This is achieved perfectly well by the polemic which Matthew reports. The notion that the disciples had stolen the body entails that Christianity is based on a lie, and that Jesus had not been raised from the dead. That was enough for some Jewish opponents of Christianity.

It is also important to take these two points together, and to put them with the major known fact about most Jews who were there at the time. One Christian source reports this particular story. There may have been plenty of other stories, for we know that most Jews rejected Christian belief that Jesus had risen from the dead, but we do not have Jewish sources to tell us how many of them cared, or what they said about it.

Matthew concludes with one major Resurrection appearance to the Eleven in Galilee (Mt. 28.16-20). This means that our second oldest narrative source follows Mark in supposing that Galilee was the main place for appearances. Apart from an appearance to ensure that the women told the disciples where to go (Mt. 28. 9–10), an untrue story because it contradicts Mark, our oldest narrative source, Mt. 28.16-20 is the earliest written narrative of a Resurrection appearance. Moreover, unlike most of the narratives of Resurrection appearances, this one may be thought to agree up to a point with one of the appearances recorded in the very old tradition passed on by St Paul. This begins its record of appearances: 'he appeared to Cephas, then to the Twelve' (1 Cor. 15.5). The question as to how much truth is to be found in this story is accordingly important. Wright comments, 'The strongest mark of authenticity in this paragraph is the jarring note: "but some doubted" (v. 17) . . . this strange comment would not have occurred to someone telling the story as a pure fiction . . .'.[43]

This is true as far as it goes. It means that some of the Eleven were not convinced by an experience which others interpreted as an appearance of Jesus. This is another piece of evidence that we must view the early list of appearances in 1 Cor. 15.3-8 with a degree of scepticism – the sole appearance of which we have a narrative account was not as straightforward as we might have believed from reading Paul's list. Secondly, this raises the question as to how many of the Eleven obeyed the ringing commands of Mt. 28.19. The most important is 'Go therefore and make disciples of all the nations'. Did the Eleven do this? No. Only Peter is even known to have travelled in the diaspora, and when Paul met the inner group of three, 'Jacob and Cephas and John' in Jerusalem, they agreed that 'we to the nations, but they to the circumcision' (Gal. 2.9). That means that

---

42   Craig, *Resurrection of Jesus*, p. 371.
43   Wright, *Resurrection of the Son of God*, p. 643.

even the inner group of three did not 'go and make disciples of all the nations'. Moreover, the rest of the Eleven are unheard of thereafter. Accordingly, whatever happened when Jesus appeared to the Eleven in Galilee, it was not a clear speech to all of them at once in which Jesus commanded them to carry out the Gentile mission. Matthew has written this into Jesus' speech because it was of central importance to the churches when he wrote.

What then of 'baptising them in the name of the Father and of the Son and of the Holy Spirit' (Mt. 28.19)? Is this what we find the Eleven doing in Acts? No. Distinctive Christian baptism is first mentioned at Acts 2.38, where Peter urges people to be baptized 'in the name of Jesus Christ', and people 'were baptised' (Acts 2.41). At Acts 8.5, Philip, one of seven Hellenists appointed to care for Christian widows, so not someone from the historic ministry, preaches the Gospel in Samaria, and people who were converted 'were baptised' (Acts 8.12). When Peter and John came down from Jerusalem, we find that these people had not yet received the Holy Spirit, 'but had only been baptised into the name of the Lord Jesus' (Acts 8.16). When Ananias, who also had no connection with the historic ministry, had cured Saul of the blindness which struck him at his conversion vision, Saul 'got up and was baptised' (Acts 9.18). At Acts 10.48, Peter orders some Gentiles, who had heard him preach and received the Holy Spirit, 'to be baptised in the name of Jesus Christ.' When Paul's party, including Timothy, Silvanus and Luke, none of whom had any connection with the historic ministry, went to Philippi, Lydia and her household 'were baptised' (Acts 16.15). In the whole of Acts, no one is baptized 'in the name of the Father and of the Son and of the Holy Spirit', Peter is the only one of the Eleven to stay in the story for any length of time as the Gospel is spread to the Gentiles, and after a while he disappears too.

We must conclude that the second major instruction in Matthew's account of this appearance was not clearly delivered by the risen Jesus. By now, the nature of Matthew's account is beginning to become a little clearer. At first sight, it appears to be the same appearance as was known to Paul's early tradition. On close examination, however, the most important quality of these traditions is that both have been rewritten. We have seen this with the Pauline tradition already.[44] Nonetheless, the fact that its list of appearances begins with an appearance to Cephas is plausible. Next, it says that Jesus appeared 'to the Twelve'. It does not say 'at once', as it does of the next appearance 'to over 500 brethren at once' (1 Cor. 15.5-6). Matthew, however, has clearly interpreted this, or a similar tradition, of a single simultaneous appearance to the Eleven, those left of the Twelve. Moreover, unlike the early Pauline tradition, Matthew has placed this supposedly single appearance in Galilee. The most important point is however the comment that when Jesus appeared, 'some doubted' (Mt. 28.17). This is a point which we would never have guessed if we had only the early tradition transmitted by St Paul, and it must be true for two reasons. One is that most of the Eleven do not turn up in the early church at all. That is why Matthew could not leave this

---

44   See pp. 456–59.

point out. The second reason follows ineluctably: this is not something which the early church would make up out of nothing. It must reflect the lack of faith in the Resurrection by some of the Eleven.

What is even more devastating is that this is the point at which the whole tradition of appearances of the risen Jesus begins to fall apart. Why do we not have accurate narrative accounts of genuine appearances of the risen Jesus? Why are we not told what happened when Jesus appeared to Cephas, over 500 brethren, and then Jacob and then all the apostles (1 Cor. 15.5-7)? Matthew has supplied us with two points which enable us to understand this. First, again, 'some doubted' (Mt. 28.17). Too much concentration on that would not make for the successful preaching of good news! Matthew can have transmitted it only if it was desperately unforgettable. Secondly, the Eleven did not obey two major commands which Matthew has the risen Jesus give them in his rather short speech.

The only way of understanding this is that Matthew has rewritten the tradition of this appearance which he received, or has invented Jesus' speech because the tradition did not tell him that Jesus made a speech, and perhaps did not tell him that he appeared to the Eleven all at once. We must take these two points together. First, some of the Eleven did not believe in Jesus' Resurrection, and did not play any significant role in the early church as Jesus was supposed to have commanded. This is what made 'some doubted' unforgettable. Secondly, we do not have accurate accounts of genuine appearances of the risen Jesus because these were not helpful enough for the needs of the churches. That is a strong argument against the genuineness of the Resurrection narratives in the Gospels, but it does not entail the genuineness of all the appearances in Paul's list.

In addition to the needs of the churches for whom he wrote, Matthew was probably inspired by traditions about Moses, as he was throughout his Gospel. Moses went up Mount Sinai to receive the Law, and made his final appearance on a mountain, so Matthew has added a mountain as the place of Jesus' final appearance (Mt. 28.16, not in earlier versions of Jesus' command). The commissioning of the Eleven is also somewhat reminiscent of the commissioning of Joshua (LXX Jesus) by Moses and by God, who tells him to 'keep and do as Moses my servant commanded you' (LXX Josh. 1.7), whereas Jesus tells the Eleven to teach all the nations to 'keep everything which I commanded you' (Mt. 28.20). Within this very basic framework, Matthew has written Jesus' speech to serve the needs of the churches for whom he wrote. This is social memory in operation.

I turn to the Resurrection narratives of Luke. I have already made the most important point. Luke *rewrote* the early tradition of appearances in Galilee, and *replaced* it with his own tradition of appearances in Jerusalem.[45] He leaves no room for the appearances in Galilee reported by Mark and Matthew, and he replaced this tradition with appearances in Jerusalem so that the risen Jesus could authorize the mission to the Gentiles, beginning from Jerusalem, and reported in Luke's second volume, Acts. Consequently, we cannot expect much early history in Luke's tradition of appearances. We must look and see whether there is any.

---

45   See pp. 463–64.

We must also consider whether Luke had any other inspiration for writing these stories. In this, we shall again receive much help from Roger Aus, who has shown that Luke was significantly influenced by Jewish traditions about Elijah.[46]

The first major appearance is to Cleopas and an unnamed disciple (Lk. 24.13-32). Cleopas is not however mentioned until v. 18, and the narrative begins simply, 'And behold! Two of them on that same day were going . . .'. This is at first sight a strange beginning, and it is only when we get to v. 18, and it turns out that one of them is Cleopas, so not one of the Eleven, nor otherwise known from the Gospel accounts of Jesus' ministry, that we must infer that these are two of 'all the rest' (Lk. 24.9). This is because Luke was inspired by the account of Elijah and Elisha in 2 Kings 2, which refers repeatedly to them as 'two of them' (2 Kgs 2.6, 7, 8, 11). Just as the two disciples were 'going' or 'walking' (v. 17), so Elijah and Elisha were 'going/walking' (2 Kgs 2.1, 6, 11), and just before Elijah's ascension they were 'walking and talking' (2 Kgs 2.11), as they were obviously doing throughout the story until that moment. Similarly, 'two of them' (Lk. 24.13) 'were conversing' (Lk. 24.14, 15).

At v. 15, Jesus suddenly 'approaching, walked with them', and at v. 31, 'he became invisible from them.' Elijah was also portrayed as suddenly appearing and disappearing. Ordinary verbs such as 'come' and 'meet' are used when he suddenly turns up. Paraphrasing 2 Kings 2, Josephus says that he 'disappeared' (*Ant.* IX, 28), a close parallel to Lk. 24.31. Josephus has an even closer parallel when he compares the disappearance of Elijah and Enoch, saying that it is written that they 'became invisible' (*Ant.* IX, 28). This is presumably because the same verb is used of God 'taking' each one of them (Gen. 5.24; 2 Kgs 2.3, 5, 9). The tradition of Elijah suddenly appearing and disappearing may readily be seen in the biblical accounts of him. For example, 1 Kgs 18.7 simply says that when Obadiah was on the way, Elijah met him. When however Elijah told him to go and tell Ahab that Elijah was there, Obadiah complained, saying, 'and it will happen that I will go from you, and the spirit of YHWH will take you to I know not where . . .' (1 Kgs 18.12). Elijah had to reassure him, saying 'I will appear to him today' (1 Kgs 18.15). This is the background for Luke's story in which Jesus just turns up, and at the end 'became invisible from them' (Lk. 24.31).

At Lk. 24.19, the two disciples describe Jesus as 'a prophet mighty in deed and word', which Elijah obviously was. One of the most important things Jesus does in this appearance story is to expound the scriptures: 'And beginning from Moses and from all the prophets, he explained to them the things concerning himself in all the scriptures' (Lk. 24.27). Luke particularly isolates for mention the central points that 'the Christ must suffer and enter into his glory' (Lk. 24.26). We have seen that the term 'Messiah' was not yet a title in the Judaism of Jesus' time.[47] Moreover, Jewish people did not expect to be delivered by a single suffering

---

46   R. D. Aus, *The Stilling of the Storm: Studies in Early Palestinian Judaic Traditions* (Binghamton, New York: Binghamton University, 2000), pp. 137–229, ch. III, 'The Road to Emmaus (Luke 24.13–35)'.

47   See pp. 392–99.

figure, and were scornful of Christian belief in Christ crucified (1 Cor. 1.23). We have also seen that scriptural witness to Jesus' Resurrection was central already to the early tradition handed on by Paul (1 Cor. 15.4). Luke has thus provided a quintessentially Christian scriptural legitimation of Christian belief in the central importance of Jesus' death and Resurrection. At the same time, he has used Jewish tradition to form his story, for Elijah expounds the scriptures in many rabbinical passages. For example, in Midr. Pss. 104.25, Elijah expounds Ps. 104.32 and Jer. 25.30 to explain to R.Nehorai why earthquakes occur. Luke also takes for granted Jewish traditions that Moses was a prophet, that there are prophecies in the Pentateuch, and that, as well as the Law, scripture contains the Former Prophets, the Latter Prophets and the Writings.

At vv. 28–29, Jesus was making as if to go on further, but the two disciples urged him to stay with them. In 2 Kgs 2.2, 4, 6 Elijah would have gone on further on his own, but Elisha insists on saying with him. The disciples recognize Jesus in the breaking of bread (Lk. 24.30-31), which is obviously a reference to the description of the Christian Eucharist in Acts. Jesus then 'became invisible from them' (Lk. 24.31), and we have seen how naturally this emerges from Jewish stories of Elijah. When Jesus had gone, the two disciples said to each other: 'Was not our heart burning in us, as he was speaking to us on the way, as he opened to us the scriptures?' (Lk. 24.32). This is natural, because Elijah appeared 'as a fire', and 'his words were as a flaming furnace' (Sir. 48.1). The fact that the disciples did not recognize Jesus until he blessed and broke the bread, and his suddenly becoming invisible (Lk. 24.30-31), also explains in story mode that his risen body was a spiritual one.

At v. 34, Luke reports that, when they returned to Jerusalem, the Eleven and those with them said that 'the Lord was raised and appeared to Simon'. This brief report is partly in Luke's style, especially in its reference to Jesus as 'the Lord', which makes his reference to 'Simon', rather than 'Cephas' or 'Peter' all the more interesting. Luke clearly intended this to be the same appearance as Paul recorded as the first of all: 'he appeared to Cephas' (1 Cor. 15.3). This underlines the importance of the fact that none of the synoptic evangelists relates this appearance. They cannot have received any tradition that it contained anything significant which suited the needs of their churches.

While they were discussing these matters, 'he appeared in the midst of them' (Lk. 24.36), which is again reminiscent of Elijah appearing. The contents of this appearance are also perfectly adapted to the needs of the Gentile churches when Luke wrote, with proof that this is really Jesus and that his spiritual body was real. After Luke has said that the disciples thought they 'were seeing a spirit' (Lk. 24.37), Jesus shows them his hands and feet (but not his side!), commenting that 'a spirit does not have flesh and bones as you see that I have' (Lk. 24.39). Before Jesus continues this demonstration by eating, Luke comments 'while they were still disbelieving from joy and being amazed . . .' (Lk. 24.41). With the tradition that 'some doubted' (Mt. 28.17) still unforgettable, Luke has rewritten it to be harmless. After eating, Jesus again expounds the scriptures. As in the appearance on the Emmaus road, this extensive presentation of 'everything written in the law of Moses and the prophets and psalms about me' (Lk. 24.44) includes the key matter of the suffering of the Christ, and this time Luke adds his Resurrection 'on the third day' (Lk. 24.46), his own careful rewriting of Jesus' original predictions. I have noted the importance of Jesus' final words, in which he vigorously commands the Gentile mission, and commands the disciples, 'stay in the city until you are clothed with power from on high' (Lk. 24.49), ensuring that there is no room for Resurrection appearances in Galilee.[48]

At the end of the appearance, Jesus 'parted from them and was taken up into heaven' (Lk. 24.51). At 2 Kgs 2.11, Elijah was separated from Elisha and 'ascended' into heaven. Luke's Ascension narrative (Lk. 24.50-53) explains why Resurrection appearances have ceased, a very important function in churches where Christians believed that Jesus had risen, but no one saw him anymore. Acts 1.3-11 clarifies this, having Jesus appear for a period of 40 days. This is not literally consistent with the Ascension narrative at the end of Luke's Gospel, and it is a traditional round figure. This underlines the story mode nature of Luke's explanation as to why Resurrection appearances have ceased.

The risen Jesus also deals vigorously with the problem of the delay of the parousia. The apostles ask whether at this time he will restore the kingdom to Israel, and the risen Jesus responds,

> It is not yours to know times or seasons which the Father fixed by his own authority, but you will receive power when the Holy Spirit comes upon you and you will be my witnesses in Jerusalem and in the whole of Judaea and Samaria and to the end of the earth.
>
> (Acts 1.7-8)

This puts aside the lengthy delay in the coming of the kingdom which Jesus had predicted. Secondly, it predicts the outpouring of the Holy Spirit which Luke relates in the following chapter, and which forms a massive display which legitimates the church as it was at this stage. Thirdly, Jesus commands the mission which would soon move out beyond Judaism into the Gentile world. Here too, therefore, matters of central concern to the churches have been written secondarily into a Resurrection appearance.

Thus Luke's appearance stories were written on a model of Elijah's appearances to meet the needs of the Gentile churches for whom Luke wrote. The major conclusion is ineluctable: these stories are not literally true. On the contrary, they are another example of the operation of social memory.

Significant conservative Christian defences of the literal historicity of these stories generally find significance in Cleopas (Lk. 24.18). For example, Bauckham comments, 'There seems no plausible reason for naming him other than to indicate that he was the source of this tradition. He is very probably the same person as Clopas, whose wife Mary appears among the women at the cross in John 19.25.' He follows the tradition attested by Hegesippus (c.160 CE) according to Eusebius, that Clopas was the brother of Jesus' father Joseph and the father of

---

48   See pp. 463–64.

Simon, who succeeded Jesus' brother Jacob as leader of the Jerusalem church (Eus. *H.E.* III, 11; IV, 22, 4). So 'Cleopas/ Clopas was doubtless one of those relatives of Jesus who played a prominent role in the Palestinian Jewish Christian movement. The story Luke tells would have been essentially the story Cleopas himself told about his encounter with the risen Jesus.'[49] Wright adds the tradition that Cleopas' companion was 'most likely his wife, one of the many Marys in the gospel story'.[50] There is no justification for any of this beyond the possibility that this rather late tradition may have led to the correct identification of Luke's character. Bauckham's argument is nothing more than an illustration of the conservative assumption that if we do not know why a particular Gospel character is named, the story must be literally true. The reasons given above for thinking otherwise remain decisive. Wright's traditional conjecture is simply arbitrary. Luke may however have met Cleopas in Jerusalem or inherited traditions about him, possibly even including some earlier version of this story, and therefore felt that he was a suitable character to put in a story in which he expressed central theological truths and encouraged church members to believe them.

Two other conservative Christian arguments of a somewhat broader kind are worth mentioning at this point. Craig defends the reliability of the Gospel Resurrection narratives by arguing that *'There was insufficient time for legend to accrue significantly'*, and that *'The controlling presence of living eyewitnesses would retard significant accrual of legend.'*[51] First, there is a fundamental difference between the traditional radical position to which Craig is responding, and the view which I have taken above. For example, in his classically influential work, Bultmann says that Lk. 24.13-35 'has the character of a true legend', that Mt. 28.16-20 'is a sort of cult legend', that Lk. 23.36-49 'seems to be an edited passage having as its basis an older legend' and describes the story of the empty tomb as 'an apologetic legend'.[52] It is this tradition with which Craig's objections engage, rather than with comments such as that Lk. 24.44-49 'is obviously in its entirety a literary production of Luke.'[53]

I have not argued that any of the Gospel stories of the empty tomb or of Resurrection appearances are legends. I have argued that they are stories, written in their present forms by the Gospel writers themselves. This view is not vulnerable to Craig's first objection, regardless of whether he is right about how long legends take to form, because stories do not necessarily take long to write. Some ten years to Mark's empty tomb story is accordingly more than long enough, and Luke's stories were written by Luke in their present form more than 50 years after whatever appearances of Jesus to his followers lay at the origin of the tradition. This is why Luke's stories reflect the needs of Gentile churches when Luke wrote. Craig's second point is not very effective against the views which I have expressed

---

49 R. Bauckham, *Jesus and the Eyewitnesses: The Gospels as Eyewitness Testimony* (Grand Rapids: Eerdmans, 2006), p. 47.

50 Wright, *Resurrection of the Son of God*, p. 652.

51 Craig, *Resurrection of Jesus*, pp. 381, 387.

52 Bultmann, *History of the Synoptic Tradition*, pp. 286, 290.

53 Bultmann, *History of the Synoptic Tradition*, p. 286.

either. Most living eyewitnesses were still in Galilee speaking Aramaic, so they were in no position to exercise any control over stories in Greek Gospels written in the diaspora, miles away from Galilee. Very few living eyewitnesses had any connection with Gentile churches, and whether, for example, Simeon the Rock would have minded Matthew's account of Jesus' appearance to the Eleven we have no idea. He might have thought that it expressed beliefs profoundly needed by the Gentile mission for which God was obviously responsible. By the time of Luke's stories, he was certainly dead, and of all the living eyewitnesses, he was the most likely to have had any influence. I conclude that Craig's objections should not be regarded as effective criticism of the approach which I have adopted.

The Johannine Resurrection narratives met the needs of the Johannine community towards the end of the first century, but since I have pointed out that this is true of this Gospel as a whole, I do not comment on them at great length, but make only some basic points.[54] One of their main functions is to legitimate belief in the Resurrection itself. This is why, for example, the empty tomb is not just found by Mary Magdalene, recalling older tradition, but witnessed to by two men (Jn 20.1-10), who would be fully qualified witnesses in a Jewish law court, a significant point in view of the community's Jewish heritage combined with its vitriolic quarrel with 'the Jews'. This is the point at which the position of women in law courts may first be thought to be relevant to the Resurrection stories, and so far from removing women from the story, it is accompanied by a highly developed story in which Mary Magdalene is the first person to see the risen Jesus, and she goes and tells the disciples 'I have seen the Lord', and passes on an important message from him (Jn 20.11-18).

Secondly, these stories clarify the nature of Jesus' Resurrection body. So, for example, Jesus appears when the doors are shut (Jn 20.26), which shows that his body was a spiritual one. Then he shows his wounds from his crucifixion (Jn 20.27), which shows that his risen body was the same one as he had before his Resurrection. Thirdly, these stories deal with concerns specific to the Johannine community. The most outstanding is Thomas's confession, 'My Lord and my God' (Jn 20.28). This is the crucial confession of Jesus' deity, contrary to Jesus' Jewish identity, absent from the synoptic Gospels, and central to the Johannine community. Like Luke's comment that the disciples 'did not believe from joy and were amazed' (Lk. 24.41), this resolution of the story of Doubting Thomas also neutralizes the once central fact that 'others doubted' (Mt. 28.17).

I have noted that John 20 is written as if its author(s) did not know the tradition of Galilaean appearances. The author(s) of the appendix however placed their appearance in Galilee. In this story the disciples do not at first recognize Jesus (Jn 21.4), which shows that his risen body was a spiritual one, but he apparently eats breakfast, which shows that his risen body was real. The story predicts Peter's death, shows that beloved disciples should always follow Jesus, and deals with the death of Christians before the parousia.

All these points show that the Johannine stories are not literally true. They

---

54   Cf. p. 464, and on the Fourth Gospel pp. 511–25.

express fundamental aspects of the faith of the Johannine community in story form. As Jesus puts it, 'Blessed are those who did not see and came to faith' (Jn 20.29). Like the whole of this Gospel, they are another classic example of social memory.

Conservative Christian defences of the literal historicity of the Johannine narratives are usually found in the context of a defence of either the historicity of the Resurrection in general, which I discuss throughout this chapter, or the historicity of John, which I discuss in the Appendix. I therefore discuss only one particular argument here. Craig comments on the 'appearance to Thomas', 'Because only John tells the story, one would be inclined to think it is not based on tradition, but rather on the reminiscences of the Beloved Disciple to the Johannine community.'[55] The first of these two points should be accepted: this appearance was not based on earlier tradition. The second is quite extraordinary. It presupposes that the deity of Jesus, totally absent from the synoptic writers and in conflict with Jesus' Jewish identity, was confessed at a Resurrection appearance, and somehow never passed on by any of the disciples to any of the synoptic writers. That is not historically plausible.

I therefore conclude that the accounts of the Resurrection appearances in the Four Gospels contain very little information that is literally true. There is some literal truth behind the accounts of Mark and Matthew. Jesus' male followers, having fled from the Garden of Gethsemane, kept out of the way and soon returned to Galilee. There some of them had experiences which they interpreted as appearances of the risen Jesus. Matthew has an account of an appearance to the Eleven which contains one vital piece of correct information: 'some doubted' (Mt. 28.17). This must be true, for neither Matthew nor the tradition before him would have made it up. It was desperately unforgettable, because some of the inner group of the Twelve did not believe in Jesus' Resurrection, and they had nothing to do with the formation of the early churches or the spread of the Gospel to the Gentiles.

All the rest of the appearances have been written for the needs of the churches for whom the evangelists wrote. This has begun already in Mark, whose story of the empty tomb is not literally true. It was written to reassure faithful Christians who believed only in *bodily* resurrection that Jesus really rose from the dead. Matthew wrote an account of a single appearance to the Eleven so that the risen Jesus commands the Gentile mission, and baptism in the name of the Father, the Son and the Holy Spirit, both requirements of Matthean churches, but alien to the behaviour of the Eleven. Luke rewrote the tradition even more completely. He replaced the earlier tradition of appearances in Galilee with his own tradition of appearances in Jerusalem, though the basic idea of appearances in Jerusalem may well reflect historical fact. In Luke's stories, the disciples did not return to Galilee. They remained in Jerusalem, waiting to be empowered by the Holy Spirit at Pentecost. After that, the Gospel would be preached to all the nations, beginning from Jerusalem. All Luke's Resurrection narratives were created by Luke. They

---

55 Craig, *Resurrection of Jesus*, p. 279.

continue the tradition of reassuring faithful Christians who believed in bodily resurrection that Jesus really rose from the dead, and further clarify the nature of his Resurrection body. They also meet other needs of the Lukan churches. So, for example, the risen Jesus explains that the Christ had to suffer, and expounds the scriptures to this effect. The stories of Jesus' Ascension, both at the end of the Gospel and at the beginning of Acts, explain why Resurrection appearances ceased relatively soon after they started. The Johannine stories similarly meet the needs of the Johannine community, including even the deity of Jesus.

Thus there is very little in the stories of Resurrection appearances in the four Gospels which is literally true. This makes it extremely difficult to find out what the original experiences, which were instrumental in causing some of Jesus' disciples to believe that he had been raised from the dead, were like. I consider what we can perhaps know in the final section of this chapter.

6. *Appearances, Visions, Apparitions and Hallucinations*

Scholars argue vigorously over the question as to whether the disciples originally experienced genuine appearances of the risen Jesus, or saw visions of him, or had hallucinations. I propose that the Resurrection appearances may reasonably be called 'appearances', because that is how those people who saw them interpreted them, and so did the early tradition about them. They may reasonably be called 'visions', because this fits everything which we know about them, in a culture in which visions were normal, and considered to be perfectly real. The term 'hallucination' should not be used of them, because it belongs to our culture, not theirs, and its pejorative implications have been almost invariably used to confuse the major issues. The term 'apparition' is not much better for the same reasons.

We have seen that the earliest evidence of appearances of the risen Jesus to some of his followers is to be found in the relatively old tradition transmitted by St Paul at 1 Cor. 15.3-7. Paul follows it immediately by equating his vision of Jesus on the Damascus Road with a Resurrection appearance. We know from the accounts in Acts that this was a vision which other people present at the time did not see or hear properly (Acts 9.3-8; 22.6-11; 26.12-18). In the third account of it, the risen Jesus gives Paul a reason why 'I have appeared to you' (Acts 26.16). Luke, who was a companion of Paul on some of his journeys, including his immediately following journey to Rome (Acts 27.1ff), represents Paul himself saying 'I was not disobedient to the heavenly vision' (Acts 26.19). Here Paul is represented as using the same word for 'vision' as Paul himself uses for 'visions . . . of the Lord' at 2 Cor. 12.1, and the same word as Luke uses for the women at the empty tomb seeing 'a vision of angels' (Lk. 24.23). It follows that Paul and Luke were both happy to think of Resurrection appearances as visions.

This is natural because Second Temple Judaism was a visionary culture, in which people believed that people saw appearances of God and angels, and had visions and dreams in which God and angels appeared to them. Appearances, visions and dreams were all regarded as means of heavenly revelations. Most of the surviving evidence comes from stories which are not literally true, but these stories are nonetheless valuable because they reflect genuine beliefs based on experiences which people had. The following is a sample of the great variety of ways in which their beliefs were expressed.

At Gen. 12.7, 'YHWH appeared to Abram'. There is no mention of a vision or a dream. At 1QApGen XXII, 27, 'God appeared to Abram in a vision, and said to him . . .'. This is a 'vision' in which Abram is able to converse with God. Isaiah's call vision begins 'In the year that Uzziah died I saw the Lord sitting on a throne high and lofty . . .' (Isa. 6.1). Seraphim, Isaiah and God all speak during the account of this experience, which is not however labelled a vision. At Dan. 8.1, 'a vision appeared to me, I, Daniel.' At Dan. 8.15, 'It came to pass while I Daniel was seeing the vision . . . behold, standing before me one like the appearance of a man . . .'. This turns out to be Gabriel, who interprets the symbolic part of the vision. At Dan. 9.21, while Daniel is praying, 'the man Gabriel whom I saw previously in a vision . . . reached me . . .'. Gabriel gives Daniel further revelation, but this time Daniel is not said to be in a vision. At Ps-Philo IX, 10, 'The spirit of God fell on Miriam at night, and she saw a dream', in which 'a man was standing in a linen garment', who predicts the birth of Moses, through whom 'I will save my people'. This is a genuine revelation by an angel in a dream. Josephus tells how, before the Roman war, 'a marvellous apparition was seen . . . was reported among those who beheld (it) . . . before sunset, around the whole country, war-chariots and armed battalions were seen high in the air, rushing across the clouds and encircling the cities' (*War* VI, 297–99).

The most important single vision was that of Ezekiel 1. In this, Ezekiel saw God's chariot, and at the top of it 'the likeness of a throne, and on the likeness of the throne a likeness like the appearance of a man . . . this was the appearance of the likeness of the glory of YHWH' (Ezek. 1.26, 28). Ezekiel says that he 'saw' this as if he was describing reality – he does not say that it was a vision. The reason this vision is so important is that Jewish people have meditated on it ever since, and have been thought to ascend into heaven and see the Chariot.

Paul is the most obvious visionary in early Christianity, and no one doubts the importance of his visionary experience on the Damascus Road. Simeon the Rock was also a visionary. Whatever we make of the Transfiguration, at the very least someone thought it appropriate to tell a story of the inner circle of three, Simeon the Rock with Jacob and John, the sons of Zebedee seeing Jesus with his clothing temporarily transformed into the whiteness characteristic of heavenly beings. Then Elijah 'appeared to them with Moses', and they held a discussion with Jesus (Mk 9.2-8). Compared with this, Peter's vision at Acts 10.10-16 is relatively straightforward. At the beginning, Luke says that 'a trance came upon him', and afterwards that he was perplexed at 'what the vision which he had seen might be' (Acts 10.17). Later, Peter begins to explain it, saying 'I saw a vision in a trance' (Acts 11.5). This makes Peter a particularly suitable candidate for 'he [Jesus] appeared to Cephas, then to the Twelve' (1 Cor. 15.5). He will not have been one of the Eleven who 'doubted' (Mt. 28.17). Jesus himself was a visionary. I have discussed his call vision at his baptism by John the Baptist

(Mk 1.9-11), and his dramatic comment 'I saw Satan fall like lightning from heaven' (Lk. 10.18).[56]

All this means that Jesus' closest followers during the historic ministry were much more likely to have visions of him after his death than normal people in our culture today. Moreover, they might relate such an event as if it were what we may reasonably call an 'appearance' of the risen Jesus.

The stories of the Resurrection appearances in the New Testament fall within the range of what was believed to be possible in Second Temple Judaism. There are no dreams. We should infer that those original experiences which were interpreted as Resurrection appearances happened when people were awake. The most ancient formulaic tradition of the earliest appearances says simply that Jesus 'appeared' or 'was seen' (1 Cor. 15.5-7), just as God 'appeared' to Abram. In Mark's account of the empty tomb, the women 'saw' an angel in the tomb (Mk 16.5), and they are told to tell his disciples that they will 'see' him (Mk 16.7). In Matthew, the angel of the Lord 'came down' (Mt. 28.2). Jesus 'met' the two Marys (Mt. 28.9). At Mt. 28.16, the Eleven 'saw' him. In Luke, two angels 'stood by' the women in the tomb (Lk. 24.4), so the women are later reported to have 'seen a vision of angels' (Lk. 24.23). In the appearance on the Emmaus road, Jesus 'approached and went along with' the two disciples, and later 'became invisible from them' (Lk. 24.15, 31). In Jerusalem, they are told that the Lord 'appeared' to Simon (Lk. 24.34). In the next appearance, Jesus 'stood' in the middle of them (Lk. 24.36). Jesus tells them 'you see me' having flesh and bones (Lk. 24.39). Thus the descriptions of the Resurrection appearances in the oldest sources, and in the stories of Luke, who knew the oldest traditions known to us, and knew Paul as well, all fall within the parameters of the descriptions of the appearances of heavenly beings in the Judaism of that time.

It is interesting that there are no trances, and no traces of any association with visions of the heavenly Chariot. We should accept these negative facts into the historical record. This is not what the Resurrection appearances were like.

All the Resurrection appearances, except for Paul's vision on the Damascus Road, were to recently bereaved followers of Jesus. For this reason, bereavement experiences are relevant for understanding the Resurrection appearances. Lüdemann was the first to make fruitful historical use of such insights, and an independent critical discussion has now been provided by Dale Allison.[57]

Appearances of dead people are part of cross-cultural experiences, so we can make careful use of them, without reading anything specific to our own culture back into the culture of the followers of Jesus. Such appearances used to be drastically under-reported in our culture, because bereaved people were afraid of being taken to be mad people hallucinating.[58] More abundant evidence

---

56   See pp. 176–77, 230, 250.
57   Lüdemann, *Resurrection of Jesus*, esp. pp. 97–100; Allison, *Resurrecting Jesus*, esp. pp. 269–99, 364–75, with bibliography. See also the important study of Dewi Rees, *Death and Bereavement: The Psychological, Religious and Cultural Interfaces* (London/Philadelphia: Whurr, 2nd edn, 2001), esp. ch. 22: 'The Bereaved and the Living Dead'.
58   Allison, *Resurrecting Jesus*, p. 271, citing A. Grimby, 'Bereavement among Elderly People:

began to accumulate with small studies, such as a 1970 study from Japan, which reported that 18 out of 20 women who had been suddenly widowed had had 'Sense of Presence' experiences, and no less than half of them had *seen* their dead husbands. Then, in 1971, Rees reported that of 293 widows and widowers whom he interviewed, 47 per cent believed that they had come into contact with their dead spouse.[59] While most of these were Sense of Presence experiences, 14 per cent saw their deceased spouse, 13.3 per cent reported hearing them, and some of these actually conversed with them, while 2.7 per cent reported being touched by their dead spouse. Fully 72.3 per cent had not mentioned their experience to anyone else before they reported it to Dr Rees, which again shows how and why such experiences were little known until the above surveys were carried out.

In general, such results have since been confirmed by a massive number of studies, which have now extended far beyond bereaved partners. The current situation is that 'all parts of the general public report a high incidence of . . . apparent contact with the dead', including 'visions while wide awake'. These included shared experiences, when 'more than one person saw an apparition'.[60] Summarizing reports as well as verified experiences, so a situation analogous to the Gospel narratives as well as the tradition in 1 Cor. 15.3-7, Allison[61] concludes, among other points, that there are numerous reports of apparitions in which departed people 'are both seen and heard', though 'they tend to say little'; 'are seen now by one person and later by another'; 'are seen by more than one percipient at the same time'; 'are sometimes seen by some but not all present'; 'create doubt in some percipients'; 'give guidance and make requests or issue imperatives'; 'are overwhelmingly real and indeed seemingly solid'; 'appear and disappear in unusual and abrupt ways'; 'are not perceived as apparitional at the beginning of the experience'; and 'are seen less and less as more and more time follows their death'.

These conclusions from abundant studies of both real experiences and stories provide a massive set of parallels to the Resurrection experiences reported in the New Testament, provided that these are treated as stories rather than literal accounts of facts. When we try to uncover what actually happened during the

---

Grief Reactions, Post-Bereavement Hallucinations and Quality of Life', *Acta psychiatrica Scandanavica* 87 (1993), p. 76; E. Devers, 'Experiencing the Deceased: Reconciling the Extraordinary' (PhD Diss., Univ. of Florida, 1994), pp. 102–14.

59 Allison, *Resurrecting Jesus*, p. 273, citing J. Yamamototo, K. Okonogi, T. Iwasaki and S. Yoshimura, 'Mourning in Japan', *American Journal of Psychiatry* 125, no. 12 (1969), pp. 1660–65; W. D. Rees, 'The Hallucinations of Widowhood', *British Medical Journal* 4 (1971), pp. 37–41; W. D. Rees, 'The Bereaved and Their Hallucinations', in B. Schoenberg *et al.* (eds), *Bereavement: Its Psychosocial Aspects* (New York: Columbia University, 1975), pp. 66–71. See now Rees, *Death and Bereavement*, ch. 22, which includes a description of the circumstances of his investigation, as well as its results in a form perfectly comprehensible to non-specialists.

60 Allison, *Resurrecting Jesus*, pp. 273–75, summarizing a lot of collected evidence of people's experiences.

61 Allison, *Resurrecting Jesus*, pp. 278–82, citing investigations and reports in extensive footnotes.

Resurrection appearances of Jesus' followers, however, some of these comments are based on comments from situations which should not be read back into the lives of normal and sane first-century Jews. The most striking example is Allison's comment that departed people 'are seen by more than one percipient at the same time'.[62] At first sight, this looks like helpful evidence for understanding the appearance of Jesus to the Eleven (Mt. 28.16-20, cf. 1 Cor. 15.5). One of Allison's major references is however to a 'Community Mail Survey of Psychic Experiences', which brings to light a modern social subgroup too different from the environment of normal first-century Galilaean Jews to be safely used to illuminate them. Another major reference is to supposedly collective visions of Jesus in an American Pentecostal church in 1954 and 1959, reported in 1965 and 1991 to the author of a 1997 book in such terms that no critical scholar should rely on the published report. Neither of these references has anything to do with the accurately reported experiences of normal and sane bereaved people described so carefully in the fine scholarship of Dewi Rees. What they do help to explain is why mainstream church authorities, and doctors, have been so suspicious and/or dismissive of such reports that normal and sane bereaved people have traditionally been reluctant to talk about their experiences of the continued presence of dead people to whom they had been close, in case they should be thought to be mad, involved in spiritualism, or both. Some people are!

However, when due allowance has been made for cultural differences and unreliable storytelling, the fact remains that bereaved people seeing appearances of the dead is a widespread cross-cultural phenomenon. This underlines the fact that, apart from Paul's vision on the Damascus Road, the Resurrection appearances were seen by bereaved people. Moreover, since Second Temple Judaism was a visionary culture, bereaved followers of Jesus, especially Simeon the Rock, were doubly liable to have experiences of the presence of Jesus after his death. There are therefore good reasons not to doubt the basic historicity of Resurrection appearances as recorded at 1 Cor. 15.5-7, and reflected in the increasingly developed stories of the canonical Gospels. Some bereaved followers of Jesus had visions of him not long after he was dead, and interpreted them as appearances of the risen Jesus from heaven, where he sat at the right hand of God.

Another major point is that when bereaved people do have experiences of dead people who speak to them, as they sometimes do, they make extremely short speeches. Most of these reassure the living that the dead are perfectly well. This makes excellent sense of the fact that the Resurrection appearances have had to be extensively rewritten, with carefully constructed speeches, to be useful for the churches.

I have described these experiences as appearances or visions without distinction, while noting that they did not have the aspect of certain visions, in that, apart from Paul's experience, they are not said to be visions, and there is no

---

62   Allison, *Resurrecting Jesus*, p. 279 with n. 321, citing especially J. Palmer, 'A Community Mail Survey of Psychic Experiences', *Journal of the American Society of Psychical Research* 73 (1979), pp. 221–51, in which 12 per cent of 'apparitional experiences were collective', and a collective vision of Jesus reported in Wiebe, *Visions of Jesus*, pp. 77–82.

trace of any of the disciples going into a trance, ascending to heaven to see these appearances, or seeing anything like the Chariot. This however defines what sort of visions they were: it does not mean that they were not visions. Conservative Christian apologists have denied that they were visions, and some discussions have suffered badly from treating the Resurrection appearances as hallucinations. I therefore consider a selection of the most important arguments.

There are two problems with the term 'hallucination'. One is that no such term is used by the primary sources, and the other is that it is a loaded term, owing to its associations in our culture. For example, Craig comments that 'the disciples were in no state of mind to hallucinate'[63]; Carrier, on the other hand, after describing the circumstances of Jesus' death and its immediate aftermath as he sees them, declares that 'All of this, as well as the confusion and grief of losing a beloved leader and the resulting crisis of faith . . . more than establishes the "emotional excitement" requirement for hallucination'[64]; Kreeft and Tacelli declare, 'Hallucinations usually happen only once, except to the insane. This one returned many times, to ordinary people'[65]; Allison, trying hard to classify the different proposals for understanding the evidence about Jesus' Resurrection, has 'Hallucinations' as his third category, and has Peter, according to this view, 'under a psychological necessity to restore his emotional equilibrium', so he 'projected exactly what he needed for healing' and 'A sort of mass hysteria, the product of emotional contagion, followed, with others as victims of their overluxuriant imaginations also claiming to see Jesus, although he was nothing but a figment of their optical delusion.'[66]

None of this is helpful in understanding the Resurrection appearances, and most of it is quite misleading. Behind such comments lies the old prejudice about hallucinations being what insane people have, the same prejudice as ensured that, for many years, bereavement experiences in our culture were drastically under-reported.[67] Bereavement visions are seen by people who are not in a particular state of mind other than what is natural to those who have been bereaved: they do not require any particular form of 'emotional excitement'; they may happen more than once, to 'ordinary people', and that is not an indication that such people are 'the insane'; and 'mass hysteria' is not required for more than one person to have such experiences, either separately or together, and nor are 'overluxuriant imaginations'. I therefore regard the term 'hallucination' as inappropriate for describing Resurrection appearances.

The use of the term 'vision' has also been criticized. For example, Craig declares that Paul 'was familiar with religious visions', which is obviously true,

63 Craig, *Resurrection of Jesus*, p. 399.
64 R. C. Carrier, 'The Resurrection of Jesus in Light of Jewish Law', in R. M. Price and J. J. Lowder, *The Empty Tomb: Jesus Beyond the Grave* (New York: Prometheus Books, 2005), pp. 369–92 (387).
65 P. Kreeft and R. K. Tacelli, *Handbook of Christian Apologetics* (Downers Grove: IVP, 1994), p. 187.
66 Allison, *Resurrecting Jesus*, pp. 204–5.
67 See pp. 490–92, with n. 47, referring to Allison, *Resurrecting Jesus*, p. 271.

but then asserts that he was 'the recipient of a genuine appearance of Jesus, not simply a vision', and he uses the term 'no mere vision' twice in his immediately following discussion.[68] Such comments have no scholarly substance. Luke has Paul refer to his experience as 'the heavenly vision' (Acts 26.19), and Luke was around at the time, and wrote up other Resurrection appearances. That Paul believed he saw 'a genuine appearance of Jesus' is true, but Craig's other comments simply show the contempt for Second Temple Judaism regrettably characteristic of many Christian scholars. Paul, and other people in his culture, believed in the reality of visions, and we must respect that if we are to have any hope of understanding them.

The next question is, who saw Resurrection appearances? The relatively old tradition in 1 Cor. 15.5-8 includes Simeon the Rock and Jacob, almost certainly Jacob brother of Jesus. There are two quite different reasons for believing this much of the tradition. One is that, in their quite different ways, they were seriously bereaved. The second is that their successive leadership of the Jerusalem church would not have been possible if they had not seen at least one Resurrection appearance. Moreover, given what we know about bereavement experiences, it is most improbable that Jesus did not appear to either of them more than once. Given also the fact that they led the Jerusalem church, it is entirely probable that some of these appearances continued when they were in Jerusalem, and that this is the ultimate basis of the tradition of Resurrection appearances in Jerusalem, before Luke rewrote it completely. Nor is there any doubt about Paul's quite different vision.

Equally, there should not be much doubt that there is some sort of truth in the stories of an appearance to the Eleven. This is however much more complicated. First, conservative scholars such as Craig can use the stories at Lk. 24.36-43, Jn 20.19-23 and even Mk 16.14-18 to suggest that this is *the same* appearance as that to 'the Twelve' at 1 Cor. 15.5, and declare this is 'the best attested appearance of Jesus after his resurrection.'[69] We have however seen that the appearance to Cleopas, his companion, the Eleven and 'those with them' at Lk. 24.36-51 is quite different from the appearance to 'the disciples', a group who did not include Thomas, at Jn 20.19-23, and that neither story is literally true. It should also be obvious that the spurious Longer Ending of Mark is dependent on these earlier Gospel traditions.[70] It follows that this is not one 'best attested appearance' at all. It is one relatively early tradition followed by three very late stories, not one of which is literally true. Accordingly, what these stories really attest very well is the need of people in the early church to believe in a single appearance to the Twelve, not the reality of such an appearance at all.

This is the point at which it matters that Paul says that Jesus appeared to over 500 brethren 'at once', but does not say this of the Twelve. Moreover, we have seen, especially from the work of Allison, that while there are *reports* of corporate visions, we do not have cross-cultural evidence of appearances of

---

68   Craig, *Resurrection of Jesus*, pp. 70–72.
69   Craig, *Resurrection of Jesus*, pp. 55–56.
70   See pp. 76–78, 462–63, 477–78.

recently dead people to as many as 11 bereaved people at once, in such a form that we can reasonably apply them to these Eleven. This brings us to the crucial evidence of Matthew: 'some doubted' (Mt. 28.17). We would never guess that from the early tradition handed on by Paul. It must reflect the fact that some of the Eleven did not believe that they saw the risen Jesus, whereas others, including the inner circle of three, Peter, Jacob and John, all of whom played leading roles in the Jerusalem church, did see visions which they believed were appearances of the risen Jesus.

At this point, the role of the Twelve in the historic ministry is of particular importance. As we have seen, Jesus chose them deliberately as a symbol of the twelve tribes of the restored Israel. He chose them both to be with him, and so that he could send them out to bring people back to God before he finally established his kingdom, and he did send them out to preach and to continue his ministry of healing and exorcism. They also accompanied him on his migratory ministry in Galilee, and on his final visit to Jerusalem. He led the Jesus movement, and he taught them that he was going to Jerusalem to die his atoning death for the redemption of Israel, as it was written in scriptures which he also taught them. Equally, he taught them that he would rise again. It is some of this entirely special group of people who doubted. Matthew does not tell us how many of them doubted. If however, several of them doubted, that would explain why they took no part in the early church, and why Matthew could not omit 'some doubted' from his largely triumphal report.

What of the 'more than 500 brethren at once' (1 Cor. 15.6)? How many of them doubted? We do not know. We do however know that neither Luke, who cannot have failed to know of this incident from St Paul, nor any of the other Gospel writers, thought this supposedly amazing incident worthy of recording. If this experience was not worth writing up, it cannot have been as unambiguous as conservative Christians like to believe. That such an event should occur is paradoxically not as improbable as an appearance to the Eleven all at once. While it is not a feature of bereavement experiences, strange experiences by large numbers of people at once have been recorded so reliably that some reports of them must be accepted. Allison is among those who would include here 'the 1968–69 sightings of the Virgin Mary at St. Mary's Coptic church in Zeitoun, Egypt; she was reportedly seen by tens of thousands, both Muslims and Christians.' She was seen, but did not speak.[71] It is entirely plausible to suppose that some of more than 500 followers of Jesus thought that they saw something on a given occasion, that the dominant interpretation was that it was Jesus, but that he said nothing. Given that the Gospel writers rewrote the appearances so that Jesus said and did more of what the churches needed, an appearance of that kind might well be what they did not choose to write up.

---

71   Allison, *Resurrecting Jesus*, p. 283 n. 333, citing J. Palmer, *Our Lady Returns to Egypt* (San Bernadino: Culligan, 1969); V. DeVincenzo, 'The Apparitions at Zeitoun, Egypt: An Historical Overview', *Journal of Religion and Psychical Research* 11 (1988), pp. 3–13; M. Carroll, *The Cult of the Virgin Mary: Psychological Origins* (Princeton: Princeton UP, 1986), pp. 211–16.

What about the women? Their absence from 1 Cor. 15.5-8 is notorious. Bauckham lists no less than five explanations from standard works of scholarship, including 'male prejudices against women's witness'.[72] There are two problems with this. One is that the empty tomb is also missing from the old tradition in 1 Cor. 15.3-8. I have moreover argued that the stories of the empty tomb are not literally true. It follows that appearances to women were not especially important to leading men in the early church. Secondly, two appearances in 1 Cor. 15.5-8 are not gender-specific. It is possible, for example, that Mary Magdalene and/ or Joanna wife of Chouza were at some stage sent by Jesus to do something important, such as to make arrangements with a Jerusalem householder to have an upper room for the Last Supper, and that they were among 'all the apostles' to whom Jesus was believed to have appeared (1 Cor. 15.7), whether or not they were among any who may have doubted too. In the absence of direct information, we have no insight into that. On general grounds, it is not probable that over 500 'brethren' to whom Jesus is said to have appeared at once (1 Cor. 15.6) were all male, however many of them may also have doubted.

It does not follow that the women did not see any individual Resurrection appearances. We have seen that all the Resurrection appearances, whether to men or to women, have been extensively rewritten. I have argued that this is partly because they were bereavement appearances, which normally involve only brief speeches when there are some. Secondly, they have been rewritten for the needs of the churches. This is why the appearances to the women are not genuine as they stand. But then, neither are the appearances to the men. The tradition of appearances to the women may be based not only on the narrative usefulness of the empty tomb stories, but also on basically sound traditions that some of the women also saw Resurrection appearances.

It follows that we know much less about the Resurrection appearances than we would like. Paul's vision on the Damascus Road was regarded by him and his followers as a Resurrection appearance, but it was different from all the others. Our two oldest narrative sources, Mark and Matthew, suppose that there was at least one appearance in Galilee. The Jerusalem tradition, as we have it, was due to deliberate rewriting by Luke, to empower the disciples for the Gentile mission which produced the Christian religion, to which Luke belonged. It is however perfectly possible that he knew an old tradition that Jesus appeared to Simeon the Rock and perhaps others when they were in Jerusalem. This makes excellent sense of the oldest tradition in 1 Cor. 15.3-7, which probably does not mention the place of the appearances because they did not happen in one place.

One further argument in favour of the empty tomb can now be dealt with. Craig argues that '*It would have been virtually impossible for the disciples to proclaim the resurrection in Jerusalem had the tomb not been empty . . . the dis-covery of Jesus's occupied grave would decisively silence his followers.*'[73] First, we have seen that the first disciples believed that God had raised Jesus from the dead, but this belief was not dependent on the story of the empty tomb. It

---

72   Bauckham, *Gospel Women*, pp. 307–10.
73   Craig, *Resurrection of Jesus*, pp. 368, 370.

is especially important at this point that the empty tomb is not mentioned in the early speeches of Acts, which were delivered in Jerusalem. I have discussed Simeon the Rock's speech reported at Acts 2.14-36, in which Simeon's arguments depend on Psalm 16, according to which God did not let Jesus go to Sheol, or the Pit, and Psalm 110, according to which Jesus was sitting at the right hand of God.[74] This was a proclamation of the Resurrection in Jerusalem, and there is no mention of the empty tomb.

Secondly, this was several weeks after Jesus' death. Contrary to Luke's version of events at the end of his Gospel and the beginning of Acts, Jesus' most important followers had been in Galilee in the meantime, so they had not been preaching the Gospel in Jerusalem. By this time, Jesus' remains would be unrecognizable. Even if someone knew where his tomb was, for example if Joseph of Arimathea was back in Jerusalem too, some of his helpers probably being there anyway, the revolting task of trying to identify which body it was would not have been decisive at all. It would not have silenced his followers, because their faith that Jesus had risen was not dependent on the missing remains of Jesus' body. They would have continued to preach the good news that God had raised Jesus from the dead in accordance with Psalm 16, and he now sits at the right hand of God in accordance with Psalm 110. Producing Jesus' remains would impress only those who did not believe in resurrection, those who believed God never took anyone to heaven, and those who believed that Jesus was a seditious criminal. Like most Jews in Jerusalem, such people did not believe in Jesus' Resurrection anyway, so producing Jesus' remains would have been a revolting exercise which had no significant effect.

We should therefore conclude that Jesus' closest followers had experiences which they interpreted as appearances of him after his death. These experiences, together with his predictions and their study of the scriptures, were instrumental in leading them to believe that God had raised him from the dead. These appearances fit into what is generally known of the experiences of bereaved people. Paul had a quite different but equally important vision on the Damascus Road.

7. *Conclusions*

The following conclusions may therefore be drawn. Jesus did not rise bodily from the dead, leaving an empty tomb behind. He was probably buried in a common criminals' tomb, where his body rotted in a normal way. He had however predicted his Resurrection in terms which did not imply bodily resurrection or an empty tomb. After his death, his bereaved followers, including Simeon the Rock and some other members of the Twelve, as well as Jesus' brother Jacob, had visions of him, which they interpreted as Resurrection appearances. They studied the scriptures and found in them predictions of his Resurrection. The passages

---

74 See pp. 459–60.

which they studied included Psalms 41 and 118, as Jesus had taught them, and Psalms 16 and 110, which, as far as we know, they studied themselves.

As time went on, accounts of Resurrection appearances, different from the original ones, were written, rewritten and rewritten. Those which we find in the Gospels have been written and rewritten with two major points in mind. One is to legitimate belief in the Resurrection of Jesus itself. It is this which led some Christians to write stories of a *bodily* resurrection. Rewriting in these terms can be seen already in the earliest of these surviving accounts, that in the Gospel of Mark. As we compare the accounts in the different Gospels, we can see more and more careful rewriting, aimed directly at ensuring that the stories could be interpreted only of a genuine bodily resurrection. The second major point of these stories is to function as revelations by the risen Jesus. For this reason, they contain brief statements and instructions which legitimate the most important beliefs and practices of the early churches. These include baptism, the mission to the Gentiles, Christological interpretation of the scriptures, the Sonship of Jesus and finally even his deity. At this level, even the synoptic Gospels are classic examples of the social memory of a large community, because they have been written with the current needs of Christian communities in mind.

It follows that we should not blindly accept the traditional Christian view that the Resurrection of Jesus was God's vindication of him. Some people will prefer the view of most Jews who were in Israel at the time, that the Resurrection did not really take place. On the other hand, there should be no doubt, even on the most rigorous of historical criteria, that some of the first followers of Jesus had genuine visions of him after his death, and that they interpreted these as appearances of the risen Lord. In other words, the historical evidence is in no way inconsistent with the belief of the first disciples, and of many modern Christians, that God raised Jesus from the dead, and granted visions of the risen Jesus to some of the first disciples, and to St Paul on the Damascus Road.

CHAPTER 13

Conclusions

I now draw together the conclusions of this account of the life and teaching of Jesus.

First, we have seen abundant evidence that Jesus was a first-century Jewish prophet. Attempts to describe him as a historical figure have however been largely so inaccurate that I felt bound to devote the opening chapter of this book to an analysis of the quest of the historical Jesus. I found that the most pervasive problem has been the inability of Christian scholars to come to terms with the Jewishness of Jesus. Consequently, I found it fruitful to consider the Nazi period, which is generally omitted, but which is illuminating because Nazi scholars *deliberately tried* to avoid the Jewishness of Jesus. This helps us to see the *social function* of most of the quest, which also avoids the Jewishness of Jesus. This is not because most investigators also try to do this, but it is a consequence of their Christian beliefs. Homing in on *social function* also enables us to understand the particular results obtained by social groups and individual investigators. For example, the unjustifiable removal of Jesus' eschatological expectations from their picture of Jesus by the American Jesus Seminar was due to their well-justified opposition to American fundamentalism. It also helps us to understand that the widespread inability of Christian scholars to come to terms with the Jewishness of Jesus is not due to lack of integrity on their part.

Equally, it does not mean that Christian beliefs cause more distortion than other ideological beliefs. This emerged with particular clarity in engaging with the opinion that Jesus did not exist. This view is demonstrably false. It is fuelled by a regrettable form of atheist prejudice, which holds all the main primary sources, and Christian people, in contempt. This is not merely worse than the American Jesus Seminar, it is no better than Christian fundamentalism. It simply has *different* prejudices. Most of its proponents are also extraordinarily incompetent.

I drew particular attention to the exceptional work of two outstanding critical scholars whose work is as free from bias as any scholars have so far become. One is the liberal Christian scholar E. P. Sanders, who has written the best life of Jesus so far, and has contributed other outstanding work to help us understand Jesus in

499

his original cultural context. The other is the Jewish scholar Geza Vermes, who
began his outstanding contributions to our understanding of the Jewishness of
Jesus as early as 1967. Their work has been widely praised, but not universally
followed. This again reflects the entrenched nature of the beliefs of the majority
of scholars, which itself is a product of their social function as scholarly representatives of (mostly Christian) social subgroups.

In this situation, I began more positive work by discussing the oldest surviving
primary sources on which an accurate picture of the historical Jesus can reasonably be based, the Gospel of Mark, the so-called 'Q' material, and the Gospels of
Matthew and Luke. I followed Crossley's dating of Mark c.40 CE, and I argued
that it was written by an unknown Christian called Marcus. I drew attention to
complex scholarly work in which I have previously argued that some parts of it
were literal translations of Aramaic sources which were perfectly accurate, and
probably written by people who were there at the time. I also argued that this
Gospel is unfinished from beginning to end. It needed thorough revision, which
was provided by the author whom we call 'Matthew', c.50–60 CE. I argued for a
chaotic model of the 'Q' material, some parts of which were also early and accurate. I followed the ancient tradition that Matthew the apostle and tax-collector
wrote down traditions about Jesus, mostly his teaching, in Aramaic, and that
different translations were made, some better than others. This may be the reason
why Matthew the Evangelist was called Matthew, for he has many early and
accurate pieces of non-Markan tradition, which could be excellent translations
of pieces originally written down by Matthew the apostle and tax-collector. Some
of these traditions were later used by Luke and hence classified with 'Q' material,
which is probably why some parts of the 'Q' material are verbally identical in
Matthew and Luke, being dependent on a single excellent Greek translation of
such material. Luke wrote much later, c.85 CE, for Gentile churches. He knew
Matthew and the 'Q' material, some of it much less well translated as well as
edited by him, and he inherited some other accurate traditions as well.

By this time, a lot of secondary material had accrued as well. In Chapter 4,
I argued that the stories of the virgin birth are entirely due to storytelling, and
in Chapter 12 I argued that the Resurrection stories are almost the same. At
various points, I also noted that Matthew and Luke rewrote correct traditions
in Mark. For example, Luke rewrote Mark's perfectly correct tradition of Jesus'
visit to Nazareth when the ministry was well under way (Mk 6.1-6, rewritten
at Lk. 4.16-30). Luke's spurious ending, according to which the inhabitants
of Nazareth threw him out and took him up to 'the brow of the hill on which
the city was built' (Lk. 4.29) misled traditional attempts to locate the site of
Nazareth, and has been abused by atheists arguing that Nazareth did not exist.

In this situation, scholars need criteria for distinguishing between authentic,
rewritten and secondary traditions. I discussed these criteria in Chapter 3. I
gave greatest weight to the criterion of historical plausibility. This is a very useful cover-all term for the main contention of this book, that the historical Jesus
should be fitted into his original cultural context in first-century Judaism. I also
fitted the criterion of Aramaisms into the context of the criterion of historical
plausibility.

To fit Jesus into his original context within first-century Judaism, we must reconstruct that culture too. I therefore surveyed the main sources which enable us to do this. I naturally drew attention to the Dead Sea Scrolls, especially those written in Aramaic. The scrolls have enabled scholars to greatly improve our knowledge of Judaism at the time of Jesus, and it is the Aramaic scrolls which have enabled me to work on Aramaic sources of the synoptic Gospels to an extent which was not previously possible. This is at the centre of the research which lies behind this book.

I also drew particular attention to some features of this culture which New Testament scholars generally overlook, because we must be aware of the way in which secondary material may occur side by side with literally accurate traditions, to help us to distinguish between the two. Authors not only repeated accurate traditions about past events from their sources, they also rewrote them in accordance with the needs of their communities. They might also add stories, also for the benefit of the communities for whom they wrote. I drew attention to the concept of 'social memory', a useful term in helping us to understand how authors, writing for communities, do repeat authentic traditions from the past, but also update them with material useful for those same communities at the time of writing, and add helpful stories of their own.

I next discussed Jesus' own background in an observant Jewish family, in a Jewish area. He spoke Aramaic. Given that both he and his brother Jacob ended up as major Jewish leaders, they will also have learnt the Torah both at home and at synagogue. They will also have attended some major festivals in Jerusalem, though we have no idea how often they went. All this necessarily entailed knowledge of the prophetic tradition, which Jesus joined when he went and was baptized by John the Baptist in the Jordan, in the general area of the Judaean desert. At some stage Jesus moved to the Jewish town of Capernaum, beside the lake of Galilee, which became the centre of his prophetic ministry. Some time after his baptism, Jesus called the Twelve, a group who symbolized the twelve tribes of Israel and who were central to his ministry. His ministry was also supported by female followers, of whom the most important was Mary from the neighbouring town of Magdala.

We do not know how long the ministry lasted, and the Gospels do not give us a chronologically successive account of it either. I therefore discussed the main points of Jesus' ministry in chapters 6–9, with Christological terms in Chapter 10, before picking up the story of the final events in Chapter 11.

I devoted Chapter 6 to God, because God was the centre of Jesus' life and ministry, at every level of his being. First, Jesus had a prayer life of his own, as we can see from the fact that he went out to pray on his own. Secondly, Jesus taught about God. I discussed the two major concepts of the Fatherhood and kingdom, or kingship, of God. I noted that these are complementary metaphors, which should be in no way opposed to each other, nor to traditional Judaism, from which Jesus drew both concepts and recreated them from his prophetic perspective. The kingship of God refers particularly to God's position as the awesome creator and ruler of the universe, whose very name was to be kept holy. I noted especially that God had always been King of the Universe, is always

King of the Universe in the present time, and will one day finally establish his kingdom. Jesus saw God's kingship powerfully revealed in the present time in his ministry of exorcism and healing. Jesus also expected God to finally establish his kingdom in the near future. Jesus was mistaken in this expectation, a common mistake which arose naturally from the Jewish culture within which Jesus lived and worked. Accordingly, it should not be regarded as a serious error of judgement in his presentation of the mighty power of God for the Jews of his time. On the contrary, it reflects the intensity of his experience of the power of God in his life and ministry.

The Fatherhood of God was the major metaphor which Jesus used to present the nearness of God to faithful Jews. For this purpose, he used the relatively intimate Aramaic word *Abba*, which everyone used for their natural fathers too. This reflects his prophetic recreation of the nearness and availability of God. Jesus also taught extensively about God's fatherly care for people. He reassured the poor that God would look after their needs. He also urged people to be like God in certain ways. In particular, as well as reassuring them that God always forgives repentant sinners, he exhorted people to forgive each other, an important feature of his ministry among ordinary Jews many of whom had many practical problems in their lives.

Jesus summed up his view of God in what we know as the 'Lord's Prayer'. This began with *Abba*, the ordinary and relatively intimate word for 'Father', which Jesus regarded as a natural way to approach God. It continued immediately with a prayer that God's name be kept holy, an indication of the awesomeness of this immediately approachable being. The next petition asked God to finally establish his kingdom. The prayer for 'bread' reflects God's care for people, especially the poor. The prayer for the forgiveness of sins reflects Jesus' awareness that God always forgives repentant sinners, and continues with a declaration that we forgive those who sin against us, which reflects Jesus' extensive teaching about how people should treat each other. The prayer ends with a plea to be delivered from the final trial which was expected to precede the final establishment of God's kingdom.

Jesus not only taught about God, his teaching was only part of the way in which he followed the prophetic tradition of acting in God's name. The most dramatic example of this throughout his ministry was his activity as the most effective exorcist and healer known to us. Like much else, this has been rewritten in the Gospel traditions, but in Chapter 7 I was for the most part able to isolate primary material from the exaggerations of secondary rewriting. This showed that, in addition to numerous exorcisms, Jesus healed a variety of illnesses including functional blindness, deafness, fever, functional curvature of the spine, paralysis and skin disorder. Jesus attributed his ability to do this to the power of God working through him. In the exorcisms, this clearly involved him in a battle with Satan, and a small number of other healings appear to be in the same category.

The overall importance of this is especially clear in two ways. One is a dispute with 'scribes who came down from Jerusalem' and perhaps other Jews, who accused him of casting out demons by the power of the devil, a dispute important enough to be transmitted by Mark and in 'Q' material as well. These opponents could not deny the effectiveness of Jesus' mighty works, which is very strong evidence of how effective he was. Jesus responded directly with the metaphors of the 'finger' and 'spirit' of God working through him. Secondly, Jesus not only performed exorcisms and other healings, he sent out the Twelve who did the same, on account of which Jesus said that he had seen Satan fall like lightning from heaven. Of course they taught as well, but nothing could better indicate the fundamental importance to the ministry of acting out the will of God for the benefit of people, and the participation of Jesus' followers in it. Jesus' teaching is more famous than that of any rabbi, but there was far more to his ministry than teaching.

Jesus is still most famous to some people as a teacher of ethics, and in Chapter 8 I sought to put his ethical teaching in its context in first-century Judaism. I began with a discussion of the controversial role of repentance in his teaching. It was of central importance, but the actual word 'repent' does not occur very often in the Gospels. I pointed out the reason for this. Whereas Greek and Hebrew both have special words for 'repent', speakers of Aramaic used the ordinary word for 'return'. Moreover, this is what Jesus called upon people to do, and then come and follow him, it was not something which his followers had to keep doing, as people should 'repent' after every misdeed. This is why for example the parable usually called 'The Prodigal Son' does not contain the word 'repent'. It portrays the son eventually giving up his dissolute way of life and going back to his father, a portrayal in parabolic form of the repentant sinner returning to God. This is the reason why the actual word 'repent' is not common in the teaching of Jesus. It is what people did when they returned to God and followed him, not something which they had to be continually urged to do.

When Jewish people who had fallen away from God returned to him, they obeyed the Torah. The Torah was the centre of Jesus' ethical teaching. That is why Jesus' ethical teaching does not provide a systematic presentation of ethics. It takes the Torah for granted, and that told first-century Jews most of what they needed to know about how to behave. Jesus told his followers what to do when the Torah was not sufficient for his purposes, as he offered them a prophetic renewal of Judaism. A significant part of his special teaching may be seen as summarized in his injunction 'love your enemies'. This did not mean 'adore the Roman imperial power', nor was it inconsistent with his extreme criticisms of chief priests, scribes and Pharisees. It was a dramatic expression of his argument that the will of God demanded that first-century Jews in Galilee should get on well together, love their neighbours and not turn each other into unapproachable enemies. On the contrary, if they quarrelled, they should always seek reconciliation. This takes us back to the importance of forgiveness, which was central enough to be found in the Lord's Prayer. Jesus continually urged people to forgive anyone with whom they had a quarrel. His prohibition of swearing to each other by all sorts of things should be seen in the same light: oaths are unnecessary in general, worse if they involve God, and liable to cause people not to get on well together.

I further argued that Jesus' prohibition of divorce should be seen within this same frame of reference. Whereas the Torah permitted divorce, Jesus argued that Moses allowed this because of people's hardness of heart, and he used fundamental texts from the Torah to argue that it was not in accordance with the will of God in creating humankind. I suggested that this should be seen in the same context as his other ethical teaching on how people should treat each other. It should be seen as urging men to be kind and considerate to their wives, and not throw them out of their homes.

Jesus' teaching on rich and poor people should likewise be seen within this frame of reference, and in the light of the massive gap between the rich and the poor in first-century Israel. His simple teaching that the poor are blessed reflects his belief that God was concerned about the welfare of people who were liable to have insufficient food, clothing and shelter for any reasonable existence. Likewise, his condemnation of the rich reflects the fact that they were so rich and oppressive that they were not doing the will of God to look after the poor and hungry. Jesus asked just one man who was that rich to sell all that he had and give it to the poor. He made no such demands on relatively well-off people whom he knew.

Jesus' extensive teaching explains why he was addressed as 'rabbi'. In his day, this term simply meant 'teacher'. I prefer to use the term 'prophet' to describe him simply because it was the more comprehensive term.

Jesus' ministry also encountered severe opposition from some of his fellow Jews, and this eventually led to his death. I discussed this opposition in detail in Chapter 9, where I particularly sought to restore the connections between the scribes and Pharisees who are mentioned as his main opponents in the Gospel accounts of his ministry, and the chief priests, elders and scribes who were responsible for arresting him and taking him to Pilate. During his ministry in Galilee, Jesus encountered serious opposition from 'scribes who came down from Jerusalem' (Mk 3.22). In the light of his ministry of exorcism, they accused him of casting out demons by the power of the devil. To have gone to this trouble, they must have been led by distinguished scribes who were in touch with the chief priests who ran Jerusalem and Judaea. Jesus' ferocious response included the accusation that in opposing the work of the Holy Spirit in his ministry they had committed an unforgivable sin. These scribes cannot have failed to report to the chief priests in Jerusalem. There was another serious dispute with 'Pharisees and some of the scribes who came from Jerusalem' (Mk 7.1). This concerned a matter of non-biblical purity Law, whether people should wash their hands before eating, so this might be of direct concern to priests as well as scribes and Pharisees. Jesus' response to this was quite ferocious too. He accused them of abandoning the commandment of God as well as holding fast to the tradition of men. This is also important because it aligns scribes with Pharisees in circumstances in which some of the scribes cannot have failed to report this situation to the chief priests in Jerusalem.

In addition to these disputes, the Gospels contain a massive amount of polemic in which Jesus attacks scribes and Pharisees, so basically the same people. He told them they were not entering the kingdom of God and accused them of stopping other people from getting into it, as well as of being 'blind guides' when they thought of themselves as guides in the observance of the Law. He also told them they ignored the main points of the Torah in their observance of additional details, such as tithing mint, dill and cumin.

All this polemic adds up to a coherent whole. Jesus was severely critical of scribes and Pharisees, and they accused him of casting out demons by the power of the devil. It is important that the scribes were significant scribes from Jerusalem who must have been in touch with the chief priests. This is a main point which enables us to connect the opposition to Jesus in Galilee during his historic ministry with the opponents responsible for his death.

On another occasion Pharisees, after two disputes about minor matters in their interpretation of the Torah, took counsel with Herodians to destroy him (Mk 3.6). As a result, some Pharisees came and warned him that Herod Antipas wanted to kill him, and Jesus responded by referring to Herod as a jackal, and declared that as a prophet he would perish in Jerusalem (Lk. 13.31-33). This shows that the Pharisees were split, as well they might be. They objected to Jesus and his disciples not conforming to their expanded regulations which were not in the Torah. When some of them resorted to Herod Antipas, the secular power who had put one major prophet to death, others came to warn Jesus. While they did not agree with his detailed halakhic judgements, they may well have approved of him bringing ordinary Jews back to God, and of his healing ministry. They may also have thought that putting him to death was murder. This is a significant point in explaining why the final action against Jesus was taken by 'elders'. The Pharisees could not be mentioned at that point because they were split, and 'elders' could include the most distinguished Herodians, as well as any other distinguished Jews who were open to persuasion by the chief priests.

All this reveals the close connection between Jesus' opponents during his ministry, and those responsible for taking him to Pilate to be put to death.

In Chapter 10, I discussed the major titles of Jesus in the synoptic Gospels. I pointed out the large argument of cumulative weight for accepting the complete appropriateness of the terms 'prophet' and 'teacher' which were applied to him, and which he also accepted. I argued that the term 'son of man' was not a Christological title during the ministry. It was an ordinary, everyday Aramaic term for 'man', 'person' (*bar* (*e*)*nāsh*(*ā*)), which was used in a particular idiom, in accordance with which an Aramaic speaker used a rather general statement to say something about himself, or himself and others made obvious by the context. They did this to speak indirectly of themselves, to avoid sounding too exalted or humiliated. So Jesus naturally used it for example to declare his authority to forgive sins, and his forthcoming betrayal. It was one of the ways in which he predicted the humiliation of his forthcoming death and the glory of his Resurrection. There is no such idiom in Greek, so all genuine 'son of man' sayings were difficult to translate. The translators adopted a strategy of using both the Greek articles when the Aramaic terms *bar* (*e*)*nāsh*(*ā*) referred to Jesus, and not otherwise. This produced a Christological title, 'the Son of man', and all the Gospel writers were very happy with this. Mark, or possibly someone before him, found this at Dan. 7.13, and used this to form new 'Son of man' sayings predicting Jesus' return on the clouds of heaven. Matthew took this up too. Other secondary 'Son of man' sayings were formed subsequently. Thus all the 'Son of man' sayings in the Fourth Gospel are very Johannine, and have no connection with the Jesus of history.

The formation of the title 'Messiah', or 'Christ', was equally complex. The major peculiarity of the evidence is that, on the one hand, Jesus never refers to himself as the Messiah in our oldest Gospel, and the word 'Christ' never occurs in the 'Q' material. On the other hand, the Greek word 'Christ' was used of him abundantly in the early church, apparently from a very early period. I argued that the solution to this problem lies with the Hebrew and Aramaic words 'Messiah', or 'anointed', (*ham*)*māshīaḥ* in Hebrew, *mᵉshīḥā* in Aramaic. Neither term was a fixed title, and Jesus had no reason to use it in order to indicate the fundamental role which he believed he was playing as God's final messenger to Israel. That is to say, his ministry was not 'non-Messianic' in the sense in which that term was used in traditional scholarship; it is simply this one word which he did not need. This also means that there was not a fixed role into which he had to fit. In particular, there was no expectation that he would be a king or military ruler, and given that he deliberately went to Jerusalem to die an atoning death for the redemption of Israel, his crucifixion did not give his followers any reason to doubt that God had sent him. On the contrary, it gave them a good reason to look forward to his Resurrection, and when some of them believed that this had indeed happened, they had good reason to want titles for him. The term 'anointed' was sufficiently flexible to be applied to him, and was found in scripture as well. As the Gospel spread in the Graeco-Roman world, it became increasingly a unique title, so much so that the term 'Christian' was eventually formed from it.

The term 'son' was important to Jesus during the historic ministry. At his call vision, he believed that he heard a heavenly voice tell him he was God's beloved son, and he used this term in indirect reference to himself in an important parable which he delivered in the Temple during his last days. In itself, however, the term meant that he was a faithful Jew, not that he was ontologically different from other people. Some other people may possibly have used it too, but it became more important to his followers after his death. In the Fourth Gospel, it does mean that he was fully divine, and ontologically different from all other human beings. That is however a secondary development, which was only possible when Christianity was splitting off from Judaism, and the Fourth Gospel reflects the Jewish criticism which it provoked.

In Chapter 11, I turned to the final events of Jesus' life. I recalled the vigorous opposition to him, and the deliberate way in which he headed for Jerusalem in order to die his atoning death. His first major action was to take over control of important aspects of Jewish behaviour in the Court of the Gentiles, the outer court of the massively expanded Herodian Temple. He threw out the money-changers and those who sold doves in this court. He prevented vessels from being carried through this court. He also preached, including exposition of texts from Isaiah and Jeremiah, in support of this action and in criticism of the chief priests who ran the Temple. The effect of this action was to turn this large court into a place for prayer rather than trade. In view of the powerful opposition to his ministry, this was bound to lead to serious action against him. There were however practical difficulties in the way of arresting him in the massive crowds which thronged the Temple shortly before the major pilgrim feast of Passover. In a significant incident, some of the chief priests, elders and scribes came to ask him by what authority he took this action. He replied with a question about the ministry of John the Baptist, which reveals that they had not accepted his prophetic ministry either, unlike most Jewish people. They could not take immediate action against Jesus, because this would have caused a major riot in a confined space. They were therefore delighted when Judah of Kerioth, one of the Twelve, offered to betray him to them.

In the meantime, however, Jesus continued to preach against them in the Temple, and made certain that he was able to celebrate the Passover with his closest followers, who will have included women such as Mary Magdalene and Salome, as well as the Twelve and others. At this meal, Jesus predicted his betrayal by one of the Twelve in accordance with the scriptures, so he knew perfectly well what was going on. He also interpreted the bread and wine with reference to his atoning death, and looked forward to God finally establishing his kingdom soon. After the meal, he went with some of his followers to Gethsemane, where he waited to be arrested, though he prayed to God to deliver him. When he was arrested by an armed group from the chief priests with Judah of Kerioth, most of his followers fled. Simeon the Rock followed in the dark when Jesus was taken to the high priest's house, but when he was identified in the courtyard by one of the high priest's servant girls, he denied knowing Jesus at all.

The chief priests, elders and scribes decided to take Jesus to Pilate, and did so the following morning. Pilate condemned him to be flogged and crucified, and the way he was mocked, and the titulus 'King of the Jews' on the cross, show that Pilate condemned him as a sort of bandit. He died about 3 p.m, and Joseph of Arimathea, who was a Jewish elder, not a disciple of Jesus, led a party who buried him to avoid the land being polluted by a corpse hanging on a tree. He was probably buried in a common criminals' tomb, the site of which was probably unknown to his followers at the time, and still is.

Jesus had predicted his death, and did much to bring it about. Consequently, there was no chance of his followers regarding him as a failure. Most of them continued to believe in the importance of his mission, and some of them came to believe that he had risen from the dead. There were three basic reasons for this. First, Jesus predicted his death and Resurrection. After his death, this gave his closest followers one good reason to trust his predictions of his Resurrection. Secondly, Jesus taught them that various aspects of his life, including his Resurrection, were foretold in the scriptures. His closest followers believed that the predictions of various aspects of his life, including his death, had been fulfilled. That gave them a second reason to believe the predictions of his Resurrection in the scriptures, especially as they continued to study the scriptures. Thirdly, some of his closest followers believed that Jesus appeared to them after his death.

This is where a central complicating factor comes into play. The stories of Jesus' Resurrection in the Gospels have been rewritten and rewritten to the point where it is extremely difficult to infer any historical facts from them at all. The most conspicuous point is that all the stories of the empty tomb are secondary. Secondly, some of the appearances in Paul's relatively early list are not written up in any of the Gospels. Thirdly, the earliest narrative account of a Resurrection appearance, Matthew's account of an appearance to the Eleven, has the extraordinary information that 'some doubted'. Moreover, whereas the inner group of three of the Twelve, Simeon the Rock and Jacob and John the sons of Zebedee, played a major role in the early church, eight of the Eleven are not recorded to have done so, except in some late legends. This underlines the fact that, apart from Paul, who had a different kind of vision on the Damascus Road, all the Resurrection appearances were to recently bereaved disciples. I concluded that they were indeed bereavement visions, of the kind known to many people in our own and other societies. This is why they had to be totally rewritten to be useful for believers in Christian churches.

This concludes my attempt to reconstruct what we can know of the Jesus of history from the surviving primary sources. I hope that readers find it as accurate and illuminating as it is possible for an independent historian to achieve. I have not made any attempt to fit it into the picture of Jesus required by any social subgroup, whether Christian, Jewish or atheist. I hope that it will be of interest to people who are genuinely committed to evidence and argument.

Further Reading

The most important lives of Jesus are discussed in some detail in Chapter 1. Others are listed at p. 4 n. 7, p. 12 n. 30, p. 21 n. 54 and p. 27 n. 82. Genuinely important scholarship on all topics is discussed in the text of each topic, and listed in the footnotes. Students and general readers may be confident that these are the most important works to turn to for further help, and for significant mistakes. I have made no attempt to catalogue the massive bibliography with which this subject area is plagued. Some indication of what is missing may be found by perusing the bibliographies and footnotes of Dunn and Meier.

Appendix. Other Gospels

1. *Introduction*

We have seen in Chapter 1 that there is no longer a universal consensus as to which Gospels are the most important for accurate information about the historical Jesus. In Chapter 2, I argued for the conventional critical view that the oldest and most reliable sources are the Gospel of Mark and some of the 'Q' material, and that there is some further historically accurate material in other parts of the Gospels of Matthew and Luke. The purpose of this appendix is to give reasons for the conventional critical view that there is very little such material in any of the other Gospels.

2. *The Gospel of John*

The Gospel According to John is conventionally dated c.85–90 CE. Its authorship is disputed. Church tradition attributed it to John, the son of Zebedee, the 'beloved disciple', an important eyewitness of the historic ministry, who wrote it in Ephesus in his old age. Many critical scholars do not believe the church tradition about its authorship, and until recently most scholars did not believe in its historical accuracy either. Partly because of its disputed authorship, it is often called the 'Fourth Gospel', for it is the fourth of the Four Gospels in the New Testament canon, and it is usually thought to have been the fourth and last of them to have been written. In 1955, Kingsley Barrett, an outstanding critical scholar, who, at the height of his fame as a New Testament scholar, was better known in the valleys of Durham as a charismatic Christian preacher, put the conventional critical view of this Gospel in a nutshell, and in 1978 he repeated it:

> It is evident that it was not John's intention to write a work of scientific history . . . It was of supreme importance to him that there was a Jesus of Nazareth who lived and died in Palestine, even though to give an accurate outline of the outstanding events in the career of this person was no part of

his purpose. He sought to draw out . . . the true meaning of the life and death of one whom he believed to be the Son of God, a being from beyond history. It is for this interpretation of the focal point of all history, not for accurate historical data, that we must look in John . . . the total effect is impressive and illuminating.[1]

This critical consensus has been challenged in recent years. Moreover, while all the arguments against the literal historicity of John, and all the reasons for regarding it as seriously anti-Jewish, could be found in scholarly works, as for example in Barrett's commentary, the scholarly community as a whole did not make these arguments readily available either in the churches, or for the interested general reader. When I obtained a permanent academic post in 1979, I assumed that a 'Johannine scholar', or possibly an author of elementary books on the Bible, would fill this obvious gap in scholarship, education and the market. However, when I began to attend national and international New Testament conferences, I discovered that none of them intended to do this. I asked why, and at this point (about 1985) our more sardonic colleagues who wrote about other things started muttering about 'careers', being dependent on churches, and not wanting to upset old ladies in pews. I therefore drafted a book tentatively entitled *The Historicity of the Fourth Gospel*, because no one else would. I did not however understand the authorship of this Gospel, nor how it came to be written, and as I worked on these problems, I became more and more perturbed by how anti-Jewish this Gospel is, and by the role it played in Christian persecutions of Jews. Eventually, I completed *Is John's Gospel True?*[2] I set out all the main arguments against the historicity of this Gospel, together with the evidence that it is seriously anti-Jewish, and I added a new theory of authorship. I concluded, 'The fourth Gospel is profoundly untrue. It consists to a large extent of inaccurate stories and words wrongly attributed to people. It is anti-Jewish, and as holy scripture it has been used to legitimate outbreaks of Christian anti-Semitism.'[3]

While most of my arguments were standard ones, a book which no other scholar would write, and which reached a conclusion most inconvenient for the bureaucratized form of Christianity which dominates the 'academic field' of New Testament Studies, was not well received by scholars. In the most conservative circles it has been seriously misrepresented. For example, in 2006, Anderson attempted to overthrow the major results of critical scholarship concerning the historicity of the Fourth Gospel.[4] While omitting my substantive arguments, he accused me among other things of 'equating the presentation of the *Ioudaioi* in John with anti-Semitism and racism'.[5] I did not do this. I demonstrated, for

---

1 C. K. Barrett, *The Gospel According to St. John: An Introduction with Commentary and Notes on the Greek Text* (London: SPCK, 1955), pp. 117–18; 2nd edn, 1978, pp. 141–42.

2 P. M. Casey, *Is John's Gospel True?* (London/New York: Routledge, 1996).

3 Casey, *Is John's Gospel True?*, p. 229.

4 P. N. Anderson, *The Fourth Gospel and the Quest for Jesus: Modern Foundations Reconsidered* (LNTS 321. London: T&T Clark, 2006).

5 Anderson, *Fourth Gospel*, p. 79 n. 47.

reasons which I summarize below, that *hoi Ioudaioi* are 'the Jews', and that this document should be regarded as seriously anti-Jewish, as it has been throughout Christian history. That is what some Christians do not wish to know. From a mainstream but seriously bureaucratized perspective, the Catholic University of Leuven put on a conference in 2000, devoted to the problem of 'Anti-Judaism and the Fourth Gospel'.[6] The contributors to papers to which my arguments were most relevant knew what to do with them: leave them out. In a profound sense, this is not a comment on me, nor on *Is John's Gospel True?* It is a comment on bureaucratized scholars, their 'careers', their involvement in churches, and not wanting to upset powerful ecclesiastical institutions and hierarchies, who mind much more than any old ladies I have encountered. At this point another of Anderson's criticisms is unintentionally devastating: 'he never clearly defines the meaning of "true".'[7] No indeed, I thought we all knew what 'true' meant. I even imagined that 'truth' was what scholarship was *for*.

I now provide an updated summary of my main arguments.

First, the authors altered the structure and chronology of Jesus' historic ministry for theological reasons. The Cleansing of the Temple took place at the end of the ministry, when it was an important event which led directly to Jesus' death.[8] The authors of the Fourth Gospel moved it to the beginning of the ministry, where it symbolizes the replacement of Judaism by Christianity. Earlier predictions of the destruction of the Temple attributed to Jesus (Mt. 24.2//Mk 13.2//Lk. 21.6, cf. Mk 14.56-59, Mt. 26.59-61) are reworded as 'Destroy this Temple and in three days I will raise it up' (Jn 2.19). 'The Jews' naturally follow the original reference of this to the Temple in Jerusalem, but the authors explain, 'he was speaking about the Temple of his body' (Jn 2.21). The distinction between 'the disciples' (Jn 2.17, 22) and 'the Jews' is historically ludicrous, because all Jesus' disciples during the historic ministry were Jewish. It reflects the split between Christianity and Judaism in Ephesus at the end of the first century. The reference to the Resurrection is equally secondary reinterpretation. Since the event has been moved to the beginning of the ministry, it has no visible consequences. On historical grounds, this is quite out of the question too, since such a disturbance at a major festival was bound to result in serious action by the chief priests, who were in charge of running the Temple.

Having removed the Cleansing of the Temple as the trigger of the Passion, the Johannine authors needed something else to set off the final events. They wrote their story of the raising of Lazarus. Lazarus is never mentioned in the synoptic Gospels, and he does not appear in John before the story of his resurrection. His resurrection is a remarkable miracle. People who are thought to be dead occasionally revive, which led to the ruling that the bereaved could visit the grave for up to three days (b. Sem 8, 1).[9] Lazarus is deliberately portrayed as

6 R. Bieringer *et al.* (eds), *Anti-Judaism and the Fourth Gospel: Papers of the Leuven Colloquium, 2000* (Assen: Royal Van Gorcum, 2001).
7 Anderson, *Fourth Gospel*, p. 79 n. 47.
8 See pp. 411–22.
9 See further pp. 240, 472.

dead for four days (Jn 11.39), so that Jesus achieves the impossible. If this story were true, it surely would not have dropped out from the synoptic tradition, and this would be doubly so if the fourth evangelist's account of its effects were true. Moreover, the story is shot through with secondary Johannine features, including its extraordinarily high Christology. At Jn 11.4, Jesus refers to himself as 'the Son of God', the term used by Martha in her confession at Jn 11.27: 'Yes, Lord, I believe that you are the Christ, the Son of God who comes into the world.' In this Gospel the term 'Son of God' indicates Jesus' full deity, an unJewish feature absent from the synoptic Gospels. Martha's confession also has the secondary title 'Christ', which she uses in the confessional manner typical of this Gospel. 'The Jews' are mentioned five times in Jn 11.1-44. John 11.8 is as external and hostile as possible: 'The disciples said to him, "Rabbi, the Jews were now seeking to stone you . . ."'. This has the drastic division between 'the disciples' and 'the Jews' which I have noted in the Johannine account of the Cleansing of the Temple. John 11.25-26 offers a classic summary of Johannine features: 'I am the Resurrection and the Life. He who believes in me will live even if he dies, and everyone who lives and believes in me will not die for ever.'

This saying is part of a major feature which this story shares with the Johannine account of the Cleansing of the Temple: it looks forward to Jesus' Resurrection. When Jesus calls on Lazarus to come forth from his tomb, he came out 'bound hand and foot with strips of cloth, and his face wrapped around with a facecloth' (Jn 11.44). It is difficult to see how this could happen too, but that is not the point! Great though this miracle is, it looks forward to the greater salvific miracle, when Jesus rose and passed through his grave clothes, leaving the facecloth rolled up separately (Jn 20.6-7).

The consequences of the raising of Lazarus are historically incredible. It leads directly to the chief priests and Pharisees plotting Jesus' death, a historically implausible reaction by faithful Jews to a mighty miracle. The Johannine authors then put Lazarus into the story of the anointing of Jesus at Bethany, a synoptic story from which he is absent (Jn 12.1-8//Mt. 26.6-13//Mk 14.3-9). This leads to a plot by the chief priests to put Lazarus to death too. And there the story of Lazarus just stops! If the chief priests succeeded in bringing about the death of Jesus, how could they fail to bring about the death of Lazarus? Yet he is not even mentioned in the rest of the Fourth Gospel. Nor does he appear in the early chapters of Acts, as he surely would have done if this story had been true.

It follows that the story of the raising of Lazarus is a Johannine invention from beginning to end.

Another significant change is that Jesus' crucifixion is placed on the wrong day. Mark gives a correct account of Jesus' final meal with his disciples as a Passover meal, held on Thursday evening after dark, when the 15th day of the Jewish month Nisan began.[10] The Johannine authors altered this. They dated the meal 'before the feast of Passover' (Jn 13.1). When Jesus was taken to Pilate, 'they did not enter the praetorium so that they should not become unclean, but

---

10 See pp. 429–37.

might eat the Passover' (Jn 18.28). The theological reason for this begins to emerge when Pilate sits to give judgement, and the revised date is stated again: 'It was the preparation of the Passover, at about the sixth hour' (Jn 19.14). This was the official time for the slaughter of the Passover victims to begin, and that is why Jesus is sent to be killed at this time. Consequently, a scripture which refers directly to the Passover victim is said to have been fulfilled in him: 'a bone of it shall not be broken' (Exod. 12.46//*Num.* 9.12 at Jn 19.36). This is part of the replacement theology of this Gospel, in which Jesus replaces Passover, and achieves far more than the Passover victims ever could, for he is presented as 'the lamb of God who takes away the sin of the world' (Jn 1.29).

This causes havoc with the narrative of the Last Supper, for Jesus' interpretation of the bread and wine as his body and blood, which subsequently became the centre of the Christian Eucharist, was originally his interpretation of two of the major elements of the Passover meal.[11] The Johannine authors accordingly do not mention this in its proper place. Instead, they wrote a complete Eucharistic discourse, and attributed it to Jesus on a separate occasion, long before the Eucharist could have been instituted, complete with more trouble from 'the Jews' (Jn 6.26-66). The connection with the original setting is that the chapter as a whole is placed near Passover (Jn 6.4).

The earlier part of the discourse, much of which could be interpreted figuratively if it were not written in a Eucharistic community, reaches a climax at Jn 6.51:

> I am the living bread who came down from heaven. If anyone eats of this bread, they will live forever, and the bread which I will give is my flesh for the life of the world

This leads to a dispute among 'the Jews', who ask an uncomprehending question because they do not believe in Johannine theology about the Eucharist: 'How can this (man) give us his flesh to eat?' (Jn 6.52). This question is never given a literal answer, because all members of the Johannine community knew that Jesus' following words referred to the Eucharist, and accordingly they give the fundamental Johannine answer to the Jewish question:

> Amen, amen I'm telling you, unless you eat the flesh of the Son of man and drink his blood, you do not have life in you. He who eats my flesh and drinks my blood has eternal life, and I will raise him up at the last day.
>
> (Jn 6.53-54)

This makes participation in the Christian Eucharist essential for salvation, a view quite remote from the Jesus of history. It does not of course mean that salvation is automatic for anyone who participates in such a meal, as Jesus says in a passage which has caused endless trouble to interpreters, to the point where I offer a new translation:

---

11   See pp. 432–35.

This scandalizes you. If therefore you see the Son of man going up where he was before, the Spirit is giving life. The flesh is no help at all. The words which I have spoken to you are spirit and life.

(Jn 6.61c-63)[12]

Jesus' Eucharistic words obviously scandalize his (Jewish) disciples, who have complained at v. 60 about his 'hard word', and who leave at v. 66, a process which symbolizes Jewish opposition to Johannine Eucharistic theology, and the split between the Johannine community and the Jewish community. Nonetheless, the Johannine authors were keen to leave open the opportunity for faithful Jews to rejoin the Johannine community with a full Johannine faith. If therefore they accept Johannine belief in Jesus' Resurrection and ascension to the Father, and accept that this is the return of the Incarnate Word to heaven where he was pre-existent before the Incarnation, it will be clear that the Spirit is giving them life. The short sentence 'The flesh is no help at all' has three levels of meaning. In the first place, 'flesh' and 'spirit' are opposite realms, 'spirit' representing God and 'flesh' aspects of life without God. It is therefore obvious that the flesh is no help – everyone needs the spirit. Secondly, the flesh of the Incarnation is no help to those who do not believe that Jesus is the Incarnate Word. Thirdly, eating Jesus' flesh in the Eucharist, essential as it is for salvation, is no help unless they believe that is what it is. If they think they celebrate a fellowship meal in memory of a great prophet, that is not enough.

All this has no connection with the Jesus of history. The date of the Passion has been changed for theological reasons, and the Eucharistic exposition in Chapter 6 is full of Johannine theology which is of much later date than the time of Jesus, and reflects the situation of the Johannine community in dispute with the Jewish community in Ephesus towards the end of the first century. The Cleansing of the Temple has been moved to the beginning of the ministry for similar reasons, to look forward to the Resurrection and to symbolize the replacement of Judaism with Christianity. Finally, these developments are the cause of this Gospel having Jesus at three Passovers rather than one. It follows that the greater length of the ministry in this Gospel, plausible though it be at first sight, is the result of theological manipulation, not a reflection of authentic tradition.

The theology found in these passages leads us to the second major reason why we should not believe in the historicity of special Johannine material: it has an extraordinarily high Christology. This includes the deity of Jesus, which is quite unJewish, for in Judaism no man can be God. Accordingly, the presentation of this high Christology is accompanied by conflict with 'the Jews', who accuse Jesus of blasphemy, a charge which is culturally appropriate even as it is historically secondary. The Gospel begins with a prologue in which Jesus' deity is openly declared: 'In the beginning was the Word, and the Word was with God, and the Word was God' (Jn 1.1) At the prologue's climax, 'the Word was made flesh and dwelt among us', and his name and title are given as 'Jesus Christ' (Jn 1.14, 17).

---

12   See Casey, *Solution to the 'Son of Man' Problem*, pp. 301–3.

The prologue ends with a brief summary of Jesus' nature and mission on earth: 'No-one has seen God. Only-begotten God, who is in the bosom of the Father, he revealed him' (Jn 1.18). Towards the end of the original Gospel, Doubting Thomas hails the risen Jesus, 'My Lord and my God' (Jn 20.28).

Throughout this Gospel, Jesus is portrayed as conscious of his position as the incarnate Son of God who is co-equal with the Father. The classic declaration is 'I and the Father are one' (Jn 10.30), a declaration so provocative that 'the Jews' immediately take up stones to throw at Jesus. At Jn 10.33, they give their reasons: 'for blasphemy, and because, although you're a man, you make yourself God.' This reaction is as important as the sayings. Not only must we explain the absence of Jesus' declaration from Matthew, Mark and Luke, we must also explain why there is no trace of such vigorous Jewish reaction to it, a reaction which takes place in public during open debate. Throughout this Gospel, Jesus refers to himself as 'the Son' (*huios*) and to God as his Father. God is the Father of others as well, but this Gospel calls other people God's children (*tekna*), never his sons, reserving the term 'son' for Jesus alone. This is another indication that the Johannine community saw an ontological difference between Jesus and other people, and its significance is brought out particularly well at Jn 5.17ff.

Chapter 5 begins with a healing on the sabbath, at which Jesus orders a man to carry his pallet. In the debate with 'the Jews' which follows, Jesus justifies his apparent breach of sabbath law by identifying himself closely with God his Father: 'My Father works until now, and I work' (Jn 5.17). Many Jews believed that God was continuously active, on the seventh day as on others. Jesus associates himself so closely with the divine activity that he effectively lays claim to divinity, claiming God as his own Father as well: 'For this reason, therefore, the Jews sought all the more to kill him, because he not only abrogated the sabbath, but also called God his own Father, making himself equal with God' (Jn 5.18). Whereas Jesus justifies his action in appearing to break the sabbath, he does not attempt to answer any charge that he called God his own Father, or made himself equal with God, and he refers to himself as 'the Son' eight times (Jn 5.19-26). Similarly at Jn 10.33ff, when 'the Jews' threaten to stone Jesus for blasphemy, and on the ground that he makes himself God, Jesus does not deny the charge but justifies his position, asserting as he does so 'I am the Son of God', and 'the Father is in me and I am in the Father'. Thus the deity of Jesus, including his position as the unique Son of God, is publicly set forth by him not only to his disciples but also in public debate with hostile contemporaries.

A significant aspect of Jesus' deity in this document is his pre-existence. I have noted how clearly it is stated in the prologue. Jesus himself states it especially clearly in his high-priestly prayer: 'And now you glorify me, Father, as well as yourself, with the glory which I had beside you before the world was' (Jn 17.5). The presentation of Jesus' pre-existence is more dramatic in Chapter 8, where it concludes a very acrimonious debate with 'the Jews'. At Jn 8.23, Jesus declares that he is 'of the above', not 'of this world'. As the discourse proceeds, he claims divine origin as well as divine inspiration. At the climax of the discourse, he declares, 'Amen, amen I'm telling you, before Abraham was, I am' (Jn 8.58). The reaction to this is as important as the declaration itself: 'The Jews therefore picked up stones to throw at him' (Jn 8.59). Stoning was the traditional penalty for blasphemy. The Fourth Gospel's Jews, in open debate, have espoused the Johannine interpretation of Jesus' pre-existence as an indication of his deity, thereby indicating the setting of this interpretation of Jesus' pre-existence in the conflict between the Johannine community and the Jewish community, in Ephesus towards the end of the first century CE.

The abundant evidence of Jesus' pre-existence in this Gospel means that its language about the sending, giving and coming of Jesus must be interpreted in a similar way. This is most obvious in passages where these descriptions form an associative complex with a clear declaration of pre-existence. The description of Jesus as 'the one who came down from heaven' at Jn 3.13 is followed by the description of him as 'the only-begotten Son' (Jn 3.16, 18), and by the statements that God 'gave' and 'sent' him (Jn 3.16-17). The same passage also offers the description 'the light has come into the world' (Jn 3.19). I have noted the secondary nature of the Eucharistic discourse of Chapter 6, which is also delivered in conflict with 'the Jews' and which has at its centre the exposition of Jesus as the bread which came down from heaven. Here Jesus also declares 'my Father gives you the true bread from heaven' (Jn 6.32), and 'I have come down from heaven' (Jn 6.38); he also describes God as 'the Father who sent me' (Jn 6.44). The pervasive nature of these descriptions entails that the whole of the exposition of Johannine Christology is secondary, a reflection of the theology of the Johannine community and far removed from the Jesus of history.

Jesus' central position is also set out in 'I am' sayings. The most central is 'I am the Way and the Truth and the Life' (Jn 14.6). This means that Jesus is central and essential for salvation, as he says explicitly: 'No-one comes to the Father except through me'. For the Johannine community, Christianity has replaced Judaism, and this is implicit at Jn 14.6, for it was the whole Jewish community who thought that they came to the Father, but not through Jesus. This verse excludes them from access to God. John 8.12 is equally central for Gentiles: 'I am the light of the world'. The occasion of this declaration was 'the feast of the Jews, Tabernacles' (Jn 7.2). Light was central to the symbolism of Tabernacles. Jesus has effectively replaced this feast, and he has become the light for everyone. The discourse ends with his rejection by 'the Jews'. In the Eucharistic discourse, Jesus twice declares, 'I am the bread of life' (Jn 6.35, 48), and then 'I am the bread of life who came down from heaven' (Jn 6.51). We have seen that such references to his pre-existence indicate his deity. In the secondary narrative of the raising of Lazarus, Jesus further declares, 'I am the resurrection and the life' (Jn 11.25).

The last 'I am' saying is remarkable for the reaction to it. When the cohort who come to arrest Jesus say that they seek Jesus of Nazareth, Jesus identifies himself with the words 'I am'.

> When therefore he said to them 'I am', they retreated backwards and fell to the ground.
>
> (Jn 18.6)

This dramatic reaction is one reason to suppose that the 'I am' statements are intended to recall Old Testament passages such as Exod. 3.14 and Isa. 52.6, in which the words 'I am' are part of God's revelation of his name, and to hint thereby at Jesus' deity. Blomberg's defence of the historicity of this incident illustrates the pathetic and unJohannine nature of the most conservative scholarship: 'the language is sufficiently vague and restrained to enable us to imagine nothing more than a small group of leaders, stunned that the man they came to arrest would step forward so forthrightly, who stepped backward on the hillside in surprise and stumbled over each other causing several to fall down.'[13] Everything is wrong with this. It is supposed to be the behaviour of a whole Roman cohort, not 'a small group of leaders'. Arrest by a whole Roman cohort is not historically plausible, whereas Mark's account of Jesus' arrest is literally true.[14] If Roman cohorts had behaved like this, they would have lost all their battles. The story *requires* Johannine theology to make sense of it. The Lamb of God sacrificed himself when he had the power of God, which he properly drew attention to by referring to God's powerful name. This had an appropriate effect, causing a whole cohort of armed soldiers to step backwards and fall to the ground, thereby showing that the Son of God was in indisputable charge of these events.

It must be concluded that the 'I am' sayings are fundamental to the picture of Jesus as this Gospel expounds him. At least the majority of them, and many of their associations, would surely have been congenial to the synoptic writers, if they had known of them. This cannot be explained on the assumption that they are genuine, but they are not difficult to understand as products of the Johannine community. Moreover, like other aspects of Johannine Christology, most of these sayings are associated with the conflict with the Jewish community.

The presentation of this conflict is another major reason for seeing all this material as a product of the Johannine community in Ephesus towards the end of the first century. During the historic ministry, all Jesus' disciples were Jewish, and his opponents were for the most part scribes, Pharisees and chief priests.[15] This document's description of the opponents of Jesus and his disciples as 'the Jews' is anachronistic, and reflects the much later conflict between the Johannine community and the Jewish community. It follows that this document is seriously anti-Jewish. Consequently, it has been used in anti-Jewish outbursts throughout Christian history. For example, in his 1543 tractate 'On the Jews and their Lies', Martin Luther used Jn 8.39 and 8.44 to characterize the Jews as children of the devil. These and other Johannine texts were prominent in his theological arguments for recommendations which included burning down the synagogues or schools of the Jews, destroying their houses, confiscating all copies of their prayer books and Talmuds, and forbidding their rabbis to teach on pain of death.[16]

---

13   Blomberg, *John's Gospel*, pp. 230–31. On Blomberg see further pp. 27–28.
14   See pp. 438–40.
15   See especially chapters 9 and 11.
16   For a translation by M. H. Bertram, ed. F. Sherman see J. Pelikan and H. T. Lehman (eds), *Luther's Works*, vol. 47 (Philadelphia: Fortress, 1971), pp. 123–306, esp. pp. 141, 170–71, 268–70, 278, 281–84, 289–91.

Recently, several scholars, influenced especially by German attempts to kill all the Jews during the Second World War, have sought to alleviate this situation by suggesting that the Johannine expression *hoi Ioudaioi* does not really mean 'the Jews'. The two major suggestions are that it really means 'Judaeans', or that it really means 'Jewish authorities' or the like, and the recent Leuven conference produced more suggestions along these lines.[17]

The rejection of traditional Christian anti-Semitism is of course to be welcomed, but telling lies about what this document says is neither good scholarship nor morally sound. None of the suggestions that *hoi Ioudaioi* means anything other than 'the Jews' is remotely plausible. In the first place, the Greek expression *hoi Ioudaioi* almost always means 'the Jews'. It means 'Judaeans' only in a few specific contexts where it is contrasted with terms such as 'Galilaeans' and 'Idumaeans'. It never *means* 'Jewish authorities' or the like. Like all ethnic terms, it may *refer* to authorities, just as speakers of English may use 'the Americans' or 'Washington' when referring to statements made on behalf of the American government. Secondly, all comments about *hoi Ioudaioi* in this Gospel make perfect sense as applied to 'the Jews', as long as we take account of the setting of this description in late first-century Ephesus, not in the ministry of the historical Jesus.

Thirdly, there are several comments which make poor sense, or nonsense, if applied to Judaeans or Jewish authorities. For example, Jn 2.1-11 tells the story of a wedding at Cana in Galilee. It follows that the stone waterpots were for 'the purification of the Jews' (Jn 2.6), not of the Judaeans. Similarly, John 6 is set in Galilee, and its Eucharistic discourse more precisely 'in a synagogue in Capernaum' (Jn 6.59). It follows that *hoi Ioudaioi* (Jn 6.41, 52) are 'the Jews', not the Judaeans. Again, Nicodemus is described as 'a ruler of the Jews' (Jn 3.1): he was not a ruler of the Jewish authorities. Following the raising of Lazarus, 'Many . . . of the Jews . . . believed in him' (Jn 11.45): these were not many of the Jewish authorities. Likewise, 'a large crowd of the Jews' went to see 'Lazarus . . . whom he raised from the dead' (Jn 12.9): this was not a large crowd of Jewish authorities. When the Johannine authors wish to refer to Jewish authorities, they call them 'the rulers' (Jn 7.48), 'the Pharisees' (e.g. Jn 9.13) or 'the chief priests and the Pharisees' (e.g. Jn 18.3). General references to Jewish customs are not compatible with *hoi Ioudaioi* being either Judaeans or Jewish authorities. For example, John 6 begins near to 'the Passover, the feast of the Jews' (Jn 6.4). Passover was not however particularly a feast of the Judaeans, nor only a feast of the Jewish authorities, and these groups were not present in Galilee for John 6, which mentions 'the Jews' again, noting their reaction to Jesus' discourse (Jn 6.41, 52).

Fourthly, the description of the Johannine community's enemies as 'the Jews' makes perfectly good historical sense. Paul converted Gentiles to Christianity in Ephesus as early as c.52–55 CE. After trouble when he preached in the synagogue, Paul 'withdrew the disciples, holding discussions daily in the school of Tyrannus' (Acts 19.9). He would obviously preach as usual to both Jews and

---

17 Bieringer *et al.*, *Anti-Judaism and the Fourth Gospel*.

Greeks, and he remained there for some two years (cf. Acts 19.10). It follows that by the end of the first century the Christian community in Ephesus, while having Jewish origins, would include Gentiles who had never been Jewish. This is why Jesus says to 'the Jews', 'I have other sheep who are not of this fold' (Jn 10.16, cf. 10.19, 22): these are Gentiles. This is also the reason why some Greeks come to see Jesus, but instead of seeing them, Jesus talks about his death, which was necessary before the Gentile mission could begin. He comments, 'if I am lifted up, I will draw *everyone* to myself' (Jn 12.20-33). Similarly, the evangelist interprets what he regards as a prophecy by the chief priest to mean that Jesus would die for the people, adding 'and not for the people only, but so that he might gather the scattered children of God into one' (Jn 11.52). This also refers to the incorporation of Gentiles into the Christian communities.

This should be analysed further with reference to the main indicators of Jewish identity.[18] Judaism was centred on the Law. On two occasions (Jn 8.17; 10.34), Jesus refers to '*your* Law', as though it belongs to an outside group, and in one of the final discourses he quotes scripture to his disciples and refers to it as '*their* Law' (Jn 15.25). This is a particularly striking example because the hostile use of 'the Jews' is absent from the final discourses after Jn 13.33. Again, after saying to 'the Jews', 'Has not Moses given you the Law?' (Jn 7.19), Jesus comments that 'on the sabbath, *you* circumcise a man' (Jn 7.22). This makes a major Jewish institution a custom of outsiders. Sabbath observance is explicitly removed: 'the Jews' sought to kill Jesus, because 'he abrogated the sabbath' (Jn 5.18). This is also the reason why even such simple terms as 'rabbi' have to be explained (Jn 1.38): some Gentile members of the community would not otherwise have known what they meant.

It is natural that some scholars have consequently been puzzled by the massive amount of Jewish culture with which this document is imbued. Moreover, this is not confined to knowledge of the written scriptures, in which Gentile Christians could be learned, then as now. For example, 'The feast of the Jews, Tabernacles, was near' (Jn 7.2). This has the typical external description, 'the feast of the Jews'. Nonetheless, Jesus cries, 'If anyone thirsts, let him come to me and drink' (Jn 7.37); he begins a whole discourse 'I am the light of the world' (Jn 8.12); and the next major incident begins with Jesus repeating 'I am the light of the world' (Jn 9.5), and telling a blind man to wash in the pool of Siloam (Jn 9.7). These three chapters were written by people who knew how Tabernacles was celebrated in Jerusalem before the destruction of the Temple. Major features were the water libation ceremony, for which the water was brought in a golden pitcher from the pool of Siloam, and light, such that when the golden candlesticks were lit in the court of the women, it was said that there was not a courtyard in Jerusalem that was not lit up by the light of the place of the water drawing (m. Sukk. 5, 3).

Such major features of Jewish culture must be taken together with another

---

18 I first suggested this in *From Jewish Prophet to Gentile God*, chs. 2–3, esp. pp. 27–31; see further *Is John's Gospel True?*, ch. 7. Dunn is the only contributor to Bieringer *et al.*, *Anti-Judaism and the Fourth Gospel*, who mentions this mode of analysis (p. 59 n. 29), and he rejects it with reference only to *From Jewish Prophet to Gentile God*.

remarkable fact. The external and frequently hostile use of 'the Jews' is absent from the final discourses after Jn 13.33 and from the Johannine epistles. We must therefore conclude that the Johannine community still contained Jewish people, and that some of them, and some of their Gentile friends, were not happy with some authors' external and hostile use of the term 'the Jews'. At the same time, however, the authors of the final discourses were not too alienated to write in the same document as the others. Moreover, despite not using the *term* 'the Jews' in this external and hostile way, they still wrote sayings such as 'no-one comes to the Father except through me' (Jn 14.6), which excludes non-Christian Jews from salvation, and 'If I had not done the works among them which no-one else did they would not have sin, but now they have seen and hate both me and my Father. But so that the word might be fulfilled which is written in their Law, "they hated me without cause"' (Jn 15.24-25), which means that non-Christian Jews hate their God. It follows that what these Jewish Christians objected to in the external and hostile use of the term 'the Jews' was not *what* this document says, but simply the identity term which it uses in saying it. They were just as opposed to the Jewish community as were their Gentile fellow-Christians.

This is what the majority of contributors to the Leuven conference were not willing to face up to. Prize comments include the following: 'Jesus' controversy with them [the *Ioudaioi*] is no uttering of hostility towards "the Jews" but an authentic form of Christian love and care for the life of "erring" brothers'; 'the polemic of the Fourth Evangelist . . . is aimed against non-Johannine Christians, not against non-Christian Jews'; '[at Jn 8.44] "the Jews" . . . are not diabolical; rather their murderous behaviour is diabolical . . . "the Jews" of the narrative represent a certain limited group of Jews, scriptural authorities in the synagogue and their followers among the rank-and-file who violently oppose the Johannine Jesus and his disciples'; 'it is wrong to describe the type of argument used in John 8.38–47 as "Johannine polemic" . . . The author is not saying that the Jewish perspective is wrong; he is saying that his opponents do not have the true Jewish perspective! . . . *hoi Ioudaioi* . . . refers to "those in Judaea".[19] In the light of the above discussion of the primary source material in its historical context, all these comments may be seen to represent quite unrealistic essays which propose to avoid the scandal of the fact of an anti-Jewish document in the Christian New Testament.

Finally, Charlesworth seeks to avoid anti-Semitism by mistranslating *hoi Ioudaioi* as 'some Judaean leaders'.[20] His arguments are extraordinarily muddled, apparently because he cannot contemplate how inaccurate this Gospel is. For example, he comments on the perfectly correct NRSV of Jn 11.54,

'Jesus therefore no longer walked about openly among the Jews . . .' This

---

19   H. Hoet, in Bieringer *et al.*, *Anti-Judaism and the Fourth Gospel*, pp. 195–96; H. J. de Jonge, pp. 239–40; M. C. de Boer, pp. 268–69; U. C. von Wahlde, pp. 440, 443.

20   J. H. Charlesworth, 'The Gospel of John: Exclusivism Caused by a Social Setting Different from That of Jesus (John 11.54 and 14.6)', in Bieringer *et al.*, *Anti-Judaism and the Fourth Gospel*, pp. 479–513.

translation inflames anti-Jewish sentiment. The reader is told, or at least given the impression, that Jesus removes himself from among the Jews. He is thus portrayed in such a way that he appears not to be a Jew. The translation also suggests that Jesus' disciples also cannot be Jews . . .[21]

Charlesworth then argues 'the regnant translation' of *hoi Ioudaioi* as 'the Jews' is 'misleading' 'because Jesus was a deeply devout Jew' and because 'each of the Twelve was a Jew'.[22] But it is not the *translation* which is misleading. It is the *text* which is misleading, for reasons including those which Charlesworth gives. He has effectively proposed that scholars should mislead everyone to protect a misleading text which is part of Christian scripture.

All suggestions such as these should accordingly be rejected. *Hoi Ioudaioi* means 'the Jews', and this document is anti-Jewish because it reflects the split between the Jewish community and the Johannine community in Ephesus towards the end of the first century.

Finally, in accordance with normal and common Jewish tradition, this document was written by several people, over a long period of time.[23] I call them 'beloved disciples', for three reasons. First, in the Fourth Gospel 'disciple' is the term which identifies followers of Jesus (e.g. Jn 2.17, 22; 12.16). Secondly, the authors of 1 John, which provides unshakeable evidence of the existence of the Johannine community and a good deal of information about it, use 'beloveds', in the plural, as a way of addressing their audience (e.g. 1 Jn 2.7; 4.1). Likewise, the unknown man who calls himself simply 'the elder', uses 'beloved' in the singular to describe and address his sole recipient, Gaius (3 Jn 1.1, 2, 5, 11). Thirdly, the fact that members of the Johannine community called themselves 'disciples', and addressed each other as 'beloved', explains why they chose descriptions such as 'the disciple whom Jesus loved' (Jn 21.20) for a narratively convenient figure who always behaves as beloved disciples should.

This character is often known as 'the beloved disciple', though this description is not found in the Gospel. He is often identified with a particular known disciple. This is due partly to overliteral interpretation of two texts, Jn 19.35 and 21.24, and to belief that both are literally true. According to this Gospel only, the soldiers broke the legs of the two men crucified with Jesus, but seeing that Jesus was already dead, one of them pierced his side with his spear, and blood and water came out:

> And he who has seen has borne witness, and his witness is true, and he knows that he speaks the truth, so that you too may believe.
>
> (Jn 19.35)

This does not identify this person. However, at Jn 19.25-27, four women 'stood beside the cross of Jesus', and Jesus could also see and speak to 'the disciple

---

21 Charlesworth, 'Gospel of John: Exclusivism', p. 483.
22 Charlesworth, 'Gospel of John: Exclusivism', pp. 483–84.
23 See Casey, *Is John's Gospel True?*, ch. 8.

standing near, whom he loved'. Christians have believed all this, and used it to identify the man at Jn 19.35 as the 'beloved disciple'. There is however no chance of it being literally true. These people would not have been allowed near the cross. We have seen the true story of the crucifixion in Mark's Gospel. The men had fled, and some women 'watched from afar' (Mk 15.40).[24] Once we have seen that John's story is not literally true, however, there is no reason to identify the figure at Jn 19.35 with 'the beloved disciple', nor to take it literally.

The person at Jn 21.24 is presented narratively as 'the disciple whom Jesus loved' (Jn 21.20). The conversation between Jesus and Peter about him appears to be concerned to refute a story that he would not die, whereas we are asked to believe that at the end of this lengthy Johannine Resurrection appearance Jesus really said 'If I want him to remain until I come, what's that to you?' (Jn 21.23). What has often been regarded as a piece of information follows:

This is the disciple who bears witness about these (things) and who wrote these (things), and we know that his witness is true.

(Jn 21.24)

This has been interpreted as a confession by 'the beloved disciple' that he was the author of the Gospel. In a Greek cultural environment, it was assumed that this must indicate a single person who was taking responsibility for the authorship of the whole Gospel, and the immediately preceding narrative was taken to mean that he wrote it in his old age. Church tradition identified him as John, son of Zebedee.

Modern scholars have produced many other suggestions for a particular individual author. Bauckham has recently argued in favour of John the Elder, a less well-known figure who appears in the earliest church tradition about the authorship of the Gospel, and who may be identified as 'the elder' who wrote 2 and 3 John (2 Jn 1.1; 3 Jn 1.1). Other scholars have recently suggested Lazarus, or Thomas.[25]

None of this should be accepted. A disciple described simply as 'whom Jesus loved' cannot be a distinctive historical figure. He is not only absent from the synoptic Gospels, he is never mentioned during Jesus' public ministry in John. He is first mentioned in the rewritten account of the Last Supper, so that Jesus

---

24 See pp. 445–47.
25 For John the Elder see especially R. Bauckham *Jesus and the Eyewitnesses: The Gospels as Eyewitness Testimony* (Grand Rapids: Eerdmans, 2006), esp. chs 14–15; *The Testimony of the Beloved Disciple: Narrative, History and Theology in the Gospel of John* (Grand Rapids: Baker Academic, 2007), esp. chs 2–3; cf. also M. Hengel, *The Johannine Question* (Trans. J. Bowden. London/Philadelphia: SCM/Trinity Press International, 1989); for Lazarus, B. Witherington III, *What Have They Done With Jesus? Beyond Strange Theories and Bad History – Why We Can Trust the Bible* (New York: HarperSanFrancisco, 2006), Part Four: 'The Disciple Whom Jesus Loved'; for Thomas, J. H. Charlesworth, *The Beloved Disciple: Whose Witness Validates the Gospel of John?* (Valley Forge: Trinity Press International, 1995).

can identify the man who will betray him. He is introduced quite simply: 'One of his disciples was reclining in Jesus' bosom, whom Jesus loved' (Jn 13.23). That could be any disciple of Jesus! When this disciple has 'leant back, on Jesus' breast' and found out that the traitor is Judas (Jn 13.25-26), he is not mentioned again in such terms during the rest of the meal. Conversation with Jesus is left to Peter, Thomas, Philip and another Judas, fading out to 'some of his disciples' (Jn 16.17) and ending with 'his disciples' (Jn 16.29). He is next found in the historically implausible scene at the foot of the cross (Jn 19.25-27).[26] A disciple 'whom Jesus loved' next occurs in a uniquely Johannine Resurrection story, in which he has a race with Simon Peter to the tomb, and comes to faith without any appearances and without even knowing the scripture that Jesus must rise from the dead (Jn 20.1-10). This reflects what beloved disciples who can no longer see Resurrection appearances, and who are not learned in the scriptures, must do. They must believe all the same. He is not mentioned again in the original Gospel. He reappears in the appendix (Chapter 21). Here Jesus appears, but the disciples do not recognize him until 'that disciple whom Jesus loved' tells Peter, 'It's the Lord!' (Jn 21.7). This again reflects the function of beloved disciples, who ensure that the Christian community knows its Lord. He continues to perform this function, being mentioned more often in this most secondary of chapters than in the whole of the rest of the Gospel. We have seen that it concludes with the much misunderstood comment, 'This is the disciple who bears witness concerning these (things) and who wrote these (things), and we know that his witness is true' (Jn 21.24). This is not a reference to a particular individual either. It reflects the fact that the whole of this Gospel was written by beloved disciples from beginning to end. They knew that their witness was true, profoundly and theologically true, including all those points at which they had deliberately rewritten the traditions which their predecessors had inherited. When the Johannine community heard this, they will all have known what it meant too.

It follows that this document does not contain any significant material about the ministry of the historical Jesus, other than that which is available in more accurate form in the Gospels of Matthew, Mark and Luke. It remains an extremely important document, both for understanding the development of Christianity in the late first century, and because of its massive influence on the theology and life of the churches. As such, it is a classic example of social memory, with which the community's traditions have been rewritten in accordance with their needs at the time of writing.

3. *The Gospel of Thomas*

The Gospel According to Thomas is a collection of sayings attributed to Jesus. It is usually dated in the second century CE. It was known to some of the Church

---

26   See pp. 445–47, 523–24.

Fathers. For example, in the early third century, Hippolytus wrote a slashing attack on many 'heretics', including Naassenes, 'who call themselves Gnostics'. He says they transmit a tradition in the Gospel entitled 'According to Thomas', which he quotes as follows (*Refutations* V,7,20):

> He who seeks me will find me in children from seven years. For there, hiding in the 14th aeon, I am revealed.

As a document considered heretical, this Gospel was not preserved in mainstream churches. It was rediscovered in two stages. The first find was in the 1890s, when some Greek fragments, to be dated in the first half of the third century, were found among a large hoard of papyri at Oxyrynchus in Egypt. At this stage, no one knew that these fragments belonged to the Gospel of Thomas. This became clear when a Coptic manuscript of the whole Gospel, complete except for some holes, was found at Nag Hammadi in Egypt in 1945, identified in 1948, and properly published in 1956. It was part of a hoard of Coptic manuscripts written in the late fourth century. Christian documents were copied in Coptic by Christian monks, who modified ancient Egyptian Demotic so that it could be written in Greek letters with a very small number of additional letters, and who added lots of Greek loanwords, such as *euangelion*, the Greek word for 'Gospel'. There is no doubt that it was translated into Coptic from Greek, as many other Christian documents were, including all four of the canonical Gospels. Most scholars think it was written in Syria in Syriac, and translated into Greek, before being translated from Greek into Coptic.

The opening of this document makes its nature quite clear (I translate from the Greek, with restorations made on the basis of the Coptic manuscript):

> These are the secret words which the living Jesus spoke, and Judas, who (is) also (called) Thomas, wrote.[1]And he said, 'Whoever finds the interpretation of these words will not taste death.'[2]Jesus says, 'Let him who seeks not cease to seek until he finds, and when he finds he will be amazed, and when he is amazed he will reign, and when he reigns he will rest.'

This establishes that this is a deliberately esoteric document, written by a Christian subgroup who declare the central importance of their knowledge of the interpretation of sayings of Jesus which are not generally known. It is therefore not surprising that many scholars accepted the orthodox patristic opinion that it is a Gnostic work, even though it lacks important features found in many advanced Gnostic documents. Unlike the four canonical Gospels, it was not a Gospel written for all Christians.

The writing down of the sayings is attributed to Judas Thomas, one of the Twelve, who is not otherwise known to have played a historically significant role after the historic ministry. In the Syrian churches, Judas Thomas was known as the twin brother of Jesus, a creative interpretation of his name *Thōmā*, the Aramaic for 'twin'. He was believed to have founded the churches of the East, especially that in the major Syriac-speaking centre of Edessa. Many of the stories about him are obviously legendary in character, but it is possible that Thomas is the central character in these stories because he originally played a significant role in the spread of the Gospel in Syria, in which case he will have played some part in transmitting sayings of Jesus which have ended up in the Gospel attributed to him.

Some of the sayings are quite remote from the ministry of the historical Jesus. There is for example nothing like Saying 114 from first-century Israel:

> Simon Peter said to them, 'Let Mary leave us, for women are not worthy of life.' Jesus said, 'Look, I myself will lead her to make her male, so that she too may become a living spirit resembling you males. For every woman who makes herself male will enter the kingdom of heaven.'

This saying obviously comes from second-, third- or fourth-century Christianity, not from first-century Judaism, and it has nothing to do with the historical Jesus, or the historical Peter. Its basic rejection of womanhood reflects the notion that femaleness means passion, earthliness and mortality, and should therefore be transcended so that a woman may return to a state of primal perfection, which may be thought of as androgyny, a being with both male and female aspects. Such notions are found in Gnosticism of the second and third centuries. This saying also reflects ascetic practices in which women sought to appear more like men. Some cut their hair, fasted enough not to menstruate, dressed like men, and entered monasteries as (male) monks. These customs were found among Christians who were not Gnostics.[27]

A few other sayings presuppose ascetic practices, and may easily be interpreted to mean that salvation is only for Christians who refrain from sex. Saying 49 is perhaps the most obvious:

> Jesus said, 'Blessed are the single (*MONACHOS*) and chosen, for you will find the kingdom. For you are from it (and) you will go there again.

The Greek word *monachos* certainly meant 'single', and may already have come to mean 'celibate', even though it did not yet mean 'monk'. The saying is clearly remote from the environment of the historical Jesus, and belongs somewhere in ascetic Christianity in Syria and/or Egypt between the second and fourth centuries.

Other sayings remote from the environment of the historical Jesus include Saying 53:

---

27 Cf. M. W. Meyer, 'Making Mary Male: The Categories "Male and "Female" in the Gospel of Thomas', *NTS* 31 (1985), pp. 554–70; E. Castelli, 'Virginity and Its Meaning for Women's Sexuality in Early Christianity', *Journal of Feminist Studies in Religion* 2 (1986), pp. 61–88; E. Castelli, '"I Will Make Mary Male": Pieties of the Body and Gender Transformation of Christian Women in late Antiquity', in J. Epstein and K. Straub (eds), *Body Guards: The Cultural Politics of Gender Ambiguity* (London/New York: Routledge, 1991), pp. 29–49.

His disciples said to him, 'Is circumcision beneficial or not?' He said to them, 'If it were beneficial, their fathers would produce them already circumcised from their mothers. But true circumcision in the spirit has become profitable in every way.'

This saying rejects one of the basic customs of Judaism. The historical Jesus said nothing like this, and it is too extreme even for St Paul. The saying must come from a considerably later period, from a Christian environment in which the split between Christianity and Judaism was felt to have taken place.

At the same time, this document contains only one saying which has a hostile use of the term 'Jew' reminiscent of the fourth Gospel. This is Saying 43:

His disciples said to him, 'Who are you to say these things to us?' 'From what I say to you, you do not know who I am, but you have become like the Jews (*Ioudaios*), for they love the tree (and) hate its fruit, and they love the fruit (and) hate the tree.'

This saying is rather difficult, but some things about it can be clearly stated. First, the hostile use of 'the Jews' places it long after the time of the historical Jesus. Secondly, it is slightly reminiscent of Jn 8.25, where 'the Jews (*Ioudaioi*)' (8.22) ask Jesus, 'Who are you?' The fact that this hostile usage occurs only once in this document also means that this Gospel as a whole came from a Christian environment long after the split with the Jewish community had taken place, so that the extreme polemic of the Fourth Gospel was no longer needed. This too would fit in with the Syriac-speaking church from the late second century onwards, and with the environment of Coptic monks.

The sayings which I have discussed are among those which provide evidence that this completed Gospel is a late composition. At the same time, this Gospel also includes some genuine sayings of Jesus, and it is not always possible to mount a decisive argument for these sayings being secondary in form. Saying 86 is one of these:

Jesus said, '[] their holes and the birds have their nests, but the Son of man does not have a place to lay his head and rest.

Apart from having a bit missing, owing to damage to the sole Coptic manuscript, this has two significant differences from the version found in 'Q' material (Mt. 8.20//Lk. 9.58). One is the interpretation of what the birds have. The 'Q' text has a very general Greek term (*kataskēnōseis*), which alludes to the fact that migratory birds have roosts in trees provided by nature.[28] Saying 86 has interpreted these as 'nests', an interpretation which is also found in some Syriac sources. This is one of a large number of small connections between this Gospel and Syriac sources. Secondly, Saying 86 has 'and rest' at the end, which Matthew

---

28   See pp. 362–63.

and Luke do not. The interpretation 'nests' is secondary, but could perhaps be early and independent of the synoptic tradition. The words 'and rest' might represent the particular Gnostic interpretation of 'rest' found for example in the opening of this document, quoted above. However, these words might be genuine, and they could have been preserved in the tradition which was incorporated in the Gospel of Thomas, and dropped in the 'Q' material, for the saying makes perfectly sound mundane sense with these words as well as without them, and it could be interpreted in a Christian sense without being particularly Gnostic.

In some cases, however, the arguments for Thomas being secondary and dependent on the synoptic tradition should be regarded as decisive. A notorious example is Sayings 65 and 66:

65 He said, 'A [usur]ious man had a vineyard. He leased it to farmers so that they would work it and he might receive its fruit from them. He sent his servant so that the farmers might give him the fruit of the vineyard. They seized his servant, they beat him, they came close to killing him. The servant went back and told his master. The master said, "Perhaps he did not know them." He sent another servant. The farmers beat that one too. Then the owner sent his son. He said, "Perhaps they will be ashamed before my son". Those farmers, since they knew that he was the heir of the vineyard, seized him (and) killed him. He who has his ears, let him hear.'

66 Jesus said, 'Show me the stone which the builders have rejected. It is the cornerstone.'

This is a shorter version of the parable of Jesus found at Mk 12.1-12//Mt. 21.33-46//Lk. 20.9-19. Several scholars have argued that the Thomas version is the more primitive, on the ground that it is in general simpler, and in particular that it has no allegorical features.[29] This has often been supported by arguing that the behaviour of the vineyard owner in Mark is unrealistic.[30] No such arguments should be accepted. We have seen that Mark's version of this parable has a perfect setting in the life of Jesus, just where Mark places it, and that it realistically portrays God's treatment of Israel, not the behaviour of an earthly vineyard owner.[31] The same cannot be said of the shorter Thomas version. Like all attempts to interpret this parable away from its original setting, it does not make significant sense. The ending found only in Thomas, 'He who has his ears, let him hear', reflects this, for the parable needs a new interpretation which Thomasine Christians could doubtless produce, as indicated in the introduction quoted above. Moreover, Sayings 63–64 are all about the unsatisfactory behaviour of the rich, and saying 64 ends 'Buyers and merchants [will]

29   E.g. J. Jeremias, *The Parables of Jesus* (Rev. trans. S. H. Hooke. London: SCM, 1963), pp. 70–77.
30   E.g. J. S. Kloppenborg, *The Tenants in the Vineyard: Ideology, Economics, and Agrarian Conflict in Jewish Palestine* (WUNT 195. Tübingen: Mohr Siebeck, 2006).
31   See pp. 417–22.

not enter the places of my Father'. Thomasine Christians are therefore likely to have interpreted their version of this parable on similar lines to the previous sayings.

This not a reasonable substitute for the original interpretation, which makes a proper connection with Jesus' criticisms of the conventional leaders of Israel, criticisms which were a significant factor in bringing about his death. The take-up of Isaiah 5, essential to the original parable (Mk 12.1-12), is no longer clear, which reflects the fact that the authors of Thomas belonged to a tradition which was not involved in the Old Testament to the extent that Jesus and the synoptic Gospels were. The next saying, clearly marked off from the parable itself in the Coptic manuscript, does not make clear the quotation from Ps. 118.22-23 either, and, without that reference, it too cannot be meaningfully fitted into the teaching of Jesus. Like some other versions of genuine sayings of Jesus in the Gospel of Thomas, Saying 66 is closer to the version in Luke, who abbreviated the quotation in Mark (Lk. 20.17//Mk 12.10-11). There are also indications of contact with the Lukan version of the parable itself, such as the word 'perhaps' (Lk. 20.13). There are also small items in common with traditions specific to the Syriac-speaking churches. For example, the word 'perhaps' is also inserted into the Sinaitic Syriac and Peshitta versions of Mk 12.6.

It should therefore be concluded that the Thomas version is entirely secondary. Snodgrass correctly characterizes it as a manifestation of 'secondary orality', which he defines with reference to this kind of example as 'a later tradition drawn from the canonical Gospels and influenced by oral transmission of the gospel stories until written down in the middle to late second century.'[32] Once we have seen this, however, there is no good reason to date the surviving version as early as this. This is an important point of method: the fact that any given saying of the historical Jesus is preserved in a different form in this Gospel is never enough to show that the Thomas version of the saying is of even relatively early date.

Basically similar comments should be made on the majority of genuine sayings of Jesus preserved in this Gospel. They are the products of secondary orality preserved in an environment which allowed them to be changed in accordance with social memory, that is, the needs of the community for whom they were eventually written down. In that sense, the Gospel of Thomas is profoundly similar to the Gospel attributed to John.

Some scholars have suggested that some sayings not found in the synoptic tradition might nonetheless be genuine sayings of the historical Jesus. Saying 82 is one of these:[33]

He who is near me is near the fire, and he who is far from me is far from the kingdom.

A Greek version of this saying, not significantly different from the Coptic, was

---

32   Snodgrass, *Stories with Intent*, p. 280.
33   E.g. J. Jeremias, *Unknown Sayings of* Jesus (Trans. R. H. Fuller. London: SPCK, 2nd edn, 1974), pp. 66–73.

known to Origen (*Hom. Lat. In Jer.* III, 3, which survives only in a Latin version), and is quoted by Didymus the Blind (*In Pss.*, on Ps. 88.8). This saying uses imaginative hyperbole, which Jesus was very fond of, and 'kingdom', which was one of his favourite terms. We might expect 'kingdom of God', but we cannot demonstrate that this was not in an original version, slightly abbreviated during a lengthy period of oral transmission, especially as the completed Gospel of Thomas does vary in terminology of this kind, with 'kingdom of heaven' (e.g. Saying 54), 'kingdom of the Father' (e.g. Saying 96), 'kingdom of my Father' (e.g. Saying 99) as well as simply 'kingdom' (e.g. Saying 49, translated above). The synoptic Gospels are very short, so there is nothing inherently wrong in suggesting that some authentic traditions have been omitted from them, but have survived elsewhere. On balance, however, it is difficult to commend this as a saying of Jesus. It has the obscurity characteristic of 'secret' sayings of Jesus which require a Gnosticizing interpretation, and it may readily be interpreted to mean that non-Christians are not saved, a view characteristic of Christianity but not of the teaching of Jesus.

Two sayings concern particular disciples. Saying 12 is certainly secondary, but it may have been formulated in the first century rather than later:

> The disciples said to Jesus, 'We know that you will depart from us. Who will be great over us?' Jesus said to them, 'Wherever you came from, you will go to Jacob (*IAKŌBOS*) the righteous (*DIKAIOS*), for whose sake heaven and earth exist.'

This saying presupposes the period of the early church. However, it presupposes the primacy of Jacob the Lord's brother in the church at Jerusalem, so it may be thought likely to have originated either before the fall of Jerusalem or relatively soon after that, rather than in later Christianity. On the other hand, Jacob continued to be greatly venerated by some Christians after his death. He was especially famous for his righteousness, Jewish Christians were especially keen on him, and they had a massive input into the Syriac-speaking church. It follows that a somewhat later origin for this saying is possible. Thomasine Christians will have been perfectly happy with it. It omits Peter, who was associated with orthodox churches, and in due course regarded by them as the first bishop of Rome. Moreover, James's primacy as the leader of the Jerusalem church, being later known as its first bishop, could easily be reconciled with stories of Thomas receiving secret revelations from Jesus and going to Edessa and such places to found churches and transmit his secret words.

Saying 13, however, originated significantly later, for it reflects the ultimate superiority of Thomas essential to this document:

> Jesus said to his disciples, 'Compare me (and) tell me who I am like.'
> Simon Peter said to him, 'You are like a righteous (*DIKAIOS*) angel.'
> Matthew said to him, 'You are like a wise philosopher.'
> Thomas said to him, 'Teacher, my mouth will not at all suffer me to say who you are like.'

Jesus said, 'I am not your [singular] teacher, since you [sg.] have drunk
(and) you [sg.] have become intoxicated from the bubbling spring which I
have measured out.' And he took him, withdrew (and) told him three words.
Now when Thomas returned to his companions, they asked him, 'What did
Jesus say to you?' Thomas said to them, 'If I tell you one of the words which
he told me, you will pick up stones (and) throw them at me, and fire will come
out of the stones (and) burn you up.'

Here Jesus' question and the verdicts of Simon Peter and Matthew have nothing
to do the ministry of the historical Jesus, but it is the comments of Jesus and
Thomas which go quite overboard. They portray Thomas as not only central
to the process of revelation, as he is throughout this document, but as receiving
from Jesus himself revelations too awesome for him to communicate them to the
other disciples. Given that stoning was the penalty for blasphemy, it is natural to
suppose that the three words have something to do with the divine name, though
we cannot be more precise. Moreover, the fire which would burn up the disciples
implies that Thomas himself was perfectly entitled to pronounce the three words.
Once again, this document might reasonably be considered profoundly Gnostic
in this sense, that it derives from a subgroup of Christians who believed that their
knowledge of secret teachings of Jesus mediated through Thomas was of central
importance. This cannot be understood except as entailing also the inadequacy
of the teachings of the mainstream churches, which had effectively canonized
all four Gospels in the New Testament by the end of the second century (though
there were still some quarrels over the Gospel of John).

We may therefore conclude that this Gospel should not be regarded as a
significant source for knowledge of the historical Jesus, as the American Jesus
Seminar has done. Some of its members have also attempted to date it, or some
of it, in the first century, and their arguments are sufficiently important for me
to comment on some of the main ones here. In 1983, they were brought together
in one book by one of the Seminar's members, S. L. Davies, who tried to show
that this Gospel should be dated c.50–70 CE.[34] One argument is from its genre.
Davies argued that documents such as the *Sayings of Amen-em-Opet*, written
in Egyptian hieroglyphs in the second millennium BCE, and the biblical book
of Proverbs, compiled in Hebrew and perhaps completed in the fourth century
BCE, established the existence of a collection of sayings as a viable genre. That is
perfectly true. Davies, however, proceeded to argue that the Gospel of Thomas
should be dated at the same time as 'Q'. There are two things wrong with this.
One is that, as we saw in Chapter 2, the 'Q' material was not a single document,
so it was not a collection of sayings comparable to the Gospel of Thomas or
any other collection of sayings. Secondly, collections of sayings were written at
many different times. Davies himself noted the *Sayings of Amen-em-Opet* and
the biblical book of Proverbs. Later examples include the rabbinical *Pirqe Aboth*,
the 'Sayings of the Fathers', compiled in Hebrew and perhaps completed in the

---

34   S. L. Davies, *The Gospel of Thomas and Christian Wisdom* (New York: Seabury, 1983).

third century CE, and the *Sentences of Sextus*, probably completed in Greek in Syria, in the second century CE. It follows that the genre of the Gospel of Thomas does not give evidence of its date.

Davies further argued that Saying 114, which I discussed above because it is so remote from the ministry of the historical Jesus, is a late addition. Moves like this, however, are not sufficient to remove the evidence of several sayings which are clearly not derived from the historic ministry.

What this move should underline, however, is the unstable nature of the text of the Gospel of Thomas. The Greek fragments from Oxyrynchus are by no means identical to the surviving Coptic sayings, which cannot have been translated from them. The saying which I quoted from Hippolytus[35] is not found in the Coptic text. Accordingly, much the best model for the compilation of this collection of sayings is the suggestion that the final Coptic text is 'probably a cumulative product which expanded over time by the interpolation of new sayings.'[36] While versions of some genuine sayings are incorporated in it, many sayings are much later in origin, and have no connection with the historical Jesus or his disciples.

The most illuminating discussion of this Gospel has recently been supplied in two fine books by April DeConick.[37] I have noted the fruitfulness of her use of recent work on secondary orality and on social memory, and some of her comments bear repeating here.

> So the formation of communal memory is not a retrieval of past traditions and history. Rather it is the 'reconfiguration' of the past, making it conform to the present experiences and future expectations of the group. 'Remembering' is not a matter of recall, but a selection and reorganization of traditions so that the present can be better understood in light of its past and a sense of continuity between the present and the past is achieved.[38]

Insights of this kind are essential to understanding the Gospels of John and Thomas, both of which include material which originated during the historic ministry of Jesus, but it has been altered in transmission, and much new material has been attributed to him, all this in the interests of the different communities which produced these two very different Gospels.

I conclude that the Gospel According to Thomas is not a significant source for understanding the life and teaching of Jesus. It is an important source for

---

35 See p. 526.

36 B. H. McLean, 'On the Gospel of Thomas and Q', in R. A. Piper (ed.), *The Gospel Behind the Gospels: Current Studies on Q* (NT. S 75. Leiden: Brill 1995), pp. 321–45, at p. 332, with similar quotations from other scholars.

37 DeConick, *Recovering the Original Gospel of Thomas*; DeConick, *The Original Gospel of Thomas in Translation: With a Commentary and New English Translation of the Complete Gospel* (LNTS 287. London: T&T Clark, 2006). This includes the Coptic text in very clear print.

38 DeConick, *Recovering the Original Gospel of Thomas*, p. 12.

understanding some later developments in early Christianity, especially those in ascetic Gnosticizing environments in Syria and Egypt.

4. *The Gospel of Judas*

The Gospel of Judas is a recent sensation. Like other apocryphal Gospels, it was lost, or rather for the most part destroyed, because it was condemned as heretical by the mainstream churches. It was already known to Irenaeus, writing c.177 CE:

> However, others again say that Cain (was) from the Power above . . . And they say that Judas the traitor was thoroughly acquainted with these things, and he alone, knowing the truth as no others did, accomplished the mystery of the betrayal. Through him all things, both earthly and heavenly, were thrown into confusion. They produce a fictitious history of this kind, calling it the *Gospel of Judas*.
>
> (*Against Heresies* I, 31, 1)

This establishes the existence of a Gospel of Judas in the second century CE, though it is less than certain that it was identical to the work which has survived. The story of its recent discovery is a shocking tale of greed and deceit.[39] It is part of the fourth-century Codex Tchacos, a Coptic manuscript which was discovered in Egypt, apparently in 1978. It was appallingly kept while attempts were made to sell it for a lot of money. By the time that it was bought by the Maecenas Foundation in 2001, and restored as far as possible by a team of scholars working under the auspices of the National Geographic Society, it was fragmentary and extremely difficult to read.

The first English translation was published in 2006, and a full critical edition of the text, with photographs and translations, in 2007.[40] Unfortunately, the photographs are difficult to read. The English translation in the critical edition begins as follows:

> The secret word of declaration by which Jesus spoke in conversation with Judas Iscariot, during eight days, three days before he celebrated Passover.

Despite significant uncertainty about the text, which is not reflected in this translation, this provides the main point; this is a Gnostic document. In so far as scholars can read it, it gives us valuable information about late second-century

---

39 H. Krosney, *The Lost Gospel* (Washington: National Geographic Society, 2006).
40 R. Kasser *et al.*, *The Gospel of Judas, from Codex Tchacos* (Washington: National Geographic, 2006); R. Kasser *et al.* (eds), *The Gospel of Judas, together with the Letter of Peter to Philip, James, and a Book of Allogenes from Codex Tchacos: Critical Edition* (Washington: National Graphic, 2007).

Gnosticism. It does not provide any new information about the historical Jesus, or about Judah of Kerioth.

When the original attempts to read this document were made public, the media fastened on the view of the original scholars working on it that this document took a favourable view of Judas, a view vigorously challenged by April DeConick, with much reason.[41] Questions of this kind are important for understanding late second-century Sethian Gnosticism, but I do not discuss them further here, because the interpretation of this document is not relevant for understanding the historical Jesus, or the historical Judah of Kerioth. From a scholarly point of view, the greed, deceit and sensationalism with which this document has been surrounded are highly regrettable.

5. *The Gospel of Mary*

The Gospel of Mary is another Gnosticizing document from the second century CE, probably the second half of that century. Like other documents which were rejected by the mainstream churches, most copies of it were destroyed, and we now have just three fragments of it. The largest has been known since 1896, though it was not published until 1955. It is from a papyrus codex, Berolinensis 8502, in which the Gospel of Mary was the first piece. This codex was written in Coptic in the fifth century CE, and it was copied from a Coptic manuscript, so the Gospel of Mary was still circulating in Egypt in the fifth century. Unfortunately, the opening part of this manuscript has been damaged. We know from the page numberings that the part which has survived starts on page 7. Pages 11–14 are missing too. So we have pages 7–10, and pages 15 to the original end at the top of page 19, with the title '*The [Go]spel according to Marihamm*', a normal Coptic form of the name of Mary Magdalene. The missing parts mean that we have to be careful about drawing conclusions from the absence of anything which might have been written in the missing pages.

Two small Greek fragments have also been found, one overlapping with 9.1–10.14 of the Coptic manuscript, the other with 17.4 to the end. Both fragments are dated to the third century CE. Moreover the Coptic version was evidently translated from Greek. This Gospel seems to have been written in Greek, probably in Syria or Asia Minor. An excellent edition, with photographs of the manuscripts, transcriptions and an English translation and commentary, has recently been provided by Tuckett.[42]

This Gospel provides secret revelations unknown to most Christians, so it is natural that most scholars have regarded it as Gnostic, even though, like the Gospel of Thomas, it lacks important features found in many later and more advanced Gnostic documents. There should be no doubt that the main character

---

41   A. D. DeConick, *The Thirteenth Apostle: What the Gospel of Judas Really Says* (London: Continuum, 2007).

42   C. Tuckett, *The Gospel of Mary* (Oxford: OUP, 2007).

is the Mary who is known to us from genuine history as Mary Magdalene, even though this epithet does not occur in the surviving parts of this document.

The part which survives begins with revelatory teaching by 'the Saviour', who is evidently Jesus. In dialogue with Peter and unnamed disciples, he gives teaching most of which has no connection with the historical Jesus, and which has an excellent setting in the second century. For example, he teaches that 'Matter [gave birth to] a passion which has no image, which came from (something) contrary to nature' (8.2-4). When he departs, Mary kisses the other disciples and becomes the central revelatory figure. After her first speech, the disciples begin to discuss what Jesus said:

> Peter said to Mary (*Mariammēn/Mariham*), 'Sister, we know that the Saviour loved you like no other woman. Tell us the words of the Saviour which you know and we do not, and which we have not heard.' Mary (*Mariham*) answered and said, 'What is hidden from you and I remember, I will tell you.'
>
> (10.1-8)

This makes Mary the central revelatory figure. Moreover, the teaching which she is to reveal is not known to the other disciples. This is a central characteristic of Gnostic texts, and it has nothing to do with the situation in the ministry of the historical Jesus. Furthermore, the bringing forth of Peter reflects his position as a leading figure in what became orthodox churches, and the whole idea that Mary knows more of the Saviour's teaching than Peter does is a deliberate criticism of them.

This is carried further when Mary's revelations are not altogether well received. Her teachings include the ascent of the soul past seven hostile powers, including for example Desire and Ignorance, two of the seven powers of Wrath. This too has nothing to do with the teaching of the historical Jesus, and fits well with what we know of Gnosticism from the second century onwards. When Mary finishes her speech, Andrew's response includes this:

> I do not believe that the Saviour said this, for it seems to be different from his thought.
>
> (17.13-15)

Mary's revelations are indeed quite different from the teachings of churches which revered the apostles and were later thought of as orthodox.

Peter accordingly joins in on Andrew's side, and when Mary weeps, Levi, who turns up in the New Testament only at Mk 2.14//Lk. 5.27, 29, defends her, and his comments include this:

> Now I see that you are arguing against the woman like the adversaries. But if the Saviour considered her worthy, who are you to disdain her? Altogether, the Saviour knows her securely. Therefore he loved her more than us.
>
> (18.8-15)

It follows that this document was produced by a subgroup of Gnosticizing Christians. They rejected the authority of what later became orthodox churches, which revered Peter as the historic leader of the Twelve, already thought by some people to have been the first bishop of Rome. These are 'the adversaries'. These Gnosticizing Christians believed in secret teaching not known to mainstream churches, and which was on the way to being developed into the full-blown Gnosticism which we know from later documents. Moreover, given the position of Mary Magdalene, deliberately picked out towards the end as more loved by the Saviour than male apostles, this was a relatively early form of Gnosticizing Christianity, in which at least some women were more highly thought of than women in the mainstream churches.

This document is therefore very important for understanding the development of Gnosticizing Christianity in the second century, and the relationship between such forms of Christianity and the mainstream churches. It has nothing to do with the historical Jesus or the historical Mary Magdalene. It is regrettable that some feminists have sought to exaggerate its significance by dating it earlier and claiming that it was more typical of early Christianity than it was.[43]

6. *The Gospel of Philip*

The Gospel of Philip has survived in one mid-fourth century Coptic manuscript, found among the Gnostic documents at Nag Hammadi in Egypt. It is a compilation of excerpts from Valentinian Gnosticism, probably put together in Greek in the third century, in a bilingual environment, probably in Syria. Philip is the only apostle to whom a saying is attributed (73, 9–19), and this, together with Philip's position in other Gnostic documents, is probably the reason why this compilation was attributed to him.[44] It is quite a valuable source for understanding Gnosticism, though its nature as a collection of excerpts, together with the nature of Gnosticism as deliberately esoteric knowledge, has made it especially difficult to understand. It became famous because of the position of Mary Magdalene in it, especially as this was misinterpreted in the *Da Vinci Code*.[45]

The compiler was especially interested in the Gnostic sacraments, which he enumerates:

> The Lord [did] everything in a mystery, a baptism and a chrism and a eucharist and a redemption and a bridal chamber.
>
> (67, 27–30)

---

43 E.g. Karen L. King, *The Gospel of Mary of Magdala: Jesus and the First Woman Apostle* (Santa Rosa: Polebridge, 2003); Esther A. De Boer, *The Gospel of Mary: Listening to the Beloved Disciple* (London: T&T Clark, 2004).

44 I follow the numbering by page and line of Nag Hammadi Codex II, as in the English translation by W. W. Isenberg in J. M. Robinson (ed.), *The Nag Hammadi Library in English* (Leiden: Brill, 4th edn, 1996), pp. 139–60.

45 On the *Da Vinci Code* see briefly pp. 25–26.

The 'bridal chamber' is asexual and metaphorical:

> A bridal chamber is not for the animals, nor is it for the slaves, nor for defiled women, but it is for free men and virgins.
>
> (69, 1–4)

'Defiled women' are simply those who have had sex, and normal human marriage is referred to as 'the marriage of defilement' (82, 4). Kissing, whether real or imaginary, need have no erotic connotations. Already Paul told people to greet each other with a 'holy kiss' (Rom. 16.16; 1 Cor. 16.20; 2 Cor. 13.12; 1 Thess. 5.26). 1 Peter 5.14 defines this as a kiss of *agapē*, so a kiss of fellowship. A Gnostic kiss may naturally involve esoteric knowledge:

> For the perfect conceive through a kiss and give birth. For this reason, we also kiss one another. We receive conception from this grace which is among us.
>
> (59, 3–6)

All this should be born in mind when considering this document's brief comments on Jesus and Mary Magdalene:

> There were three who always walked with the Lord: Mary his mother and her sister and Magdalene, the one who was called his companion (*koinōnos*). His sister and his mother and his companion were each a Mary.
>
> (59, 6–11)

There is a problem with the text of this, and it is natural that some scholars would read 'his' rather than 'her' sister in line 8. Epiphanius also records a tradition that one of Jesus' sisters was called Mary (*Haer.* 78, 8). Be that as it may, it should be obvious that this means that Mary Magdalene has been accorded the same kind of importance as she has in the Gospel of Mary, not that she is being portrayed as his wife.

The same applies to the second passage:

> And the companion of[]Mary Magdalene[]her more than []the disciples[]kiss her []on her[] The rest of[] They said to him, 'Why do you love her more than all of us?' The Saviour answered and said to them, 'Why do I not love you like her? A blind man and one who sees, when they are in the darkness, the two do not differ from one another. When the light comes, he who sees will see the light, and he who is blind will remain in darkness.'
>
> (63, 32–64, 9)

It will be obvious that there are several significant gaps in the only manuscript at this point. The part with gaps must be interpreted in the light of what follows. The first main point is that, as in the Gospel of Mary, it is clearly said that the Saviour loves Mary Magdalene more than he loves the other disciples, who must include those held in the highest regard in more orthodox churches. Moreover, this time the Saviour confirms that this is the case. The second main point is that the Saviour proceeds to interpret this in terms of the basic imagery of light and darkness. It follows that the reason for the saviour's exceptional love of Mary Magdalene is that she is a figure for the advanced knowledge of Gnostics, which they believed exceeded the knowledge of mainstream churches, just as it was they who believed that salvation was by knowledge anyway. Hence she could take up the position of the central revelatory figure, just as she does in the Gospel of Mary.

These two main points are much more important than which words should be restored in the holes in the manuscript. It is entirely plausible that we should read, '[He used to] kiss her [often] on her [lips]'. One reason why this is plausible is that this imagery was used in ascetic Gnostic circles, so it is plausible that this document should say this, meaning to symbolize the importance of Mary as an insightful revelatory figure, as she is so clearly in the Gospel of Mary, as indicated in the following lines of this passage.

Finally, all this has nothing to do with the ministry of the historical Jesus, or his historical relationship with Mary Magdalene. It was invented by second- and third-century Gnostics, and it is quite illegitimate to read any of it back into the ministry of Jesus at the beginning of the first century CE.

7. *The Secret Gospel of Mark*

The last document in this appendix of falsehood is the weirdest of all, for none of us can read any manuscript of it.[46] In 1960, Morton Smith announced to the annual meeting of the Society of Biblical Literature that he had discovered a letter of Clement of Alexandria, which discussed three versions of the Gospel of Mark, his original version which we have in our New Testament, a second version, 'a more spiritual Gospel for the use of those who were being perfected' (I, 19–22), and a third version, expanded from the second by the heretic Carpocrates. Smith did not publish this letter until 1973, which is quite extraordinary.[47] It contains two short excerpts from the *Secret Gospel*, and one phrase attributed to the Carpocratians. This is the only part of the *Secret Gospel* to have survived, if it

---

46   For a recent account of the main points see P. Foster, 'Secret Mark', in Foster (ed.), *Non-Canonical Gospels*, pp. 171–82. The most important recent books about it are S. G. Brown, *Mark's Other Gospel: Rethinking Morton Smith's Controversial Discovery* (Waterloo, Ontario: Wilfrid Laurier Univ., 2005); S. C. Carlson, *The Gospel Hoax: Morton Smith's Invention of Secret Mark* (Waco: Baylor Univ., 2005); P. Jeffery, *The Secret Gospel of Mark Unveiled: Imagined Rituals of Sex, Death, and Madness in a Biblical Forgery* (Yale: Yale Univ., 2007).

47   M. Smith, *Clement of Alexandria and a Secret Gospel of Mark* (Cambridge, MA: Harvard UP, 1973); M. Smith, *The Secret Gospel: The Discovery and Interpretation of the Secret Gospel* (New York/London: Harper and Row/Gollancz, 1973/1974), of which I have used the 2005 edition (Middletown: Dawn Horse), which affects the pagination. This edition is readily available.

is genuine, and there are no other copies of the letter which Smith attributed to Clement. It has been argued that Smith forged it, and a vigorous debate about this continues. The book in which it was written has disappeared, so proper scientific texts on the sole manuscript, which Smith did not attempt to arrange, are now impossible. This is extremely regrettable, even though 'scientific' discussions of such matters as the Turin Shroud, the James ossuary, and the existence of Nazareth and Capernaum, show how biased 'scientists' can be.[48]

The longer excerpt is said in the letter attributed to Clement to have been placed after Mk 10.34 (II, 21–2). It contains one incident, in which Jesus raises a young man, after rolling the stone from the door of his tomb, going in and seizing him by the hand (II, 23–III, 4):

> But the young man looked at him and loved him, and began to implore him that he might be with him. And going out of the tomb they went into the house of the young man, for he was rich. And after six days, Jesus commanded him, and when it was evening, the young man came to him, wearing a linen garment over his naked (body). And he remained with him that night, for Jesus taught him the mystery of the kingdom of God.
>
> (III, 4–10)

The young man then returned to the other side of the Jordan (III, 10–11).

The second piece is very short. It is placed after the opening sentence of Mk 10.46, 'And they came to Jericho' (III, 11–14).

> And there were there the sister of the young man whom Jesus loved and his mother and Salome. And Jesus did not receive them.
>
> (III, 14–16)

The phrase 'naked to naked' is said in the letter (III, 13–14) not to be part of the 'more spiritual Gospel', so it belongs to the falsifications of the Carpocratians.

Smith interpreted 'the mystery of the kingdom of God' as baptism administered by Jesus. His most explicit description is in his more popular book:

> It was a water baptism administered by Jesus to chosen disciples, singly and by night. The costume, for the disciple, was a linen cloth worn over the naked body. This cloth was probably removed for the baptism proper, the immersion in water, which was now reduced to a preparatory purification. After that, by unknown ceremonies, the disciple was possessed by Jesus' spirit and so united with Jesus. One with him, he participated by hallucination in Jesus' ascent into the heavens, he entered into the kingdom of God, and was thereby set free from the laws ordained for and in the lower world. Freedom from the law may have resulted in completion of the spiritual union with physical union.[49]

---

48 See pp. 127–32.
49 Smith, *The Secret Gospel*, pp. 106–7.

In a separate description, after arguing that many people criticized by New Testament writers inherited a genuine libertine tradition which went back to the historical Jesus, Smith was more definite about sex.

> Jesus therefore developed the Baptist's rite by adding to it an ascent into the kingdom, which gave his followers supernatural powers like his own and freed them, too, from the law. Finally, he added another rite, derived from ancient erotic magic, by which his followers were enabled, they believed, to eat his body and drink his blood and be joined with him, not only because possessed by his sprit, but also in physical union.
>
> By use of these rites Jesus made himself the center of a libertine circle.[50]

Everything is wrong with this. Nothing in it belongs to the ministry of the historical Jesus, as that may reasonably be reconstructed from the earliest primary sources. Moreover, the homoerotic sex at the end of the first passage simply completes an exercise in sensationalist falsehood, as does making Jesus the centre of a libertine circle. Nothing resembling the nocturnal initiation into mysteries described by Smith is known until more than a century after Jesus' death. The inappropriate nature of 'unknown ceremonies' is further indicated by Smith's footnote on the 'unknown ceremonies' to which he referred in the first of the above passages:

> To judge from the *hekalot* and Qumran texts, the magical papyri and the Byzantine liturgy, these will have been mainly the recitation of repetitive, hypnotic prayers and hymns. The magical tradition also prescribes, in some instances, interference with breathing. Manipulation, too, was probably involved; the stories of Jesus' miracles give a very large place to the use of his hands.[51]

None of these sources are relevant for understanding the ministry of Jesus, except for the stories of his miracles, in which his use of his hands has nothing to do with masturbation, as appears to be implied here.

Possession by Jesus' spirit, this kind of union, and ascent into the heavens, are all unknown in the earliest sources for Jesus' ministry. The kingdom of God was central to the ministry of Jesus, but all this had nothing to do with entering it. Jesus and his earliest followers were all faithful Jews who lived their lives within the framework of Jewish Law, from which they neither wished nor endeavoured to set themselves free. Gay sex was not part of the ministry either, nor was there a libertine movement with Jesus at the centre.

Women, however, were of central importance and one of them was called Salome (Mk 15.40).[52] 'Jesus did not receive them' (III, 16) is improbable and unmotivated. At this point, Smith launches one of several unsatisfactory attacks

---

50 Smith, *The Secret Gospel*, p. 131.
51 Smith, *The Secret Gospel*, p. 107 n. 12.
52 Cf. pp. 192–98.

on canonical Mark. He translates the opening of Mk 10.46 'And *they* come into Jericho', and the next bit 'And when *he* was leaving Jericho' (Smith's emphasis). He continues, 'It is clear that something has been cut out of Mark at this place . . .'.[53] There is no justification for this. Mark's participle 'leaving' (*ekporeuomenō*) is singular because, in accordance with normal Greek grammar, it agrees with the nearest subject, 'he', whereas the whole subject is 'he and his disciples and a considerable crowd'. Mark's text makes perfectly good sense, and all we should infer from it is that Mark did not receive a useful tradition about anything significant happening while Jesus was in Jericho. Smith, however, knew that the word 'receive' does not occur in canonical Mark, so he attributed it to Clement as he cut out a conversation between Jesus and Salome, whom Smith describes as 'a very shady lady', on the basis of her role among later 'heretics'. This gave him another argument that his *Secret Gospel* 'was part of the original material and that our present text of Mark was produced by abbreviation, not expansion.' All this creative fiction is no evidence for anything.

In addition to unconvincing attacks on passages of canonical Mark, Smith grossly misinterprets other passages. For example, Jesus' parables are sometimes difficult to interpret, because they are stories with little or no reference. One such is the parable of the sower (Mk 4.3-8), for which Mark supplied a secondary interpretation (Mk 4.14-20), all part of his collection of parables (Mk 4.2-34). This is the context in which Mark attributes to Jesus a saying in which he explains to 'those around him with the Twelve': 'To you has been given the mystery of the kingdom of God, but to those outside everything happens in parables' (Mk 4.11-12). In this context (cf. also Mk 4.33-34), it should be clear that this is a somewhat lame explanation of the church's difficulty in understanding the parables, a problem which is still with us. Smith removes it from this context completely, and interprets it in the light of his *Secret Gospel of Mark* as 'a baptism', which 'was "taught" by night to a disciple who came "after six days," "wearing a linen cloth over his naked body".'[54] This has nothing to do with the interpretation of the parables, the context of the expression in canonical Mark.

Smith passes to the Passion narrative, and gets to the young man who 'was following him with a linen garment over his naked (body), and they seized him, but he left the linen garment and fled naked!' (Mk 14.51-52). Smith declares that 'nobody has ever been able to explain what that young man was doing alone with Jesus in such a place, at such a time, and in such a costume.'[55] But the young man was *not* 'alone with Jesus'. He was simply the last of Jesus' followers, other than Simeon the Rock, to flee from the scene.[56] Smith, however, interprets the story to mean that the 'business in hand was baptism; the youth wore the required costume.' As an interpretation of part of the Passion narrative, this has no plausibility whatever.

Moreover, these are the main points. Smith's handling of supposedly primary

---

53   Smith, *The Secret Gospel*, p. 65.
54   Smith, *The Secret Gospel*, p. 73.
55   Smith, *The Secret Gospel*, p. 75.
56   See pp. 439–40.

source material, whether genuine or forged, is fraudulent from beginning to end. This is central to a complete argument of cumulative weight, too long to be presented in its entirety here, that Smith should never have been believed by anyone, and that he forged this document himself.[57] This is coherent with the appalling quality of his subsequent book, *Jesus the Magician*.[58]

8. *Conclusions*

It is regrettable that this appendix needed to be written. In Chapter 2, I gave reasons for taking the conventional view that the major sources for the life and teaching of Jesus are the Gospels of Matthew, Mark and Luke. I also gave reasons for taking less conventional views of the dating of Mark and Matthew, and I took a view of the nature of the 'Q' material which, though widespread among New Testament scholars, is unusual in publications about 'Q'. That is what anyone writing a life of Jesus should have to discuss.

It is little short of tragic that I should have had to discuss the historicity of other Gospels, because critical scholars have already given ample reasons for their conventional belief that none of them contains significant material about the historical Jesus, other than that already found in the synoptic Gospels. Scholars have known for more than a century that the Gospel attributed to John does not contain a significant amount of additional material which is literally true, though it contains a lot of theology which good Christian theologians have had good reasons to consider spiritually profound. The resurgence of a contrary view is due to a resurgence of Christian fundamentalism, emanating especially from the American Bible Belt: it has nothing to do with new evidence or new arguments.

It was natural that the discovery of the Gospel of Thomas should have caused great excitement among scholars, and that it should have provoked scholarly discussion as to how important a source for the teaching of Jesus it should be considered to be. The original critical scholarship on this subject was valuable, and so is some recent work, notably the books of April DeConick. The excessive importance of this Gospel in recent scholarship about Jesus is however due largely to the American Jesus Seminar, who attached far too much historical importance to a late source. This helped them to form a picture of Jesus who was like a cynic philosopher, which suited their intellectual ambience.

It is even more regrettable that any of the other Gospels discussed in this appendix should have been taken seriously as sources for the life and teaching of the historical Jesus. Most of them are Gnostic, or Gnosticizing, documents

---

57 See further Carlson, *Gospel Hoax*; Jeffery, *Secret Gospel of Mark Unveiled*. I do not wish to imply that all their arguments are convincing, but that those of their arguments which are convincing, taken together with my comments here, and on *Jesus the Magician*, together form an overwhelming argument of cumulative weight.

58 See pp. 275–78.

of much too late a date. They are valuable sources for our understanding of the development of Christianity in the second to fourth centuries, but they have nothing to do with the historical Jesus. Some of the falsehoods surrounding them are due primarily to American feminists who wish to believe that Mary Magdalene was a major figure in the ministry of Jesus and in early Christianity. Others are due to pure sensationalism, some but not all of it centring on an American novel. The last one is a forgery by Morton Smith.

In one sense, however, it is fitting that this appendix should end on this note. As I argued throughout Chapter 1, and at intervals throughout this book, the major fault of the whole quest of the historical Jesus is that scholars have sought to find a Jesus who reflects their own concerns, not the historical figure of a first-century Jew. In a profound sense, therefore, this appendix merely catalogues extreme examples of that major fault. The rest of this book has been devoted to trying to correct it.

Index